Europe in the Contemporary World
1900 to the Present

A Narrative History
with Documents

Europe in the Contemporary World
1900 to the Present

A Narrative History
with Documents

Bonnie G. Smith

RUTGERS UNIVERSITY

BEDFORD/ST. MARTIN'S

Boston ◆ New York

For Bedford/St. Martin's

Executive Editor for History: Mary Dougherty
Director of Development for History: Jane Knetzger
Senior Developmental Editor: Louise Townsend
Production Editor: Kendra LeFleur
Senior Production Supervisor: Joe Ford
Executive Marketing Manager: Jenna Bookin Barry
Editorial Assistant: Holly Dye
Production Assistants: Kristen Merrill and Lidia MacDonald
Copyeditor: Patricia Herbst
Text Design: Anna Palchik
Indexer: Jacqueline Brownstein
Cover Design: Billy Boardman
Cover Art: (Front cover) Reichstagskuppel, Berlin, Germany: © Blaine Harrington III/CORBIS. (Back cover) Reichstag with glass dome in Berlin, Germany: © Svenja-Foto/zefa/CORBIS.
Cartography: Mapping Specialists Ltd.
Composition: Pine Tree Composition, Inc.
Printing and Binding: R. R. Donnelley & Sons Company

President: Joan E. Feinberg
Editorial Director: Denise B. Wydra
Director of Marketing: Karen Melton Soeltz
Director of Editing, Design, and Production: Marcia Cohen
Managing Editor: Elizabeth M. Schaaf

Library of Congress Control Number: 2006933436

2 1 0 9 8 7
f   e   d   c   b   a

For information, write: Bedford/St. Martin's, 75 Arlington Street, Boston, MA 02116 (617-399-4000)

ISBN-10: 0–312–40699–1
ISBN-13: 978–0–312–40699–8

To my graduate students—
past and present—
who have so many original insights
into the European past
and even more
about the contemporary world

P R E F A C E   F O R
I N S T R U C T O R S

What a privilege to teach today's globally connected students. They are technologically astute, self-aware beyond our understanding, and able to acquire their education in one of the world's most diversified societies. This book was written to engage these twenty-first-century students, introducing them in up-to-date ways to one of the world's most complex and important regions.

The first goal of *Europe in the Contemporary World* is to present a vivid, accurate, and well-rounded portrait of Europe and Europeans since the beginning of the twentieth century. It strives to give equal weight to all facets of experience over a century of European history, presenting essential political events while describing principal developments in the economy, society, and culture of Europe. It aims to show the ways in which social, cultural, and economic changes connect with politics, often driving political change and not just reflecting it. *Europe in the Contemporary World* thus offers a fuller and more accurate portrait of Europe's past than other works on the subject. The book's format is ideally suited to this purpose in that its chapters combine narrative with primary documents and picture essays, offering students an even richer, multidimensional experience.

A POST–COLD WAR PERSPECTIVE

This book has a unique perspective—and an important one, I think—in that it is told from a post–World War II, post–cold war, and twenty-first century vantage point. It provides a fresh and balanced account, allowing for the unmistakable impact of both world wars and the cold war but also offering readers a look at Europe's ongoing innovations in the political, economic, cultural, and social spheres throughout the period since 1900 and beyond. For example, not only did Europeans pioneer modernism (drawing extensively on influences from abroad) in the early twentieth century, they also formed the vanguard of a particularly twentieth-century brand of globalization, evident in the 1920s with the establishment of large multinational corporations like Nestlé and the Royal Dutch Shell oil company. Europeans continue to innovate in transport and communications (Europe had the first commercial Internet and worldwide Web system in the early 1980s). They have also been at the forefront of advancing social citizenship, integrating immigrants, and charting new political and economic, not to mention artistic, paths. Students focused mostly on the world wars and the cold war may overlook both the path-breaking, prewar developments as well as the more recent dynamic of the Common Market, European Union, and 2004 integration of eastern European countries into the EU. Without shortshrifting the importance of world warfare during the twentieth century, then, this book surveys Europe's striking panoply of social, political, and cultural structures and institutions across the decades from 1900 to the present and beyond—from the art nouveau of the "Belle Epoque" to a common economic currency—the Euro—in an era of increasing globalization. Taken together, these structures and institutions constitute Europe's rich and diverse legacy to the twenty-first-century world, one that will continue to affect our students' lives as workers and citizens. Thus the twenty-first-century perspective of this book aims to provide students with tools they need for understanding past and current issues that will continue to be important to all Americans.

EUROPE IN THE WORLD

Crucial to this perspective and the book's approach is the recognition that many of our students have a greater awareness of the world than we did in the past. Internationally famous sports and film stars, global messaging on the Internet, and the greater presence of world events in all the media are regular parts of students' lives. This book confronts the challenges and opportunities of our ever more connected world by situating European history within its true global context. Read any European newspaper or watch European news programs to see how deeply Europe's peoples engage the world and are enmeshed in its developing political, economic, and cultural history. The story of this engagement has evolved over the course of the twentieth century. In 1900, some rural folk, village dwellers, and inhabitants of remote mountain regions or northern parts of Scandinavia were just beginning to enjoy regularly imported products like sugar, chocolate, and coffee. By 2010, reggae music, Asian bubble teas, and Latin American soccer stars would be just as familiar in Europe's most remote areas as in its metropolises. *Europe in the Contemporary World* chronicles this growing exposure to the outside world and the concomitant shifts in European attitudes and policies toward the rest of the world, while it also presents the consumer culture and dramatic changes in the composition of society that Europe witnessed over the past century owing to that exposure. Thus colonialism, cultural importation, and migration are integral parts of the story and receive significant attention in the narrative and the textual and visual sources.

OLD EUROPE OR NEW EUROPE?

Is the history of this single continent obsolete? Is the history of Europe too old and irrelevant in a globalizing and high-tech world to be worth our attention? Viewing Europe's recent history from the vantage point of a global, twenty-first-century perspective would seem to suggest otherwise, since these approaches allow us to revisit the subject with fresh eyes. Europe looks different when we examine its contemporary history in its totality, paying equal attention to its many successes and failures across time. Its history becomes at once more complicated and more interesting, and certainly more relevant, when we look at politicians and foreign soldiers fighting in the world wars; when we look at race riots in which new immigrants are demanding jobs from government officials of ever-evolving political institutions. These are the complex interactions of modern life—whether in Europe, Asia, or North America. If the history of a single continent can be called "obsolete," it is only because it is being told from an old-fashioned perspective. There can be no simple history of this continent, for, like most of the world's regions, Europe is a fluctuating entity not just in its physical geography but also in the minds of its own citizens—the diverse builders of contemporary Europe. This book attempts to show that Europe's history is woven with many threads—global, regional, national, local, religious, ethnic, and individual—that sometimes connect and sometimes separate. In joining these diverse ways of thinking about European lives and about Europe itself, the story starts to be interesting.

A HOST OF COMPELLING WRITTEN AND VISUAL PRIMARY SOURCES

This volume also allows your students to connect more meaningfully with the past by offering a rich array of textual and visual documents that will excite and engage readers while reinforcing the importance of primary sources to the study of history. Each narrative chapter is followed by three or more written sources selected to allow students to experience the historian's task of dealing with the evidence from past events and to give them the opportunity to consider not just predigested facts but the fascinating raw source material of history. Simultaneously, the documents are chosen to illustrate that same range of political, social, economic, and cultural topics covered in the narrative, allowing students to dig deeply into all the major facets of the European past. For example, Chapter 4 on the 1920s provides a substantial excerpt from Adolf Hitler's *Mein Kampf* alongside Aleksandra Kollontai's vision of a new relationship between men and women under socialism, while Mohandas Gandhi's critique of European civilization rounds out that chapter's primary sources. Questions for analysis are included after each document or set of documents to encourage historical thinking. These questions can also serve as the basis for class discussion and debate.

To make the best use of contemporary students' strong visual sense, each chapter contains a picture essay derived from the period at hand. Several of the picture essays examine the relationship between art and politics, while others look at the ways in which the world wars have shaped thinking through propaganda and racial stereotyping. As with the documents, these picture essays help students to make connections between politics and culture, for example, and to hone their skills in analyzing sources—in this case images as evidence that have much to reveal about the past. The picture essay can even be an entry point into the chapter, something to be considered first or along the way toward understanding the material. Here too, questions for analysis help guide student appraisal of what they are seeing and can facilitate classroom discussion.

Just as I have provided these sources to enrich students' experience of the sometimes distant and unfamiliar European past, so, too, I have tried to make the narrative more immediate by using true life stories and pointed detail to reach this vital audience more effectively. The voices of an array of Europeans echo through this book as they present their own stories. Students will encounter moments from history as diverse as an anxious Winston Churchill watching post-Munich celebrations to immigrant women in the 1970s adapting their cultural rituals to their new surroundings. These plentiful voices, represented in brief quotations, are yet another aspect of the rounded picture this book intends to draw.

USEFUL PEDAGOGY

To aid in the task of presenting a complex Europe that is at once regionally and culturally diverse and at the same time deeply implicated in global events, each chapter offers the following pedagogic features: chapter-opening timelines that interweave local with global events; a broad array of maps that help build students' global geographic literacy by showing Europe in the context of the broader world; vivid opening vignettes that invite readers into the chapter and reinforce central chapter themes; in-text images that illustrate the multifaceted European experience both at home and abroad; and footnotes and an extensive bibliography of suggested references and selected Web sites that offer further opportunities for exploring themes and topics covered in the chapter. Finally, I open the book with an Introduction for Students that discusses my global and twenty-first-century approach and the ongoing debates over Europe's legacy, explains the book's structure and the importance of the primary sources that are included, and provides a rationale for the value of studying this complex and influential region of the world.

ADDITIONAL RESOURCES

Bedford/St. Martin's has published both online and print resources relevant to the twentieth-century European history course that complement this textbook.

Book Companion Site at bedfordstmartins.com/smitheurope   This site extends the goals of the text by integrating maps, primary documents, links to relevant Web sites, and online research resources at a single Web address. Resources can be selected and stored for later use or published to a unique Web address.

Suggestions for Teaching with the Documents and Picture Essays in *Europe in the Contemporary World*   Located on the instructor's side of the Book Companion Site, these suggestions offer helpful ideas about teaching with the textual and visual sources at the end of each chapter.

Bedford Series in History and Culture   European titles in this highly praised series, including several focused on twentieth-century Europe, combine first-rate scholarship, historical narrative, and important primary documents for undergraduate courses. Each book is brief, inexpensive, and focused on a specific topic or period. Package discounts are available.

ACKNOWLEDGMENTS

This book resulted from the generous assistance of many people—editors and publishers, college teachers who reviewed the work, my graduate students past and present, and a supportive family. Special thanks go to the reviewers who teach in universities and colleges across the country. They have provided a wealth of insights, detailed corrections and comments, and lists of good new books to consult. The manuscript benefited from close readings by Thomas Adam, The University of Texas at Arlington; Nina Bakisian, University of San Francisco; Melissa Bokovoy, University of New Mexico; Robert W. Brown, University of North Carolina at Pembroke; Jose R. Canoy, University of Oklahoma; Mark Choate, Brigham Young University; Carole Fink, The Ohio State University; Richard S. Fogarty, Bridgewater College; V. Lyle Haskins, Northeastern State University; Jeffrey H. Jackson, Rhodes College; Padraic Kenney, University of Colorado at Boulder; Alexis Pogorelskin, University of Minnesota Duluth; Diethelm Prowe, Carlton College; Nathan Stoltzfus, Florida State University; Eric Strahorn, Florida Gulf Coast University; A. Martin Wainwright, University of Akron; and Judith Walden, University of the Ozarks. The book also owes a great deal to special Rutgers colleagues Belinda E. Davis and Paul Hanebrink, who contributed their expert knowledge of central and eastern Europe in the twentieth century. Thanks go to them for taking the time to review a large portion of the book-in-progress.

Bedford/St. Martin's has the best publishing team an author could hope for. The inspiring leadership of Joan E. Feinberg, president, and Denise Wydra, editorial director, is a marvel to behold as they discuss in detail what will make the best book for students. With publisher for history Mary V. Dougherty and executive editor Katherine Meisenheimer rounding out the discussion of how to produce good books and then helping to make those ideas a reality, any author has to be grateful for such persistent and thoughtful guidance. Many thanks to them as well. Jane Knetzger, director of development, oversaw the macro and micro development of the book with a rationality and calm that are enviable. Amy Leathe, editorial assistant, ran the review program, turned over most of the manuscript to production, and provided a lead for one special document as well as other helpful tips. When Amy left Bedford, Holly Dye took over seamlessly and has been enormously helpful in developing the book companion Web site. Kendra LeFleur, patient and saintly production editor, expertly put the book through production and helped out with all the glitches that so complex a book inevitably generates. Thanks, too, to Pat Herbst who copyedited this work, making the book's interior flow more smoothly, as well as to freelancer Arthur Johnson for his meticulous proofreading. Billy Boardman and Donna Dennison created what has to be the most beautiful textbook cover ever! Photo researcher Connie Gardner labored long and hard over the illustration program. We hope it will help Jenna Bookin Barry, executive marketing manager for history, promote the book, but then Jenna needs no help as she has so many ideas for getting books into the hands of readers. From the very beginning, she also provided thoughtful ideas for how to develop this work. Tisha Rossi was also there at the beginning, devising the plan for *Europe in the Contemporary World* and convincing me that it was the right book to do.

There are some people one can never do without. The first is the talented, expert, imaginative, and infinitely supportive senior editor for the book, Louise Townsend. Louise has had so many terrific ideas and turns of phrase that *Europe in the Contemporary World* is very much her work too. Her own historical expertise fills its pages, while her cheerleading through tough revisions literally made the book happen. The second is a cluster of incomparable scholars—my graduate students, past and present, whom I worship for their talent, creativity, and devotion to teaching and writing. Some did specific research that shows up on these pages: Louisa Rice, Tamara Matheson, Cynthia Kreisel, and Michal Shapira. All, however, have contributed intellectually and emotionally to the final product. Finally, my family—Don, Patrick, John, Patience, and Denise—are, in a word, the best. I love and value them more than it is possible to say, especially in a history book.

BRIEF CONTENTS

C O N T E N T S

CHAPTER **10**
Postindustrial Europe and
Its Critics, 1965–1979
554

MAPS AND CHARTS

INTRODUCTION FOR STUDENTS

Twenty-first-century Europe is, by most accounts, a great place to live. It contains the most highly educated workforce in the world. Broad stretches of the continent enjoy the world's best-run cities, excellent systems of roads and public transportation, and an effective civil service system, the training for which comes in special schools. The countries of Europe have drawn closer together, moving toward complete unification, in the European Union—an event that would bring even greater efficiency and competitiveness to a region that already composes a mighty economic unit with a dense and active population. To judge by European newspapers, Europeans know more about the rest of the world than the average Chinese person and are certainly better informed than Americans. Europeans regularly sit in cafés and coffeehouses discussing current events rather than the latest celebrity gossip—though they are perfectly capable of that too. European states have some of the lowest crime rates in the world as well as the lowest rates of infant mortality. The twenty countries where life expectancy is longest are almost all European (the United States is not among this group). Thus an observer might be justified in thinking Europeans must have done something right to enjoy such a relatively high level of prosperity and well-being. For this reason alone, Europe's history merits investigation for the lessons in the arts of living it might bring.

And yet the story of Europe and Europeans over the last hundred years or so has tended toward extremes—fluctuating between incredibly difficult times of war, mass murder, and destruction and years of marked prosperity, hope, and health. *Europe in the Contemporary World* tells that story in all its richness, horror, and complexity. It narrates the violence that shaped Europe's history as well as the vast array of accomplishments of which Europeans can rightly boast. It presents momentous political and military events alongside the activity of everyday life and production in the arts that has made Europe so renowned for its culture, industry, and innovation. Since the agents of all this activity—Europeans themselves—are incredibly diverse in backgrounds and points of view, this book also includes their testimonies and perspectives. Primary source texts and images by and about a variety of figures, both little known and famous, provide you with a vivid glimpse of Europe's recent past.

BEACON OF CIVILIZATION OR "DARK CONTINENT"?

Travelers, not to mention Europeans themselves, have always recognized that Europe has important political and cultural lessons to offer. Even in the eighteenth century, a writer on Europe believed that, though the smallest of the world's regions, Europe was "the most considerable for its commerce, navigation, fertility, for its enlightenment and industry, for its knowledge of the arts, sciences and trades."[1] Today more people from around the globe visit countries like France and Great Britain than travel to the United States. Throngs of tourists take in wondrous sights, from the ancient temples of the Acropolis in Athens or the Coliseum in Rome to the sweeping skyscrapers of the new Berlin and the extraordinary modern museums of Madrid, London, and St. Petersburg. Visitors are eager to see where old masters such as the playwright Shakespeare or the composer Mozart lived and worked, but the lure of modern Europe is just as great. From the all-glass pyramids that dot the landscape around the Louvre Museum to the Prague home of Franz Kafka, who brought us our first fictional imaginings of the unseen power of the modern state, the magnetism of European culture is overpowering. It has produced much that is valuable to the world today and indeed seems to serve as the foundation of a Western civilization.

And yet, if you are a regular browser of bookstores' history sections, you know that their shelves are filled with gripping best sellers on Europe's tragic history during World War I and World War II, with their massive casualties and incredible innovation in the tools of mass destruction. The Europeans who perpetrated and suffered from the horrific events of the world wars, including the Holocaust, are also very familiar from movies and television. The Russian Revolution and the cold war, too, fold into the story of a Europe whose history is nothing but disastrous — a cluster of countries that seem to bring only brutal suffering to the world. Stalin's purges and the vicious prison camp system of the USSR reach the mass history market, playing to an audience that is rightly stirred by the bloodshed and suffering of the past. We are fascinated by Adolf Hitler, Joseph Stalin, and Benito Mussolini — dictators with a striking ability to get things done — even, or especially, mass murder.

Alongside violence on its own soil, the Europe we tend to know also ruled large portions of the world through colonization, and it brought hardship and catastrophe to many in Africa, Asia, and the Americas. And when the European rule of distant lands was overturned through decolonization, horrific suffering and countless deaths often followed. In our own era, violence has returned to Europe itself as neighbors have killed one another in huge numbers because they were Muslim, Jewish, Croat, Serb, or simply — like Sweden's prime minister Olof Palme, assassinated in 1986 — because they had unpopular ideas. Europe, it must be admitted, has had a bloody, militaristic past, especially since 1900. For many, it is "the dark continent," as one historian has recently put it.

---

[1] Chevalier de Jaucourt, quoted in "Europe," in *Encyclopédieou Dictionnaire raisonné des sciences, des arts et des métiers*, vol. 6, Denis Diderot, ed. (Stuttgart-Bad Cannstatt: Frommann-Holzboog, 1966–1967 [reprint of 1756 edition]), 211.

HUMAN AGENCY AS READ FROM THE SOURCES

For those who study the history of Europe today, the picture is at once more complicated and more interesting than simple formulations of Europe as an endlessly bloody battleground or, alternatively, Europe as the source of all enlightenment and culture. The amazing variety of actions and of participants that make up Europe's history during this period moves us beyond such easy characterizations. Shaping the twentieth century, Europeans banded together in mass movements to promote environmentalism, civil equality, feminism, gay liberation, ethnic pride, refugee security, political ideologies, and peasant rights. Laborers, farmers, housewives, soldiers, and citizen activists reduced the birth rate, changed marriage patterns, established networks for migration, promoted public education, voted, went on strikes, diversified society, and undertook countless inventions and discoveries. Across the century they pursued a wide range of livelihoods: blue-collar work, white-collar work, technocratic and bureaucratic work, postindustrial work—all of which you will read about in this book. They created the generation gap, the gender gap, the sexual revolution, and race relations—both bad and good. The story of Europeans in the twentieth-century world is above all the story of people making history.

To allow you a closer look at these individuals, each chapter in this book contains human voices and first-person accounts, both in the narrative and in the primary documents. For example, you can read an account from a young migrant worker in early-twentieth-century France as well as the stories of late-twentieth-century immigrants newly arrived in Europe. You hear from Mikhail Gorbachev of the Soviet Union and Alva Myrdal of Sweden justifying their new governmental policies, and from Simone de Beauvoir on the role of women and a gay liberation manifesto from the United Kingdom. In addition to how Europeans viewed themselves, you will also encounter the perspectives of non-Europeans on Europe, such as Mohandas Gandhi's view of Europeans toward the beginning of the twentieth century and the visions of Japanese military leaders of the late 1930s and early 1940s for defeating the great imperial powers, including Great Britain, France, and Russia. You will get to feel the past through these documents, gaining insights that might be missed in the distilled accounts of written histories, and you will get to judge for yourself the actions and beliefs of Europeans great and ordinary.

In this book you will also *see* history through a picture essay at the end of each chapter. These essays focus on subjects as diverse as European modernism in the arts, everyday life in wartime, politics in the streets in the 1960s, and urban architecture in the twenty-first century. The idea is that visual sources bring the same kind of immediacy to understanding history that written sources do. Photographers and artists provide striking records that we can judge with our eyes and then put in the context of written European history. Like the written documents, these visual records serve to enliven our understanding of people in the past, even those as distant as Europeans in 1900.

EUROPE IN THE WORLD

Historians can better understand the contradictions of the European past by telling the story of both the "dark continent" and a brilliant, even path-breaking civilization in the revelatory context of world history. These contradictions appear most starkly when we look at Europe's relationships with the rest of the world as an inseparable part of its identity. Long the major force in the modern phase of globalization, Europe began its contemporary relationship with other continents around 1450, when direct contact began with Asia and Africa and subsequently with the Western Hemisphere. From these early contacts new products, ideas, and institutional examples flooded Europe. Europeans learned about free trade, public education, and a civil service system based on merit and came to enjoy a vast array of products from chocolate, tea, and coffee to waterproof rain gear and rubber tires. Along the way they developed, with Arab and African traders, an extensive slave system across the Atlantic world. From there they determined by the mid-nineteenth century to conquer and rule the rest of the world; this process continued past World War I. As our story opens, Europeans were slaughtering peoples around the world in order to rule them, and this violence continued past World War II through the middle of the twentieth century. Indeed, historians believe that imperial conquest helped develop the mentality for mass slaughter of European civilians in the twentieth century.

Products, ideas, and interactions with the world's peoples helped fashion the West's twentieth-century identity, specifically its sense of being modern. Beyond everyday cultural imports, philosophical ideas and themes in modern art, dance, theater, and music came from imitating Asian, African, and Latin American styles, as did theories of racial liberation and tactics of massive civil disobedience. Vast migrations—both temporary and permanent—of Europeans to the rest of the world occurred from the mid-nineteenth century on, but so did global migration from the rest of the world to Europe, accelerating after World War II to encompass tens of millions of people.

Ethnic, cultural, and intellectual mixture became more apparent than ever before as the twentieth century drew to a close, and Europeans rethought ideas of public welfare, expanding public education, housing, transport, and the very notion of citizenship. Europe exercised global power in the twentieth century, but the process of wielding its economic and political might around the world continued the progression of making Europe's heritage a mixture of global influences. European multiculturalism has been a constant in our contemporary world and has continued to grow with the advent of the twenty-first century.

A BALANCE OF POLITICAL, ECONOMIC, SOCIAL, AND CULTURAL EVENTS

Set in a world context, European history involves a complex story with many plots and subplots. Through both narrative and primary sources, this book treats the full range of events included in that intricate tale, investigating politics and social and cultural life through both good times and bad. You will witness the actions of politicians operating at the highest reaches of government and determining grand issues of war and peace, the development of Europe's economic and technological expertise—including the earliest computers—and the unfolding of Europe's many intellectual accomplishments. This text also pays close attention to the habits and customs of everyday life in the context of momentous events like global warfare and the worldwide Great Depression. For if political leaders made the decisions to fight World Wars I and II and to conduct the cold war, the European population as a whole was the flesh and blood of those decisions. By the same token, ordinary people helped make Europe's novel-reading, newspaper-buying, film-going, television-viewing, and computer-using public one of the most up-to-date in the world.

WORLD CITIZENS: PAST, PRESENT, AND FUTURE

Concerned Europeans, like their counterparts in the United States and around the world, think deeply about the past in order to make better choices in the future. Europeans today are engaged in a wholesale debate over their tragic twentieth-century past, their current place in the world, and the future directions the region will take in this new century. They are fully aware that Europe has some of the most successfully run cities, social programs, and national governments in the world, while its citizens live longer and are healthier than in any other region. How did Europe get this way, they legitimately ask themselves, and will it stay so prosperous, healthy, and innovative in the future? How did this prosperity emerge amidst the slaughter of tens of millions in warfare, persecution, genocide, and famine that gripped many parts of Europe in the twentieth century and even beyond?

The challenges that Europe faces at the moment include maintaining its economic and political dynamism among a population that is statistically older than that of other regions of the world. Europeans discuss issues of multiculturalism, looming nationalism, brutal ethnocentricism, and even lingering anti-Semitism—all of these presented in this book. My hope is that after reading it, students will look at European society as well as their own in a more informed and reflective manner. I write this book for you as if you were students in my own classroom trying to comprehend Europe's past and present and what lessons its history offers. Understanding the European past can be a training ground for understanding the world today—a task that is more imperative than ever before as you face the challenge of becoming an informed citizen facing a complex future.

Europe in the Contemporary World
1900 to the Present

A Narrative History
with Documents

1

Imperial Europe at the Dawn of the Twentieth Century

IN THE SUMMER OF 1898 A GROUP OF PROMINENT DUTCH women held an industrial fair in The Hague, capital of the thriving imperial nation of the Netherlands. Their goal was to showcase the nation's achievements and in particular to display women workers in modern industry, the arts, and crafts. The fair also featured Dutch life beyond Europe, making the exposition an act of national pride—a "national cause," the sponsors called it. Outside the main buildings the fair offered to viewers a model Indonesian village, complete with local peoples imported from the prosperous Dutch colony to display folkways and indigenous life. They played Indonesian music on the traditional percussion instruments of the gamelan, cooked Indonesian food using peanut and other novel sauces, and dyed the celebrated batik fabric under the curious eyes of Dutch and other visitors. Such a display brought the colonies to the *metropole,* or European homeland—in this case the Netherlands. It testified not only to Dutch imperial holdings at the turn of the twentieth century but to the global reach of Europe in general.

International fairs with exhibits from around the world were a regular feature of imperial life in Europe, which defined itself in terms of its global power at the dawn of the twentieth century. Europe's colonial holdings

◆ **Indonesian Women Demonstrating Batik Dyeing**
Much of the splendor of European life in 1900 depended on the importation of resources, including designs, productive techniques, ideas, art, music, and natural materials from around the world. Textile designers were eager imitators of global patterns, and public demonstrations of global knowledge really helped them. The Indonesian women showing how to make batik fabric at expositions such as the one at the Hague in 1898 advanced globalization and fostered European progress. *Courtesy of Universiteit Utrecht.*

abroad during this time were extensive. Great Britain, France, and other European powers controlled great swaths of territory from Africa and the Middle East to India and the Pacific islands. These fairs provided an opportunity to showcase the cultural fruits of empire and often had a profound effect on those who attended them. From the Crystal Palace Exhibition in 1851 in London to the Universal Exposition in Paris in 1889, where the Eiffel Tower was first open to the public, millions of Europeans attended these fairs, often astonished at what they saw. Sir William Gilbert, the English librettist, found his world turned "topsy-turvy" after viewing an exposition that featured Japanese products, and he wrote the renowned operetta *The Mikado* in 1885 in response. Gilbert was among a vast number of Europeans who wove the materials that came from beyond Europe—whether manners, musical sounds, patterns in art and poetry, or products like chocolate—

into their culture at home. In so doing he along with his collaborator Sir Arthur Sullivan became celebrated—both of them knighted by Queen Victoria. Achieved in the metropole, their accomplishments, combined with global expositions of products and folkways from around the world, enhanced pride in the individual nations that exhibited them—whether in Paris, London, Rome, or Berlin. The age of empire in Europe was also a period of soaring patriotism and intense, even militant nationalism.

The world's fairs at the turn of the century took place in a Europe that was modern and complex. The expansion of industry produced class divisions between the wealthy, who sponsored world's fairs, and the workers, who labored in them and who—as in the case of women workers at the fair in The Hague—sometimes protested the long hours and very low pay. From the diamond cutters who processed the gems produced by the Dutch company de Beers from company mines in South Africa to the hands in textile factories, the women operatives displaying their skills at the fair represented the large and vocal working classes of the time. To make matters more complex, gender roles were changing along with the development of this kind of class awareness. The Dutch women who orchestrated this fair were a sign of the gradual evolution of gender roles by which middle-class women were taking on public responsibilities. Changing gender roles and the swelling of working-class protest that veered into calls for socialist revolution and the overthrow of the capitalist system of private property upset many. Thus, although the industrial fair in the Netherlands attracted tens of thousands of proud, admiring, and curious visitors, it inadvertently showcased some of the burning issues of the day.

Even as the fair was in full swing, discontent arose over the economic downturns that accompanied European industrial and agricultural modernization. Not only did hard-pressed workers organize strikes and political parties for working people, but millions migrated to find opportunities elsewhere. New nation-states such as Australia, Argentina, Canada, and the United States attracted newcomers seeking economic opportunity outside Europe. Experiences of migration were not always success stories, however. Many a mournful emigrant from Europe found his or her treatment no better elsewhere, although many millions more were glad to escape. At the Dutch women's fair, the Indonesians who served luscious local food or who played Indonesian instruments fell homesick and demanded to return even before the fair was over.

In 1900, still another international fair took place in Paris to open the new century. Buildings rose to house the exhibition, many of them in the experimental "art nouveau" style that remains a vivid architectural element of the city today. The year 1900 was part of a period that later came to be called the "Belle Epoque" or the "good old days." Europe was at the top of its game. Its prosperity was rising; the bicycle, the telephone, electric appliances, and other inventions were making life even better; and city life offered amusements found in newspapers, café leisure, vaudeville shows, and even the young film industry. Population soared as prosperity helped people live longer.

Yet Europeans, leading the way in inventions and new ideas, were entering one of the most destructive periods in history. As the century opened, militants assassinated a frightening number of heads of state and bombed stock exchanges and other institutions of European power, terrifying the ruling classes. Many nations teemed with militant nationalists demanding more conquests, and relationships among the great powers were increasingly raw because of competing imperial ambitions. Militants and ordinary people in colonized regions around the world chafed with resentment at European pretensions to power, which caused them to explode in violent resistance. National ambitions, bitter differences among classes, and growing violence are as much parts of Europe's story in the early twentieth century as is Europe's prowess in technology and innovation as displayed in the Dutch women's and other festive world's fairs.

EUROPE'S PEOPLES AND NATIONS IN THE GLOBAL ORDER

In 1900 Europe had already embarked on the course that eventually would make it more densely populated and urbanized than any other of the world's regions (see Map 1.1). It had healthy industrial and agricultural sectors, which experienced continuing economic growth despite mounting global competition. Benefiting from sufficient food and from rapidly expanding industrial power, the European population came to live longer but also to demand an even better standard of living. Leaders of the great powers of Europe had increasingly to address working-class aspirations even as they simultaneously engaged in a contest among the nations for the commercial markets and global influence that they believed crucial to maintaining national strength abroad and social peace at home.

Prosperity for States and Society

Industrial and agricultural progress of the previous century formed the backbone of Europe's burgeoning population of 450 million in 1900. Europe's innovators had piled invention upon invention to foster mechanized agriculture; create modern transportation and communications systems; and mount chemical, steel, and electrical power plants—all of which served to support a growing number of people. Advances in medicine increased life expectancy nine years between 1850 and 1900. The largest in Europe, Russian population more than doubled, rising from 73.6 million in 1861 to 165.1 million before World War I. German population also rose dramatically, growing by 25 percent between 1890 and 1910 to reach 65 million. Great Britain's population grew from 34 million to 42 million during the same period. Only France bucked this trend, with a population that had increased only 40 percent over the entire course of the nineteenth century in contrast to the quadrupling of citizens in Britain. France's failure to grow at the same rate as the rest of Europe had several causes, among them its consistently shaky politics, including a series of tumultuous revolutions that began in 1789 and continued for almost a century.

◆ Map 1.1 **Europe in 1900**

Europe in 1900 was a collection of relatively small nation-states that only in the late nineteenth century had become more economically powerful than India and China. Compact and relatively unified, each of the great European powers was armed with destructive modern weaponry and fortified by mass armies. Most rulers believed in their nation's superiority and successfully promoted nationalism among their people.

The European countryside could not absorb the extra population. Machinery reduced the number of hands needed on small farms and large estates alike. Thus, cities like Berlin grew from 1.5 million to 2.5 million between the 1890s and the outbreak of war in 1914, as people sought opportunity in urban life.

Modern industry and agriculture brought unprecedented prosperity, although this prosperity was spread very unevenly among socioeconomic groups or classes. Most European countries had aristocracies with immense privileges and economic wealth, and they not only controlled vast landed estates but under their property lay natural resources such as the ore and coal that industry craved. At the other end

◆ **The Working Poor**
In 1900 the working-class family was often large because health was improving and infant mortality declining. Urban parents used their young children in household tasks such as fetching water, scavenging for discarded goods, and minding young siblings. Concerned about national strength in an age of intense international rivalry, reformers worried about the medical care, education, nutrition, and parenting that poor children received. Many wealthy young adults went "slumming" to fulfill what some saw as the exciting mission of rescuing poor families and instructing them on how to improve themselves. Would you say that this family needs improvement? *Brown Brothers.*

of the social ladder stood the vast majority of Europeans employed on the land, in the mines, and in the factories that processed these materials into goods like steel. It was the ups and downs of advancing industrialization that put people out of work and underemployed them at varying moments in their lives. Out to make profits for themselves, the wealthy classes often paid far less than a living wage to their workers. Even the aristocratic Queen Victoria, who died in 1901 as the century opened, was appalled at the poverty of her people. Early in her regime she had noted on visiting one industrial region: "In the midst of so much wealth, there seems to be nothing but ruin." Depressed at the sight, she remarked on the "wretched cottages" and sickening "black atmosphere" of factory towns in which "a third of a million of my poor subjects" live.[1] Still, the vast majority of the population deferred to the aristocracy and revered the monarchy: the young Queen Wilhelmina of the Netherlands was the prized visitor to the Dutch women's industrial fair.

Europeans were divided by class, and they were also divided into competing nations. Rich or poor, the majority of them inhabited the six major, strikingly different empires that dominated the international scene as the twentieth century opened. Each of the empires actually had an emperor, except for France, which was a republic with a president and prime minister (though its nobility remained rich and influential). The Ottoman Empire, ruled by a sultan from Constantinople, had a system of powerful ministers running different regions of its extensive Mediterranean holdings. France, Germany, Austria-Hungary, and Britain allowed the majority of white men to vote in national elections before 1914, while the Ottoman and Russian empires remained autocracies. The empires of the Ottomans, the Habsburgs of Austria-Hungary, and the Romanovs of Russia comprised mostly adjacent lands, while the French, British, and Germans ruled over territories that were oceans away from the metropole. Smaller states like the Netherlands, Portugal, and Belgium held significant territory abroad. The empires also differed in the extent of industrial modernization and in the size of their armies and navies. The Ottomans, Russians, and Habsburgs lagged far behind their western neighbors. The only common denominator to all the empires was that each was multiethnic and the various ethnicities often were held in place by the threat of force or by actual brutality.

Great Britain: Greatest of the European Powers

Britain was foremost among these powers. At Queen Victoria's death in January 1901, Great Britain claimed to rule 25 percent of the world's landmass and 20 percent of its population. Its proudest achievement was its empire in India, although British colonies in Africa were becoming increasingly important with the discovery of extensive natural resources such as rubber, gems, and gold and other precious metals. Britain also had controlled Ireland for two hundred years and Egypt for twenty, but nationalist movements in each region were rising to contest British exploitation. The need for fuel for home lighting and in the growing automobile industry spawned a drive into the Middle East in pursuit of oil. In the nineteenth century Britain had been an industrial pioneer in textiles, railroads, and metallurgy, and it traded its manufacturing goods around the world in exchange for raw materials. However, despite the imperial quest for raw materials, the British had lost their lead in innovation, falling behind in the advances taking place in electricity, chemicals, and transport. Nonetheless, Britain's worldwide trade sustained the nation's position as the leading global banker, with London an international hub that would remain powerful into the twenty-first century. As control of capital became increasingly important to the progress of industry, Britain's lead in global finance ensured that its upper class would remain wealthy for the entire century, whatever happened to the country's manufacturing might.

Headed by a constitutional monarch, Britain had a well-defined social structure, topped by an aristocracy with incredible staying power despite the wealth of the industrial and financial classes. Its power based in vast holdings of land and political patronage, the aristocracy received excellent government jobs and served at the highest reaches of the imperial services abroad. Decked out in special uniforms—bristling with medals, ribbons, and imperial crosses—the aristocracy enjoyed both the trappings and the high positions of power. Empire thickened the aristocratic crust of society, as the monarchy brought sultans, rajahs, and other high officials outside England proper into its systems of honors, responsibilities, and imperial patronage. Wealthy industrial and banking families were also assimilated into the aristocracy and its values through the marriage of nonaristocratic sons and daughters to titled children of the aristocracy and the constant creation of new peers by the monarch. In this way, as the industrial and manufacturing classes expanded their wealth, aristocracy remained vibrant in England and indeed across Europe, making status and family lineage important values in administering empires. Even the House of Commons, the lower house of the English parliament, was an aristocratic bastion: 75 percent of its members came from the titled class. Thus, although Britain's parliament, selected by the male electorate, appeared representative of the people in its making of laws, it was largely the political arm of a single social class.

Aristocratic political and economic domination made Britain, like other European societies, profoundly conservative. The ruling class tended to value a person's lineage above all else. This aristocracy became, as one English conservative put it, "a fortress of society's security in a changing world."[2] Aristocracies were balanced to a certain extent by a growing industrial culture, which valued individualism, promoted a voice for everyone, and honored individual achievement especially in the form of personally earned wealth. Imperial prejudice on the basis of race as well as rank was part of this system. Even as imperial rulers granted titles and privileges to sultans and other sovereigns in the colonies as a means of cementing a worldwide order of privilege and political status, they considered these colonial elites inferior because of their race. As one aristocrat put it, when setting out for Asia or Africa he felt "very Tory and pre-Tory Feudal"—a reference to the former name of the Conservative Party, which most vigorously defended monarchy, aristocratic privilege, and centuries-old traditional values.[3]

At the other end of the social scale, working-class people, growing in literacy, worker activism, and participation in government, often paid a price for British industrial and imperial expansion even as many proudly supported the imperial enterprise and looked up to their social "betters." Economic downturns struck them hard, and industrial innovation displaced workers, often making their skills obsolete. Many skilled craftsmen were forced to become day laborers and underemployed rural farmhands. Some one million low-paid and often ill-treated workers toiled long hours as domestic servants for the upper classes. Job security became increasingly precarious with the advent of technology and new managerial practices. As a result, unions grew in membership, and in 1900 they helped form the Labour Party (initially called the Labour Representation Committee) to address working people's needs. People left the British Isles in search of opportunity around the world when they failed to find it at home: by the late nineteenth century more people had left Britain than had left any other European country. Others joined the army while many among the middle classes joined the civil service abroad in hopes of bettering their lot in the wider empire.

France: Britain's Rival and Germany's Enemy

Across the English Channel, France was Britain's obvious rival, for the two had fought one another for more than two centuries to gain colonies and global resources. France controlled Indochina—modern-day Vietnam, Cambodia, and Laos—in the Far East, making it a competitor for Asian trade, and it held a rich assortment of colonies in north and west Africa. By 1900 France had sent many settlers to Algeria, which it divided into official French departments, or governing units. Unlike other French possessions, Algeria was considered not a colony but a part of France. The French central government sent officials to Indochina and to France's other overseas regions on deliberate missions to "civilize" the peoples over whom it held sway. The government saw the inculcation of French "values," language, literature, and the history and geography of France as essential to expanding not just its political but its cultural power around the globe.

As this cultural mission expanded in the French colonies, Britain and France struggled with one another for international trade and influence in Africa and the Middle East. In 1898, the two countries narrowly averted war at Fashoda, a village in southeastern Sudan, as the French army's east-west expeditions across the African continent ran up against the British drive to control the continent from north to south—that is, "from Cairo to Capetown," as the slogan supporting British expansion went. On the eve of a showdown, the French and British generals sat together drinking whiskey, awaiting orders from their respective governments about whether to engage in battle. Ultimately French officials decided that war between the two countries would not be worth the price. In the aftermath of this standoff at Fashoda, many observers of the political scene saw the heated global contest between France and Great Britain as the most likely source of any future war. Yet many French leaders harbored a burning resentment against Germany, France's neighbor, which had taken the rich provinces of Alsace and Lorraine after winning the Franco-Prussian War of 1870–1871. French enmity thus swung in two directions.

On the domestic front, the French government seemed perpetually in turmoil, and the French themselves looked revolutionary and tumultuous, having changed the form of their government repeatedly over the previous century. The only major republic in Europe, France had allowed universal male suffrage for more than half a century. Since the French Revolution of 1789, French republicans had tried to counter the centuries-old influence of the Catholic Church by instituting a compulsory and secular public education system and by further democratizing the civil service and armed forces through curtailing the access of royalist aristocrats to preferred positions. As in the colonies, the "civilizing mission" of education aimed to gain the allegiance of a diverse population that spoke different languages such as Breton and northern French dialects and that often favored monarchical rule and the authority of priests over the rule of law. Secular education became increasingly important, for in 1900 France was still emerging from the Dreyfus Affair in which an aristocratic and antirepublican military elite and the Roman Catholic clergy had joined forces in 1894 to convict an innocent Jewish army officer, Alfred Dreyfus, of treason. In the face of actual espionage, the army leadership, representing the old Catholic and monarchical aristocracy, had forged documents and commited perjury to build a case against a Jew. Those loyal to the French republic had with great difficulty defeated these stubborn forces of the old regime, who had aimed to keep their privileges from becoming further democratized while claiming to protect the country from a "Jewish menace." The cost for all involved in the Dreyfus Affair was high: France in 1900 was plagued by civil strife. The upper classes were pitted against one another over Dreyfus, and the socialist parties, with their ideology of an international brotherhood of workers, were winning seats in local and even national government. Steadfast republican anticlericals in charge of the government drove Catholics out of the officer corps and Catholic religious orders out of teaching.

Germany: Europe's Rising Star

The rising star of Europe in 1900 was Germany, and there was hardly a European politician who did not look nervously over his shoulder to see what the Germans might do next. Germany's nationalism, imperial ambitions, and industrial might soared as the century opened. In the Franco-Prussian War of 1870–1871 the modernizing Prussian army had swiftly defeated the French to force all the individual German states into a single national entity (the Second Reich, or Empire). It was not only the French who feared the next move, however. Unification provided the impetus for rapid industrialization, population growth, and colonial expansion, making the Germans rivals to nearly every other European power. By 1900 the Germans were everywhere, establishing businesses in the Ottoman Empire, setting up colonies in East and central Africa, exploring the Pacific, and creating ties with Japan, China, and countries in Latin America. Germany's heavy industry was booming, and Germany was a leader in the production of chemicals, electricity, and new kinds of consumer goods like automobiles, far outstripping Great Britain in adapting to the twentieth-century climate of fast-paced industrial innovation.

Unlike in Britain, where parliamentary rule neutralized the monarchy as a political force, in Germany the emperor, Kaiser William II, and his conservative cohort of aristocrats had the commanding political voice. Their wealth built on vast agricultural holdings and their position guaranteed by high military and government service, these influential leaders found urban life, modern culture, and the elements of liberal democracy such as a free press and elections vile. They despised the increasingly wealthy entrepreneurs who rivaled them, but they abhorred the industrial working classes even more. The Social Democratic Party, which emerged

◆ **Kaiser William and His Entourage**
In 1900 Germany was the European continent's foremost military power. Its standing army was well disciplined; its arms producers were among the most advanced in the world; and the amount invested in new weaponry, battleships, and other military equipment was soaring. German military men had long held important positions as trusted and influential advisers; those most faithful to Kaiser William II are shown with him here. In the first decade of the century, scandal rocked this close-knit and powerful group when evidence of cross-dressing and homosexuality caused the downfall of many of the kaiser's most intimate colleagues. *The Granger Collection, New York.*

in the 1860s to advocate socialism, had become the most powerful force at the polls despite the rigged electoral system in Prussia—the dominant state in the Reich—that apportioned votes by wealth. Traditionalists accepted modern technology only insofar as it would increase military power, linking their interest in battleships, heavy artillery, and modern rail transport to their desire to expand German might around the globe. Likewise they valued the working class only to the extent that it built the weaponry to buttress the military ambitions of the aristocracy. A growing hatred of Jews only added to the profound social tensions in Germany.

Scandal plagued the public legitimacy of this ruling aristocratic class, however. In 1908, Kaiser William II's entourage, comprising the most powerful of these military aristocrats, was dismissed for homosexuality and cross-dressing. These were the kaiser's confidants, and he shared their military values, even to the point of sitting on a saddle rather than a chair when he worked at his desk. William II, related through marriage to most of the ruling houses of Europe, found himself mired in the military's disgrace. Sharing the aristocratic insecurities in the face of modern life, he brashly tried to push Germany into the global limelight, blustering and bullying to acquire world power instead of employing a more skillful diplomatic style. Because of the centrality of Germany's industrial power to its international stature, he, like his preferred companions in the aristocracy, had to accommodate industrial leaders and entrepreneurs. He gave them honors and sponsored the advance of capitalism through colonies and the promotion of international business.

Austria-Hungary: The Clash of Ethnicities

The Austro-Hungarian monarchy to the east of Germany was an empire built on the House of Habsburg, a Germanic dynasty that since the thirteenth century had expanded its holdings in central Europe to include present-day Slovakia, the Czech Republic, Hungary, and parts of Poland. The monarchy and its bureaucracy administered the many ethnicities that comprised it as distinct entities rather than create a unified nation of common beliefs, language, and rights (see Map 1.2). In the place of commitment to a single culture, loyalty during this era went to the person of the emperor, Francis Joseph (r. 1848–1916), who had ruled long enough to inspire obedience if not devotion among his subjects. People remained ethnically defined subjects of the monarch—Hungarians, Poles, Czechs, and Croats, for example—rather than participants in a constitutional union of equal citizens governed equally.

When an industrially and militarily more powerful Prussia had defeated Austria in the 1860s, the Hungarian elite had forced the Habsburg emperor to acknowledge Hungarian wealth by creating a "dual" Austro-Hungarian monarchy that allowed Hungary virtual home rule. As a result, Hungarians had more privileges than the Slavs to the south. The dominant ethnic Germans in the empire, however, had the most privileges of all. What bound these unequal groups together was the ruling Habsburg dynasty. Subjects followed its every move as today viewers follow soap operas, paying particular attention to the glamorous though tragic progress of Francis Joseph's family life. His son, the crown prince, and his mistress committed suicide; his wife, the beautiful empress Elizabeth, was assassinated in 1898.

The empire lagged behind its western neighbors economically, with only a patchy industrial development. The Czechs developed heavy industry, and in parts of Austria proper the ethnic Germans owned and operated textile and other factories, allowing the empire to rival the French and Russians in the production of steel. Other parts of the empire, however, remained steeped in traditional agrarian ways. Industry had not permeated the Habsburg realm in a uniform way but rather was connected to the activities of particular ethnic groups and regions. This uneven development of modern production further marked ethnicities from one

◆ **Map 1.2 Principal Ethnic Groups in Austria-Hungary, c. 1900**
Much of Europe was a mixture of ethnicities, merged over the course of many centuries. People in the Balkans, for example, had intermarried with invaders since classical times, and many Balkan people spoke several languages to deal with the neighbors around them. Yet this map shows distinct ethnicities inhabiting the various regions of eastern Europe. Given this mixture, what accounts for the pre–World War I sense among a great many people that they were "Poles," "Slovaks," "Serbs," "French," or "Russians"?

another, fragmenting political life even more into those with economic wealth and thus political clout and those with neither economic nor political influence. Thus, Austria-Hungary was a dynastic empire in which economic solidarity was elusive and nationalism was a divisive rather than a unifying force because of the empire's many nationalities. Failing to develop either economic or political mechanisms for integrating its multiple ethnicities—as the United States, for example, learned to do—the Austro-Hungarian monarchy was seen as a "ramshackle realm" by the early twentieth century.

Owing to these ethnic divisions and extreme economic inequalities, the potential for social conflict was great, even though the Habsburgs did not covet lands beyond Europe. Some families in Hungary owned hundreds of villages in the confines of a single estate on tens of thousands of acres of land. As elsewhere in Europe, the discovery of mineral wealth on family lands allowed aristocrats to enhance their agricultural wealth with extractive and other industries. Peasants on these estates were desperately poor, their ethnicity used as an excuse for oppression and exploitation. In Hungary, for instance, the upper classes viewed the Croats and Ruthenians who tilled the soil for them as ethnically inferior. Hungarians, also known as Magyars, used the prerogatives they gained not only for this kind of economic exploitation but also for cultural and social dominance over other ethnic groups. Through a policy known as Magyarization, the Hungarians forced the use of the Hungarian language on other ethnicities to the point of forbidding tombstone inscriptions in any language other than Hungarian. Their successes provoked other ethnicities in the empire to demand rights of their own so forcefully that in 1897 the government accorded to the prosperous Czechs rights such as the use of their language in schools and in the civil service. The policy caused riots and further promoted animosity among other ethnicities. Some observers wondered how long the empire could survive intact: "a land of ruins," one high official characterized the Habsburg domain.[4]

Paradoxically, Habsburg bureaucrats saw the solution to their troubles in the expansion of the empire into the Balkans. Such expansion would bring in groups of South Slavs who for centuries had lived under the dominion of the Ottoman Empire. Adding more ethnicities was seen as a way to dilute the power of any single group, especially the Hungarians. Fearing a takeover by the Habsburgs, the South Slavs and other groups in the Balkans sought to block this kind of imperialism *within* Europe. They turned to Russia for support, citing their common heritage as Slavs—a concept known as pan-Slavism. The combination of the Habsburg dynasty's ambitions in the Balkans and Russia's connections to the Slavs increased the likelihood of a clash of empires in the region.

Russia: The Imperial Colossus

Russia, Austria-Hungary's neighbor to the northeast, was a sprawling but even more extensive empire, straddling the Eurasian landmass. Comprising more than 140 ethnicities, Russia had long been ruled by an absolute monarch, the tsar. Nicholas II (r. 1894–1917) firmly believed that God had given him his mandate as tsar of all the peoples of his realm. A leader of limited ability, Nicholas was nonetheless sincere in this and several other foundational beliefs: the centrality of the Russian Orthodox faith, the need to Russify all other ethnicities, and a determined hatred of Jews. Ideas for reform such as the evolution of Russia into a constitutional monarchy with truly representative government or an end to police terrorism, which were occurring to the west, he called "senseless dreams," and on this point most of the powerful members of the centralized bureaucracy agreed.[5]

This bureaucracy, acting as an adjunct to the monarchy to perform all the administrative acts that such an extensive empire required, believed in autocracy as much as Nicholas did, especially given the agrarian foundation of wealth and the illiterate condition of the tens of millions of peasants. Yet oddly enough, this combination of tsar and bureaucracy did not serve Russia well. A more adept monarch might have used his absolute power to effect significant changes, but Nicholas was so convinced of his unique abilities mandated from heaven that he did not. For its part, the bureaucracy continually intrigued its way through policy making despite the skill and sincerity of many administrators who might have helped the imperial order evolve.

Given the rapidly changing conditions of early-twentieth-century life, rule by a bureaucratic autocracy that unleashed pogroms on Jews and sent political activists to lethal prisons had its dangers, and many in the upper classes were all too aware of them. Russia had begun to modernize, building an industrial infrastructure and introducing its agricultural products into the global marketplace. Often industrial workers were treated like prisoners, however, marched to barracks after work under armed guard and then locked in until work began the next morning. Activists with talk of revolution moved among these workers. There were also masses of discontented peasants, burdened with the debt forced on them as a condition of their emancipation in 1861 and tied to the communal agricultural structure called the *mir*. The law prevented them from freely moving from the mir to towns and cities in search of opportunity without permission. Facing the need to improve their land and modernize in an increasingly competitive and global agricultural market, many peasants were open to the influence of a variety of political revolutionaries. One novelist captured the sudden intensity of peasant resentment: "They've fenced in our earth, our mother, with spiked collars and wire [barbed wire]. Sit here, they say, with your rags—there's no freedom for you."[6]

Not only workers and peasants but also members of the rising industrial and commercial bourgeoisie chafed at their lack of influence and at Russia's glaring political and administrative backwardness. Even within the bureaucracy itself there were liberal reformers, albeit conservative by Western standards, who admired what they saw in their travels to Germany, France, and Britain. Visiting Germany, one high official found "the Germans have a calm, even attitude to business, they are orderly both within and without, disciplined in their habits, their minds and their hearts."[7] This report was in marked contrast to the generally held view within the aristocratic ruling class that Russia was spiritually more advanced than the money-grubbing, egoistic, and unruly industrial societies in the rest of Europe. The health of the Russian Empire thus depended on a precarious balance of social forces. On the one hand, autocratic, police-state rule kept a population that was being buffeted by change submissive, while on the other hand, the push of economic and social modernity kept those same people open to rebellion.

The Ottoman Empire: Sick Man of Europe?

The Ottoman Empire, in contrast to the other imperial regimes, appeared to be openly disintegrating, mostly at the hands of European imperialism and the incursions of Western business. Indeed, observers dubbed it "the sick man of Europe," highlighting how far this empire's fortune had fallen compared to the fortunes of its neighbors to the west and north. Its apogee had come several centuries earlier, when it comfortably controlled parts of southeastern Europe, western Asia, Asia Minor, and North Africa, including Egypt—all of these constituting parts of a single multiethnic empire. Its subjects excelled in crafts and trade, while the government itself tolerated all ethnicities and religions. Late in the eighteenth century, the empire's weaknesses became glaringly apparent with the Napoleonic invasion of Egypt followed by British pursuit of Egyptian cotton and other raw materials once Napoleon had been driven from the scene. In the nineteenth century, the Ottoman Empire, ruled by the sultan from Constantinople, had surrendered most of North Africa to the Europeans, while the eastern Mediterranean was fast becoming a European sea. Under the nationalist banner, Greece and Serbia gained their independence in the first half of the century while Austria and Russia worked to erode Ottoman strength in southeastern Europe in the second half. Despite efforts to modernize its administration and economy, the Ottoman Empire was defeated in the Balkans by the Russians and Balkan nationalists in the Russo-Turkish War (1877–1878), after which the Congress of Berlin of 1878 confirmed the independence of Serbia and Montenegro and recognized Romania and Bulgaria as free states. Austria-Hungary received the right to administer Bosnia-Herzegovina, and secret accords gave France and Britain the right to colonize Tunisia and Egypt respectively.

Defeat at the hands of the Russians forced the sultan's hand internally. He granted a constitution, broadening the access to power by elite groups. Despite the slow erosion of the empire's political cohesion, Ottoman culture developed the accoutrements of modernity—an active press, nationalist movements for independence, railroads, and a thriving commerce, much of the last, however, financed and controlled by European powers. Pan-Arab and pan-Islamic movements took shape in the modern ferment stirring across the Ottoman lands, and these movements also threatened the cohesion of the empire's various religions and ethnicities. A distinctly Western urbanism flourished: Cairo and Constantinople had lively business and intellectual elites, and chic clubs, theaters, nightspots, and other secular institutions mushroomed in the cities. Watching the West, a feminist movement also arose, while the multiplicity of ethnicities and the wealth generated by straddling commercial crossroads made Ottoman culture among the most cosmopolitan and sophisticated in the world. As the traditional trading prowess of Ottoman subjects adapted to the demands of the European-dominated global commerce, the pull of modernization and nationalism pushed both the people and the institutions of the Ottoman Empire toward transition or decay—depending on one's point of view.

SOCIETY IN THE AGE OF EMPIRE

Whether laboring on a sugar-beet field in northern France (see Document 1.1) or lounging in a Viennese coffeehouse, Europeans across the continent participated in an interlocking global economy. Steamers covered the world's oceans, transporting people, manufactured goods, and raw materials. Although there had been global economic interactions along Indian Ocean, trans-Saharan, or central Asian routes for millennia, the scale of early-twentieth-century trade was unprecedented, and the interdependence of people thousands of miles from one another was more pronounced. Economic cycles of booms and busts circled the world: people around the globe had felt the downturn of the last quarter of the nineteenth century from which the economy recovered early in the twentieth century. Simultaneously the benefits of trade were global, as traders from every continent had opportunities for profit and cultural contact. Except for the railroads, large ocean liners, and some heavy industrial machinery, there was no simple divide between regions that exported only raw materials and those that had technology. Japan produced many of the same goods that the European powers did; India, China, and Africa had had a long lead in textile production over the West; the engineering of roads and bridges was known globally; and advanced art and architecture existed almost everywhere. These techniques and products circulated worldwide more thoroughly than at any time in the past, although some groups of people living in remote regions still had little direct contact with international trade and culture.

Social and Cultural Influence of Empire

Because of this diversity, empire transformed European habits and ways of life even as it transformed the lives of those Europe colonized. Sheer military might enabled European empires to maintain colonies across the globe; seizing land and controlling trade enriched many Europeans and exposed them to a wide array of goods. (See the Picture Essay.) At the highest ranks of society, the rich enjoyed more gold, diamonds, and other precious gems from newly opened African mines. Queen Victoria—at one end of Europe—gave cashmere shawls from the Indian subcontinent's province of Kashmir and other imperial products as gifts, and she employed Indian soldiers as her honor guard. At the other end of Europe, the Russian imperial palaces featured Turkish lounges and Chinese summer houses filled with Chinese furniture. In Germany, palaces housed porcelain rooms to display coveted dishware and figurines from the Far East, and lodges and chateaus alike featured trophy rooms displaying the mounted heads of exotic animals shot on African or Asian hunting trips.

The fruits of empire transformed life lower down on the social ladder as well, especially eating habits. Diets in early-seventeenth-century England, for example, were based mostly on beef, beer, bread, and cheese. Ordinary people at the beginning of the twentieth century enjoyed coffee, tea, sugar, potatoes, tomatoes, and other foods that did not originate in Europe. The poor ate an orange as a great treat and even enjoyed the occasional chocolate candy. Cookbooks for middle-class households featured an ever expanding list of raw ingredients and foreign dishes. Coconut cakes and pies, chutneys of dates, mangoes, and pineapples, meat and fish curries, corn puddings and bread, gingerbread and candies, rice-based main dishes and rice puddings had all entered the middle-class diet, and this nutritional variety offered by food products from around the world improved health.

Influences from outside Europe had a long history, extending from the food that was eaten to household furnishings, but now they affected even the lower classes because industrial prosperity increased Europeans' buying power and the number of things they owned. Dishware that could withstand the heat of tea and coffee at first came from Asia and was later imitated by Europeans. Copying Asian techniques, European potteries arose in vast numbers to meet a huge demand for dishes—called "china" for good reason—and employed tens of thousands of workers. Sofas, ottomans, and divans—comfortable, cushioned furniture—were also imported from abroad and later became copied and mass-produced in European factories and workshops. Oriental carpets and imitation ones were prized, as were lacquered furniture, African statuary, and decorated screens from Japan. Potted palms, a large variety of trees and shrubs, and the very flowers that decorated homes and gardens came from beyond Europe for the most part. In fact, decorative gardens except for medicinal herbs were nearly unknown until the iris, tulip, lilac, rhododendron, and many other species reached flower-poor Europe in the sixteenth to nineteenth centuries. Greenhouses, based on architectural designs and engineering knowledge from southwestern and southern Asia, were attached to homes of the wealthy, while nurseries and scientific farms built larger greenhouses to improve the food supply and to extend the growing season.

By the twentieth century most Europeans had access to cotton clothing, thanks to the textiles that first came from Africa and Asia. Brightly decorated, lightweight garments became available only after sustained contact beyond Europe, and these textiles caught the public imagination. Muslins and chintzes joined the taffetas, satin, and mohair that had originally come from beyond the West. Cotton, however, was destined to become the most useful and popular of these fabrics. By the early twentieth century an indigenous cotton industry, begun in Britain, had spread to Poland and other parts of eastern Europe, although in rural areas people continued to spin and weave flax and wool by hand. More lightweight than other fabrics and easy to wash, cotton spawned the use of changeable underwear, bed linens, dishtowels and dustcloths, and a variety of other products that contributed to increased longevity through better hygiene, especially in the twentieth century. Palm, coconut, and other oils from Africa allowed for the making of soap that operated to the same end. Rubber from Africa and Asia, newly vulcanized after the middle of the nineteenth century, protected Europeans from the wet and cold in the form of raincoats and galoshes. The same rubber made possible some of the new machinery that ordinary people enjoyed—bicycles with rubber tires and sewing machines run with rubber belts.

Daily Life and Leisure Time

Contact with the rest of the world had helped form the public sphere and especially shaped the phenomenon of growing leisure time that accompanied the development of industrialization. In imitation of non-Westerners, Europeans imbibed foreign products like coffee and chocolate in public spaces such as cafés and tearooms, where they discussed current affairs and news. Café life was so booming as the century opened that it was a favorite theme of artists and photographers. These coffeehouses imitated those first found in parts of the Middle East, while the new department stores of the late nineteenth century—a standard feature of urban life in the twentieth—took as their model the massive bazaars found in thriving Middle Eastern cities. Workers with increased leisure time spent Sundays in public gardens, many of them modeled after Chinese gardens. Vincennes Park in Paris, the Prater in Vienna, and the gardens of Drottningholm in Sweden contained winding pathways, irregularly shaped lakes, and craggy rock formations—all in imitation of Chinese landscapes. As further evidence of the Chinese inspiration, most of these pleasure gardens offered merry-go-rounds, an array of stone seats, and small gazebos or other miniature buildings that invited people to quiet contemplation.

Nations prided themselves on their global accomplishments, showcasing imperialism in a variety of ways made for the newly leisured citizenry. Zoos increased in number and in size, displaying animals captured around the globe. Anthropological, colonial, and natural history museums offered exhibits on the evolution, customs, arts and crafts, and living conditions of the world's peoples. Strollers in botanical gardens like those at Kew looked at offerings from around the world, and world fairs were incredibly popular.

Daily activities centered on celebrating empire in even more direct ways. Schoolchildren in Britain observed Empire Day—in fact, Queen Victoria's birthday—and school curricula taught children national histories built on pride in conquest of peoples seen as inferior. Everyone celebrated empire: observances of Empire Day were held in Hong Kong, Lagos, Nairobi, Montreal, and Sydney—all of them part of the extensive British holdings. More mundane activities also bred a greater degree of cosmopolitanism among Europeans. Non-Western classics like *Tales of the Arabian Nights,* the *Rubaiyat of Omar Kayyam,* and the *Kama Sutra* were translated for a varied readership. People relaxed with imported games of checkers, parcheesi, polo, backgammon, and mahjong, and playing cards—a widespread pastime that had also come from China some centuries earlier. Music halls featured humorous or patriotic songs about the progress of explorers and armies. Operas—a popular art form among all classes—centered on characters from Japan, China, Egypt, India, and a variety of other non-European locales. *Aida, Turandot,* and *Madame Butterfly* were but some of the favorites. Popular entertainment such as Gilbert and Sullivan's *Mikado* gave Europeans hummable tunes mimicking foreign melodies.

Ideas from around the world saturated high culture, providing its verve and innovative edge. The operas of Richard Wagner had become the backbone of the German repertoire and even promoted German nationalism. The most popular, such as *Tristan and Isolde,* featured lovers going to their death gladly as they believed that the consuming fires of their passion would take them to a higher, purer realm. Wagner and other composers took this motif from Hindu beliefs surrounding the Indian custom of cremating corpses on funeral pyres, sometimes with wives willingly joining their dead husbands in the flames. Famed artists, using print techniques learned from Japan, created bright poster art that advertised cocoa, soap, vaudeville shows, and steamships while their high art, whether painting or sculpture, by the end of the century had come to borrow the compositional style and colors of Japanese prints or African sculpture. The French composer Claude Debussy, who had heard Indonesian music played by the gamelan at the Universal Exposition of 1889, reworked his own musical scores to make them less lyrical in the Western manner, instead adopting the gentle, circular, repetitive music of Asia. As other composers followed Debussy's lead, musical forms from

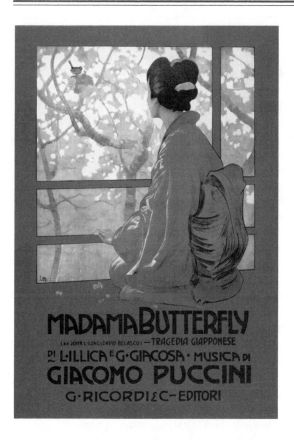

◆ **Poster for the Italian Production of**
Madame Butterfly
Giacomo Puccini's opera *Madame Butterfly* premiered
in Italy in 1904, enthralling audiences with its lyrical
music accompanying the tragic love story of an
American sailor and a Japanese woman. Europeans
flocked to performances of *Madame Butterfly* and many
other theatrical and musical productions describing
encounters of Westerners with people around the world.
Puccini would later compose *Turandot,* a story set in
China, for which he drew musical inspiration by
listening to a Chinese music box. *Photo by Buyenlarge/
Time Life Pictures/Getty Images.*

around the world definitively made their way into European compositions in the
twentieth century, forever transforming the musical arts.

European architects drew on designs from other countries, borrowing Chinese
wooden cutwork on buildings to create the gingerbread on Victorian houses. The
glass and iron railroad stations and domes of department stores derived from
Middle Eastern and Indian engineering of light and airy glass supported by delicate iron ribs adorned with arabesque designs. By the beginning of the twentieth
century, several other global styles were shaping new construction projects, primarily in cities. Urban apartment houses—in Latvia's capital, Riga, or in Paris, for instance—adopted the curving arabesque lines of *art nouveau,* a style that featured
floral patterns, leaves, vines, and other graceful ornaments from nature in imitation of Persian, Arab, South Asian, and Japanese models. The avant-garde of
European designers, however, turned from these ornate patterns to those of Japan,
favored for clean lines and structural simplicity, right down to the joints and other
details of construction. A few neighborhoods in Bucharest, Paris, and Vienna
started to adopt the plain, geometric forms found notably in Japan but also in the
architecture of North and sub-Saharan Africa.

EUROPE IN AN AGE OF MIGRATION

The expansion of the European powers produced worldwide economic change that had a dramatic effect on the lives of families and communities. More food, improved sanitation, and better medicine boosted the population beyond what the traditional farm community could support, helping to cause a wave of migration both within and out of Europe. Diasporas of Italians, Slovaks, Irish, and other Europeans took shape in both the Western and the Eastern hemispheres. Some hard-pressed peasants turned against their neighbors, inflicting violence especially on Jews and minority ethnic groups in their communities. Jews by the millions thus joined the migration, and European families fanned out around the globe. As the century opened, then, dramatic changes in the structure and size of the population posed dilemmas, resulting in one of the most extensive migrations in human history.

Changing Families and Family Economies

In the past, the farm family had taken pains to limit fertility to correspond to the low population levels that traditional agriculture could support. Late marriage, abstinence, and even infanticide were all methods of population control. High infant mortality rates also kept the size of the population down. But the nineteenth century saw an accelerating increase in population in villages and cities alike due to a better standard of living that improved longevity. Better sanitation because of safer water supplies and sewage removal cut down on water- and waste-born illnesses. A new understanding that germs produce disease led to such benefits as the pasteurization of milk, the use of antiseptics to treat wounds, and the sterilization of medical instruments. Europeans had many more products and a larger food supply thanks to their access to goods from around the world. Rubber from the Congo, for example, provided condoms that helped cut the alarming spread of venereal disease. Soap, as noted earlier, added to personal and household cleanliness that also reduced the occurrence of illness. Although childhood diseases like measles and whooping cough remained killers, infant mortality declined by 10 to 20 percent across Europe. These improvements almost single-handedly produced Europe's population boom. This boom in turn pressed hard on the resources of rural families and communities.

Interestingly, the boom in population was accompanied by a trend toward limiting the size of families that would continue throughout the coming century. Whereas the middle of the nineteenth century saw families of six or more children, at the beginning of the twentieth century many urban couples, particularly in western Europe, were reducing the size of their families to four children. In most cases the rise of the middle and professional classes encouraged this trend. These families were upwardly mobile, did not need large numbers of children to work fields or perform artisanal labor, and wanted to protect family resources. For example, simply educating a middle-class child was growing more expensive as secondary school and even university training became prerequisites for a successful career and even—in the case of women who remained at home—for the education of one's own children in the early childhood years. Urban working-class families tended to reduce family size more slowly, for children performed useful household work such as fetching water and earned money for the family economy by taking jobs at a relatively early age.

Whatever one's family size and circumstances, the global economy of which Europe was now a driving force had dramatic repercussions on ordinary household economies. While more and varied products improved the quality of life for many, competition from global forces brought hardship to many families, especially those engaged in agriculture and other rural occupations. By the early twentieth century, grain and other agricultural products from the United States were driving down prices for European produce, causing distress in Russia, Prussia, and other areas where innovation had not reached. The introduction of refrigeration late in the nineteenth century also drove down the prices of local goods as it allowed meat and other perishables to compete across vast distances. All this reduced the cost of food and other necessities for city dwellers but hurt the rural family, whose income dropped. Textiles and metal products from around the world competed with local goods, as did raw materials like iron, copper, and tin. Also, the global population explosion that was building steam drove down the price of labor in some occupations and sectors of the economy, especially as large numbers moved from farms to cities, from country to country, and from continent to continent. Paradoxically migration also helped ease the crisis in the family economy caused by globalization.

Regional Migration and Urbanization

Although migration has existed over millennia, in the twentieth century it amounted to a flood, especially from the most agricultural parts of Europe such as Russia, Austria-Hungary, Scandinavia, Ireland, and southern Italy. As population expanded because of increased longevity, rural areas became overcrowded and unable to support their inhabitants. A large percentage of agricultural workers was simply superfluous, given the efficiencies provided by new equipment such as mechanical reapers and dairying machines. Local artisans faced daunting competition from large-scale manufacturing of shoes and tools. Some artisans and agricultural workers sent their daughters away to work in textile factories to help support their own way of life as farmers or craftsmen, proletarianizing them. While sons often remained at home to keep the farm or the trade within the family, huge numbers of both women and men left the countryside to search for work in the city. Cities thus absorbed some of the rural poor, making internal migration on the continent a striking feature of early-twentieth-century life. For example, Poles lived as a divided ethnic group in Russia, Germany, and the Habsburg Empire before World War I, and 80 percent of the ten million who migrated between the end of the nineteenth century and 1914 went to large Polish cities such as Warsaw or to prosperous regions of Germany to find work. Only 20 percent went abroad to the United States. Not wanting to quit farming or their traditional crafts, four million peasants and artisans in the western Russian empire migrated, with government encouragement, to Siberia, Turkestan, Kazakhstan, the Transcaucasus, and other areas newly accessible to them by road and train. These and other migrants also hoped for opportunities in mining, metallurgy, and other industries that were part of Russia's ongoing attempts at modernization.

Newcomers swelled the size of cities, and urbanization began to tip the balance against the countryside. The agrarian way of life lost its dominance as an oversupply of rural workers was drawn to the city in search of a livelihood. Berlin in the first decade of the twentieth century reached close to four million inhabitants. In 1856 there were fewer than six million people living in Russian cities, but by 1914 there were more than twenty-six million, the bulk of them in Moscow and St. Petersburg, though Kiev, Riga, Baku, Odessa, Tiflis, and other cities also were thriving. In northern Italy, Milan, Turin, and Genoa formed a concentration of industrial cities, attracting workers from the countryside to their automobile and textile factories, the latter coming to surpass French cotton production. Villages like Bilbao in Spain grew into industrial centers as deposits of iron led to rapid development at the turn of the century of both mining and metallurgy. In the distant past, the population in China's cities had passed the million mark. For Europe, the early twentieth century was the great age of urbanization, with more and larger cities exerting their pull on rural peoples.

Global Migration

The globalization of markets thus brought the globalization of labor in the form of migration. The global economy that drove people from their traditional livelihoods also offered opportunities for work in more distant parts of the world, inspiring a growing trend toward transnational migration beyond Europe. Myths of gold-paved streets in Sydney, New York, or Buenos Aires circulated in remote villages among populations that often had no source of information other than rumor. These myths made certain areas—notably Canada, the United States, Argentina, Australia, and New Zealand—magnets for emigrants (see the Picture Essay, Figure 1.6). For example, in the first decade of the twentieth century alone, some two million people left Austria-Hungary for the United States. When relatives or fellow villagers moved to a certain region across the seas, others tended to follow the same migratory path.

Migration was also a big global business built on a network of entrepreneurs needing labor for railroads, road-building projects, and industry. Shipping lines, government officials, and various other institutions, such as churches concerned with the well-being of parishioners, facilitated the transcontinental movement of workers. Adding to the incentives and to the distorted reports of easy wealth, their agents—more than five hundred in southern Italy alone—traveled to the most impoverished and isolated regions to sign up workers. Agents aimed to fill specific occupational needs, such as finding young women for domestic service or recruiting young men for construction work, or they simply received bounties from companies for a designated number of healthy and able recruits. The early-twentieth-century literature from eastern and southern Europe abounds in criticism of recruiting agents who broke up families with promises of easy wealth. "We could pay off our debts," a mother is first persuaded by the agent to believe in the 1909 Slovak novel *The Magnet-like Country*. But after her son goes off to America, no money ever materializes.[8]

Political as well as economic circumstances swelled the tide of migration from Europe. Many in the Austro-Hungarian monarchy fled brutal treatment by Hungarians bent on Magyarizing the other ethnicities in their region. Jews were forced out of Russia by late-nineteenth-century legislation forbidding them to live in Moscow and St. Petersburg. In the fifteen years before World War I, some 2.8 million Russians migrated to North America, 1.1 million of them Jews. Although many Jews with professional and business skills were welcome to take part in Russia's drive to industrialize and modernize, others faced incredible poverty because of the limited amount of lands Jews were allotted and because their artisanal occupations were under attack from industrialization. Jews faced pogroms and other forms of violence and discrimination because of rising anti-Semitism, and this situation caused Jewish intellectuals to advocate *Zionism*—the movement to establish a Jewish state. Russian and Austrian competition over the Balkans drove people from the region.

The imperial powers also sponsored migration—for instance, offering tracts of land to Europeans willing to settle in Algeria, Indochina, and elsewhere. In the aftermath of the South African War (discussed later in this chapter), the British government hoped to break the back of Boer claims to power by encouraging emigration, especially by women, whose presence as wives and mothers would encourage permanent settlement and produce children who would become "loyal subjects of the crown." Without women, officials declared, the men who had flocked to the area to obtain wealth "would remain transients and do nothing to ensure the future loyalty of South Africa."[9] Encouragement for women to migrate was couched in terms of their high-minded contribution to national well-being. "The *man* can conquer and subjugate territories in the world for the German idea," one woman journalist claimed, "but only the persistence of *woman* can implant and preserve the German idea abroad over the long term!"[10]

Both global and regional migration affected family life, gender roles, and individual well-being. Migration was often seasonal, or it involved temporary relocation for a five- or six-year period. In hard times, regional migration often entailed backbreaking agricultural work: members of an artisanal family in northern Europe whose livelihood in weaving was precarious because of mechanization worked as seasonal laborers in rural sugar-beet fields (see Document 1.1). The children, of nursery school and primary school age, worked alongside their parents so relentlessly that they were usually too tired to eat at night. Community leaders sent Russian youth to cities to work in factories, but they were obliged to return home to do fieldwork in the summer and help bring in the harvest. A household economy thus continued to exist even when children moved away and even when they crossed oceans. Young men from Sicily and from Croatia, Dalmatia, and other areas of the Balkans would migrate to the United States to earn enough money to marry a predetermined fiancée, to provide a dowry, or to buy available land when they returned. In these cases, the migrant was still considered part of the extended family, even being consulted on decisions in his absence. The "golden dollars" helped Europeans remaining behind survive the agricultural crisis brought on by global competition. Around the turn of the century, Italy's emigrants sent an estimated 100 million dollars to Italy—an incredible sum that went toward alleviating the poverty in the southern region of the country.

Still, despite the economic rewards migration could bring, many recruits experienced the modern conditions of migration as the most brutal time of their lives. Russian workers arriving from the countryside lived far from families, packed together in slumlike barracks, with meager food and iron discipline. Entering the United States or other farflung ports of call was usually a chilling experience, for a person's name could be changed, an immigrant could be subjected to quarantine, and various agents and agencies sought to profit from immigrants' dislocation by paying low or even no wages at all for their work. Unless a person migrated within an extended family or ethnic network, his or her native tongue, agricultural skills, and artisanal know-how were often useless, even laughable. Thus, reports of economic hard times elsewhere and of the exploitation of immigrant labor around the world emerged. "Our fate is no better here," one Slovak worker wrote from the United States. "The life of a poor worker is the same everywhere."[11]

Nonetheless, migration within and beyond Europe continued on a vast scale in the twentieth century, creating a culture of flexible people able to adapt to a broad range of work opportunities. When money was returned to the family back home, it often had transformative power, allowing women to set up small businesses or buy more property and helping children to improve themselves by staying in school instead of trying to find work. Providing wider knowledge of the world and money to build family resources, migration despite all its difficulties proved a mighty tool of economic growth.

NATIONALISM AND THE EVOLVING NATION-STATE

Even as the European continent experienced the force of globalization, the countries that composed it were at the apex of their power, and people's commitment to the nation-state often grew along with the expansion of national might. For some five hundred years, European states like France and England had consolidated their administrative, political, and economic rule, spreading the state's authority and unifying various peoples. The central government made mounting demands on its people through a growing bureaucracy of competent administrators. For example, the civil service of would-be great power Italy went from 50,000 employees in 1861 to almost 378,000 in 1910. Throughout the nineteenth century, European states claimed new prerogatives and had continued to add to the central government's regulatory and taxing powers. For instance, roadways went from being private to public thoroughfares, and censuses, fingerprinting, the issuing of passports and work permits, the setting of criteria for citizenship, and the regulating of labor all became governmental tasks. The state increasingly came to sponsor and regulate education so that citizens could better understand their responsibilities to the nation as a whole and support the government that ran it.

The Growth of Nationalist Feeling

The early twentieth century saw the rise of nationalist feeling that increasingly was more than simple patriotism. In the eighteenth century, people had been loyal subjects of a king; by the twentieth century, Europeans shared a greater sense of commonality as citizens of a nation. In eastern Europe people still expressed loyalty to a monarch or dynasty, but this loyalty was tempered by various national groups' recognition of their common origins, traditions, and languages.

The French in the late eighteenth century produced an early justification and explanation for cohesive nation-states. Emerging after the French Revolution of 1789, this early nationalism centered on pride in the rule of law embodied in France's Declaration of the Rights of Man and its Napoleonic Code. In contrast to the arbitrary rule of aristocracies and monarchs over subjects, these fundamental laws and principles stated that everyone enjoyed the same rights as citizens, had the same duties to the state, and would suffer the same consequences in case of crimes and misdemeanors—all because an overarching nation-state stood watch over those laws in the name of all citizens. In France, the modern concept of "citizenship," defined in law, replaced unquestioning subjection to a king or to a privileged aristocracy and became one foundation of modern nationalist sentiment.

In reaction to what at the time seemed a radical formulation, German states and other countries advanced ideas of citizenship based on common blood or ethnicity. The traditions, shared history, and common sentiments of people of the same ethnicity provided a counterweight to the human rights and legal traditions. Both Italians and Germans had unified in the mid-nineteenth century around the idea of shared blood and shared history, Italians pointing to their roots in the Roman Empire and the Germans invoking the medieval empire of Charlemagne, and it was this countervailing notion that added a layer of complexity to the twentieth-century understanding of nationalism.

At first the state did not demand that the various peoples it brought under its dominion surrender their own identities, be they religious, local, or ethnic. However, the modern "nation," as opposed to a kingdom, required not only administrative integration but social and cultural integration as well. By the early twentieth century, nation-states were working in various ways to achieve it. Within the Russian Empire were more than a hundred ethnic groups. The tsar's government attempted to impose unity on them through Russification. This policy entailed promoting the Russian Orthodox religion, the Russian language, and Russian culture through strict programs in schools and churches. Changing traditional cultures and patterns of everyday life proved difficult, if not impossible, however, in so diverse an empire. Russification on the empire's western borders in Poland, Ukraine, and Finland, and to the east and south in central Asia with large

◆ **German Olympic Athletes**
The modern revival of the ancient meeting of athletes in the Olympic Games took place in 1896 in Athens, Greece. The sponsors intended to highlight international cooperation and to mute increasingly militaristic nationalism. Critics judged the physical competition among national teams as a less lethal form of warfare, but a preparation for war nonetheless. Which interpretation does this picture of German Olympic athletes in the 1890s suggest? *The Granger Collection, New York.*

Turkic populations, faced serious challenges. Educated Jews preferred the German Empire's emphasis on secular culture, philosophical thought, and classical literary artistic values to the emphasis in states like Russia and Austria-Hungary that promoted religious culture—Russian Orthodoxy or Roman Catholicsm—to achieve unity, for one by-product was violent anti-Semitism.

Most Western governments gradually introduced compulsory public education, which built secular skills such as counting, reading literature, writing, and the basics of being a citizen. Education taught peasant, migrant, and working-class children the ways of the industrializing and commercializing world: how to tell time; how to figure the cost of individual items; how to measure; how to calculate interest on a savings account. Citizens came to believe that they owed it to their government to develop skills that would allow them — and their country — to get ahead. But there was more than one path to this modern knowledge. In an attempt to build on the formidable strength of Islamic schools in many of its Asian sectors, the tsarist government of Russia introduced Russian-language instruction and the teaching of math and science alongside religious training. In contrast, the French republic in 1905 drove Catholic teaching orders from the country, so threatening did republicans believe religion to be to democratic and modern institutions and especially to the advance of science and technology.

Schools were pillars not only of modernity but of nationalism. Knowledge of the basic laws of the state helped forge a civic identity and a sense of belonging. In schools most children learned a standard set of customs such as rituals of politeness and hygiene. They studied their nation's history — much of it consisting of the monarchy's deeds and the state's important wars. A sense of belonging was fortified by learning geography — not only the outer boundaries of the nation but the distinctive features of individual cities and regions within the nation. "My child," began one grade-school geography book, "you should love France because nature has made her beautiful and her history has made her great."[12] Finally, schools taught a national language to peoples who most generally as the century opened spoke dialects of Italian, German, or French. Memorizing poetry or reading prose classics, students confronted an enduring abstract beauty that was said to resemble the destiny of the nation.

Patriotic songs, military parades through capital cities, and the construction of monuments and public buildings provided recognizable signs of national unity. The Russian emperor Nicholas II patronized such events as Borodino Day, which celebrated France's failure to conquer Russia in 1812, and he sponsored the Russian Boy Scouts to build their civic pride. The Germans celebrated Sedan Day in commemoration of Prussia's victory over the French in 1870, an event that led to the formation of the German Empire. Those peoples aspiring to independent nation-state status worked to invent similar traditions through the recovery of folk songs and folklore, which intellectuals then published and political groups sang or recited.

The South Slavs of Serbia, Bosnia-Herzegovina, and Croatia, for example, chafing under Austro-Hungarian domination, celebrated songs, poetry, and sculpture depicting a history distinct from that of their Habsburg rulers. So important did national culture become that Austria-Hungary stymied the display at the 1911 Rome exhibition of the Croatian artist Ivan Mestrovic's "Kosovo Temple." The design for the temple commemorated the heroic resistance of South Slavs in a famous battle against the Ottomans in 1389. As one patriot put it: "What the pyramids were for the Egyptians, pagodas for the Indians, the Parthenon for the Greeks, the Coliseum for the Romans, what the Gothic cathedrals were for the Middle Ages, the luxurious palaces for the Renaissance, what the National Gallery is for today's Englishmen and the Louvre is for the French, that is what Mestrovic's temple is for the Southern Slavs."[13] From London to St. Petersburg common rituals, symbols of unity, and sites of national pride worked their nationalizing magic, integrating many ethnic groups but also setting them against others.

The Nation-State versus the Ethnic Nationalism of Minorities

A unifying force early in the nineteenth century, nationalism spontaneously became a powerfully divisive force as the twentieth century opened. The nationalism of the dominant group in a nation often confronted the fierce separatist nationalism of smaller groups submerged in the nation. Nationalism fortified ethnic groups to resist states like the Habsburg Empire, and it developed a unified national ideal among people of the dominant ethnicity, such as the English, who ruled over the Irish, Welsh, and Scottish ethnicities. Because the dominant ethnicity in the nation-state ruled in its own interest, often denying political power and economic opportunity to other ethnic groups, minorities like the Irish, Czechs, Poles, and Croats organized pressure groups demanding everything from full independence, to home rule, to economic justice.

In some cases, such as that of the various ethnic Slavs of the Austro-Hungarian monarchy, pressure groups sought transnational unity. The ethnic Slavs, all the while demanding greater ethnic autonomy in the Habsburg Empire, looked to the Slavic powerhouse, Russia, as a possible unifier of all Slavs and thus their liberator from the ethnic German domination of the Habsburgs. In the Ottoman Empire, which was not a nation-state as the century opened, an administration that had traditionally let ethnicities go their own way in religion and language as long as taxes were paid on time soon felt nationalist pressures from the various ethnicities of the Balkans—many of them demanding independence or the right to merge with other Slavic groups.

The resistance of minorities to the advance of the nation-state opened the century and remains a powerful, even determining force in European history. In Russia, Ukrainians, Poles, and other groups each built a nationalist base, hoping to win independence to the west of the empire. To the east, the Tatars and other (usually Islamic) peoples along the Volga, along with Koreans, Japanese, Mongolians and peoples of the Far East, and the northern peoples of Siberia, were also actively asserting their ethnic rights against the expanding Russian central government. In the vast area conquered from the sixteenth through the late nineteenth century, Russification as a strategy to create unity was complex and hotly disputed. Russian Orthodox missionaries, often acting on their own, aimed to convert minorities from Islam. However, resistance to Russian cultural nationalism was growing. The early twentieth century saw massive rates of return to Islam, the perpetuation of Islamic dress, and growing contempt for Russian culture in favor of tribal dress and grooming. Even the local clergy who had been converted to Russian Orthodoxy, according to one observer, were unable to keep their relatives from returning to Islam. Why is it, a baffled Russian priest asked, that "the hearts of Tartars are not touched by the sound of church bells?"[14] The Russian case well indicates the difficulties a central government might encounter in its effort to create a uniform, single culture for the modern state.

The Growth of Militant Nationalism

Another type of nationalism had as great an impact as the welling up of powerful ethnic identities across Europe. This was the increasing tendency to consider the nation-state's military power and the exercise of that military power against other nations as nationalism's primary purpose. A century earlier, nationalism was a concept implying unity among citizens on the basis of shared rights or cultural or ethnic solidarity. By the twentieth century, nationalism had become the stuff of power politics and a means by which politicians whipped up the masses to support arms buildups and imperial rivalry. According to this emerging definition, people existed as a nation in order to dominate other nations and to exercise power on the international scene. Increasingly nationalism was acquiring a military cast as the realization grew that a unified army of soldiers wielding the latest military hardware could win the imperial game, conquer more territory, and provide citizens back home with more goods to enjoy.

Popular culture made heroes of colonial warriors, adventurers, and military leaders. Advertising was developing at the time, and it too touted fighters and nationalistic wars: an ad for a particular brand of scotch whiskey in 1900 featured military leaders such as Lord Kitchener and General Buller and other newsworthy fighters in the colonies seated somberly around a whiskey bottle in an informal war council.[15] A war spirit associated with imperialism was building even as ads showing soldiers consuming beverages, cigarettes, and other products increased sales of those products (see the Picture Essay, Figure 1.4). For every newspaper article conveying the horrors of colonial warfare there were other articles glorifying soldiers and the military and increasing the acceptability and normality of war for the average reader.

In this charged, nationalistic, and empire-building atmosphere that Europeans sought to integrate diverse groups of non-European people. The process involved coordinated military and nationalistic development. The goal was for far-flung peoples to acquire a feeling of belonging to a mighty empire sufficient to make them want to give their lives for the conquering imperialists. The imperial nations made local officials in Africa and Asia into administrators for the empire, and they built mass armies of indigenous men, who learned to shoot their own people with the same powerful European weaponry that had enabled imperialists to take over these regions in the first place. Improving ports and harbors and building railroads facilitated the rapid deployment of troops, the movement of goods to market, and the rapid spread of Western culture and ideas. Because Europeans had amassed capital from the profits of domestic industrialization and international trade with a growing number of regions, they could afford not only to build railroads and support armies but to pour in the vast sums of money needed to develop mines in Africa and plantations around the world. Guns, steamships, and railroads used to create empire were sources of pride and power, not only to Europeans back home but to a certain segment of the colonized population.

EMPIRES IN JEOPARDY

Empires expanded in these prosperous times, as governments, adventurers, and traders sought greater wealth and influence. In this climate the perils of empire grew (see Map 1.3). Despite evidence that some colonized people at the highest reaches of their respective societies profited from political and economic connections with the imperial powers, resistance in the colonies mounted. International competition also plagued every attempted conquest, and as the twentieth century opened, the powers were almost daily mired in struggles to control lands and peoples.

Conflict and Conquest in Africa

In 1899 Britain became engaged in a shockingly bloody, even desperate fight for control of South African wealth—principally in diamond and gold mines and other natural resources—against descendants of Dutch settlers called the Boers. The Boers, who controlled the Transvaal and the Dutch Free State, ruling over a number of African groups including the Zulus, contested the arrival of adventurers from Britain and elsewhere who hoped to share in South Africa's bounty. Cecil Rhodes, a talented and ruthless adventurer backed by accumulated capital that could develop the mines, had tried to stir up a war in hopes that the British could lay claim to the Dutch-held lands. In 1896 the Boers easily routed a dispatch of Rhodes's raiders, leading to the outbreak of the South African or Boer War in 1899. Both sides used African troops; the British also brought in the Indian colonial army. Outnumbering the Boers by seven to one, the British nonetheless struggled to win. The Boers engaged in simple guerrilla-style warfare, taking advantage of their knowledge of the territory and the British lack of a planned-out offensive.

The war dragged on, causing unease and even outrage in Britain. The foreign correspondents who flocked to South Africa reported appalling bloodshed, heavy casualties, and the unfit condition of the average British soldier. Most alarmingly to those who liked to think of Britain as the most civilized country in the world, news arrived back in London of rampant disease and the inhumane treatment of South Africans, who were being herded into a new institution—the concentration camp. The concentration camps alone became the graveyard of tens of thousands,

▶ **Map 1.3 Europe in the World, c. 1900**
Europeans controlled colonies in many parts of the world. Their military prowess and cheap products helped them advance as traders, while individual Europeans became wealthy through investment abroad. Is the vast range of colonization historically understandable as the natural undertaking of countries with military power? Does the extent of European colonization look to be an example of overreach?

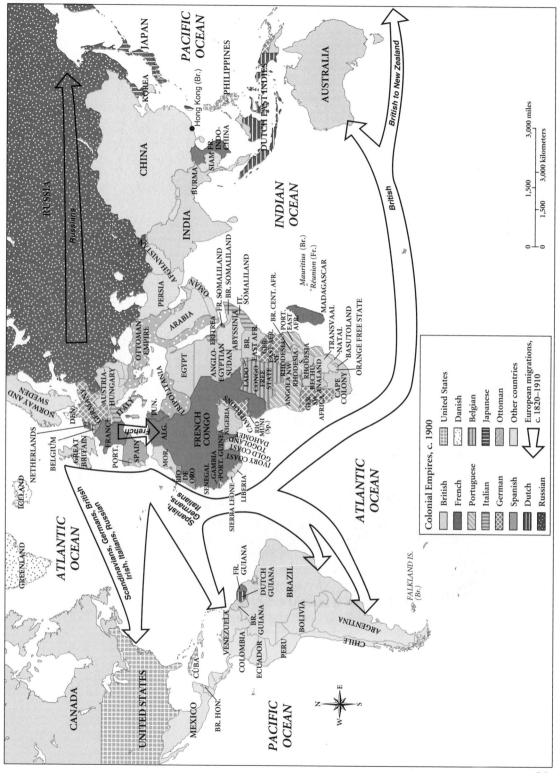

Colonial Empires, c. 1900

British
French
Portuguese
Italian
German
Spanish
Dutch
Russian

United States
Danish
Belgian
Japanese
Ottoman
Other countries

European migrations,
c. 1820–1910

ATLANTIC OCEAN

PACIFIC OCEAN

INDIAN OCEAN

GREENLAND

ICELAND

CANADA

UNITED STATES

MEXICO

BR. HON.

CUBA

COLOMBIA

VENEZUELA

ECUADOR

PERU

BOLIVIA

BRAZIL

FR. GUIANA

DUTCH GUIANA

BR. GUIANA

CHILE

ARGENTINA

FALKLAND IS. (Br.)

Scandinavians, Germans, British
Irish, Italians, Russian

Spanish, Germans, Italians

NORWAY AND SWEDEN

NETHERLANDS

BELGIUM

GREAT BRITAIN

DEN.

GERMANY

FRANCE

AUSTRIA-HUNGARY

ITALY

PORT.

SPAIN

MOR.

ALG.

TUN.

TRIPOLITANIA

RIO DE ORO

SENEGAL

PORT. GUINEA

GAMBIA

SIERRA LEONE

LIBERIA

IVORY COAST

GOLD COAST

TOGOLAND

DAHOMEY

NIGERIA

CAMEROONS

RIO MUNI (Sp.)

FRENCH CONGO

ANGOLA

GER. SW. AFRICA

SW. RHODESIA

NW. RHODESIA

BECHU ANALAND

CAPE COLONY

ORANGE FREE STATE

TRANSVAAL

NATAL

BASUTOLAND

GER. EAST AFR.

BR. EAST AFR.

PORT. EAST AFR.

BR. CENT. AFR.

CONGO FREE STATE

LADO

UGANDA

ABYSSINIA

ANGLO-EGYPTIAN SUDAN

EGYPT

ERITREA

FR. SOMALILAND

IT. SOMALILAND

BR. SOMALILAND

MADAGASCAR

Réunion (Fr.)

Mauritius (Br.)

OTTOMAN EMPIRE

ARABIA

OMAN

PERSIA

AFGHANISTAN

RUSSIA

Russians

INDIA

BURMA

SIAM

FR. INDO-CHINA

CHINA

Hong Kong (Br.)

KOREA

JAPAN

PHILIPPINES

DUTCH EAST INDIES

AUSTRALIA

British to New Zealand

British

PACIFIC OCEAN

0   1,500   3,000 miles
0   1,500   3,000 kilometers

N E S W

33

and some people in England began to worry about the daily threats to international peace and about the barbarism that increasingly accompanied imperialism. Critics, such as members of the vocal socialist parties of Europe, called imperialism "a policy of robbery and conquest." Even so prominent a member of the establishment as the British poet Rudyard Kipling, author of the poem "The White Man's Burden" (see Document 1.2), condemned the bluster and bragging of imperialists. "Recessional," a much-recited poem of his, set British world dominion in a succession of doomed empires and called on a higher being to protect the British from their many follies: "For heathen heart that puts her trust / In reeking tube and iron shard, / All valiant dust that builds on dust, / And guarding, calls not Thee to guard, / For frantic boast and foolish word— / Thy mercy on Thy People, Lord!"

Imperialism brought an ever rising level of violence against the indigenous peoples of Africa. Between 1904 and 1907, German inroads into East and Southwest Africa provoked local resistance to the unfair trading practices and outright confiscation of property. The Germans countered this resistance with the best

◆ **Starving Hereros**
In the first decade of the twentieth century the German army drove the Herero people from their traditional lands, leaving them to starve. The tactic of leaving people without basic means of support and shelter was used during this and later periods against Armenians, Russian peasants, Jews, and other ethnic and religious groups. Anti-imperial activists produced this photo as well as others documenting atrocities across Africa. Does the origin of this photo in a human rights cause reduce its reliability as evidence? *Permission of the publisher, Cornell University Press.*

in weapon technology. In East Africa, where the Germans were trying to gain control of the local ivory trade, enforce the growth of cotton, and collect money through levying taxes, local peoples united in 1905 to stage an uprising against German attempts to take their resources. The Maji-Maji revolt, so named after the magic water the Tanzanians hoped would protect them, ended in massacre and German destruction of all villages, crops, and other provisions, leading to famine and near genocide.

Between 1904 and 1906 the Germans pursued a similar policy of devastation against the Herero people, who resisted the inroads on their cattle trade and grazing lands in Southwest Africa. German soldiers wielding machine guns mowed down the Hereros—a tactic that one German general defended as an appropriate display of "iron firmness."[16] Although exact figures are uncertain, the Herero population was reduced from about one hundred thousand to approximately eight thousand, the survivors driven from their territory (see Document 1.3). The colonial powers' use of mass slaughter has led historians to see imperialism as the training ground for future devastating wars and genocide of the twentieth century.

The Russian and Ottoman Empires in Crisis

Russia's main vehicle for expanding and consolidating its empire was the railroad, and the construction of a trans-Siberian line brought the country into a catastrophic confrontation with Japan—itself a rising imperial power. Sergei Witte, minister of finance under tsars Alexander III and Nicholas II, provided the major rationale for modernizing from the top down. Descended from colonizers, Witte firmly endorsed colonization and economic development, primarily to strengthen the autocratic state. A transcontinental railroad would open markets and reverse the power equation between Russia and powers to the west. Once built, he maintained, the railroad would make Russia the dominant market in the world: "The silk, tea, and fur trade for Europe, and the manufacturing and other trade for the Far East, will likely be concentrated in Moscow, which will become the hub of the world's transmit movement," he predicted.[17] Nicholas II, like his counterparts across Europe, was an enthusiastic imperialist. In the Russian case, the tsarist state rather than a variety of individual entrepreneurs such as Cecil Rhodes directed economic modernization and imperial expansion.

The trans-Siberian railroad provided a different benefit when the tsar's government decided to move peasants—some five million between 1890 and 1914—from western Russia to Siberia. The hope was that as the peasants intermingled with indigenous peoples, not only would the Tatars and other ethnic groups become Russified but these remote regions would benefit from the infusion of true Russian stock. Russian imperialists used the same justification employed by white settlers in the United States as they moved westward and occupied Indian lands: it was said that these "open" or "empty" lands would suddenly be populated and made fruitful. The government of the tsar thus designated millions of acres of land used by the nomadic foraging peoples of central Asia for Russian, Ukrainian, and Belorussian settlers. Schools and churches went up overnight, and agricultural experts took on the assignment of replacing foraging traditions with market agriculture, advancing the economic as well as the cultural Russification of Siberia.

This expansion both disturbed local peoples and inflamed international politics. Passing through Manchuria, the trans-Siberian railroad alerted Japan and Britain to the extent of Russian ambitions in Asia and especially in the Far East. Matters came to a head in the winter of 1904 when the Japanese, smarting not only from Russian expansionism but also from great-power interference in the region, attacked and defeated the Russian Pacific fleet at Port Arthur on the Liaotung peninsula. The trans-Siberian railroad, whose development had provoked the Japanese in the first place, now proved its incapacity to meet wartime demands for transport: it could not move sufficient troops and supplies rapidly enough or efficiently extricate the wounded. The trans-Siberian railroad was too poorly built for heavy use. Shoddy construction caused the infrastructure to fall apart along the length of the railroad and obstructed the war effort. In 1905, the Japanese defeated the Russian Baltic fleet at the Tsushima Strait, effectively ending the war (see Document 1.4).

The shock of Russia's defeat was worldwide, and Russia itself erupted in revolution. Colonized peoples reveled in Japan's victory, which seemed to promise that non-Westerners could defeat the great powers. Ordinary Russians were crushed by the sacrifices they bore to pay for the collapsing war effort, and one Sunday in January 1905 a crowd of protesters gathered outside the tsar's Winter Palace in St. Petersburg to make the tsar aware of their distress. Instead of allowing the people to express their grievances, troops shot into the crowd, killing hundreds and wounding thousands. In spreading the news of this and other resistance to increasing wartime burdens, the railroad proved all too efficient. Hearing of the massacre of "Bloody Sunday," urban workers rebelled, striking over wages and factory conditions and demanding parliamentary representation. They organized workers' councils called *soviets* to set their own policies. Violence escalated: in February, the tsar's uncle, Grand Duke Sergei, was assassinated; in June, sailors on the battleship *Potemkin* mutinied; in the fall, railway workers struck, bringing transportation to a halt; and the Baltic states, Transcaucasia, and workplaces in Moscow broke out in rebellion. The tsar's policy of sending his troops to assault protesters only provoked more activism.

The Revolution of 1905 forged an alliance among artisans, industrial workers, peasants, professionals, and liberal members of the upper classes against the autocracy represented by the tsar and the most privileged aristocrats. Amid the tide of rebellion, wealthy liberals from the local councils and the well-educated elites demanded the creation of a constitutional monarchy and a representative legislature to replace the autocratic government. They also wanted an end to censorship and to public scrutiny by the secret police. Nicholas refused, hoping that the military could restore order, but continuing protest and social chaos forced him to create a representative body—the Duma. Although few Russians could vote for representatives, the very existence of the Duma along with the lifting of censorship prompted the creation of political parties, promoted open discussion of political matters, and liberalized the atmosphere somewhat.

Japan's victory over Russia inspired further opposition to the status quo and caused modernizers outside Europe to believe that they too could bring about change. After a period of reform in the Ottoman Empire, Sultan Abdülhamid II (r. 1876–1909) had turned back the clock by canceling the constitution and thus restoring power to his personal coterie. In response Turkish modernizers, many of them in the military elite, staged a coup in Constantinople in 1908, driving out the sultan and his retainers. "The whole empire burst forth in universal rejoicing," an American missionary on the scene in Beirut reported. "The press spoke out. Public meetings were held, cities and towns decorated, Moslems were seen embracing Christians and Jews."[18] Like the Japanese with their interest in the rapid modernization of Germany, the Young Turks, as the new rulers styled their group, turned westward, employing borrowed German funds, partnerships with German businesses, and ties with the German government to strengthen the economy and thus their hold on power. Aiming to build Turkic might, the Young Turks had no interest in the self-determination of other peoples in the Ottoman Empire. Instead, wherever possible the new ruling group repressed demands for a greater say in government and greater autonomy.

The success of Turkish nationalism aroused a range of feelings among the Muslim peoples controlled by the Russians. Educated in Muslim schools, residents of the Crimea and central Asia found themselves drawn to pan-Islamic and pan-Turkic movements though they shunned outright activism. Pyotr Stolypin, Russia's new minister of the interior, feared "a national revival" that was spreading "in the building of mosques even in the smallest villages, as well as the opening of schools and the publication of literary works."[19] Even though the Muslims launched no movements during the 1905 Revolution, Stolypin and other members of the tsar's government saw the development of pan-Islamism and pan-Turkism as a looming menace, to the point of forbidding the teaching of "modern" subjects — seen as frightening in themselves — in Islamic schools. Tsarist Russia added a heavy dose of repression to its half-hearted postrevolutionary reform. The sum of these policies did little either to improve the political climate or to provide more effective institutions of government.

CONCLUSION

Russia's defeat by Japan in 1905 marked a major turning point in world events — one that reformers in Asia and Africa hailed as a sign of their own future freedom. "We who are hated as cowards and imbeciles," one Indian paper wrote, "are proud of this triumph of the East in its terrible struggle with the West."[20] Imperial Europe was on notice; its right to control the world's peoples and cultures, under challenge.

The globalization of trade had made many Europeans wealthy, and control of the terms of trade had generally improved Europeans' standard of living. Yet the spread of prosperity and power was uneven, not only abroad but in Europe itself, leading to migration in search of economic and political opportunity. The division of society into classes remained highly visible despite migration, even though class divisions were often downplayed in calls for a common nationalism that would transcend the socioeconomic divide. Various types of nationalism swept across every level of European society, bringing calls for imperial expansion, ethnic independence, and military buildup. Russification was the way in which one central government tried to foster national allegiance and unity.

Russia was not alone in facing political and social challenges. Revolution and violence were widespread as the century opened. Enjoying the fruits of empire, the peoples of Europe wanted more—more democracy, more territory, and a better economic future—from their aristocratic elites. Non-European peoples in the rest of the world wanted the same. Having imbibed nationalism from Europeans, they were laying the groundwork for challenging the imperial powers, and this resistance added to the pressures that would test imperial Europe. The progress of modernity in combination with international rivalries made the opening decades of the twentieth century both highly combustible and dense with amazing inventions and rapid social change.

DOCUMENTS

Migrant Life in 1900

A
T THE TURN OF THE CENTURY, Europeans' lives followed a less professionalized
path than they do today, and there were fewer if any of the health, educational,
and unemployment benefits to provide a safety net to meet the hazards ordinary
people faced. In this document, Marie-Catherine Gardez, born in 1891 in the north
of France, recalls the challenges encountered and the resilience shown by her family struggling to survive at the turn of the century. Gardez went to work in earnest
when she was ten, after four years of schooling. The family occupation was hand-
loom weaving, and even though Marie-Catherine, two of her sisters, and both parents worked at it, the Gardez family could not fully support itself by this trade
alone. While the Gardez produced fine quality handkerchiefs and household
linens, which they sold to a wholesaler in town, their goods could not compete with
cheaper factory-made textiles.

Many such seemingly outmoded occupations remained even up to the middle
of the twentieth century: handcutters of velvet, individuals who specialized in
slaughtering pigs, workers in slate, and many more. Such artisans pieced their income together by doing odd jobs in villages near and far. Credit from local merchants allowed the Gardez family to survive until summer, when they traveled several hours to eastern Normandy to work on sugar-beet and wheat farms, where
they performed menial but necessary tasks. Migrant labor was specialized in its
own way, as Marie-Catherine Gardez's encounter with the reapers shows. At the
end of the summer the family received a collective payment, which allowed them
to pay their bills from the previous winter.

Each member of an artisanal family had a well-defined role and followed traditional rituals and behavior, and this document makes clear the importance of
children to the family economy. Even though France had imposed compulsory education in the 1880s, the state simply could not enforce its policy when families
needed children to make ends meet. For the rest of her life, Marie-Catherine
Gardez worked, no longer as a weaver but as a domestic on a farm and at various
odd jobs.

A French journalist who made Gardez's acquaintance in a nursing home in the
1970s recorded this account of her life. When reading Gardez's recollections, consider what features of the modern world are reflected in them. Gardez's account is
based on her memories, some of them more than fifty years old. This raises questions about whether we can consider oral histories reliable as evidence of past
experience. "Even today . . . there is nothing better than the chicory of my memories," Marie-Catherine Gardez observes.

Document 1.1

MARIE-CATHERINE GARDEZ SANTERRE
Oral History, early 1970s

. . . Everyone in the village wove during the winter months for eighteen hours each day. Once I had finished my schooling, I too had "my" loom. (Being the youngest, I had the most opportunity to go to school, and I went for [four] years.) I was still so tiny when I first wove that I had to have wooden "skates" attached to my feet so I could reach the pedals. My legs were too short!

We got up at 4:00 in the morning, each day. We washed with water that came from the court fifty meters away, where a well served all the families in our *coron,*° and dressed. Hop! we went down the ladder to the cellar, with its two coal-oil lamps. In the meantime, my mother lit the round stove that heated the main room. The stove had niches in its main section where we could warm our frozen feet when she called us, around 10:00, to come upstairs and get our "coffee." It was a long time to wait after waking before we got our hot drink, so it seemed delicious to us.

Even today—really—there is nothing better than the chicory° of my memories. While we were weaving, Maman straightened the house, scoured the floor, scraped the table with a shard of glass, threw fresh sawdust on the tiles, and boiled potatoes. At the same time, she wound the yarn we would weave the next day onto bobbins that fit into our shuttles. My sisters and I wove linen cloth for handkerchiefs, which we rolled into bolts. My father, who was stronger and more skillful, made wider pieces of linen. These wide lengths of cloth

were more difficult to manage, but much sought after at that time.

Come Saturday, we would run one at a time to the merchant's agent, a neighbor in the *coron*. We tried to waste as little time as possible. He would collect our completed work and pay us for it. My earliest memory is earning two francs a week. When my handkerchiefs were perfect, as I learned to make them, the boss gave me five sous for a tip. Later, I earned up to five francs a week. But I always ran home and gave the money to my mother. My sisters would go then, one after another, and finally Papa, to take their work and get their pay.

We couldn't make ends meet with these pitiful earnings. All winter long, we lived on credit. Only when we came back from the season in the country were we able to pay our bills. Each year we worked for six months on a farm in the Seine-Inférieure, far from home. . . .

. . . One day my father announced that I knew enough and that I would have to work at a loom like my two sisters.

That was the end of my lazy mornings. No more sleeping until 7:00. I began my difficult apprenticeship when I was only knee-high to a grasshopper. For eight years, and after, when I was married, I took my place in the big cellar, which was only dimly lit by coal-oil lamps. Later, these were replaced with kerosene lamps.

In the cellar there were four looms, two on one side and two on the other. The big one was reserved for Papa; my sisters and I worked on the three smaller ones.

My sisters Emérance and Anatolie were the only ones still at home. My brother Léandre and all the others were married. Their names were Louise, Zulma, Palmyre, Lucie, Edwige, Espérance. . . .

It was a long trip to the department of the Seine-Inférieure, where we went to work. We paid

---

° *coron:* A small row of houses.
° *chicory:* A perennial herb, cultivated for its edible leaves. The dried, roasted, ground roots of this plant are used as a substitute for coffee.

SOURCE: Serge Grafteaux, *Mémé Santerre: A French Woman of the People,* trans. Louise A. Tilly and Kathryn L. Tilly (New York: Schocken, 1985), 6–7, 14, 18–28.

four francs each for the train, and I remember we changed at least twice on the way.

People often ask why we didn't stay and work on the farms in the region where we lived. It was impossible, because the farms there weren't big enough. Near Avesnes, the properties were tiny; they had been subdivided many times, and the farmers could barely live on what they grew. The proof was that every now and then they had to slaughter an animal, butcher it, and sell it in order to make ends meet.

Because there was no work closer to home, we had to emigrate in the month of May. For us kids, the move to new horizons was a joy, but for my parents, what a pain! They had to pack our baggage. Each of us had a bundle of clothes, larger or smaller depending on the size of its owner. Papa and Maman were weighed down like donkeys. Maman hid a little gray purse in her corset, in which she kept the family money. She rarely had more than three or four francs left after we paid for the railroad tickets. Sometimes we had to borrow to pay for the tickets and send a money order when the farm at Saint-Martin reimbursed us for our voyage, which was part of the deal.

. . . All the families left together, or almost together, for the big farms in Normandy. They were expected. Most of them—families like ours that were serious and hard-working—returned to the same farm year after year. In those days we didn't bother with the paperwork that people do today. A person's word was as good as a signed contract. Of course, under these conditions we couldn't be too particular about our pay. But sometimes we managed to get a little more money for a little less work.

There would be a long procession of us walking to the nearest railroad station, which was at Cambrai, twelve kilometers away. Every morning, a horse-drawn cab, which we called "the mail," would go by, but it cost too much. Papa said, "When you're lucky enough to have good legs, you ought to know how to use them. Carriages are for the rich, my little ones; walking will give you round calves so you will find good husbands more quickly."

So we walked with our bundles on the ends of sticks, and it seemed a long, long time before we could see the clock tower of the town in the distance. When we finally arrived, we settled in the railroad-station waiting room and devoured two hunks of bread that my mother had spread with plenty of fresh white cheese. This was washed down with a cup of clear water dipped from the station's fountain in the freight room. Then the train would come puffing in. Each father would settle his brood as best he could. As we pulled out of the station, our heads instinctively turned back toward our village, already far behind. Our feelings were divided between our anticipated joys in the country and the sorrow of leaving home.

Avay was a village in the Seine-Inférieure with houses clustered around its church and cemetery. The Saint-Martin farm where we were going to work was about a kilometer from the village. We were thankful that it wasn't farther, because we had to attend mass and vespers there on Sunday. During the harvest or the sugar-beet–picking season, we sometimes missed church when our work was pressing. The priest told my father that we were excused, for God preferred strong people who missed mass because of their work to those weaklings who went because they didn't know how to use the ten fingers He gave them. Nevertheless, Papa hated not being able to go to church on Sunday. "It seems like I'm missing something to make my joy complete," he would say to Maman. . . .

As soon as we got out of the four-wheeled carts that met us at the Dieppe railroad station, we had to move into the lodgings that were assigned to us. We would live there for the next months. Our home was smaller than the one in Avesnes. The beds were squeezed one against the other because each family lived in a single room. Sometimes there was a wood stove; sometimes a fireplace. Maman always went directly to that part of the room, because it was "hers." There she would cook the vegetables for our meals. We had to buy these vegetables, in addition to bread and cheese. The farmers gave us bowls of a good thick soup made from meat at noon and in the evening. Sometimes we even found little pieces of meat in the soup. They were good but, unfortunately, we didn't find them very often.

Before my marriage, five of us worked: my father, my mother, my sisters Emérance and Anatolie, and I. Other families had more workers. Seven or eight children would go to the fields, even the little ones. Papa said it was shameful to put five- or six-year-olds to work. "There is a time for everything in life," he explained. "Just because a father was forced to work with kicks on the behind at an early age, he shouldn't do the same to his little kids." In our family, we waited until we were eleven, because he said that that was quite young enough.

The Saint-Martin farm produced only wheat and sugar beets. It belonged to a big company in Paris which owned many farms throughout France. We only saw the agent, who wasn't a bad sort. Anyway, for most of the work, it didn't matter. We were paid by the job, for example, for the wheat harvest. The more one did, the more one got. And each person in a family had to work his own assigned plot of ground. We were paid by the row for thinning the sugar beets and by the pound for the harvest. Wheat was toted up in bales, made up of two sheaves. We were paid by the day only for working in the farmyard or house and for spreading night soil.

We received our entire pay when we left in November. It was a substantial amount of money, as much as we ever saw at one time. In some seasons, we had to ask for small advances in order to pay for our vegetables, bread, and lard. Families that liked fancy living got many advances, so they didn't receive much when they left. "When one drinks wine, when one smokes, you can't make it," said Papa. "Also, you must have the luck of marrying a thrifty wife, which is rare," he added. Maman blushed under her piped bonnet at this indirect compliment, one of the few he paid her.

That year, like all the others, we moved in and started to work the very next day at 6:00 A.M. I could never believe the extent of the fields, which seemed to spread on forever. At the beginning of May, they were covered with fine green sprouts. Wheat fields undulated in the distance. These were the fields that we would keep free from thistles. We sliced through the thistles with one clean blow of the hoe; they would ooze a greenish milk from their sliced stalks. "That's good for colic," Maman said.

Marcel, the surveyor, would arrive at the same time as we, with a clinking of rods against his hundred-meter iron chain. He surveyed each plot of the field to be harvested. When we had finished our plot, three, four, or five days later, the agent would inspect to see that the work was done thoroughly and to record the number of the field and plot. Then we knew that we had earned forty sous. But we had to have all the pricklers killed. If one thistle was still standing, the agent complained loudly.

In some families, he was called "the big squealer." I noticed that he hardly said anything when inspecting our plots. There was never a thistle left. That was because Papa made us understand that no matter what we did, we had to do it well. No doubt it's because of this that the company employed my parents, and later me and my husband, all our lives, with no complaints about any of us. Still, this sort of work was hard for a little girl! When I saw the plot I was assigned, it seemed as if I would never reach the end of those long, long rows.

Once we got to the end of a row, we had to turn right away, without standing up. From time to time I stopped to look at a bird or to observe a motionless toad in front of me, staring at me with gold-circled eyes. The toads bothered me. It seemed that they were there to watch me. But Papa didn't tolerate daydreams. He would bring me back to reality. "Your sister will finish her plot before you if you laze about like that all the time," he would yell. He didn't say it meanly and his tone was never angry. He just said it, but that was enough to get my hoe moving again, chopping each green thistle with one clean blow.

Around 10:00 A.M., everyone stopped for a bit. From our smock pockets we would pull out pieces of bread, spread with the cheese Maman made from the whey the farm sold her. A mouthful of warm chicory, drunk from Papa's canteen to wash it down, and we resumed work until noon. Heat or rain never stopped our work unless it rained extremely hard or there was a thunderstorm. . . .

After chopping out the thistles, a job which lasted to the end of May, we had to remove rocks from the same wheat fields where we had spent the preceding weeks. The stones that threatened to dull the sharp blades of the scythes had to be picked out of the earth. We placed them in baskets that we carried on our backs and emptied into the nearby roads. There they helped the oxcarts get through the mire of wet weather. This job, too, was long, tiring, and monotonous. When we reached the end of the field, the road was far off and we had to jump over the furrows, straining under the weight of the basket, to avoid crushing the tender, green shoots. We dared not trample the shoots! We knew that in August they would be big stalks heavy with grain that was made into flour and then bread. And bread was precious and good.

Gathering the stones was poorly paid, exhausting work, but my sisters and I weren't in a hurry, because what followed was even worse. Papa wasn't that cheerful either when he announced in the evening, "Tomorrow, my little ones, we begin spreading fertilizer." The fertilizer, what a nightmare! Of all the things I've had to do in my life, none took so much out of me. The oxcarts would arrive in a long parade, beginning early in the morning—slowly but surely. They had left in the night for the railroad station at Dieppe, where night soil would arrive by the carload. The oxen would stolidly pull them to the fields where we would be waiting for them. Once there, they turned off the road and, with their necks extended and eyes bulging out of their heads, pulled their heavy loads into the cultivated fields. Their drovers spurred them on by yelling,

"Ah oua, my big Clairon! Come on, dia Alexandre, my good beast!"

The carter would quickly pull out the pin and release the wooden bar so that the dump wagon could tip its evil-smelling contents into an enormous pile that it seemed we could never finish spreading. It had to be spread with pitchforks. The whole family worked together on this job. That way, each cartful was spread out more quickly.

When we returned, exhausted, we still had to face the ordeal of the pump. Maman washed us with green soap right in the trough to remove the long dirty streaks from our short legs. Despite this scrubbing, our evening soup didn't taste very good. An awful odor of spoilage, of rot, stuck to us. It still filled our nostrils long after we had finished that foul task.

When it was done, Papa would say to Maman, "Well, Marie-Catherine, we worked hard; with the manure-spreading we will pay the baker's accounts when we return." In fact, we did earn more for manure-spreading, so we were satisfied that we were helping pay for the six-pound loaves. . . .

A couple of days before the harvest, strapping, hairy men arrived at the farm, talking and laughing loudly: they were the reapers, come from Flanders, with their scythe blades, gleaming like silver, in their sacks. They would sharpen them with sweeping strokes against the whetstones which they soaked in horns full of water attached to their waists. They brought not only their blades, but also the wooden handles which shone like waxed furniture, worn smooth by their hands.

One of the reapers explained to Papa that these tools were precious. Without his own scythe, the best reaper was clumsy. By balancing his tool, before beginning, he could find the curve in the wood that the left hand melded to, while the fingers of the right hand fit into the little indentations that hours of work had worn.

We were always a bit scandalized by the life of the reapers, always ready with an off-color joke. The seasonal laborers didn't like to leave their wives and daughters alone for long when the reapers were around, for fear they would prowl into the farmyard. At the farm, they all lived in the same barn, sleeping in the straw. In the morning, they would sing while they washed and shaved at the pump, splashing themselves with water. They sang a lot and ate as much. The farm fed them, and we were stunned to see how much they ate at a single meal.

In the morning, they had large bowls of coffee and milk with bread and cheese when they rose. At 8:00, they had a thick, boiling soup; then, at 10:00, small loaves of bread and meat washed down with beer. At 1:00, their lunch would consist of salt pork, boiled potatoes, an enormous quantity of cheese, and a pot of steaming coffee. In the afternoon, around 3:00, they returned to the farm for big loaves of bread sliced into enormous salad bowls of raw milk. And at 10:00 P.M., when work ended, they dined—with meat, eggs, and broth this time. It looked like an orgy to us, who were not used to such quantities of food!

But reaping was grueling and difficult work. The farmers paid well because, as they said, "a good reaper is not easy to find." Those big, laughing, blond men were solid as rocks. In the evenings after dinner, as they smoked their pipes in the farmyard, they still had the strength to sing the songs of their homeland in rough and joyous voices.

My father respected the reapers. He admired their spirit, although he himself was no sloucher, of course. His only reservation was that they were too inclined to fool around with women. He never approved of that.

Although they went to bed late, they were up promptly and faithfully at their posts the next day. Lined up in rows like a battle formation, they were ready to go as the skies brightened after dawn. At the signal of the foreman, they began to cut the golden waves of wheat. Their scythes flashed in front of them like shining dancers; as they sliced the stems, there was an odd, whistling sound. They stopped from time to time; the whetstones resonated clearly on the metal that each reaper

honed in his own way. Then the ballet would continue, the sharpened scythes whistling even more beautifully, continuing their work among the heavy golden stalks.

Ah, the reapers! I missed them when they left never to return. They were replaced by the enormous mechanical beast that arrived in later years. It did the work of ten reapers. But it didn't sing! When I walked behind the machine, I was deafened by the noise of the knives coming and going and nauseated by the smell of the gasoline that the driver poured into the green-painted flanks of his machine.

For the moment, though, we seasonal laborers followed the reapers across the long fields of wheat. Sometimes "mine"—the one who preceded me—would turn toward me after sharpening his blade and smile under his blond mustache. "*Godfordom!* You aren't very big for this sort of work!"

And it seemed that he sometimes went more slowly on purpose in order to give me time to catch up. I gathered all the wheat that he cut into big armfuls, which were called sheaves. With two sheaves we made a bale, which we tied together and dragged to a stack where the wheat dried.

We worked quickly in order to avoid being outdistanced by the great devils moving so swiftly ahead of us with the whistling, crunching sound of the blade on the wheat. When I could overtake "my" reaper, I was very pleased. I played a game that flattered me. I wasn't tall or well-rounded for my thirteen years, but I imagined that, if he slowed down, it was because he was in love with me! The poor man! No doubt his thoughts were far from that sort, but this little romance made my work less tedious. Sometimes I got so close to him that I smelled the strong odor of sweat from his naked and muscle-knotted torso. When I stopped for a breath, I watched his muscles ripple with the movement of the scythe, in perfect harmony with the tool. Then suddenly, ashamed of watching him like that, I would blush and bend quickly to gather the wheat. . . .

QUESTIONS FOR ANALYSIS

1. In what ways was the Gardez family affected by the forces of modernization and industrialization? In what ways was the Gardez family untouched?

2. How accurate do you think Marie-Catherine Gardez's memories are?

3. What hesitations if any should we have about the value of Marie-Catherine Gardez's account as historical evidence?

Imperial Dreams, Imperial Realities

EUROPEANS POPULATED THE WORLD BEYOND EUROPE in a variety of capacities. Some, like British poet Rudyard Kipling (1865–1925), were born into families of colonial officials. Kipling grew up in India and served as a sharp-eyed journalist there before returning to England to write complex poetry about his experiences, the British Empire, and army life. Others voyaged to the colonies as missionaries, travelers and scientists, or traders and businessmen. All these sojourners had different opinions about life in colonial realms and about the relationship of the non-Europeans they encountered there to the white imperialist population. Among the harshest opinions were those of military leaders like aristocrat Lothar von Trotha (1848–1920), the general in charge of German Southwest Africa. Many missionaries genuinely wished to deliver colonized people from their "pagan" beliefs. Trotha genuinely believed, as he wrote in his diary in 1905, that "The natives must give way—look at America. Either via the bullet, or the mission, with alcohol."[21]

Both Kipling and Trotha wrote extensively during this period of heightened European imperial activity and competition at the turn of the century. In 1898 the United States went to war with Spain over Cuba and took the Philippines as part of the spoils of victory. Kipling wrote "The White Man's Burden" in 1899 to mark the event and alert Americans to their newfound responsibilities. His complex judgments about imperialism are partially revealed in this poem (Document 1.2). A few years later, in 1904, Trotha issued a proclamation accompanied by a letter to his German troops and another letter to his superiors on the General Staff back in Germany. He called for and justified the complete destruction of the Hereros of Southwest Africa, a pastoral people who were rebelling against the German takeover of the lands they needed for their cattle. The Hereros had killed male German settlers, and German newspapers prompted calls for revenge by saying (falsely) that the Hereros had also killed women and children. Some civilians, including German missionaries who reported atrocities suffered by the Hereros, had sympathy for these pastoral people, but Trotha did not. He was one of those who had them slain or driven into the desert to starve (see Starving Hereros on p. 34) His rationale appears in Document 1.3.

Document 1.2

RUDYARD KIPLING

The White Man's Burden, 1899

Take up the White Man's burden—
    Send forth the best ye breed—
Go, bind your sons to exile
    To serve your captives' need;
To wait, in heavy harness,
    On fluttered folk and wild—
Your new-caught sullen peoples,
    Half devil and half child.

Take up the White Man's burden—
    In patience to abide,
To veil the threat of terror
    And check the show of pride;
By open speech and simple,
    An hundred times made plain,
To seek another's profit
    And work another's gain.

Take up the White Man's burden—
    The savage wars of peace—
Fill full the mouth of Famine,
    And bid the sickness cease;
And when your goal is nearest
    (The end for others sought)
Watch sloth and heathen folly
    Bring all your hope to nought.

Take up the White Man's burden—
    No iron rule of kings,

But toil of serf and sweeper—
    The tale of common things.
The ports ye shall not enter,
    The roads ye shall not tread,
Go, make them with your living
    And mark them with your dead.

Take up the White Man's burden,
    And reap his old reward—
The blame of those ye better
    The hate of those ye guard—
The cry of hosts ye humour
    (Ah, slowly?) toward the light:—
"Why brought ye us from bondage,
    Our loved Egyptian night?"

Take up the White Man's burden—
    Ye dare not stoop to less—
Nor call too loud on Freedom
    To cloak your weariness.
By all ye will or whisper,
    By all ye leave or do,
The silent sullen peoples
    Shall weigh your God and you.

Take up the White Man's burden!
    Have done with childish days—
The lightly-proffered laurel,
    The easy ungrudged praise:
Comes now, to search your manhood
    Through all the thankless years,
Cold, edged with dear-bought wisdom,
    The judgment of your peers.

SOURCE: Rudyard Kipling, "The White Man's Burden," in *The Bedford Anthology of World Literature: The Twentieth Century,* ed. Paul Davis et al. (Boston: Bedford/St. Martin's, 2003).

Document 1.3

LOTHAR VON TROTHA
Proclamation to the Herero People and Accompanying Letters to German Troops and to the German General Staff, October 1904

[PROCLAMATION TO THE HERERO]   I, the great general of the German soldiers, send this letter to the Herero people. Herero are no longer German subjects. They have murdered, stolen, cut off the ears and noses and other body parts from wounded soldiers, and now out of cowardice refuse to fight. I say to the people: anyone delivering a captain to one of my stations as a prisoner will receive one thousand marks; whoever brings in Samuel Maherero will receive five thousand marks. The Herero people must leave this land. If they do not, I will force them to do so by using the great gun [artillery]. Within the German border every male Herero, armed or unarmed, with or without cattle, will be shot to death. I will no longer receive women or children but will drive them back to their people or have them shot at. These are my words to the Herero people.

[LETTER TO GERMAN TROOPS]   . . . This proclamation is to be read to the troops at roll-call, with the addition that the unit that catches a captain will also receive the appropriate reward, and that shooting at women and children is to be understood as shooting above their heads, so as to force them to run [away]. I assume absolutely that this proclamation will result in taking no more male prisoners, but will not degenerate into atrocities against women and children. The latter will run away if one shoots at them a couple of times. The troops will remain conscious of the good reputation of the German soldier.

SOURCE: Lothar von Trotha, Proclamation and letters, in Isabel V. Hull, *Absolute Destruction: Military Culture and the Practices of War in Imperial Germany* (Ithaca: Cornell University Press, 2005), 56–59.

[LETTER TO CHIEF OF GENERAL STAFF].   For me, it is merely a question of how to end the war with the Herero. My opinion is completely opposite to that of the governor and some "old Africans." They have wanted to negotiate for a long time and describe the Herero nation as a necessary labor force for the future use of the colony. I am of an entirely different opinion. I believe that the nation must be destroyed as such, or since this was not possible using tactical blows, it must be expelled from the land operatively and by means of detailed actions.

. . . Because I neither can treat with these people, nor do I want to, without the express direction of His Majesty, a certain rigorous treatment of all parts of the nation is absolutely necessary, a treatment that I have for the present taken and executed on my own responsibility, and from which, as long as I have command, I shall not detour without a direct order. My detailed knowledge of many Central African tribes, Bantu and others, has taught me the convincing certainty that Negroes never submit to a contract but only to raw force. Yesterday before my departure, I had the warriors who were captured in the last several days, [and who were] condemned by court-martial, hanged, and I have chased all the women and children who had gathered here back into the desert, taking with them the proclamation to the Herero people. This proclamation (enclosed), which will unavoidably become known, will be attacked. I only ask that it be explained to His Majesty that these means are absolutely necessary, and that my order to the troops (who are [still] excellently disciplined and with three characters like Deimling, Estorff, and Mühlenfels will surely remain so) gives the necessary instruction and guarantee for the execution of the order. On the other hand [*sic*] accepting women and children, who are mostly ill, is an eminent danger to the troops, and taking care of them is impossible. Therefore, I think it better that the nation perish rather than infect our troops and affect our water and food. In addition, the Herero would interpret any kindness on my side as weakness. They must now die in the desert or try to cross the Bechuanaland border. This uprising is and remains the beginning of a race war, which I already predicted in 1897 in my reports to the chancellor on East Africa. . . . Whether this uprising was caused by poor treatment [of the Africans] remains irrelevant to its suppression. . . .

QUESTIONS FOR ANALYSIS

1. What attitudes toward colonized peoples and toward imperial rulers do Kipling and Trotha share?

2. What differences do you find in Kipling's and Trotha's ideas about imperialism?

3. Imagine yourself a Filipino or a Herero. What might your reaction have been to either the poem or the proclamation?

Japan's Challenge to the West

THE JAPANESE MILITARY DEALT THE MIGHTY RUSSIAN EMPIRE a stunning blow in the Russo-Japanese War of 1904–1905. Japan had modernized its military to a high level of effectiveness since the Meiji Restoration in 1868, when reformers among the Japanese elite—including Shigenobu Okuma, the author of Document 1.4— restored the emperor to power and themselves set the economy of the country on a modernizing path. As a result, Japanese forces fought more efficiently and had better equipment than their Russian adversaries. The Russian generals were disorganized, and their brash and boastful behavior could not compensate for their lack of skill. Despite Russia's failure, the great powers—including the United States, which had both Pacific and Atlantic trading interests—stepped in and forced Japan to return some of its conquests. This intervention strengthened the belief among the Japanese and among reformers in the colonies that the Western powers were determined to rule the rest of the world single-handedly and not allow non-Westerners to enjoy the fruits of their own victories.

Japan's victory over the massive Russian Empire shocked the world, pleasing colonized peoples and alarming the Western powers. "The Tragedy of Russia in the Pacific" was the title of one British account. A "stupendous spectacle," noted another Westerner; "Asia advancing, Europe falling back." But in the Ottoman Empire, India, and Africa many people were elated. The surprising victory gave colonized peoples courage and resolve. It challenged Western domination not just militarily but psychologically as well.

Japanese leaders, expressed no surprise about their nation's victory over Russia but rather saw in it the culmination of Japan's national development. They gave credit to the "emperor system," in which a special culture promoting the Japanese traits of upright character and respect for established social order had developed. The emperor system took shape as an ideology with the Meiji Restoration of 1868, when Japan once again opened itself up thoroughly to foreign influences. Paradoxically the restoration of the emperor in 1868 signaled Japan's rapid modernization, including the development of a bureaucratic and industrially focused central government. The emperor system celebrated values that would propel the country toward military domination of the government—a trend at odds with modern ideas of democratic politics. The emperor system also justified Japan's increasingly imperialistic actions. During the next few decades Japan would fight with China for influence in East Asia, occupy Korea and Formosa, and seek to take over most of the Pacific.

In Document 1.4 Shigenobu Okuma (1838–1922), a high government official, explains his lack of surprise at Japan's ability to defeat Russia, recalling the course of Japanese cultural policies over the past centuries. Speaking to an audience in 1904, he contrasts Japan's fidelity and activism with European decadence. In describing Europe as decadent, Okuma drew on a characterization that would grow in appeal to movements then developing against the domination of the West.

Document 1.4

Shigenobu Okuma
The Rise of Japan Was Not Unexpected, 1904

The recent development and prosperity of the Japanese Empire is no sudden and unexpected event which has come before the world without any adequate cause or reason for its coming into existence. It is the necessary outcome of certain causes well known to all who have studied our national history.

If we turn to the history of Europe we shall find one rule, to which there is absolutely no exception. Any nation, no matter what its constitution or form of Government may be, will prosper so long as it keeps itself swimming with the great current of human thought: to attempt to stem the current or swim against it, involves national ruin. There is no exception to this rule.

At the end of the Middle Ages, we find the people of Spain and Portugal full of a vigorous spirit of adventure: the discovery of America, the circumnavigation of the Cape of Good Hope, the opening of the new trade routes to India, were all due to their energy, and brought them into intimate relations with the peoples of the Far East. Spanish settlements were to be found in every quarter of the globe, and the name of Spain was feared and respected over the whole continent of Europe.

But her ruin soon came. The whole extent of her power scarcely covered two centuries of pleasant but profitless dreams. A few great nobles held the whole power; neither at home nor in their colonies were the people allowed the slightest voice or interest in the management of their own affairs; the most clear and distinct lessons of contemporary history were neglected by a despotic and blinded oligarchy—progress was hindered, the nation stood still, and stagnation brought decay—Spain's power fell as quickly as it had risen.

The same phenomenon may be observed in the case of Holland, more distinctly still in that of Turkey. Turkey was a great power in the fifteenth century, when she destroyed the Eastern Empire of Rome, and took Constantinople; but the Renaissance and Revival of Learning, which her arrival at Constantinople brought to Western Europe, she rejected for herself. She turned her back deliberately on the modern civilization and culture that was coming into prominence around her, and the result was easy to foresee. It is a long time since it has been possible to compare Turkey to anything but a sick man in a hospital, waiting for the hour of dissolution, and only saved from it by the disagreements of European powers.

But it would be wrong, in the case of any of these countries, to lay the blame for their decay on to the shoulders of the people in general. In Spain and Portugal, a grossly superstitious form of religion, administered by avaricious ecclesiastics and an ignorant hierarchy, on the one hand, and on the other an ostentatious court and despotic aristocracy had combined to poison the wells of national life, and it was owing to these that the Spanish Colonial Empire of which it could once be said that "the sun never set on its dominions" had dwindled and dwindled until the loss of Cuba, Porto Rico, and the Philippines had reduced it to one or two insignificant islets in the Atlantic. The same causes had been at work in Turkey, and had produced precisely similar results. Russia is now following the bad examples of these countries: the same poison is at work in her political and social system, and the same symptoms of disease are manifesting themselves. An ignorant and arrogant hierarchy, an ostentatious Court, a corrupt moral atmosphere in the aristocracy, in the military and naval services, in the very

SOURCE: Speech of Count Shigenobu Okuma in *The Russo-Japanese War Fully Illustrated* (Tokyo: Kinkodo Publishing Co., 1904), 347–354.

entourage of the Czar himself, this is the poison that is destroying her life. Russia is trying to swim against the stream of human enlightenment; she cannot well escape from the punishment that inevitably follows upon such a line of action.

If now you will turn to the history of Japan, you will be able to see at a glance why it is that this Empire has always been so successful in all her undertakings. It is because our nation has always acted from the beginning on the principle, which has been so clearly enunciated for us in the Imperial Rescript at the time of the Great Restoration, of "seeking knowledge throughout the world,"° i.e. of adopting what is good from every country, and entering into an honourable rivalry in culture and civilization with all nations throughout the world.

This is the fundamental principle which accounts for the rise of Japan in the world; she has never hesitated to adopt anything that she has found to be good; she has ever tried to swim with the tide of human progress; she has never shrunk from any sacrifice in eradicating what she has found to be bad. The voice of the people can make itself heard in the management of public affairs, and it was the same Imperial Rescript, in a phrase which gave us the keynote of a liberal form of governmental administration, that bade us "settle affairs by public opinion—." This principle of appealing to a public opinion illuminated and guided by knowledge sought throughout the world, has rendered possible the granting of a

wise and just Constitution and Body of Laws, and Representative Government co-existent with a large measure of local autonomy, the execution of Juridical Reforms, the abolition of vexatious restrictions on commerce and the free development of every form of national life. It has, in other words, enabled and encouraged the people of Japan to swim prosperously with the stream of human progress.

If this principle, of keeping abreast with the tide of human progress, is to be made effective, it requires that the intellectual faculty should be applied to all the concerns of human life, and that cannot be done without education. For more than thirty years, the Government of Japan has devoted a very large amount of attention and energy to the question of education, and the best training that could be procured has been given with a generous hand to students of political, social and military affairs, as well as for those preparing themselves for humbler but no less important walks of life in commerce, industry, and agriculture. The country has also stepped out into the wider arena of the world of reality and has become a formidable competitor in the field of international trade and commerce, her free-trade policy during the last thirty years having greatly assisted her development along this line. The Japanese people is not merely a nation of fighters: it has no mean skill in agriculture, industry, and commerce, and if you will take the trouble to investigate the statistical tables of progress throughout the Empire, you will find that the national wealth has increased six or seven fold during the last thirty years, and that if you compare the present wealth of the country with what it was at the conclusion of the Japan-China War ten years ago, it has, even during that short period, more than trebled itself. The utilization of the Chinese War indemnity added immensely to the permanent wealth of the nation. This may be seen by looking at the great increase of capital and deposits in banks, at the increased circulation of money evidenced by the bill-exchanges at Tokyo, Osaka, and other places, at the increased revenue derived from the Post and

---

°The original words of this important Imperial Rescript are as follows: (1) In administering the business of the State, We shall settle affairs by public opinion which shall have an opportunity of expressing itself in public representative assembly. (2) Our administration shall be in the interests of the whole people, and not of any particular class of Our subjects. (3) No person, whether official or private citizen, shall be hindered in the prosecution of his legitimate business. (4) The bad customs of past ages shall be abolished, and Our Government shall tread in the paths of civilization and enlightenment. (5) We shall endeavour to raise the prestige and honour of Our country by seeking knowledge throughout the world. [Note in document.]

Telegraph Services, at the development in the amount of foreign trade and the growing number of merchant vessels, at the vastly increased investments in mining, spinning, and manufacturing industries. Japan's victories are not confined to the fields of military and naval glory. She has conquered in every direction, and it speaks volumes for her credit that in a young nation which has only emerged into the world during the last thirty years, the national wealth should have trebled itself in ten years.

And now, you will ask me, what will be the effect of the present war?

I think that at the conclusion of the present struggle we shall have far better times than we had after the war with China; for our people have much increased in wisdom since then, and there is far more practical knowledge and *savoir-faire*. Our commercial organs are far greater than they were then, we shall be able to take in and digest larger quantities of additional wealth, make it productive in larger amounts and in a far shorter time. Our credit and means of communication will be much improved: in short, I look forward to a period of great national prosperity.

So far, I have tried to sketch the progress which Japan has made by carrying out her fundamental principle of "seeking knowledge throughout the world," and swimming with the tide of human progress. The object which her statesmen have had before them has been to bring Japan in every respect up to the present-day level of European and American civilization, and in doing so they have deliberately excluded the question of religion, as not coming within their purview. When Japan was first opened to foreigners, some fifty years ago, she already possessed two religions, the *Buddhism* and the *Shintoism*; but in accordance with her Constitution, which allows her subjects absolute freedom of religious faith and worship, Christianity has also been able to come in, and establish itself by the side of the ancient national creeds of the country. In the history of Europe, we find that the introduction of a new religion has rarely, if ever, taken place without a collision, accompanied by bloodshed, be-

tween the old faith and the new. The Thirty Years' War was a war of religion (not of religions, for the combatants only represented two forms of the same faith); it lasted for a whole generation; brought to an end by a conference of the powers concerned, it continued to bear its evil effects in Europe, for over a century more, and the questions which it raised were not finally solved, till the law stepped in which proclaimed toleration and the freedom of the conscience.

In Japan, you will find nothing of the kind; for the principle underlying our national life is very different from that which underlies Western countries. It has always been our principle to seek the good by seeking knowledge throughout the world; we have never had a religious war,° because every religion is free to enter our country.

Nor must it be supposed that the history of Japan is, as some foreigners perhaps think, at all analogous to the history of other Oriental nations. Japan has had a history quite her own, and quite distinct from that of the peoples of Central Asia such as China, Mongolia, Persia, or Turkey. No analogy can be drawn from the history of these nations to that of Japan.

The origin of our modern Japanese development must not be sought in the opening of the country half a century ago. If you read her history for the last two thousand five hundred years you will find that her people have always possessed in a very high degree the power of assimilation. Japan came into contact first with the civilization of China, and assimilated it, without any trouble. When some years later the Buddhism of India invaded Japan through China, her native Shinto found a way to make room amicably for the newcomer, though in China a fierce feud arose between the followers of Buddha and those of Confucius. It

---

° The destruction of the Roman Catholic Missions in the sixteenth century was carried out, not because they were Christian, but because they were considered to be inseparably bound up with the aggressive policy of Spain, which was at that period a serious menace to the independence and integrity of Japan. [Note in document.]

is worthwhile noting that fifteen hundred years ago Japan understood and appreciated the principle of religious toleration. She was ready to welcome all that was good.

In the 16th century, when Spain and Portugal opened intercourse with Japan they brought with them their Christian faith. The most famous of the Jesuit missionaries, St. Francis Xavier, tells us in his memoirs that though the Spaniards interested themselves in the propagation of their faith wherever they went he had found no country in which it was embraced so readily and willingly as in Japan. In the course of some forty years, over six millions of converts had been made, and there had been no hostile collision between the promoters of the new religion and the defenders of Shintoism and Buddhism. A few years later Tokugawa Iyeyasu, the greatest of Shoguns, banished all Christian missionaries and absolutely prohibited the profession of Christianity. The reason was entirely a political one. Ambitious and intriguing Spanish priests had caballed with disaffected barons and officials of the Government to get political power into their own hands. Had they succeeded, their action could have had but one result, the dismemberment of Japan, and its eventual absorption by Spain, and the stern action of Iyeyasu finds abundant justification in the political circumstances of the times. Iyeyasu's age was the age which in Europe witnessed the fierce religious wars of the Reformation in Germany, the Wars of the Huguenots, and the Massacre of St. Bartholomew's Day in France, the religious troubles of England, and the establishment of the Spanish Inquisition —

reasons enough to justify him in closing the country against the introduction of such a spirit.

During the 216 years of her seclusion from the world, Japan was quietly developing her internal resources, and her treasures of national literature and vigour. It was with well husbanded stores of energy and activity that she at length emerged once more from her seclusion to attain to eminence by strides of unparallelled rapidity.

When peace shall have crowned the efforts which Japan is making in the present war, the effect upon herself will be that she will be able to make still greater progress in the paths of civilization, and that the true spirit of the Japanese nation will have more room to display itself. Japan has never been an advocate of war, and will never draw her sword from its sheath unless compelled to do so by the pressure of foreign powers. We are fighting now for peace and not for war; and when peace is secured we shall be only too glad to put by the sword and devote ourselves to the promotion of the higher interests of our country.

I think, Gentlemen, that if you will study the history of the country, you will find that the present eminence of our country is no mushroom growth. It has its roots in the past, and finds its true explanation in historical causes which anyone may understand that reads them. I hope, too, that many foreigners may be induced to devote attention to the history of Japan. They will then understand that the present war is not one of race against race or religion against religion, but that the victory of Japan means the fusion into one harmonious whole of the civilizations of East and West.

QUESTIONS FOR ANALYSIS

1. What is the nature of Japanese superiority in Okuma's view?
2. How does Okuma draw on European history to make his arguments? What empires does he mention? Why, in his opinion, did they decline?
3. What effect might Okuma's speech have had on his audience and on readers around the world?

PICTURE ESSAY

Europe's Global Aura
in an Age of Nationalism

TODAY IT IS SOMETIMES BELIEVED that globalization is exclusively a phenomenon of the late twentieth and early twenty-first centuries. In 1900, however, Europeans were linked to a global economy and imbibed global products and influences to an impressive degree even as they became increasingly organized in centralized national states. A range of parades and commemorative ceremonies worked to inspire patriotism in ordinary folks. The monarchs who often led such ceremonies had wider experience of the world and relied for their own amusements and social interactions on ties to members of the nobility outside their borders. Members of the upper classes including royal families often chose their partners from

◆ Figure 1.1 **Aristocrats and Their Retinue on a Grand Tour of Egypt**

◆ Figure 1.2 **Louis Mountbatten in a Sailor Suit**
Hulton Archive/Getty Images.

a transnational network of prospective, suitable spouses. The result was a very international upper class.

No longer content with the traditional grand tour of Europe, members of the upper class broadened their cultural outlook by crossing oceans and continents. Aside from state visits to other European countries, some monarchs voyaged far afield, not simply on official visits but on trips that provided a broader range of experience and information. Unlike his parents and grandparents, Nicholas II, tsar of Russia (r. 1894–1917), traveled in his youth to Japan, India, China, and Egypt. In Figure 1.1 Nicholas stands close to the center of the group dressed in a light suit and bowler hat and holds a cane next to his identically clad brother. Photographers snapped his picture in many of these places, capturing his image in Chinese rickshaws and also showing him wearing traditional Russian monarchical garb dating back centuries. At home, Nicholas II endorsed the eradication of languages other than Russian and religions other than Russian Orthodoxy, which may strike us as paradoxical given his exposure to a variety of cultures. Looking at this picture, speculate about how Nicholas II reconciled his penchant for traditional ceremonies with his modern travel around the world.

The experience of empire, a prerequisite for membership in the elite, meant crossing oceans, and high and low, male and female alike sported the global fashion of the day: the sailor suit, in this case worn by Lord Mountbatten of the British royal family (Figure 1.2), who also carries a small bear, which became popular because of the imperial hunt. A "teddy bear" also designated a great U.S. imperialist, Theodore Roosevelt. Shipbuilding constituted a big part of defense budgets, and ministries of war lobbied to persuade members of parliament and other power brokers to approve budgets for huge battleships. Tourism began to flourish in this age of prosperity and empire for the major powers. Did wearing sailors' garb encourage the elite to support the vast naval expansion at the turn of the century? Or did sailor suits and pictures of prominent individuals like the young Mountbatten wearing them encourage love of the seas, the sporting life in sailboats, and perhaps even internationalism?

Amid rising calls to celebrate national identity, Europeans embraced foreign customs like tea parties, imported over the centuries from Japan. In both Russia and Britain, tea became a drink associated with distinctive national customs.

Families such as these well-to-do travelers in India employed servants from around the world (Figure 1.3) and even brought them to Europe to make teatime appear authentically cosmopolitan and imperial. Queen Victoria was committed to having servants from South Asia in her English residences, perhaps to indicate her status as empress of India. In this photo of teatime in India, what markers of difference do you see among the various individuals? Does teatime in this photo look English or Japanese—that is, does this custom from outside Europe look British by this time?

Even to the patriotically minded, foreignness sold products and was widely used in the growing business of advertising in magazines and posters. Photos of elephants were used to sell tea, and black-faced caricatures of Africans were used to sell chocolate. An advertisement for Pears' soap (Figure 1.4) shows a white, apparently European, woman emerging from a shell to ask a startled young African whether he has bathed. This question replicates the justification for imperialism:

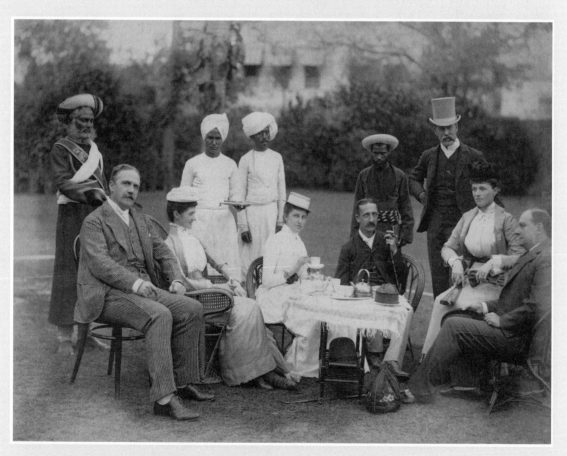

◆ Figure 1.3 **A British Tea in India with Native Retinue** *The British Library.*

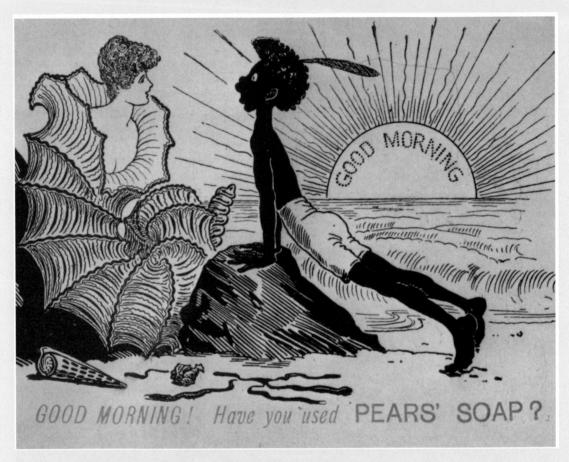

◆ Figure 1.4 **An Advertisement for Pears' Soap, c. 1890** *Hulton Archive/Getty Images.*

that Europeans were cleaning up "dirty" natives. Consider the visual elements of this ad. How are the woman and the African portrayed and what might this reveal about Europeans' attitudes toward both colonized peoples and toward themselves? Why did the artist depict the woman encased in a shell? Why does the African wear a feather in his hair?

So imperialized and globalized had culture become that knowledge of the world was more readily available than ever before. People enjoyed amazing variety, and displaying global fashion and global knowledge became important. What travelers found in Southeast Asia also inspired a move toward unisex dressing in continental Europe. In some parts of the temperate non-West, lightweight and nonconstricting styles were almost uniform, and men and women wore the same pajama-type garments. European imitation produced trousers and loose-fitting, slim attire that made it easier for women to take up sports such as bicycle riding, tennis, and soccer. A preference for simplicity of style in clothing—especially comfortable, less confining clothing for women—was strong at the beginning of the century. The Liberty store, still in existence in London today, had opened in 1875 to sell the new styles as well as an array of fabrics from South, East, and West Asia. By the end of the nineteenth century, less restrictive undergarments became the norm, and casual dresses had a straighter, more fluid cut unlike the style of but a few decades earlier (Figure 1.5). This theater coat was said to copy a kimono by its designers. Although it does not have the *obi*, the restrictive wide belt worn with the kimono in Japan, it does have the kimono's straight lines. What other ingredients make us think of Japan when we look at this image? Why does the manufacturer use Japanese images to market this design?

The poor and oppressed such as Europe's Jews and landless workers also became global, traveling around the world to Shanghai, Buenos Aires, New York, and elsewhere to seek their fortunes or escape persecution. Many, however, maintained their traditional ways and their ties to their homelands. A large number returned to Europe for visits and even for resettlement, indicating that their homelands still had a strong influence on their lives. In an era of rapid globalization, identities became more complicated than ever before. These immigrants to the United States arriving at Ellis Island (Figure 1.6) may have had only a temporary stay in mind. What if

◆ Figure 1.5 **A Kimono-style Coat, c. 1912, Influenced by Oriental Design** *Mary Evans Picture Library/The Image Works.*

◆ **Figure 1.6 Immigrants at Ellis Island** *Culver Pictures.*

anything does the image convey about these people's attitudes and intentions? What class do these immigrants represent, and why does the gender balance look so skewed toward men?

QUESTIONS FOR ANALYSIS

1. Why in an age of rising nationalism were foreign travel, foreign products, and foreign customs and styles so popular and even necessary?

2. What do these figures indicate about European identity? Do you sense a global identity? Or is national identity still evident in these images?

3. In what ways are nationalism and globalism mutually exclusive? In what ways do they work together?

NOTES

1. Quoted in John Montgomery, *End of an Era* (London: George Allen and Unwin, 1968), 20.

2. David Cannadine, *Ornamentalism: How the British Saw Their Empire* (London: Penguin, 2001), 124.

3. Ibid., 131.

4. Joseph Baernreither to Baron Alois Lexa von Aehrenthal, September 11, 1899, quoted in Solomon Wank, "Pessimism in the Austrian Establishment at the Turn of the Century," in *The Mirror of History: Essays in Honor of Fritz Fellner*, ed. Solomon Wank et al. (Santa Barbara: ABC Clio, 1992), 299.

5. Quoted in Paul Dukes, *A History of Russia: Medieval, Modern, Contemporary*, 3rd ed. (Durham: Duke University Press, 1998), 176.

6. Andrey Biely [Boris Bugáyev], *The Silver Dove*, trans. George Reavey (New York: Grove, 1974 [1909]), 60.

7. Prince Aleksei Obolensky, quoted in Dominic Lieven, *Russia's Rulers under the Old Regime* (New Haven: Yale University Press, 1989), 273.

8. Bozena Slanciková-Timrava, quoted in Frantisek Bielik, Horst Hogh, and Anna Stvrtecká, "Slovak Images of the New World: 'We Could Pay Off Our Debts,'" in *Roots of the Transplanted*, vol. 1, ed. Dirk Hoerder and Inge Blank (New York: Columbia University Press, 1994), 387.

9. Joseph Chamberlain, quoted in Brian Blakeley, "Women and Imperialism: The Colonial Office and Female Emigration to South Africa, 1901–1910," *Albion*, 13 (1981), 2: 132–134.

10. Quoted in Lora Wildenthal, *German Women for Empire, 1884–1945* (Durham: Duke University Press, 2001), 168.

11. Quoted in Bielik, Hogh, and Stvrtecká, "Slovak Images of the New World," 382.

12. Ernest Lavisse, *Petit Manuel d'histoire*, quoted in Jean-Pierre Rioux and Jean-Francois Sirinelli, *Histoire culturelle de la France: Le Temps des masses* (Paris: Seuil, 1998), 24.

13. Quoted in Andrew Baruch Wachtel, *Making a Nation, Breaking a Nation: Literature and Cultural Politics in Yugoslavia* (Stanford: Stanford University Press, 1998), 56.

14. Quoted in Robert P. Geraci, *Window on the East: National and Imperial Identities in Late Tsarist Russia* (Ithaca: Cornell University Press, 2001), 113.

15. Described in John Gooch, ed., *The Boer War: Direction, Experience, Image* (London: Frank Cass, 2000), 41–55.

16. German General Staff report, quoted in I. Goldblatt, *History of South West Africa from the Beginning of the Nineteenth Century* (Capetown: Juta, 1971), 132.

17. Quoted in Stephen G. Marks, *Road to Power: The Trans-Siberian Railroad and the Colonization of Asian Russia, 1850–1917* (London: I. B. Tauris, 1991), 117.

18. H. H. Jessup, *Fifty-Three Years in Syria*, vol. 2 (New York: Fleming H. Revell, 1910), 786–787.

19. Quoted in Robert Geraci, "Russian Orientalism at an Impasse: Tsarist Education Policy and the 1910 Conference on Islam," in *Russia's Orient: Imperial Borderlands and Peoples, 1700–1917*, ed. Daniel Brower and Edward J. Lazzerini (Bloomington: Indiana University Press, 1997), 142.

20. Quoted in Bonnie G. Smith, *Imperialism: A History in Documents* (New York: Oxford University Press, 2000), 131.

21. Lothar von Trotha, diary, January 19, 1905, quoted in Isabel V. Hull, *Absolute Destruction: Military Culture and the Practices of War in Imperial Germany* (Ithaca: Cornell University Press, 2005), 30.

GENERAL WORKS

Bayly, C. A. *The Birth of the Modern World, 1980–1914: Global Connections and Comparisons.* 2004.
Hobsbawm, Eric. *The Age of Empire, 1875–1914.* 1987.
Keylor, William R. *The Twentieth-Century World.* 2001.
Kohn, Hans. *Nationalism.* 1955.
Mazower, Mark. *The Dark Continent: Europe's Twentieth Century.* 1999.
McNeill, J. R., and William H. McNeill. *The Human Web: A Bird's-Eye View of World History.* 2003.

SUGGESTED REFERENCES

Europe's Peoples and Nations in the Global Order   A look at the major empires, their rulers, and peoples appears in the following books. Among the most fascinating is Wortman's study of imperial ceremonials in Russia.

Berghahn, Volker R. *Imperial Germany, 1871–1918: Economy, Society, Culture, and Politics.* 2005.

Cannadine, David. *The Rise and Fall of the British Aristocracy.* 1990.

Clark, Christopher. *William II.* 2000.

Held, Joseph, ed. *The Columbia History of Eastern Europe in the Twentieth Century.* 1992.

Kupchick, Dennis. *Culture and History in Eastern Europe.* 1994.

Lieven, Dominic. *Russia's Rulers under the Old Regime.* 1989.

Popkin, Jeremy D. *A History of Modern France.* 1994.

Sked, Alan. *The Decline and Fall of the Habsburg Empire, 1815–1918.* 1989.

Wortman, Richard. *Scenarios of Power: Myth and Ceremony in Russian Monarchy: From Alexander II to the Abdication of Nicholas II.* 2000.

Society in the Age of Empire European society was diverse in terms of class, with large gaps between the aristocracy at the top of the social ladder and the rural peasantry at the bottom. Imperialism further complicated the social order and came into play in Europe's social structure as well as in the social structure abroad.

Cannadine, David. *Ornamentalism: How the British Saw Their Empire.* 2001.

Conklin, Alice. *Mission to Civilize: The Republican Idea of Empire, 1895–1930.* 2000.

Cox, Jeffrey. *Imperial Fault Lines: Christianity and Colonial Power in India, 1818–1940.* 2002.

Davis, Mike. *Late Victorian Holocausts: El Niño Famines and the Making of the Third World.* 2001.

Gilmour, David. *The Long Recessional: The Imperial Life of Rudyard Kipling.* 2002.

Grever, Maria, and Berteke Waaldijk. *Transforming the Public Sphere: The Dutch National Exhibition of Women's Labor in 1898.* 2004.

Koven, Seth. *Slumming: Sexual and Social Politics in Victorian London.* 2004.

McClintock, Anne. *Imperial Leather: Race, Gender, and Sexuality in the Colonial Contest.* 1995.

Sowerwine, Charles. *France since 1870: Culture, Politics, and Society.* 2001.

Troy, Nancy J. *Couture Cultures: A Study of Modern Art and Fashion.* 2002.

Europe in an Age of Migration One of the oddities of history is that wealthy European countries provided millions of migrants to the rest of the world. The collection of letters and stories edited by Hoerder and Blank contains some of these migrants' stories as does the engaging book by Reeder.

Burds, Jeffrey. *Peasant Dreams and Market Politics: Labor Migration and the Russian Village, 1861–1905.* 1998.

Engel, Barbara. *Between the Fields and the City: Women, Work, and Family in Russia, 1861–1914.* 1994.

Green, Nancy. *The Pletzl of Paris: Jewish Immigrant Workers in the "Belle Epoque."* 1986.

Hochstadt, Steve. *Mobility and Modernity: Migration in Germany, 1820–1989.* 1999.

Hoerder, Dirk, and Inge Blank, eds. *Roots of the Transplanted,* 2 vols. 1994.

Moch, Leslie Page. *Moving Europeans: Migration in Western Europe since 1650.* 2003.

O'Sullivan, Patrick, ed. *The Irish World Wide: History, Heritage, Identity,* 6 vols. Vol. 1: *Patterns of Migration.* 1992.

Reeder, Linda. *Widows in White: Migration and the Transformation of Rural Italian Women, Sicily, 1880–1920.* 2003.

Ristaino, Marcia R. *Port of Last Resort: Diaspora Communities of Shanghai.* 2001.

Slezkine, Yuri. *Arctic Mirrors: Russia and the Small Peoples of the North.* 1994.

Nationalism and the Evolving Nation-State National feeling was surging in 1900 despite globalism, and nationalism took varying forms whether in the Balkans, as in Wachtel's book, or in Ireland, as in McDevitt's.

Burns, Michael. *Dreyfus: A Family Affair.* 1992.

Chickering, Roger. *We Men Who Feel Most German: A Cultural Study of the Pan-German League, 1886–1914.* 1984.

Geraci, Robert P. *Window on the East: National and Imperial Identities in Late Tsarist Russia.* 2001.

Gooch, John, ed. *The Boer War: Direction, Experiences, Image.* 2000.

Greenfield, Liah. *Five Roads to Modernity.* 1992.

Hull, Isabel. *Absolute Destruction: Military Culture and the Practices of War in Imperial Germany.* 2005.

Jansen, Marius B. *The Making of Modern Japan.* 2000.

Kansu, Aykut. *The Revolution of 1908 in Turkey.* 1997.

Kornberg, Jacques. *Theodor Herzl: From Assimilation to Zionism.* 1993.

McDevitt, Patrick. *"May the Best Man Win": Sport, Masculinity, and Nationalism in Great Britain and the Empire, 1880–1935.* 2004.

Sinha, Mrinalini. *Colonial Masculinity: The "Manly Englishman" and the "Effeminate Bengali" in the Late Nineteenth Century.* 1995.

Wachtel, Andrew Baruch. *Making a Nation, Breaking a Nation: Literature and Cultural Politics in Yugoslavia.* 1998.

Weeks, Theodore R. *Nation and State in Late Imperial Russia: Nationalism and Russification on the Western Frontier.* 1996.

Wildenthal, Lora. *German Women for Empire, 1884–1945.* 2001.

Selected Web Sites

Two Web sites maintained by U.S. universities are Russian Studies, <**bucknell .edu/Russian**>, and The Victorian Web, <**victorianweb.org**>. To see what France launched at its Universal Exposition in 1889, see <**tour-eiffel.fr/teiffel/uk**>. Fascination with the major non-Western contender for empire—Japan—can be traced on the Japanese history Web site, <**csuohio.edu/history/japan/index .html**>. The University of Leiden in the Netherlands maintains a Web site for migration history; it includes helpful statistics and breaks down migrants by country of origin and destination: <**www.let.leidenuniv.nl/history/migration/**>. The Anglo-Boer War Museum maintains a helpful Web site on many aspects of the South African War: <**anglo-boer.co.za/**>.

2

Modernity and the Unsettling of Europe

1900–1914

IN THE SUMMER OF 1908, WILBUR WRIGHT SUCCESSFULLY piloted his motor-powered airplane for one minute and forty-five seconds over western France. Because American investors were uninterested in the further development of what appeared to be a creaking, unpromising contraption, Wright had come abroad to sell his and his brother Orville's invention. The Wright brothers were eager to provide a viable machine for European amateurs who piloted gliders, hot air balloons, and dirigibles. Wilbur ate, slept, and spent almost all of his time in France with his precious plane in clear view. By the end of the year he was taking 125-mile flights, winning hundreds of thousands of francs in prize money offered by wealthy European businessmen with "a passion for wings." Despite mishaps and even a fatality involving one of his planes, the French so lionized Wilbur—"the man of the century," they called him—that he and his brother concluded a sale of their design to the French. "The future lies in the air," a leading British journalist announced, and indeed with the Wright brothers the age of the airplane was born.[1]

At a time of rising competition among nations, new technology had a complicated impact in Europe, promoting both nationalism and internationalism and inspiring both fear and optimism. In July 1909, one year after

◆ The Wright Brothers' Flying Machine

Technological innovation determined Europe's power in the modern age, but there were technological transfers across national borders and around the world. The first successful airplane was built by U.S. innovators Orville and Wilbur Wright, shown here piloting their plane in Pau, France, in 1909. Wealthy European individuals and governments snapped up the flying machine, and writers and artists heralded the dawning of a new age now that humans could break free of the earth's confines. *Hulton Archive/ Getty Images.*

Wright's first flight in France, the French aviator Louis Blériot flew across the English Channel. "England is no longer an island," ran the elated if alarmed commentary. Given the heated nationalist atmosphere, Blériot was immediately equated in French newspaper stories with military heroes from the mythical past: "You could easily take him for one of those robust defenders of ancient Gaul," read an editorial in the French daily *Le Matin*.[2] In *The War in the Air* (1908) British novelist H. G. Wells predicted that airplanes would soon dominate warfare, terrorizing civilians. The air force in Wells's novel was German; its target, New York: "As the airships sailed along they smashed up the city as a child will shatter its cities of brick and card. Below, they left ruins and blazing conflagrations and heaped and scattered dead."[3] Though unimaginable to the average reader, the scene was inspired by a 1908 flight of more than two hundred miles made by a German dirigible—a

1908	Wilbur Wright pilots motor-powered plane over western France.
1908	British novelist H. G. Wells predicts in *The War in the Air* that airplanes will soon dominate warfare.
1908	Young Turks stage revolution in Ottoman Empire.
1908	Austria-Hungary annexes Bosnia-Herzegovina.
1908– 1909	Gustav Klimt paints *Embrace of Isis and Osiris.*
1909	French aviator Louis Blériot flies across English Channel.
1909	F. T. Marinetti issues "Manifesto of Futurism."
1910	Germany devotes 45 percent of national budget to defense.
1910– 1911	Working-class activism and strikes erupt across Europe.
1911	British House of Lords gives up right to veto legislation.
1911	Wassily Kandinsky publishes *Concerning the Spiritual in Art.*
1912	British government introduces bill to enact home rule for Ireland.
1912	Montenegro, Bulgaria, Serbia, and Greece defeat Ottoman Empire in First Balkan War.
1913	Igor Stravinsky's ballet *Rite of Spring* performed in Paris.
1913	Irish women separate from London-based WSPU to protest England's control of Ireland.
1913	Second Balkan War erupts.
1913	Most European men (outside of Russia) have right to vote.
1913	Germany's Social Democratic Party wins elections.
1914	France manufactures 45,000 automobiles—up 300 percent from 14,000 in 1905.
1914	Austrian painter Oskar Kokoschka employs expressionist techniques in *The Storm.*
1914	Madame Caillaux' trial for murder frequently front-page news across Europe.

torpedo-shaped hot air balloon designed by the German aeronaut Count Ferdinand Zeppelin and later named after him. This feat heightened tensions in the international arms race already underway among the great powers. A German bureaucrat had already predicted that the creation of an air force would enable Germany to invade Britain by landing half a million soldiers in a single night's flight. From bureaucrats to novelists to newspapermen, the airplane symbolized modernity; but, given the international tensions of the day, such modernity sometimes seemed to presage destruction and cataclysm.

Optimists viewed the airplane as an invention that would benefit human society: it would convey people and goods, and someday perhaps everyone would own a plane. Aviation symbolized for many the democratic potential of Europeans' advanced modernity. A new sense of the speedup of time, inspired by railroads and automobiles as well as airplanes, gripped the imagination. The potential benefit of telephones, mass transit, airplanes, and fast cars—with their vigor, speed of communication and movement, and sheer force—challenged pessimists. In fact, many envisioned a future of action that would replace dreary bourgeois morality and the grim rhythms of industrial society. The new technology inspired intellectuals and artists known as "Futurists" to think new thoughts, dream new dreams, and create new poetic forms (see Document 2.5). The airplane itself inspired visions of universal transformation, with humans liberated from the confines of earth. Air travel might allow people the freedom to soar, to escape the limits of everyday life, and lead to the rebirth of spirituality. The promise offered by the airplane challenged all previous understandings of human potential.

Europeans pioneered contemporary modernity. This much-debated term alluded to more than the dizzying pace of innovation embodied by inventions such as the airplane. The sense of being modern also arose from the contrast between the bustling innovation of the present and the sluggish status quo of the past. Individuals viewed rapid change from different standpoints—as a harbinger of decline, violent clash, or a brilliant utopian future. Some statesmen and reformers who equated modernity with a new rationality launched peace conferences at the beginning of the century in the belief that societies had become so rational as to be able forever to avoid war. Modernity inspired confidence that the whole world would want to be modern like Europe; it seemed to confirm the imperialist conviction that Western accomplishments needed to be spread abroad. Europeans pursued their drive to influence the rest of the world with confidence that technology would improve and pacify other regions.

The political and social realities in Europe and abroad were far from pacific, however. The great powers increased their production of ever larger battleships and more destructive artillery, fueling the Europe-wide arms race. Modern politics were shrill and harsh, and modern politicians attracted votes by patriotically menacing other countries with the threat of war. Women began asserting their rights, insisting that discrimination was an outdated remnant of superstitious and less educated societies. The working classes, often influenced by socialist thought, wanted better working conditions and a higher standard of living, given the promise of technology. In the colonized world, national liberation groups added theirs to the voices raised for rights, autonomy, and equal access to the fruits of progress. To these groups, technology seemed a force for democratization because it had the potential to help everyone, not merely the elite. But many upper-class leaders, especially in the aristocracy, disdained these forces for change, ordering the police to shoot strikers and to throw suffragists in jail. In some colonies schools were closed because they bred independent thinkers, not servile laborers. The clash of aspirations inflamed social and political worlds alike, pushing technological progress away from peace and toward war.

THE MANY FACES OF MODERNITY

An important aspect of modernity in the early twentieth century was the rapid pace of technological change. Factory workers experienced the frequent introduction of new types of machinery, and the very wealthy could tinker with their new cars and even private planes. The hustle and bustle of urban life, with its trams, electricity, and crowds, made for a life utterly different from the tranquil pace of rural living. Single workers new to city life, many of them unmarried women, headed for jobs in the morning rush and then on weekends relaxed with leisure-time activities. Hawkers for the daily press bellowed out scandalous headlines, jolting the senses with the rapidly changing "news." Modern life undermined long-standing traditions, bringing excitement and not a little anxiety.

Modern Technology

In the late nineteenth and early twentieth centuries, bicycles, sewing machines, and typewriters, as well as telephones and lamps powered by electricity, brought new technology into the home and into other private spaces and contributed to people's sense of modernity. Unlike the airplane, which only the wealthiest had access to, many of the things developed during these years were for individual use and were affordable to lower-income people. At the beginning of the twentieth century Germany alone was producing some 250,000 bicycles. The ease that technology introduced into everyday life encouraged many people to feel optimistic about humanity's future.

German engineers had pioneered the automobile with the invention of the internal combustion machine, but in 1911 German manufacturers produced only 11,000 cars, and German consumers were not rushing out to purchase them. It was France that led the way in the manufacture of automobiles, producing 14,000 in 1905 and 45,000 in 1914—a 300 percent increase in less than a decade. Thanks to the early centralization of the French state and the invention of the mass army during the Napoleonic wars, the French excelled in civil engineering and enjoyed an excellent system of roads, which encouraged long-distance automobile travel and tourism. The French also led in producing and exporting airplanes before World War I, having understood the significance of the Wright brothers' invention early on. Early automobiles were bought mostly by the wealthy, the avant-garde, and

◆ **Embarking on a Road Trip**

The automobile was some fifteen years old when Madame Lockart and her daughter set out in 1903 on their Paris–to–St. Petersburg journey. Departing in their ultramodern machine from in front of the medieval Notre Dame Cathedral, they were in for an adventure as they made their way across a continent not yet criss-crossed with paved roads. In addition to adventure, the automobile generated new enterprises such as filling and repair stations, road-building, and the sale of protective clothing to shield travelers from the dust of travel on dirt roads. *Hulton Archive/Getty Images.*

people such as doctors who needed to travel extensively. Like the plane, the auto was indicative of the French talent for designing innovative luxury items. France exported one-third of its cars to Britain. Shortly before World War I the United States began to overtake French auto production.

Cars spawned a host of new industries—road construction, service stations, roadside cafés, map and guidebook publishing, and travel clothing and accessories, to name a few. Roads were key. "The great national highroads connecting St. Petersburg, Moscow, Warsaw, and Kiev are admirably adapted for motoring and are kept in good condition," one guidebook to Russia assured would-be tourists, though it advised against attempting to venture beyond these major thoroughfares into the countryside. Tourism flourished, and automobile clubs and racing competitions with large cash prizes also promoted automobile travel (see Documents 2.1, 2.2, and 2.3). Because many races were international, the belief that the automobile would promote good relations among nations was widespread. Because drivers had an opportunity to learn about other cultures as well as their own, many commentators believed that the automobile would bring the peoples of a nation or a continent closer together.

Technological advance transformed a variety of fields besides transportation. The chemical industry was a leading sector, producing everything from superior gunpowder and explosives to chemical fertilizer and medicines and pain relievers such as aspirin. Because of its high level of funding for technical education, Germany became an innovator, developing celluloid, bakelite, and other early synthetic materials from which Ping-Pong balls, buttons, dishes, and other products were made. The electric industry joined the surge in technological advance at the beginning of the century. Almost half its growing capacity provided electricity to municipal buildings and transport systems such as trams and railroads. Office buildings, factories, and even some individual homes acquired electricity, but the main impetus for development of the industry came from rapid urbanization and thus from municipal projects.

Despite competition among the great powers to advance the technological sophistication of their respective industries, the high costs of technology were starting to lead to international cooperation among individual entrepreneurs and institutions. Building railroads—whether in Europe, in the colonies, or in individual nations around the world—cost millions, and banks from several powers often teamed up to provide governments the capital needed for railroad construction. Belgian and French banks are one example of such an alliance in international finance. With the advent of oil as an important source of energy, financiers and entrepreneurs like the Nobels of Sweden poured money into the development of Romanian and Russian drilling. Here, too, the costs were enormous, and to meet them as well as to prevent wasteful competition, countries and enterprises combined their efforts. The East Asiatic Petroleum Company, for instance, was formed in 1903 with British, Dutch, German, and Russian capital as well as money from the Rothschild, Nobel, and Mantachov firms. Under these conditions, it was possible to predict—as some Europeans did—that the economic development of industrial technology would foster globalization and international cooperation.

Life in the Modern City

Technology at the turn of the century increased the fast pace of city life, which in turn came to symbolize modernity. Cities expanded because they incorporated outlying regions, extended sewer lines and other services into suburbs, and provided tramways, trains, and subways to bring suburban residents into the urban workforce. The wonders of this urban technology produced a rush of excitement about modernity, and cafés, parks, and urban street life offered a richer recreational life than people had enjoyed before. The decades before World War I were called the "Belle Epoque" in part because of the vibrancy of urban life, especially enjoyed by men and women with wealth and the leisure time to experience it. But ordinary workers also saw some rise in their real wages in the last decades of the nineteenth century, and the workday diminished enough to provide them with a few extra hours for relaxation and urban pleasures.

Modern city life, however, was not without its critics. Some, distressed by the anonymity and crowds that replaced the intimacy of village life, claimed that urban

◆ **The State Opera Platz in Vienna**
Built between 1861 and 1869, the Vienna Opera House at the time symbolized the expanding
reach of the modern state into cultural and social life. In the early twentieth century it was
also a landmark of urban vitality. Busy people dodged bicycles, trams, and even automobiles
by day. By night they frequented the opera, theater, burlesque, dance and music halls, cafés,
and beer gardens. Urban life stood in contrast to rural ways experienced by many Europeans,
especially in the eastern part of the continent, where urbanization occurred more slowly.
Brown Brothers.

life caused personality disorders. Berlin-based sociologist George Simmel be-
moaned what he saw as the emptiness and instability of city life, which appeared
to him "as the mania for traveling, as the wild pursuit of competition and as the
typically modern disloyalty with regard to taste, style, opinions and personal relationships."[4] Events were said to occur too quickly in the modern commercial city
with its electric and gas lighting and rapid transport and rushing crowds. New-
fangled automobiles, trams, and bicycles made crossing streets ever more dangerous. Indeed, in 1906 a horse-drawn wagon struck and killed the great French scientist Pierre Curie. Critics complained that department stores held too many
overly stimulating goods. Simply window-shopping could produce uncomfortable
sensations of longing and desire, critics warned.

Crowds of strangers jostled the modern city dweller, and some individuals were bothered by the stare of unfamiliar eyes on public transport. Passengers on trains, subways, and trams almost single-handedly created a booming market for pulp books and newspapers. They could satisfy their urge to be up-to-date and at the same time avoid intimate contact with other passengers by burying their noses in the latest best seller. These moments of privacy, however, ended quickly when commuters exited onto city streets filled with migrants wearing strange clothing and speaking foreign languages and later returned home to apartment houses filled with strangers with whom they had no social intimacy or even casual contact.

Paradoxically, even as it gave rise to feelings of isolation, anonymity, and alienation among many city dwellers, urban modernity also fostered provincialism and ethnic solidarity, especially among working-class newcomers. Cities displayed segregation by occupation and by nationality or ethnicity. Furniture makers, garment workers, and workers in other crafts often chose to live and work with their fellow artisans in the same part of town. To find job security and support, newly arrived migrants often moved to quarters where others of the same nationality lived. Jews from rural areas of Europe, for instance, settled and remained together in the same neighborhoods, though many assimilated into the broader urban society. Before radio and television, news from one part of the city did not necessarily penetrate another, to say nothing of news from abroad. Thus, among city workers, knowledge of the wider world was often vague, sometimes even nonexistent. Although the children of migrant workers learned in school that their homelands controlled empires, that knowledge was as "unreal as a story from *Grimm's Fairy Tales*," as one British woman remembered.[5] The demands of work and neighborhood, where one hid truant children, scavenged for discarded items, and shared local gossip, formed an important mental boundary within even the most bustling capital city.

While many criticized the sense of isolation fostered by urbanization, others applauded the modern advances prompted by population growth, migration, and mass society. Modern apartment buildings of brick and concrete allowed more family privacy and intimacy, and they were built in great numbers for the lower-middle and upper-working classes, complete with a water closet, separate bedrooms, gas and running water for each unit, and other amenities. Efforts were made to improve personal hygiene and sanitation in cities by restricting the location of slaughterhouses, dyeworks, tanneries, and other enterprises that generated noxious odors and other kinds of pollution to nonresidential areas. Reform groups promoted garden apartments and green areas to make home life more pleasant, and they sponsored worker gardens in poor parts of the city so that family members could spend leisure time together in what the reformers deemed "uplifting" activity.

Another outcome of urban modernity was a growing secularism and a related interest in nonreligious sources of self-improvement. Once guided by priests, ministers, rabbis, and other clergy, the working classes tended to neglect religious activities in favor of secular ones such as reading newspapers and books. Literate because of compulsory education or because of their own desire to read, workers turned, as one recent historian has put it, "from the Good Book to the Great

Books." In the case of British readers, these included Shakespeare, John Stuart Mill, George Eliot, and the Brontë sisters. At the end of the workday many laborers attended night schools, read in cafés, and formed societies for mutual instruction in the classics. They borrowed books from public libraries or circulated books among neighbors. Historians estimate that in the early twentieth century almost half the working families in England read aloud in the family on a regular basis and that as many owned considerable numbers of books, often protecting them with great care and regularly washing hands before reading. In 1913 the sale of books in comparatively illiterate Russia reached 100 million copies in the Russian language alone.

Political modernizers such as the Russian revolutionary leader V. I. Lenin saw great promise in this turn to reading: "Millions of cheap editions on political themes were read by people, by the masses, by the crowd, more greedily than ever before,"[6] he noted, commenting on the change after the turn of the century. Ramsay MacDonald, a working man who would become prime minister of England in the 1920s, remembered that reading Sir Walter Scott's heart-stopping adventures of medieval knights "opened out the great world of national life for me and led me on to politics."[7]

Many in the upper classes feared the effects that reading would have on the lower classes, and they were right to do so. Workers often equated villains in classics like Scott's *Ivanhoe* with the modern-day capitalists and large landowners who they thought were exploiting them. Some workers simply enjoyed reading about the upper classes in Scott's novels, which glorified monarchical government and aristocratic deeds in the past. In either case, whether readers were fans of Walter Scott or of Shakespeare, the very experience of reading often led them to think for themselves. Many found that reading opened their minds to critical ideas and encouraged militant activism to bring social and economic justice for the lower classes. Many read Karl Marx, Friedrich Engels, and German socialist August Bebel, all of whose writings led the way to the socialist parties or to trade union activism.

Newspapers were another important guide to modern urban life. Their circulation soared, and their content changed to meet the demands of modern urban dwellers. A century earlier, newspapers carried lengthy articles featuring political commentary, their circulation was limited, and many were printed only weekly (so comparatively leisurely was the pace of life). By the early twentieth century, as one reporter noted, "Every hour in Berlin flings millions of newspaper pages onto the streets, into houses, into offices, banking suites, factories, taverns, and theaters." Newspapers "completely changed the face of the street," he continued, with their kiosks and readers in taverns and cafés, their faces hidden by blaring front-page headlines.[8] In an increasingly impersonal environment where word of mouth could no longer be counted on to keep people informed, newspapers provided crucial information in the form of advertisements for jobs, accommodations, and useful items for sale. They also brought news of people—great and ordinary—in columns and articles devoted to scandals, murders, burglaries, and the doings of high society. On the eve of World War I, most French dailies ignored the news of the assassination of the heir to the Habsburg throne and his wife and the diplomatic maneuverings that preceded the outbreak of war. Instead, the front page of most papers carried news of the burning scandal of the day: the trial of Madame Caillaux, the upper-class wife of a high government official, who had murdered a newspaper baron for publishing accounts of her husband's love affairs. Perhaps paradoxically, given newspapers' capacity for reducing citizens' isolation and ignorance of events, many critics saw the newspaper with its hodgepodge of news, gossip, ads, sports, and serialized fiction as emblematic of modern life's fragmentation.

Gender Roles and Sexual Life

The attention to personal scandal highlighted some of the transformations altering intimate and family relationships. New patterns of social interactions, rapidly taking shape because of urbanization and technological development, modified family and gender roles. The migration of rural workers to cities, for instance, involved married men and their families, single men, and increasing numbers of single women. On the eve of World War I, women constituted 48 percent of the population of St. Petersburg; two decades earlier, they had been 30 percent. Single men endured long factory hours—sixty hours a week on average by the turn of the century but often higher. These men sometimes lived in squalid barracks and at other times packed into boarding houses where they were forced to share the rental of a bed. Some women coming to cities had to turn to prostitution to earn a living, contributing to the impression that urban modernity was a danger rather than a blessing and that the social order was falling apart.

Whether danger or blessing, economic opportunities available in modern cities increased the proportion of women and men in white-collar and blue-collar jobs at the expense of the agricultural sector in the late nineteenth and early twentieth centuries. The rise of modern commercial facilities—most notably the department store—and the development of a managerial sector in business created the white-collar sector, in which people worked as stenographers and secretaries in insurance companies, industrial firms, and banks and as department store clerks and shopkeepers' assistants. Government jobs also increased for both men and women with the growing bureaucratization of nation-states. Between 1891 and 1910 the number of employees in the Italian civil service rose from 126,000 to 376,000; the French civil service counted 451,000 employees in 1901 and 699,000 in 1911. This growth opened a segment of the labor market to young women able to read, write, and do arithmetic as a result of compulsory education. The growing need for educated white-collar workers tapped all available literate candidates— both men and women. Thus, in the Austrian sector of Austria-Hungary, the number of men in the professions and in white-collar public sector jobs rose from 151,000 in 1890 to 291,000 in 1910, and the number of women went from 30,900 to 79,000, most of them in postal, telegraph, and telephone work. Women also worked as schoolteachers and librarians, jobs that appealed to women of the lower-middle and upper-working classes who would have shunned factory work for reasons of propriety. By the early twentieth century, women were beginning to dominate school teaching across Europe, except in Germany and Russia.

The expanding presence of women in the white-collar workforce angered some men because the women seemed to be moving out of their familiar, subordinate place. Also, the presence of low-paid women threatened to drag down white-collar wages, and for this reason men in clerical jobs were hostile to the women in their midst, seeing them not as coworkers but as competitors. In response to a Dutch questionnaire of 1903, one man responded that although he had never worked with a woman clerk, "I am against female colleagues on principle."[9] There also were protests about women working in well-paying jobs such as at British potteries.

Despite all evidence to the contrary, reformers and labor unions joined forces to limit women's jobs in well-paying industrial work on the grounds that it would make women ill and harm their unborn children. Almost no one contested women's working in menial, poorly paid jobs such as laundry work or sewing long hours at home. And there were few protests about the working conditions endured by the rural women who streamed into the city and became domestic servants — one of the most exploited sectors of the workforce — to serve the increasingly prosperous middle class. As the century opened, some 20 percent of the female workforce in Spain toiled up to twenty hours a day in domestic service, 30 percent in the city of St. Petersburg.

Whatever their profession or class, single people migrating to cities escaped the patriarchal control that shaped rural life. Observers were especially struck by the increasing numbers of independent working women in cities. New opportunities for single middle-class women in white-collar work helped erode the Victorian mentality that prized female ignorance and chastity and relegated women to the "separate sphere" of the home. Single women became associated with modernity, particularly the modernity of city life. No longer supervised by their families, many lived by themselves in boarding houses and apartments and walked the streets unescorted. Signs of their modernity included working outside the home in respectable jobs and behavior that polite society deemed scandalous: sexual relations outside of wedlock and single parenthood. Some highly educated women like the Italian doctor and innovator in early childhood education Maria Montessori had children outside of marriage; other prominent women like Alma Mahler, wife of famed composer and conductor Gustav Mahler, had multiple lovers. The growing presence of women in the workforce and the willingness of some women to ignore social propriety are indications of the ongoing unfolding of individualism and independence as social and political values.

New technology expanded sexual freedom for women as well as for men. Physicians helped perfect new birth control devices. Rubber diaphragms and condoms protected both sexes from venereal disease, allowed them greater sexual independence, and contributed to the reduction in family size. Bicycles and cars permitted leisure-time travel by the unmarried, and trains and steamships transported people hundreds and sometimes thousands of miles from the watchful eyes of families and neighbors. Butterfly collector Margaret Fountaine, an unmarried Englishwoman, had love affairs with the local guides she met in the Middle East and elsewhere. In a 1901 diary entry, she described a passionate encounter with Khalil

Neimy, her guide in Lebanon and Palestine: "He carried me across the room, and laid me on my bed, and when he lay over me the weight of his body was sweet to me now because I loved him."[10] Middle-class women like Fountaine and Montessori were in the forefront of developing women's independence, which itself was emblematic of educational, artistic, scientific, and sexual modernity.

Men's roles changed in tandem with the decline of the agricultural household, where men had long exercised independent decision making, sometimes for vast extended families laboring as a unit. The power of men diminished as they moved away from the land and became workers at the mercy of foremen and bosses. Family size decreased, and this also reduced the extent of men's influence, especially as children came under the sway of teachers and took jobs in industry themselves. Yet men gained stature as soldiers in citizen armies, as wage earners with money, and as citizens because of the expanding right to vote. They themselves gained new skills in schools and factories, and the growing popularity of team sports, along with service in the army, taught them to prize a rugged masculinity. Some in the elites saw technology such as planes offering a training ground for the further development of masculine prowess and heroism. It would help overcome the softening feminization of culture they saw resulting from the abundance of goods provided by trade and industry. Unprecedented prosperity along with the more visible presence of women in public was wearing away the hardy male spirit that had built Europe. To their minds, fast planes and cars and sports would contribute to shaping a new man, making masculinity emblematic of modernity (see Document 2.2).

Another manifestation of modern life was the increasing visibility of women and men who lived as same-sex couples. Many same-sex couples inhabited informally defined homosexual sections of cities, working and socializing with their neighbors. There were cafés and clubs for meeting people with same-sex proclivities, special social circles in homes, and rituals of belonging such as nicknames and common jokes. In the early twentieth century some high-society people were also prominently "out" as homosexuals. To celebrate female homosexuality, socialites Nathalie Barney and Renée Vivien made a very public trip to the Greek island of Lesbos—birthplace of the classical Greek poet Sappho, who wrote beautiful odes to her female lovers. Vivien wrote *A Woman Appeared to Me,* a novel celebrating lesbian love. Although some people announced their homosexuality as a distinct sexual orientation during these years, people continued, as they had in past centuries, to practice a more polymorphous sexuality than would later be the case. Both up-and-coming politician Harold Nicholson of England and writer Thomas Mann of Germany were married and had male lovers. Nicholson's wife, the writer Vita Sackville-West, also had same-sex relationships that were integral to her life. In some cases, homosexuals, like the aristocrats in Kaiser William II's circle who were the scandal of Europe at the time, saw their same-sex love as a higher way of being.

In keeping with the growing value placed on scientific explanation and the pattern of increasing secularism, some of the leading psychologists declared that same-sex love was not amoral but rather a fact of nature. Homosexuals themselves developed a range of explanations for their lifestyle, including calling themselves a "third sex," and a few prominent physicians like Havelock Ellis maintained that homosexuality should be regarded as an ordinary, natural phenomenon. Still, scandals about homosexuality increased in number. For example, in 1910, hard on the heels of the scandal about the cross-dressing of Kaiser William's military entourage, the German press threatened to expose munitions magnate Frederick Krupp's liaisons with boys, and the possibility of scandal led to Krupp's suicide. Such incidents produced a heated journalistic defense of heterosexuality and the family even as social change was taking place in the realm of familial and sexual mores. Sexual behavior and gender roles entered the political sphere as never before, providing fodder for those who wanted to gain support of the voting masses.

MODERNITY AND THE RISE OF MASS POLITICS

As Europe prospered and became more modern, it also experienced waves of political protest and rising discontent. Modernity entailed the waning power of the aristocracy because of the spread of suffrage to men of all classes. Not only did the population demand the vote, politicians increasingly accepted theories of political liberalism that expanded concepts of natural rights beyond the right to free speech and fair trials to include the right to participate in one's political destiny by voting. By 1913 most of the men in Europe outside of Russia had the right to vote, making the early twentieth century an age of mass politics.

What that meant for the control of government in a culture where traditional agrarian elites were used to ruling unchallenged differed from country to country, but the first years of the decade saw unprecedented and heated debate over the role of traditional wealth and influence in politics. In some countries the old ruling classes aggressively aimed to maintain their grip on political institutions, while the avant-garde also saw itself as constituting an elite (see Documents 2.5 and 2.6). The spreading wave of political voices—encompassing working-class men, women of all classes, and eventually the utterly disenfranchised in the colonies—indicated the coming to maturity of the "masses." Some historians have seen in the rise of the masses a "crisis of liberalism," especially in the turn of many working people to socialism. In their view, these new claimants to a say in representative government challenged not only the old aristocratic power but also the liberal power of middle-class male elites who reaped the benefits of constitutional government, parliamentary institutions, and capitalist economic development.

Working-Class Politics

In the last third of the nineteenth century, it was the rise of national working-class parties that most threatened the old order. These parties had developed, paradoxically, at a time of slowly rising wages and of gradually declining hours at work. Unions were thus partly a manifestation of workers' strength and prosperity, not simply their oppression. Workers were all too aware, however, of the insecurity that they all faced. Technological change was regularly making some workers obsolete or superfluous as new machines replaced them. Machines speeded up work processes, increasing fatigue rather than minimizing it even as a new layer of authoritarian managers often demanded ever greater levels of productivity because of the new technology. Workers demanded better pay and more control over work itself. They sought to achieve their gains by forming unions and working-class political parties. Significantly, women workers were largely excluded from these early worker organizations. When introducing new machines and procedures, bosses often hired low-paid women to bear the brunt of change. Thus, most unions felt that the presence of women in factories put them out of work and pulled their wages down. Instead of inviting women to join them in worker solidarity against such practices, they adopted the bosses' view that women were menials. Many men demanded the exclusion of women from factories.

Industrialized countries such as France, Britain, Italy, and Germany had the most powerful worker organizations and political parties, complete with bureaucracies, labor newspapers, and permanent offices located in most major cities. Because of migration, these parties had a rare opportunity to capture the allegiance of newcomers to the city and to integrate them into working-class activism. Nonetheless, they had to struggle against strong opposition from elites for their right even to exist—especially in Russia, where worker organization was illegal, and in Germany, where only beginning in the 1890s did William II permit the formation of workers' parties. Worker parties and unions also had to compete against one another for the votes of Catholics, Protestants, craftspeople, factory and office workers, and peasants. Nonetheless, despite external opposition and internal struggles among the parties themselves, by the beginning of the twentieth century working-class parties had become so popular that one—Germany's Social Democratic Party, which adhered to Marxist socialism—surpassed all others, including the elite parties, in Germany's 1913 elections.

The rise of socialist parties was not exclusive to Germany but had been occurring across Europe since the last third of the nineteenth century as worker dissatisfaction and worker solidarity grew. The upper classes feared these worker parties in general for their vote-getting capacity, but it was their ideology based on the writings of Karl Marx (1818–1883) and Friedrich Engels that most threatened elites. In the spirit of nineteenth-century social science, Marx and Engels had announced their analysis of the economics and social organization of contemporary Europe as "scientific," and they called their program "socialism" to indicate its concern for the state of society. Their many books and articles described society as organized among competing economic classes. Instead of adhering to the liberal political view of the virtues of holding and protecting private property, Marx and Engels believed that the capitalist system with its private property in land, capital, and factories was in decline. Marxist thought argued that the working poor—the "proletariat"—were being exploited, unjustly deprived of the fruits of their labor in the form of the unearned profits of the bourgeoisie, or owners. The proletariat, composed of those who lacked property in the means of production (factories, land, capital), would join together to overthrow this unfair system. All of this Marx and Engels demonstrated by showing through statistics that profit was actually the "alienated" labor or being of a worker and that the bourgeois owner statistically provided less in material terms to the productive process than he was taking away from it. Marx and Engels added a revolutionary thrust to their analysis by denouncing the nation-state as an institution that pitted workers against one another in nationalist rivalries, whipped up as later socialists would claim by jingoistic politics, to divert them from their common ills generated by capitalist exploitation. "The working man has no country" became the slogan of international socialist parties.

Marxism was utopian because it "scientifically" promised a fully just society in the future once workers had ended the reign of the capitalist owners of the means of production. This combination of utopianism and science proved attractive. By the early twentieth century, labor leaders and socialist politicians were engaged in hot debate within the Second International (a transnational organization of representatives from the socialist parties of the different nations founded in 1889) about how best to hasten the arrival of this new future. In meeting halls of both the Second International and the socialist parties across Europe workers brought forth both complex analysis and bitter arguments over the situation of labor. Where would capitalists fall first to a socialist uprising, the delegates speculated. Most thought this likely to occur in Britain or Germany, where concentrations of industrial workers were heaviest. However, peasant Russia was not far from their minds either, thanks to its program of industrialization, the turbulent Revolution of 1905 that swept nearly all classes to revolution, and the persistent efforts of its various protest parties. Finally, debates raised the question of a reformist rather than revolutionary road to a utopian and socialist future. Given the rising numbers gained by workers' parties in elections, was it not possible that the working class could come to power simply by winning elections? Those who advocated the more gradual road to socialism were called "revisionists." All of these issues kept socialist and other worker parties in productive ferment—a ferment that absolutely terrified many members of the ruling elite.

At the level of individual life, crowded urban living facilitated the development of a distinctly working-class politics, and solidarity often began at the neighborhood level. Sharing facilities such as common toilets, water supplies, and laundry areas, working women exchanged news of neighbors in financial distress or ill health, the arrival of officials to execute evictions, and the arrest of friends for activism, drunkenness, or petty crime. Neighbors served as character witnesses for one another, and news of labor troubles such as wage cuts or layoffs swept through neighborhoods. Many working-class families took in boarders such as migrants from the countryside and initiated them into the community of workers and its concerns. Passing time together sitting in front of doorways on pleasant evenings or in cafés and beer gardens, neighbors, despite the alleged anonymity of modern life, built up a degree of solidarity. Strikes brought communities together in mutual aid, providing food and child care. In these ways neighborhoods provided a baseline of support without which mass politics would not have taken place.

◆ **Striking Van Boys**
From the oil fields of Baku to the streets of London where these English newsboys are on strike, in 1913 workers around the globe protested long hours, dangerous tasks, cold and damp factories with polluted air, insufficient wages, and abusive treatment. Strikes also produced camaraderie and solidarity, powerful assets for hard-pressed workers. *Topical Press Agency/Getty Images.*

Working-class political parties enhanced this solidarity with an assortment of clubs and special events for workers. Choral societies were among the most popular in the days before radio, television, and more recent sources of entertainment. As unions succeeded in getting the workweek cut to five or five-and-a-half days, workers formed special clubs to go hiking or bicycling together. In the days before radio, television, or widespread secondary education for laborers, working-class cafés and party libraries offered a large selection of reading material to intellectually hungry workers, and the political parties across Europe set up evening classes to teach an array of subjects but also to build solidarity. By these latter means, workers came to know the fine points of Marxism, which shaped their thinking about politics and labor activism.

Europe's workers experienced improvement in their condition in the first decades of the twentieth century, as business picked up after a three-decade-long slump and as new jobs developed around new technology and industry. Nonetheless, violence against political and business leaders escalated in a wave of assassinations that dominated the headlines. At the turn of the century the premier of Spain (1897), the empress of Austria-Hungary (1898), King Umberto of Italy (1900), and President William McKinley of the United States (1901) were all assassinated. Some four thousand officials were attacked or assassinated in Russia, foremost among them Prime Minister Pyotr Stolypin (1911), whose home had earlier been bombed. Political activists, among them anarchists and anarcho-syndicalists who believed in the creative political force of mass violence, were eager to bring down the elite. They bombed stock markets and country homes alike, while workers across Europe began a round of strikes demanding better wages and working conditions. From labor strikes in French vineyards, in the oilfields of Russia, and in the railway yards of Bulgaria to general work stoppages in Sweden, the working classes politically, vocally, and sometimes violently expressed their grievances against low wages, obsolescence due to the introduction of technology, and dangerous working conditions, especially in mines and factories.

A faction in the upper classes fought back hard. By 1900 parties representing agrarian elites used militant nationalism and imperialism to contest the socialist appeal for international brotherhood and justice. Invoking militant patriotism, pride in empire, hatred for Jews, and the necessity of dominance at home and overseas, they were able to gather support at the polls. In Vienna at the turn of the century, political candidates found vicious anti-Semitic rhetoric effective in corralling the votes of artisans, office workers, and ethnic Germans facing competition for jobs from recently arrived ethnic groups, especially the flood of Jewish poor migrating to the city. The most successful opportunist of this type and a hero of Adolf Hitler was mayor of Vienna Karl Lueger, who combined sweeping programs to help lower-middle-class urban craftsmen hurt by modernization with speeches referring to Jews as "vermin" and "slime." Elsewhere landowners and industrialists used veiled and not so veiled threats to influence their tenant farmers, day laborers, and factory workers to vote the right way. Many employers directed foremen to march their workers to the polls. Mass politics were so passionate and even violent at times that they could threaten the very existence of the state.

Feminists on the March

Like workers active in prolabor and socialist parties, women presented themselves forcefully during the early twentieth century as a new political constituency. Instilled with the Enlightenment belief in human rationality and equal rights to citizenship, the feminist movement gained strength in the early years of the twentieth century until there were millions of female and male activists on its behalf. The movement had a wide-ranging program encompassing property rights, the right to divorce, the right of working women to keep their wages, and the right to enter exclusively male professions such as law and finance: "The women's movement demands *not alms, but justice* for the female sex," German activist and newspaper editor Lily von Braun announced. "It demands open access to the universities, changes in the laws that treat women as second-class people, and constitutional recognition of the woman as a citizen with equal rights."[11] Acting on both the local and the national scene in individual countries, the movement spawned many, sometimes competing organizations, representing specific issues such as protective legislation and the right to divorce. In the face of rising nationalist, socialist, and prolabor movements often based on rights for men of a single nation, the activists defended their efforts as broadly majoritarian. "The woman question is without doubt the most important movement in our century," a manifesto of Ukrainian women announced. "While other issues relate to some one part of society, this movement touches half of the whole human race."[12] In this spirit, the women's movement spawned several international groups consisting of organizations from around the world. The most notable of these, the International Woman Suffrage Alliance formed in 1902, convened regularly in congresses held in major cities.

The International Woman Suffrage Alliance represented a consensus among many though not all feminist activists that the only way to speed up the process of gaining rights for women was to obtain the vote. In 1906, through backroom deal making, Finnish women obtained the vote in what was then a semi-autonomous duchy of Russia. Despite victory in Finland and the burgeoning support for suffrage, some feminist organizations, such as the major groups in France and Germany, held the vote to be too unladylike and radical, but even in those countries a few activists bravely agitated despite the reluctance of their contemporaries in the movement. While some continued to work for access to jobs, equal pay, and legal rights, others surged forward in subordinating all other issues to the suffrage cause. Frustrated by the slow progress of social and economic reform, some turned to desperate measures.

The most militant and visible was the Women's Social and Political Union in Britain, which began mass marches in 1907 to dramatize women's demands for political representation (see Document 2.4). Taking politics to the streets, the marchers were mostly from the middle class, but working women from the northern textile factories formed a strong contingent among them. These "suffragettes," as this group came to be called, were headed by the respectable, middle-class activist Emmeline Pankhurst and her daughters. Crowds gathered, and some men assaulted the marchers, grabbing their breasts and mauling them. Taking up a new kind of protest, the suffragists chained themselves to the gates of the parliament building and blocked entryways in "passive resistance." In 1909 the campaign itself turned violent, as women, disguised as proper ladies, slashed works of art in museums, set off bombs, and carried hammers in their clothing to smash store windows, all to demonstrate that men in power cared only for the protection of their private property. "We have tried to be womanly," Emmeline Pankhurst noted in her trial in 1908. "We have tried to use feminine influence, and we have seen that it is of no use. . . . We are here, not because we are law-breakers; we are here in our efforts to become law-makers."[13] As bills to give women the vote met defeat, some

◆ **Suffragists Released from Prison**

English suffragists engaged in vigorous marches and protests to obtain for women the right to vote. The government often responded with equal vigor, jailing them for "disturbing the peace." Emmeline Pankhurst and her daughter Christabel are shown here with supporters on their release from prison in 1908. This would not be Emmeline's last stint in jail. In 1912, the government had her arrested a dozen times, releasing her when she went on a hunger strike and then arresting her again as soon as her condition improved. Activism for equal rights was common across Europe before 1914. In the aftermath of World War I, when women finally received the vote, politicians claimed that such activism had not influenced their decision. Rather, they insisted that granting the vote to women was a reward for women's patriotism during wartime. © *Hulton-Deutsch Collection/CORBIS.*

turned to even more desperate measures. On Derby Day in 1913 one of the suffragists, Emily Wilding Davison, threw herself in front of the king's horse and was trampled to death in the tradition of those willing to die for a higher cause.

Like other popular movements at the time that sought to expand rights to a broader range of people, the suffrage movement met fierce opposition. With fertility rates plummeting across the West, some prominent politicians accused women of launching a birth strike in order to gain rights, and they firmly opposed any moves to grant women the legal privileges that men enjoyed. Others felt that equality would bring about the collapse of the natural gender order. Italian premier Francesco Crispi maintained that "women's hands are meant for kissing not for voting." Women themselves were often the most vocal antifeminists: "Woman is made for love, before being made for knowledge," one French woman novelist declared.[14] Law codes continued to uphold the principle that women owed obedience to their husbands. Despite some modifications, such as according women in a few countries the right to own their wages, these codes mostly remained in force until after World War II. Education was another area that remained segregated by sex. Although women gained admission to some universities and often surpassed men in their studies, distinguished male intellectuals repeatedly voted to deny them degrees no matter how well they scored on university exams. Cambridge and Oxford universities, for instance, did not accord women degrees until after World Wars I and II respectively.

A final kind of dissent came from among suffragists themselves. In 1913 Irish women, determined to strike an independent blow for their suffrage within the context of the struggle for Irish home rule, separated from the London-based movement. As one leader put it: "we had no desire to work under English women leaders: we could lead ourselves."[15] In this case feminist unity fell victim to battles for national liberation.

Like socialism, feminism was a transnational movement, and it reflected both the increasing communications across the globe made possible by new technology and the unifying potential of urbanization. The growth of capital cities provided venues for international meetings of workers and women alike, with public transport, hotels, and even women's clubs at the delegates' disposal. Books, letters, and reports with the latest ideas on the condition of women circulated widely, and individual speakers and organizers traveled the world. Ellen Key, a celebrated Swedish activist, inspired movements in Japan and elsewhere around the world with her ideas for improving the material conditions of motherhood as the basis for good marital and family relationships. Likewise, European feminists imbibed philosophies from Asia advocating a balance of male and female forces to effect harmony in society and the universe alike. As women attended meetings unchaperoned and traveled independently, a model of women's political modernity—like a model of working men's political modernity—was taking shape.

THE ARTS AND PHILOSOPHY EMBRACE MODERNITY

The arts and philosophy so effectively embraced new methods and ideas that the term *modernism* has clung to the painting, literature, and thought of the early twentieth century ever since. Caught in the whirlwind of modern life, artistic and theoretical styles changed rapidly, like so many inventions crowding out earlier ones. Modernists emphatically rejected all that had gone before as hopelessly out-of-date and wrongheaded, making traditional ideas the butt of ridicule. "Make it new!" American expatriate poet Ezra Pound clamored from his adopted home in Europe. Pound made Western poetry "new" by studying Chinese ideograms and applying the principles of Chinese poetry to his own. As imperialist travelers returned home with examples of non-Western art and thought, many an artist borrowed from styles around the world in the quest for modernity and the "new." The result was an unprecedented period of innovation in the arts and philosophy and a cornucopia of novel, even shocking works that disturbed traditionally minded Europeans. Oddly enough, many of these shocking modern works contained statements against modernity itself. This paradox leads historians to see in this prewar period not only the advance of modernity but simultaneously a revolt against aspects of the dramatic changes that were sweeping Europe.

Innovation in the Arts

Practitioners of the visual, musical, and literary arts in the early twentieth century produced works in many styles, unlike their more traditional predecessors, who followed an established artistic canon. Mocking both past styles and the status quo, modern artists were brash in their denunciations. Futurist art and literature thrived on insults to public taste, foul and ungrammatical language, and hatred of women, whose changing status was in their creators' opinion an appalling aspect of contemporary life. Artists marketed these attributes of futurism to potential buyers as urban, technological, and modern. The young Russian poet Vladimir Maiakovsky explained it this way: "The poetry of futurism is the poetry of the city, of the modern city. The city replaces nature and becomes itself an element of nature. Telegraphs, airplanes, express trains, elevators, rotatives [printing presses], sidewalks, and factory smokestacks—these are the elements of the beautiful in urban nature. The regular, calm, slow rhythms of older poetry no longer speak to the psyche of the city dweller. Everything is now angles, broken lines, zigzags. Poetry must adapt itself to these new forms."[16] Such was one manifesto for the cult of the new, and others soon followed (see Document 2.5).

In the early twentieth century, artistic pioneers abandoned the realism of great novels such as *War and Peace,* the harmonious melodies of composers such as Beethoven, and pretty impressionist scenery that had generated pride in European civilization. Constituting themselves as an avant-garde of forward-thinking people, painters like Pablo Picasso and composers like Arnold Schoenberg began deliberately shocking their audiences with portraits of grotesque bodies and symphonies full of dissonant sound. In some cases, such as that of the Spanish-born Picasso, the reasons were as much political as artistic. Picasso had grown up in anarchist Barcelona, where there were frequent protests against government, industrialist, and landowner power. Avant-garde painters in Germany rejected the triumphalist paintings of historical scenes so much loved by William II and his officials. In the search for a new style, painters in Russia turned to folk motifs to show faith in the utopian future of a liberated and flourishing peasantry; they turned away from detailed realism toward "primitivism," a deliberately unsophisticated style of painting that looked like the work of children or people without artistic training. Other artists were struck by the highly stylized sculpture and sounds that arrived from Africa and other parts of the imperialized world. (See the Picture Essay.) Whatever the particular influence, they were determined to make art anew. "We were possessed," wrote a German poet reflecting on the years at the beginning of the twentieth century. "In cafés, on the streets, in our studios, day and night, we were 'on the march,' at a cracking pace, to fathom the unfathomable: poets, painters and musicians all working together to create 'the art of the century,' an incomparable art towering timelessly over the art of all past centuries."[17]

Modern style varied, but one influential school that flourished across the various artistic genres adopted the term *expressionist*. Expressionist painters formed a movement of many different techniques but shared a unifying belief in the healing, spiritual, and expressive power of color. They took their ideas of color's symbolic and emotional significance from the theosophists—Europeans who practiced a version of Hinduism mingled with Buddhism. Expressionists like Norwegian painter Edvard Munch used a variety of muted pastels to show pleasure, turmoil, and ease—all of these feelings emanating from within the self. Artists wanted to depict nature not as it conventionally appeared but as an "inner impression" of an inner truth that they captured and expressed outwardly in their work—thus the term *expressionism*.[18] Another expressionist, the Austrian Oskar Kokoschka, lived a tormented life of poverty and neuralgic pain, which he drew on to create powerful portraits that today are considered masterpieces. Yet he made many of his subjects appear so tortured in the final product that they mostly refused to purchase them. His depiction of his relationship with his lover Alma Mahler (*The Storm*, 1914) achieved its powerful effects through the expressionist use of swirls of color.[19]

There was something incredibly jarring about expressionism, and indeed the bizarre depictions, the intense or odd colors, and the movement away from realism were meant to unsettle audiences. Only by "shaking the inner self" of viewers could expressionist art do its work. Expressionist artists, whether in the visual, theatrical, dance, musical, or literary arts, held to this creed. "Astonish me," exhorted the composer Arnold Schoenberg, announcing the need for artists and their audiences to throw off the shackles of conventional middle-class taste with its beloved repertoire of easy and harmonious, genteel and melodious tunes. To replace harmony, tonality, and the use of classically recognized chords, Schoenberg and other contemporary composers turned to atonality—a system of using all the notes of the chromatic scale without prioritizing them. When it first appeared in Schoenberg's and others' work, the impression conveyed was of musical chaos. One critic wrote of the modernist operas of Richard Strauss that they "spit and scratch and claw each other like enraged panthers." The Russian composer Aleksandr Scriabin wanted to incorporate expressionism's powerful sense of color into his musical works. In his sonata *A Poem of Fire* (1908) he employed a new invention, the color organ, which along with sound emitted lights of varying hues within the concert hall. His performances aroused strikingly different reactions in his audiences, but this was the intent of expressionism. Instead of merely duplicating reality, expressionist music was intended to awaken the internal self and cause it to reflect on its emotional and spiritual state. The question was how much of this jarring society could stand.

◆ **Oskar Kokoschka,** *Self-Portrait* **(1917)**

The great Austrian expressionist painter Oskar Kokoschka continually experimented with depicting inner feelings, dissonance, and turmoil on the canvas. He professed to have developed expressionist techniques by visiting an ethnographic museum, where he "learned how primitive peoples . . . had decorated the skulls of the dead with facial features with the play of expressions, the lines of laughter and anger, restoring them to the appearance of life." Wanting to lessen Kokoschka's poverty, a sympathetic official hired the artist to teach painting to sixth-grade girls but fired him after a year. Instead of teaching artistic techniques, Kokoschka had encouraged his young pupils to paint from their imaginations and feelings—like good expressionists. *Giraudon, Art Resource, New York.*

Like the visual and musical arts, musical drama and theater churned people's emotions with their content. Leoš Janáček from Czechoslovakia, considered the best composer of opera of the twentieth century, captured the jarring nature of ethnic divisiveness and rural migration in his song cycle *Diary of One Who Vanished,* the story of a young Slavic man who runs off with a gypsy and becomes dead to his village. The fragility of the patriarchal family in modern times drove the plot of his tragic opera *Katya Kabanova,* in which the heroine strays from her traditional husband for a stranger from the city. Janáček's music, like that of his contemporaries such as Hungarian Béla Bartók, combined folk tunes and natural sounds imitating the songs of birds and human voices with the dissonant strains of musical modernism.

The final blow for many viewers was the emergence of abstract art within expressionism, because abstraction boldly dispensed with any attempt to convey the material world. Wealthy Russian painter Wassily Kandinsky, perhaps the first to reject realism altogether, explained the turn toward abstraction as an attempt to capture the "spiritual" in art (see Document 2.6). Instead of catering to the ill-educated and materialist bourgeois, Kandinsky explained, avant-garde artists would appeal to the soul and to higher values. He found examples of the kind of art he espoused in the work of South Asian and African artists flooding European markets, in which there was no attempt merely to copy a "real" object. The artist who rejected capturing the realism of objects had thus shown "our sympathy, our spiritual relationship, with the Primitives. Like ourselves, these artists sought to express in their work only internal truths, renouncing in consequence all consideration of external form."[20] Simultaneously in the first decade of the century, cubists like Pablo Picasso were making realistic forms more angular and distorting their surfaces. But the radicals were the purely abstract artists, who painted geometric forms such as triangles, circles, arcs, and straight lines as signs of the spiritual purity to which they aspired.

Here was the paradox of modern art: it aimed at once to be jarring and healing. If the industrial world had brought fragmentation, abstract and expressionist artists hoped to restore the viewer to spiritual wholeness, in part by drawing on models they found in non-Western art (see the Picture Essay). As if to counter this modern fragmentation, expressionist artists collaborated to an impressive degree on theatrical and musical productions, pooling their talents. Painters painted scenery, much of it full of mystical symbolism; composers created scores meant to capture in music the expressionism of the visual arts; and dramatists wrote librettos and scripts addressing the deep mysteries of a unified cosmos. Scenery was redrawn in the expressionist style — sometimes grotesque and shocking, at other times geometric and abstract — while the repertoire of classical opera received an expressionist facelift with an infusion of the mystical palette in stage lighting. Composer Gustav Mahler's style of direction in opera or symphonic music was expressionist: Mahler demanded an outpouring of intense emotion from his choruses. He set his music to Chinese and other non-Western poetry. Dancers tried to recapture the vivid emotions they imputed to the indigenous peoples of Africa and the Americas. Their motions were jerky, they wore frightening masks, and they moved to dissonant music (see the Picture Essay, Figure 2.6). These innovators gave birth to modern dance. Irish playwright and Nobel laureate William Butler Yeats modeled his works after the Noh plays of Japan, in which actors wore stylized masks. Moreover, many of these artists worked in multiple genres, most notably Schoenberg as a painter and Kandinsky as a musician. Indeed the latter characterized many of his abstract paintings as "improvisations" and "compositions." They refused personally and artistically to be fragmented by the society around them. In the process, however, they created an art that to viewers seemed stylistically fragmented and deeply unsettling.

Modernism in Thought

Similar disturbances and profound reformulations were taking place in the world of thought, many of them evident in the writings of a younger generation disillusioned with the claims of science and the social sciences to certainty and predictability. Their precursor in this questioning was Friedrich Nietzsche (1844–1900), a German classicist and philosopher who died as the new century was being born but whose ideas remained among the most germinal for the future. Influenced by a range of non-Western beliefs, especially by the Hindu idea of *maya*, which posited that the world of our senses or what we call "reality" is an illusion, major thinkers like Nietzsche denied our ability fully to know the natural world. Instead, they maintained, all we have of the natural world are our own representations or interpretations of it. Nietzsche also rejected the "herd morality" he saw in Western society, much of it handed down by institutionalized Western religion, notably Christianity and Judaism. "Good" and "evil" were simplistic concepts, Nietzsche believed, relating only to the gross materialism of commercial and imperial Europe. Bypassing such materialist-driven banalities, he advocated living "beyond good and evil" in a joyful existence honoring the vital life forces that endow all creation. He presented a model for this zestful and spiritually oriented life in the character Zarathustra in his epic work *Thus Spake Zarathustra*—the name is the Greek form of the name of the Persian religious leader Zoroaster, who seemed to embody some of Nietzsche's own ideals.

Nietzsche called his prescription for living the "gay science," indicating the new and boundless future that awaited those who turned away from the world of materialism and science. But some thinkers used his ideas to tinge Enlightenment optimism with pessimism. If the world was unknowable, what rules would guide humans who needed knowledge to help them? How would leaders determine policy, doctors determine cures, and reformers make life better, if none of the old measures had meaning? The notable social scientist and pioneer of modern sociology, Max Weber (1864–1920), stepped up to address some of these difficult issues. A prominent German intellectual and a student of Western and non-Western religions, Weber found mass society too complex to be governed easily no matter how advanced social thinking was. By the time all the elements of a social policy were calculated, he said, conditions would have changed and the proposed policy would be hopelessly out-of-date. To replace the lumbering bureaucracy of modern government, Weber suggested, the most effective leader would be a charismatic figure acting improvisationally and zestfully. Such a leader would confront society's problems with Zarathustra-like verve. This was not a hopeful answer for people who believed in a democracy governed rationally by deliberative civil servants. Like the works of Nietzsche and Marx, Weber's writings proved influential for the rest of the century.

Equally disturbing to the status quo and enduring in his influence was Viennese doctor Sigmund Freud (1856–1939), who shaped modern understanding of the human mind and personality. Trained in neuroscience, Freud devised a "talking cure" in which his patients, many of them middle- and upper-class women suffering from hysteria, recounted fragments of troubling dreams, symptoms of physical maladies, and experiences from family life. Freud believed that by correctly interpreting these various disturbances with the help of an analyst, patients would not only gain insights into their condition but also feel powerful emotions in the process, thus experiencing something resembling a cure. He called this new therapy *psychoanalysis.*

Like expressionists, Freud saw the human self as fragmented, with three different parts of the psyche at war with one another. The *ego* wants to confront reality but is hampered in its efforts both by the unruly erotic drives of the *id* and by the moralizing of the *superego*—a cluster of do's and don'ts that harps on parental or societal rules. According to Freudian theory, the ego and the superego carve themselves out in the course of an individual's maturation, for in infancy the human psyche is nothing more or less than a bundle of erotic impulses. The development of a more mature and rational personality—that is, one guided by an ego—necessitates the repression of childish desires in favor of realistic skills and character formation. The price of all this repression of free-wheeling infant behavior may be disturbing symptoms such as psychosomatic pains, hysteria, twitching, nightmares, and obsessive behavior in everyday life. It was these symptoms that a patient could overcome by discussing dreams and experiences with the analyst.

Freud's talk therapy was oddly unscientific and strangely reminiscent of the trances and talking cures used by witch doctors and shamans in non-Western cultures. Freud focused on practices such as fetishism toward shoes, gloves, and other items of everyday life—healing practices in a range of societies including many in Africa. Portraits and photographs of Freud's work space show a vast collection of art, including paintings and statuary from North and sub-Saharan Africa, Asia, and other parts of the world beyond Europe. He professed to "actually have read more archeology than psychology,"[21] and in so doing he fell in with the globalizing intellectual spirit of the time. Imperialism provided information about therapies and cures from around the world such as the interpretation of dreams, and these helped shape the new "sciences" of the mind.

Because Freud's therapy was so oriented toward uncovering and talking about the sexual roots of neurosis, his ideas were not palatable to everyone. Many people found the emphasis on sexuality distasteful. However, those who appreciated his ideas and practices—the numbers influenced by Freud grew in the twentieth century—accepted as modern the idea that the self has powerful sexual and irrational components. After Freud, the sciences of the mind began to prosper, undertaking studies of personality and intelligence that were increasingly divorced from considerations of the individual as an entity with a spiritual or divinely ordained core. Psychologists increasingly saw people as maladjusted, neurotic, and controlled by their drives rather than judging them to be sinful or evil. Such a diagnosis gave food for thought as Europe's leaders dragged the world into the catastrophic violence of World War I.

THE ROAD TO WAR

By the beginning of the twentieth century, Europeans had developed technologically sophisticated weaponry capable of wreaking unprecedented destruction on people in far-off lands and at home. A warlike spirit arose in the colonies with the unblinking slaughter of Asians and Africans—resisters, ordinary civilians, and even children among such people as the Hereros (see Document 1.3). Tensions within European society—including tensions unleashed by the West's own technological, social, and artistic modernity—were near the surface, waiting to erupt. Occasions for war were also omnipresent, whether in the competing aspirations of the various powers or in the pent-up political grievances of Europe's ethnicities and interest groups. Even seemingly innocuous events like the revival of the Olympics in 1896 contributed to war fever: "Sport calls for endurance and sangfroid, the military virtues," one journalist explained, "and it keeps youth in a warlike frame of mind."[22] A major European war was already planned for and even hoped for by nationalist groups and generals alike. "I consider a war to be inevitable," the chief of the German General Staff announced in 1912, "and the sooner the better."[23] By 1914, the leading European countries had vast armies, enhanced military budgets, more destructive weaponry, and a complex alliance system—one ensuring that if war broke out, neutrality would not be an option. All that was needed to ignite a major international conflagration was a spark.

Military Buildup amid Shifting Alliances

Imperial conquest, militaristic nationalism, and economic competition brought about a massive buildup of civilian armies and materiel among the European powers before World War I (Chart 2.1). By 1914 France and Germany called up 250,000 men and Russia 450,000 or more for military training each year, while maintaining active peacetime military forces of 910,000, 891,000, and 1,352,000 respectively. During the nineteenth century, armies had remained relatively constant in both size and cost. Between 1905 and the outbreak of war, however, as the costs of innovation in weaponry and the maintenance of complex general staffs and large armies grew, military budgets soared. A whopping 45 percent of Germany's national budget was devoted to defense in 1910. Although all the powers increased their expenditures, some could better afford to do so than others, but even wealthy European countries became financially overextended.

The most striking and costly military innovation was the dreadnought—a class of massive battleships with unprecedented firepower. Made possible by new developments in metallurgy, these armored ships essential to conducting imperial adventures and war made shipbuilding one of the leading industries. The launching of the first of these behemoths, the HMS *Dreadnought* in England in 1905, was part of Britain's campaign to upgrade the Royal Navy by building at least seven of

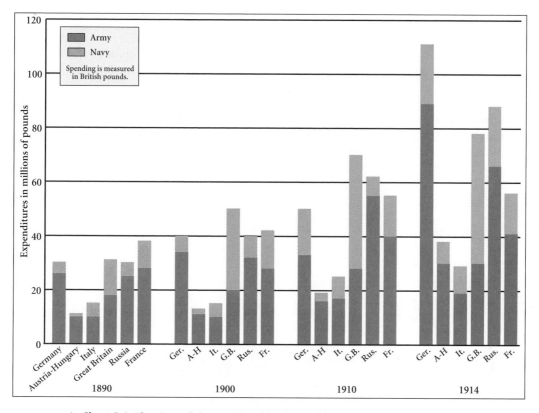

◆ Chart 2.1 **The Growth in Armaments, 1890–1914**
As the twentieth century opened, nationalism was intertwined with pride in military and imperial power, as the leading European nations engaged in a massive arms race. This graph shows the amounts spent on both armies and navies during these fateful years. Only in 1914 did the Germans outspend everyone. Historians often ask whether better diplomacy could have prevented the outbreak of war in 1914, but people living at the time believed that the military buildup made war inevitable. What is your judgment of this question? Which countries could best afford modern warfare?

these ships a year. Other countries then decided that they could do no less, but the costly undertaking had to be sold to the public. Defense officials hired public relations firms—a new player in the growing service economy—to promote huge expenditures for battleships, and right-wing nationalist parties took the battleship campaign into politics. The German Naval League and other groups in other nations lobbied parliaments and voters to beat the drums of war and call for a naval buildup. They were financed by businesses that stood to profit—in the case of the German Naval League, by the munitions manufacturer Krupp. Spokesmen and publicity agents inspired fear in the populace, warning about massive unemployment if military expenditures did not increase and predicting the utter annihilation of nations that lacked dreadnoughts and other sophisticated weapons of war.

They thus raised the temperature of nationalism and war fever across European societies.

Diplomatic preparations for war accompanied the military buildup, as international relations became more bellicose. In an attempt to prevent further violence after he had successfully conducted Germany's wars of unification, Otto von Bismarck, the first chancellor of the united Germany, had negotiated a series of defensive alliances in the 1870s and 1880s. The Triple Alliance (1882) among Austria-Hungary, Italy, and Germany and the Reinsurance Treaty (1887) between Russia and Germany promised assistance in the event that one of the signatories was attacked (Map 2.1). Kaiser William II turned German foreign policy in a more ag-

◆ **Map 2.1 Pre–World War I Alliances**
Otto von Bismarck, architect of German unification in the nineteenth century, had constructed a set of defensive alliances with the Habsburg Empire, Russia, and Italy. His aim was to protect Germany from war on two fronts and, if possible, to prevent the country from going to war again. Kaiser William overruled this strategy, letting the alliance with Russia lapse and letting his advisers change the alliance with Austria-Hungary to an offensive one. Early in the twentieth century, England and France developed an "understanding" and were soon joined by Russia. Historians judge this alliance system, mostly formed in secrecy, as a crucial element leading to war. Do you?

gressive direction with his mission to expand the German Empire no matter how provocative his actions seemed to the rest of Europe. He allowed the Reinsurance Treaty to lapse, driving Russia to ally with France in the 1890s, and his riposte to the British claim that the sun never set on its empire was to demand for Germany "a place in the sun." In the early twentieth century, he contested French claims to North Africa, especially Morocco, which the British had secretly promised France in 1904 in return for a dominant position in Egypt. In 1905 and again in 1911 William stirred the international pot with aggressive maneuverings, most notably his dispatch of a gunboat to Morocco in 1911 to menace the French. Two international conferences rejected Germany's claim for some award of new territory to compensate for French gains. Their ambitions thwarted, German policy makers looked to the European continent itself as a place to expand. To the detriment of its other alliances Germany drew closer to Austria-Hungary as part of a vision to create a greater Mitteleuropa, or Central Europe. In so doing, German military leaders jettisoned the security provided by Bismarck's careful cultivation of a wide array of diplomatic ties.

Confronted with rising German bellicosity, Britain and France set aside their own rivalry over colonial territory to form an *entente cordiale* (1904), a series of agreements that they strengthened in 1906. Not only did these agreements settle their competing imperial claims, but the military leadership of the two countries began sharing information and devising common military strategies. In 1907 British and Russian diplomats also reached an understanding or *entente*, turning the entente cordiale into a Triple Entente. Hardened plans for war soon replaced supple alliances on both sides.

Internal Problems of the Great Powers

Domestic crises further fueled the march toward war. Among the looming social problems were ethnic tensions in Austria-Hungary, movements for political and labor reforms across Europe, and the dislocation and alienation produced by modernity, including migration and dizzying urban growth. Working-class activism soared after 1910, and strikes erupted everywhere. In France workers shut down the railway system in 1911; in Russia strikes paralyzed the gold mines, oil fields, textile factories, electric works, and rubber companies. As northern Italy rapidly industrialized, labor and socialist groups prospered, but in the underdeveloped agrarian south, a thriving criminal class, commonly known as the brotherhood, joined wealthy landowners in exploiting the poor. In Russia, along with the assassination of thousands of public officials, a general strike erupted in St. Petersburg in 1914. Public protest dogged the footsteps of the tsar as he continually stymied Russian citizens' calls for more effective representative government. In Germany the Social Democratic Party gained a huge following, and some of its leaders actively opposed Germany's militarism and its conservative ruling elite. Germany, one statesman announced in response to growing socialist success, needed to build its military resources "to prepare for the unavoidable battle against the Social Democratic movement."[24] Domestic strife and international contests kept nerves on edge and politicians unhinged.

The greatest of the imperial powers, Britain enjoyed neither domestic harmony nor peace across its empire. Like the Austrian monarchy, the British were thrown off balance in the early years of the century, not only by the South African War and the Boxer Rebellion of 1900, in which famine-ridden Chinese began a violent movement to slay foreigners, but by uprisings far closer to home. The House of Lords became so antagonistic toward taxation that the government had to curtail some of its powers. In 1911, under threats to dilute aristocratic privileges almost out of existence, the House of Lords gave up its right to veto legislation.

In Ireland protests against two centuries of British rule intensified. A veritable flood of Irish emigrants poured from the British Empire, and people who remained in Ireland became increasingly impatient with all aspects of what was effectively Britain's colonization of their country. The Irish Land League, formed in 1879, protested the practice of English landowners driving tenants from their farms in order to increase rents on new farmers who replaced them. The 1903 Land Act accelerated the process of providing funds so that tenants could purchase land from absentee English landlords. Other Irish men and women protested quasi-colonial political rule: although the Irish were represented in the British parliament, Ireland was administered by non-Irish officials appointed in London.

Activists gave this cause political shape with the founding in 1905 of Sinn Fein ("We Ourselves"), a group committed to complete Irish independence. Pro-independence leaders organized Irish members of the House of Commons so that they voted as a block, awarding their votes to whichever party supported Irish home rule. In 1912 the British government introduced a bill to enact home rule for Ireland. The prospect of independence, however, met with resistance not only in England but in some parts of Ireland, notably the northern province of Ulster, where many were Unionists—that is, they considered themselves British and favored retaining ties with England. In response to the proposal for home rule, rallies of tens of thousands took place, and competing independent armies sprang up in support of those favoring an independent Ireland and those opposing a break with Britain on the grounds that it would lead to economic disaster. In 1914, despite an amendment to allow any Irish county to remain united with Britain should it wish to, Ireland stood on the brink of civil war.

Based on the belief that Ireland was "a distinct nation," the "de-Anglicizing" of Ireland was at the top of the nationalist agenda. Cultural leaders such as the poet W. B. Yeats and the activist Maud Gonne sponsored schools, magazines, and clubs and advocated the use of the Gaelic language to fortify Irish cultural traditions. Yeats worked in a group that founded Dublin's Abbey Theatre to produce Irish rather than English plays. To counteract English materialism—the insatiable drive for money and power, as Yeats saw it—he infused works based on Irish lore with idealist messages and literary devices found in Buddhist and Hindu writings and Japanese plays. These fresh and uncontaminated styles from outside the West, he believed, could help renew Ireland's own cultural heritage. Irish nationalists, led by Gonne and Yeats, countered parades, ceremonies, and other special events sponsored by the British to foster Ireland's allegiance to the empire with events of their own meant to block the influence of British culture. Sporting events grew in popularity as celebrations of an independent Irish masculinity. In 1914 the spread of cultural and political nationalism inflamed Ireland's people—both those who favored home rule and those who opposed it. The issue perilously divided Britain itself on the eve of World War I.

Balkan and Great-Power Instability

In the Balkans all the tensions of political and cultural modernity came to a head in the early twentieth century as the great powers intervened in the political dynamics of the region. Located on the eastern Mediterranean, the mountainous region had for centuries lain squarely in the path of powerful empires eager to expand their territories and increase their wealth. The Ottomans looking westward, the Russians and Austrians to the south, and the British, French, and Germans to the east—all of them benefited from stirring up antagonisms in the Balkans. The peoples of the Balkans have been characterized as an assemblage of ethnic groups whose millennia-old hatreds and perpetual vendettas keep the region chronically unstable. This reputation, created after World War I to dim the responsibility of the powerful European nations for the horrendously destructive war, obscures the political manipulation and vicious fighting that the great powers engaged in to control the region. As successive Balkan territories such as Greece and Serbia became quasi-independent principalities and then independent states, the great powers played an active role in setting the boundaries of the new nations. This intervention was often at the expense of ethnic groups seeking independence and political recognition as the twentieth century opened. In this way, the major powers laid the foundation for the conflicts in the Balkans that continue to the present day.

Amid this interference, Balkan intellectual and political leaders in the nineteenth century tried to promote a degree of cultural unity in the region. Although the multiple languages and religions practiced in the Balkans were said to make regional unity impossible, as the twentieth century opened many people embraced the idea that they might band together to resist their common imperial masters, especially Austria-Hungary and the Ottoman Empire. To that end, intellectuals compiled a Serbo-Croatian dictionary and developed and promoted a common Serbo-Croatian literary language for the expression of South Slav nationalism. Serbian poet and writer Vuk Karadžíc, who had sponsored programs for the reconciliation of the languages in the mid-nineteenth century, also collected poetry, folk songs, and epics on the history of the region, all in an effort to demonstrate a common heritage. A palace coup in Serbia's capital of Belgrade in 1903 brought to power Peter Karadjordjevic, a foe of Austro-Hungarian influence. Suddenly local peoples took hope in the possibility of unity for the South Slavs under a strong leader, and they kept the spirit of a united and independent region alive in the politics and art of the period. As one novelist described the scene before 1914: "Those were the days of the sudden flowering of the Yugoslav idea, and it was Belgrade which, through a series of royal celebrations, transformed into a true South Slavic stage of fiery patriots."[25] Although ethnic and religious infighting and Serbian aspirations to dominate any South Slav state that would emerge posed serious obstacles, hope for Balkan unity flourished.

Cultural modernity developed in the context of economic and social change. Peasant agriculture dominated much of the region, making rural people vulnerable to the declining prices for produce on the world market. Industrialization occurred, but it did so under onerous conditions such as high interest rates imposed by France, Germany, Britain, Russia, and others who financed railroad and other modernizing projects. In Bulgaria, for example, German financiers of the railroad levied tariffs that raised prices and cut profits for local people, and a large French loan early in the century was made on condition that the proceeds from tobacco production go not to finance public works but to French bankers as a guarantee of the loan. Inspired by the uprising in 1904–1905 of Russian workers against the tsarist system, the Bulgarian industrial and municipal workers went on strike, and farmers formed peasant parties to fight high taxes on produce and to obtain pro-agrarian policies. Discord mounted, leading to assassinations, political coups, and abrupt changes of leadership. The social tensions erupting in the midst of foreign manipulations worsened the instability in the region, making the great powers both fearful that a rival power might take advantage of the unstable situation and all the more eager to exploit the Balkans' vulnerability.

Two major events in 1908 — the Young Turk revolution and the Austro-Hungarian military annexation of the Balkan province of Bosnia-Herzegovina — further destabilized the region and led to the First and Second Balkan Wars in 1912 and 1913. Instead of posing as liberators or bringing about liberal reforms, the Young Turk revolutionaries in Constantinople aimed to restore a portion of the Ottoman Empire by regaining control of the Balkans. Building on the anger that existed among the people, the Balkan governments of Montenegro, Bulgaria, Serbia, and Greece went to war against the Ottoman Empire to secure land — particularly in strategically located Macedonia — and to assert their independent policies. These allies easily routed the Turks and were thwarted only when they attempted to advance as far as Constantinople.

The quick victory in that First Balkan War masked looming tensions among the Balkan states especially over land. Also, Russia and Austria-Hungary were hovering menacingly in the wings to block any advantage that might accrue to the other. The peace settlement reached in the spring of 1913 quickly fell apart, and the Second Balkan War erupted among the victors themselves. The main issue was the territory awarded Bulgaria in the earlier settlement. The Bulgarian army swung into action against Greece and Serbia before the troops were to demobilize for the summer harvest and before Russia could impose an unfavorable rollback of Bulgarian gains in Macedonia. Having remained neutral in the First Balkan War of 1912–1913, the Romanians mobilized to ensure that they too won territory, and even Turkey invaded. The Bulgarians surrendered within a few weeks. The resulting settlement of the Second Balkan War took territory from Bulgaria and enhanced Serbia, a client of Russia. With great consternation, Austria-Hungary and Germany watched this mounting threat to their ambitions for sustained influence in the Balkans and in the Middle East. The Habsburgs also felt that they needed to stop Serbian expansion in order to maintain the loyalty of Austria-Hungary's Poles, Czechs, and other Slavs, who often looked to the might of fellow Slavs in Russia and, now, Serbia, which was growing in stature. Supporting their Habsburg ally, the German emperor and his advisers whipped up public sentiment against the rising Slavic menace.

The situation was becoming dire for the Habsburgs. The Hungarian leadership in the government obstructed financial and foreign policy in a show of ethnic force, and this strategy increased the importance of the Slavs to the Habsburg dynasty as a countervailing force. In 1896 the thousand-year celebration of the Magyar conquest and settlement on the Danube had incited an outburst of nationalism that threatened the Austro-Hungarian status quo and thus the country's status as a great power. By the early twentieth century the Magyar leadership was objecting to the use of German as the language of command in the Austro-Hungarian army. Faced with the stirrings of the South Slavs and the claims of the Czechs and Germans, officials of the empire in 1913 felt a need for real change.

One proponent of change—albeit of a reactionary kind—was the heir to the Habsburg imperial throne, Archduke Franz Ferdinand. Supported by an influential coterie of aristocrats, he wanted to overturn parliament and return to the absolutism of former times. He also favored "trialism"—the creation of a three-pronged balance of power in the empire by boosting Slav unity to offset Magyar power. In the year leading up to World War I, Franz Ferdinand was joined by Habsburg officials in the belief that a "courageous thrust" was needed, one that would bring about a "new order." "The parliamentary form of government has outlived its usefulness," an adviser to Franz Ferdinand had written as early as 1898. "The so-called individual freedoms must be curtailed."[26] At the top levels of government the idea of a coup d'état to restore absolutist rule had real appeal—even urgency—to counter the modern political forces of socialism and the self-determination of ethnic groups. As 1914 opened, a third Balkan war was on the minds of Habsburg officials, this time one in which Austria-Hungary would fight against Russia's ally Serbia in order finally to resolve divisive ethnic aspirations and modern social issues. In fact, this so-called third Balkan war was about to erupt—but in the unimaginable form of World War I.

CONCLUSION

"Time is increasingly against us," the German chancellor Theobald von Bethmann Hollweg warned as Europe moved closer to war.[27] His message came in the summer of 1914 during diplomatic negotiations over whether to go to war. In the modern age, the fast pace of life and rapid change influenced not only issues of everyday life and economic innovation but also crucial questions of war and peace. People's nerves were on edge, and the tenor of life made some foresee catastrophe. The young Winston Churchill witnessed the rise of mass politics and mass armies of the day: "The wars of peoples will be more terrible than those of kings," he accurately predicted.[28] His fellow countryman Herbert Asquith, Britain's liberal prime minister from 1908 to 1916, agreed: "We are within measurable, or unimaginable, distance of a real Armageddon."[29] Asquith no doubt had in mind the technological advances in weaponry that made such an Armageddon a real possibility and a modern mind-set that valued speed and quick action rather than negotiation and calm.

Yet although globalization of the economy pitted nations against each other in an often bitter rivalry for profit and power so that the threat of war loomed large, these same powers were simultaneously tied more closely together than ever before. Even as these warnings occurred, even on the eve of the most destructive war in human history to date, the British and Germans were negotiating their joint financing of the Baghdad Railway, and the International Tribunal at The Hague was adjudicating disputes among nations. New artistic and intellectual trends and movements such as socialism and the fight for women's suffrage crossed oceans and continents to bind people together. The modern age was thus charged with possibility, both positive and negative: able to promote simultaneously peace and war, unity and fragmentation, technological innovation and mass destruction. Given the military buildup of the preceding decades, an alliance system that fostered aggression, and competition for control of the Balkans, in the summer of 1914 the forces of war and destruction gained the upper hand.

D O C U M E N T S

The Automobile

NEW PRODUCTS OFTEN TAKE SOME TIME TO WIN ACCEPTANCE, and as cars became more and more common on the roads—many of them made for horses and carriages—opinions as to their utility and purpose abounded. Were they good or bad, and, more important, were their drivers outlaws and miscreants? What uses would automobiles serve in society as a whole? One of the first uses people made of automobiles was to chase after speed as they had done in bicycle races of the late nineteenth century. Among the most dramatic spectacles, giving great publicity to early-twentieth-century automobiles, were city-to-city car races, such as the Paris-to-Madrid race of 1903, described in Document 2.1. Millions of people followed the course of these races, many of them lining the route that the cars would take and getting in the way of the drivers, often with tragic results. Early automakers themselves, such as Louis Renault, founder of the Renault autoworks in France, participated, and governments watched these phenomena of mass society with a wary eye. Louis Renault's brother Marcel was killed in the 1903 Paris-to-Madrid free-for-all, described here. Racing captured the spirit of the times and took Europeans across the continent and into Asia, Africa, and beyond in search of greater and greater speed.

Commentaries about the automobile and ideas about its use filled newspapers and advice books on how to be modern. Drivers themselves were sometimes unsure why they were driving, and there were various justifications for buying and operating these expensive, disruptive vehicles. In the opinion of an article written for a German book of conversational topics (Document 2.2), automobiles actually promoted health as much as walking briskly or mountain climbing. Although Futurists (see Document 2.5) appreciated the strength and speed of machines, arguments for the health benefits of driving were equally modern in that they provided a rationale for the growing amount of leisure time that the middle classes devoted to walking, hiking, and generally "taking the air."

In 1914, an article written for a German automobile magazine explained the importance of the automobile to camping (Document 2.3). The writer claimed that camping was but one of many national differences in the use of leisure time. This writer connects ownership of his vehicle with an array of upper-class values, habits, and pastimes. Few car owners in the very early days saw their automobiles as the workhorses they later would become.

Document 2.1

ANTHONY RHODES
Louis Renault: A Biography, 1969

In 1903 the Paris–Madrid race was organized with greater difficulty than the Paris–Vienna. The Automobile Club de France suspected that some of the vehicles, the Mors, Panhard and Dietrich of the 80–100 hp class, were now capable of speeds of over 90 mph. . . . The cars went much faster; but the roads on which they travelled were exactly the same. Although the Route Nationale 10 to Bordeaux was the fastest in France, it still belonged to the age of carriages, and its curves were designed to deal with nothing faster than a galloping horse. Its hump-backed bridges dated from the seventeenth century, and if its gutters did not harm springless carriages, they were dangerous to car wheels.

The Spanish authorities had readily agreed to the race and arranged elaborate festivities in Madrid for those who completed it. It was the French Government, under pressure from socialists in Parliament as well as from certain public bodies and the Press, which objected. . . . But then, after many representations from the Automobile Club de France, authorization was obtained from Paris. The race was to last three days. . . .

The start took place at Versailles on Sunday 24 May at 4 A.M.; but such was the enthusiasm of the crowd that they had begun assembling there the day before. . . . It was afterwards calculated that more than a hundred thousand people spent the night in the open-air near Versailles, sleeping on benches or wherever they could lay their heads. Small fortunes were made by itinerant food and wine vendors. The local inns were full, the price of hard-boiled eggs increased hourly, and all the bread in Versailles was sold out before the start; by 4 A.M. there was not a slice of ham or cup of coffee left.

Amid a blaze of fire caused by the multicoloured flames of several hundred exhausts, in an aroma of petrol, acetylene and alcohol, over six hundred strange creatures clad in black leather and goggles strode about beside their vehicles, nervously puffing at their last cigarettes and sipping from small glasses of cognac. The competitor who caused the most interest was the only female in the race, the famous Amazonian Madame du Gast, who was driving a Benz, wearing her celebrated corseted leather armour. A hideous cacophony, the back-firing of dozens of differently designed engines, the varied horns and cries of the spectators split the air and woke up the local inhabitants. One hundred and sixty policemen on foot and sixty mounted police tried vainly to keep some order in the unruly, half-intoxicated mob. Marcel Renault must have had a presentiment of what was in store, because he said some days before that he would have preferred not to compete this time. But the future of Renault Frères was at stake, and they required services of their best driver. . . .

Along the highway to Bordeaux about a million people lined the route; and in spite of earlier fears, the Government had taken inadequate security precautions to control them. . . .

Louis and Marcel Renault were driving their light, 1,430 lb. four-cylinder vehicles; and even on the tremendously fast roads of the great French plain it was soon clear that they were more than holding their own. . . . Marcel passed many cars during the morning; and it was not until after Poitiers, near Couhè-Verac, that disaster came. He attempted to pass a cloud of dust containing the famous Léon Théry. Théry, who had good visibility, saw the turning ahead, but Marcel did not. Within a second, he was no longer on the road but

SOURCE: Anthony Rhodes, *Louis Renault: A Biography* (New York: Harcourt, Brace and World, 1969).

crossing a ditch at 80 mph. His front wheel caught in it, and the car did three somersaults before landing a hundred feet away on its back with the bonnet facing Paris. Underneath, unfortunately not thrown out in the somersault, lay Marcel Renault. . . . He was taken to hospital where he did not regain consciousness, and he died the following morning. . . .

. . . Marcel Renault's accident was only one of many. Throughout the afternoon as survivors struggled to the finish of the first stage at Bordeaux, they brought tales of crashes, deaths and injuries to drivers, mechanics and spectators. . . .

During the night of 24/25 May the French Government telephoned the Prefect of Bordeaux and ordered the race to be stopped. . . .

Document 2.2

"Motorwagen" article, 1909

HYGIENIC CONSIDERATIONS. Driving in a motorcar, like all mechanical calisthenics, effects a brisk activization of the entire organism, but, in comparison with other calisthenic methods, possesses notable qualities of its own. In contrast to indoor calisthenics, the flow of fresh air in particular must be considered, which stimulates the activities of the skin and lungs in a pleasant manner and, in so doing, initiates an extremely advantageous unburdening of the internal organs, which are quite excessively gorged with blood. Horseback riding seems to many persons too rigorous, and driving in a normal wagon without air-filled tires too rough; in contrast, driving in a motorcar consists of a light and gentle floating motion, which makes itself felt in a pleasant manner, rather like riding in a skiff on calm water. With the vehicle's low center of gravity, the rough bumps of the road are almost entirely absorbed by the pneumatics and the springs, so that there is no feeling of inflexibility and stiffness after a long drive, as one often has stepping out of a normal carriage or railroad car. Rather, one has the feeling of being pleasantly tired, much as after a breezy climb out of doors one feels intensified sleepiness and hunger. A highly advantageous effect on the nerves goes hand in hand with the beneficial relaxation caused by scenic landscapes and the unburdening of the internal organs. To be sure, several prerequisites must be fulfilled: neither dawdle along your way, nor race, but proceed rather at a moderate tempo, and, indeed, systematically, mornings and afternoons, in summer and winter, outfitted when necessary with glasses, leather gloves, a fur wrap, etc. As a result of the beneficial effect on the nerves, we find motorcar enthusiasts particularly among those devoted to the performance of mental labor.

SOURCE: "Motorwagen," *Meyers Grosses Konversationslexikon,* 6th ed., vol. 14 (1909), quoted in Wolfgang Sachs, *For the Love of the Automobile: Looking Back into the History of Our Desires* (Berkeley: University of California Press, 1992), 5.

Document 2.3

"Camping" article, 1914

We Germans have become leaders in the automotive industry; we also gave the significance of reliability trials its rightful due. In short, we have taken a big, perhaps the biggest, part in the victorious and portentous development of the automobile. But certain things involved in imparting to it the art of living we have heedlessly passed by. That is simply in our nature as a working people. Just as the French are always gratifying their effervescent, explosive temperaments in sensational high-speed races, so will we always remain in principle a basic, goal-oriented nation. The English, in contrast, are not unfortunate in their ability to lighten some of the strictness of sporting activities through a genial, almost quaint sense of humor, through a joy in calm, agreeable living. We Germans immediately recognize this English talent, the more so whenever an Englishman has sought out such hours of friendly existence in nature. For that reason, our healthy capacity to conform—which, as is well known, we possess more than any other nation—might bestow upon us a side of motorism that is attractive and worthy of imitation: "camping." The English understand "camping" as a free and easy style of pitching tents in the wild; the experience stretches over days, often even weeks, and is an original connection between culture and nature.

Hidden deep in the silent landscape, in a forest meadow full of tall grass, near a gentle little stream, sits the motor car. A rainproof awning is stretched over it. Beside it are the "wigwams," likewise made of a friendly light grey or white cloth. A wood fire flickers under a humming blue enamel kettle being tended by a lady's delicate hand. In her city apartment she would not make the tea. Here, however, she does; for one does not take the domestics along on a "camping" trip. It is just as obvious that they are left at home as that the otherwise customary and valuable jewelry is deposited in the bank vault—unless, of course, one is traveling in refined company. White and airy, too, is the thoroughly informal attire; one might even go barefoot or wear straw slippers. The children leap about in the freest style conceivable, their joy fluttering in friendly competition with the loose hair of the girls in the breeze.

The "chief" of the camp is just approaching. His sleeves are rolled up, revealing two suntanned forearms; in one hand he carries a fishing rod, in the other a small collapsible aluminum bucket, in which the patiently angled dinner (fried fish is on the menu) flops. He—one of the most significant figures in the upper elite—carries his sustenance with pride, the fruit of his own labor. In just a few minutes the folding furniture is removed from the bottom of a large suitcase and set up; a little table cloth is spread over it, and now, from deep within the attractive picnic basket, which holds all of the delicious, sweet secrets and found a convenient spot beside the spare tire on the drive out, many delightful treats emerge: the cookie tin, the sugar bowl, a little bottle of rum. . . .

No, one truly misses nothing in this corner of the world, completely isolated though it is, because such a significant means of assistance—as the motor car—belongs to it.

SOURCE: "Camping," *Allgemeine Automobil-Zeitung* (April 1914), quoted in Wolfgang Sachs, *For the Love of the Automobile: Looking Back into the History of Our Desires* (Berkeley: University of California Press, 1992), 158–159.

QUESTIONS FOR ANALYSIS

1. What early motivations for the use of the automobile do these writers express?

2. In what ways do the writers show their appreciation for the automobile's contribution to modern life?

3. Given that the automobile at this point in European history was a luxury item used by professionals and the upper classes, what indications of class identity do you find in these writings about automobile ownership?

The Politics of Women's Suffrage

THE WOMEN'S SUFFRAGE MOVEMENT advanced everywhere in Europe in the early twentieth century, helped by urbanization and improved communication. In Britain, the movement gained real impetus when Emmeline Pankhurst and her daughters Christabel and Sylvia founded the Women's Social and Political Union (WSPU) in 1903. Pankhurst (1858–1928), a widowed activist, had tried to get a number of organizations to take up the cause of women's suffrage but without success. While supporting herself and her family, she started the new suffrage organization out of frustration with the glacial pace of change in women's rights. Based in militant activism, the WSPU transformed suffragism, employing dramatic forms of appeal to the public and to politicians. Acting on their slogan "Deeds not words" in the early years of the twentieth century, members of the WSPU undertook a series of parades and large public meetings to dramatize their conviction that women deserved the right to vote.

The creation of the WSPU expanded the appeal of the suffrage movement, leading to the adherence of hundreds of other societies. Organizations of women workers and women professionals joined. So did actresses and artists, florists and bartenders. Their rationale for the vote was varied, but many objected, as men had in an earlier era, to being taxed without having representation in parliament. In the first decade of the twentieth century, the WSPU actively lobbied parliament for the vote, sending dozens of its women to attempt to meet the delegates face-to-face.

Middle-class women were an important source of free labor for the political parties. So when they took to lobbying on their own behalf instead of voluntarily doing publicity for the party and signing up new members, the level of anger rose and violence against the women increased. At least one woman is known to have died from the beatings she received. In several attempts to meet with members of parliament described here, the women appeared whenever a suffrage bill was on the agenda. As upper-class men became increasingly angry at women marchers from their own class, they handed out harsh jail sentences. When the jailed women went on hunger strikes, they were force-fed, a practice that ruined the health of many. Pankhurst's "My Story" recounts in dramatic detail the treatment of women and the ideals for which they were struggling. Published in 1914, the account itself helped publicize the story of suffrage politics to a broader audience.

The violence against women and the hostile response that women eventually mounted in return have been interpreted as part of the "crisis of liberalism" before World War I. Classical liberal doctrine foresaw a balanced and harmonious society in which reason would prevail in political discussions. It advocated rights and opportunity. The intense anger aroused by women's political discussion symbolized liberalism's crisis in the prewar period, as did such differing political events as revived anti-Semitism, anarchist and working-class politics, imperialist violence, and growing ethnic conflict. For their part, women invoked history, saying that their activism on behalf of the vote simply duplicated the measures men had used in the past to gain the franchise. Emmeline Pankhurst was still frustrated with the failure to gain the vote when she penned her account.

Document 2.4

EMMELINE PANKHURST
My Story, 1914

[On February 13, 1907, a deputation of women marched on the House of Commons to present a resolution on behalf of women's suffrage. Emmeline Pankhurst describes what happened.]

. . . The Government, it appeared, had decided that not again should their sacred halls of Parliament be desecrated by women asking for the vote, and orders had been given that would henceforth prevent women from reaching even the outer precincts of the House of Commons. So when our deputation of women arrived in the neighbourhood of Westminster Abbey they found themselves opposed by a solid line of police, who, at a sharp order from their chief, began to stride through and through the ranks of the procession, trying to turn the women back. Bravely the women rallied and pressed forward a little farther. Suddenly a body of mounted police came riding up at a smart trot, and for the next five hours or more, a struggle, quite indescribable for brutality and ruthlessness, went on.

The horsemen rode directly into the procession, scattering the women right and left. But still the women would not turn back. Again and again they returned, only to fly again and again from the merciless hoofs. Some of the women left the streets for the pavements, but even there the horsemen pursued them, pressing them so close to walls and railings that they were obliged to retreat temporarily to avoid being crushed. Other strategists

took refuge in doorways, but they were dragged out by the foot police and were thrown directly in front of the horses. Still the women fought to reach the House of Commons with their resolution. They fought until their clothes were torn, their bodies bruised, and the last ounce of their strength exhausted. Fifteen of them did actually fight their way through those hundreds on hundreds of police, foot and mounted, as far as the Strangers' Lobby of the House. Here they attempted to hold a meeting, and were arrested. Outside, many more women were taken into custody. It was ten o'clock before the last arrest was made, and the square cleared of the crowds. After that the mounted men continued to guard the approaches to the House of Commons until the House rose at midnight.

The next morning fifty-seven women and two men were arraigned, two and three at a time, in Westminster police court. Christabel Pankhurst was the first to be placed in the dock. She tried to explain to the magistrate that the deputation of the day before was a perfectly peaceful attempt to present a resolution, which, sooner or later, would be presented and acted upon. She assured him that the deputation was but the beginning of a campaign that would not cease until the Government yielded to the women's demand. "There can be no going back for us," she declared, "and more will happen if we do not get justice." . . .

[On October 21, 1908, Emmeline Pankhurst appeared in court to address charges of inciting the public to "do a certain wrongful and illegal act, viz., to rush the House of Commons at 7:30 P.M. on October 13th."]

SOURCE: Emmeline Pankhurst, *The Suffragettes: Towards Emancipation* (London: Routledge, 1995), 82–83, 128–130, 178–181, 187–188.

"Before you decide what is to be done with us, I should like you to hear from me a statement of what has brought me into the dock this morning." And then I told of my life and experiences, many of which I have related in these pages of what I had seen and known as a Poor Law Guardian° and a registrar of births and deaths; of how I had learned the burning necessity of changing the status of women, of altering the laws under which they and their children live, and of the essential justice of making women self-governing citizens.

"I have seen," I said, "that men are encouraged by law to take advantage of the helplessness of women. Many women have thought as I have, and for many, many years have tried, by that influence of which we have been so often reminded, to alter these laws, but we find that influence counts for nothing. When we went to the House of Commons we used to be told, when we were persistent, that members of Parliament were not responsible to women, they were responsible only to voters, and that their time was too fully occupied to reform those laws, although they agreed that they needed reforming.

"We women have presented larger petitions in support of our enfranchisement than were ever presented for any other reform; we have succeeded in holding greater public meetings than men have ever held for any reform, in spite of the difficulty which women have in throwing off their natural diffidence, that desire to escape publicity which we have inherited from generations of our foremothers. We have broken through that. We have faced hostile mobs at street corners, because we were told that we could not have that representation for our taxes that men have won unless we converted the whole of the country to our side. Because we have done this, we have been misrepresented, we have been ridiculed, we have had contempt poured upon us, and the ignorant mob have been incited to offer us violence, which we

°*Poor Law Guardian:* An official overseeing public welfare programs.

have faced unarmed and unprotected by the safeguards which Cabinet Ministers enjoy. We have been driven to do this; we are determined to go on with this agitation because we feel in honour bound. Just as it was the duty of your forefathers, it is our duty to make the world a better place for women than it is to-day.

"Lastly, I want to call attention to the self-restraint which was shown by our followers on the night of the 18th, after we had been arrested. Our rule has always been to be patient, exercise self-restraint, show our so-called superiors that we are not hysterical; to use no violence, but rather to offer ourselves to the violence of others.

"That is all I have to say to you, sir. We are here, not because we are law-breakers; we are here in our efforts to become law-makers."

The burly policemen, the reporters, and most of the spectators were in tears as I finished. But the magistrate, who had listened part of the time with his hand concealing his face, still held that we were properly charged in a common police court as inciters to riot. Since we refused to be bound over to keep the peace, he sentenced Mrs. Drummond and myself to three months' imprisonment, and Christabel to ten weeks' imprisonment. It was destined to be a kind of imprisonment the authorities had never yet been called upon to deal with. . . .

[Here, Pankhurst describes the violence that occurred on November 18, 1910, thereafter referred to as "Black Friday," when suffragists marched on the House of Commons to demand passage of the Conciliation Bill, a bill to give the vote to taxpaying and property-owning women.]

How to tell the story of that dreadful day, Black Friday, as it lives in our memory—how to describe what happened to English women at the behest of an English Government, is a difficult task. I will try to tell it as simply and as accurately as possible. The plain facts, baldly stated, I am aware will strain credulity. Remember that the country was on the eve of a general election, and that the Liberal Party needed no help of Liberal women.

This fact made the wholesale arrest and imprisonment of great numbers of women, who were demanding the passage of the Conciliation Bill, extremely undesirable from the Government's point of view. The Women's Liberal federations also wanted the passage of the Conciliation Bill, although they were not ready to fight for it. What the Government feared, was that the Liberal Women would be stirred by our sufferings into refraining from doing election work for the party. So the Government conceived a plan whereby the Suffragettes were to be punished, were to be turned back and defeated in their purpose of reaching the House, but would not be arrested. Orders were evidently given that the police were to be present in the streets, and that the women were to be thrown from one uniformed or ununiformed policeman to another, that they were to be so rudely treated that sheer terror would cause them to turn back. I say orders were given and as one proof of this I can first point out that on all previous occasions the police had first tried to turn back the deputations and when the women persisted in going forward, had arrested them. At times individual policemen had behaved with cruelty and malice toward us, but never anything like the unanimous and wholesale brutality that was shown on Black Friday. . . .

The Government very likely hoped that the violence of the police towards the women would be emulated by the crowds, but instead the crowds proved remarkably friendly. They pushed and struggled to make a clear pathway for us, and in spite of the efforts of the police my small deputation actually succeeded in reaching the door of the Strangers' Entrance.° We mounted the steps to the enthusiastic cheers of the multitudes that filled the streets, and we stood there for hours gazing down on a scene which I hope never to look upon again.

At intervals of two or three minutes small groups of women appeared in the square, trying to join us at the Strangers' Entrance. They carried

little banners inscribed with various mottoes, "Asquith Has Vetoed Our Bill," "Where There's a Bill There's a Way," "Women's Will Beats Asquith's Won't," and the like. These banners the police seized and tore in pieces. Then they laid hands on the women and literally threw them from one man to another. Some of the police used their fists, striking the women in their faces, their breasts, their shoulders. One woman I saw thrown down with violence three or four times in rapid succession, until at last she lay only half conscious against the curb, and in a serious condition was carried away by kindly strangers. Every moment the struggle grew fiercer, as more and more women arrived on the scene. Women, many of them eminent in art, in medicine and science, women of European reputation, subjected to treatment that would not have been meted out to criminals, and all for the offence of insisting upon the right of peaceful petition.

This struggle lasted for about an hour, more and more women successfully pushing their way past the police and gaining the steps of the House. Then the mounted police were summoned to turn the women back. But, desperately determined, the women, fearing not the hoofs of the horses or the crushing violence of the police, did not swerve from their purpose. And now the crowds began to murmur. People began to demand why the women were being knocked about; why, if they were breaking the law, they were not arrested; why, if they were not breaking the law, they were not permitted to go on unmolested. For a long time, nearly five hours, the police continued to hustle and beat the women, the crowds becoming more and more turbulent in their defence. Then, at last the police were obliged to make arrests. One hundred and fifteen women and four men, most of them bruised and choked and otherwise injured, were arrested. . . .

[Pankhurst hoped to move her readers with stirring accounts of the indignities and violence individual suffragists underwent in their quest for the vote. Here, she describes British aristocrat Lady Constance Lytton's ordeal of being force-fed after

°*Strangers' Entrance:* Entrance for visitors to parliamentary sessions.

her arrest at a protest (her second of that year) on October 11, 1909.]

Smarting under the sense of the injustice done her comrades in this discrimination, Lady Constance Lytton did one of the most heroic deeds to be recorded in the history of the suffrage movement. She cut off her beautiful hair and otherwise disguised herself, put on cheap and ugly clothing, and as "Jane Warton" took part in a demonstration at Newcastle, again suffering arrest and imprisonment. This time the authorities treated her as an ordinary prisoner. Without testing her heart or otherwise giving her an adequate medical examination, they subjected her to the horrors of forcible feeding. Owing to her fragile constitution she suffered frightful nausea each time, and when on one occasion the doctor's clothing was soiled, he struck her contemptuously on the cheek. This treatment was continued until the identity of the prisoner suddenly became known. She was, of course, immediately released, but she never recovered from the experience, and is now a hopeless invalid.

I want to say right here, that those well-meaning friends on the outside who say that we have suffered these horrors of prison, of hunger strikes and forcible feeding, because we desired to martyrise ourselves for the cause, are absolutely and entirely mistaken. We never went to prison in order to be martyrs. We went there in order that we might obtain the rights of citizenship. We were willing to break laws that we might force men to give us the right to make laws. That is the way men have earned their citizenship. Truly says Mazzini° that the way to reform has always led through prison.

° *Mazzini:* Italian politician and revolutionary Giuseppe Mazzini (1805–1872).

QUESTIONS FOR ANALYSIS

1. What were the goals of Emmeline Pankhurst and her followers?
2. What are the most important political concepts in Pankhurst's account?
3. How are Pankhurst's actions and ideas related to the other political currents of her day?

Elites and the Spiritual Future of Europe

MODERN ARTISTIC THOUGHT HAS MANY FACES, and some of the most influential thinkers saw early-twentieth-century society entering an era of growing spirituality. Oddly enough, they saw breakthroughs in science and technology as offering new potential for aesthetic and spiritual progress, building higher values that would carry people beyond ordinary materialism and middle-class morality. According to a range of avant-garde thinkers, in the midst of growing democracy a new elite would emerge with aims far superior to those of the noisy denizens of crowded cities, who threatened aristocratic distinction and dominance. The tireless capacity of machines would allow individuals to soar spiritually.

In 1909, the wealthy Italian writer and founder of the Futurist movement in the arts, Filippo Tommaso Marinetti (1876–1944), issued his Futurist manifesto (Document 2.5) about the importance of humans attaching themselves spiritually to the machine. Conquering time and space, elite thinkers espousing a "futuristic" vision would become hard, like machines themselves, and infinite in their capacities, he predicted. In another work, "Let's Murder the Moonshine," Marinetti proposed that machine-oriented artists could stamp out the lyrical and romantic heritage of the past to usher in a new art. Luigi Russolo, a follower of the Futurist program, issued *The Art of Noises* in 1913, calling for music that more accurately reflected the sounds of modernity—the sounds "that fall dissonantly, strangely, and harshly upon the ear." The "music of noise," he called it and proceeded to invent instruments to create mechanical noises that would advance the language of music in the twentieth century.[30]

Wassily Kandinsky (1866–1944), a Russian-born artist who worked in Munich, also predicted a new future for the arts and for the world as a whole, and his view of the future was even more spiritually inclined and elitist than Marinetti's. Influenced by Asian thought and trained in ethnography, Kandinsky saw realism in the arts as a sign of Western naïveté, and he founded with fellow enthusiasts the Blue Rider movement in the arts. Anyone could imitate nature, the Chinese had long ago recognized, and those in the Blue Rider agreed. The lofty goal of art, they insisted, should be to capture higher values that were hardly apparent in the realistic depiction of people and things and that eluded ordinary citizens who settled into simply following a religious creed, a political faith such as socialism, or a routine method such as the scientific one. Such people, in Kandinsky's words, "had never solved any problem independently, but are dragged as it were in a cart by those the noblest of their fellowmen who have sacrificed themselves."[31] Believing that humanity needed to progress to higher realms, Kandinsky introduced what has since become known as "abstract art." Kandinsky was a great colorist, and his use of color was taken from color codes used by the Theosophist movement. He saw the goals realized in African art—a "metaphysical art" he called it—as important to the West. The movement of art in his day was upward, Kandinsky wrote in *Concerning the Spiritual in Art* (Document 2.6), toward concerns and values far loftier than those of the realist and historical art of the past. Like similarly minded thinkers in this age of the airplane, he used images of rising in space to explain his ideas about art and the future movement of society as a whole to new heights. And he believed, as the excerpt here shows, that only an elite few would be pulling humanity upward.

Document 2.5

F. T. MARINETTI
Manifesto of Futurism, 1909

1. We intend to sing the love of danger, the habit of energy and fearlessness.

2. Courage, audacity, and revolt will be essential elements of our poetry.

3. Up to now literature has exalted a pensive immobility, ecstasy, and sleep. We intend to exalt aggressive action, a feverish insomnia, the racer's stride, the mortal leap, the punch and the slap.

4. We say that the world's magnificence has been enriched by a new beauty; the beauty of speed. A racing car whose hood is adorned with great pipes, like serpents of explosive breath—a roaring car that seems to ride on grapeshot—is more beautiful than the *Victory of Samothrace.*°

5. We want to hymn the man at the wheel, who hurls the lance of his spirit across the Earth, along the circle of its orbit.

6. The poet must spend himself with ardor, splendor, and generosity, to swell the enthusiastic fervor of the primordial elements.

7. Except in struggle, there is no more beauty. No work without an aggressive character can be a masterpiece. Poetry must be conceived as a violent attack on unknown forces, to reduce and prostrate them before man.

8. We stand on the last promontory of the centuries! . . . Why should we look back, when

what we want is to break down the mysterious doors of the Impossible? Time and Space died yesterday. We already live in the absolute, because we have created eternal, omnipresent speed.

9. We will glorify war—the world's only hygiene—militarism, patriotism, the destructive gesture of freedom-bringers, beautiful ideas worth dying for, and scorn for woman.

10. We will destroy the museums, libraries, academies of every kind, will fight moralism, feminism, every opportunistic or utilitarian cowardice.

11. We will sing of great crowds excited by work, by pleasure, and by riot; we will sing of the multicolored, polyphonic tides of revolution in the modern capitals; we will sing of the vibrant nightly fervor of arsenals and shipyards blazing with violent electric moons; greedy railway stations that devour smoke-plumed serpents; factories hung on clouds by the crooked lines of their smoke; bridges that stride the rivers like giant gymnasts, flashing in the sun with a glitter of knives; adventurous steamers that sniff the horizon; deep-chested locomotives whose wheels paw the tracks like the hooves of enormous steel horses bridled by tubing; and the sleek flight of planes whose propellers chatter in the wind like banners and seem to cheer like an enthusiastic crowd.

It is from Italy that we launch through the world this violently upsetting, incendiary manifesto of ours. With it, today, we establish *Futurism* because

° *Victory of Samothrace:* An ancient Greek statue.

SOURCE: F. T. Marinetti, *Let's Murder the Moonshine: Selected Writings,* trans. R. W. Flint (Los Angeles: Sun and Moon Press, 1991), 49–52.

we want to free this land from its smelly gangrene of professors, archaeologists, ciceroni,° and antiquarians. For too long has Italy been a dealer in secondhand clothes. We mean to free her from the numberless museums that cover her like so many graveyards.

Museums: cemeteries! . . . Identical, surely, in the sinister promiscuity of so many bodies unknown to one another. Museums; public dormitories where one lies forever beside hated or unknown beings. Museums; absurd abattoirs of painters and sculptors ferociously macerating each other with color-blows and line-blows, the length of the fought-over walls!

That one should make an annual pilgrimage, just as one goes to the graveyard on All Souls' Day—that I grant. That once a year one should leave a floral tribute beneath the *Gioconda,*° I grant you that. . . . But I don't admit that our sorrows, our fragile courage, our morbid restlessness should be given a daily conducted tour through the museums. Why poison ourselves? Why rot?

And what is there to see in an old picture except the laborious contortions of an artist throwing himself against the barriers that thwart his desire to express his dream completely? . . . Admiring an old picture is the same as pouring our sensibility into a funerary urn instead of hurling it far off, in violent spasms of action and creation.

Do you, then, wish to waste all your best powers in this eternal and futile worship of the past, from which you emerge fatally exhausted, shrunken, beaten down?

In truth I tell you that daily visits to museums, libraries, and academies (cemeteries of empty exertion, calvaries of crucified dreams, registries of aborted beginnings!) is, for artists, as damaging as the prolonged supervision by parents of certain young people drunk with their talent and their ambitious wills. When the future is barred to them, the admirable past may be a sol-

° *ciceroni:* Guides.
° *Gioconda:* Leonardo da Vinci's painting, the *Mona Lisa.*

ace for the ills of the moribund, the sickly, the prisoner. . . . But we want no part of it, the past, we the young and strong *Futurists!*

So let them come, the gay incendiaries with charred fingers! Here they are! Here they are! . . . Come on! set fire to the library shelves! Turn aside the canals to flood the museums! . . . Oh, the joy of seeing the glorious old canvases bobbing adrift on those waters, discolored and shredded! . . . Take up your pickaxes, your axes and hammers, and wreck, wreck the venerable cities, pitilessly!

The oldest of us is thirty: so we have at least a decade for finishing our work. When we are forty, other younger and stronger men will probably throw us in the wastebasket like useless manuscripts—we want it to happen!

They will come against us, our successors, will come from far away, from every quarter, dancing to the winged cadence of their first songs, flexing the hooked claws of predators, sniffing doglike at the academy doors the strong odor of our decaying minds, which already will have been promised to the literary catacombs.

But we won't be there. . . . At last they'll find us—one winter's night—in open country, beneath a sad roof drummed by a monotonous rain. They'll see us crouched beside our trembling airplanes in the act of warming our hands at the poor little blaze that our books of today will give out when they take fire from the flight of our images.

They'll storm around us, panting with scorn and anguish, and all of them, exasperated by our proud daring, will hurtle to kill us, driven by hatred: the more implacable it is, the more their hearts will be drunk with love and admiration for us.

Injustice, strong and sane, will break out radiantly in their eyes.

Art, in fact, can be nothing but violence, cruelty, and injustice.

The oldest of us is thirty: even so we have already scattered treasures, a thousand treasures of force, love, courage, astuteness, and raw will power; have thrown them impatiently away, with fury, carelessly, unhesitatingly, breathless and un-resting. . . . Look at us! We are still untired! Our hearts know no weariness because they are fed with fire, hatred, and speed! . . . Does that amaze you? It should, because you can never remember having lived! Erect on the summit of the world, once again we hurl our defiance at the stars!

You have objections?—Enough! Enough! We know them . . . we've understood! . . . Our fine deceitful intelligence tells us that we are the revival and extension of our ancestors—perhaps! . . . If only it were so!—But who cares? We don't want to understand! . . . Woe to anyone who says those infamous words to us again!

Lift up your heads!

Erect on the summit of the world, once again we hurl defiance to the stars!

Document 2.6

WASSILY KANDINSKY
Concerning the Spiritual in Art, 1911

[The] all-important spark of inner life today is at present only a spark. Our minds, which are even now only just awakening after years of material-ism, are infected with the despair of unbelief, of lack of purpose and ideal. The nightmare of mate-rialism, which has turned the life of the universe into an evil, useless game, is not yet past; it holds the awakening soul still in its grip. Only a feeble light glimmers like a tiny star in a vast gulf of dark-ness. This feeble light is but a presentiment, and the soul, when it sees it, trembles in doubt whether the light is not a dream, and the gulf of darkness reality. This doubt, and the still harsh tyranny of the materialistic philosophy, divide our soul sharply from that of the Primitives. . . .

The life of the spirit may be fairly represented in diagram as a large acute-angled triangle divided horizontally into unequal parts with the narrow-est segment uppermost. The lower the segment the greater it is in breadth, depth, and area.

The whole triangle is moving slowly, almost invisibly forwards and upwards. Where the apex was today the second segment is tomorrow; what today can be understood only by the apex and to the rest of the triangle is an incomprehensible gib-berish, forms tomorrow the true thought and feel-ing of the second segment.

At the apex of the top segment stands often one man, and only one. His joyful vision cloaks a vast sorrow. Even those who are nearest to him in sympathy do not understand him. Angrily they abuse him as charlatan or madman. So in his life-time stood Beethoven, solitary and insulted. How many years will it be before a greater segment of the triangle reaches the spot where he once stood alone? Despite memorials and statues, are they re-ally many who have risen to his level?

In every segment of the triangle are artists. Each one of them who can see beyond the limits of his segment is a prophet to those about him, and helps the advance of the obstinate whole. But those who are blind, or those who retard the movement of the triangle for baser reasons, are fully understood by their fellows and acclaimed for their genius. The greater the segment (which is the same as saying the lower it lies in the triangle) so the greater the number who understand the words of the artist. . . .

The solitary visionaries are despised or re-garded as abnormal and eccentric. Those who are not wrapped in lethargy and who feel vague long-

SOURCE: Wassily Kandinsky, *Concerning the Spiritual in Art,* trans. M. T. H. Sadler (New York: Dover, 1992 [1911]), 1–2, 13–14, 19.

ings for spiritual life and knowledge and progress, cry in harsh chorus, without any to comfort them. The night of the spirit falls more and more darkly. Deeper becomes the misery of these blind and terrified guides, and their followers, tormented and unnerved by fear and doubt, prefer to this gradual darkening the final sudden leap into the blackness.

At such a time art ministers to lower needs, and is used for material ends. She seeks her sustenance in hard realities because she knows of nothing nobler. Objects, the reproduction of which is considered her sole aim, remain monotonously the same. The question "what?" disappears from art; only the question "how?" remains. By what method are these material objects to be reproduced? The word becomes a creed. Art has lost her soul.

In the search for method the artist goes still further. Art becomes so specialized as to be comprehensible only to artists, and they complain bitterly of public indifference to their work. For since the artist in such times has no need to *say* much, but only to be notorious for some small originality and consequently lauded by a small group of patrons and connoisseurs (which incidentally is also a very profitable business for him), there arise a crowd of gifted and skilful painters, so easy does the conquest of art appear. In each artistic circle are thousands of such artists, of whom the majority seek only for some new technical manner, and who produce millions of works of art without enthusiasm, with cold hearts and souls asleep.

Competition arises. The wild battle for success becomes more and more material. Small groups who have fought their way to the top of the chaotic world of art and picture-making entrench themselves in the territory they have won. The public, left far behind, looks on bewildered, loses interest and turns away.

But despite all this confusion, this chaos, this wild hunt for notoriety, the spiritual triangle, slowly but surely, with irresistible strength, moves onwards and upwards.

The invisible Moses descends from the mountain and sees the dance round the golden calf. But he brings with him fresh stores of wisdom to man.

. . . The number is increasing of those men who put no trust in the methods of materialistic science when it deals with those questions which have to do with "non-matter," or matter which is not accessible to our minds. Just as art is looking for help from the primitives, so these men are turning to half-forgotten times in order to get help from their half-forgotten methods. However, these very methods are still alive and in use among nations whom we, from the height of our knowledge, have been accustomed to regard with pity and scorn. To such nations belong the Indians, who from time to time confront those learned in our civilization with problems which we have either passed by unnoticed or brushed aside with superficial words and explanations. . . .

QUESTIONS FOR ANALYSIS

1. What are the specific goals of Marinetti and Kandinsky? What is their overall vision of society and of their role in it?

2. Why, given the development of mass society, the presence of poverty, the rise of insistent nationalism, and the violence of imperialism, did these artists find so much hope in Europe? Who or what was going to help Europe advance?

3. Do you find Marinetti's and Kandinsky's elitism arrogant and irresponsible or important for progress in the arts and in society? How is this elitism related to the structure of society as a whole at the opening of the twentieth century?

4. In what ways might this elitism be connected to the fear of democracy expressed by conservative politicians in the first decade of the twentieth century? In what ways is it unrelated to politics?

PICTURE ESSAY

Cross-Cultural Borrowing in Modern Art

MODERN ART WAS PROFOUNDLY AFFECTED at the turn of the twentieth century by influences beyond the West. Ethnologists and imperialist adventurers brought back statues and objects from Africa, Asia, and Latin America. Artists quickly incorporated features from these objects into their own work—much of it highly valued today. Using traditional forms, colors, compositional patterns, and subject matter from these imported works, European artists constructed an art that has come to be seen as "modern" or "modernist"—that is, markedly different from all that came before it. These works departed from traditionally realistic styles that valued the exact replication of nature, people, or historical subjects on the canvas or in sculpture. Instead, artists at the beginning of the century distorted faces, objects, and nature itself so that they looked geometrical, asymmetrical, or lacking in visual perspective. Soon, artists did away with any connection to reality whatsoever by creating nonrepresentational, abstract art. Modern art also featured "low" or ordinary subjects that earlier artists had rejected because they were not high-minded enough—slums, prostitutes, and people laboring to exhaustion, for example.

Most prominent was the art of Spanish painter Pablo Picasso (1881–1973), who from 1904 on settled in Paris, the art capital of the world at the time, and mingled with other resident artists or visitors attempting the same kind of cultural borrowing. News from Africa filled Parisian newspapers, and objects including sculpture from Africa could be found in Paris flea markets and museums. Picasso was riveted by what he saw: "I understood what the Blacks used their sculpture for. . . . *They were weapons* . . . to help them become free."[32] Using non-Western forms was thus a kind of weapon by which Picasso freed himself from the confines of traditional art. In his painting *Les Desmoiselles d'Avignon* (1907) (Figure 2.1), he borrowed the forms of African masks to shape the heads of his "Desmoiselles," a word that can mean "prostitutes" in French. By using prostitutes in this major work of art, the artist hurled a challenge at the polite art-viewing world and the critics who dismissed innovation. What elements in this artwork can you pick out as potentially disturbing to a viewer from a century ago?

The Italian artist Amedeo Modigliani (1884–1920) was more extreme than Picasso in his adaptation of the highly stylized forms of African sculpture. He featured smooth, nonrealistic, often elongated figures, as in this two-foot-high *Head*

117

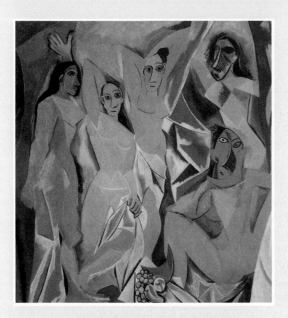

◆ Figure 2.1 **Pablo Picasso, *Les Demoiselles d'Avignon*, Paris, June–July 1907** *Oil on canvas, 8′ × 7′8″. The Museum of Modern Art, New York. Acquired through the Lillie P. Bliss Bequest. Photograph © The Museum of Modern Art/Licensed by SCALA/Art Resource, New York. © Estate of Pablo Picasso/Artist Rights Society (ARS), New York.*

of limestone, sculpted in 1911–1912 (Figure 2.2). In such borrowings there was a sense for the artist of returning to meaningful, primal forms and rejecting the realistic and materialistic art beloved by the middle classes. Modigliani also painted portraits using the same elongated styles, stretching his subjects visually until they were exaggerated in their slenderness and height. He painted the Russian poet Anna Akhmatova in this style (see Document 5.2). Many in the public found Modigliani's sculpture "humorous" and even "insane." Look-ing at the sculpture, what is your reaction to the finished work and to some of the ideas behind it?

In his Paris workshop, Romanian-born sculptor Constantin Brancusi (1876–1957) created "modern" sculptures that appeared as if they might be figures of Africans or Pacific Islanders done by artists from the region. Brancusi's "Socrates" (1922) (Figure 2.3) exemplifies this adaptation of forms that look simple to the Western observer and that aim to demonstrate "pure form." Why do you think that he used such an abstract and apparently primitive style to portray the legendary thinker Socrates? Brancusi went on to create smooth, almost abstract birds and other forms from brass and other metals that looked as if they might have been made far from his Parisian workshop. He was followed by scores of sculptors, including famed British artists Henry Moore and Barbara Hepworth, trying to express eternal truths in their use of basic, primal forms such as circles. For them, as for Wassily Kandinsky (see Document 2.6), realistic depiction was a lower, materialistic form of art, and artworks from places like Africa were hardly "primitive" at all.

Influences came from a variety of sources. Viennese artist Gustav Klimt (1862–1918) was the son of a goldsmith, and he inserted flecks and patches of gold into his paintings, many of them eagerly sought by high society in prewar Vienna—a city of vast experimentation, including that of Sigmund Freud. Many of Klimt's works have a mosaic-like look, displaying the influence of artworks in early Christian churches in Asia Minor and in Ottoman buildings, some of which Klimt saw firsthand and others of which he viewed in highly prized photographs. Klimt also found inspiration in the Egyptian Book of the Dead, an ancient

◆ **Figure 2.2** **Amedeo Modigliani,** *Head,* **1911–1912** *Tate Gallery, London/Art Resource, New York.*

collection of illustrated chants and magic formulas to be used by the dead to guide their way through the underworld. The Book of the Dead gave him a series of motifs that he placed in the background of his paintings, as we see in Figure 2.4, his celebrated *Embrace of Isis and Osiris* (1908–1909), whose very title suggests foreignness. Klimt also used Egyptian motifs to decorate garments, including his own clothing, but his experimentation drew mixed reactions. For every high-society family that wanted a portrait by him there were other members of that same social

◆ **Figure 2.3 Constantin Brancusi, *Socrates*, 1922** *Digital image © The Museum of Modern Art/Licensed by SCALA/Art Resource, New York.*

class who were outraged by his break with tradition. What characteristics in this painting qualify the work as modern? What about the painting might have appeared shocking to some viewers?

German artist Paula Modersohn-Becker (1876–1907), using a nonrealistic and "primitive" style—a term often applied to nonrealistic art—painted *Self-Portrait with Amber Necklace* (1906), portraying herself as a woman from the South Seas (Figure 2.5). Modersohn-Becker moved from her rural home to work in Paris, where she was influenced by the work of such great painters as Paul Cézanne, Vincent van Gogh, and Paul Gauguin, who painted many Tahitian women, similar to Modersohn-Becker's self-portraits. Unlike those male artists, however, she cast herself as the naked subject, perhaps pointing to the fact that even in the transition to modernism nude women remained a favored topic and that things had not changed all that much. During her lifetime her work received little praise. After her death in childbirth at age thirty-one, her paintings became celebrated as part of the "expressionism" of modern art. In other ways, her work also appears

◆ **Figure 2.4 Gustav Klimt, *Embrace of Isis and Osiris*, 1908–1909** *Austrian Museum of Applied Arts.*

quintessentially modern, imitating the style of a child in its lack of good perspective and its thick, awkward lines. What do you think of the paradox apparent in Paula Modersohn-Becker's work—namely, that to look "modern," the artist had to borrow from societies that in technology could not match Europe?

Non-Western motifs were appearing in many artistic genres but in none more so than dance. Igor Stravinsky's ballet *Rite of Spring* caused a scandal when it was presented in Paris in 1913 by the Russian Ballet. Stravinsky (1882–1971) rejected the choreography, costumes, music, and story of the classical ballet (Figure 2.6). Individual dancers, such as the star Vaslav Nijinsky, shown here, developed entire routines in which they imitated Native American, Egyptian, or African steps or poses of a "primitive" fertility dance. Although audiences protested, even screaming insults and stomping out of performances, modern dance almost in its

◆ **Figure 2.5** **Paula Modersohn-Becker,** *Self-Portrait with Amber Necklace,* **1906**
Erich Lessing/Art Resource, New York.

entirety developed from experimentation, especially with what some people called "primitivism," much of it derived from research into dance from Asia, Africa, and the Americas and from subsequent development of new movements and steps. The relationship between seemingly incompatible ideas—traditional, primitive, realistic, and modern—is a topic to consider when you examine these images.

◆ **Figure 2.6 "Primitives" in the Ballet *The Rite of Spring* by Igor Stravinsky, 1913**
Bettmann/CORBIS.

QUESTIONS FOR ANALYSIS

1. What outside influences can you discern in the works of these modern artists? Why do you think so many images of women were used to create "modernity"?

2. When you look at these works of art by European artists, do you think of them as "primitive" or "modern," as emanating from "traditional" or "advanced" societies?

3. Given all these outside influences, what can you say about a distinctive "European" style in art?

NOTES

1. Alfred Harmsworth, Lord Northcliffe, quoted in Robert Wohl, *A Passion for Wings: Aviation and the Western Imagination, 1908–1918* (New Haven: Yale University Press, 1994), 38.

2. *Le Matin,* quoted ibid., 61.

3. H. G. Wells, *The War in the Air* (London: George Bell and Sons, 1908), 207.

4. Quoted in Peter Fritzsche, *Reading Berlin 1900* (Cambridge: Harvard University Press, 1996), 32.

5. Quoted in Jonathan Rose, *The Intellectual Life of the British Working Classes* (New Haven: Yale University Press, 2001), 342.

6. Quoted in Paul Dukes, *A History of Russia: Medieval, Modern, Contemporary,* 3rd ed. (Durham: Duke University Press, 1998), 199.

7. Quoted in Rose, *The Intellectual Life of the British Working Classes,* 40.

8. Hans Brennert, quoted in Fritzsche, *Reading Berlin 1900,* 16.

9. Quoted in Francisca de Haan, *Gender and the Politics of Office Work: The Netherlands, 1860–1940* (Amsterdam: University of Amsterdam Press, 1998), 53.

10. Margaret Fountaine, *Love among the Butterflies: The Diaries of a Wayward, Determined, and Passionate Victorian Lady* (London: Collins, 1980), 139.

11. Quoted in Karen Offen, *European Feminisms, 1700–1950* (Stanford: Stanford University Press, 2000), 205.

12. Quoted ibid., 218.

13. Quoted in Susan Groag Bell and Karen Offen, eds., *Women, the Family, and Freedom: The Debate in Documents, 1750–1950,* vol. 2 (Stanford: Stanford University Press, 1983), doc. 61.

14. Colette Yver, quoted in Theodore Zeldin, *France, 1848–1945,* vol. 1 (Oxford: Clarendon, 1973), 354.

15. Margaret Cousins, quoted in Maria Luddy, ed., *Women in Ireland, 1800–1918: A Documentary History* (Cork: Cork University Press, 1995), 273.

16. Quoted in Pierre Pascal, *Les grands courants de la pensée russe contemporaine* (Paris: Fischbacher, 1977), 44.

17. Johannes R. Becher, quoted in Wolf-Dieter Dube, *The Expressionists* (London: Thames and Hudson, 1972), 21.

18. Wassily Kandinsky, quoted ibid., 20.

19. From Dube, *The Expressionists,* 179–188.

20. Wassily Kandinsky, *Concerning the Spiritual in Art,* trans. M. T. H. Sadler (London: Dover, 1977 [1911]), 1.

21. Stefan Zweig, quoted in Peter Gay, *Freud: A Life for Our Times* (New York: Norton, 1988), 171.

22. Quoted in Marc Ferro, *The Great War, 1914–1918,* trans. Nicole Stone (London: Routledge, 1973), 15.

23. Quoted in David G. Herrmann, *The Arming of Europe and the Making of the First World War* (Princeton: Princeton University Press, 1996), 179.

24. Quoted in James Joll, *The Origins of the First World War* (London: Longman, 1984), 111.

25. Quoted in Andrew Baruch Wachtel, *Making a Nation, Breaking a Nation: Literature and Cultural Politics in Yugoslavia* (Stanford: Stanford University Press, 1998), 53.

26. Prince Karl Schwarzenberg to Aehrenthal, February 1898, quoted in Solomon Wank, "Pessimism in the Austrian Establishment at the Turn of the Century," in *The Mirror of History: Essays in Honor of Fritz Fellner,* ed. Solomon Wank et al. (Santa Barbara: ABC Clio, 1992), 299.

27. Quoted in Ferro, *The Great War,* 49.

28. Quoted in Martin Gilbert, *The First World War: A Complete History* (New York: Henry Holt, 1994), 3.

29. Quoted in John Charmley, *Splendid Isolation? Britain, the Balance of Power, and the Origins of the First World War* (London: Hodder and Stoughton, 1999), 301.

30. Luigi Russolo, *The Art of Noises,* trans. Barclay Brown (New York: Pendragon Press, 1986), 24.

31. Wassily Kandinsky, *Concerning the Spiritual in Art,* trans. M. T. H. Sadler (New York: Dover, 1997), 10.

32. Quoted in Natasha Staller, *A Sum of Destructions: Picasso's Cultures and the Creation of Cubism* (New Haven: Yale University Press, 2001), 334.

SUGGESTED REFERENCES

The Many Faces of Modernity Technology, urbanization, changing gender identities, and new ways of life made up European modernity. But there were also moves to block these changes, as can be seen in Malone's and Haan's work.

Duberman, Martin, et al. *Hidden from History: Reclaiming the Gay and Lesbian Past.* 1989.

Forth, Christopher. *The Dreyfus Affair and the Crisis of French Manhood.* 2004.

Fritzsche, Peter. *Reading Berlin 1900.* 1996.

Haan, Francisca de. *Gender and the Politics of Office Work: The Netherlands, 1860–1940.* 1998.

Healy, Kimberly. *The Modernist Traveler: French Detours, 1900–1930.* 2003.

Malone, Carolyn. *Women's Bodies and Dangerous Trades in England, 1880–1914.* 2004.

Marks, Steven. *Road to Power: The Trans-Siberian Railroad and the Colonization of Asian Russia, 1850–1917.* 1991.

Rappaport, Erica. *Shopping for Pleasure: Women in the Making of London's West End.* 2000.

Roberts, Mary Louise. *Disruptive Acts: The New Woman in Fin-de-Siècle France.* 2002.

Rose, Jonathan. *The Intellectual Life of the British Working Classes.* 2001.

Sachs, Wolfgang. *For Love of the Automobile: Looking Back into the History of Our Desires.* 1992.

Wohl, Robert. *A Passion for Wings: Aviation and the Western Imagination, 1908–1918.* 1994.

Modernity and the Rise of Mass Politics   Mass politics, with which we are familiar today, disturbed many, and governments tried to deal with newly educated and urbanized workers. Judson's work shows how the Habsburgs addressed this issue in a complicated multiethnic state, while Weitz looks at the development of socialism in Germany.

Di Scala, Spencer, ed. *Italian Socialism between Politics and History.* 1996.

Dixon, Joy. *Divine Feminism: Theosophy and Feminism in England.* 2001.

Eley, Geoff. *Forging Democracy: The History of the Left in Europe, 1850–2000.* 2002.

Hause, Steven. *Hubertine Auclert, the French Suffragette.* 1987.

Judson, Pieter. *Exclusive Revolutionaries: Liberal Politics, Social Experience, and National Identity in the Austrian Empire, 1848–1914.* 1996.

Kent, Susan. *Gender and Power in Britain, 1640–1990.* 1999.

Lekan, Thomas M. *Imagining the Nation in Nature: Landscape Preservation and German Identity, 1890–1945.* 2004.

Luddy, Margaret, ed. *Women in Ireland, 1800–1918: A Documentary History.* 1995.

Marks, Steven. *How Russia Shaped the Modern World: From Art to Anti-Semitism, Ballet to Bolshevism.* 2003.

Miller, James E. *From Elite to Mass Politics: Italian Socialism in the Giolittian Era.* 1990.

Offen, Karen. *European Feminisms, 1700–1950: A Political History.* 2000.

Weitz, Eric. *Creating German Communism, 1890–1990: From Popular Protests to Socialist State.* 1997.

The Arts and Philosophy Embrace Modernity   Art and ideas changed as rapidly as social customs did. Because physicians believed in Enlightenment values such as rationality, they were fascinated by the appearance of the criminal, as Gibson's work shows, and they pursued a number of paths to understand the human condition, as Owen's work demonstrates.

Eksteins, Modris. *Rites of Spring: The Great War and the Birth of the Modern Age.* 1989.

Everdell, William R. *The First Moderns: Profiles in the Origins of Twentieth-Century Thought.* 1997.

Gay, Peter. *Freud: A Life for Our Times.* 1988.

Gibson, Mary. *Born to Crime: Cesare Lombroso and the Origins of Biological Criminology.* 2002.

Kaplan, Temma. *Red City, Blue Period: Social Movements in Picasso's Barcelona.* 1992.

Kern, Steven. *The Culture of Time and Space, 1880–1918.* 1983.

Marchand, Suzanne, and David Lindenfeld, eds. *Germany at the Fin de Siècle: Culture, Politics, and Ideas.* 2004.

Owen, Alex. *The Places of Enchantment: British Occultism and the Culture of the Modern.* 2004.

Safranski, Rüdiger. *Nietzsche: A Philosophical Biography.* 2002.

Staller, Natasha. *A Sum of Destructions: Picasso's Cultures and the Creation of Cubism.* 2001.

Zaretsky, Eli. *Secrets of the Soul: A Social and Cultural History of Psychoanalysis.* 2004.

The Road to War Could World War I have been avoided? Historians keep looking for new clues, and the books on the steps toward war are expert in showing both clear missteps and murkier issues.

Berghahn, Volker R. *Germany and the Approach of War in 1914.* 1993.

Charmley, John. *Splendid Isolation? Britain, the Balance of Power, and the Origins of the First World War.* 1999.

Cornwall, Mark, ed. *The Last Years of Austria-Hungary: A Multi-National Experiment in Early Twentieth-Century Europe.* 2002.

Herrmann, David G. *The Arming of Europe and the Making of the First World War.* 1996.

Hewitson, Mark. *Germany and the Causes of the First World War.* 2004.

Hobson, Rolf. *Imperialism at Sea: Naval Strategic Thought, the Ideology of Sea Power, and the Tirpitz Plan, 1875–1914.* 2002.

Joll, James. *The Origins of the First World War.* 1984.

Nolan, Michael E. *The Inverted Mirror: Mythologizing the Enemy in France and Germany, 1898–1914.* 2005.

Stevenson, David. *The Outbreak of the First World War: 1914 in Perspective.* 1997.

Williamson, Samuel. *Austria-Hungary and the Origins of the First World War.* 1991.

Selected Web Sites

The Trans-Siberian Railway has a very engaging Web site, complete with photos of engineering pioneers and the many different railroad stations along its routes: <**transsib.ru/Eng**>. An informative Web site for art nouveau is <**nga.gov/feature/nouveau/nouveau.htm**>. Nineteenth- and twentieth-century philosophy is explored in <**epistemelinks.com/index.asp/**>. The BBC (British Broadcasting Company) has many historic components to its Web site and covers the Pankhursts and other feminists of the early twentieth century: <**bbc.co.uk**>. Trenches on the Web looks at military conditions before war erupted: <**trenchesontheweb.com**>.

3

World War I and the Russian Revolution

1914–1922

O N JUNE 28, 1914, IN THE BOSNIAN CAPITAL OF Sarajevo, an assassin fired two shots into the royal car carrying the heir to the Habsburg throne, Franz Ferdinand, and his wife, Sophie. Moments later, both were dead. Their killer, a nineteen-year-old Bosnian Serb, Gavrilo Princip, had fulfilled a youthful dream—killing any Habsburg he could locate. Princip had been a student and bookworm who loved reading Sir Walter Scott's sagas of medieval knights and following the adventures of Arthur Conan Doyle's detective Sherlock Holmes. But the Habsburg subjects from the north who flooded his homeland of Bosnia after its annexation by Austria-Hungary in 1908 essentially colonized the region, seizing land and opening factories where they exploited local labor—all with the approval of the government in Vienna. Poverty among Muslims and Slavs in Bosnia increased, strikes broke out, and ethnic nationalism mounted. With help from military officials in neighboring Serbia, who directed a terrorist organization called the "Black Hand" from within the Serbian government, a secret society called the "Young Bosnians" was formed. Princip joined this group, which aimed to track the Habsburgs and, by killing them, eventually to free Bosnia from the Austrians. The group wanted to unite Bosnia with Serbia and perhaps even cre-

♦ **Assassination of the Austrian Archduke and His Wife**
Headlines worldwide announced Gavrilo Princip's daring assassination of the heir to the Habsburg throne, but few people foresaw that a cataclysmic world war would soon follow. Yet little more than a month later, as July turned to August in 1914, the great European powers divided into two antagonistic camps and then for four years fought one another, expending the lives and resources of millions of Europeans and other peoples around the world. *The Granger Collection, New York.*

ate a federation of South Slavic states under Serbian leadership. Princip got more than his wish, for the assassination unexpectedly set in motion the events that led to the tragedy of World War I.

At the time, world leaders were hardly shocked and expected a measured response to the murder. Assassination had become a kind of occupational hazard for major political figures over the past decades. In Austria-Hungary some officials even breathed a sigh of relief at Franz Ferdinand's death because they disliked his abrasive style and his policies toward the Hungarians, whose disruptive power he had brusquely aimed to curtail. Habsburg government officials who had long opposed Franz Ferdinand's conciliatory moves toward the Slavs — the flip side of his anti-Hungarian disposition — saw an opportunity to put down the Serbs once and for all. This move would strengthen the Hungarian hold on and influence in the Balkans generally. Shortly before the assassination, William II of Germany had urged Austria-Hungary to take definitive action. After the assassination, German military and diplomatic leaders encouraged the Habsburgs not to deal with the Serbs and guaranteed full German military support to back up Austrian intransigence — a "blank check," this assurance of unconditional support was called. Sure of German backing, Austria-Hungary issued an ultimatum, all of which Serbia accepted save Austria-Hungary's demand to participate in the investigation of the assassination. This one issue became the excuse for a war that would plunge Europe into unprecedented catastrophe.

In less than five weeks after the assassination, full-scale war broke out. Nationalist ambitions and counterambitions, old feuds and rivalries, alliances and counteralliances brought all the great European powers to the battlefield. First, Austria-Hungary declared war on Serbia in an attempt to solve its problems in the Balkans, and Germany encouraged this aggression as part of its own plan for creating a German-dominated Mitteleuropa, or Central Europe. Russia mobilized to support its Slavic ally Serbia and extend its own influence. France mobilized to fulfill the terms of its alliance with Russia but also to get revenge on Germany for its defeat in the Franco-Prussian War in 1871. Britain followed its allies France and Russia into a war against Germany and Austria-Hungary, who became known as the Central Powers, when Germany violated Belgian neutrality in its haste to invade France. Many soldiers and civilians welcomed the challenge, but there were others who faced the war with fear and even protest.

Although war had been foreseen, nothing went according to plan. Because of their large armies and huge supplies of powerful weaponry, both sides envisioned a short war with limited casualties. Instead, the war dragged on and on, and the death toll became staggering. Few predicted the need to militarize the home front, but that was precisely what happened. By November 1914, both sides had less than several weeks' supply of ammunition left, so the ratcheting up of production became crucial. As resources were diverted to the war effort, civilians began to suffer real deprivation in addition to the horrendous loss of loved ones on the battlefield. Rebellion broke out among soldiers and civilians alike, and soon Russia was embroiled in full-scale revolution.

As the war drew to a close in 1918, four major monarchies collapsed, leaving political uncertainty if not chaos in their wake, and revolution threatened everywhere. Amid turmoil, the victorious powers met to construct the Peace of Paris, a peace that many thought problematic. New, unstable nations were created; the victors extended their sway over more of the world; and the emotional toll of the conflict went unrelieved. What became known as the "Great War" significantly transformed European society as well as politics. When it was all over, the South Slavs were free from the Habsburgs, united into an independent state. Gavrilo Princip died a broken man in 1918, but his actions had the outcome he desired. For everyone else, World War I left a legacy of bitterness, death, destruction, and sorrow.

WORLD WAR I BEGINS

At the end of July 1914, mobilization for war occurred with lightning speed—the result of years of military buildup and planning. Hours and days mattered, given the speed that railroads made possible, and generals and armies alike were eager to test the new firepower in spirited offensives that formed the stock-in-trade of military strategy at the turn of the century. The combination of new weaponry and outdated ideas of strategy helped give World War I its unprecedented casualties, and the resulting stalemate colored many a soldier's searing experience of the war. Unprecedented destruction changed civilian life too, forcing the militarization of entire populations, including women and old men. Propaganda campaigns and intense deprivation, however, took their toll in disbelief, leaving governments in fragile condition. Although the German kaiser at the last minute demanded a war limited to Russia to avoid fighting the British, German military planners vetoed him because of their inflexible plan based on a rush to war.

The Opening Battles

German strategy was based on the Schlieffen Plan, named after its author, a former chief of the German General Staff. The plan outlined for German forces a way to combat antagonists on two fronts by concentrating on one foe at a time: first, a rapid and concentrated blow to the west against France, leading to that nation's defeat in six weeks, accompanied by a light holding action against France's ally Russia to the east; then, deployment of Germany's western armies to the east against Russia, which, German planners believed, would mobilize far more slowly than France. The German strategy, however, hit an unexpected snag in the form of Belgian resistance. On August 2, the Belgian government rejected an ultimatum to allow the uncontested passage of the German army through neutral Belgium on its way to attack France. Germany's subsequent violation of Belgian neutrality brought Britain into the war on the side of Russia and France, which had mobilized against Germany on August 1. The conflict became global in late August, when Japan, eager to expand its empire in the Far East, declared war on Germany.

The first months of the war squelched expectations of quick victory. Deceived by German diversionary tactics on France's eastern borders, the main body of French troops attacked the Germans in Alsace and Lorraine instead of meeting the invasion from the north. Despite this initial success, the Schlieffen Plan disintegrated in part because Belgian resistance bought time for British and French troops to reach the northern front. Unused to marching under fire in the summer heat, the fatigued German reservists were redirected to the east of Paris instead of taking the plan's longer way around, which would have led to the encirclement of the capital. The German detour ground to a bloody halt when British and French armies engaged their enemy along the Marne River in France. Neither side could prevail, and the fighting continued late into the autumn of 1914 along the Marne and up to Ypres in Belgium. In the first three months of fighting there were more than 1.5 million casualties on the western front alone.

On the eastern front the "Russian steamroller"—so named because of the twelve million men mobilized—drove far more quickly than expected into East Prussia and parts of the Austro-Hungarian Empire. The Russians had so much faith in their mass army that they had ignored all advice to modernize their strategy, weaponry, or communications. "If the War Minister himself boasted that he had not read a single military textbook in . . . thirty-five years . . . why should anyone else?" notes a character in Aleksandr Solzhenitsyn's novel *August, 1914.*[1] Thus, the Russian success was short-lived, as the Germans intercepted messages that the Russians failed to send in code and crushed the tsar's army in East Prussia by the end of August. The Germans then turned south to aid their Austro-Hungarian allies in Galicia. These victories made heroes of the military leaders Paul von Hindenburg and Erich Ludendorff and allowed them to demand more troops for the eastern front and thus finally wreck the Schlieffen Plan, whose premise was a light defense in the east until the western allies had been defeated.

Outdated military concepts guided both sides. Officers believed in a "cult of the offensive," in which spirited attacks and high troop morale would be decisive. "Train others and prepare yourselves: we must foment the spirit of the offensive everywhere, even in the smallest details of training," one French military leader announced.[2] Despite the availability of new, powerful war technology, such as more deadly artillery, an old-fashioned vision of warfare persisted, and officers were unwilling to abandon their sabers, lances, and bayonets. "Neither numbers nor miraculous machines will determine victory," a general insisted. "This will go to soldiers with valor and quality—and by this I mean superior physical and moral endurance, offensive strength."[3] Given the destructive potential of the technology available to the industrialized powers, the war opened on a completely unrealistic note: Napoleonic weaponry and strategy, uniforms, polished swords, and cheerful military plans were seen as central to victory. Even the Schlieffen Plan, considered by some the height of military brilliance, has been called "a work of fiction" because, among numerous reasons, it did not take into account that France had an excellent railway system that could quickly transport troops to meet a northern invasion.[4]

As a result, on both European fronts what the German planners expected to be an offensive war of movement settled into a stationary, defensive war (Map 3.1). On the western front, the two sides faced off along a line stretching from the North Sea through Belgium and northern France to Switzerland. There, millions of soldiers dug in parallel lines of trenches up to thirty feet deep that would serve as their nightmarish homes for the next four years. The lack of a decisive victory brought trench warfare to the eastern front too, though combat was more mobile there. Facing the firepower of sophisticated weapons such as heavy artillery and rapid-firing machine guns, soldiers paid dearly if ordered to leave their trenches for the cult of the offensive.

◆ **World War I Gas Masks**
The German army made the first effective use of chlorine gas against French and British forces in 1915 at Ypres, causing painful injury and death. Gas masks for man and beast alike provided protection when troops saw clouds of chlorine gas rolling toward them. The subsequent use of mustard gas gave no such warning and took some time to take effect. Both sides developed chemical agents that disabled surviving soldiers so severely that in 1925 an international agreement banned their use. Still in existence, the ban is mostly ignored by the world's powers. *The Granger Collection, New York.*

War at sea proved equally indecisive, despite decades of confidence about its crucial role. Relying on Britain's superior naval powers, the Entente blockaded the entry to the Mediterranean and North seas to prevent supplies from reaching the Central Powers. Nonetheless, neutral countries, notably the Netherlands, Switzerland, Sweden, and Norway, kept trading with them. William II and his advisers launched a massive submarine, or U-boat (*Unterseebot*), campaign against Allied and neutral shipping around Britain and France. In May 1915, German submarines sank the passenger ship *Lusitania,* killing more than twelve hundred people including 128 Americans. Although the atmosphere in the United States crackled with outrage, President Woodrow Wilson maintained a policy of neutrality. Not willing to provoke Wilson any further, the Germans called off unrestricted submarine warfare. In May 1916 the navies of Germany and Britain clashed in the Battle of Jutland. Although the outcome was inconclusive, the battle demonstrated that the German fleet could not dislodge British power on the sea.

In the fall of 1914, Turkey entered on the side of the Central Powers and prevented much-needed Allied supplies from reaching Russia via the Black Sea. Ottoman armies forced the Entente powers to shift troops from Europe to protect their oil interests in the Near East, which Turkey threatened to seize. In 1915, Italy, which at first had allied with Germany and Austria-Hungary, sold its support to the Entente, opening a third front against the Central Powers in the south in exchange for the promise of territory in Africa, Asia Minor, the south Tyrol, the Balkans, and

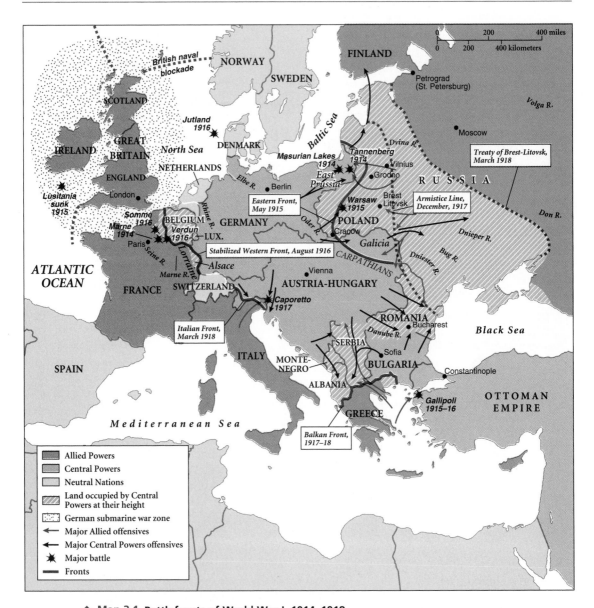

◆ Map 3.1 **Battlefronts of World War I, 1914–1918**

Battlefronts in World War I stretched across thousands of miles. European villages, farms, and even cities were devastated by the punishing artillery fire. In the west, the front remained fairly stationary, and soldiers settled into deep trenches that offered some protection. The eastern front was more mobile, and many civilians suffered repeated invasions by armies on both sides. While noting their own inhuman conditions in diaries and letters, soldiers often expressed dismay at the plight of villagers in their army's path.

elsewhere at the end of the war. Bulgaria, hoping to defeat Serbia and to annex Macedonia, joined the Central Powers in October 1915.

Colonies provided massive assistance and also served as battlegrounds. Some one million Africans, another million Indians, and more than a million people in the British commonwealth countries served on the battlefronts. The imperial powers also conscripted countless numbers of colonized people and consigned them to forced labor on both the home front and the battlefield. A million Kenyans and Tanzanians are estimated to have been used for portage and other menial labor in the battle for East Africa. Colonial troops played a major role in the fighting that occurred across sub-Saharan Africa. The long and vicious campaign for East Africa alone resulted in loss of life not only among African troops confronting each other on behalf of the imperialist powers but also among civilian populations, who saw their resources confiscated and villages burned. Relying on Arab, African, and Indian troops, the British successfully waged war on the Ottoman Empire and menaced Germany's longtime interests in the Middle East with the fall of Baghdad in 1917 and fighting in Palestine, Syria, and Mesopotamia. In 1917, when revolution again broke out in Russia, the war moved into the Caucasus in a fight for the rich Baku oil fields, expanding the British theater of war to a dangerous extent.

War Aims and the Struggle for Victory, 1915–1916

Each side envisioned a triumph followed by territorial gains that would justify the bloodshed. While German troops sat mired in trenches, the General Staff, many high-ranking politicians, leading industrialists, respected university professors, and groups such as the Pan-German League continued to foresee a far-flung German Empire. Germany aspired to annex Russian territory, to incorporate parts of Belgium and an industrialized slice of France and Luxembourg, and to turn the Netherlands and the rest of Belgium into a satellite zone. Some German leaders hoped to annex Austria-Hungary as well and to take Poland and other territory from Russia. The dual monarchy of Austria-Hungary sought victory to consolidate its control of the Serbs, Germans, Hungarians, Croats, Czechs, Poles, and other nationalities who lived together but were increasingly resistant to rule by the Habsburg crown. The acquisition of more land in the Balkans was seen as a way of permanently establishing Austria-Hungary's credibility and strength as a multiethnic empire.

On the other side, Russia wanted to reassert its status as a great power and as the Slavs' protector by taking all three portions of Poland partitioned by Germany, Austria, and Russia itself in the eighteenth century, and by annexing a reunified Poland to the Russian Empire. It also aimed to annex Habsburg territory peopled by Ukrainians and to reorganize the rest of Austria-Hungary into a *triple* monarchy that would recognize Slavic political claims in the entire region. France and Britain fed Russia's dreams of expansion by promising it Constantinople and the long-desired Dardenelles — the strait between European and Asian Turkey and a crucial trade and military route — at the end of the war. The French too craved territory, especially the return of the provinces Alsace and Lorraine, lost to Germany after the Franco-Prussian War of 1870–1871. And France desperately wanted new boundaries with Germany to guarantee French national security. The British sought to keep the North Sea coast from falling to another great power and to cement their hold on Egypt and the Suez Canal, as well as to secure the rest of their empire. In 1916, in the Sykes-Picot agreement, France and Great Britain divided Ottoman lands in the Middle East among themselves.

Although ideas for a negotiated peace were proposed from the middle of the war on, neither side could envision peace without substantial territorial gains and absolute surrender by the enemy. "No peace before England is defeated and destroyed," the kaiser railed against his cousin King George V. "Only amidst the ruins of London will I forgive Georgy." Politician and powerful journalist Georges Clemenceau, who became premier of France for the second time in 1917, called for a "war to the death." General staffs continued to prepare fierce attacks several times a year. Campaigns opened with heavy artillery pounding enemy trenches and gun emplacements. Troops then scrambled "over the top" of the trenches, usually to be mowed down by machine-gun fire from defenders secure in their own trenches.

Still, indecisive offensives continued. On the western front, the French desperately wanted to oust the Germans from France's northern industrial regions. Throughout 1915 they assaulted the enemy at Ypres, Loos, and Artois but accomplished little; casualties of 100,000 and more in a single campaign became commonplace. On the eastern front, troops on both sides fared no better than their counterparts in Belgium and France. In the spring of 1915, Russian armies captured parts of Galicia and lumbered toward Hungary, only to be driven back by the Central Powers later that year, bringing the front closer to St. Petersburg, the Russian capital. Austro-Hungarian armies routed the Serbs in 1915 and then engaged the newly mobilized Italian army.

The catastrophic casualties continued to mount in 1916, as the military situation became even more disastrous. Hoping that a definitive blow against the French would induce the British to withdraw from the war, German troops attacked the fortress at Verdun, the fall of which, they calculated, would break French morale. Launching massive assaults from February through April 1916, the Germans fired as many as a million shells in a single day. Combined French and German losses totaled close to a million men. Nonetheless, the French held.

In June 1916, hoping to relieve their allies, the British unleashed in the Somme region of France an artillery pounding of German trenches that was supposed to ensure an easy victory for Britain. On July 1, twenty thousand British soldiers died going "over the top"—the artillery had failed to penetrate the deeply dug German fortifications. In several months of battle at the Somme River, 1.25 million men were killed or wounded, but the final result was stalemate. "The incompetence, callousness, and personal vanity of those high in authority" struck soldiers from all nations. "A raving lunatic could never imagine the horror of the last thirteen days," an Australian officer wrote in his last letter before he was killed in combat on the Somme.[5] By the end of 1916, the French had absorbed more than 3.5 million casualties. To help the Allies engaged at Verdun and the Somme, the Russians struck again, driving once more into the Carpathian Mountains, recouping territory, and menacing the Habsburg Empire. As Habsburg forces faltered, the German

◆ **Soldiers Felled by Gas and Flame Attack**
Powerful weaponry and chemical attacks killed and wounded soldiers by the millions in
World War I. Brief truces allowed competing sides to gather up thousands of dead soldiers
and bury them in mass graves near the battlefields. This photo of dead troops killed in a gas
attack gives some idea of the scale of the medical tasks involved in total war. Often there was
no respite in battle for days. Other pictures show soldiers in trenches fighting alongside the
bodies of their fallen comrades and even using those corpses for protection. *Hulton
Archive/Getty Images.*

army was able to stop the Russian advance. Suffering huge losses, the Habsburg
army resorted to recruiting men in their mid-fifties, and the German General Staff
was impelled to take over Austrian military operations. The war was sapping
Europe's strength and undermining individual countries' sovereignty.

The Soldier's War

From the point of view of soldiers in the trenches, the war had a distinctive look.
When men in the trenches engaged in combat, they experienced a veritable hell of
shelling and sniping, flying body parts, rotting cadavers, and blinding gas — a new

weapon resulting from breakthroughs in the chemical industry. The average life span of a machine gunner during an attack was thirty minutes, and under these conditions soldiers were often reduced to hysteria or succumbed to shell shock through the sheer stress and violence of battle. The powerful shells of the German cannon "Big Bertha," (named after Bertha Krupp, owner of Germany's largest munitions establishment) not only pulverized the sturdiest fortress but utterly undid the mental stability of men under fire. Many soldiers living in these conditions felt alienated from civilization and became cynical: "It might be me tomorrow," a young British soldier wrote his mother in 1916, adding "Who cares?"[6] War was often a deeply alienating and impersonal experience, (see Document 3.1) depending less on swords and spirit than on wire cutters, artillery shells, gas masks, and tanks. Having gone to war for a bracing escape from ordinary life in industrial society, soldiers learned, as one German put it, "that in the modern war . . . the triumph of the machine over the individual is carried to its most extreme form."[7] Bombs, machine guns, and poisonous gas made old-fashioned notions about swordsmen bravely wielding their sabers obsolete if not ridiculous. Soldiers took this hard-won knowledge into battle, pulling their comrades back when an offensive seemed foolhardy or too costly.

This was not the only face of war, however. Whereas governments and officers tended to see war as "kill or be killed," troops at the front often put into effect their own practice of "live and let live." Despite the generals' commitment to the cult of the offensive, some battalions went for long stretches with hardly a casualty. Diaries and letters show that throughout the war, and despite the increasing threat of severe punishment, these low rates stemmed from agreements among troops to avoid battle at certain times. For example, troops facing each other across the trenches frequently allowed their enemies to eat their meals in peace, even though the trenches were within a hand grenade's reach. A German soldier described trenches "where friend and foe alike go to fetch straw from the same rick [stack] to protect them from cold and rain—and never a shot is fired."[8] Throughout the war, enemy soldiers fraternized on both fronts. They played an occasional game of soccer, yelled and sang together across the trenches especially at Christmas and Easter, and occasionally exchanged mementos. A British veteran of the trenches explained to a new recruit that the Germans "don't want to fight any more than we do, so there's a kind of understanding between us. Don't fire at us and we'll not fire at you."[9]

Burying enemy dead in common graves with their own fallen comrades, many ordinary soldiers came to feel more warmly toward enemies who shared the trench experience than toward civilians back home. One infantryman wrote: "It is only on the home front that the atmosphere is still warlike. . . . At the [battle]front there is far too much mutual understanding of one for the other." At times the military command turned a blind eye to fraternization in hopes that it might lead to defection, especially on the eastern front, where armies were composed of many ethnicities and people often felt competing allegiances. In the late autumn of 1917, amid war weariness and revolt across Europe, fraternization increased. Austro-Hungarian soldiers, for example, reported going over to talk to the Russians:

"Music, singing, dancing. Then all 15 of us were treated to a cup of tea. . . . We exchanged our treasures; I got at least a kilo of sugar and a nice piece of coarse soap. Then we crawled back under the wire."[10]

Camaraderie among one's own troops alleviated some of the misery of trench life and aided survival. Sharing the danger of death and the deprivations of front-line experience weakened traditional class distinctions. In some cases upper-class officers and working-class draftees became friends in that "wholly masculine way of life uncomplicated by women," as one soldier put it. According to diaries and letters, soldiers picked lice from one another's bodies and clothes, revered section leaders who tended their blistered feet, and came to love one another, sometimes even sexually. The high command—distant, privileged, and hierarchical—maintained aristocratic ways such as holding horse shows behind the lines and enjoying lavish meals. They were often viewed with contempt by those in the trenches, both ordinary soldiers and ranking officers. British poet Siegfried Sassoon, himself an officer, expressed the not infrequent contempt for those at the top in his poem "The General":

> "Good-morning; good-morning!" the General said
> When we met him last week on our way to the line.
> Now the soldiers he smiled at are most of 'em dead,
> And we're cursing his staff for incompetent swine.
> "He's a cheery old card," grunted Harry to Jack
> As they slogged up to Arras with rifle and pack
> But he did for them both by his plan of attack.

There were, however, distinctly positive memories of this front-line community, where issues of gender and class identity tended to recede, and these memories survived the war to influence postwar politics.

Colonial troops from Asia and Africa had different experiences of the trenches. They were often put in the very front ranks, where the risks were greatest. "Splendid Achievements" ran one appreciative headline in a British newspaper commenting on the valor of colonial soldiers and endeavoring to raise money to help the wounded ones. European observers noted that these soldiers suffered particularly from the strange food they were given and the rigors of a totally unfamiliar, cold climate even when enveloped in mufflers and heavy gloves. Like class divisions, racial barriers sometimes fell—for instance, whenever a European took steps to alleviate the distress that cold inflicted or to comfort homesickness. Some colonial soldiers found much to admire in European institutions (see Document 3.2), but the horror experienced by many matched that of their European comrades: "Am I dead, am I alive?" one corporal from Dahomey in western Africa wrote of trench warfare. "What miserable crowned head was able to order such horrors?"[11] Colonial troops developed second thoughts about the sometimes respectful obedience they gave imperialists, for in this war they got to see their "masters" completely undone and "uncivilized" in the most shocking ways.

THE HOME FRONT

World War I has been called the first total war. As such, it was a fight to the finish in which neither side could envision a negotiated peace. In addition, it was "total" because the home front played as important a role as the battlefield. Based on heavy weaponry, the war could proceed only with the heightened productivity and sacrifices of civilians. Although fought most dramatically and tragically on battlefields, the war was one of economics in which each side sought to strangle the other's trade and productive capacity, even to the point of starving entire nations. Civilians thus gradually became targets over the course of the war, marking another first in modern warfare. Close to the end of the war, the Germans developed a cannon whose shells could accurately strike targets some ninety miles away, making the masses of people living in capital cities such as Paris viable targets. To maintain a high level of productivity and sacrifice in the face of growing danger, governments bombarded the home front with propaganda calling for total allegiance and correct thinking about the war and imprisoned critics. Another striking change on the home front was the state's absorption of the economy. This added to the human toll in the slow deterioration of people's health, because food was efficiently shifted from the home front to the battlefield and because nitrates for fertilizers needed to boost agricultural productivity were allotted to the manufacture of munitions. By 1917 starving civilians on both sides yearned for peace.

Politics End

War muted the clash of classes, economic interests, and social visions that had driven politics before August 1914. Suddenly there developed a sense that everyone supported his or her nation at war and indeed that war would smooth out social and political tensions: "After a war, everything is better," one British politician trumpeted. Even as political discontent over the conditions of work and everyday life increased as the century opened, the propaganda for imperialism and the arms race whipped up patriotic war fever among European peoples, and when war broke out, there were spontaneous parades of singing civilians, a rush of young men to the enlistment office, and an apparent end to the contentious prewar political spirit. Socialist parties in France and Germany voted for war budgets instead of opposing them. As a result, the international labor movement mostly disintegrated, morphing from a transnational organization powered by defiant, antinationalist rhetoric to collections of individual nationalists participating en masse in the war effort and clamoring for the death of those whom they formerly considered brother workers. For decades socialist parties had preached that "the worker has no country" and that nationalism was an artificial ideology meant to keep workers disunited and subjected to the will of their employers. Socialists had envisioned that their deputies would vote against military budgets and that their members would refuse to fight. However, the enthusiasm of the working class for the war in 1914 was no less than that of the military and upper classes. Political debate at the heart of democratic government ceased, and working-class support of the war ended the Second International's role as an opposition force.

Political and social leaders of every stripe fostered a sense that there was now only a single political will. "I no longer recognize political parties," Kaiser William announced on August 4, 1914. "I recognize only Germans."[12] Thus was born the idea that citizens were unanimous in their support of the nation and that the nation consisted of like-minded people. In the name of unity the German government put aside its plan to arrest prominent social democrats. Feminists, too, got behind the war effort, although many had been pacifists before the war. Christabel Pankhurst, who had declared the outbreak of war to be "God's vengeance upon those who held women in subjection," soon became fiercely patriotic and prowar like other suffrage leaders. The Pankhursts even changed the name of their suffrage paper to *Britannia* in support of the nation. Labor leaders backed the war in the belief that it would usher in an era of equality and social justice, as did others who had been at the receiving end of discrimination and at the bottom of the social hierarchy: "In the German fatherland there are no longer any Christians and Jews, any believers and disbelievers, there are only Germans," one rabbi proudly claimed.[13]

This solidarity on the home front sometimes took the form of an unshakable belief that people were fighting not over Serbia or colonies or trade but for a spiritual cause. A *union sacrée,* or sacred union, the French called their political unanimity. The war took on apocalyptic meaning for everyone from kings to poets. The Russian writer Mikhail Bulgakov believed that it pitted Western decadence, especially of the German variety, against Russia's superior Orthodox religion and innocent peasant tradition, and that "Russia bears the frightening responsibility for the spiritual destiny of humanity." Another Russian patriot saw the war similarly, as "a struggle of West versus East, Russianism versus Germanism, in which the Slavic race, with Russia in the lead, is called on to play the determining role in the fate of humanity."[14] Germans believed the same: "We felt ourselves placed completely in the service of a higher task, a task which we ourselves had not sought, but which had been placed upon us by a higher power," one German intellectual claimed during the war.[15] The belief that in wartime the nation was at its best, fulfilling not only a political but a divine destiny, remained vivid even after the war and into the years that followed. Motivated by these myths, people rejected rational political debate in favor of belief in and obedience to the government.

Propaganda and Censorship

Belief in the righteousness of the nation's cause—whichever that nation might be—was thus widespread in 1914, fostered in previous decades by vigorous arguments and publicity for nationalism, imperialism, and arms buildup. Most combatant governments initially directed their propaganda at neutral countries such as the United States, the Scandinavian countries, and the Netherlands to gain their support. After several months of massive casualties with no victory in sight, however, governments realized that a questioning mood was growing among their own citizens at home and that a concerted and centralized propaganda effort was needed on the home front and in the colonies too (see the Picture Essay). In England, Rudyard Kipling, H. G. Wells, and other prominent authors worked with the British Department of Information to promote the war throughout the empire. Arthur Conan Doyle, author of the wildly popular Sherlock Holmes detective stories, wrote recruitment tracts such as "To Arms" to encourage men to enlist. Journalists targeted housewives, especially those with male servants, to sacrifice their domestic comforts for the war. One British government pamphlet on food rationing proclaimed that "The kitchen is the key to victory."[16] "Eat less Bread and Victory is Secure" ran a poster displayed prominently on London streets. German propaganda warned that French African troops would rape German women if Germany were defeated, and in Russia, Nicholas II changed the German-sounding name of St. Petersburg to the Russian "Petrograd" in 1914.

Censorship went hand in hand with propaganda once unanimous popular enthusiasm for battle appeared to be waning. Convinced that workers and social democrats were enemies of the state, the German military demanded immediate censorship, suspending "the right to express opinion freely by word, print or picture."[17] The social democratic newspaper *Vorwärts*, like other papers, was encouraged to write only positively about conditions on the home front. A conservative paper was closed down simply for having paraphrased the German prime minister's remark in December 1914 that "We must tighten our belts if we are going to hold out."[18] Heavy censorship was applied to films, an increasingly popular medium made possible by new technology and offering real opportunity for governments to get across powerful images. Lighthearted and foreign films were outlawed in Germany. Instead, the public, eager for news from the front, lapped up newsreels showing troops on the battlefield, members of the royal family visiting the wounded, the training of new recruits, and other inspirational scenes. Governments' practice of allowing only staged battles to be screened brought whoops of irreverent laughter from moviegoing soldiers on leave.

The aim of propaganda was twofold: to instill patriotism and loyalty in the citizenry at home and to foster hatred for the enemy's culture and society. Allied propagandists depicted the Germans as barbarian Huns gleefully spearing babies with their bayonets. German propagandists portrayed the French, British, and Russians as uncivilized illiterates, cruelly withholding treatment to wounded enemy soldiers (see the Picture Essay). The British press called for the internment or deportation of all individuals of foreign birth or even foreign extraction: "The only safe plan," wrote a British newspaperman, "is to arrest and deport every German. . . . The only safe place for all Germans is a concentration camp."[19] All governments excelled at inventing stories of atrocities such as the rape of women, the murder of children, the mutilation of the clergy, nurses, and doctors, and the deliberate starvation and ill treatment of prisoners of war. "It never occurred to me that newspapers and statesmen could lie," wrote one intellectual after the war.[20] Although civilian suffering in the war was very real, many of the most outrageous tales of cruelty, as well as tamer slurs and insults attributed to the enemy, were later discovered to be the fabrications of propaganda offices.

War Transforms Society

Just as governments used propaganda and censorship to boost morale and curtail criticism of the war, so too did they seek to control and coordinate the economic activities of the entire society to meet the needs of prolonged industrial warfare. As early as mid-November 1914, German artillery on the western front had been reduced to a four-day supply of ammunition. All combatants lacked ready replacements for weapons and materiel. Thus, at different rates in the various countries, bureaucracies began to oversee factories, transportation systems, and the allocation of resources ranging from food to coal and steel and textiles. They shifted resources away from civilian needs and toward those of the military. Under centralized direction in France, the daily production of 75-millimeter shells rose from 13,500 at the beginning of the war to 212,000. Factories making civilian goods—household items, luxury clothing, and amenities such as pianos—were converted to supply munitions and other military hardware. In Germany, the Krupp factories, which had produced a wide range of goods before 1914, shifted entirely to military production. Governments also mandated in many instances that jobs could no longer be done by men, thus increasing the number available for frontline duty on the battle field. The British government stipulated that contracts for the manufacture of shells, for instance, had to be carried out by a workforce consisting of at least 80 percent women. By 1916 the German General Staff passed a law permitting the conscription of women into the industrial workforce—a regulation that would have been utterly unthinkable before the war.

Military stalemate, the need for mass armies of young men, and the vast quantities of munitions essential to waging industrial warfare brought an unprecedented number of women into the workforce, transforming wartime society. Nations needed their labor, and with husbands, brothers, and sons gone and support uncertain, women had to work to feed their families and themselves. Many women with children found the tasks of caring for a family and undertaking repetitive, backbreaking work exhausting: "Always repeating the same motions, constantly bending over the same machine," one worker described the routine in a defense factory.[21] Others saw the work as an adventure, as they took on entirely new and sometimes challenging roles as streetcar conductors, ambulance drivers, or postal workers. Many single women, unused to having money of their own, enjoyed earning wages and spending them. They got their hair cut to a more practical and increasingly fashionable length, bought dresses with shorter skirts—even up to mid-calf—and ventured out alone to "the pictures." The suddenly improved appearance and circumstances of lower-class young women struck observers as frivolous and even unpatriotic. Other women worked at home or on the front lines as nurses (see Document 3.3), and some even served as soldiers alongside their husbands or other male relatives. The Women's Battalion of Death in

Russia became notorious for conducting trench warfare, replacing men who had deserted.

The integration of women into the labor force facilitated changes in industrial production already underway before the war began. It permitted the ongoing simplification of tasks implicit in the evolution of mechanization, which made it possible for machines to handle many operations formerly done by workers or broke a job down into its component steps—a phenomenon called rationalization. In one British instance, a job that took one craftsperson a day or more to complete was broken down into twenty-two distinct operations, which were given to twenty-two women working side by side, who were able to finish the job in a small amount of time. Unions resisted the eradication of skill resulting from mechanization or rationalization, but factory owners used the wartime emergency to introduce women onto the shop floor to perform the simplified tasks. They justified the elimination of skilled jobs by claiming that women could not perform difficult work and by pointing to the looming national peril that called for all able-bodied people to work no matter what the shop floor circumstances. War also stimulated the development of a place for women in well-paid male bastions such as metallurgy and munitions. In western Europe, they went from being 5 or 6 percent of the prewar workforce in metallurgy to composing 10 percent in the postwar period and 15 to 20 percent of metallurgical workers in 1939.

The supposedly masculine enterprise of war actually advanced changes in gender roles already on the horizon in 1914. Many men viewed these developments with alarm. At first the war had appeared to reinforce traditional gender roles, throwing women out of work as textile factories and the retail and luxury trades went out of business and sending men off to defend the fatherland and protect its weakest citizens—namely, women and children. But as the war progressed, men returned from the front weakened and wounded physically as well as emotionally and saw that many women had become employed and had taken on men's family responsibilities. "The war itself, as a great economic force . . . is giving their chance to working women," a Scottish periodical reported. "Employment can and will never be the same again."[22] These developments gave men much food for thought. Some men believed that women's employment contributed to keeping the war effort going, perhaps even sending men to their own deaths. Many men resented what they sensed would be a permanent change in gender roles that would affect their ability to earn a living as well as their dominance at home.

FROM WAR FEVER TO REVOLUTION

These changes in society and the economy, the stress of life on the home front, and the dire conditions experienced by soldiers in the trenches turned the spirit of war to a spirit of revolt. In the spring of 1917, the United States entered the war on the side of the Allies, but it took a year for this unprepared but growing industrial power to send the kind of reinforcements the Allies needed to break the stalemate. In the meantime, political opposition to the war grew and quickly became menacing. "We are living on a volcano," warned an Italian politician in the spring of 1917.[23] In May and June, the French army mutinied, and the Austro-Hungarian and Italian armies began to experience massive desertions—over two million in 1918. At the beginning of the war, most armies had little trouble attracting enthusiastic and patriotic reservists, but when the Germans redeployed men from the eastern to the western front, some 10 percent deserted, and in later offensives soldiers simply refused to go over the top. By 1917 soldiers on both sides felt alienated from their nations' military leaders and from men who stayed safely at home—"shirkers" with enough influence to avoid the front lines, privileged munitions workers, and government officials who prolonged the war with no understanding of what frontline soldiers were experiencing. In Russia the alienation was intensely felt across the civilian population too, paving the way for full-scale revolution.

Containing Revolt during Wartime

The deterioration of morale forced governments to remilitarize both civilians and military personnel in the middle of the war—that is, they had to restore everyone's will to fight. The French were most successful in appeasing army mutineers while disciplining them by listening to the soldiers' complaints. The soldiers said they had revolted "not to bring about a revolution," as one wrote, "rather to attract the attention of the government in making them understand that we are men, and not beasts to be led to the slaughterhouse."[24] The French high command succeeded in getting soldiers to return to combat by promising to avoid costly offensives and meting out milder punishments to deserters. Remarkably few soldiers were executed for what was essentially a capital military crime committed by tens of thousands. This outcome was in distinct contrast to events in Germany, where the plan for remobilizing the armies that were balking in 1917 and 1918 called for "authority on the one hand, and subordination on the other."[25] Harsh punishments followed. The German army never regained full, voluntary trust in the cause or the state, creating a situation ripe for even greater mutinies in the final, crucial hours of the war and ultimately for revolution thereafter.

Civilian protests occurred too and were equally threatening to the combatants' ability to wage total war. Initial protests on the home front were a response to the fall in the standard of living caused not only by the backbreaking work in factories and on farms but by increasing prices and food shortages. "Wages are not rising [but] food prices have risen by 100 and 200 percent," a Budapest paper complained in the summer of 1915. "We cannot bear this any longer."[26] In the fall of 1916 failed harvests in Austria-Hungary left people so hungry that they hardly mourned Emperor Francis Joseph, who died that year after a reign of sixty-eight years. Matters became worse when the 1917 harvests in the Hungarian breadbasket fulfilled only 53 percent of the need for grain. Food shortages in the major cities across Europe left women standing in long lines in an often futile attempt to feed their families. In 1915 and 1916 police in Berlin reported women's anger at the unavailability of staples such as pork and potatoes. "Mistrust . . . is growing rapidly throughout the masses," a newspaper warned.[27] Women united around this crisis, eventually engaging in strikes and political riots against government policy.

Protest grew bitter because of the visible discrepancy between the condition of the wealthy and the middle and lower classes, thus dividing citizens even as governments tried to maintain the fiction that everyone suffered equally. While workers toiled longer hours on less food, many in the upper classes bought abundant food and fashionable clothing on the black market and lived conspicuously well. "Equality—Equality—Equality for those who are suffering," a banner in a working-class neighborhood of Paris proclaimed in 1916. "Over the seventeen months of this horrible war, not all women have suffered."[28] Instead of controlling prices and profits, governments allowed many businesses to charge what they wanted in exchange for following economic centralization, a step that resulted in sustained military production but also led to a surge in the cost of living and thus in social strife. In 1918 a German roof workers' association pleaded for relief: "We can no longer go on. Our children are starving."[29] Fissures developed in the spiritual unity the war had promised, as war brought some people starvation and others profit—sometimes enormous wealth. Craftspeople producing nonessential consumer goods suffered most. In some countries white-collar employees, accustomed to being a notch above manual workers, endured falling wages in comparison with the earnings of munitions workers.

In an effort to avoid responsibility for myriad domestic crises, government officials often blamed internal enemies for causing the shortages that were undermining the unity of the nation. It was "the word in Berlin," one policeman reported as early as Christmas 1916, "that only Jewesses and the wives of munitions workers can afford goose now."[30] The search for and persecution of internal enemies operated in the name of defense of the national community. In 1915 Ottoman forces killed more than a million members of the empire's long-standing Armenian community, justifying the genocide by accusing the Armenians of loyalty to the Russian enemy. "Hunger, death, despair shout at me from all sides," wrote one German officer who documented the ejection of Armenians from their homes and the massacre of many of them.[31] Although Jews sprang to the national cause in Germany, the conservative high command, which had supported anti-Semitism before the war in patriotic and agrarian leagues, began inciting anti-Semitism in an effort to weld the fragmenting consensus for war back together.

As governments were distracted by the effort to mobilize the army and simply to feed the population, independence and protest movements sprang into action. In Ireland political strategists judged conditions ripe to achieve their independence from Britain. On Easter Monday in 1916, a group of Irish nationalists attacked government buildings in Dublin in a poorly coordinated effort to wrest Irish independence from Britain. The rebels, a band of between one and two thousand, declared an independent Irish Republic and constituted themselves as the Irish Republican Army (IRA). They held out for some six days against government forces, which pounded away at the city of Dublin and the rebels in it (see the Picture Essay, Figure 3.5). When the Easter Rebellion was over, the British, who could not tolerate sedition amid the mounting problems of war, dealt harshly with the participants, executing fifteen and incarcerating many more. The rebels' martyrdom captured Irish hearts and minds, and the Easter Rebellion marked a major step on the bitter road to independence and the partitioning of their island (see the Picture Essay).

In Austria-Hungary similar struggles by nationalist groups agitating for self-determination hampered the empire's war effort. The Czechs undertook a vigorous anti-Habsburg campaign at home, while in Paris, Tomáš Masaryk and Edvard Beneš established the Czechoslovak National Council, from which they lobbied the Allied powers for recognition of their rights. For Poles, Józef Piłsudski set up the Polish Military Organization in Austrian Galicia and trained members to become the basis for an independent Polish army after the war. The People's Party, representing peasants and the National Union of Workers, formed underground political movements that hoped to unify the Russian, Habsburg, and German portions of an independent Poland after a century and a half of partition. In the Balkans a committee representing the three dominant groups—Serbs, Croats, and Slovenes—aimed to create a South Slav nation carved from Habsburg and Balkan territory despite the push by many Serbs for an enlarged Serbia. All of these nationalists were buoyed by U.S. president Woodrow Wilson's Fourteen Points, a statement of principles for ending the war without vengeance and creating a durable peace. Promulgated in January 1918, it advocated national self-determination of peoples in any postwar settlement. Moreover, the Allies encouraged many of these groups with direct aid in hopes of weakening the Habsburg monarchy and Germany.

In most cities by 1916 bands of strikers and protesters had become disruptive, singing protest songs, waving red flags, and engaging in acts of civil disobedience such as destroying property or failing to pay rent or café bills. These and other disturbances brought severe retribution from the government. Amid growing revolt, pacifists and principled critics of war in general were so great a thorn in the side of the state that they were often prosecuted for sedition and even imprisoned. In 1915 women from combatant and noncombatant countries alike held a peace conference at The Hague in the Netherlands, site of two earlier international meetings to persuade the major powers to move toward peace. Several governments on both sides were so alarmed that they did not allow women from their countries to attend. In that same year Marxist women, at the instigation of the exiled Bolsheviks Inessa Armand, Nadeshda Krupskaya, and V. I. Lenin, convened to draw attention to the war as a conflict that pitted worker against worker. This movement denounced members of the Second International for having signed a "class truce" when they voted budgets for the world war.

The Russian Revolution

The breakdown in support for the war was most consequential in Russia, for it led to the Russian Revolution of 1917 and the first in a dramatic series of collapses in monarchical rule across Europe. Conditions in Russia were more dire than elsewhere, and allegiance to a war fought mostly by the peasantry quickly deteriorated. Russia's cities had urbanized and industrialized rapidly owing to the development of large, state-sponsored factories. In 1917 more than two-thirds of Petrograd's workforce was employed in factories with more than a thousand workers. Such huge concentrations of workers built solidarity and working-class political awareness, but under those conditions of forced industrialization work life was especially hard and living in barracks the norm. In the summer of 1914 workers had conducted so threatening a general strike in St. Petersburg that authorities feared that Russia's war industry might shut down completely. Although men outnumbered women by approximately 10 to 7 when war broke out, the number of women migrants had picked up in the prewar period, and married women had moved into the workforce during the war to support their families. Thus, there were many politicized women workers, ready to mobilize against the wretched conditions of everyday life and failure to win the war.

Conditions in rural areas were also grim, especially with the enormous loss of agricultural manpower due to the primarily peasant army raised by the state. Industrial workers were in too short supply in Russia to be sent to the front. Because the economy was transformed to eliminate the production of civilian goods, peasants had little incentive to produce food, for there was little they could buy with their profits. The traditionally obedient peasantry was heard to say, "hang ten or fifteen generals and we might start to win."[32] The inferior weapons available to the army meant that death stalked every family, making people furious with the lack of progress in the war. Though Russia had mobilized with the same patriotic fever as elsewhere, the wrenching changes brought by defeat in the Russo-Japanese War of 1904–1905, revolution in 1905, and rapid industrialization and agrarian reform all combined with the deprivations of wartime to ignite a revolutionary explosion.

In Russia as elsewhere, hard-pressed civilians and soldiers looked for internal enemies. At the top of their list was the monarchy, which commanded little respect by 1917 because Nicholas II stubbornly refused to reform his autocratic government to meet the needs of total war. Russia enjoyed no smooth coordination of production with military needs; rivalries were simply too powerful and the ability to cooperate was undeveloped, with Nicholas providing little leadership. He bypassed or ignored advisers, industrial leaders, and representatives to the Duma because of his unswerving belief in his divine right to rule absolutely and his talent to do so. Of an increasingly mystical bent, the tsar and his German-born wife, Alexandra, were held in thrall by Grigori Rasputin, a holy man/charlatan who claimed to be able to control the hemophilia of their son and heir. When government ministers challenged Rasputin's influence on state matters, Nicholas sided with Rasputin. "Is this stupidity or treason?" one influential member of the Duma asked of the impotent wartime administration. People on the streets saw Rasputin and the foreigner Alexandra as internal enemies contributing to Russia's travails—especially the catastrophic casualties and the failure to win the war.

In March 1917 the situation came to a head when crowds of working women demanding relief from harsh conditions swarmed into the streets of Petrograd on what was International Women's Day. One metalworker described the scene: "We could hear women's voices in the lane overlooked by the windows of our department: 'Down with high prices!' 'Down with hunger!' 'Bread for workers!' I and several comrades rushed at once to the windows. . . . The gates of No. 1 Bol'shaia Sampsonievskaia mill were flung open. Masses of women workers in a militant frame of mind filled the lane. Those who caught sight of us began to wave their arms, shouting: 'Come out!' 'Stop work!' Snowballs flew through the windows. We decided to join the demonstration."[33] It seemed like a repeat of 1905, as the strikers grew to several hundred thousand the next day. The tsar was their target as in the Revolution of 1905, but conditions had fatally changed since that time: after three years of a devastating and losing war, the army revolted too, leaving the monarchy defenseless.

Nicholas II returned from the front in his private railroad car. The news that Moscow workers and soldiers had joined the Petrograd strikers forced his decision to abdicate, toppling the three-hundred-year-old Romanov dynasty. The momentous event opened floodgates of hope that now the presumed culprits in Russia's string of defeats were gone: "Now, everything is possible," the poet Aleksandr Blok wrote his mother on the abdication of the tsar. Like others he extolled the revolution as a triumph and the beginning of a new era. Middle- and upper-class politicians from the old Duma formed a new governing entity called the Provisional Government, but continuing hardships and the competing aspirations of many groups—workers, homemakers, students, liberal politicians, and soldiers, all active politically—made it difficult for the new body to govern. Despite these competing forces, at first hopes were high that under the Provisional Government, as Blok put it, "our false, filthy, boring, hideous life should become a just, pure, merry, and beautiful life."[34]

The revolution, as it unfolded throughout 1917, took place in two arenas: one was in the Provisional Government, composed essentially of moderates; the other was in the factories and on the streets. The Provisional Government faced the difficult tasks of pursuing the war successfully and improving the management of domestic affairs. It also had to establish a new constitutional government to ensure the regime's credibility among people who had a hard time envisioning life without a tsar. The Provisional Government competed for allegiance with the spontaneously elected soviets—councils of workers and soldiers that had first sprung up during the Revolution of 1905 and that were quickly revived in 1917. Holding heated debates during their meetings, the elected members of the soviets pressed for improved living conditions, a speedy resolution of the war, and change in the direction of work life to further the creation of a totally new and more just society.

Lively and informal, the soviets contrasted the people's needs with the privileges of the upper-class men who ran the Provisional Government. In the first euphoric rush of revolution, the soviets ended deferential treatment for industrialists and officers and urged respect for workers and the poor. In so doing they worked for a fundamental change in Russian mentality and habits. Factory leaders of the soviets were usually skilled workers or those in metallurgy who knew that the government could not afford to retaliate against them, so needed were the munitions and other war necessities they produced. Acting together, workers drove hated supervisors from their midst and demanded a say in the conduct of work processes.

The atmosphere in these first days of reform was lighthearted, giving an air of carnival and celebration to the profound social transformations taking place. But when the factory owners resisted, workers used their newfound autonomy to challenge them, and when the Provisional Government issued unpopular edicts, especially connected with the conduct of the war, workers were capable of shutting down restaurants, transportation, and other facilities to the elites.

The Provisional Government and the soviets generally agreed that Russia had to jettison its old agrarian and aristocratic system to become modern and middle-class—or bourgeois. At the outset they thus cooperated more than might have been expected given the diverging and even antagonistic interests. However, the arrival in Petrograd of political exile V. I. Lenin in April 1917 was like the planting of a time bomb in the unfolding political scene.

Variously described by contemporaries and biographers as humorless, uncompromising, and brilliant, Lenin had spent his life promoting socialism by maneuvering his small band of Bolsheviks in meetings of the Second International and of other exiled Russian socialists and by publicizing his theories in his political writings. He had no experience with mass politics, but he quickly sprang into action once back in Russia, issuing the "April Theses" (see Document 3.4). This document called for Russia to withdraw immediately from the war, for the soviets to seize power on behalf of the workers and poor peasants, and for all private land to be nationalized.

Led by Lenin, the Bolsheviks boldly challenged any compromise with the Provisional Government and instead devised a set of demanding slogans: "All power to the soviets" and "Peace, Land, and Bread." Definitively breaking with the legacy of the social democrats and socialists who had voted for war, the Bolsheviks adopted the name Communists. While the Provisional Government reassured Russia's allies of Russia's firm commitment to fighting the Central Powers, workers in the large Petrograd factories took up the Communists' slogans, demanded an end to the death and deprivation, and issued a call for a change in government. Lenin's agitation succeeded in tearing the fragile revolutionary coalition apart: "We recognize that power must belong only to the people itself, i.e., to the Soviet of Workers' and Soldiers' Deputies as the sole institution of authority enjoying the confidence of the people."[35] The government's continued support for war and the growing muscle of the Bolshevik minority caused a crisis in the Provisional Government. Influential leaders from the old Duma resigned, several socialists entered the government, and a new leader emerged in Minister of War Aleksandr Kerensky.

Kerensky undertook a major offensive against the Germans in June and July of 1917. War weariness and outright rebellion, however, were rife in the army, and the Russians were defeated once again. This loss was followed by more urban riots and peasants confiscating land in the countryside. Kerensky became prime minister, using his commanding oratory to arouse patriotism, but he lacked the political skills to fashion an effective wartime government. During the "July Days" of 1917 groups of workers, soldiers, and sailors—many of them Bolsheviks—agitated for the soviets to replace the Provisional Government. When in August, however,

◆ **V. I. Lenin Addressing a Crowd in Moscow**
Lenin had spent much of his adult life organizing fellow Bolshevik revolutionaries while in exile and maneuvering among competing groups to dominate the Russian revolutionary movement. In April 1917, the German leadership arranged his return to Russia in hopes that this antiwar activist would somehow pull Russia out of the war and thus bolster Germany's chance for victory. Lenin led a successful coup against the Provisional Government, which had taken charge after the fall of the Romanov dynasty, and then sued the Central Powers for peace. Here Lenin rallies supporters in Moscow on May Day—a traditional holiday that the working-class movement made its own. *The Granger Collection, New York.*

General Lavr Kornilov launched a coup to bring the revolution under the control of a military dictatorship, the Provisional Government enlisted Bolsheviks and other leaders of the people to stop him. Factory and railway workers disrupted the movement of Kornilov's troops, and other ordinary people pitched in to halt the coup.

In part because of their role in preventing the coup, the Bolsheviks' popularity in the cities rose, while the stature of other politicians fell, especially that of the Provisional Government. It had neither called for a popular assembly nor enacted land reform. Some believed it had secretly backed the Kornilov coup, and its conduct of the war remained disastrous. The soviets likewise had no accomplishments to their credit, and the condition of their constituency—the urban poor and the armies—remained dire. But Lenin cleverly used the discredit of his opponents to seize the day, driving his supporters to a final confrontation with the Provisional Government in November 1917. To prevent Kerensky from holding elections that might have stabilized politics and thus the government, the Bolsheviks seized key facilities (including the former tsar's Winter Palace, home of the Provisional Government), drove out the government, and presented supreme power to a congress of soviets while claiming the right of the Bolsheviks to head a government. In elections held late in the fall, the Bolsheviks received only 25 percent of the vote, and the Socialist Revolutionary Party—the party that had agitated longest in Russia on behalf of peasants and workers alike—gained a substantial plurality of 40 percent. To consolidate their position, the Bolsheviks simply drove these and other opposition delegates out of the first meeting of the elected representatives in January 1918.

Civil War Begins in Russia

Lenin and his party were now in power but had little experience at doing anything other than agitating for change. Few had thought out what it actually would mean to govern, conduct diplomacy, or run an economy. The new government legislated the abolition of private property and allowed peasants to keep all the land they had seized during wartime revolt and revolution. The government nationalized factories (though many had already been taken over by workers themselves, their owners driven out). Under the Provisional Government, both men and women had received the vote, making Russia the first great power to legalize universal suffrage. The right to vote soon became a hollow privilege, however, once slates were limited to candidates from the Communist Party. Finally the Bolsheviks sued for peace, thinking that the German army would look kindly on their Russian working-class comrades and that the German government would thus pull back from Russian soil and negotiate fair terms.

The Germans did nothing of the kind, refusing the Bolsheviks' peace terms, taking the city of Riga, and advancing on Petrograd. Not only did German policy envision the acquisition of vast amounts of land in eastern Europe as spoils of war, but the German high command viewed Russians with loathing: "The whole of Russia is no more than a vast heap of maggots—a squalid swarming mass," the German commander of the eastern front wrote in his diary. If victorious, he claimed in a characterization that would resurface with the Nazis, the Russian people would "turn the whole of Europe into a pigsty."[36] Threatened with the invasion of Petrograd, the new government moved to the more secure internal city of Moscow, where the capital remains to this day, and made peace with the Germans, accepting a massive transfer of territory to Germany that was formalized in the 1918 Treaty of Brest-Litovsk. "Obscene," Lenin called the German landgrab, but in the long run it meant little to true Bolsheviks, for they believed that revolution would erupt across Europe and in that moment of working-class brotherhood such things as national boundaries would be swept away.[37]

Acceptance of the Bolsheviks also sprang from the disastrous conditions across Russia. The economy had collapsed, and the army high command had mobilized the remaining armies in the field to wage civil war against the revolution. These counterrevolutionaries, or "Whites," as they are known, enlisted various nationality groups—such as Ukrainians and the Baltic states—to fight against Lenin's government. The goal of these nationalists, however, was their own independence, and this aspiration often put them at odds with the White Russian generals, whose goal was restoration of the tsar. The Whites, who opposed the Communist "Reds," also benefited from the support of Russia's former allies—Britain, the United States, and Japan, foremost among them. Some of the Allies simply hated the Bolsheviks, and others wanted to keep supplies out of German hands or even make it possible for Russia to rejoin the Great War against Germany. The crucial factor was the peasantry: they composed the bulk of the armies, and their allegiance made a vast difference. Rural people had little appreciation for a party committed to the triumph of the urban proletariat, but because they knew that the Whites would return confiscated land to the original aristocratic owners, large numbers of peasants sided with the Communists. Nonetheless, faced with the specter of the Whites and their allies rescuing the tsar and his family, the Bolsheviks executed the Romanovs in July 1918.

Even though the Whites had competing and even contradictory goals, the Bolsheviks had a tough time of it, as industrial and agricultural productivity alike continued to plummet in the ever deepening chaos and uncertainty. To be able to wage war, the Bolsheviks needed to supply and feed their armies. They did so by instituting "war communism," a policy that sent troops and workers into the countryside to confiscate grain for the army and urban workforce. War communism initiated the centralization of the production and distribution of food—a policy that would last until the collapse of the Soviet Union late in the twentieth century. It worsened food shortages and even contributed to famines throughout the 1920s.

Alongside Lenin, the architect of war communism was Leon Trotsky, who enjoyed support among factory workers and the armed forces. Trotsky helped mold the new Red Army into an effective fighting force of some five million people who endured harsh discipline but received more respect than aristocrats had ever given recruits from the peasantry. As the untried Bolshevik administration improvised these dramatic policy changes, the civil war progressed, bringing great uncertainty and even greater suffering for the ordinary citizen of the new, revolutionary Russia.

THE GREAT WAR ENDS

Both sides drew different messages from the Russian surrender to the Germans. The Central Powers viewed it as hopeful for their victory. Worried at first, Britain and France were reassured as U.S. troops began to arrive in Europe in 1918. No matter how alliances shifted, however, both sides confronted continuing war protest, and the lesson of the Russian Revolution was there for all to see. Still determined to win, leaders in every combatant country faced the possibility that their nation would succumb to revolution and collapse at home no matter how the war turned out. In this atmosphere of uncertainty and spreading disorder, the Central Powers collapsed, leaving the future of Europe in the unsteady, often vengeful hands of the victorious Allies as they negotiated a complicated and bitter peace.

The Struggle to End the War

Amid civilian and military revolt in 1917 and 1918, negotiations for an end to the Great War were at last taking place among the combatants. The new Habsburg emperor, Karl, secretly asked the Allies for a peace settlement in order to prevent the total collapse of his empire. When the United States entered the war, President Woodrow Wilson issued his Fourteen Points—a call for a "peace without victory" and for an end to the conditions, such as militarism and secret alliances, that had made for war. In 1917, the German Reichstag passed a resolution announcing its desire for a "peace of understanding and permanent reconciliation of peoples."[38] Outraged, Ludendorff and Hindenburg sent out propagandists to whip up anti-Semitism and prowar feelings against what they characterized as the traitorous behavior of the Reichstag.

In the fall of 1917 at Caporetto, Italy, the German high command tried a new tactic, concentrating forces that would pierce single points of the enemy's relatively thin defense lines and then wreak havoc along the defenses from the rear. Believing this new type of offensive would be the key to a breakthrough victory, the Germans launched a major assault on the Allies on the western front. Although the territorial gain was significant, the offensive ground to a bloody halt within weeks, dashing the hopes of the weary and demoralized German troops that their massive losses would end. By then the British and French had started making limited but effective use of tanks supported by airplanes—a combination that would later dominate military tactics. An Allied offensive in the summer of 1918, for which the American forces were now sufficiently built up to make an important contribution, pushed back the Germans all along the western front. Allied troops advanced toward Germany, and the German armies rapidly disintegrated. But the relentless German high command asked for further sacrifices beyond the two million casualties of the spring and summer. As rumors of a final sea battle leaked out, German sailors at the naval base at Kiel mutinied against what they saw as a suicide mission. Their rebellion capped years of indignities from high-ranking officers whose champagne-filled diet contrasted with the meager fare of the sailors and of their families back home.

The German high command had been cynically and secretly preparing for defeat when in October 1918 it helped create a civil government, headed by the liberal Prince Max of Baden. The intention of the military command, led by Ludendorff and Hindenburg, which had taken over the civilian government and run it dictatorially, was to let this new administration sue for peace so that civilians rather than the military would take the blame for the defeat and be discredited. As peace negotiations took place, the generals proclaimed themselves fully capable of continuing and winning the war. The home front, they maintained, had defeated Germany, delivering a "stab in the back." As Ludendorff put it, civilians "must now eat the soup they have served us."[39] Indeed, in the fall of 1918 the home front was in full revolt against the war and unfeeling monarchical rule. The sailors' revolt spread to working people in Berlin and other cities. In an attempt to prevent the outbreak of a full-fledged revolution, government officials proclaimed Germany a republic, and on November 9 the kaiser fled the country, later officially abdicating.

The Central Powers collapsed on all fronts. Since the previous winter, Austria-Hungary, where starvation was rampant and an influenza epidemic was taking its grim toll, had kept many combat divisions at home simply to maintain civil order. Desertions from Habsburg armies mounted into the hundreds of thousands, and by the fall of 1918 anti-Habsburg ethnic activists, urged on by the Allies, were in full revolt, tearing down imperial insignia from public buildings and taking over government offices. At the end of October, the Czechs and Slovaks declared the independent state of Czechoslovakia, and the Croatian parliament simultaneously announced Croatia's independence. As Germany's social order collapsed and its armies withdrew, delegations from the two sides signed an armistice on November 11, 1918, in a railroad car in France, and the guns on the western front at long last fell silent.

Conservative figures put the battlefield toll at a minimum of ten million deaths; thirty million more people were wounded, were incapacitated, or eventually died of their wounds (Table 3.1). In every European combatant country, industrial and agricultural production had plummeted from prewar outputs. Those

Country	Standing armies and trained reserves	Total mobilized	Killed or died of wounds	Total military casualties
Austria-Hungary	3,000,000	7,800,000	1,200,000	7,020,000
British Empire	975,000	8,904,000	908,000	3,190,235
France	4,017,000	8,410,000	1,363,000	6,160,800
Germany	4,500,000	11,000,000	1,774,000	7,142,558
Italy	1,251,000	5,615,000	460,000	2,197,000
Russia	5,971,000	12,000,000	1,700,000	9,150,000
Ottoman Empire	210,000	2,850,000	325,000	975,000

◆ Table 3.1 **World War I Casualties**
These figures convey some idea of the loss of life and the disabilities inflicted by World War I. Notice in particular the high number of total casualties compared to the number mobilized. Added to these grave losses were the indebtedness of the combatant countries and the costs of reconstruction that some countries would bear. Memories of the Great War and the peace settlement shape European history down to the present.

parts of Asia, Africa, and the Americas dependent on Europe for supplies and trade had also felt the impact of Europe's declining capabilities. From 1918 to 1919, the world's weakened populations suffered another devastating blow when influenza rampaged across the globe, leaving an estimated one hundred million more dead.

Making Peace in the Midst of Revolution

In January 1919 the peace conference to craft a settlement to the war opened in Paris. While Woodrow Wilson advocated a peace without the spoils of conquest, the European allies were preoccupied with the horrendous toll of death and destruction, fear of advancing revolution, and the fact of starvation and disease spreading around the world. The victors arrived with vast retinues of diplomats and experts amid the looming threat of even more chaos. All participants in the conference had to sort through the multiple war aims and the accumulation of promises and agreements desperately cobbled together during the war. France, Italy, Great Britain, and the ethnic groups of eastern and southeastern Europe hoped for territorial gains at the expense of Germany, Austria-Hungary, and the Ottoman Empire. British and French statesmen came to the negotiating table goaded by the fury of electorates demanding that the Germans be held fully accountable for the horrors of the war. To them, Wilson seemed utterly naïve, and the American people seemed to have little appreciation of European wartime suffering. In France especially, where thousands of villages and bridges, millions of acres of agricultural land, and thousands of miles of roads had been devastated, numbness and sorrow turned to rage at the thought of a peace without victory. In Great Britain, David Lloyd George had been elected prime minister with slogans such as "Hang the Kaiser."

Alongside the victors, a variety of interests sought recognition and redress from the statesmen at the Paris meeting. Representatives of colonized countries and regions once under the Ottomans flocked to the peace conference because they believed in the sincerity of Wilson's Fourteen Points. They clung especially to the promised "self-determination of peoples." Seeking reform if not outright independence, these included princes from the Middle East, such as Prince Faisal, whose father Husayn had helped the Allies take Syria and Palestine from the Ottomans, as well as more modest representatives from other regions. The former had received guarantees of future rights, even written agreements for complete autonomy in exchange for their help in the war effort. The latter included not only soldiers but tens of thousands of conscripts who had been forcibly taken from Southeast Asia and elsewhere to work as slave laborers in European factories. In 1919, Nguyen Ai Quoc (Nguyen the Patriot), residing in Paris, wrote a widely distributed pamphlet calling for Vietnam's independence from French colonial rule. The result was that this political fledgling, soon to call himself Ho Chi Minh, was tailed by the police. He soon turned to socialist politicians as perhaps the only allies responsive to oppressed peoples. More prosperous countries, even allies, appeared almost as supplicants too: the Japanese, hewing to the wishes of the other

◆ **King Faisal and the Arab Delegation at the Paris Peace Conference**
The Arab delegation, headed by King Faisal (1885–1933), attended the Paris Peace
Conference fully expecting independence on the breakup of the Ottoman Empire. The
economically strapped victors, however, had other plans—namely, to expand their empires
into the oil-rich Middle East. At first, a regional congress elected Faisal king of "Greater
Syria," but the charter of the new League of Nations gave different parts of the region to
France and Britain, allowing the French to oust him. Britain, which carved out the kingdom
of Iraq, was forced to make Faisal king of that country in order to maintain control, so great
was the resistance to the League's mandate system. One prominent member of the Arab
delegation was the colorful British colonel and adventurer, T. E. Lawrence, third from right.
Lawrence had aided Faisal in the Arab Revolt of 1916 against the decaying Ottoman
government, a revolt in exchange for which the Allies had informally promised Syria
independence. © *Bettmann/CORBIS.*

victorious allies, made few requests but pushed hard and unsuccessfully for a final
statement from the peace conference renouncing racism. Such disappointments at
Paris would push colonized people even further toward radical action.

In May 1919, at about the same time as the peace settlements were being
forged, the Bolsheviks set up the Third International or Comintern to replace the

old Second International. To counter Russia's exclusion from the peace process, the Comintern proselytized for the spread of socialist revolution around the world and agitated among former socialists to persuade them to adhere to Moscow in the postwar tumult. Although Europeans in the Comintern aimed to bring socialism to their industrialized countries, Lenin, who had written his "Theses on the National and Colonial Question," had also addressed the revolutionary potential of peoples oppressed by Western imperialism. Thus a "green comintern" was also organized to address issues of colonial and agricultural societies as potential sites of revolution and to educate the peasantry. The green comintern put the negotiators from the imperial countries of France and Great Britain on notice that they had more to fear than simply a revived Germany or the Bolsheviks in Russia. The Comintern brought Ho Chi Minh and other Asian representatives to Moscow for training. For others, Confucianism provided the groundwork for activism to escape Western domination and materialistic values: "One need not fear of having little," Confucius had taught, "but of not having equal distribution of goods."[40] Such activity, menacing to the diplomats in Paris and sometimes unacknowledged, swirled around the conference and would bear fruit in the years to come.

After six months the statesmen and their teams of experts produced the Peace of Paris, which effectively redrew the map of Europe and the Middle East. Germany, Austria-Hungary, and the Ottoman elite were stunned by the extreme terms, which separated Austria from Hungary, reduced Hungary by almost two-thirds of its inhabitants and three-quarters of its territory, and treated Germany severely. The treaties replaced the Habsburg Empire with a group of small, internally divided and relatively weak states (Map 3.2). Treaty provisions established the boundaries of the new states of Czechoslovakia, Poland, and the Kingdom of the Serbs, Croats, and Slovenes (later renamed Yugoslavia). Cutting three million Germans away from Austria, the treaties clustered these Germans in Czechoslovakia and reduced Austria's economic base. Many Austrians, their empire gone, fervently hoped to merge with Germany, but the settlement expressly forbade such a union. After a century and a half of partition, Poland was reconstructed from parts of Russia, Germany, and Austria-Hungary; one-third of its population was ethnically non-Polish. The statesmen in Paris also created a Polish corridor that connected Poland to the Baltic Sea; the corridor separated East Prussia from the rest of Germany, although the city of Danzig was granted the status of a free city. These arrangements satisfied no one, and the boundaries of Poland remained in dispute, provoking outright fighting in border regions. Even as these and other rivalries developed among both new and old states, the Allies had high hopes that the new eastern Europe would be stable. Many experts, however, feared that the seeds of dissent had been planted by the peacemakers.

The Treaty of Versailles, which settled Germany's future, only partially quenched the French thirst for revenge. France recovered the provinces of Alsace and Lorraine, and Belgium received a strip of German land. The victors would temporarily occupy the left, or western, bank of the Rhine and the coal-rich Saar basin. President Wilson bowed to his allies' expectations that, as France had done after its defeat by Germany in the Franco-Prussian War, Germany would pay sub-

0 200 400 miles
0 200 400 kilometers

Ceded by Germany	
Ceded by Austria-Hungary	
Ceded by Bulgaria	
Ceded by Russia	
British mandates	
French mandates	
Demilitarized zone	
Boundaries of German, Russian, and Austro-Hungarian empires in 1914	

NORWAY
Oslo
SWEDEN
Stockholm
FINLAND
Helsinki
Petrograd (St. Petersburg)
ESTONIA
North Sea
GREAT BRITAIN
DENMARK
Copenhagen
Baltic Sea
Memel
LATVIA
LITHUANIA
Moscow
NETHERLANDS
London
Amsterdam
Brussels
Danzig
East Prussia
Warsaw
U S S R
BELGIUM
GERMANY
Weimar
Ruhr
Frankfurt
POLAND
Kiev
Volga R.
LUX.
Saar
Lorraine
Rhine R.
Versailles
Paris
Prague
CZECHOSLOVAKIA
Galicia
Bessarabia
Caspian Sea
Loire R.
FRANCE
Alsace
Vienna
Geneva
SWITZ.
AUSTRIA
Budapest
HUNGARY
ROMANIA
Po R.
Tyrol
Genoa
Venice
Bucharest
Black Sea
Rhône R.
CROATIA
Belgrade
Danube R.
SPAIN
ITALY
YUGOSLAVIA
SERBIA
BULGARIA
Rome
Sofia
Constantinople
ALBANIA
TURKEY
PERSIA
GREECE
Athens
SYRIA
IRAQ
Baghdad
TUNISIA (Fr.)
Mediterranean Sea
Beirut
Damascus
PALESTINE
Jerusalem
ALGERIA (Fr.)
TRANS-JORDAN
KUWAIT (Gr. Br.)
Cairo
LIBYA (It.)
EGYPT (independent 1922)
SAUDI ARABIA
NORTH AFRICA

◆ Map 3.2 **Europe and the Middle East after the Peace Settlements of 1919–1920**
The Russian Revolution and the Peace of Paris altered the political landscape of Europe dramatically. The German, Russian, and Austro-Hungarian empires were either broken up altogether into multiple small states or saw their territory reduced considerably. The Ottoman Empire, which had sided with Germany and Austria-Hungary, also collapsed at the end of World War I, in part owing to Allied encouragement of Arab uprisings against the Ottomans by promising independence at the war's end. But once victorious, France and Britain gained control of Syria, Iraq, and Transjordan through the mandate system, by which the individual Allied countries were allowed to govern former German colonies and Ottoman territory.

159

stantial reparations for the civilian damage. The specific amount was established not by the peacemakers in 1919 but by Allied commissions, which only in 1921 agreed on the sum of 132 billion gold marks. Germany also had to surrender the largest ships of its merchant marine, reduce its army, almost eliminate its navy, stop manufacturing offensive weapons, and deliver a large amount of free coal each year to Belgium and France. Furthermore, it was forbidden to have an air force.

To the average German, these terms were an undeserved humiliation made worse by Article 231 of the Treaty of Versailles. This article stipulated that the victors would collect the bulk of reparations from economically viable Germany rather than from decimated Austria. It spoke of Germany's "responsibility" for damage done during a conflict "imposed on [the Entente] by the aggression of Germany and her allies." To outraged Germans, this was no "peace without victory," as Wilson had promised. They interpreted the article as a "war guilt" clause, and the government set up a special propaganda office to refute it and to contest the terms. This imposition of war guilt made many Germans feel they were outcasts in the community of nations, and their resentment and anger over it would have ominous implications for future relations within Europe.

Finally, at Woodrow Wilson's strong urging, the Peace of Paris set up the League of Nations, whose deliberations and collective security were to replace the divisive secrecy of prewar power politics. The peacemakers also put in place a cluster of commissions and councils to oversee such matters as the redrawing of boundaries, the determination of reparations, and the status of ethnic minorities in the newly created countries. The League would be responsible for guiding the world toward disarmament, arbitrating its members' disputes, and monitoring labor conditions. While some European politicians cynically accepted the League as "Wilson's toy," ironically and perhaps tragically, the United States, returning to its prewar isolation, failed to ratify the peace settlement and refused to join the League. Americans' growing sense that the United States was special and the rest of the world hopelessly corrupt resulted in the U.S. withdrawal from all international commissions and organizations for the collective resolution of problems. Moreover, Germany and Russia were not allowed into the League until 1928 and 1933 respectively and were thus blocked from acting in legal concert with other nations. The wartime mentality of allies and enemies, of victors and losers, the virtuous and the evil, haunted the interwar years and ultimately would undermine chances for a sustainable peace.

The situation was similarly discouraging in the settlement of questions beyond Europe (see Map 3.2). Instead of liberating the subjected peoples in the former colonies and territories of Germany and the Ottoman Empire, the victors snatched them up, devising an administrative system of mandates overseen by the League of Nations (see Document 3.5). In the Near East, Great Britain acquired a mandate over Mesopotamia (present-day Iraq) and Palestine, and France received a mandate over Lebanon and Syria. Germany's territories in Africa were mandated to Great Britain, South Africa, France, and Belgium. Japan, Australia, and New Zealand held mandates over Germany's former colonies in the Pacific. The League Covenant justified the mandate system as providing governance by "advanced nations" over territories "not yet able to stand by themselves under the strenuous conditions of the modern world." The war, however, had depleted the Great Powers' financial resources and mental resolve, if not their appetite for colonies. They simply could not afford the cost of ruling people increasingly determined to be free. Colonized and other people of color, many of whom had served as cannon fodder at the front, were challenging the claims of their European masters. "Never again will the darker people of the world occupy just the place they had before," the African American leader W. E. B. Du Bois predicted in 1918. Many other leaders of oppressed peoples had reached the same conclusion.

CONCLUSION

"One has only to be patient," up-and-coming Indian activist Mohandas Gandhi said of European civilization in 1909, "and it will be self-destroyed."[41] The peace conference at Paris ended what the economist John Maynard Keynes called the first "European civil war"—a war in which Europe seemed on the verge of self-destruction. Four major dynasties disappeared in this conflagration, and the social order based on the dominance of landed elites and the "best circles" was sorely tried and in many cases, such as Russia, wounded beyond revival. While men at the front fell by the millions, society at home changed dramatically. Citizens on the home front rebelled at the slaughter and deprivation. The masses came into their own in these demonstrations despite their suffering from shortages, blockades, and the ravages of influenza. Women made a dramatic showing as workers and heads of households, even though the autonomy of most people seemed suffocated by increasing government control of the economy and communications.

Beyond the physical and human destruction involved, World War I and the peace treaties that followed reduced the moral credibility of Europe. Not just the toppling of kingdoms and empires but the innovation of total war designed to destroy entire states and their citizens seemed to call into question the values and traditions of European "civilization." The peace settlement resolved some matters such as the long-sought-after independence of ethnic groups in central Europe, but it left a legacy of bitterness and instability. In some ways it seemed as if Europeans had learned no lessons. The mandate system continued the practice of apportioning the globe among European powers, boosting resentment and fueling costly struggles against this domination. Having overthrown the Romanov dynasty, the Russians at war's end were immersed in deadly civil strife over the terms of their new government. World War I had bankrupted Europe and left the task of rebuilding civil society and entire nations to people totally numbed by tragic loss. At the same time, unnoticed by many in the face of so much suffering and confusion, the war had advanced productivity, innovation, and industrialization. It remained to be seen whether in a climate of lingering hatred these forces could be harnessed to provide peacetime benefits and to serve humanitarian ends.

DOCUMENTS

War and the Individual

W ORLD WAR I WAS A TOTAL WAR because it showed the possibility for total destruction with the use of modern industrial weaponry and because it involved both the battlefront and the home front. Men went to war thinking the battlefront was theirs—a place that would allow a respite from domesticity and the femininity that increasingly shaped public life. Most of them young, they were also looking forward to adventure, experiences out of the storybooks. Once at the front, however, these young warriors felt the shock of modern technological warfare. They were engulfed in death, dismemberment, and the exhausting, debilitating conditions of trench warfare.

In the lulls of fighting, there was time for reflection, and many soldiers set down their thoughts in diaries, letters, and even poetry and stories. German university student Johannes Haas noted the beauty of the countryside—the singing of the larks, the bright blue sky—and the good comradeship of his mates in letters to his brother on the eastern front (Document 3.1). Haas pondered the meaning of the war and decided that he might change his plan of study once the war was over. But like so many young men whose lives were cut short by World War I, Haas (1892–1916) never had the chance to alter his plans. He was among the tens of thousands killed at Verdun in 1916.

Many colonial soldiers gained a revised sense of European life once they participated in the slaughter on the western front. They came to question whether people in the West were at all "civilized"—cultural superiority being the rationale that Europeans, Japanese, and Americans presented for conquering and occupying foreign countries and ruling them by force. Other colonial soldiers found positive qualities and institutions to write home about. Some found the condition of women and marriage admirable and urged that improvements be made in their own cultures' customs. Khan Mahomed Khan, an Indian Muslim, noted from his post in France that his opinion of Europe had changed for the better. In a letter written to his father in 1917, he discusses his newfound admiration and change of heart (Document 3.2).

The war's heavy casualties changed the masculine nature of war that men at the time craved so much. Women were soon being recruited to drive ambulances, tend to the wounded and dying on the battlefield, and serve as nurses in field hospitals. In this setting, traditional gender roles were reversed, with men weakened and sometimes hysterical and women commanding and rational. Battlefield experience often changed women's perspective on many things too, especially their view of men. Many women came from middle- and upper-class families in which they had been protected from contact with men outside the family circle. Moreover, whatever their relationship to men, most women saw them as commanding presences; even those of the lower classes had skills and experience of the world unknown to women. Women's knowledge of men's physiology was also more limited then than it is now. So caring for wounded soldiers provided women with new knowledge and new understanding of men and their vulnerabilities.

Some women who came to the battlefield hospitals were trained health-care workers, but far more had scant knowledge of medical procedures, biology, and science. At frontline hospitals these women became more knowledgeable about and competent in performing some medical procedures. Instruction in the sciences and human physiology opened new terrain to many of them.

Their experiences differed so profoundly from all that had gone before that memoirs from battlefield nurses—whether Serbian, Russian, English, or German—abound. Like the war poets, war nurses became important interpreters of World War I. According to some historians, war nurses held opinions different from those of the majority of women, who remained on the home front. Women who knew of war only from a distance tended to mythologize what was happening, even to see warriors as bloodthirsty murderers—a view reinforced by propaganda. Nurses, in contrast, saw soldiers for what they often were on the industrialized battlefield—victims of cannons, poison gas, grenades, machine guns, and the bombs dropped from that new invention, the airplane.

Maria Luisa Perduca (1896–1966), an Italian nurse, had worked as a teacher of French before the war. Her published accounts of hospital life show her deep feelings about the plight of wounded soldiers (Document 3.3). In the postwar years, those nurses who entered public life were unafraid of interacting with men as colleagues. They supported women's right to participate in public life alongside men; they regularly voted and were active in a far wider range of undertakings. Perduca served as a battlefield nurse again in World War II and gained recognition for her public activism in the Red Cross.

Document 3.1

JOHANNES HAAS
Letter, 1915

In the afternoon I had to play "skat"° with some comrades, but I was rather absent-minded over it. Pictures of old days were passing through my mind. One of the players is Bergman of the Mansfelds, and he is talking about Rostock— Rostock, where I spent a winter of seeking and doubting! That little bookseller with the spectacles and the many books, I wonder what has become of him? . . . The corner there, just like the beach at Heiligendamm. Heiligendamm, one morning, an icy-cold wind, rain, snow, and myself, bare-headed, because I didn't know what I was doing, wandering for seven hours along the coast. I did not come home till 1 o'clock in the morning, having had nothing to eat all day, and how tired I was!—tired out, but "no forrarder"!°

Skat again. A passing comrade shows some French postcards which he "captured" in Belgium; their vulgarity sickens me; that sort of thing even here! A monoplane in the sky; one of the skat-players, an artificer, begins telling once again the story of his monoplane: the German Government refused it; the French bought it, but only paid half the money. That gives one pecuniary and patriotic reflections. At last the skat is finished and we go home. Our afternoon coffee is diluted with "Love-Gift" rum.

Towards evening. I must be alone for a bit. I'll go out. There is little W. looking like a gipsy. "Yes, yes, Comrade, my eldest. Born in the middle of August. We hadn't a bite in those days, and always Englishmen, Frenchmen, or black devils on top of us. Yes, yes, if it were but all over! Otherwise he'll be able to walk before I see him!" W. is war-weary

like most of those who have been here from the start. There is no enthusiasm, such as you at home imagine—no enthusiasm, but blind fury which makes no prisoners and yet is sorry for those who have also got a wife and children at home.

. . . I am alone in the fields. My thoughts keep wandering homewards and dwelling on the past and the future. And what about the present? Oh, at present it is delightful to be alone! I feel just as you do, my dear little brother, shivering out there in Russia with your machine-gun. We agree in that as we do in everything else. I have never been so much alone as I am here, except in Berlin, when I was absolutely by myself, struggling through the crowded corridors of the University to Erich Schmidt's lectures. One feels equally solitary as one marches along with the rank and file, hour after hour, abandoned to one's own thoughts. And I sometimes felt like that in the students' cafés— as if the whole atmosphere were somehow alien to me. If I could only begin my student-days all over again! But I won't let myself think that. After the war everything will be different, and then I *must* begin again, anyhow.

The question is: shall I be a clergyman or not? The old question, the old uncertainty, the old struggle! Here one has time to examine oneself, to prove one's attitude towards God. Many people have found themselves able to make up their minds about such things here, but I find myself more doubtful than ever. . . .

It is getting cold outside now. I will go into my tent. I am thinking over the great ethical problem of the war. Preachers in the pulpits at home dismiss the question much more easily; for us here the war remains a most difficult matter for one's conscience to decide about. When one is actually fighting the instinct of self-preservation and the excitement drown every other feeling, but when one is in rest or doing nothing in the trenches, then it is dif-

---

° *skat:* Three-person card game.

° *no forrarder:* No further ahead.

SOURCE: A. F. Wedd, *German Students' War Letters*, trans. Philipp Witkop (Philadelphia: Pine St. Books, 2002), 198–201.

ferent. One looks with astonishment and horror at the more and more cunningly elaborate means devised for destroying the enemy. One is torn between the natural instinct which says, "Thou shalt do no murder," and the sacred obligation, "This must be done for the sake of the Fatherland." This conflict may be temporarily suspended sometimes, but it always exists. It often occupies my mind after we come in in the evening. The opposition between the two principles is emphasized when one looks out upon such a peaceful valley as this that lies before me. The white-owl, the "bird of death," screeches from the alder-clump, and the thunder of the guns grows louder again. Then all is still. It is night. Slowly I prepare for bed.

April 1915

The most trying part of this *mole's* war is that one can never have a real straightforward fight. When the first larks soar and, undisturbed by shells and whistling bullets, sing their morning hymn, then the guns begin firing aimlessly into the dawning

day. This murdering is so senseless. The one consolation is that one is doing one's duty. I do think that we Germans have, more than any other nation, a stern sense of duty. And we stick to that in this ghastly war. The justification for militarism, which from the ordinary human point of view is detestable, is that it has helped to encourage and strengthen this sense of duty. Of course there are some shirkers here as everywhere else — "it takes all sorts to make a world" — but those who have this sense of duty do not ask: "Is it dangerous? Are the guns firing?" No: one shoots, one stays awake, one is constantly on the watch, burrows in the ground till 12 or 1 o'clock, and is at it again by 5 the next morning, simply because it's one's damned duty and obligation. And all that is done just as a matter of course — neither willingly nor unwillingly — naturally, simply, just because it has got to be done. One may be a little braver or a little more skilful than another, but the same cheery tone prevails all through. Everybody does his best, one working for all and all for one.

Document 3.2

Khan Mahomed Khan
Letter, October 11, 1917

36th Jacob's Horse
France

11th October 1917

Get Gul Sabab, Mahomed Zaman and Allah Nawaz as much teaching as you can, because that age is coming — in fact it has already come — in which the educated will be highly esteemed. This war has caused an upheaval of the times, and has opened the eyes of the careless. The people of Europe live in ease and comfort simply through education. Both men and women are sufficiently

educated to know wherein lies their profit and loss, and to plan and secure their advantage. My own eyes have been opened since I came to Europe, and I have entirely altered the views which I held before. I wring my hands with regrets that I did not set myself to acquire learning, but regrets are of no avail now. I missed my chance and I am now well in years. If I live to return, and if God gives me children, I will fashion their lives according to my new ideas. Please God, I will give them a good education, whether they be sons or daughters. When I was in Hindustan and used to hear of anyone going to England for education, or even of anyone setting himself to acquire complete education in Hindustani, I used myself to say

SOURCE: David Omissi, ed., *Indian Voices of the Great War: Soldiers' Letters, 1914–1918* (London: Routledge, 1999), 324.

"these people lose their religion and return as Christians." Now that I have come here, I realize how wrong I was in my ideas. There is no question at all of religion—it is education alone which makes them wise, and teaches them to hate and abandon those habits and customs in our country which are improper, and to live according to their new ideas. Such people, however, are only one in a thousand, and have to contend with great difficulties at the hands of the majority who treat them as if they had lost their senses, whereas in reality it is the majority who are blinded by ignorance.

Document 3.3

MARIA LUISA PERDUCA
A Hospital Year, 1917

AN AMPUTATION

This too; after all the horrors that have torn our souls, that have sunken us in a mute, sour anguish, one that stupefies us.

Angelo, brother, poor foot-soldier from the Marche region, your face thin, your eyes sad as though you could foresee the end; these words are for you, they are like the flowers that I send to your tomb.

He had come here from another hospital, accompanied by his father, who had always taken care of him after he was wounded; not for love, but so that the military mess would remember to nourish him.

His knee had been shattered by a grenade; was it a knee or was it a shapeless mass of bleeding ground flesh, from which greenish pus ran? No one could look at it for long.

Every attempt was made to save him from amputation; but all failed. One evening the surgeon asked us to make a decision.

Nothing could be more difficult or more painful than this, to persuade a creature of twenty to either die or be deformed for the rest of his life.

None of us had the courage, none of us knew how to find the proper words; but the matron and chaplain gradually convinced him.

He let them speak looking at us sadly, as though thinking:

—Yes, go ahead, I'm going to die anyway.

The next morning, before the operation, we found him calmly chatting with his family; two obtuse laborers who seemed not to understand, not to hear, confused by their bestial daily existence.

The operating room was ready.

Around the glazed iron bed stirred the white garments of the surgeon, his assistant and the matron all busily occupied with sterilizing.

On the tables the scalpels, the gouges, the tubes, the scissors, the needles for stitching, the bobbins of silk and rubber all gleamed; the corporal nurse had sharpened the knives and the saws.

Two soldiers carried him away from his room; he glanced at his mother once more, touched her hand, then sank on their powerful shoulders.

They placed him on the bed, he trembled like a leaf calling us softly:

—Stay near me, stay near me.

He desperately grabbed at my arms.

—Yes, dear, yes, I'm here, Angelo.

The assistant put the mask in place and let a few drops of chloroform fall.

His hollow torso rose and fell quickly; they held his wrist, his arteries pulsed dizzily.

SOURCE: Margaret R. Higonnet, ed., *Lines of Fire: Women Writers of World War I* (New York: Plume, 1999), 217–219.

He breathed with difficulty, his pupils began to shrink.

He fell asleep.

Only the very center of his brain continued to work; the man vegetated, lived mechanically, insensitive; it was nearly death.

In his narcotic sleep he seemed to complain gasping incomprehensibly; every now and then I would look at the orb of his inert eyes.

The surgeon examined the horrible knee, pierced here and there by tubes. He removed them one by one; he asked that a tourniquet be applied to the thigh, washed his hands once again, picked up the amputating knife, and began to mark a circle in the nude flesh as far as the femur.

The blood gushed from the cut vessels; he dried; he stopped again, put down the amputating knife; the matron handed him the saw, he grasped it ordering that I inject the patient with morphine. He placed the tool between the torn limbs and began to saw.

A long creak, a blunt blow, it was over.

That instant penetrated us, our brains, our nerves, our flesh, our spirits, and did not abandon us for many days.

The leg fell by sheer force into the basin placed below, like an object that was dead, finished.

A soldier wrapped it in a wax sheet and took it away; and by a strange contrast, we felt as though something alive were being taken away, a person.

The stump resembled the trunk of a tree that had been sawn, within which we could see the nerves and the white circle of the marrow. The flaps of the skin were stretched to cover the red of the flesh and the white of the bone; the matron handed over the curved and threaded needles, the surgeon stitched.

Angelo continued to sleep, unconscious.

The assistant removed the mask. His pupils enlarged gradually; as soon as he was in his warm bed, surrounded by the affectionate eyes of his companions, he woke up, looked at us, and smiled. He could not remember.

—I'm fine—he said.

We had to look the other way to hide our faces.

QUESTIONS FOR ANALYSIS

1. Describe the different subjects treated by these battlefield authors, and account for the diverging concerns among these young people.

2. Despite the different subjects, do you sense any shared attitudes about war and society among these writers?

3. What values emerge from these battlefield accounts, and how do they connect with the war aims of the different powers?

Lenin's "April Theses":
A Program for Immediate Action

In the spring of 1917 Bolshevik leader V. I. Lenin (1870–1924) returned to revolutionary Russia after years in exile as a propagandist and journalist. To develop his political ideas and skill, he had read widely, not only Karl Marx but also Niccolò Machiavelli, Charles Darwin, Aristotle, and Harriet Beecher Stowe. Although he was from a prosperous and respected upper-class family, Lenin was committed to bringing down, as he put it, "the hated Old Russia" from an early age, especially after the execution of his brother for plotting to kill the tsar. Lenin was exceptionally gifted, politically astute, and so driven on behalf of revolution that even his fellow Bolsheviks thought him slightly mad. In the spring of 1917 he had an opportunity to direct his programs toward the masses at home. One of his first acts on arriving was to issue the "April Theses," a program for immediate action to determine Russia's future.

Instead of being a grateful returnee to postimperial and reform-minded Russia, Lenin scolded and complained about his compatriots on the left. The "Theses" gave them no credit for toppling the Romanov dynasty or for setting up workers' and soldiers' soviets that within a few months had become politically powerful in Russia. At the time of Lenin's return, the soviets were determining factory policy, working on social welfare issues, and cooperating with the Provisional Government, which had replaced the monarchy. The cabinet of the new government was headed by Prince Georgii Lvov, who had directed the prerevolutionary system of councils called *zemstvos,* which concerned themselves with education and public welfare. Also included in the cabinet were professionals and businessmen. The aftermath of revolution thus saw both the Provisional Government and the soviets putting aside some of their differences to solve the immense problems faced by an essentially rural society fighting an industrial war.

The situation outraged Lenin, whose Bolshevism precluded proletarian compromise with the middle classes. Moreover, Lenin fumed that Bolsheviks were outnumbered in the soviets themselves, ceding leadership to an array of worker parties. The "April Theses" addressed the composition of the Russian government, its policies, and Russia's continued participation in the war. The solution for everything, in Lenin's opinion, would be a heavy dose of Marxism-Leninism. Instead of cooperation he demanded that workers break with bourgeois politicians and with workers in the soviets who continued to support the war. Instead of pragmatic solutions to the problems at hand, he demanded immediate social revolution. His followers were stunned at his extreme position; many believed that the "April Theses" sounded a call for civil war. "Peace, land, and bread" was a platform, however, that appealed to those who had been serving as cannon fodder and suffering from shortages. "All power to the Soviets"—another of Lenin's slogans—sounded the call for the masses finally to take power.

Document 3.4

V. I. LENIN
April Theses, 1917

1. In our attitude towards the war, which under the new government of Lvov and Co. unquestionably remains on Russia's part a predatory imperialist war owing to the capitalist nature of that government not the slightest concession to "revolutionary defencism" is permissible.

The class-conscious proletariat can give its consent to a revolutionary war . . . only on condition: (a) that the power pass to the proletariat and the poorest sections of the peasants aligned with the proletariat; (b) that all annexations° be renounced in deed and not in word; (c) that a complete break be effected in actual fact with all capitalist interests.

In view of the undoubted honesty of those broad sections of the mass believers . . . who accept the war only as a necessity, and not as a means of conquest, in view of the fact that they are being deceived by the bourgeoisie, it is necessary with particular thoroughness, persistence and patience to explain their error to them, to explain the inseparable connection existing between capital and the imperialist war, and to prove that without overthrowing capital *it is impossible* to end the war by a truly democratic peace, a peace not imposed by violence.

The most widespread campaign for this view must be organised in the army at the front.

Fraternisation.

2. The specific feature of the present situation in Russia is that the country is *passing* from the first stage of the revolution—which, owing to the insufficient class-consciousness and organisation of the proletariat, placed power in the hands of the bourgeoisie—to its *second* stage, which must place power in the hands of the proletariat and the poorest sections of the peasants.

This transition is characterised, on the one hand, by a maximum of legally recognised rights (Russia is *now* the freest of all the belligerent countries in the world); on the other, by the absence of violence towards the masses, and, finally, by their unreasoning trust in the government of capitalists, those worst enemies of peace and socialism.

This peculiar situation demands of us an ability to adapt ourselves to the *special* conditions of Party work among unprecedentedly large masses of proletarians who have just awakened to political life.

3. No support for the Provisional Government; the utter falsity of all its promises should be made clear, particularly of those relating to the renunciation of annexations. Exposure in place of the impermissible, illusion-breeding "demand" that *this* government, a government of capitalists, should *cease* to be an imperialist government.

4. Recognition of the fact that in most of the Soviets of Workers' Deputies our Party is in a minority, so far a small minority, as against *a bloc of all* the petty-bourgeois opportunist elements, from the Popular Socialists and the Socialist-Revolutionaries down to the Organising Committee . . . who have yielded to the influence of the bourgeoisie and spread that influence among the proletariat.

The masses must be made to see that the Soviets of Workers' Deputies are the *only possible* form of revolutionary government, and that therefore our task is, as long as *this* government yields to the influence of the bourgeoisie, to present a patient, systematic, and persistent *explanation* of the errors of their tactics, an explanation especially adapted to the practical needs of the masses.

As long as we are in the minority we carry on the work of criticising and exposing errors and at

---

° *annexations:* Taking territory as spoils of wartime victory.

SOURCE: V. I. Lenin, *Collected Works: April–June 1917*, vol. 24 (Moscow: Progress Publishers, 1964), 21–25.

the same time we preach the necessity of transferring the entire state power to the Soviets of Workers' Deputies, so that the people may overcome their mistakes by experience.

5. Not a parliamentary republic—to return to a parliamentary republic from the Soviets of Workers' Deputies would be a retrograde step—but a republic of Soviets of Workers', Agricultural Labourers' and Peasants' Deputies throughout the country, from top to bottom.

Abolition of the police, the army and the bureaucracy.°

The salaries of all officials, all of whom are elective and displaceable at any time, not to exceed the average wage of a competent worker.

6. The weight of emphasis in the agrarian programme to be shifted to the Soviets of Agricultural Labourers' Deputies.

Confiscation of all landed estates.

Nationalisation of *all* lands in the country, the land to be disposed of by the local Soviets of Agricultural Labourers' and Peasants' Deputies. The organisation of separate Soviets of Deputies of Poor Peasants. The setting up of a model farm on each of the large estates. . . .

7. The immediate amalgamation of all banks in the country into a single national bank, and the institution of control over it by the Soviet of Workers' Deputies.

8. It is not our *immediate* task to "introduce" socialism, but only to bring social production and the distribution of products at once under the *control* of the Soviets of Workers' Deputies.

° I.e., the standing army to be replaced by the arming of the whole people. [Note in document.]

9. Party tasks:
   (a) Immediate convocation of a Party congress;
   (b) Alteration of the Party Programme, mainly: (1) On the question of imperialism and the imperialist war; (2) On our attitude towards the state and *our* demand for a "commune state"; (3) Amendment of our out-of-date minimum programme. (c) Change of the Party's name.

10. A new International. . . .

I write, announce and elaborately explain: "The Soviets of Workers' Deputies are the *only possible* form of revolutionary government, and therefore our task is to present a patient, systematic, and persistent *explanation* of the errors of their tactics, an explanation especially adapted to the practical needs of the masses."

Yet opponents of a certain brand present my views as a call to "civil war in the midst of revolutionary democracy"!

I attacked the Provisional Government for *not* having appointed an early date, or any date at all, for the convocation of the Constituent Assembly, and for confining itself to promises. I argued that *without* the Soviets of Workers' and Soldiers' Deputies the convocation of the Constituent Assembly is not guaranteed and its success is impossible.

And the view is attributed to me that I am opposed to the speedy convocation of the Constituent Assembly!

I would call this "raving," had not decades of political struggle taught me to regard honesty in opponents as a rare exception.

QUESTIONS FOR ANALYSIS

1. What specific changes does Lenin call for in the "April Theses"? How do the changes relate to the situation in which Russians found themselves in 1917?

2. In what senses was this document politically and socially divisive?

3. What parts of the "April Theses" seem most powerful and persuasive and why?

The Mandate System

L ATE IN THE NINETEENTH CENTURY, the European powers became concerned about the violence inflicted on the peoples of Africa. One specific culprit was King Leopold II of Belgium, who had personally claimed the resource-rich Congo and was determined to use whatever brutality was necessary to force the local people to harvest rubber from indigenous rubber trees. Leopold's agents cut off hands and even murdered those who failed to meet regular quotas. In 1885 the imperial powers met in Berlin, ultimately issuing the Berlin Congo Act, which explicitly endorsed the common protection of native rights. Five years later the powers issued the General Act of Brussels, which set up international agencies to monitor the sale of alcohol in Africa and to push for the abolition of slavery there. In the process of creating these agencies, the powers began discussing imperialism in terms of native peoples' need for protection even though the powers themselves were foremost in abusing the native peoples. They also talked about shared responsibility for that protection. In several instances before World War I, international conferences suggested that the powers collectively administer territories. In 1898, for example, Britain, France, Italy, and Russia awarded Prince George of Greece a "mandate" over the island Crete after an Ottoman official had massacred inhabitants.

During World War I several politicians and theorists suggested mandates as a way of administering lands held by the defeated Ottomans and Germans. Advisers to President Woodrow Wilson suggested his proposed League of Nations would be the proper collective body for overseeing Mesopotamia (Iraq) and the territories taken from Germany. A single government would act as a "mandatory" of the League, and the League itself, in Wilson's mind, would acquire these territories as its "common property." The principles of the mandate system were laid out in 1920 in Articles 22 and 23 of the Covenant of the League of Nations.

Despite the great powers' lofty moralistic rhetoric, the mandate system justified a postwar land grab of immense proportions. Great Britain, including its dominions Australia and New Zealand, acquired almost a million square miles of territory; France, a quarter of a million; and Belgium and Japan, smaller but still significant areas. Some twenty million people were suddenly subjected to their political rule. By this system instituted during the Paris peace talks, "advanced" nations, including Australia and Japan, exercised political and economic control over mandated territory, though local leaders in some cases retained limited authority. This was, in effect, a kind of recolonization sanitized as "a sacred trust of civilisation," as Article 22 expressed it, and outrage mounted among the local rulers and peoples who suddenly acquired new masters. Instead of the independence they had been promised in exchange for their crucial help in the war, they were to be subjected to a new kind of domination by imperial powers who, despite their own barbarism during World War I, saw as their mission the civilizing and stabilizing of "uncivilized" regions. The statement that some regions were closer to civilization than others provided still further proof of the imperial powers' condescension. The system provided a visible focal point for resistance and sparked armed uprisings in South West Africa (1922), Syria (1925), Palestine (1929, 1936), and Samoa (1926, 1933). Although the hard-pressed British and French intended that mandates would shore up Britain and France and help meet their wartime outlays, it may be argued that the greed and duplicity manifest in the mandates prepared the way for colonial liberation.

Document 3.5
Articles 22 and 23 of the Covenant of the League of Nations, 1920

ARTICLE 22

To those colonies and territories which as a consequence of the late war have ceased to be under the sovereignty of the States which formerly governed them and which are inhabited by peoples not yet able to stand by themselves under the strenuous conditions of the modern world, there should be applied the principle that the well-being and development of such peoples form a sacred trust of civilisation and that securities for the performance of this trust should be embodied in this Covenant.

The best method of giving practical effect to this principle is that the tutelage of such peoples should be entrusted to advanced nations who by reason of their resources, their experience or their geographical position can best undertake this responsibility, and who are willing to accept it, and that this tutelage should be exercised by them as Mandatories on behalf of the League.

The character of the mandate must differ according to the stage of the development of the people, the geographical situation of the territory, its economic conditions and other similar circumstances.

Certain communities formerly belonging to the Turkish Empire have reached a stage of development where their existence as independent nations can be provisionally recognised subject to the rendering of administrative advice and assistance by a Mandatory until such time as they are able to stand alone. The wishes of these communities must be a principal consideration in the selection of the Mandatory.

Other peoples, especially those of Central Africa, are at such a stage that the Mandatory must be responsible for the administration of the territory under conditions which will guarantee freedom of conscience and religion, subject only to the maintenance of public order and morals, the prohibition of abuses such as the slave trade, the arms traffic and the liquor traffic, and the prevention of the establishment of fortifications or military and naval bases and of military training of the natives for other than police purposes and the defence of territory, and will also secure equal opportunities for the trade and commerce of other Members of the League.

There are territories, such as South-West Africa and certain of the South Pacific Islands, which, owing to the sparseness of their population, or their small size, or their remoteness from the centres of civilisation, or their geographical contiguity to the territory of the Mandatory, and

SOURCE: Covenant of the League of Nations in *League of Nations Official Journal,* 1 (February 1920).

other circumstances, can be best administered under the laws of the Mandatory as integral portions of its territory, subject to the safeguards above mentioned in the interests of the indigenous population.

In every case of mandate, the Mandatory shall render to the Council an annual report in reference to the territory committed to its charge.

The degree of authority, control, or administration to be exercised by the Mandatory shall, if not previously agreed upon by the Members of the League, be explicitly defined in each case by the Council.

A permanent Commission shall be constituted to receive and examine the annual reports of the Mandatories and to advise the Council on all matters relating to the observance of the mandates.

ARTICLE 23

Subject to and in accordance with the provisions of international conventions existing or hereafter to be agreed upon, the Members of the League:

(a) will endeavour to secure and maintain fair and humane conditions of labour for men, women, and children, both in their own countries and in all countries to which their commercial and industrial relations extend, and for that purpose will establish and maintain the necessary international organisations;

(b) undertake to secure just treatment of the native inhabitants of territories under their control;

(c) will entrust the League with the general supervision over the execution of agreements with regard to the traffic in women and children, and the traffic in opium and other dangerous drugs;

(d) will entrust the League with the general supervision of the trade in arms and ammunition with the countries in which the control of this traffic is necessary in the common interest;

(e) will make provision to secure and maintain freedom of communications and of transit and equitable treatment for the commerce of all Members of the League. In this connection, the special necessities of the regions devastated during the war of 1914–1918 shall be borne in mind;

(f) will endeavour to take steps in matters of international concern for the prevention and control of disease.

QUESTIONS FOR ANALYSIS

1. What attitudes among the victors in World War I does the mandate system display? What signs, if any, does the mandate system give that the attitudes of imperialists were changing?

2. What kinds of protection for the mandatory powers do these articles allow?

3. What grievances do you see within the system itself?

PICTURE ESSAY

The Home Front

A T THE TIME THE WAR BROKE OUT, Europe was one of the most prosperous regions of the world. Although there was an uneven distribution of wealth, many Europeans enjoyed the technological advances of the day and a sparkling urban life. People in general were healthier and living longer. During the war, much of that changed as the great powers were bankrupted by the war's great cost and as civilian discontent threatened central governments. Beleaguered by disruption and disorder, the combatant powers sought both to ensure the maintenance of social order on the homefront and the full mobilization of able-bodied young men for the battlefront. This left women and older men responsible for staffing the homefront industries.

Both the social changes engendered by the war and the attempts of governments to bring to society the orderliness and efficiency of machines were captured in posters, newspapers, and photograph albums of the times. The ability to provide widely distributed images of war was a sign of Europe's complex situation during the Great War: photography, newspapers, and mass-produced posters represented technological advances bringing people together just as technology itself was simultaneously mobilized to blow them to bits.

Changes in society, politics, and public culture occurred rapidly during the war. The most obvious change was women working outside the home (Figure 3.1), and photographs captured both spontaneous and carefully staged images of women workers to use in publicity. In this case the workers are miners, carrying heavy bags of coke, a coal residue. We do not know who captured this particular image, and whether or not it was simulated, but in general women were shown as capable and enthusiastic about the new tasks they undertook, even arduous ones in mining, metallurgy, and munitions. This publicity could both encourage support for the war and help accustom people to the unfamiliar and, to some, disturbing sight of women in traditionally male occupations. What image of British women do you take away from viewing this wartime photo? Do you think it was staged or not and why? Does it make a difference? How do you imagine citizens on the home front reacted to similar photos in newspapers or to seeing actual women performing dirty, strenuous tasks?

Governments filled public spaces with propaganda posters to bolster civilian support as casualties mounted, everyday necessities grew scarce, and protests erupted (Figures 3.2 and 3.3). Like soldiers, civilians on both sides were encouraged to accept mass killings and the loss of loved ones to achieve victory. Propaganda posters had several purposes. One of them was to inspire love of homeland and motivate the viewers, no matter how poor, to give money to offset

◆ Figure 3.1 **Women Coke Workers**
Imperial War Museum.

◆ **Figure 3.2 German Poster of a Teutonic Knight**
Swim Ink 2, LLC/CORBIS.

the enormous costs of the war. This poster of a Teutonic Knight, intended to raise money for Germany's Seventh War Loan, imitates the style of traditional wood-cuts, and the knight brings to mind Germany's historic strength and heritage of steadfastness. Evaluate the likely effectiveness of this image of the Teutonic knight as propaganda for raising funds and boosting patriotism.

Another purpose of propaganda was to arouse hatred for the enemy. Propaganda specialists created posters depicting the enemy's barbarism and reinforcing in the public's mind the stories of atrocities supposedly committed by enemy soldiers and their leaders. Images of women and children being raped, tortured, and killed outraged people on the home front and strengthened their already

◆ Figure 3.3 **British Poster, "The Gentle German"**

RED CROSS OR IRON CROSS?

WOUNDED AND A PRISONER OUR SOLDIER CRIES FOR WATER.

THE GERMAN "SISTER"
POURS IT ON THE GROUND BEFORE HIS EYES.

THERE IS NO WOMAN IN BRITAIN
WHO WOULD DO IT.

THERE IS NO WOMAN IN BRITAIN
WHO WILL FORGET IT.

◆ Figure 3.4 **British Poster, "Red Cross or Iron Cross?"**
Imperial War Museum.

negative views of the enemy. Governments made the public space horrific with terrifying images such as the one in Figure 3.3. What feelings does this British poster, ironically titled "The Gentle German," elicit in you, and what elements cause you most concern? This is a drawing, not a staged photograph. Why was a cartoon-like graphic used in this instance of anti-German propaganda?

More subtle because they played to popular misogynist stereotypes were depictions of women luring men to their doom. The temptress and spy Mata Hari was so vividly used to portray feminine evil that long after the war the term *Mata Hari* was applied to women criminals and traitors. A British poster showing a German nurse refusing water to a wounded British prisoner of war (Figure 3.4) was meant to stir outrage at the enemy's betrayal of feminine values and to strengthen support at home for Britain's own compassionate nurses at the front, even though British civilians might abhor the idea of women taking a more prominent role in society. Which of the poster's elements seem most striking and why? In what ways does this poster seek to engage women in the war effort?

Governments held newspapers to strict standards for describing and photographing the war, prohibiting realism in portraying the actual destruction and violence of the battlefield. Depictions of decaying corpses or body parts such as limbs dangling from trees were forbidden; any dead soldier whose photograph was published had to be intact bodily and peaceful of expression. Battles were carefully staged in films to avoid portraying actual carnage. But soon it was impossible to escape the grim images from the home front itself (Figure 3.5). Revolution broke out in Ireland and Russia, and by the end of the war the people of Germany were massing in the streets, threatening to overthrow first the monarchy and later their new republican government. In Ireland, leaders of the movement for home rule were angry because the outbreak of World War I stalled the achievement of Irish sovereignty. Many of those working for independence hoped Germany, not Britain, would win the war, and on the Monday following Easter in 1916 they staged an uprising and declared Ireland's independence. Dublin became the scene of pitched

◆ Figure 3.5 **British Soldiers at a Barricade in Dublin**
Hulton Archive/Getty Images.

battles when British government forces took steps to put down the movement. Artillery shells shattered homes and public buildings in Dublin, and to this day bullet holes mar the surfaces of those that remain standing. As you look at the image of these British forces, consider the different reactions viewers in Ireland, Britain, Germany, and the United States might have had to this photo if it appeared in a newspaper during the war.

The war transformed millions of people into refugees, especially on the eastern front, where the fighting was more mobile. As armies moved back and forth through farmland, villages, and cities in eastern and east-central Europe, they laid waste to people's homes and resources, forcing entire families to move to escape the carnage and civil war that surrounded them. After the war, enforcement of Wilson's principle of self-determination led to majority populations driving out the minority ethnicities among them. The victorious Allies, including the United States, approved of this compulsory and often deadly migration of civilians. The family in Figure 3.6 is ethnically Greek and moved from Turkey after the war as part of a forced transfer of populations between the two countries. This family may in fact have lived in the Ottoman Empire for generations going back centuries, and it is likely that Turkish was their first language. Now, like thousands of other refugee families in Greece and Turkey and across Europe who were compelled to abandon their homes, sometimes only able to take with them what they could carry, they face an uncertain future. What dangers might this family have faced along their journey? What problems and possibilities—social, cultural, economic—might have awaited them and other refugees across Europe in their new homeland?

◆ **Figure 3.6 Greek Refugees from Turkey**
Bettmann/CORBIS.

QUESTIONS FOR ANALYSIS

1. Some military historians believe that modern warfare is equally a phenomenon of both battlefield and home front and that knowing about the home front is as important as knowing about the battlefield. Based on figures from the Picture Essay and elsewhere in the chapter, to what extent do you agree or disagree with this idea.

2. Use these illustrations to explain what "militarizing" the home front means.

3. In what way do these images show the civilians' war to be different from the soldiers' war?

NOTES

1. Aleksandr Solzhenitsyn, *August, 1914,* trans. Michael Glenny (New York: Farrar, Straus and Giroux, 1972), 106.

2. Colonel de Grandmaison, quoted in Marc Ferro, *The Great War, 1914–1918,* trans. Nicole Stone (New York: Routledge, 1973), 33.

3. Quoted in Paul Kennedy, *The Rise and Fall of the Great Powers* (New York: Vintage, 1989), 223.

4. Bernadotte E. Schmitt and Harold C. Vedeler, *The World in the Crucible, 1914–1919* (New York: Harper and Row, 1984), 65.

5. Quoted in B. H. Liddell Hart, *The Real War, 1914–1918* (Boston: Little, Brown, 1930), 225–248.

6. Ivor Gurney, *War Letters,* ed. R. K. R. Thornton (Ashington, Northumberland: Carcourt New Press, 1983), 171.

7. Quoted in Eric J. Leed, *No Man's Land: Combat and Identity in World War I* (Cambridge: Cambridge University Press, 1979), 30.

8. Quoted in Tony Ashworth, *Trench Warfare, 1914–1918: The Live and Let Live System* (London: Macmillan, 1980), 26.

9. Quoted ibid., 26.

10. Quoted in József Galántai, *Hungary in the First World War* (Budapest: Akadémiai Kiadó, 1989), 272.

11. Quoted in Bonnie G. Smith, *Imperialism* (New York: Oxford University Press, 2000), 140.

12. Quoted in Gordon Craig, *Germany, 1866–1945* (New York: Oxford University Press, 1978), 340.

13. Quoted in Jeffrey Verhey, *The Spirit of 1914: Militarism, Myth, and Mobilization in Germany* (Cambridge: Cambridge University Press, 2000), 160.

14. Pascal, 47–48.

15. Rudolf Eucken, quoted in Verhey, *Spirit of 1914,* 4.

16. Quoted in Cate Haste, *Keep the Home Fires Burning: Propaganda in the First World War* (London: Allen Lane, 1977), 43.

17. Quoted in David Welch, *Germany, Propaganda, and Total War, 1914–1918: The Sins of Omission* (New Brunswick: Rutgers University Press, 2000), 30.

18. Quoted ibid., 33.

19. Quoted in Haste, *Keep the Home Fires Burning,* 109.

20. Quoted ibid., 87.

21. Quoted in Laura Lee Downs, *Manufacturing Inequality: Gender Division in the French and British Metalworking Industries, 1914–1939* (Ithaca: Cornell University Press, 1995), 134.

22. *Scottish Law Courts Record,* n.d. quoted ibid., 46.

23. Quoted in Christopher Seton-Watson, *Italy from Liberalism to Fascism, 1870–1925* (London: Metheun, 1967), 470.

24. Quoted in Leonard V. Smith, "Remobilizing the Citizen-Soldier through the French Army Mutinies of 1917," in *State, Society, and Mobilization in Europe during the First World War,* ed. John Horne (Cambridge: Cambridge University Press, 2000), 153.

25. Quoted in Wilhelm Deist, "The German Army, the Nation-State, and Total War," ibid., 169.

26. Quoted in Galántai, *Hungary in the First World War,* 83.

27. *Breslauer Tagewacht,* quoted in Belinda J. Davis, *Home Fires Burning: Food, Politics, and Everyday Life in World War I Berlin* (Chapel Hill: University of North Carolina Press, 2000), 123.

28. Dubesset et al., *Parcours de Femmes: Réalités et Representations,* 254.

29. Quoted in Jürgen Kocka, *Facing Total War: German Society, 1914–1918,* trans. Barbara Weinberger (Leamington Spa: Berg, 1984), 25.

30. Quoted in Davis, *Home Fires Burning,* 133.

31. Armin Wegner, diary entry, quoted in *The Great War and the Shaping of the Twentieth Century* at www.pbs.org/greatwar/chapters/ch2_voiceszhtml.

32. Report of the chief of police of Petrograd Province, quoted in Ronald Kowalski, *The Russian Revolution, 1917–1921* (London: Routledge, 1997), 29.

33. Quoted in Steve A. Smith, "Petrograd in 1917: The View from Below," in *The Workers' Revolution in Russia, 1917: The View from Below,* ed. Daniel H. Kaiser (Cambridge: Cambridge University Press, 1987), 62.

34. Quoted in Richard Stites, *Revolutionary Dreams: Utopian Vision and Experimental Life in the Russian Revolution* (New York: Oxford University Press, 1989), 38.

35. Quoted in Smith, "Petrograd in 1917," in *The Workers' Revolution,* 66.

36. Quoted in Sheila Fitzpatrick, *The Russian Revolution,* 2nd ed. (Oxford: Oxford University Press, 1995), 72.

37. Quoted in Mark D. Steinberg and Vladimir M. Khrustalëv, *The Fall of the Romanovs: Political Dreams and Personal Struggles in a Time of Revolution* (New Haven: Yale University Press, 1995), 288.

38. Craig, *Germany, 1866–1945,* 387.

39. Quoted in V. R. Berghahn, *Modern Germany: Society, Economy, and Politics in the Twentieth Century* (Cambridge: Cambridge University Press, 1987), 59.

40. Quoted in William J. Duiker, *Ho Chi Minh: A Life* (New York: Hyperion, 2000), 75.

41. Mohandas Gandhi, "Hind Swaraj," in *The Collected Works of Mohandas Gandhi,* vol. 10 (Ahmedabad: Navajivan Trust, 1963), 21.

SUGGESTED REFERENCES

General Works Audoin-Rouzeau, Stéphane, and Annette Becker. *14–18: Understanding the Great War.* 2004.

Keegan, John. *A History of Warfare*. 1993.

Schmitt, Bernadotte E., and Harold C. Vedeler. *The World in the Crucible, 1914–1919*. 1984.

Strachan, Hew. *The First World War: To Arms*. 2004.

Winter, J. M. et al eds. *The Great War and the Twentieth Century*. 2000.

World War I Begins The extensive literature on World War I provides a look at the grand strategy of generals on both sides, but it also examines the world of soldiers in the trenches. Particularly interesting are the varied reactions of colonial soldiers and their descriptions of life in the trenches, as provided in Omissi's collection of their letters.

Asprey, Robert B. *The German High Command at War: Hindenburg and Ludendorff Conduct World War I*. 1991.

Brown, Ian Malcolm. *British Logistics on the Western Front, 1914–1919*. 1998.

Echenberg, Myron. *Colonial Conscripts: The "Tirailleurs Sénégalais" in French West Africa, 1857–1960*. 1990.

Gatrell, Peter. *Russia's First World War: A Social and Economic History*. 2005.

Hašek, Jaroslav. *The Good Soldier Schweik*. 1920.

Holquist, Peter. *Making War, Forging Revolution: Russia's Continuum of Crisis, 1914–1921*. 2002.

Horne, John, ed. *State, Society, and Mobilization in Europe during the First World War*. 2000.

Karau, Mark D. *"Wielding the Dagger": The MarineKorps Flandern and the German War Effort, 1914–1918*. 2003.

Morrow, John J. *The Great War: An Imperial History*. 2005.

Omissi, David, ed. *Indian Voices of the Great War: Soldiers' Letters, 1914–1918*. 1999.

Verhey, Jeffrey. *The Spirit of 1914: Myth, Militarism and Mobilization in Germany*, 2000.

Williams, John Frank. *Anzacs, the Media, and the Great War*. 1999.

The Home Front The war on the home front involved cultural adjustment, as described in Robb's book, as well as a barrage of propaganda and even light-hearted antics (as found in Roshwald and Stites). The political aspects of the home front experience are well-told by Davis.

Davis, Belinda J. *Home Fires Burning: Food, Politics, and Everyday Life in World War I Berlin*. 2000.

Downs, Laura Lee. *Manufacturing Inequality: Gender Division in the French and British Metalworking Industries, 1914–1939*. 1995.

Grayzel, Susan R. *Women's Identities at War: Gender, Motherhood, and Politics in Britain and France during the First World War*. 1999.

Gullace, Nicoletta F. *The Blood of Our Sons: Men, Women, and the Renegotiation of British Citizenship during the Great War*. 2002.

Higonnet, Margaret R. *Lines of Fire: Women Writers of World War I*. 1999.

Kocka, Jürgen. *Facing Total War: German Society, 1914–1918.* 1984.

Robb, George. *British Culture and the First World War.* 2002.

Roshwald, Aviel, and Richard Stites, eds. *European Culture in the Great War: The Arts, Entertainment, and Propaganda, 1914–1918.* 1999.

Welch, David. *Germany, Propaganda, and Total War, 1914–1918: The Sins of Omission.* 2000.

From War Fever to Revolution Revolt against war was widespread, and as a serious political phenomenon it extended from Ireland to Russia. Fitzpatrick provides a classic account of the Russian Revolution.

Cornwall, Mark. *The Undermining of Austria-Hungary: The Battle for Hearts and Minds.* 2000.

Dickinson, Frederick R. *War and National Reinvention: Japan in the Great War, 1914–1919.* 1999.

Fitzpatrick, Sheila. *The Russian Revolution.* 1995.

Hennessey, Thomas. *Dividing Ireland: World War I and Partition.* 1998.

Jahn, Hubertus. *Patriotic Culture in Russia during World War I.* 1995.

Johnson, Nuala. *Ireland, the Great War, and the Geography of Remembrance.* 2003.

Richter, Donald C. *Chemical Soldiers: British Gas Warfare in World War I.* 1992.

Smith, Leonard. *Between Mutiny and Obedience: The Case of the French Fifth Infantry Division during World War I.* 1994.

Steinberg, Mark, and Vladimir M. Khrustalëv. *The Fall of the Romanovs: Political Dreams and Personal Struggles in a Time of Revolution.* 1995.

Wrigley, Chris, ed. *The First World War and the International Economy.* 2000.

The Great War Ends The end of the war was as tumultuous as the war itself. It involved privation, pandemic, and widespread violence. Healy offers a particularly vivid account of life in the Austro-Hungarian monarchy as it collapsed, leading to decades of tumult in the region.

Barry, John M. *The Great Influenza: The Epic Story of the Deadliest Plague in History.* 2004.

Bruce, Robert B. *A Fraternity of Arms: America and France in the Great War.* 2003.

Cooper, John Milton. *Breaking the Heart of the World: Woodrow Wilson and the Fight for the League of Nations.* 2001.

Dobson, Sean. *Authority and Upheaval in Leipzig, 1910–1920: The Story of a Relationship.* 2001.

Dunn, Seamus, and T. G. Fraser, eds. *Europe and Ethnicity: The First World War and Contemporary Ethnic Conflict.* 1996.

Healy, Maureen. *Vienna and the Fall of the Habsburg Empire: Total War and Everyday Life in World War I.* 2004.

Liulevicius, Vejas Gabriel. *War Land on the Eastern Front: Culture, National Identity, and German Occupation in World War I.* 2000.

Mackaman, Douglas, and Michael Mays, eds. *World War I and the Cultures of Modernity.* 2000.

Roshwald, Aviel. *Ethnic Nationalism and the Fall of Empires: Central Europe, Russia, and the Middle East, 1914–1923.* 2001.

Strachan, Hew. *Financing the First World War.* 2004.

Zeman, Zbynek. *The Masaryks: The Making of Czechoslovakia.* 1990.

Selected Web Sites

There are many useful Web sites about World War I. Both the BBC and PBS offer reliable material on the Web: <**bbc.co.uk/history/worldwars/wwone**>; <**pbs.org/greatwar**>. Information about military leaders and battles is available at <**www.spartacus.schoolnet.co.uk/FWW.htm**>. Documents may be found at the World War I Document Archive, <**lib.byu.edu/~rdh/wwi**>. Cornell University Library has an interesting site that presents the rising authoritarian leaders of the interwar and post–World War II periods: <**cidc.library.cornell.edu/DOF/fathers.htm**>.

4

A World Transformed

1920–1929

IN 1928 THE BRITISH NOVELIST VIRGINIA WOOLF published *Orlando*, a novel depicting an extraordinary character who moves through hundreds of years of history, observing wars, meeting interesting monarchs, and dealing with shady characters. Orlando's saga opens with the youth swinging his saber at the lifeless head of a Moor—a North African—dangling from the rafters of the family's estate. Orlando's forbears had "struck many heads of many colours off many shoulders" and by so doing were representative of the bloody and imperialist lineage of Britain. The frightening first page, showcasing Orlando's blithe games with the skull of an African, constitutes Woolf's clarion call against war and imperialism that had cost so many lives, but the unconventional book also sealed Woolf's place among modernist writers of the time. The novel stressed transformation, not only in the hero's long life span of centuries, during which Orlando experiences the entirety of world history in "the immensely long tunnel in which she seemed to have been traveling for hundreds of years. . . ."[1] More astonishingly, as that quotation suggests, by the end of the novel Orlando has metamorphosed from a bellicose young man into a strikingly intelligent and peace-loving woman.

◆ Virginia Woolf
Virginia Woolf was a brilliant presence in London literary circles. She wrote novels with intriguing characters such as Orlando and Clarissa Dalloway. She also produced stinging indictments of war and women's poverty during the interwar years. *Time Life Pictures/ Getty Images.*

The 1920s were years when many people, like Woolf, craved peace and hoped to distance themselves from Europe's legacy of destruction. World War I had brought years of suffering that was unprecedented for modern Europeans, though perhaps not so unfamiliar to Europe's colonized people. After the war, transformation appeared a distinct possibility. The old order of monarchs and aristocrats had fallen,

1923	Adolf Hitler and Paul von Ludendorff attempt to overthrow Weimar government in Beer Hall Putsch.
1923	Ruinous inflation in Germany.
1923	First Exposition of Household Arts held in Paris.
1924	Dawes Plan reduces German reparations and restores value of German currency.
1924	First Labour Party prime minister elected in Britain but loses ten months later to Conservative Party candidate.
1924	Lenin dies.
1925	Franz Kafka publishes *The Trial*.
1925	Virginia Woolf publishes *Mrs. Dalloway*.
1925–1926	Hitler uses jail time after Beer Hall Putsch to write *Mein Kampf*.
1926	Józef Pilsudski takes over Polish government in a coup.
1926	Miners and other unions in Britain declare a "General Strike" to protest wage cuts.
1927	Theodor van de Velde publishes *Ideal Marriage: Its Physiology and Technique*.
1927	American pilot Charles Lindbergh completes first nonstop solo flight across Atlantic Ocean.
1928	Virginia Woolf publishes *Orlando*.
1928	Egyptians found Muslim Brotherhood to revive Islam and halt Westernization.
1929	Young Plan further reduces German reparation payments.
1929	"Yugoslavia" becomes official name of Kingdom of the Serbs, Croats, and Slovenes.
1929	Erich Maria Remarque publishes *All Quiet on the Western Front*.
1929	Virginia Woolf publishes *A Room of One's Own*.
1929	Mussolini signs Lateran Agreement with papacy.

creating new states in eastern Europe and making room for a more just society that would benefit more people, it was hoped. Some believed that the Bolshevik regime in Russia would realize these dreams. There was also a sense that warlike impulses needed curbing: institutions such as the new League of Nations would facilitate a lasting peace by ending international disagreements through negotiations instead of bloodshed. As leaders of colonial liberation movements became more vocal in their anti-imperial protests in light of their own troops' experience in the Great War, some Europeans began to acknowledge openly that non-Western values, including those of Indian leader Mohandas Gandhi, had much to offer (see Documents 4.2 and 4.3). Orlando's metamorphosis into a woman was inspired by the Hindu spiritual belief that as one lives out one's karma through the ages, the soul is reincarnated into a different body. Gender is thus less important than one's state of spiritual enlightenment. Some saw in this search for inspiration beyond Europe an "Asiatic fever," especially among the young, who believed that a "decadent" postwar Europe hovered on the eve of "a great transformation in the entire spiritual adjustment of the Western world," as one German writer put it.[2]

Even as they tried to cope with the bloody wartime legacy, some leading Europeans came to see the future in utopian terms. The advance of technology during and after the war provided rayon and other synthetic fabrics, which lowered the cost of textiles, while radios and phonographs rolled out of manufacturers' doors. As sales soared, the everyday life of ordinary people promised to improve after wartime sacrifice and suffering. Progress and even perfection stood in the wings, for it seemed that society could be as smoothly running as a machine. Women finally gained the vote in Britain, Germany, and the newly independent countries of eastern Europe, affirming the democratic potential of the modern nation-state. Politicians sponsored the construction of more and more modern housing in hopes that veterans would be satisfied and that good relationships between the sexes might be restored. The Swiss architect Le Corbusier claimed, "The house is a machine for living in," and it was believed that the new and harmonious designs would promote peaceful living. The war actually brought the people of formerly hostile nations closer together, and the increased availability of technology such as radio, film, and cars accelerated this process. Manufacturers touted efficient production for its ability to transform the impoverished workers of the prewar years into well-paid citizens with purchasing power to fuel a burgeoning consumer economy.

Postwar technology sparked a Europe-wide quest to improve society and perhaps achieve utopia, although some visionaries thought this could be achieved only by violence and conquest. The Bolshevik triumph led to the birth of the USSR in 1922 committed Marxists, Lenin and his successor Joseph Stalin believing, that their violent suppression of class enemies and dissent was justified by the final triumph of comunism. Also in 1922, Benito Mussolini came to power in Italy with the help of his fascist bands of Black Shirts. His intention was to restore manly vigor and the mighty Roman Empire through war and conquest. Waiting in the wings in Germany was Adolf Hitler, who admired the violent Mussolini, while across Europe other fascistic groups hewed to a similarly militaristic line about the need to make society more martial and strong. As authoritarian forces triumphed, and as "totalitarian" dictatorships developed, Virginia Woolf wrote other, more explicitly antiwar books. Plagued by depression and the horror of another world catastrophe, she would commit suicide in the early years of World War II.

THE SEARCH FOR STABILITY

Violence continued from Ireland to Russia as well as in Europe's dealings with colonized peoples. Personal stability was hard to come by because wartime industries shut their doors, leaving millions without jobs. Moreover, soldiers returning from the front had a difficult time laying down their arms. Their rage at the experience of unbearable slaughter kept society in turmoil as veterans turned their anger against civilians and politicians. Civil war in Russia and elsewhere advanced in these disturbing years, while not unexpectedly the Peace of Paris left a huge legacy of ill will and instability that further fed civilian discontent. President Woodrow Wilson even admitted during the peace negotiations that his principle of ethnic self-determination was proposed in ignorance—"without the knowledge," as he put it, "that nationalities existed, which are coming to us today."[3] Compounding the ignorance embedded in the Peace of Paris, the victors in this war failed to provide effective leadership to ensure the peace. The United States, a major world economic power, adopted a stance of isolation in political matters, leaving the League of Nations—its invention—to fend for itself. Britain and France were too bankrupt, bitter, and distracted by their own domestic and imperial problems to calm the international waters.

An Unsettled Peace

In the immediate postwar years a warlike atmosphere persisted. As the Whites fought the Bolsheviks for control of the Russian government, continuing civil war in Russia disrupted lives and productivity, leading to famine that ultimately killed five million people. In Germany, even in the early 1920s, half a million men, many of them recently conscripted youth, still in battlefield units, roamed the nation. They fought on German-Polish borders, aiming to recover lost territory for the defeated fatherland, and they intervened in local politics, assassinating thousands of revolutionaries, reformers, and middle-of-the-road politicians. In Hungary, stunned by the loss of territory, leftist militants proclaimed a soviet republic in the winter of 1919. Their leader, Béla Kun, widened his support to include the nationalist middle class when he announced a plan to overturn the hated Trianon Treaty of the Peace of Paris, which had reduced Hungary by 70 percent. Army officers temporarily supported his coup, as did the landowners whom he put in charge of many large tracts of land. However, Kun also nationalized industry and used terrorist secret police tactics on the population. Opponents overthrew his regime late in the summer. In 1920 the new Polish government successfully resisted Poland's reincorporation into Russia by beating back an invasion by Russian soviets who believed that Polish workers would welcome Bolshevism.

In Ireland the British government's brutal repression of the Easter Uprising in 1916 had left such a bitter legacy that moderates on both sides who wanted compromise on the issue of Irish independence lost all credibility. Instead, Sinn Fein, the organization most committed to a free Ireland, became the dominant political force and waged a violent campaign against British institutions, burning buildings, attacking British officials, and generally wreaking havoc. In 1919 republican leaders in Ireland announced the country's independence from Britain and created a separate parliament called the Dáil Éireann. The British government refused to recognize the Dáil and sent in the Black and Tans—a volunteer army of demobilized soldiers named for the color of their uniforms—to subdue the pro-independence forces. Terror reigned in Ireland, as both sides waged guerrilla warfare, taking hostages, blowing up buildings, and shooting into crowds of fans at soccer matches. An outraged British public left the government no option but to stop the bloodshed and settle, which it did by overturning the Irish declaration of independence and by creating the Irish Free State—a self-governing dominion but one still answerable to the British crown. Ulster, a group of six northern counties containing a majority of Protestants, gained a different status as self-governing but with representation in the British parliament. The settlement was so unsatisfactory to the Irish that fighting soon resumed. The quest for full independence for the Irish Free State and for the rights and well-being of Catholic minorities in the northern counties of Ulster would ensure that violence remained intense in the years to come.

Nor were the victorious Allies on the continent pacific or united in their diplomacy. They followed a divided policy after the war, as any shred of consensus quickly vanished. France, hit hardest by wartime destruction and billions of dollars in debt to the United States, estimated that Germany owed it at least $200 billion. A vengeful spirit born of massive reconstruction costs and loss of life made the French determined to punish Germany and claim reparations. "The Germans will pay!" echoed through the Chamber of Deputies whenever deliveries of goods or cash slowed.[4] The British, by contrast, had suffered little damage on their soil and thus showed more financial leniency toward Germany by adopting a conciliatory tone and even arguing that the Versailles Treaty needed immediate revision. Britain worried more about maintaining its expanded empire and restoring prosperity through trade with Germany than about exacting huge reparations. Nevertheless, both France and Britain depended on some monetary redress to pay their war debts to the United States because Europe's share of world trade had plunged dramatically during the war. Although the United States wanted the debts paid, it treated Germany's fragile Weimar Republic gently and adopted a harsher stance toward its Allied debtors. In the postwar American climate of isolation, dwindling U.S. sympathy for Europe caused the growing industrial giant to withdraw from almost all bodies for global cooperation, despite the United States' role in shaping the postwar settlement and its emergence as a great Western power. The United

◆ Verdun

The French town of Verdun was a ruin in January 1918, when these soldiers passed through it. After the war Verdun remained a burning memory because of the months of relentless battle and the massive loss of life. Veterans, families of the dead and wounded, and curious tourists began visiting the battlefield in the 1920s, while the French government built an ossuary to preserve the bones of many who had fallen there. Private companies organized tours as the decade wore on; hotels and restaurants sprang up; and Verdun, like Europe as a whole, was reborn in a dramatically new form. *Hulton Archive/Getty Images.*

States' lack of participation crippled the international commissions and other organizations intended to replace the prewar system of secret alliances and backdoor diplomacy with mechanisms for collective security. The Peace of Paris would break down at crucial moments in the 1930s because of insufficient muscle and will.

Germany claimed that the demand for reparations strained its government, already beset by political upheaval. Indeed, as early as 1919 British economist John Maynard Keynes had predicted a chain of disasters for the entire continent if the German economy were to collapse from the burden of reparations: "An inefficient, unemployed, disorganized Europe faces us, torn by internal strife and international hate, fighting, starving, pillaging and lying."[5] The difficult German situation, however, was not the result of the Peace of Paris alone. The kaiser had refused to control prices or raise taxes, especially on those whose wealth was growing because of soaring profits, to cover the immense costs of the struggle. Thus, the new Weimar Republic simultaneously had to deal with soaring inflation, pay reparations, and finance the staggering domestic war debt. It thus faced a dilemma, because as an experiment in democracy, the fledgling Weimar Republic, established in 1919, also needed to woo the citizenry, not alienate the German people by hiking taxes. In 1921, when Germans refused to present a realistic payment scheme, the French occupied several cities in the Ruhr. Germany then accepted a payment plan that amounted to only $12.5 billion over thirty-six years.

Embroiled with France and other powers to the west, the Weimar government deftly sought economic and diplomatic relations in eastern Europe and reached agreements in 1922 and 1926 that fostered economic ties with Russia, desperate for western trade. As Germany's relations with the powers to the west continued to deteriorate, Germany began secretly rearming. In 1923, after Germany defaulted on coal deliveries, France and Belgium sent troops into the Ruhr basin, planning to seize its abundant resources to recoup their wartime expenditures. Urged on by the Weimar government, Ruhr citizens fought back, shutting down industry and services by staying home from work. At the Krupp factories in Essen, the avid French occupiers shot into a crowd of factory hands who refused to work, killing more than a dozen and further enraging the German population. The German government gave the workers state funerals and, more significant from an economic point of view, printed trillions of marks to support the workers, to provide funds to the closed industries, and to pay its own war debts with practically worthless currency. Soon Germany was experiencing a staggering rate of inflation, which further demoralized its citizens and posed a grave threat to the international economy.

In the postwar spirit of peaceful diplomacy, the League of Nations (Map 4.1) sought to resolve the ongoing acrimony and economic chaos through negotiations. Two League-sponsored agreements, the Dawes Plan (1924) and the Young Plan (1929), reduced payments to the victors and restored the value of German currency. These plans also evened the balance of Germany's trade with east and west, a balance that Germany's economic agreements with Russia had threatened. Only the French were unhappy, but their postwar weakness forced them to accept the reductions, and in the end a diplomatic resolution was reached. Some people took heart from the settlement. In Germany, however, anger remained intense because

▶ **Map 4.1 The League of Nations and the World in 1929**
Founders intended the League of Nations to serve as an institution for collective security. Meeting together regularly, nations would present a united front to prevent war by dealing collectively with issues of aggression. The organization was flawed in several ways, however. It endorsed colonialism, even expanding the grip of the European powers at a time when anticolonial opposition was growing. Still more problematic, three major powers— Germany, the USSR, and the United States—were initially not members of the League and did not participate in its undertakings.

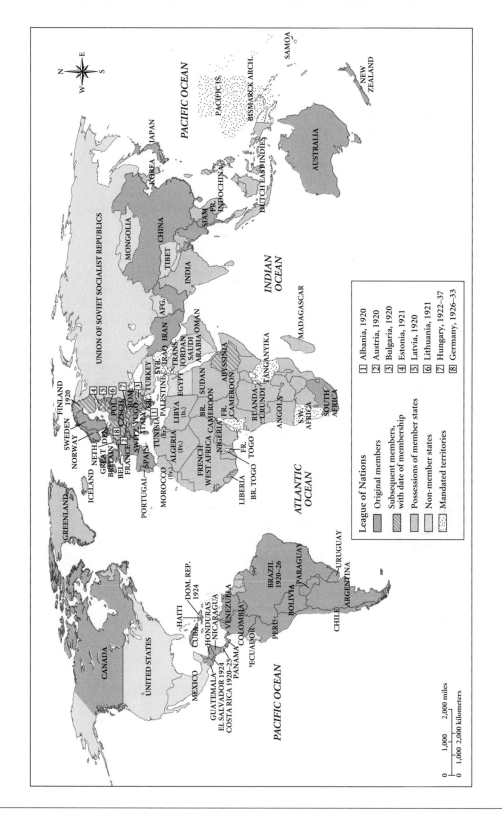

League of Nations

- Original members
- Subsequent members, with date of membership
- Possessions of member states
- Non-member states
- Mandated territories

1 Albania, 1920
2 Austria, 1920
3 Bulgaria, 1920
4 Estonia, 1921
5 Latvia, 1920
6 Lithuania, 1921
7 Hungary, 1922–37
8 Germany, 1926–33

of the widespread belief that any reparation payments at all were unjust. Gustav Stresemann, the German statesman who negotiated the downward revisions in German payments as well as improving his country's standing in the world of nations, became a hated figure and whipping boy for extremist politicians in Germany.

The Weimar Experiment

Defeat and inflation following on four years of unbearable suffering tested the political soundness of Germany—a country that was only half a century old. Intense division followed the abdication of the kaiser and the creation of the Weimar Republic, which was led by the Social Democrats headed by party chief Friedrich Ebert. The Weimar Republic established a parliamentary, federal government with a president elected for seven years. This post, though largely ceremonial, had two important powers: the right to dissolve parliament and the right to issue emergency orders. A chancellor administered the government, after being nominated by the president and approved by the parliament, whose members served four-year terms.

Both reactionaries who wanted a restoration of the imperial political order and Communists who favored a Bolshevik-style revolution in Germany opposed this system precisely because it was parliamentary and appeared to favor a liberal, middle-class consensual form of government. Critics on the right insisted that defeat and the Versailles settlement had brought the downfall of their conservative agrarian and military leaders, because the treaty reduced the size of the officer corps, which had provided them with jobs. The creation of a republican government curtailed their influence and put the hated civilian classes in power. A republic, according to these critics and the demobilized soldiers allied with them, was "an attempt of the slime to govern."[6] They called civilian politicians "November criminals"—a reference to the government responsible for signing the armistice in November 1918. During the first years of the Weimar regime, the military, including leaders like Ludendorff, and demobilized soldiers, like the budding politician Adolf Hitler, staged coups to overturn the government. Hitler and Ludendorff's failed "Beer Hall Putsch"—launched in 1923 in a Munich tavern—is the best-known attempt. Critics on the left, inspired by the Communist takeover in Russia, also wanted to overthrow the Weimar government and held many a raucous protest. Both the right and the left taunted republican politicians in the mass media in order to destroy Weimar's legitimacy. The ensuing turmoil brought street violence, a string of demonstrations, and the assassination of republican politicians by the reactionaries.

Through it all, Weimar politicians in the 1920s gradually consolidated the new system, achieving a downward revision of reparations payments, the establishment of trade relationships to the east, the diplomatic isolation of France, and successful mobilization of the masses to resist attempts to overthrow constitutional government. The daily battering from the political extremes hurt Weimar's credibility, however, and the natural allies of representative government moved to less middle-of-the-road politics because of the wartime experience and the ruinous inflation of

1923. The government had to cut jobs and pay during the crisis, putting teachers, clerks, and government employees out of work. Those who had savings were ruined, as runaway inflation made those savings utterly worthless. Some farmers prospered because they could repay loans on land and modern equipment for the price of a potato. The downward spiral of the middle classes, however, gave the impression that society was being turned upside down and that the "scum" was rising as the respectable classes declined. One critic urged his fellow Germans to "wander through the parlours and fancy eating establishments — everywhere, in every lousy corner you will smack up against the same plump face of the potbellied profiteers of war and peace."

In the 1920s the middle-of-the-road parties lost around a third of their middle-class constituency at the polls even though by the end of the decade the German economy had stabilized and prosperity had reemerged. Instead of receiving praise for its accomplishments, the republic was vilified as the humiliating triumph of all that was bourgeois and Jewish. Among the vilifiers was Adolf Hitler, who used his jail time after the abortive Beer Hall Putsch to write his hate-filled, anti-Semitic *Mein Kampf* (see Document 4.1). As in the case of Hitler, anti-Semitism, which had flourished to explain wartime suffering, became the accepted political rhetoric of peacetime too. In 1925 the war hero Paul von Hindenburg was narrowly elected president, a victory that many saw as a reminder that a "real Germany" persisted beneath the "whorish" facade of the republic.[7]

New Nations in Eastern and Southeastern Europe

Different but equally difficult dilemmas from Germany's plagued the nations emerging from the ruins of defeated Austria-Hungary and those on the fringes of the former Russian Empire. Destroying the Habsburg Empire, the war left the region divided into a host of new states, all of them desperately needing to succeed in nation building. Though exhilarating to Czech, Polish, Serb, and other nationalists, the settlement created daunting problems. The new political entities had to set up effective governments, ensure economic well-being, and create solidarity among a citizenry composed of multiple ethnicities, many living in isolated rural areas. Vast migrations occurred. A million people escaped the civil war in Russia; eight hundred thousand soldiers from the defeated White army demobilized. Two million more people fled Turkey, Greece, and Bulgaria because the postwar settlement stated that the new nations should be built along ethnic lines — "a great unmixing of populations" one statesman reportedly called the trend. Hundreds of thousands more people sought safety in emerging nations with those most closely representing their own ethnic group. Hungary, for example, had to receive three hundred thousand people of Magyar ethnicity who were no longer welcome in Romania, Czechoslovakia, and Yugoslavia. Other refugees, often displaced and landless peasants, crowded into economically devastated areas with no concern for ethnicity, simply looking for support. Without land or jobs, they had nothing to do "but loaf and starve," as an English reporter observed of soldier-refugees in Bulgaria.[8]

Civil wars ensued in various parts of eastern Europe. Romania, Czechoslovakia, and the Kingdom of the Serbs, Croats, and Slovenes invaded Hungary, for instance, to gain more land. Finland and the Baltic states, where refugees also settled, freed themselves from Russian domination but with continuing turmoil. Above all, instability reigned because the new nations lacked a political consensus; rural and urban people often were driven by different concerns. As a result, long-standing and powerful institutions such as the Catholic Church, left in place after the collapse of the Habsburgs, reasserted their own competing authority and values, most notably in Poland and Hungary. Peasant groups were also active because of the land redistribution, carried out fitfully in most of these eastern European countries and posing another challenge to the nation-building process. In theory, aristocratic landowners would surrender tens of thousands of acres to the landless and small peasants who had formerly worked for them as virtual serfs. Despite the mandate for redistribution, however, there was much unevenness to the process, which only intensified animosities. Social and cultural divisions came to the fore, slowing the development of political consensus and stable institutions.

Political conditions both within and among the new nations were shaky. The immediate postwar scramble for territory among citizens meant that even such well-endowed states as Czechoslovakia, which benefited from a strong industrial base, had problems reducing internal conflicts. Adding to their difficulties, the new governments threw up tariff walls against one another, replacing a unified economic region—Austria-Hungary—with small antagonistic economies. Authoritarian figures were not long in gaining power in response to the waves of discontent and disunity especially manifested in the anger of peasants who acquired land just as bumper crops around the world were causing prices to sink. In 1920 in Hungary, Admiral Miklós Horthy ended the postwar chaos caused by the 1919 Communist takeover by Belá Kun and the invasion and occupation of Budapest by the Romanians. Using support from the church and old elites eager to regain power, the authoritarian government under Horthy trampled on the basic rights of non-Hungarian minorities with the excuse that they were foreign to the Hungarian soul. The church and intellectuals turned away from the secularism on which many states to the west had built national unity, instead celebrating the Hungarian nation as the bulwark of Christianity and thus casting Jews as dangerous outsiders despite the centrality of liberals, Jews, and other ethnicities to reviving the Hungarian economy.

Anti-Semitism became a preferred mechanism for fostering unity in several other new nations, a prominent example being Poland. During the war the patriotic leader of the "Polish legions," Józef Pilsudski, had started fighting for the Central Powers but changed sides when he saw that they would lose. In 1926 he took over the government of Poland in a violent coup d'état, deftly working to pull his country out of its economic difficulties by selling coal and gaining new economic allies. Like leaders of other new countries, he had to deal with class divisions. Large landowners and urban business elites banded together in support of Pilsudski in hopes of controlling peasants and workers. Anti-Semitism fused these competing groups into a national whole by uniting them in blaming Jews for the common problem of economic hardship. Although ethnic conflict existed and rural life was deteriorating, the poorly developed and badly coordinated economic infrastructure was of greater concern to urban, modernizing nation builders. Having formerly been divided among three countries, Poland had neither a uniform currency nor uniformly spaced train tracks.

Declared on December 1, 1918, independently of the peace conference, the Kingdom of the Serbs, Croats, and Slovenes faced similar nation-building problems. Its very name contained the seeds of discontent, for it preserved the primacy of the Serbs and made no mention of many of the other ethnicities residing in the kingdom. Those groups constituted some 20 percent of the population because the Balkans for centuries had been a crossroads of conquerors and migrants. The most recent settlers had come from the Habsburg Empire. Hundreds of thousands of demobilized soldiers from the peasantry also had complicated mixtures of ethnic and regional loyalties—not national ones. Nonetheless, unification into a single nation was not a totally new idea. Shortly before the war, young and well-educated members of the urban middle class had helped foster a climate favoring the merger of all the region's peoples into a state to be called "Yugoslavia"—literally "country of the South Slavs." Many Serbs, however, having borne the brunt of Austrian force in World War I and emerging as one of the victors, favored a centralized state based on Serbian leadership—a greater Serbia. Although the popular "Yugoslavia" became the official name in 1929, Serbs dominated the new government, and their power fostered bitter division and led almost immediately to calls for secession by the Slovenes, Croats, Montenegrins, and other ethnic groups.

Dominating the parliament, administration, and monarchy, the Serbs worked to achieve national cohesion through the institutions of a centralized government. Simultaneously, newspapers and novels promoted an active debate about the best ways to fuse the many Balkan cultures into one. "If we accustom our people truly to look at our literature as a single whole," one editor claimed, "all of that would be a great deed. In this way greater assimilation would occur all by itself."[9] Educators were often successful in introducing the sense of a "Yugoslav" cultural tradition into primers and anthologies, but government officials gave scant support to the nation-building effort, little sensing its importance to their own success. Squabbles among politicians from the varying factions escalated in severity and erupted into such violence that ultimately one of them was shot by a colleague in the floor of the parliament in 1928. As a result of the utter failure to reach a consensus on the form of rule or even to maintain minimal political tranquillity, the monarch, Aleksandar I, declared himself dictator but compromised by officially changing the name of the kingdom to Yugoslavia. Based in the Yugoslav ideal, Aleksandar's political solution failed to quell the bitter strife, and he himself was assassinated in 1934.

Political and Economic Recovery in Great Britain and France

Like most people in Germany and the new states of eastern Europe, the bulk of ordinary British and French citizens, many of them grief-stricken and worn, wanted national politics and their lives restored to a peacetime status quo. But for the victorious Allies too, civil and political unrest followed in the wake of World War I. In Britain continuing violence by returning soldiers and by armies in the colonies, a sinking postwar economy, and the embittered climate surrounding Irish independence so tarnished the reputation of David Lloyd George's Liberal government that in 1924 the first Labour Party prime minister, Ramsay MacDonald, was elected. The belief that he would give workers a fair deal brought him to office, but his working-class background made him too eager to please and deferential to the upper classes. MacDonald believed in parliamentary institutions rather than revolution; however, he failed to win over the business community and lost the support of his natural working-class constituency. After only ten months in office, in late 1924 the Conservative Stanley Baldwin was elected prime minister in a campaign noted for his effective use of radio. Baldwin was the first British politician to bone up on the new medium's requirements and defeat his opponent with what would become the well-worn ploy of calling a political enemy "soft on communism." Baldwin built on postwar anxieties: "Democracy has arrived at a gallop in England," he warned of MacDonald's followers, ". . . it is a race for life; can we educate them before the crash comes?"[10]

Economic problems shaped the political landscape, as the foundations of British industrial wealth cracked with old age. In 1912 the British textile industry produced 8 million square yards of goods; in 1930 as the Great Depression was beginning, only 3.3 million. The coal industry faced intense pressure, not only from more efficient producers elsewhere but from stagnating demand for coal because of new fuels such as oil. Manufacturers of iron, steel, and other products were increasingly uncompetitive because of their failure to modernize procedures, and the deterioration in these industries bred political discontent. There were gains in new sectors such as synthetics and automobiles, but workers in older sectors felt real distress. In 1925 mine owners announced that the only way to keep the coal mines open was to cut wages. Unions countered that the owners needed to modernize and make the business more efficient. The miners themselves were irate. They and many other workers were expecting increased concern for their well-being in return for their contributions to the war effort. Many were in sympathy with the Bolsheviks. To their chagrin, in 1926 a government commission endorsed the wage cuts. The miners went on strike, joined by other major unions. To the amazement of many strikers, the declaration of this "General Strike" roused the ire and the determination of the middle classes that Britain would not be shut down. Students, housewives, businessmen, and professionals kept the country running by driving trains and loading ships as if they were back in wartime. Anti-union legislation followed, breaking the strength of the unions without addressing the causes of persistent economic deterioration.

Even more than in Britain, the postwar political leadership in France seemed unable to address postwar problems with vigor and commitment. Although France had modern automobile and aircraft industries and a robust heavy manufacturing sector, it was still less developed industrially than either Germany or Britain, and faced grave financial problems resulting from the war—including the costs of rebuilding devastated regions of the country. Unlike countries where loss of life and devastation were less, France experienced not only full employment but an actual labor shortage that attracted migrant workers from the entire Mediterranean region. Yet paying for everything was an obstacle that successive administrations met by simply printing money and demanding more from the Germans. The first postwar French government was a coalition of conservative and right-leaning parties—the "blue horizon" it was called because so many of its leading figures wore uniforms. It was hard for these men to overcome the bitterness of the war experience, so their main policy initiative was to press Germany hard in the Ruhr. Fearing the outbreak of another war, the French public threw these leaders out and brought to power a coalition of left-leaning politicians from the Radical and Socialist parties. These groups focused on boosting population. To make sure that women reproduced after the incredible loss of life, the Radical leadership helped pass draconian legislation against the spread of information about birth control, the sale or dissemination of birth-control devices, and the practice of abortion. By the early 1940s abortion was a capital crime. Utterly incapable of resolving the crucial economic problems of debt management and industrial modernization, these politicians became absorbed with old-fashioned political maneuvering, which gradually but also dangerously reduced confidence in parliamentary democracy.

SOCIETY RECOVERS

Profoundly shaken, Europeans expanded rituals of commemoration after the war; but even as they mourned, consumers turned to restocking their households after four years of wartime shortages, and governments set out to repair wartime damage. Industrialists and planners had improved productivity during the war, and these improvements shaped the postwar return to consumer manufacturing. To calm a rebellious citizenry, politicians and businessmen worked to provide greater leisure, better housing, and somewhat more economic security for the average person. Mass culture flourished, and the mass entertainment of radio, films, and books reached millions, perhaps distracting some of them from the lingering pain of the Great War.

Remembering the Great War

Europeans filled the continent with cemeteries for the war dead, but the massive loss of life changed even the most traditional rituals of mourning. His son killed on the battlefield, author Rudyard Kipling was among those who influenced the decision that all tombstones for individual soldiers—rich or poor—would be the same. Wealth, he maintained, should not allow some to "proclaim their grief above other people's grief" when rich and poor had died the same death in the same cause.[11] Buried side by side in common graves, rich and poor were commemorated with simple markers such as small crosses. To preserve the memory of war, towns and even tiny villages erected costly monuments, often quarreling over the representational style and the images to be used. Such commemoration could divide but it could also bring together people who had experienced the war differently—home front and battlefront, protesters and militants, deserters and decorated veterans—minimizing conflict and class issues in the creation of a common national memory.

As the population remained haunted by the war, both returning soldiers and the civilian population found outlets for expressing rage and softer sentiments about their wartime experiences. Veterans hastened to publish their war memoirs in the hope that the memory of their experience would live on: some twenty-five hundred war poets published in Britain alone. Battlefield tourism arose, aided by trains and buses, printed guidebooks, and the construction of restaurants and hotels near every major battleground. People flocked to churches for comfort, and in more bizarre behavior, many professed to see traces of dead soldiers in shadows on photographs, for example, or floating through public spaces. Occult practices such as séances peaked, spreading into the rhetoric of politics, which acquired a sacred, glorified tone. While some people criticized the war as a horrific waste of humanity and resources resulting from the actions of big business and power-hungry governments, others sanctified the killing, seeing in the deaths of soldiers a spiritual event—a holy sacrifice in the service of an equally holy nation. Polish soldiers, for instance, who fought against one another for the Habsburg, Russian, and German empires, nonetheless mythologized: "Poland has not yet perished, / So long as the Riflemen live / . . . God's grace is with you, / We shall build Poland from sea to sea."[12] The spiritualization of murder, especially by veterans and fledgling politicians, shaped fascism, communism, and nazism, inspiring a cult of violence and murder as sacred. To sell newspapers on street corners and in train stations, the mass media carried accounts of battlefields as sacred places of sacrifice. The head of the Soviet Cheka (the first of many Soviet secret police organizations) in these same years called the ideal secret police agent "pure in spirit" and saw in the murders committed by the Cheka a spiritual "cleansing" or "purge" of the nation.[13] The tendency to sanctify war and murder in the 1920s redefined the nature of patriotism.

There was also bitter disagreement over how to understand the war. Some soldiers considered the war to be essentially meaningless, an incoherent four years—neither sacred nor romantically tragic. One Frenchman wrote that at the beginning of the war his "heart skip[ped] a beat" when he encountered a cadaver but thereafter he quickly felt "a hard coldness, a dry indifference, a kind of shrinking of the spirit" at the sight of dead comrades.[14] German novelist Erich Maria Remarque described his best-selling *All Quiet on the Western Front* (1929) as a "report on the generation that was destroyed by the war—even if they escaped the grenades."[15] Veterans in the postwar years often resorted to satire, irony, and flippancy to express their rage and revulsion at the collapse of civilization the war represented. The German artist George Grosz depicted maimed soldiers and brutally murdered women in his drawings and paintings. He also caricatured the fat-cat businessmen and bankers who had profited handsomely from the war, showing them cavorting with grotesque women decked out in sleazy finery. The drawings of Grosz's countryman Otto Dix showed the hideously maimed faces of dead soldiers, worms and insects eating away at the remaining flesh; Dix too produced vivid paintings of women hacked to death. Käthe Kollwitz, another artist in defeated Germany, executed unforgettable woodcuts and sculpture of starving children, blinded veterans of war, and bereft parents of fallen soldiers.

From Wartime to Peacetime Productivity

The need to rebuild and to restock empty cupboards fueled some sectors of the postwar economy. Several million migrants, moving to escape civil war and to find opportunity, contributed to the work of reconstruction. Peasants from eastern Europe, plagued by the turmoil of civil war and the uncertainties of land redistribution, sought jobs in urban areas or moved to western Europe, where farmhands were needed. Polish workers went to France, where more than a million farmers had been killed or incapacitated in the war and where the work of rebuilding was vast in the northwestern part of the country. Migration from the colonies also increased, as the rebuilding of European commerce shut down colonial businesses that had grown up during the war. Before World War I, around five thousand Algerians worked as migrants in France. Between 1920 and 1925, approximately twenty times that number came, many of them as conscripts and forced laborers, because all opportunity had evaporated in their homeland. "Is this Africa or still France?" one popular song went. "The Arabs bow as if you're a mullah." A trend started taking shape in which colonization and globalization would make Europe more multicultural and multiethnic.

Although it took European industry as a whole a decade to return to prewar levels of productivity, there were immediate success stories: the electrical industry across Europe, for instance, grew at a rate of 7 percent annually, and European automobile manufacturers began setting the pace in small automobiles. The balance sheet, however, was uneven. Some industrialists had learned lessons in efficiency, innovation, and management, but others simply drove their workers harder. Artisanal rather than factory production of furniture, clothing, and household goods remained strong, leaving the biggest gains in productivity to occur outside Europe. In the United States car manufacturer Henry Ford had introduced assembly-line production before the war, and many European entrepreneurs thus looked to the United States for models of how to streamline output. They also imported the methods of U.S. efficiency experts such as Frederick Taylor to improve the operation of the workforce. Ford's innovations allowed for costs to be cut and wages raised, transforming his workers into consumers even of expensive goods such as the very automobiles they produced. In 1912, there were some 900,000 automobiles in the United States; by the end of the 1920s, over 23 million.

Some industrialists traveled to the United States to gain firsthand knowledge of the new techniques. They found an array of new practices to increase worker productivity, including time-motion studies pioneered by Taylor that changed the bodily movements of workers performing specific tasks. Capitalism in America, one analyst wrote, "is not ethically better than in Germany but is economically much smarter."[16] Europeans saw in the United States an efficient economic system that allowed for high wages and thus mass consumerism. Participating in such transatlantic research was a group of increasingly internationalized entrepreneurs who joined together in ventures for oil exploration, shipping, and the development of pharmaceuticals. Mergers created gigantic globalized industries in the interwar years, but at the same time industrialists also kept their cultural distinctiveness. European efficiency experts studied mental fatigue as well as physical efficiency, insisting that mental not physical activities were key and that breaks and vacation time would increase productivity. The upshot of this idea was the gradual introduction of vacation days in Europe, far beyond the number allotted U.S. workers. Many union officials approved of the changes because wartime cooperation with managers had led them to make productivity a top priority. Many agreed that increased productivity would improve the lot of European workers as it was improving that of Americans. Efficiencies on the factory floor and in organizing production, marketing, exploration for resources, and attention to working-class leisure, marked the cutting edge of business and union leadership in the 1920s.

Nonetheless many workers found that these new procedures intensified their work, and in an uncertain economic climate, many were afraid to complain. As in the past, new machines put people out of work, and in areas of declining industries such as coal, unemployment was becoming permanent, and families were struggling to survive. Some who remained employed found that the machines reduced their fatigue, and they appreciated this aspect of change. To pay for the machines, however, bosses often reduced wages. "Everything is agitated, everything is hurried. American methods—without American wages or prices," one German metalworkers' newspaper put it.[17] Workers' movements, even their bathroom breaks, were regulated. Some workplaces forbade talking altogether. "When I left the factory, it followed me," wrote a French metalworker. "In my dreams I was a machine." One response was renewed worker activism, and union membership soared right after the war and into the early 1920s. Socialist and communist activism also flourished in the expectation that the day of the veteran and the worker was at hand.

Social Change in the Postwar Years

Governments faced a rebellious citizenry at the end of the war, and to dampen the revolutionary spirit, politicians focused on providing a better standard of living and a return to family life. Improved housing—including what the British called "homes for heroes"—was at the top of many a postwar agenda because both wartime destruction of housing stock and the failure to build civilian housing during the war had created shortages. From Bucharest to Stockholm and Vienna an unprecedented building boom took place across Europe in the 1920s (see the Picture Essay). The city government of Vienna built large apartment complexes with laundry rooms, common cooking facilities, and day care centers; the apartments featured high-quality heating and plumbing systems. An adjunct to urban living, suburbanization also occurred, facilitated by ever improving mass transit, increasing numbers of roads, and the wider distribution of the automobile. Rising

◆ **London Flappers**

These 1929 "flappers"—photographed paying for a taxi—represented the new freedom many women found after the war. Wartime shortages made skimpier clothing for women a necessity, and many women workers cut their hair short to avoid accidents in the workplace and because maintaining it was easier. Men's clothing changed too, as uniforms became drab rather than displayed flashy colors, and men and women alike dressed in the relaxed clothing that grew more fashionable with the spread of sports and vigorous leisure activities. *The Granger Collection, New York.*

global productivity in agriculture freed up land for residential use around European cities. Suburbanization spawned chic neighborhoods with massive houses but also gave rise to an even greater number of neighborhoods filled with modest single-story houses or bungalows modeled on the small rectangular buildings that Europeans had marveled at when they first started colonizing South Asia (see the Picture Essay).

While the snug nest of the bungalow represented something of a refuge for postwar heterosexual couples, the separation of home front from battlefront had generated suspicion between the sexes. Some veterans returned to find women unappealingly transformed by bobbed hair and tailored clothes, smoking, holding jobs, and spending money of their own. For their part, many women had a hard time welcoming men whom they saw as hardened killers who had lived with filth, decay, and death. Young men in England returned to vandalize university classrooms and to brutalize women working as conductors and holding factory jobs, and veterans on the continent, refusing to disband, continued to terrorize and even murder civilians. The population of Europe had declined, and marriage had dropped to astonishingly low rates. Despite a mini-marriage boom at the war's end, an alarming number of men and women seemed to prefer a return to separate spheres, and glamorous same-sex couples attracted attention. The youthful energy that singles expended in jazz clubs and cinemas did not augur well for a sustained rebound in the marriage and birth rates. The flapper, a sexually liberated and single working woman, took center stage in films, pushing the dedicated housewife to the side. It was not that norms had totally changed, but rather those living outside the norm were prominently featured in the press and other mass media.

Alongside the program for family housing, in the private sphere marriage and sex manuals appeared, ushering in the turn to books rather than to clergy or family for advice and giving dramatic evidence that the war had undermined Victorian reticence in sexual matters. In 1918, British scientist Marie Stopes published the best seller *Married Love*, which featured frank discussions of sexual relations. In 1927, the wildly successful *Ideal Marriage: Its Physiology and Technique* by Dutch author Theodor van de Velde appeared. Translated into dozens of languages, van de Velde's book, like Stopes's, described sex in rhapsodic terms, crediting it with being the centerpiece of a successful relationship. Information about physiology and birth control educated couples about how to limit family size now that urban living had made the large farm family obsolete. New women's magazines touted the pleasures of married life and taught women of all classes how to make the home more inviting. Screwball comedies about the perils of marriage poked fun at the institution while making it entertaining to millions of filmgoers. The job of social recovery reached deep into the intimacy of the home.

Leisure and Consumerism

New leisure activity in the 1920s, including consumerism, also helped erase memories of the war. Rising productivity and increased time off from work allowed people to escape to the mountains and seaside for skiing and swimming vacations.

The healing and revivifying properties of sunshine, exercise, and seawater were touted to an urban population. Small bungalows also made possible cheap sojourns at the shore, in the forests, and in the mountains of Europe, where nature—increasingly remote—could be enjoyed. The war had made people thinner and pushed endurance to the limit, making it easier to identify with public figures in sports. Heroes with physical prowess came to the fore, as they swam the English Channel, excelled at team sports, climbed ever higher mountains, and skied faster. The American pilot Charles Lindbergh typified the craving for larger-than-life heroes. Europeans wildly celebrated his nonstop solo flight from the United States across the Atlantic to Paris in 1927. People made their bodies sleek and buff, like those of heroes, and they wore trimmer, more revealing clothes as if they were athletes or were in training to become athletes. Women bobbed their hair, wore deodorant, sported suntans, and underwent cosmetic surgery to fit popular images of fitness, youth, and beauty.

For many, youth symbolized the new postwar beginning, and there was a temporary focus on youth as emblematic of future hopes. The state, more effectively centralized because of the war, enforced the school-leaving age with new vigor. Thus, more boys and girls tended to stay in school until the age of approximately fourteen to sixteen. A broader array of social programs—such as pensions for veterans, old-age assistance, and subsidies to families to provide for medical care and necessities such as milk—somewhat reduced the burden on youth wages to support the family, giving some young people with jobs new spending power. Young people became important consumers of the mass cinema, modern fashions in clothing, and the sociability found in dance halls, pubs, and cafés. Advertisers started to tap into this new market, and political parties recognized the electoral potential of the youth vote. Communist, socialist, fascist, and religiously based political parties started programs for young people.

Trendsetters in culture and consumption began looking to America, which embodied the youthfulness of postwar civilization. The United States flourished in the 1920s thanks to the wealth it made from the war. Whether in advertising, popular music and film, or business methods, the United States had had the opportunity to innovate while Europeans were mired in battles. Europeans loved American films and pulp stories devoted to the Wild West. The carefree modern "girl" fascinated them, and journalists fixated on "Girlkultur" or the prominence of young women in everyday American life. Jazz was especially attractive to the young and avant-garde. "The shakening and loosening of bodies. Only that can help us," wrote a German critic, praising the cultural energy that seemed to have passed to the United States. Others saw jazz as akin to the war in its effect because it demolished middle-class hypocrisy: "it knocks down every hint of dignity, correct posture, and starched collars."[18] Entranced by the United States, European artists, engineers, and architects visited and even migrated permanently. But Americans continued to value European culture, some choosing to become expatriates like Gertrude Stein and Ernest Hemingway. The internationalization of style intensified around the adoption by European and other societies of American consumer goods and culture.

The machine age, as some began to call the postwar era, featured the public consumption of small appliances—electric toasters, irons, radios, phonographs—that enhanced domestic life. The war had been mechanical and modern, creating a desire for those characteristics in home furnishings. Charlotte Perriand, a furniture designer of lower-class origins who with the architect Le Corbusier would introduce chairs made of tubular steel, early in the 1920s started the trend of ridding the household interior of sofas and overstuffed chairs. She replaced hers with nothing but a metal bar for drinks and sleek bar stools. In 1923 in Paris the first Exposition of Household Arts took place to publicize all sorts of gadgets and modern appliances for wealthy and more modest homes alike, and displays of new equipment for the household soon became a regular and highly popular attraction, drawing audiences from across Europe and North America. The Bauhaus movement began in Germany in 1919 to consider the design of machine-made objects, including furniture. Among its many streamlined products was a "modern" kitchen, with all white cabinets and counters imitating those of a scientific laboratory. Spare, utilitarian, and stripped of Victorian curlicues, Bauhaus style influenced the interior design of government-sponsored housing for workers, allowing housewives to become efficient like their husbands working in factories.

RESURGENCE OF EMPIRE IN AN AGE OF UNREST

Despite the trauma of war, Europeans reasserted their imperialist goals. The war strengthened Europeans militarily, if not politically or economically, and in the 1920s they expanded their imperialist activity. The mandate system gave Britain, France, and other victors access not only to Germany's colonies in Africa but to the riches of the fallen Ottoman Empire in the Middle East. Improved military hardware, faster steamships, and renewal of worldwide business activity raised Britain and France to the height of their global power despite postwar problems at home. Here was a paradox: enjoying an expanded imperial base, Europeans were also culturally more dependent on foreign goods and economically more reliant on the proceeds from foreign taxation and profits. In the face of Europeans' reasserted domination and simultaneous dependency, colonial people around the world grew angrier and more resentful. Leaders of independence movements harnessed that anger, reaching out to the masses instead of confining their activism to the elites.

A Growing Imperial Appetite

Though bankrupted and shell-shocked in the years following 1918, Britain and France along with the Netherlands, Belgium, Japan, and Australia profited from an expanding network of global enterprises. European owners controlled the major petroleum companies, which extracted Middle Eastern and Indonesian oil to fuel growing numbers of automobiles, airplanes, trucks, ships, and buses and to heat homes. Along with oil, Europeans more regularly enjoyed foreign products such as hot chocolate and tropical fruit—items provided by the Swiss food giant Nestlé and other global firms. Marketed to the rest of the world, European films were often set in the newly fashionable areas of North Africa and the Middle East; the desert was a common backdrop for operettas and movies. Sporting events such as cricket and boxing were internationalized as big business in the interwar years. British cricket teams competed with teams from the West Indies, New Zealand, and other parts of the Commonwealth. From the economy to the dinner table to leisure activities, global ties were tightened in the interwar years, and renewed colonial bureaucracies monitored the extension of business and influence into new areas.

Popular and high culture continued to flourish under the influence of the world outside Europe. Dance halls across Europe welcomed the African American exotic dancer and singer Josephine Baker, who wore skirts made of bananas and imitated "savages" in her performances. White performers wore blackface makeup to make themselves appear as if they came from societies that Europeans had depicted as "barbarian." American jazz and blues performers were said to represent a more intuitive, less rational musical tradition because of its African heritage. Composers produced operas and ballet scores about Africans, African Americans, and people of color in the Caribbean. In Paris, Darius Milhaud wrote the score for *The Creation of the World*, a ballet that enacted an African creation myth and took its choreography from an anthropological film of African ceremonies. Couples learned the tango and other Latin American dances and sang pop songs such as "My Tonkin Woman," after the French colonial city in Vietnam. Interest in the colonies led to more extensive tourism and more colonial expositions and ethnographic museums. Thus Europe's global ties significantly enriched and expanded Europeans' cultural experiences.

Postwar Imperial Policies and Colonial Unrest

The balance of power among the imperial nations was changing, however. One major development was increasing competition with Japan for markets, resources, and influence. During the war, Japanese industrialization had altered dramatically from the production of textiles to heavy industry such as shipbuilding and metallurgy. Japan's industrial development advanced because of the Western powers' outsourcing the production of industrial goods for their wartime needs. As Japan took shipping, financial, and other business from Britain and France, Japanese prosperity skyrocketed, intensifying the challenge to Britain as the dominant power in China. The Japanese government touted its success across the region and pointed to its achievements as a sign of the political and economic ascent of Asia after years of subservience to and exploitation by Western imperialists. Japanese politicians claimed that Japan's prosperity would pull neighbors such as Indonesia and Indochina from their oppression. Strongly nationalist, the government of Japan was nonetheless accommodating toward the Western powers because it could not afford to compete militarily with them at that moment. Thus, although outraged by the Western powers' refusal officially to condemn racial discrimination in the Peace of Paris, the Japanese government cooperated in the Anglo-American-dominated peace settlement, even agreeing at the 1921 naval conference in

Washington to a treaty that set the tonnage ratio of English, American, and Japanese battleships at a disadvantageous 5:5:3. "Rolls Royce, Rolls Royce, Ford," a Japanese official commented bitterly.[19]

Most exploited colonial peoples expected imperialism's contraction not its expansion after the war. For in order to gain colonized people's wartime sacrifice of life and resources, European combatants had promised them new rights and freedoms. The postwar broadening of the victorious powers' exploitative activity thus seemed especially galling. Rebellion erupted and political turmoil followed in the wake of the Peace of Paris. On May 4, 1919, Chinese students in Beijing protested the awarding of Germany's territorial holdings in the Pacific to Japan, especially Japanese control over the Shandong Peninsula. Labor unions joined the protesting students, and merchants closed their businesses in solidarity as a boycott of Japanese goods took shape. In Syria, supporters of King Faisal fought a series of battles in 1920 against the French army sent to occupy the new French mandate. Motivating many of these rebellions was the promise of self-determination enshrined in Wilson's Fourteen Points, which the victors were now ignoring.

The attitude of superiority among the French and British entering the new mandate areas of the Middle East, and the betrayal of wartime promises, angered local rulers and members of the merchant and financial classes. After forcing Faisal to abdicate in 1920, the French high commissioner in Syria, General Henri Gouraud, called the people of the mandate France's "adopted children," freed from "a bad prince" by a country that would be a "true mother" to them.[20] As the French pitted Christian against Muslim and rich against poor, hundreds of opposition societies took shape despite improvements to schooling, public health, and infrastructure such as roads that came with the occupation. Opposition groups sensed the weakness of the occupying powers. In Egypt a nationalist movement led by a political party called the Wafd, and backed by a populace, outraged at the confiscation of property and forced labor during the war staged ongoing demonstrations against the British. The anger was so pervasive that the British agreed to grant Egypt independence in 1922. The continuing presence of British troops across the country, however, showed that the old colonial relationship remained in place.

Also feeding anger in the Middle East was the British-sponsored settlement of European Jews in Palestine. Influenced by rising nationalist and Zionist sentiment and reeling from the rising tide of anti-Semitic violence across Europe, Jews had only recently come to settle on Palestine as the homeland that Zionist leaders had urged them to seek. In 1920 Britain was awarded the region as a mandate, and British imperialists renewed their efforts to create a white and reliable state there that would reinforce the safety of the Suez Canal and the increasingly important oil pipelines. To justify Jewish settlement, they used the arguments they had employed when colonizing parts of Africa, Asia, and North America earlier: they claimed that the territory was nearly uninhabited and thus waiting for settlers to populate it, and they argued that the arrival of European capital, technology, and advanced ideas would "civilize" the tens of thousands of Palestinians whose lands would be taken. In 1920 and 1921 the Palestinians rebelled against what to them was only the latest phase of imperialist overreach. The situation was especially bitter because they had been promised autonomy as a reward for their contributions to the Allied war effort. Britain shrugged this promise off, while Zionists hoped that Palestine really was their "promised land."

Mass Resistance Grows

Resistance mounted in the colonies, as Europeans, driven by the need to restore their war-devastated economies, became more entrenched and more demanding even as their armies and resources were stretched thin. Having promised reforms in the administration of India, the British gave India very little of substance when it came to self-rule and only allowed a place in the League of Nations as a nonindependent member. Britain even selected the Indian delegates. Under the guise of reform, the British enacted laws that increased the penalties for speaking out against British rule and that assigned more responsibilities to local leaders in an obvious ploy to make them appear responsible for tax increases by the imperial government. These insulting measures led to the refusal by the India National Congress—the organization formed in 1885 by elite Indians to lobby for greater autonomy—to cooperate with Britain's schemes. Protest erupted. At Amritsar in 1919, the British massacred civilian pilgrims whose ranks contained nonviolent protesters against the new laws. Even citizens back in England were shocked by the number of casualties—close to four hundred dead and twelve hundred wounded. The Amritsar Massacre galvanized the activist lawyer Mohandas Gandhi to use the strategy of satyagraha, or nonviolent protest, against British rule and to continue the boycott of British goods that other Indian leaders had started before the war.

Gandhi's tactics hit Britain where it hurt. During the war, independent Indian manufacturers had prospered by making textiles for uniforms and parts for munitions because the British themselves could not keep up with the insatiable demands of total war. After the war, the British not only wanted the trade back for British businesses but also wanted to maintain the high level of taxes they had imposed on India to pay for the European war. Educated in England, Gandhi (1869–1948) understood Britain's economic weakness and sensed its moral vulnerability. He urged his fellow citizens to forgo alcohol on which the British imposed high taxes: "Many problems can be solved," Gandhi wrote early in his career, "by remembering that money is their God."[21] He fostered civil disobedience with the clear knowledge of the propaganda value of British forces beating and arresting people who simply stood silently demonstrating their commitment to basic human rights. Whenever his followers began to resort to violence, the authoritarian and austere Gandhi would call the demonstration off until self-discipline returned. Despite his conservatism when it came to maintaining the hierarchical and grossly unequal caste system among Indians themselves, Gandhi's leadership appealed to millions, and armed with this support, he became a formidable foe (see Documents 4.2 and 4.3). Frustrated by strikes and nonviolent protests, the British arrested Gandhi in 1922 and sentenced him to six years in prison. Headquartered in a colonial jail, Gandhi's movement for Indian independence now gained real momentum.

◆ **Gandhi Spinning**
Mohandas Gandhi, a sophisticated Indian lawyer trained in Britain, became an icon of
colonial resistance to Europe. He built his reputation by refusing to show deference to
Western values that he deemed materialistic and warlike. Instead Gandhi sought to display
the spiritual strength of non-Western peoples through simple practices like growing his own
food and here, in 1925, spinning cloth for his own clothes. Eschewing Western values and
technologies, he believed, would develop the inner discipline he and his followers needed
to support his program of nonviolent resistance. *Hulton Archive/Getty Images.*

In 1921 a pan-African congress took place, part of a rising tide of activism by
people of African descent. The congress brought together hundreds of Africans,
Europeans, and Americans in three meetings in London, Brussels, and Paris—the
heart of imperialist Europe. From the London meeting, African American intellectual W. E. B. Du Bois issued "To the World," a ringing indictment of the oppression
of Africans particularly by the British and Americans. "The world must face two
eventualities," the manifesto proclaimed, either the assimilation of Africans as
completely equal citizens into the West or the achievement of a free "great African

state" so developed that it could stand on its own.[22] Du Bois condemned the imperialist looting of African wealth and human resources, which, he warned, diminished the ability of Africans to shape their own destiny. Simultaneously, in the United States Marcus Garvey, the Jamaican-born founder of the Universal Negro Improvement Association, inspired African Americans with his support for the migration of black Americans to Africa and his message of "Africa for the Africans." The French West African poet Léopold Senghor and other intellectuals founded a literary and political movement based on "Négritude," awareness of and pride in the traditions, arts, and cultures of Africa. Embracing "blackness," intellectuals in the Négritude movement laid the groundwork in the late 1920s and 1930s for later attempts to move beyond civil rights alone and toward a positive valuation and appreciation for the achievements of people of color.

In the 1920s the European powers in Africa accelerated their exploitation and development of the continent, bringing prosperity to local producers of cocoa, palm oil, coffee, and other agricultural products. Developing railroads and other infrastructure with forced African labor, the Europeans also oversaw the construction of institutions such as schools and hospitals to combat the spread of disease. Africans often had contradictory responses to this complex legacy. Some, notably Blaise Diagne, the West African delegate to the French National Assembly, challenged Du Bois's position. Like other African American intellectuals also living in Paris at the time, Diagne found admirable elements in French culture and society. Africans, he argued, wanted to remain French, not gain second-rate status as an independent state. Some Egyptian nationalists wanted to adopt European dress and construct a Western-style state, but others turned to the Muslim Brotherhood, founded in 1928 to revive Islam and halt Westernization. Across the globe colonized peoples were seeking justice and freedom. They may have had differing agendas, but they all were part of the political resistance sweeping the colonial world after World War I.

AN AGE OF EXTREMES

Postwar society was swirling with cultural and political debates about the future. The bitterness with which many viewed the war was matched by the glorification and spiritualization of the war by nationalist politicians, writers, and ordinary citizens. Fascist and Nazi movements arose, promising perfectly run societies, and Communists in the Soviet Union promoted their own vision of a workers' paradise. Artists and writers were enthralled by the possibilities in modern society for machine-like perfection and deeper insights into the human psyche. Simultaneously, however, writers such as Franz Kafka saw the reverse side of the coin—the overwhelming power of government and bureaucracy, thought control, and the decline of freedom. Ideas and politics alike swung between optimism and despair, pacifism and militarism, making the 1920s an age of extremes.

Utopias and Dystopias

Pessimism gripped some writers in the 1920s. The German writer Oswald Spengler published *The Decline of the West* (1918–1922)—a two-volume work explaining the historical decline of many great empires such as China and predicting that the West would take the same path to ruin. Other writers had high hopes for the kind of elite direction that the military had brought. The Spanish philosopher and writer José Ortega y Gasset warned of the predominate desire for "mass" amusements and material goods and lack of ethical and cultural values in mass society. Instead of succumbing to the leveling effect of mass democracy, Ortega y Gasset believed, elites needed to take charge and use their high intelligence and superior values to direct society.

While elitist thinkers like Ortega y Gasset gained ground, the utopian aura of the machine age surrounded the arts. The popular French modernist painter Fernand Léger filled his canvases with machine-like forms; even the humans resembled fat, rounded pipes. Musical compositions such as *Ballet Mécanique* (1924) and *The Age of Steel* (1927) evoked and celebrated work on the factory floor. In Arthur Honegger's ballet *Skating Rink* (1922) the dancers were supposed to move "as regularly and monotonously as pistons or wheels."[23] Cars, airplanes, and telephones formed the background for advertising and poster art, their sleek perfection inspiring consumers to make purchases.

Some artists were not thrilled by the vision of a benign mechanical future, nor could they maintain optimism after the wartime assault on civilized values. Thus, one strand of postwar literature prominently featured the elite aesthete—a person who lives for aesthetic experience and is untroubled by the tawdry issues of economic and social reality. French author Marcel Proust in his multivolume novel *Remembrance of Things Past* (1913–1927) explored the workings of memory, the passage of time, and sexual modernity through the life of the narrator. Proust's portrayal of the inner life as dominated by obsessions and haunting memories paralleled Freud's very similar concerns. For Proust the re-creation of raw life within an artistic work of imagination provided redemption. He valued beauty and aestheticism over both rational analysis and conventional morality.

Contemporary writers James Joyce and Virginia Woolf shared Proust's and Freud's interest in the memories and sensations of the interior self. Joyce's novel *Ulysses* (1922) presents the fast-moving interior monologue of the character Leopold Bloom on a single day in Dublin, illuminating what Bloom reads in the paper, local characters, popular music, and events important to Irish history. Bloom's mind wanders over "the coincidence of meeting, discussion, dance, raw, odd sort of the here today and gone tomorrow type, night loafers, the whole galaxy of events all went to make up a miniature cameo of the world we live in, if taken down in writing, especially as the lives of the submerged tenth, viz. coalminers, divers, scavengers, etc. were very much under the microscope lately."[24] The oral traditions and insider knowledge roaming the protagonist's consciousness would have been foreign to the English imperialist reader whose own government oppressed Ireland. For Virginia Woolf, the effect of war and imperialism had been to dissolve the solid society from which absorbing stories and realistic characters were once fashioned. Readers of her novel *Mrs. Dalloway* (1925), whose protagonist's inner life on a single day also forms the basis of the plot, gain the impression of a British Empire disintegrating into incomplete relationships, fragmented conversations, and momentary sensations. In her extended essay *A Room of One's Own* (1929), Woolf advocated for women artists a private space so isolated from the demands imposed by society and households alike that they would feel free to create.

The most gripping literary depictions of the modern citizen's predicament appear in the writings of Franz Kafka, an insurance claims lawyer in Prague. Kafka portrayed helpless individuals manipulated by vast, impersonal bureaucracies such as the state, large-scale businesses, and the military. Kafka's novels *The Trial* (1925) and *The Castle* (1926) show the hopeless condition of a bewildered individual whose fate is determined by an omniscient bureaucracy that keeps the protagonist in a state of utter confusion as he attempts to fulfill the state's wishes. Kafka's short story "In the Penal Colony" tells a gruesome tale of a prisoner whose sentence, carried out at the whim of unseen leaders, entails having the law that he broke and his punishment incised on his body by a lethal machine in which he is suspended as in a rotisserie. Kafka's stories, many of them begun during the war, evoked frightening dystopias at a time when others across Europe—both politicians and the artists they attracted—were envisioning a postwar political utopia.

Utopian Dreams in the Soviet Union

The recognized leader of the Bolsheviks, Lenin drove the Red Army to put down the counterrevolutionary White forces led by tsarist generals, ethnic nationalists, and the Allied forces who invaded Russia. The Red Army was successful against these units with their disorganized and even mutually antagonistic programs. When the civil war ended in 1922 with the defeat of the tsarist armies and the withdrawal of Allied forces, Lenin continued to centralize the government under a Bolshevik elite because of his utter lack of faith in the capacity of the "inadequately enlightened" peasants and workers. He also bore down on the middle class and the aristocracy and used violence to crush anyone who stood in his way, employing equally committed and ruthless party members such as Leon Trotsky and Joseph Stalin to direct purges and executions. Lenin had little use for the liberal traditions of freedom and rights and thus did not hesitate to terrorize peasants who hid their grain from the starving people in the cities. On occasion, Lenin simply executed people who disagreed with him, but other violence occurred because Bolshevik rule was in dire straits. In the early 1920s, Communist Russia continued to be plagued by disease and starvation, and industrial production stood at a mere 13 percent of prewar output.

Bloody uprisings followed on the heels of the Bolsheviks' own ferocity. Peasant bands called Green Armies revolted against war communism and against prohibitions on the private trade of their agricultural produce. In 1921 workers in Petrograd and sailors at the naval base at Kronstadt revolted, calling for "Soviets without Communists." Workers protested their short rations and the privileged lives of Bolshevik supervisors. Sailors, whose Kronstadt community was a model of cooperative socialism, wanted a return to the early promises of the Bolsheviks for a truly proletarian society. The pressure caused Lenin to compromise, not by instituting the sort of socialism the workers wanted but by reinstating elements of the old capitalist economy through a new economic program. The democratic left, to his eyes, posed a greater threat to Communist centralization than the right.

Announced in 1921, the New Economic Policy (NEP) substituted a fixed tax on production for seizure of grain. The partial return to the free market allowed peasants to control their grain sales and to profit from free trade in consumer goods. The state still controlled large industries and banking, but the NEP encouraged people to produce, to sell, and even, in the words of leading Communist Nicholai Bukharin, to "enrich themselves."[25] More food and the availability of goods alleviated the plight of the average person, but many continued to live in poverty. The rise of "NEP-men," who bought and furnished splendid homes and cared only about improving their standard of living, belied the Bolshevik goal of a classless utopia. Yet it fit with many a prewar socialist analysis that saw Russia as unready for socialism until it developed a capitalist marketplace and a large pool of proletarians.

Many sincere Communists protested vociferously against the NEP. At the 1921 party congress a group called the Worker Opposition objected to the party's usurpation of economic control from worker organizations. The group favored trade-union leadership of industry and pointed out that the NEP was an agrarian program, not a proletarian one. Communist activist Aleksandra Kollontai, who strongly opposed centralization and the party's apparent move backward toward capitalism, wrote critical novels aimed at raising the consciousness of working people. She portrayed NEP-men as greedy and superficial, seeking out beautiful women who lived as sexy parasites in the household instead of as workers contributing to the welfare of society. With behind-the-scenes help from loyalists like Stalin, Lenin put down the Worker Opposition and urged Stalin and others he trusted to begin grooming a new generation of Communists to replace these opponents. Thus, Lenin articulated what became a fundamental tenet of the Communist system—that opposition within the party was not allowed.

At the local level, however, debate flourished and was even encouraged because it accorded with the idea that revolution had to touch everyday life. Lenin called for widespread participation in creating the Soviet utopia: "Get to work right there, at the grass roots, without waiting for orders,"[26] he urged. Appalled by peasants' lack of education, party cadres flocked to the countryside to set up classes, and volunteers harangued the public about the importance of literacy—only 40 percent on the eve of World War I. To facilitate social equality between the sexes, a core ingredient of the Marxist utopia, the state made birth control, abortion, and divorce readily available. Feminist activists and intellectuals like Aleksandra Kollontai foresaw a new morality wherein the "inequality between the sexes and the dependence of women on men will disappear without trace."[27] Communism would create for men and women "a background of joyful unity and comradeship [where] Eros will occupy an honourable place"[28] (see Document 4.4). As commissar for public welfare, a post she received before beginning to write novels critical of government policies, Kollontai promoted birth-control education among the masses and programs to offer day care for children of working parents.

The bureaucracy swelled to bring modern culture to every corner of life, and *hygiene* and *efficiency* became watchwords, as they were among officialdom in the rest of Europe. Yet the situation under the Bolsheviks was grave because of wartime deprivation and because the Russian Empire, as a peasant society, had lacked the basic tools to undertake sanitary measures in the countryside. Nonetheless, agencies such as the Zhenotdel (Women's Bureau) sought to teach women about the principles and practices of modern sanitation and about their rights under communism. "Americanization" was viewed favorably because it provided methods for sweeping away the past. Thus, semiofficial institutes and associations brought the methods of Henry Ford and Frederick Taylor into factories, the army, the arts, and everyday life. *Timeists,* as the efficiency experts were called, aimed to replace tsarist backwardness with technological modernity. The League of Time, a group of experts founded in 1923, sought out and punished "embezzlers of time"—late or dawdling workers and even officials.[29]

Cultural change was on the Bolshevik agenda because the Bolsheviks and their followers—many of them semiliterate and uneducated—resented intellectuals and other cultural leaders from the past who stood in the way of creating a new "Communist person." Lenin himself was conflicted: steeped in the classics, he nonetheless despised literary people and artists. Some writers, such as the young Vladimir Nabokov in 1919, went into exile. Other artists, like the composer and pianist Dmitri Shostakovich, remained and endured privation—in his case, being denied access to his piano, which authorities considered an item signifying privilege and luxury. Writers and artists along with workers argued heatedly about whether it was possible to integrate the old elite culture into Communist culture or whether the former had to be thrown out, as some avant-garde intellectuals believed. The short-lived government agency Proletkult aimed to develop proletarian culture through such undertakings as workers' universities, a workers' encyclopedia, a workers' theater, and workers' publishing. But in the 1920s the rebelliousness of elite prewar experimental theater, abstract art, and free verse could be seen in Bolshevik culture.

Intellectuals saw technology as key to producing utopian art as well as a utopian society. Composers punctuated their music with the sounds of train and factory whistles. They wrote ballets about robots and cement factories. Electricity was another common theme of new work. Technology was to play a part in redirecting human spirituality toward faith in communism and away from orthodox religion. The premier painter, sculptor, and architect of the revolution, Vladimir Tatlin, built a model of the Monument to the Third International made of intricate metalwork and featuring a spiral staircase (see image on page 216). The proletarian ascending the staircase symbolized the quest to reach the heights of Communist instead of religious truth. The design of textiles and ordinary objects also took on a special, spiritualized meaning, as journals promoted the utopian and artistic

◆ Model of the Monument to the Third International

Soviet artist Vladimir Tatlin enthusiastically reacted to the formation of the Third International, or Comintern, by designing a monument that would also house its offices. With this model, created in 1920, Tatlin envisioned a structure that would also have restaurants and an office that would beam messages onto the clouds for people to read. The mock-up is open-ended at the top, pointing skyward in a swirling upward movement — perhaps Tatlin's vision of the future under communism. *Digital Image © The Museum of Modern Art/Licensed by SCALA/Art Resources, NY.*

nature of every level of design. The poet Vladimir Mayakovski wrote poetry praising his Soviet passport and essays promoting toothbrushing as a meaningful act.

Like other movements of the postwar period, Bolshevism held great attraction for the young. The triumph of Marxism and its application to every field of endeavor let young people break through established power structures in the arts and sciences. Communism meant opportunity for youthful careers, since the old ways had to go. Young avant-gardists used their skills to advertise the revolution and promote modern education. Acting on their belief that abstraction embodied pure and forceful ideas, many became leading commercial artists on behalf of Bolshevism. These young intellectuals branded people who stuck with older paradigms in the arts and social sciences as bourgeois or class enemies; in classic works of literature, they insisted, "there was nothing worthy of life."[30]

Amid factional fighting among the Bolsheviks and struggles to recover from a decade of war, revolution, and civil war, Lenin suffered a debilitating stroke in 1922 and died two years later. Even before Lenin's death, Bolsheviks were thinking in quasi-spiritual terms about his stature. "Lenin is alive in the soul of each individual Party member. Every member of our Party is a particle of Lenin," the Central Committee announced.[31] This kind of thinking served practical ends, building unity and allegiance to a new political regime that was failing to provide peace and prosperity for its citizens. Those who controlled the Lenin cult would thus wield as much power as the cult of Lenin contained. So Lenin's death led to his apotheosis not only as a political leader but as a godlike character. His embalmed body was put on display in a public mausoleum in Moscow's Red Square. Although this ritual was crucial to the rise of the Lenin cult, peasant religiosity—part of the broader postwar religious awakening across Europe—gave flesh, bones, and feeling to it. Connected with the perpetuation of Bolshevik power, the arrangements for Lenin's funeral became a web of intrigue and infighting for the authority that control of the cult would bestow. Stalin put himself in charge of mobilizing cultural fervor around Lenin as part of a move to outflank Trotsky and other hated rivals. Clad in the high-necked tunic that would become the unofficial uniform of Soviet communism, he styled himself as the chief mourner.

Beginning with the arrangements for Lenin's funeral, Stalin (1879–1953), who held the powerful post of general secretary of the Communist Party, quickly consolidated his grasp on power. Organizing the Lenin cult and dealing with thousands of local party officials gave him enormous national patronage. He also gained credit for welding the non-Russian regions into the Union of Soviet Socialist Republics (USSR) by shaping the constitution that was ratified in December 1922—still another example of executive accomplishment. Although Lenin had become wary of Stalin's growing influence and ruthlessness and in his last political testament was critical of Stalin, Stalin allowed the will to be read among a core group of Bolsheviks, who, in an act of solidarity, ordered the document's suppression. Stalin then proceeded to discredit his chief rival, Leon Trotsky, as an unpatriotic internationalist insufficiently devoted to culturally and economically modernizing the Soviet Union. With the blessing of Trotsky's other rivals, Stalin had him exiled and later murdered in Mexico. Bringing in several hundred thousand young new party members, who personally owed their positions in the party, government, and industry to him, Stalin by 1928–1929 had achieved nearly complete power in the USSR.

Fascist Triumph in Italy

Benito Mussolini (1883–1945) rode a powerful tide of postwar discontent and utopian dreams to become Italy's sole leader—*il Duce*—in 1922. Italian ire first rose when the Allies at Paris refused to honor the territorial promises of the 1915 Treaty of London. Gaining little despite being on the winning side, Italy then suffered the dire consequences of war as manufacturing plummeted and as conditions in agriculture deteriorated. Peasants protested their serflike status in Italian society, while workers inspired by socialism and anarchism engaged in strikes for better wages to catch up with wartime inflation. Mussolini, a socialist journalist who hated the kind of government based on guaranteed rights and constitutions, built a personal army of veterans (the Black Shirts) and the unemployed to overturn what he saw as a corrupt and utterly ineffective parliamentary system. In 1922 his supporters, known as Fascists, started a march on Rome, threatening a coup. Mussolini himself waited in safety on the sidelines. The prospect of the bullying and violent Fascist troops causing destruction and loss of life and overturning the constitutional monarchy provoked King Victor Emmanuel III (r. 1900–1946) to invite Mussolini to become prime minister and restore order and prosperity to the country.

Fascism did not have an elaborate ideology; it was about seizing and using state power. A country of extremes with severe rural poverty and thriving modern businesses such as the automobile industry coexisting side by side, Italy welcomed Mussolini's promise to achieve unity and his vow to overcome the contradictions of modernity. The nation-state had become the focus of attention for many during the war—the hero of a sacred wartime drama. Mussolini vowed to bring the state closer to the people. Prior to the coming of Fascist rule, individuals had been isolated, Mussolini claimed. His regime would help them "enter the State and come to be part of the State."[32] Fascism would quell chaotic modernity and the alienation it brought with a return to tradition—that of the Roman Empire, artisanal production, and the simple, self-sufficient, and orderly life directed by a restored patriarchal family. Fascism would end the disorder of mass society and protect the individual by restoring traditional hierarchies. One Fascist intellectual announced that Fascism "allows each personality to retain its perfect contours, because we assign each person in the social scale a specific place."[33]

Mussolini's regime depended on the violent eradication of opposition; both free speech and labor activism, for example, were considered harmful to the state's preeminence. Yet Mussolini had an appreciation of the global stage on which he wanted a bigger role. He believed that Italy had to develop a modern high culture whose products would be as influential in the international cultural marketplace as those of France, Germany, and the United States. Thus, in contrast to the political conformity demanded of the population at large, politics should not impinge on cultural accomplishments. The Duce himself promoted this idea in 1928: "Just as it must be permissible to say that Mussolini, as a violin player, is a very modest dilettante, it must also be permissible to advance objective judgments on art, prose, poetry and theater. . . . Here party discipline has no place."[34] Avant-garde artists and intellectuals were encouraged to think freely and experiment—often to the dismay of committed Fascists. Because Fascism was an avant-garde political movement, calling for daring and for an end to bourgeois blandness and individual freedom, the administration saw the Fascist value in promoting artists who could advance Italy's reputation for being on the cutting edge in all arenas of human endeavor.

Thus, somewhat paradoxically, Mussolini harnessed the power of culture and especially of cultural modernity, while touting a return to obedience and tradition. A rhetoric of cultural freedom papered over vicious acts against individuals by the Fascist government. Modern artistic accomplishments drew admirers to Italy, boosting lucrative tourism and international consumption of Italian products, as Mussolini hoped. In 1929, the wealthy young writer Albert Moravia published *The Indifferent Ones,* a novel of moral corruption and apathy. Moravia's social critique, hailed for its "truthful" realism, was interpreted as supporting the Fascist project of reinvigorating Italy by eliminating the influence of such decadent types in the upper classes. Films such as *Mother Earth* promoted a different kind of reinvigoration by unabashedly glorifying life in the countryside. Seductresses, city life, and American-style materialism made their appearance in these films to attract audiences while being condemned and ultimately failing at the end of the story to tempt the "true Italian" hero.

Fascists ruled by spectacle, making the modern city a stage complete with modernist buildings to house the Fascist bureaucracy and the party's museums. Old residential neighborhoods fell to the wrecking machines to make room for broad avenues for Fascist parades. People were given time off from work to attend welcoming ceremonies for Fascist officials, fill public squares to hear Mussolini speak, and participate in parades of athletes, war widows, and veterans. Participants generally wore uniforms and appeared en masse to convey the impression of the state's power and citizen solidarity. Public ceremonies featured celebrities such as ace aviators or Guglielmo Marconi, inventor of the radio, pledging their allegiance to Mussolini to illustrate that even prominent individuals were subservient to the grandeur and power of the state. Planes roared overhead, newsreel cameras whirled, and loudspeakers blasted the Fascist message to promote the mass participation of citizens in Fascist activities, thus creating what historians have called the "culture of consent."

Fascism was not all parades and speeches, however. Mussolini consolidated his power by putting himself at the head of government departments, by making criticism of the state a criminal offense, and by violently steamrolling parliamentary opposition. Tactics were part of the message: "Fascism is not a church," Mussolini announced upon taking power in 1922. "It is more like a training ground."[35] Fascism depended on an elite minority of brutal followers to smash the internationalist socialist movement and to destroy the parliament and bureaucracy. Fascist

◆ Mussolini and Fascist Spectacle

Benito Mussolini took over the Italian government in 1922 after a show of military force—the "March on Rome," in which he himself did not participate. A citizenry emerging from the traumas of war found military displays like this one, repression of opposition, and loud-mouthed boasting reassuring. They hoped that a strong hand would right all of society economic and social wrongs. Fascists sold militarized politics in the form of a dictatorship as far preferable to a politics based on citizens' rights, consensus and debate, and the rule of law. In hard times, millions agreed. *Farabolfoto.*

bands demolished socialist newspaper offices, beat opposition politicians, attacked striking workers, and used their favorite tactic of forcing castor oil (which causes diarrhea) down the throats of socialists on the streets or anywhere else they could be found. Fascists murdered certain powerful opponents such as the moderate Socialist parliamentary deputy Giacomo Matteotti without hesitation. Despite this brutality, the sight of the Black Shirts marching through the streets like disciplined soldiers paradoxically signaled to many Italians that social order would be restored. From the beginning, large landowners and businessmen approved Fascist attacks on strikers and generously supported the movement, their ample funding allowing Mussolini to build a huge Fascist Party bureaucracy and put thousands of the unemployed back to work. Mussolini created the impression that Fascists had rescued Italy's failing economy when no one else could. Mussolini, people boasted, made the trains run on time; they stopped worrying about the cost in human lives because the state, not individuals, mattered.

Italian Fascism's relationship with the Catholic Church constituted the final paradox of Mussolini's rule in Italy. Although Mussolini was an atheist, he recognized the importance of Catholicism to most Italians and thus found a way to accommodate traditional religion within Fascism's modernist framework. In 1929 he signed the Lateran Agreement with the church, resolving tensions with the papacy that dated from the nineteenth-century wars of Italian unification. The Lateran Agreement established the permanent borders of Vatican City and put it under papal sovereignty. The government recognized the church's right to determine marriage and family doctrine. In return the church ended its criticism of Fascist tactics.

Mussolini also rebuilt the old "corporate" state in which individual rights were denied in favor of a system that emphasized people's duty to the state and their fixed place in society. Corporatist decrees in 1926 organized employers, workers, and professionals into groups or corporations resembling medieval guilds. These groups would settle grievances and determine conditions of work through state-controlled channels. The decrees, which drew applause from business leaders, outlawed independent labor unions and eliminated peasant political groups, effectively ending political or workplace activism and curtailing workers' freedom of expression. Mussolini also cut women's wages by decree; in the late 1920s he won the approval of civil servants, lawyers, and professors by banning women from those professions. The thrust of Fascism was antifeminist in that Mussolini did not want women out of the workforce altogether but wanted to ensure that men had the better jobs. As Fascism strengthened men's social and economic privilege while curtailing their civil and political rights, it eliminated any vestiges of workplace well-being for women.

CONCLUSION

The end of World War I made people hope for a new era of peace and well-being based in part on the creation of democratic nations in eastern Europe during the peacemaking process. Technology promised to improve the conditions of everyday life by providing an array of new products and good jobs. The urban young revived people's spirits as they gaily patronized films, dance halls, and cafés. Experimentation in the arts continued, inspiring utopian visions of a better life. Nowhere was this experimentation more pronounced than in the new Soviet Union, with its outsized promises of fairness and future happiness for everyone. Yet conditions in the Soviet Union were far from perfect. The end of the bloody Russian civil war brought only more starvation and the spread of disease. Under the leadership of Lenin, a Communist dictatorship took shape based on violence and the elimination of political freedoms.

The dictatorial state, as it emerged in the 1920s in the Soviet Union and Italy, was one that took priority over individual human rights while it professed to confer great benefits on everyone. Under the guise of militant nationalism, the Fascist government of Mussolini that came to power in 1922 promoted state violence as an end in itself. In claiming to create a utopia, it papered over all the problems of modern life. After years of wartime deprivation, citizens flocked to leaders who promised them a rapid end to their suffering through a victorious state.

World War I had heightened nationalist sentiment, and it was further fueled by the Fourteen Points principle of national self-determination. Europe, however, was a continent of extreme ethnic mixture where wartime and postwar changes battered many people's sense of stability. Democratic governments in France and Great Britain floundered when faced with the task of postwar recovery. For up-and-coming dictators like Mussolini and Stalin the postwar era offered unprecedented opportunity to seize on discontents and shape the future. When a global depression loosened social ties and eroded human decency, Hitler's politics of hatred was next in line to find an audience among the disillusioned.

DOCUMENTS

Hitler's Creed

WHILE MUSSOLINI AND OTHER AUTHORITARIAN LEADERS were trying their hand at wielding power, some attempts at the same kind of takeover of government were thwarted in Germany. In 1923 Hitler tried an unsuccessful coup against the Weimar Republic—the Beer Hall Putsch—and landed in jail, where he wrote *Mein Kampf* (*My Struggle*). The book is not only a diatribe against people whom he perceived to be Germany's enemies but also a blueprint describing how those enemies, notably Jews and the disabled, should be eliminated. These ideas were fundamental to the National Socialist German Workers' Party—the Nazi Party—which Hitler came to lead during the 1920s. Nazis and Communists were rivals for the support of working people in the troubled postwar period, and Hitler's hateful message against Jews and the financial elite, who according to Nazi ideology were identical, made *Mein Kampf* the bible of this movement. When Hitler came to power, he forced the Nazi Party to purchase this work for new members and encouraged industrialists and others who sought influence with him to buy it for their workers. As a result of the forced sales of *Mein Kampf* and other funds that he extorted from those wanting to do business with the Nazi government, Hitler ended his life a billionaire.

The first excerpt presented here is a small sample of Hitler's obsession with Jews—an obsession that leads him to see Jews in total control of every aspect of society, from unions to business, and responsible for all of Germany's ills from the defeat in World War I to the spread of diseases and epidemics. Besides hate-filled chapters about Jews, *Mein Kampf* contains Hitler's uncanny psychological insights into the mass mind and how to manipulate it, as the second passage reveals. Hitler understood ordinary people so well as to sense their weaknesses and vulnerabilities. Of the masses, he wrote, "their intelligence is small. . . . In consequence of these facts, all effective propaganda must be limited to a very few points and must harp on these in slogans." Hitler intuitively understood the importance of what we know as "sound bites." In addition, he simultaneously encouraged lying to the masses, not on the small scale of everyday white lies but on a large scale with a "big lie"—a falsehood so huge that no one would dream that it was not the truth.

Hitler knew the value of his oratory. In the 1920s he was the fledgling Nazi Party's most popular speaker, able to attract mass audiences who despite their modest circumstances were willing to pay admission to be mesmerized and perhaps healed of their war wounds by Hitler's rhetoric. In preparation for these performances, Hitler studied the speeches of current and past politicians. David Lloyd George, former prime minister of Britain, earned high praise from Hitler:

"Precisely in the primitiveness of his language, the primordiality of his expression, and the use of easily intelligible examples of the simplest sort lies the proof of the towering political ability of this Englishman."[36] Hitler checked out halls in advance of his speeches to ensure that he would achieve the right rapport with his audience. Posing for photographers, he practiced dramatic physical gestures, and he perfected his electrifying demagogic style, which made it possible for the National Socialists to raise money from thousands of ordinary people to support the party's ragtag armies and finance Nazi activities. Hitler's takeover of the German government in 1933 was not so much achieved by violence (though it played a large role in his rise to power) as it was the outcome of a shrewd marketing by a media-savvy writer and speaker.

Document 4.1

ADOLF HITLER
Mein Kampf, 1925–1926

. . . Since the Jew is not the attacked but the attacker, not only anyone who attacks passes as his enemy, but also anyone who resists him. But the means with which he seeks to break such reckless but upright souls is not honest warfare, but lies and slander.

Here he stops at nothing, and in his vileness he becomes so gigantic that no one need be surprised if among our people the personification of the devil as the symbol of all evil assumes the living shape of the Jew.

The ignorance of the broad masses about the inner nature of the Jew, the lack of instinct and narrow-mindedness of our upper classes, make the people an easy victim for this Jewish campaign of lies.

While from innate cowardice the upper classes turn away from a man whom the Jew attacks with lies and slander, the broad masses from stupidity or simplicity believe everything. The state authorities either cloak themselves in silence or, what usually happens, in order to put an end to the Jewish press campaign, they persecute the unjustly attacked, which, in the eyes of such an official ass, passes as the preservation of state authority and the safeguarding of law and order. . . .

The Jew's domination in the state seems so assured that now not only can he call himself a Jew again, but he ruthlessly admits his ultimate national and political designs. A section of his race openly owns itself to be a foreign people, yet even here they lie. For while the Zionists try to make the rest of the world believe that the national consciousness of the Jew finds its satisfaction in the creation of a Palestinian state, the Jews again slyly dupe the dumb *Goyim.*° It doesn't even enter their heads to build up a Jewish state in Palestine for the purpose of living there; all they want is a central organization for their international world swindle, endowed with its own sovereign rights and removed from the intervention of other states: a haven for convicted scoundrels and a university for budding crooks.

SOURCE: Adolf Hitler, *Mein Kampf* (Boston: Houghton Mifflin, 1971), 324–327, 179–181.

°*Goyim:* Yiddish for "Gentiles."

It is a sign of their rising confidence and sense of security that at a time when one section is still playing the German, Frenchman, or Englishman, the other with open effrontery comes out as the Jewish race.

How close they see approaching victory can be seen by the hideous aspect which their relations with the members of other peoples takes on.

With satanic joy in his face, the black-haired Jewish youth lurks in wait for the unsuspecting girl whom he defiles with his blood, thus stealing her from her people. With every means he tries to destroy the racial foundations of the people he has set out to subjugate. Just as he himself systematically ruins women and girls, he does not shrink back from pulling down the blood barriers for others, even on a large scale. It was and it is Jews who bring the Negroes into the Rhineland, always with the same secret thought and clear aim of ruining the hated white race by the necessarily resulting bastardization, throwing it down from its cultural and political height, and himself rising to be its master.

For a racially pure people which is conscious of its blood can never be enslaved by the Jew. In this world he will forever be master over bastards and bastards alone.

And so he tries systematically to lower the racial level by a continuous poisoning of individuals.

And in politics he begins to replace the idea of democracy by the dictatorship of the proletariat.

In the organized mass of Marxism he has found the weapon which lets him dispense with democracy and in its stead allows him to subjugate and govern the peoples with a dictatorial and brutal fist.

He works systematically for revolutionization in a twofold sense: economic and political.

Around peoples who offer too violent a resistance to attack from within he weaves a net of enemies, thanks to his international influence, incites them to war, and finally, if necessary, plants the flag of revolution on the very battlefields.

In economics he undermines the states until the social enterprises which have become unprofitable are taken from the state and subjected to his financial control.

In the political field he refuses the state the means for its self-preservation, destroys the foundations of all national self-maintenance and defense, destroys faith in the leadership, scoffs at its history and past, and drags everything that is truly great into the gutter.

Culturally he contaminates art, literature, the theater, makes a mockery of natural feeling, overthrows all concepts of beauty and sublimity, of the noble and the good, and instead drags men down into the sphere of his own base nature.

Religion is ridiculed, ethics and morality represented as outmoded, until the last props of a nation in its struggle for existence in this world have fallen.

Now begins the great last revolution. In gaining political power the Jew casts off the few cloaks that he still wears. The democratic people's Jew becomes the blood-Jew and tyrant over peoples. . . .

If we pass all the causes of the German collapse in review, the ultimate and most decisive remains the failure to recognize the racial problem and especially the Jewish menace.

The defeats on the battlefield in August, 1918, would have been child's play to bear. They stood in no proportion to the victories of our people. It was not they that caused our downfall; no, it was brought about by that power which prepared these defeats by systematically over many decades robbing our people of the political and moral instincts and forces which alone make nations capable and hence worthy of existence. . . .

The function of propaganda does not lie in the scientific training of the individual, but in calling the masses' attention to certain facts, processes, necessities, etc., whose significance is thus for the first time placed within their field of vision.

The whole art consists in doing this so skillfully that everyone will be convinced that the fact is real, the process necessary, the necessity correct, etc. But since propaganda is not and cannot be the necessity in itself, since its function, like the poster, consists in attracting the attention of the crowd, and not in educating those who are already educated or who are striving after education and knowledge, its effect for the most part must be aimed at the emotions and only to a very limited degree at the so-called intellect.

All propaganda must be popular and its intellectual level must be adjusted to the most limited intelligence among those it is addressed to. Consequently, the greater the mass it is intended to reach, the lower its purely intellectual level will have to be. But if, as in propaganda for sticking out a war, the aim is to influence a whole people, we must avoid excessive intellectual demands on our public, and too much caution cannot be exerted in this direction.

The more modest its intellectual ballast, the more exclusively it takes into consideration the emotions of the masses, the more effective it will be. And this is the best proof of the soundness or unsoundness of a propaganda campaign, and not success in pleasing a few scholars or young aesthetes.

The art of propaganda lies in understanding the emotional ideas of the great masses and finding, through a psychologically correct form, the way to the attention and thence to the heart of the broad masses. The fact that our bright boys do not understand this merely shows how mentally lazy and conceited they are.

Once we understand how necessary it is for propaganda to be adjusted to the broad mass, the following rule results:

It is a mistake to make propaganda many-sided, like scientific instruction, for instance.

The receptivity of the great masses is very limited, their intelligence is small, but their power of forgetting is enormous. In consequence of these facts, all effective propaganda must be limited to a very few points and must harp on these in slogans until the last member of the public understands what you want him to understand by your slogan. As soon as you sacrifice this slogan and try to be many-sided, the effect will piddle away, for the crowd can neither digest nor retain the material offered. In this way the result is weakened and in the end entirely cancelled out.

Thus we see that propaganda must follow a simple line and correspondingly the basic tactics must be psychologically sound.

For instance, it was absolutely wrong to make the enemy ridiculous, as the Austrian and German comic papers did. It was absolutely wrong because actual contact with an enemy soldier was bound to arouse an entirely different conviction, and the results were devastating; for now the German soldier, under the direct impression of the enemy's resistance, felt himself swindled by his propaganda service. His desire to fight, or even to stand firm, was not strengthened, but the opposite occurred. His courage flagged.

By contrast, the war propaganda of the English and Americans was psychologically sound. By representing the Germans to their own people as barbarians and Huns, they prepared the individual soldier for the terrors of war, and thus helped to preserve him from disappointments. After this, the most terrible weapon that was used against him seemed only to confirm what his propagandists had told him; it likewise reinforced his faith in the truth of his government's assertions, while on the other hand it increased his rage and hatred against the vile enemy. For the cruel effects of the weapon, whose use by the enemy he now came to know, gradually came to confirm for him the "Hunnish" brutality of the barbarous enemy, which he had heard all about; and it never dawned on him for a moment that his own weapons possibly, if not probably, might be even more terrible in their effects. . . .

QUESTIONS FOR ANALYSIS

1. What are the elements of Hitler's anti-Semitism?

2. How do Hitler's ideas about human character and potential relate to the European tradition of human dignity, the importance of reason, and the commitment to human rights?

3. Account for the appeal of Hitler's ideas to postwar Germans and to others in Europe in the 1920s.

4. Some people found Hitler's ideas utterly ridiculous and therefore hardly threatening to society. Referring to the selections presented here, explain why they might have held this opinion.

Gandhi's Attack on European Civilization

Indian activist Mohandas Gandhi, a London-trained lawyer, took his first steps toward notoriety in South Africa. His experience of racism there helped him formulate his appeal to the Indian masses that they liberate themselves from British imperialism. He returned to India and began to organize and agitate for "Hind Swaraj"—Indian home rule. His methods included journalism, speeches, and especially nonviolent protest, a potent symbol of India's difference from the violent, even genocidal Europeans, who, as he noted in his writings, during World War I massacred one another by the millions. Eventually Gandhi gained the allegiance of the Indian masses and transformed the Indian National Congress from a genteel reformist party into a potent political movement.

Gandhi focused on many issues in his massive outpouring of journalistic writing. Document 4.2 appeared soon after the 1919 Amritsar Massacre of a gathering of Indians for a religious festival. In writing for journals and newspapers such as *The Hindu* and *Young India,* he was particularly intent on undermining the view of many in the Indian leadership that Britain was to be emulated. Indians who worked for the British and even those who aspired to be liberated from imperialism had great respect for British "civilization." They also accepted the British view that Indians, in contrast to Westerners, lacked civilization and a cultural tradition. In Document 4.3, Gandhi takes pains to dispel that idea in an interview with the American journalist Drew Pearson. To Gandhi's way of thinking, his fellow citizens had the story backward: South Asia had a very long tradition of civilization, and Britain and other Western countries valued only one thing: material wealth. He preached that Indians should take none of these nations as a role model in their drive for independence.

Gandhi's program was utopian. He envisioned an India of small self-sufficient communities in which people grew their own crops and spun the cloth for their own clothes. Gandhi himself wore a loincloth and shawl to embody this ideal. Indians, however, had built factories for textiles and metallurgy, and the country had both railroads and motorized vehicles. There was a modern proletariat, and ambitious Indian industrialists worked their laborers as hard as Westerners did. Gandhi judged such "progress" to be the root cause of India's subjection: Indian merchants wanting trade and modern commerce had essentially handed the country over to the West, and Indians were adopting the ways of materialism and turning away from a life of contemplation, humility, and good values.

To be civilized, Gandhi believed, men and women had to avoid the "satanic" world of modern industry and urban society. This notion led him to oppose modern technology such as advances in birth control and modern values such as individualism. Gandhi essentially left the Indian caste system intact, although he tried to alleviate its hardships, and he seemed unconcerned that his opposition to birth control was one factor in soaring Indian birthrates. His views, some of them expressed in the two documents that follow, have led many people to consider Gandhi a traditionalist, but he did transform world politics, eventually making it impossible for the British to continue to rule India.

Document 4.2

MOHANDAS GANDHI
The Inwardness of Non-co-operation, 1920

. . . The movement of non-co-operation is neither anti-Christian nor anti-English nor anti-European. It is a struggle between religion and irreligion, powers of light and powers of darkness.

It is my firm opinion that Europe today represents not the spirit of God or Christianity but the spirit of Satan. And Satan's successes are the greatest when he appears with the name of God on his lips. Europe is today only nominally Christian. In reality it is worshipping mammon. "It is easier for a camel to pass through the eye of a needle than for a rich man to enter the Kingdom." Thus really spoke Jesus Christ. His so-called followers measure their moral progress by their material possessions. The very national anthem of England is anti-Christian. Jesus, who asked his followers to love their enemies even as themselves, could not have sung of his enemies, "Confound his enemies, frustrate their knavish tricks." . . . The last War however has shown, as nothing else has, the Satanic nature of the civilization that dominates Europe today. Every canon of public morality has been broken by the victors in the name of virtue. No lie has been considered too foul to be uttered. The motive behind every crime is not religious or spiritual but grossly material. But the Mussulmans and the Hindus who are struggling against the Government have religion and honour as their motive. Even the cruel assassination° which has just shocked the country is reported to have a religious motive behind it. It is certainly necessary to purge religion of its excrescences, but it is equally necessary to expose the hollowness of moral pretensions on the part of those who prefer material wealth to moral gain. It is easier to wean an ignorant fanatic from his error than a confirmed scoundrel from his scoundrelism.

This however is no indictment against individuals or even nations. Thousands of individual Europeans are rising above their environment. I write of the tendency in Europe as reflected in her present leaders. England through her leaders is absolutely crushing Indian religious and national sentiment under her heels. England under the false plea of self-determination is trying to exploit the oilfields of Mesopotamia which she is almost to leave because she has probably no choice. France through her leaders is lending her name to training cannibals as soldiers and is shamelessly betraying her trust as a mandatory power by trying to kill the spirit of the Syrians. President Wilson has thrown on the scrap-heap his precious fourteen points.

It is this combination of evil forces which India is really fighting through non-violent non-co-operation. . . .

SOURCE: Mohandas Gandhi, "The Inwardness of Non-co-operation," *The Collected Works of Mahatma Gandi,* vol. 22 (Ahmedabad: Navajivan Trust, 1963), 235–236.

° *assassination:* The Amritsar Massacre.

Document 4.3

MOHANDAS GANDHI
Answers to Drew Pearson's Questions, 1924

[DP] Mr. Gandhi is recuperating in the mountain air of Poona, just a few miles from Yeravda prison in which two years of confinement so broke his health that unconditional release by the British Government was necessary. His first statement, when interviewed, was:

[MG] I shall resume my activities for the attainment of swaraj just as soon as I am restored to complete health.

[DP] What course would he take? He answered quietly:

[MG] I still believe it possible for India to remain within the British Empire. I still put implicit faith in non-violence, which, if strictly followed by India, will invoke the best in the British people. My hope for the attainment of swaraj by non-violence is based upon an immutable belief in the goodness which exists deep down in all human nature.

I have always maintained that India had no quarrel with the English. Jesus denounced the wickedness of the Scribes and Pharisees, but he did not hate them. So we need not hate Englishmen, though we hate the system they have established. They have given India a system based upon force, by which they can feel secure only in the shadow of their forts and guns. We Indians, in turn, hope by our conduct to demonstrate to every Englishman that he is as safe in the remotest corner of India as he professes to feel behind the machine gun.

[DP] What do you mean by swaraj?

[MG] A full partnership for India with other parts of the Empire, just the same as Canada, South Africa and Australia enjoy. Nor shall we be satisfied until we obtain full citizens' rights throughout the British Dominions for all the King's subjects, irrespective of caste, colour or creed.

[DP] I asked Mr. Gandhi if he still believed in boycotting the Councils.

[MG] Yes, I still believe that we should not participate in the Councils until Britain suffers a change of heart and acts squarely with us. However, I do not wish to express any opinion on the action of the Nationalist party in participating in the Councils, until I have talked with the leaders. This I have already started to do.

[DP] When asked if imprisonment had changed his views on politics and religion, Mr. Gandhi replied:

[MG] They have undergone no change, but have been confirmed by two years of solitude and introspection. I have been experimenting with myself and friends by introducing religion into politics, and now I believe they cannot be divorced. Let me explain what I mean by religion. It is not Hinduism, which I prize most highly, but the religion which transcends Hinduism—the basic truth which underlies all the religions of the world. It is the struggle for truth—for self-expression. I call it the truth-force—the permanent element in human nature, constantly struggling to find itself, to know its Maker. This is religion.

I believe that politics cannot be divorced from religion. My politics can be summed up in two words—non-violent non-co-operation. And the roots of non-co-operation are buried in the religions of the world. Christ refused to co-operate with the Scribes and Pharisees. Buddha fearlessly refused to co-operate with the arrogant priesthood of his day. Mahomed, Confucius, most of our great prophets have been non-co-operators. I simply and humbly follow in their footsteps.

Non-co-operation means nothing less than training in self-sacrifice. And this again was prac-

SOURCE: Mohandas Gandhi, "Answers to Drew Pearson's Questions," *The Collected Works of Mahatma Gandhi,* vol. 23 (Ahmedabad: Navajivan Trust, 1963), 195–197.

tised by the great teachers of the world. Strength does not come from physical capacity. It comes from indomitable will. I have ventured to place before India the ancient law of self-sacrifice — the obedience to the strength of the spirit.

By non-violence I do not mean cowardice. I do believe that, where there is only a choice between cowardice and violence, I would advise violence. But I believe that forgiveness adorns a soldier. And so I am not pleading for India to practise non-violence because she is weak, but because she is conscious of her power and strength. The *rishis,*° who discovered the law of non-violence, were greater geniuses than Newton. Having themselves known the use of arms, they realized their uselessness and taught a weary world that its salvation lay not through violence, but through non-violence.

Therefore, I respectfully invite Americans to study carefully the Indian National Movement and they will therein find an effective substitute for war.

° *rishis:* Sages who set down the Vedic scriptures.

[DP] Before his imprisonment Mr. Gandhi was a most severe critic of modern civilization and I asked if his views had suffered any change.

[MG] They remain unchanged. My opinion of modern civilization is that it is a worship of materialism, resulting in the exploitation of the weak by the strong. American wealth has become the standard. The United States is the envy of all other nations. Meanwhile, moral growth has become stunted and progress measured in pounds, shillings and pence.

This land of ours, we are told, was once the abode of the gods. But it is not possible to conceive of gods inhabiting a land which is made hideous by the smoke and din of mill chimneys and factories, and whose roadways are traversed by rushing engines, dragging cars crowded with men who know not for the most part what they are after, do not care, and whose tempers do not improve by being uncomfortably packed together like sardines in boxes. Factories have risen on the corpses of men, women, and children to create what we call civilization.

QUESTIONS FOR ANALYSIS

1. Judging from these two selections, what do you see as the main tenets of Gandhi's program?

2. Why were traditional ideas and pacifist ideas so powerful in challenging imperialism?

3. What flaws or pitfalls might Gandhi's colleagues in the fight for home rule have identified in his program and in his personal lifestyle?

Love and Sexuality in Postwar Society:
The Communist Case

A MONG THE SOCIAL CHANGES THAT World War I ushered in was heightened concern for stable relationships between the sexes. Although the Bolsheviks' main goal was to secure political power, some revolutionaries in the Soviet Union proposed a wide array of cultural and social changes. Aleksandra Kollontai (1872–1952), the revolutionary daughter of a prominent general, focused on maintaining worker democracy, promoting the welfare of women and children, and constructing a new sexual morality. To this end she poured out a stream of journalism and wrote engaging novels in simple Russian to help working women grasp the changes under way in the 1920s. Her work addressed the new "modern woman" or "flapper" from the working class, who had made her appearance on the wartime stage as a factory worker, frontline nurse, and white-collar employee, replacing the men who had gone to the battlefront.

Kollontai was addressing, in "Communist" terms, issues that were being dealt with across postwar Europe. She described the transformation in sexual relations that she hoped would accompany the transition from capitalism to socialism. Under capitalism, the scrutiny of women's sexuality was based on preserving the legitimate transfer of fortunes from one generation to another. Tough capitalist law codes, even giving husbands and families the right to kill an unfaithful wife, aimed to preserve a propertied society. They did not, however, make society more moral, Kollontai maintained. When private property was eliminated under the Bolsheviks, a new morality would come into being—one based on authentic human relationships rather than on a concern for property. The idea may have been Communist, but it acknowledged the condition of men and women in an urbanizing world, in which agriculture employed fewer people and increasing numbers of people were propertyless workers employed in industry and the service sector.

Kollontai wrote extensively about sexuality, even producing a memoir about her experiences as a "sexually emancipated woman." She had sexual relationships with several revolutionaries, but in her work she criticized the passage from partner to partner of the early days of the Russian Revolution. With Communist goals in the process of being realized, Kollontai envisioned a new morality in the making, and "Make Way for Winged Eros" (1923) expresses her vision. Kollontai was also addressing moral questions that were challenging people across postwar Europe: Were any values left in Europe? After so much violence and slaughter, could people ever reestablish loving relationships? Kollontai's answer was specific to the Soviet Union but pertinent to the entire postwar world.

Because Kollontai also agitated for worker democracy during the Bolsheviks' drive for elite leadership, a campaign which Lenin helped spearhead took shape to denounce her as an amoral and loose woman. As Kollontai was discredited, so eventually were many of the reforms in the condition of women that she helped promote. The literature of sexual emancipation and partnerships based on love flourished less in the revolutionary USSR than in capitalist Europe and the United States.

Document 4.4

ALEKSANDRA KOLLONTAI
Make Way for Winged Eros:
A Letter to Working Youth, 1923

LOVE AS A SOCIO-PSYCHOLOGICAL FACTOR

You ask me, my young friend, what place proletarian ideology gives to love? You are concerned by the fact that at the present time young workers are occupied more with love and related questions than with the tremendous tasks of construction which face the workers' republic. It is difficult for me to judge events from a distance, but let us try to find an explanation for this situation, and then it will be easier to answer the first question about the place of love in proletarian ideology.

There can be no doubt that Soviet Russia has entered a new phase of the civil war. The main theatre of struggle is now the front where the two ideologies, the two cultures—the bourgeois and the proletarian—do battle. The incompatibility of these two ideologies is becoming increasingly obvious, and the contradictions between these two fundamentally different cultures are growing more acute. Alongside the victory of communist principles and ideals in the sphere of politics and economics, a revolution in the outlook, emotions and the inner world of working people is inevitably taking place. A new attitude to life, society, work, art and to the rules of living (i.e. morality) can already be observed. The arrangement of

sexual relationships is one aspect of these rules of living. Over the five years of the existence of our labour republic, the revolution on this non-military front has been accomplishing a great shift in the way men and women think. The fiercer the battle between the two ideologies, the greater the significance it assumes and the more inevitably it raises new "riddles of life" and new problems to which only the ideology of the working class can give a satisfactory answer.

The "riddle of love" that interests us here is one such problem. This question of the relationships between the sexes is a mystery as old as human society itself. At different levels of historical development mankind has approached the solution of this problem in different ways. The problem remains the same; the keys to its solution change. The keys are fashioned by the different epochs, by the classes in power and by the "spirit" of a particular age (in other words by its culture).

In Russia over the recent years of intense civil war and general dislocation there has been little interest in the nature of the riddle. The men and women of the working classes were in the grip of other emotions, passions and experiences. In those years everyone walked in the shadow of death, and it was being decided whether victory would belong to the revolution and progress or to counter-revolution and reaction. In face of the revolutionary threat, tender-winged Eros fled

SOURCE: *Selected Writings of Aleksandra Kollontai*, trans. Alix Molt (New York: W. W. Norton, 1980), 276–279, 285–292.

from the surface of life. There was neither time nor a surplus of inner strength for love's "joys and pains." . . . And in Russia, for a time, the biological instinct of reproduction, the natural voice of nature dominated the situation. Men and women came together and men and women parted much more easily and much more simply than before. They came together without great commitment and parted without tears or regret.

Prostitution disappeared, and the number of sexual relationships where the partners were under no obligation to each other and which were based on the instinct of reproduction unadorned by any emotions of love increased. This fact frightened some. But such a development was, in those years, inevitable. Either pre-existing relationships continued to exist and unite men and women through comradeship and long-standing friendship, which was rendered more precious by the seriousness of the moment, or new relationships were begun for the satisfaction of purely biological needs, both partners treating the affair as incidental and avoiding any commitment that might hinder their work for the revolution.

The unadorned sexual drive is easily aroused but is soon spent; thus "wingless Eros" consumes less inner strength than "winged Eros," whose love is woven of delicate strands of every kind of emotion. "Wingless Eros" does not make one suffer from sleepless nights, does not sap one's will, and does not entangle the rational workings of the mind. The fighting class could not have fallen under the power of "winged Eros" at a time when the clarion call of revolution was sounding. It would not have been expedient at such a time to waste the inner strength of the members of the collective on experiences that did not directly serve the revolution. . . .

But now the picture changes. The Soviet republic and the whole of toiling humanity are entering a period of temporary and comparative calm. The complex task of understanding and assimilating the achievements and gains that have been made is beginning. The proletariat, the creator of new forms of life, must be able to learn from all social and psychological phenomena, grasp the significance of these phenomena and fashion weapons from them for the self-defence of the class. Only when the proletariat has appropriated the laws not only of the creation of material wealth but also of inner, psychological life is it able to advance fully armed to fight the decaying bourgeois world. Only then will toiling humanity prove itself to be the victor, not only on the military and labour front but also on the psychological-cultural front.

Now that the revolution has proved victorious and is in a stronger position, and now that the atmosphere of revolutionary élan has ceased to absorb men and women completely, tender-winged Eros has emerged from the shadows and begun to demand his rightful place. "Wingless Eros" has ceased to satisfy psychological needs. Emotional energy has accumulated and men and women, even of the working class, have not yet learned to use it for the inner life of the collective. This extra energy seeks an outlet in the love-experience. The many-stringed lyre of the god of love drowns the monotonous voice of "wingless Eros." . . .

In the life of the Soviet republic an undoubted growth of intellectual and emotional needs, a desire for knowledge, an interest in scientific questions and in art and the theatre can be observed. This movement towards transformation inevitably embraces the sphere of love experiences too. Interest is aroused in the question of the psychology of sex, the mystery of love. Everyone to some extent is having to face up to questions of personal life. One notes with surprise that party workers who in previous years had time only for Pravda editorials and minutes and reports are reading fiction books in which winged Eros is lauded.

What does this mean? Is this a reactionary step? A symptom of the beginning of the decline of revolutionary creativity? Nothing of the sort! It is time we separated ourselves from the hypocrisy of bourgeois thought. It is time to recognise openly that love is not only a powerful natural factor, a biological force, but also a social factor.

Essentially love is a profoundly social emotion. At all stages of human development love has (in different forms, it is true) been an integral part of culture. Even the bourgeoisie, who saw love as a "private matter," was able to channel the expression of love in its class interests. The ideology of the working class must pay even greater attention to the significance of love as a factor which can, like any other psychological or social phenomenon, be channelled to the advantage of the collective. Love is not in the least a "private" matter concerning only the two loving persons: love possesses a uniting element which is valuable to the collective. This is clear from the fact that at all stages of historical development society has established norms defining when and under what conditions love is "legal" (i.e. corresponds to the interests of the given social collective), and when and under what conditions love is sinful and criminal (i.e. contradicts the tasks of the given society). . . .

LOVE-COMRADESHIP

The new, communist society is being built on the principle of comradeship and solidarity. Solidarity is not only an awareness of common interests; It depends also on the intellectual and emotional ties linking the members of the collective. For a social system to be built on solidarity and co-operation it is essential that people should be capable of love and warm emotions. The proletarian ideology, therefore, attempts to educate and encourage every member of the working class to be capable of responding to the distress and needs of other members of the class, of a sensitive understanding of others and a penetrating consciousness of the individual's relationship to the collective. All these "warm emotions"—sensitivity, compassion, sympathy and responsiveness—derive from one source: they are aspects of love, not in the narrow, sexual sense but in the broad meaning of the word. Love is an emotion that unites and is consequently of an organising character. The bourgeoisie was well aware of this, and in the attempt to create a stable family bourgeois ideology erected "married love" as a moral virtue; to be a "good family man" was, in the eyes of the bourgeoisie, an important and valuable quality. . . .

What is the proletariat's ideal of love? We have already seen that each epoch has its ideal; each class strives to fill the conception of love with a moral content that suits its own interests. Each stage of cultural development, with its richer intellectual and emotional experiences, redefines the image of Eros. With the successive stages in the development of the economy and social life, ideas of love have changed; shades of emotion have assumed greater significance or, on the other hand, have ceased to exist.

In the course of the thousand-year history of human society, love has developed from the simple biological instinct—the urge to reproduce which is inherent in all creatures from the highest to the lowest—into a most complex emotion that is constantly acquiring new intellectual and emotional aspects. Love has become a psychological and social factor. Under the impact of economic and social forces, the biological instinct for reproduction has been transformed in two diametrically opposed directions. On the one hand the healthy sexual instinct has been turned by monstrous social and economic relations, particularly those of capitalism, into unhealthy carnality. The sexual act has become an aim in itself—just another way of obtaining pleasure, through lust sharpened with excesses and through distorted, harmful titillations of the flesh. A man does not have sex in response to healthy instincts which have drawn him to a particular woman; a man approaches any woman, though he feels no sexual need for her in particular, with the aim of gaining his sexual satisfaction and pleasure through her. Prostitution is the organised expression of this distortion of the sex drive. If intercourse with a woman does not prompt the expected excitement, the man will turn to every kind of perversion.

This deviation towards unhealthy carnality takes relationships far from their source in the biological instinct. On the other hand, over the centuries and with the changes in human social life and culture, a web of emotional and intellectual experiences has come to surround the physical attraction of the sexes. Love in its present form is a complex state of mind and body; it has long been separated from its primary source, the biological instinct for reproduction, and in fact it is frequently in sharp contradiction with it. Love is intricately woven from friendship, passion, maternal tenderness, infatuation, mutual compatibility, sympathy, admiration, familiarity and many other shades of emotion. With such a range of emotions involved, it becomes increasingly difficult to distinguish direct connection between the natural drive of "wingless Eros" and "winged Eros," where physical attraction and emotional warmth are fused. The existence of love-friendship where the element of physical attraction is absent, of love for one's work or for a cause, and of love for the collective, testify to the extent to which love has become "spiritualised" and separated from its biological base.

In modern society, sharp contradictions frequently arise and battles are waged between the various manifestations of emotion. A deep intellectual and emotional involvement in one's work may not be compatible with love for a particular man or woman, love for the collective might conflict with love for husband, wife or children. It may be difficult for love-friendship in one person to coexist with passion in another; in the one case love is predominantly based on intellectual compatibility, and in the other case on physical harmony. "Love" has many faces and aspects. The various shades of feeling that have developed over the ages and which are experienced by contemporary men and women cannot be covered by such a general and inexact term. . . .

We are talking here . . . of the complexities of "winged Eros"; this should not be confused with sexual relations "without Eros," where one man goes with many women or one woman with a number of men. Relations where no personal feelings are involved can have unfortunate and harmful consequences (the early exhaustion of the organism, venereal diseases etc.), but however

entangled they are, they do not give rise to "emotional dramas." These "dramas" and conflicts begin only where the various shades and manifestations of love are present. A woman feels close to a man whose ideas, hopes and aspirations match her own; she is attracted physically to another. For one woman a man might feel sympathy and a protective tenderness, and in another he might find support and understanding for the strivings of his intellect. To which of the two must he give his love? And why must he tear himself apart and cripple his inner self, if only the possession of both types of inner bond affords the fullness of living?

Under the bourgeois system such a division of the inner emotional world involves inevitable suffering. For thousands of years human culture, which is based on the institution of property, has been teaching people that love is linked with the principles of property. Bourgeois ideology has insisted that love, mutual love, gives the right to the absolute and indivisible possession of the beloved person. Such exclusiveness was the natural consequence of the established form of pair marriage and of the ideal of "all-embracing love" between husband and wife. . . .

Proletarian ideology cannot accept exclusiveness and "all-embracing love." The proletariat is not filled with horror and moral indignation at the many forms and facets of "winged Eros" in the way that the hypocritical bourgeoisie is; on the contrary, it tries to direct these emotions, which it sees as the result of complex social circumstances, into channels which are advantageous to the class during the struggle for and the construction of communist society. The complexity of love is not in conflict with the interests of the proletariat. On the contrary, it facilitates the triumph of the ideal of love-comradeship which is already developing. . . .

The hypocritical morality of bourgeois culture resolutely restricted the freedom of Eros, obliging him to visit only the "legally married couple." Outside marriage there was room only for the "wingless Eros" of momentary and joyless sexual relations which were bought (in the case of prostitution) or stolen (in the case of adultery). The morality of the working class, on the other hand, in so far as it has already been formulated, definitely rejects the external forms of sexual relations. The social aims of the working class are not affected one bit by whether love takes the form of a long and official union or is expressed in a temporary relationship. The ideology of the working class does not place any formal limits on love. But at the same time the ideology of the working class is already beginning to take a thoughtful attitude to the content of love and shades of emotional experience. In this sense the proletarian ideology will persecute "wingless Eros" in a much more strict and severe way than bourgeois morality. "Wingless Eros" contradicts the interests of the working class. In the first place it inevitably involves excesses and therefore physical exhaustion, which lower the resources of labour energy available to society. In the second place it impoverishes the soul, hindering the development and strengthening of inner bonds and positive emotions. And in the third place it usually rests on an inequality of rights in relationships between the sexes, on the dependence of the woman on the man and on male complacency and insensitivity, which undoubtedly hinder the development of comradely feelings. "Winged Eros" is quite different.

Obviously sexual attraction lies at the base of "winged Eros" too, but the difference is that the person experiencing love acquires the inner qualities necessary to the builders of a new culture— sensitivity, responsiveness and the desire to help others. Bourgeois ideology demanded that a person should only display such qualities in their relationship with one partner. The aim of proletarian ideology is that men and women should develop these qualities not only in relation to the chosen one but in relation to all the members of the collective. The proletarian class is not concerned as to which shades and nuances of feeling predominate in winged Eros. The only stipulation is that these emotions facilitate the development and strengthening of comradeship. The ideal of love-comradeship, which is being forged by proletarian ideology to replace the all-embracing and

exclusive marital love of bourgeois culture, involves the recognition of the rights and integrity of the other's personality, a steadfast mutual support and sensitive sympathy, and responsiveness to the other's needs.

The ideal of love-comradeship is necessary to the proletariat in the important and difficult period of the struggle for and the consolidation of the dictatorship. But there is no doubt that with the realisation of communist society love will acquire a transformed and unprecedented aspect. By that time the "sympathetic ties" between all the members of the new society will have grown and strengthened. Love potential will have increased, and love-solidarity will become the lever that competition and self-love were in the bourgeois system. Collectivism of spirit can then defeat individualist self-sufficiency, and the "cold of inner loneliness," from which people in bourgeois culture have attempted to escape through love and marriage, will disappear. The many threads bringing men and women into close emotional and intellectual contact will develop, and feelings will emerge from the private into the public sphere. Inequality between the sexes and the dependence of women on men will disappear without trace, leaving only a fading memory of past ages.

In the new and collective society, where interpersonal relations develop against a background of joyful unity and comradeship, Eros will occupy an honourable place as an emotional experience multiplying human happiness. . . .

But at the present moment we stand between two cultures. And at this turning-point, with the attendant struggles of the two worlds on all fronts, including the ideological one, the proletariat's interest is to do its best to ensure the quickest possible accumulation of "sympathetic feelings." In this period the moral ideal defining relationships is not the unadorned sexual instinct but the many-faceted love experience of love-comradeship. In order to answer the demands formulated by the new proletarian morality, these experiences must conform to three basic principles: (1) Equality in relationships (an end to masculine egoism and the slavish suppression of the female personality). (2) Mutual recognition of the rights of the other, of the fact that one does not own the heart and soul of the other (the sense of property, encouraged by bourgeois culture). (3) Comradely sensitivity, the ability to listen and understand the inner workings of the loved person (bourgeois culture demanded this only from the woman). But in proclaiming the rights of "winged Eros," the ideal of the working class at the same time subordinates this love to the more powerful emotion of love-duty to the collective. However great the love between two members of the collective, the ties binding the two persons to the collective will always take precedence, will be firmer, more complex and organic. Bourgeois morality demanded all for the loved one. The morality of the proletariat demands all for the collective. . . .

The blind, all-embracing, demanding passions will weaken; the sense of property, the egoistical desire to bind the partner to one "forever," the complacency of the man and the self-renunciation of the woman will disappear. At the same time, the valuable aspects and elements of love will develop. Respect for the right of the other's personality will increase, and a mutual sensitivity will be learned; men and women will strive to express their love not only in kisses and embraces but in joint creativity and activity. The task of proletarian ideology is not to drive Eros from social life but to rearm him according to the new social formation, and to educate sexual relationships in the spirit of the great new psychological force of comradely solidarity.

QUESTIONS FOR ANALYSIS

1. What distinctions does Kollontai draw between bourgeois love and proletarian love?
2. Describe the importance of love to the socialist collective as expressed in Kollontai's writing.
3. How do Kollontai's ideas fit with the evolution of Communist policies in the 1920s?

PICTURE ESSAY

Building the Future

AFTER YEARS OF MILITARY BUILDUP AND INVESTMENT IN WAR, politicians in the 1920s turned their attention to civilians, their dwellings, and the urban environment. During the war, population had continued to rise, despite wartime losses, but investment in civilian needs such as housing and transport had suffered in this war as in all other wars. Infrastructure in public buildings such as libraries and schools had deteriorated because the military had first claim to taxpayers' money. Postwar planners determined that citizens who had suffered so greatly during the war, even to the point of rebelling against their governments, needed to be made more comfortable in their surroundings, including their private living space. Wartime products were thus directed to civilian use, and industrial materials such as metal went into the design of sleek, modern furniture for the household. Public planners felt that the public landscape needed to be made aesthetically pleasing as an expression of democracy. "Art should *interpret* industry, as art once interpreted religion," a character in D. H. Lawrence's novel *Women in Love* (1920) announces.[37] The drive to beautify public space in a modern way with modern materials shaped architecture and urban planning in the interwar years.

The pervasive beauty of the urban landscape would bind society together, Francis Pick, head of the London Underground system in the interwar years, believed. "Bare living [is] not life," he wrote. "Everyone is entitled to something more. Public institutions: Museums, art galleries. Higher education."[38] Acting on this belief, Pick hired leading modernist architects to redesign the subway stations. The new design was far different from the dark Victorian style common when the London Underground had opened some seventy years earlier with a jumble of ads and an often muddled presentation of information about the system on station walls. According to Francis Pick, the stations needed to reflect the modernity of the urban environment, and one of his first acts was to hire graphic artists who could provide the clear, modern lettering and vibrant abstract symbols for the Underground that we see in the sign for Hammersmith station (Figure 4.1). Large avant-garde art posters decorated the subway walls in an orderly fashion.

Many modern artists engaged in commercializing art for the public. They believed that abstract art conveyed a higher, more spiritual truth than realist images did and that the public would imbibe these messages if they were visible in the environment—whether in subway posters, in advertising, or in the streamlined appearance of new public buildings. What indications of modern life does the photo of Hammersmith station provide, and how did the redesign of this station serve postwar goals?

239

◆ **Figure 4.1 Hammersmith Underground Station, London, 1933**
London Transport Museum/© Transport for London.

In the Soviet Union and elsewhere, some modern subway stations were conceived and designed to symbolize the intertwined power of the mass society and its government. Massive and ornate both inside and outside, metro stations in Moscow dwarfed their users, providing cavernous space along with efficient service. Designed by prominent artist Alexei Dushkin and named after the famed poet of the 1920s Vladimir Mayakovski, the Mayakovski station in Moscow (shown in Figure 4.2) is one of the most grandiose anywhere. In one section, its ceiling celebrates such aspects of modern life as aviation and sports. Even though the interior decoration also depicts events in the day of an ordinary worker, the gigantic proportions of the station suggest other values. What feelings might this design have evoked in an ordinary person entering the metro system?

Officials made a major effort to construct residences for the masses who had endured the horrors of industrial war. Utopianism fueled by feelings of hope at the war's end and by the revolutionary changes in Russia fostered progressive planning

◆ Figure 4.2 **Mayakovski Metro Station, Moscow**
Peter Arnold, Inc.

for the use of space. Architects and urban planners grew in prominence as modern apartment buildings rose in cities from London to Moscow. Many of these buildings were prefabricated and constructed in what came to be called the "International Style," a spare and unadorned design that was associated with modernity and became popular around the world. According to the modern architect Le Corbusier, this style eliminated the "falsity, make-up, and tricks of the courtesan" of Victorian-era carvings, curlicues, wrought-iron, and other popular decorations.[39] Critics, however, mocked the unadorned German apartment buildings as the "Arab Village Housing Project" and "a suburb of Jerusalem," suggesting their resemblance to the streamlined and plain styles of North Africa and the Middle East.[40]

The Sandleitenhof complex built in Vienna in the interwar years provided 1,587 apartments for workers (Figure 4.3). As the photo of an interior courtyard shows it was massive. Each apartment offered electricity, cold running water, gas for cooking, a kitchen, a bathroom, and hardwood floors. The apartments were small, ranging

◆ Figure 4.3 **Workers' Housing in Vienna**
Bettmann/CORBIS.

from 400 to 600 square feet. Residents had access to common laundry facilities and to the interior courtyard. The new housing for workers had striking features, such as the monumental scale of the balconies and curved walls of Germany's worker housing (Figure 4.4). What might have been the drawbacks of living in the apartment complexes shown in Figures 4.3 and 4.4? What advantages might families have enjoyed?

Suburbs with cute bungalows also appeared throughout the 1920s. The bungalow, whose name derives from the former northeast Indian province of Bengal, was by one account "the most revolutionary new dwelling type" of the twentieth century (Figure 4.5).[41] More isolated from neighbors than either apartment building flats or row houses, the bungalow sheltered the family from community eyes.

◆ Figure 4.4 **Workers' Housing in Berlin, c. 1930**
© *Austrian Archives/CORBIS.*

Despite a brief postwar upsurge in the birthrate, family size was dropping and smaller houses suited that trend. Bungalows were sold to the middle-classes as practical solutions to the servant problem—that is, a smaller and more compact house required fewer or no servants to clean and maintain it. The upper-working classes, for their part, could aspire to an affordable home of their own, often subsidized by governments. People needed less kitchen space because of the availability of canned foods. Other space- and time-saving conveniences like washing machines cut down the room needed to complete household tasks, further lessening the overall need for space as well as the need for servants. Women could be tempted to leave the postwar workforce, handing their jobs over to veterans, in return for a

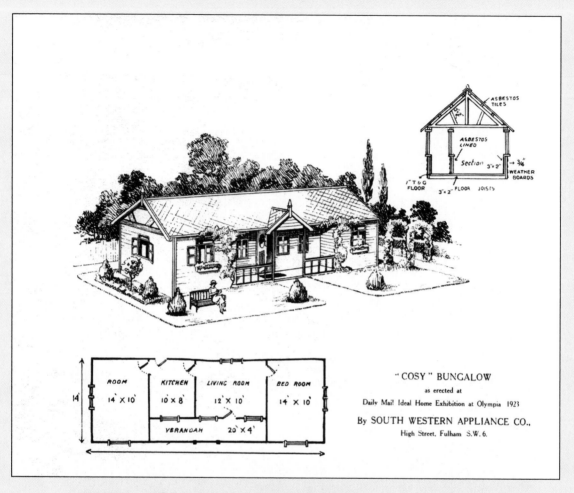

◆ Figure 4.5 **Building Plan for a British Bungalow, 1923**

snug little bungalow. Given these advantages the bungalow itself became one of the most popular styles of housing across Europe and the United States. The construction of rectangular bungalows in planned developments gave rise to the prefabricated housing industry. Features such as private porches reflected the postwar emphasis on family intimacy and the resocialization of men and women as couples after their separation during the war. Songs about the coziness and romance of the bungalow proliferated in music halls and on the new radio stations: "Our little love nest, Beside a stream / Where red, red roses grow, Our bungalow of dreams."[42]

It was thought that people who owned their own homes and spent time with their families in suburban living would be less likely to mass together in urban protest movements. Suburbanization, however, brought its own special problems, for alternating with neighborhoods of bungalows were the new, concrete multi-

◆ Figure 4.6 **Stockholm Public Library Designed by Gunnar Asplund, 1928**
© *Alex Farnsworth/The Image Works.*

◆ Figure 4.7 **Interior of the Stockholm Public Library**
© *Alex Farnsworth/The Image Works.*

story buildings looming like a ring of fortifications around cities. The situation led to urban planning that paid less attention to boulevards, transport, and sanitation facilities and devoted more effort to the construction of amenities outside of cities to offset the starkness of the new high-rise apartment buildings. Planners promoted the building of garden apartments, public libraries (Figures 4.6 and 4.7), and parks to improve the quality of life beyond the city center.

Stockholm's imposing public library, designed in 1921 and completed in 1927, was built of steel and concrete. As the design evolved, the building became increasingly simple and modernist in style with its interior giving a sense of openness and space. The interior was spare and functional with its floor replicating the geometric design of the exterior. One of the notable public buildings of the 1920s, the Stockholm Public Library, like many across Europe, was built to meet the growing needs of an educated mass public in the postwar period. This library's monumental grandeur made it one of the city's major institutions in which citizens could take pride. What message might the architectural features—inside and out—of this building have conveyed to Stockholm's citizens about books and study? In what ways did this building serve both public and individual needs?

QUESTIONS FOR ANALYSIS

1. Which design features of these very different architectual interiors and exteriors do you find most striking?

2. What do the architectural features indicate about postwar European society and its values?

3. What political elements can you discern in the design and function of these buildings?

NOTES

1. Virginia Woolf, *Orlando: A Biography* (New York: Penguin, 1946 [1928]), 1, 193.

2. Adolf Reichwein, *China and Europe: Intellectual and Artistic Contacts in the Eighteenth Century,* trans. J. C. Powell (New York: Knopf, 1925), 4.

3. Woodrow Wilson, quoted in Aviel Roshwald, *Ethnic Nationalism and the Fall of Empires: Central Europe, Russia, and the Middle East, 1914–1923* (London: Routledge, 2001), 160.

4. Edouard Bonnefous, *Histoire politique de la Troisième République,* vol. 3 (Paris: Presse universitaire de France, 1959), 34.

5. John Maynard Keynes, *The Economic Consequences of the Peace* (London: Macmillan, 1920), 233.

6. Quoted in Michael Burleigh, *The Third Reich: A New History* (New York: Hill and Wang, 2000), 36.

7. Burleigh, *The Third Reich,* 83.

8. *Morning Post,* April 5, 1921, quoted in Claudia M. Skran, *Refugees in Inter-War Europe* (Oxford: Clarendon Press, 1995), 39.

9. Quoted in Andrew Baruch Wachtel, *Making a Nation, Breaking a Nation: Literature and Cultural Politics in Yugoslavia* (Stanford: Stanford University Press, 1998), 84.

10. Quoted in H. Van Thal, ed., *The Prime Ministers,* vol. 2 (London: Allen and Unwin, 1975), 269.

11. Quoted in David Gilmour, *The Long Recessional: The Imperial Life of Rudyard Kipling* (London: John Murray, 2002).

12. Quoted in Harold B. Segel, "Culture in Poland during World War I," in *European Culture in the Great War: The Arts, Entertainment, and Propaganda, 1914–1918,* ed. Aviel Roshwald and Richard Stites (Cambridge: Cambridge University Press, 1999), 68.

13. Feliks Dzerzhinsky, quoted in Mark D. Steinberg and Vladimir M. Khrustalëv, *The Fall of the Romanovs: Political Dreams and Personal Struggles in a Time of Revolution* (New Haven: Yale University Press, 1995), 286.

14. Maurice Genevoix, quoted in Daniel J. Sherman, *The Construction of Memory in Interwar France* (Chicago: University of Chicago Press, 1999), 22.

15. Quoted in Anton Kaes et al., eds., *The Weimar Republic Sourcebook* (Berkeley: University of California Press, 1994), 24.

16. Quoted in Mary Nolan, *Visions of Modernity: American Business and the Modernization of Germany* (New York: Oxford University Press, 1994), 69.

17. Quoted ibid., 175.

18. Quoted in Uta G. Poiger, *Jazz, Rock, and Rebels: Cold War Politics and American Culture in a Divided Germany* (Berkeley: University of California Press, 2000), 17, 21.

19. Quoted in Sally Marks, *The Ebbing of European Ascendancy: An International History of the World, 1914–1945* (London: Arnold, 2002), 219.

20. Quoted in Elizabeth Thompson, *Colonial Citizens: Republican Rights, Paternal Privilege, and Gender in French Syria and Lebanon* (New York: Columbia University Press, 2000), 40.

21. Mohandas Gandhi, "Hind Swaraj," in *The Collected Works of Mahatma Gandhi,* vol. 10 (Ahmedabad: Navajivan Trust, 1963), 23.

22. Quoted in David Levering Lewis, *W. E. B. Du Bois: The Fight for Equality and the American Century, 1919–1963* (New York: Henry Holt, 2000), 41.

23. Quoted in Carol Oja, *Making Music Modern: New York in the 1920s* (New York: Oxford University Press, 2000), 65.

24. James Joyce, *Ulysses,* ed. Danis Rose (London: Picador, 1997 [1922]), 561.

25. Quoted in William G. Rosenberg, "Introduction," in *Russia in the Era of NEP,* ed. Sheila Fitzpatrick et al. (Bloomington: Indiana University Press, 1991), 8.

26. Quoted in Geoffrey Hosking, *A History of the Soviet Union* (London: Fontana, 1985), 58.

27. Quoted in Alix Holt, trans., *Selected Writings of Aleksandra Kollontai* (New York: W. W. Norton, 1980), 290.

28. Quoted ibid., 290.

29. Quoted in Richard Stites, *Revolutionary Dreams: Utopian Vision and Experimental Life in the Russian Revolution* (New York: Oxford University Press, 1989), 156–157.

30. Stites, *Revolutionary Dreams,* 71.

31. Quoted in Nina Tumarkin, *Lenin Lives! The Lenin Cult in Soviet Russia* (Cambridge: Harvard University Press, 1997), 148.

32. Quoted in Mabel Berezin, *Making the Fascist Self: The Political Culture of Interwar Italy* (Ithaca: Cornell University Press, 1997), 110.

33. Umberto Bernasconi, quoted in Ruth Ben-Ghiat, *Fascist Modernities: Italy, 1922–1945* (Berkeley: University of California Press, 2001), 3.

34. Quoted ibid., 23.

35. Quoted in Adrian Lyttelton, *The Seizure of Power: Fascism in Italy, 1919–1929,* 2nd ed. (Princeton: Princeton University Press, 1987), 44.

36. Adolph Hitler, *Mein Kampf,* ed. D. C. Watt (London: 1990). 433.

37. D. H. Lawrence, *Women in Love* (Cambridge: Cambridge University Press, 1987 [1920]), 424.

38. Francis Pick, quoted in Michael T. Saler, *The Avant-Garde in Interwar England: Medieval Modernism and the London Underground* (New York: Oxford University Press, 1999), 35.

39. Quoted in Peter Gössel and Gabriele Leuthäuser, *Architecture in the Twentieth Century* (Cologne: Taschen, 1991), 165.

40. Quoted in Janet Ward, *Weimar Surfaces: Urban Visual Culture in 1920s Germany* (Berkeley: University of California Press, 2001), 61.

41. King, *The Bungalow,* 156.

42. Ibid., 258.

SUGGESTED REFERENCES

General Works

Golby, John, et al., eds. *Between Two Wars.* 1990.

Spiering, Menno, and Michael Wintle, eds. *Ideas of Europe since 1914: The Legacy of the First World War.* 2002.

The Search For Stability Europe was crowded with an unprecedented number of refugees, and dealing with them as well as with other postwar problems often surpassed politicians' and statesmen's capabilities. Skran's book captures the situation well.

Ambrosius, Lloyd E. *Wilsonianism: Woodrow Wilson and His Legacy in American Foreign Relations.* 2002.

Berend, T. Ivan. *Decades of Crisis: Central and Eastern Europe before World War II.* 1998.

Fink, Carole. *Defending the Rights of Others: The Great Powers, the Jews, and International Minority Protection, 1878–1938.* 2004.

Hanebrink, Paul. *In Defense of Christian Hungary: Religion, Nationalism, and Antisemitism in Hungary, 1890–1944.* 2006.

Hessler, Julie. *A Social History of Soviet Trade: Trade Policy, Retail Practices, and Consumption, 1917–1953.* 2004.

King, Jeremy. *Budweisers into Czechs and Germans: A Local History of Bohemian Politics, 1848–1948.* 2002.

Siegel, Mona L. *The Moral Disarmament of France: Education, Pacifism, and Patriotism, 1914–1940.* 2004.

Skran, Claudena M. *Refugees in Inter-War Europe: The Emergence of a Regime.* 1995.

Wright, Jonathan. *Gustav Stresemann: Weimar's Greatest Statesman.* 2002.

Society Recovers The rich literature on the postwar period is wide ranging, covering social and political movements as well as the growth of consumer life. Among challenging interpretations is that by Watson, who shows that bitterness about the war arose after it was over, when economic and social conditions were precarious for many veterans.

Brenner, Michael. *The Renaissance of Jewish Culture in Weimar Germany.* 1996.

Dean, Carolyn. *The Frail Social Body: Pornography, Homosexuality, and Other Fantasies in Interwar France.* 2000.

Dinerstein, Joel. *Swinging the Machine: Modernity, Technology, and African American Culture between the World Wars.* 2000.

Gruber, Helmut. *Red Vienna: Experiment in Working-Class Culture, 1919–1934.* 1991.

Lerner, Paul. *Hysterical Men: War, Psychiatry, and the Politics of Trauma in Germany, 1890–1930.* 2003.

Mosse, George. *Fallen Soldiers: Reshaping the Memory of the World Wars.* 1990.

Nolan, Mary. *Visions of Modernity: American Business and the Modernization of Germany.* 1994.

Northrup, Douglas. *Veiled Empire: Gender and Power in Stalinist Central Asia.* 2004.

Rabinbach, Anson. *The Human Motor: Energy, Fatigue, and the Origins of Modernity.* 1992.

Sherman, Daniel J. *The Construction of Memory in Interwar France.* 1999.

Søland, Birgitte. *Becoming Modern: Young Women and the Reconstruction of Womanhood in the 1920s.* 2000.

Watson, Janet S. K. *Fighting Different Wars: Experience, Memory, and the First World War in Britain.* 2004.

Resurgence of Empire in a Time of Unrest We often forget that the interwar period—not just the years before World War I—was also an era of empire. Huda Sharawi's memoirs describe the struggle of Egyptians against Britain in the 1920s.

Balderston, Theo. *The World Economy and National Economics in the Interwar Slump.* 2003.

Buettner, Elizabeth. *Empire Families: Britons and Late Imperial India.* 2004.

Collett, Nigel. *The Butcher of Amritsar: General Reginald Dyer.* 2005.

Gouda, Frances. *Dutch Culture Overseas: Colonial Practice in the Netherlands Indies, 1900–1942.* 1995.

Marks, Sally. *The Ebbing of European Ascendancy: An International History of the World, 1914–1945.* 2002.

Peabody, Sue, and Tyler Stovall, eds. *The Color of Liberty: Histories of Race in France.* 2003.

Roy, Tirthankar. *The Economic History of India, 1857–1947.* 2000.

Sharawi, Huda. *Harem Years: The Memoirs of an Egyptian Feminist (1879–1924).* 1987.

Thompson, Elizabeth. *Colonial Citizens: Republican Rights, Paternal Privilege, and Gender in French Syria and Lebanon.* 2000.

Wilder, Gary. *The French Imperial Nation-State: Negritude and Colonial Humanism between the Two World Wars.* 2005.

An Age of Extremes In this age of extremes, extraordinary thinkers and tragically unforgettable dictators produced an array of political and cultural ideas. These books give a sampling of their thoughts and deeds. Kirschenbaum shows the impact of communism on young children, while Helstosky provides a look at the ways in which Fascism shaped the food Italians ate.

Adamson, Walter L. *Avant-Garde Florence: From Modernism to Fascism.* 1993.

Ben-Ghiat, Ruth. *Fascist Modernities: Italy, 1922–1945.* 2001.

Bonnell, Victoria E. *Iconography of Power: Soviet Political Posters under Lenin and Stalin.* 1997.

Gruber, Helmut, and Pamela Graves, eds. *Women and Socialism, Socialism and Women: Europe between the Two World Wars.* 1998.

Helstosky, Carol. *Garlic and Oil: Politics and Food in Italy.* 2004.

Jackson, Jeffrey H. *Making Jazz French: Music and Modern Life in Interwar Paris.* 2003.

Kirschenbaum, Lisa. *Small Comrades: Revolutionizing Childhood in Soviet Russia, 1917–1932.* 2001.

Koenker, Diane. *Republic of Labor: Russian Printers and Soviet Socialism, 1918–1930.* 2005.

Lyttelton, Adrian. *The Seizure of Power: Fascism in Italy, 1919–1929.* 1973.

McGreevy, Linda F. *Bitter Witness: Otto Dix and the Great War.* 2001.

Saler, Michael. *The Avant-Garde in Interwar England: Medieval Modernism and the London Underground.* 1999.

Service, Robert. *Lenin: A Biography.* 2000.

Stites, Richard. *Revolutionary Dreams: Utopian Vision and Experimental Life in the Russian Revolution.* 1989.

Selected Web Sites

Indiana University maintains a richly informative site on the League of Nations: <**www.indiana.edu/~league/**>. The Schomberg Center of the New York Public Library has digitized documents on African American culture and its influence in the Jazz Age; see <**nypl.org/research/sc/sc.html**>. For an exhibit on Harlem and its influence in the 1920s, see<**si.umich.edu/CHICO/Harlem/text/exhibition .html**>. There is also an informative Web site on the Bauhaus: <**bauhaus.de/ english/**>. The following site provides an array of archival information, photos, biographical facts, and other digitized material on Mohandas Gandhi: <**mkgandhi.org**>. Cornell University Library has an interesting site that presents the rising authoritarian leaders of the interwar and post–World War II periods: <**cidc.library.cornell.edu/DOF/fathers.htm**>.

5

Facing Global Economic Depression

1929–1939

O N A COLD DECEMBER NIGHT IN BERLIN IN 1931, AN audience watched enraptured as the first act of the *Rise and Fall of the City of Mahagonny,* Bertolt Brecht and Kurt Weill's experimental opera, unfolded on the stage. The enthusiastic throng shouted "Bravo!" and applauded wildly when the curtain went down. Members of Adolf Hitler's powerful Nazi Party, which fancied itself an expert critic of the arts, howled at the performance, however: it was "decadent," it was "filth," they screamed. In fact, the opera's message was hardly uplifting: the inhabitants of the city of Mahagonny settle into lives of thievery, prostitution, gluttony, and double-dealing as the city's economy crashes. As bad, to Nazi viewers, composer Kurt Weill was Jewish, and the score combined jazz and the blues from an "inferior" African American tradition with lyrical songs as well as modern atonal music. To the Nazi way of thinking, theater and music should represent classical ideals of beauty and national greatness.

Berlin's thriving art world featured cosmopolitan productions influenced in part by the sophisticated avant-garde arriving from Russia and other eastern European countries. Berlin's cabarets, theater, and film flourished between the wars, attracting gifted artists and enthusiastic audiences, and the Nazis viewed them all with hatred and

◆ **Lotte Lenya and Harald Paulsen in *The Rise and Fall of the City of Mahagonny,* 1931**
These actors play the cynical adventurers in the Berlin production of this pathbreaking opera. Hustlers and whores traveling the United States, the characters would do anything for a dollar. The talented Lotte Lenya escaped Nazi Germany to continue a successful and eventful career in the United States, even playing villains in James Bond films. *Courtesy of the Weill-Lenya Research Center, Kurt Weill Foundation for Music, New York.*

1936	Charlie Chaplin's film *Modern Times* debuts.
1936	General Francisco Franco stages uprising against republican government in Madrid; civil war begins in Spain.
1936	Hitler sends troops into Rhineland.
1936	Ethiopian capital, Addis Ababa, falls to Italy.
1936	Arabs in Palestine undertake general strike to protest migration of Jews.
1936–1937	French Popular Front forms government.
1936–1937	Rome-Berlin Axis brings Italy and Germany together as allies.
1936–1938	Show trials in USSR result in mass purges.
1937	Gold Coast cocoa producers withhold cocoa until they are paid more for their crops.
1937	Swedish government inaugurates welfare state policies.
1937	George Orwell publishers *The Road to Wigan Pier.*
1938	70 percent of German households have radios.
1938	Virginia Woolf publishes *Three Guineas.*
1938	March: Germany annexes Austria—the Anschluss.
1938	September: European leaders meet with Hitler in Munich.
1938	November 9–10: *Kristallnacht:* Nazis attack synagogues, Jewish-owned stores, and homes and imprison more than 20,000 Jews.
1939	More than 9 million households wired for electricity in Britain.
1939	Franco's troops defeat republicans in Spain.
1939	March: Hitler occupies the rest of Czechoslovakia.
1939	May: Hitler and Mussolini form Pact of Steel.
1939	August 23: Germany and USSR sign Nazi-Soviet Nonaggression pact.

255

contempt. In the case of *Mahagonny*, this negative opinion was somewhat ironic given that in the libretto the left-wing Brecht critiqued materialism and the commercialization of human relationships in a spirit not at odds with Nazi beliefs. After Hitler came to power in 1933, Weill fled Germany, and the works of Brecht were among those the Nazis burned in vast bonfires to eliminate critical and avant-garde views.

The Marxist-inspired Brecht wrote in an era of economic collapse dramatized by the crash of the United States' stock market in 1929. He was one of many writers in those rocky years who looked to the Soviet "experiment" for inspiration, and his harsh message about the decay produced by capitalism inspired many a working-class person to join the Communist party. Both Communist and Fascist parties, including the Nazis, continued to grow with the coming of the Great Depression, and the political scene became increasingly violent across Europe as Communists, Fascists, and Nazis used physical force to terrorize and intimidate their fellow citizens. Social life was turbulent too: decay caused by evictions, the collapse of small businesses, and challenges to traditional gender roles, such as that of the male breadwinner, threatened families and neighborhoods. Governments fought desperately but too often used misguided policies to boost their economies and restore prosperity. A drive for conquest both inside and outside of Europe was a common strategy, one that Nazis and Italian Fascists employed most in the fateful depression years. Expansion, they promised a demoralized, even desperate citizenry, would solve *all* problems and bring national greatness.

In an era of economic depression and lingering postwar malaise, cultural and political values clashed, as the reaction to Brecht and Weill's opera showed. Perhaps the greatest values under attack were embodied in the notion of human rights—the right to free speech, to a humane standard of living, and to security from physical attack. Amid cries for quick solutions to economic hard times, democracies such as France and Britain, to say nothing of the fledgling states of eastern Europe, were hard-pressed to preserve those rights, though fight for them many citizens did. The countries that turned to a militarized style of leadership—Italy and Germany leading the pack—saw human freedoms as outdated and effeminate ideals. Germany joined Italy and the Soviet Union in setting up violent dictatorships; governments in Spain, eastern and central Europe, and as far away as Japan did the same. By the late 1930s democratic values had fallen even more out of favor. In the democracies, many people criticized free speech as too messy, and even in republican France parliamentary debate turned into furious shouting matches. Incivility became a political style touted as "manly" by the Nazis. When violent incivility began to permeate the international sphere, it set the stage for another world war. Although Stalin outpaced everyone in slaughtering the masses in the 1930s—some twenty million by one horrific estimate—Adolf Hitler led the way toward the outbreak of another catastrophic war. His stage was a globalized European society, suffering from economic depression and at odds with democratic and representative government, which had expanded in the earlier part of the century. The Great Depression starved democratic traditions while it fed the advance of dictatorship, war, and genocide.

CRASH AND DEPRESSION

Economic difficulties plagued Europe after World War I. Many people were thrown out of work by the swift reduction of military needs, and some countries such as Britain never returned to robust employment. Agricultural prices declined as mechanization increased farm output. Bumper crops around the world, especially in Asia late in the 1920s, added to the calamitous crash in prices. Japan, Latin America, and eastern Europe were already feeling an economic downturn as the decade wound down. In western Europe financial turmoil over reparations and dislocation caused by industrial modernizing such as the switch from coal to oil also added to the perils facing postwar workers and entrepreneurs. Although the war had slowed some aspects of globalization while the great powers were locked in combat, economies around the world remained connected to one another. The wartime advances made in non-European economies contributed to the failure of the European powers to reestablish peacetime prosperity with dispatch. There was some stabilization of the European economy after 1924, but the complete collapse of the U.S. stock market in the fall of 1929 took place in circumstances that were hardly auspicious for a quick rebound. Instead, the world reeled from this event in distant New York. Its impact was felt in the highest reaches of government and in the modest homes of ordinary people, where it affected family life, physical well-being, and morale around the globe.

The Depression Comes to Europe

The stock market crash in the United States was a global event; its effects were far-ranging. Exuberant Americans, confident as their economy rose to new heights of prosperity, had invested enthusiastically in the stock market during the "Roaring Twenties." Despite a few naysayers, some nine million Americans had played the market on credit, with which they borrowed money in brokerage accounts. Their faith that the market would continue to rise and thus allow them to repay their brokerage debts had been unshakable. But then the U.S. Federal Reserve tightened the availability of credit in hopes of curbing what it considered an unhealthy mania. In response, brokers demanded that their clients immediately pay back the borrowed money, and investors rushed to sell stocks to cover their loans, causing the market to plummet. Between October and mid-November 1929 the value of businesses listed on the New York Stock Exchange dropped from $87 billion to $30 billion. As a leading international creditor, the United States had increasingly financed the development of enterprises globally since 1914. Suddenly strapped for credit, U.S. financiers cut back on investments and called in short-term debts. These moves undermined industry and finance around the world.

The United States was not only a leading creditor but a leading producer and consumer; its troubles intensified the world's troubles as American households cut spending and as output rapidly declined. Commerce slowed both nationally and internationally, leaving the United States with an estimated 14 million workers unemployed and five thousand banks ruined. The savings of millions were wiped out. In Germany the official number of unemployed was 6.12 million, one-third of the workforce in 1932, but the real number—including uncounted people working in "off-the-books" jobs—was probably at least 7.5 million. France had a more self-sufficient economy with a larger ratio of peasant proprietors to industrial workers than the rest of western Europe, but by early 1932 manufacturing output had dropped some 25 percent, and by the mid-1930s more than 800,000 French people had lost their jobs. Great Britain with its aging industries had close to 3 million unemployed in 1932.

The depression was uneven in its movement across Europe. Economies in eastern and east-central Europe were particularly hard hit but in different ways. The breakup of the Austrian Empire had created small economic units, most of them undeveloped industrially except for Czechoslovakia. Declining prices for agricultural produce left the region's many farmers without money to buy the chemical fertilizers and motorized machinery they needed to remain competitive, and they too went under. The situation was especially bitter for peasants in Hungary and Poland because they had pressed for and obtained land redistribution from the massive estates of the Magyars, Russians, Germans, and Catholic Church. The depression curtailed these farmers' ability to operate their newly acquired farms, for profit in agriculture increasingly depended on efficiency and the consolidation of holdings. In Poland, for example, the Sejm, or parliament, had taken more than six million acres from the vast estates of the Catholic Church and the nobility and awarded the acreage to some seven hundred thousand new landholders. Many of these peasants quickly fell into debt trying to make their land viable—a fatal situation to be in during the credit crunch. Meanwhile, the fledgling governments of eastern and east-central Europe tried to make their national economies prosper by creating new industries and building infrastructure. Bureaucrats found no funds left to alleviate the farmers' plight. In eastern Europe, welfare relief during the Great Depression was out of the question.

Responding to the crisis, governments in the industrial countries often followed policies that actually worsened the misery of the unemployed. Germany did not expand coverage in its old system of unemployment relief, which benefited less than a million of those without jobs and provided aid for only half a year. As tax revenues fell, funds for assistance were almost unobtainable and were far less than the amount a single person let alone an entire family needed to survive. The inability of the Weimar and other national governments to deliver on their promises of welfare benefits ate away at faith in republican government in Germany and elsewhere. The British responded to unemployment by cutting allocations to the unemployed— the "dole"—because of traditional wisdom that attributed the economic downturn to unbalanced budgets and overspending. Britain's termination of the gold standard in 1931 deflected Britain's problems onto other countries by devaluing its own currency and thus making British goods cheaper. Other countries followed. The result was disorder in the currency markets both on the continent and abroad.

The depression was additionally an uneven experience given that many new industries continued to experience growth. Automobile manufacturing expanded,

◆ **Unemployed Protest outside Labour Exchange**
The Great Depression in the democracies lasted until the outbreak of war in 1939. These unemployed British men chained themselves to a railing outside the London Labour Exchange, demanding some kind of governmental relief. Their plight and the experiences of others out of work helped shape the benefits eventually offered by the welfare state. Joblessness attacked men's self-esteem, undermining their identity as breadwinners and making them receptive to fascism. © *Hulton-Deutsch Collection/CORBIS.*

spawning output in glass, tires, and machine tools, and in road construction, roadside stands and restaurants, and automobile repair and servicing. Bakelite, rayon, celluloid, and other synthetic materials were used to make affordable dishes, clothing, film, buttons, and Ping-Pong balls. People in the lower middle class snapped up cheap versions of formerly expensive products such as cameras and radios. The electric industry extended power lines to greater numbers of customers, who then purchased light bulbs, irons, toasters, and vacuum cleaners. In Britain the number of households wired for electricity went from under three million in 1929 to more than nine million by 1939. As household modernization progressed, falling rents and lower prices for food and for manufactured goods during the Great Depression increased the prosperity of some segments of the working population.

Consumerism received a boost during the 1930s from several innovations. Retail outlets selling inexpensive goods—the American five-and-dime store Woolworth's and its European counterparts—sprang up in cities. These stores brought to the purchase of thread, small household wares, and hardware the same large range of products and convenient one-stop-shopping that the large department stores had brought to furniture, draperies, tailored clothing, and household linen several generations earlier. Also, in the 1930s governments passed laws providing for paid worker vacations—a reward for rising productivity and an acknowledgment of the need for regularly scheduled leisure time. As the prosperous working classes now joined the middle and upper classes going to beaches, mountains, and forests to relax, industry benefited from orders for small trailers, tents, hiking shoes, and bathing dress, and new leisure-oriented businesses were established and prospered. Thanks to these innovations in mass marketing during the depression years, many sectors bucked the downward trend.

Governments fought the depression by channeling the consumerism that did exist into purchasing goods made or grown within the nation. Mussolini, for example, sought to make Italy self-sufficient in food, and Italian bureaucrats churned out recipes that used only Italian products. However, individuals desiring coffee, sugar, tea, and other products not available in Italy undermined the strict observance of this kind of economic nationalism, for trade was too tightly interconnected globally to sustain economic isolation.

Governments also jettisoned any remaining attachment to the doctrine of free trade. They erected high tariff walls—rates sometimes exceeded 50 percent on imported goods in order to promote the purchase of domestic goods and thus boost employment at home. To the countries of eastern Europe, the tariffs were especially damaging obstacles to the traditional trade with former neighbors in the Austrian Empire. Countries resorted to bartering with one another, trading resources such as coal, steel, and grain rather than buying and selling for cash, especially given the turmoil in exchange rates. Germany, for example, bartered its coal for coffee from Brazil and its chemical fertilizer for cotton from Egypt. Germany's bartering with the struggling new eastern European states tied their well-being to that of their far more powerful neighbor. The dire repercussions for these small and fledgling economies would soon unfold.

Pressures on Society

No matter what governments could or could not do, the widespread postwar unemployment proved psychologically shattering, especially to men who had been active as soldiers and saw themselves as virile breadwinners able to support their families. Unemployment was so dire because it brought men home to the "women's sphere." Some simply took to their beds; others undertook domestic tasks. The psychological burden was so great that some men pretended that they were employed while they looked for odd jobs.

Young men had more difficulty getting jobs than older ones, and young women had an even harder time. In Germany 38.5 percent of unemployed women were between ages fourteen and twenty-five, whereas young men constituted 24.1 percent of the male unemployed. The public, however, was concerned with the men. Most who failed to find work were not entitled to any kind of public relief and thus were thrown into poverty. As unemployed young men rode subways, played cards in parks, and stood around in groups on street corners, a sense of unease mounted. "We used to stay in bed late in the mornings," one former gang member from Lancashire, England, recalled of the 1930s, "so as not to need breakfast."[1] Because of falling revenue, governments cut programs for youth set up in the 1920s. Employment in Fascist or Nazi armies was thus a boon to these young people, giving them a sense of purpose and a way to air their grievances.

Across Europe news commentators and politicians blamed men's unemployment on women, even when modernization of industry was the culprit: "the unskilled woman worker is taking over the job of a skilled male worker; men—fathers of families—are being sacked and very young girls are being engaged in their place," wrote one German journalist.[2] The accusations against women were particularly vicious because they picked on vulnerable people earning low wages, including the millions of women whose chance for a better standard of living, marriage, and family had evaporated with the death of an entire generation of eligible men in World War I. Moreover, in the electrical industries such as radio, employers used the excuse of tough economic times to introduce new cost-cutting procedures. In a normal economy the elimination of skilled male workers would have produced crippling union protest, but the depression allowed the rearrangement of work to look like a response to hard times by substituting cheap and tractable female labor for expensive and unionized male labor. Nonetheless, politicians, labor leaders, and journalists held the "low woman competitor," not employers' push to modernize the economy, responsible for male unemployment, fracturing the underpinnings of social harmony.

Neighborhood solidarity suffered too. Cafés and taverns and other spots where workers socialized lost much of their clientele as people cut back on spending. In the first four years of the depression, German beer drinking dropped by 43 percent. Small local groceries, also places of sociability and stability, lost business. The departure of evicted tenants, often neighbors of long standing, left holes in the fabric of neighborhood life. Social order was further disturbed as young children increasingly took on odd jobs after school to help out their families or quit school altogether. Women, whose housekeeping funds dropped, had to spend more time mending, shopping for bargains in food, and soliciting welfare agencies for family relief. Their sociability declined simply for lack of time. Family breakup and child abandonment rose. Crime increased, especially among the young. What were once social clubs for youth, such as biking societies, turned into gangs foraging for food and other resources that the young might sell on urban streets alongside unemployed men and crippled war veterans. Men's sense of sociability and self was thus devastated too. As one U.S. observer reported of men congregating on streets, "Men stood alone more often than in groups. . . . The middle-aged men were perfectly willing to talk . . . but more often than not, I found them alone."[3] As peaceful social interaction disintegrated, the popularity of politicians agitating for violent change, among them fascists and communists, increased.

During times of economic uncertainty many couples postponed marriage and practiced birth control, accelerating the trend toward small families. Much information about birth control had already spread by word of mouth among rural and urban workers, but by the 1930s pamphlets on family planning and contraception had increased the flow of information. Clinics like those established by sexologist Marie Stopes and other reformers who founded Britain's Family Planning Association helped families space the birth of children, and soon there were hundreds of clinics across Europe. These trends were welcomed by some, but many others worried about the impact of declining population on national strength. For instance, French political and economic leaders were shocked to hear that in 1929 there were nine thousand more deaths than births in the country. In Italy the median family size among professionals (including parents) was 3.28 people in the mid-1930s. A "horrible crime," Italian officials shrieked. Birth control, according to one Italian intellectual, allowed people to "enjoy oneself without paying the price."[4] Birthrates dropped everywhere and among all classes, but urban workers conspicuously cut family size in these lean years. The deficit in births became a constant, fueling vague accusations that at some times women, at other times men or immigrants, and at still other times single people were dragging down entire nations. Political rhetoric about the decadence of modern life heated up and helped demagogues rise to power.

Thus, the depression directly fostered hatred among social and ethnic groups. In Germany workers who joined political parties — Social Democrat, Communist, and Nazi — were all violently opposed to one another and thus unable to pursue a common interest. Parties of the right and of the left used the economic crisis to emphasize the ineptitude of representative institutions and consensus politics. Communists, on the left, argued that the depression showed the bankruptcy of the capitalist system and vied with Nazis, on the right, for the allegiance of the masses. In Germany these two parties clashed violently, even causing deaths. In the countryside of the new eastern European nations, where depressed prices devastated farming, people rioted against Jews, who, they insisted, controlled the banks that had loaned them money; against the commerce in grain, which was paying them less; and against government bureaucrats, who insisted on collecting taxes in such hard times. Anti-Semitism also flourished in cities and among elites and workers alike; citizens across Europe blamed Jews for every social ill. Anti-Semitic slurs replaced substantive political debate: "Nazi leaders sit with Thyssen and his Jewish bankers," wrote a German social democratic journalist in 1932, referring to industrial magnate Fritz Thyssen, who had long funded Hitler, "in order to destroy working-class organizations."[5] Elites in England and France fashioned their distaste for modernity into hatred for Jews, whom they accused of embodying modern materialism and thus causing the depression. The prize-winning French author Louis-Ferdinand Céline and other writers produced works whose hate-filled anti-Semitism was excused as aesthetically vigorous literature. Like the harsh rhetoric about population decline, anti-Semitism did nothing to solve the depression. The rhetoric provided for some the comforting illusion that they knew which group was responsible for Europeans' economic plight, even though the vast majority of Europe's Jews were incredibly poor.

The Impact Abroad

The economic crash and the instability that followed were no less devastating to non-European populations. As the Western powers cut production, the demand for primary resources such as tin from Latin America plunged, leaving local workers unemployed and starving. Farmers in the United States, Argentina, Australia, and other countries where agriculture had flourished during the war found their profits plummeting as prices fell from oversupply. Consumers cut their purchases of imported luxuries such as coffee, sugar, and meat, further depressing prices. As in Europe, demand for some goods dropped because of new processes. The development of synthetic fabrics hit the producers of raw cotton and silk with special force, and the discovery of procedures to recycle rubber reduced the amount needed from Asia and Africa. Wherever people had transformed their economy to concentrate on a single cash crop such as cotton for the Western market, the imposition of tariffs by the Western powers paralyzed trade by further discouraging demand. People in these regions could not fall back on their traditional practice of growing many crops for their own use, because years earlier the colonial powers had insisted that farmers produce large quantities of whatever single commodity European industry needed.

The depression hit the colonies' productive capacity with unprecedented force. Many colonies had set up industries to fill the gap left by Europe's wartime turn to the manufacture of military goods. In India, for instance, jute mills, cotton factories, and steel manufacturing, begun by local entrepreneurs in the mid-nineteenth century, took off during the war. Modern, large-scale farming had also developed, with middle-class owners investing in land alongside the foreign landlords of plantations. The depression caused a collapse in agricultural and manufactured goods alike, leaving those who had invested in new enterprises and modern equipment—both agricultural and industrial—with an unpayable burden of debt and their workers without a livelihood. To make matters worse, the imperial powers maintained, and even increased, their demands for taxes and charges, and individual European investors continued to draw profits out of the colonies. For example, during the depression one-sixth of all British profits in finance, shipping, and other enterprises came from India. Although Britain devalued its own currency, it did not allow the colonies to take the same protective action. As a result, the colonies paid their taxes in highly valued currency while the British paid their bills and pensions at far lower cost.

Protests in the colonies increased because of the depression, and these included strikes and political demonstrations, often met by brutal force. In 1930 the

British first used strafing from the air on Indian civilians attending a nonviolent protest rally. African farmers organized to counter the falling prices paid them by European traders. In 1937 Gold Coast producers of cocoa withheld cocoa for some seven months until they were paid more for their crops. Young people, hit by the depression in the colonies as they were elsewhere, became increasingly politicized, especially as Marxist, pan-Arab, pan-African, and Gandhian ideas spread. Commitment to building local economies while rejecting goods from the imperial powers actually had the effect by the mid-1930s of bolstering local industries and worsening the trade slowdown in Europe. Reformers and revolutionaries called on their own peoples to join together as never before to throw off colonialism.

THE TRIUMPH OF DICTATORSHIP

In the midst of the Great Depression three men towered above the rest, pronouncing themselves uniquely capable of stemming the tide of economic and social disaster. Using old-fashioned terror and styling themselves as marshals of men, Hitler, Mussolini, and Stalin vowed to pull their countries out of the misery plaguing the rest of the world. They used the mass media, along with unprecedented violence, to create the illusion that they were effective and in charge. Their impact was so great that the trio remains fascinating, and many people continue to see them as upholders of values—whether utopian, social, or gendered.

The fascist dictators Mussolini and Hitler announced that the days of union agitation in the factory were over and said they would restore, in Mussolini's words, "the tranquil rhythm" of labor of an earlier age.[6] They claimed to be restoring human dignity to men; they promised to modernize life while eliminating the materialist corruption of the old ruling classes. Mussolini, Hitler, and Stalin were the inheritors of the military ethos of World War I and the modern ethos of the machine age, and they aimed to close the gap between the individual and the nation-state by having the state direct everyday life (see the Picture Essay). The word often used to define such societies is *totalitarian* because of the unparalleled violence they employed to align everyone's thought and action with the modern state. Because Italy and Germany lacked colonies and global influence, Mussolini and Hitler promised to invade and colonize beyond their borders. They vowed that such vigorous activity would make men be men and women be women again and that enemies—Jews in the case of the Nazis—would be crushed.

Hitler's Rise to Power

Adolf Hitler rose to power in a climate of national defeat, psychological trauma, and economic depression, all of it the more deeply felt because of Germany's economic capacity and international pariah status. Although a ne'er-do-well before the war—someone who fancied himself a great artist but ended up living in the flophouses of Vienna—Hitler gained a fresh identity and sense of purpose while a German soldier in World War I, and he personally felt the rage of the average veteran at the humiliation of the Versailles Treaty. Hitler was a brawler, part of the rough, criminal male underworld of postwar Germany made up of pimps, hustlers, gangsters, and disoriented veterans. Developing into a commanding speaker and even leading the failed Beer Hall Putsch in 1923, however, he came to head the National Socialist German Workers' Party—the Nazi Party—of angry, disillusioned young men eager to overturn lawful, representative government that was said to have caused their defeat. His speeches—"Why We Are Anti-Semites" was first delivered in 1920—often drew hundreds and even thousands, and the admission price helped finance the party. Popularity and his own political tactics transformed him from being a down-and-outer into *der Führer*, leader of his party.

The Nazis, one of several fledgling political groups of malcontents and veterans, called both Communists and big business enemies. Nevertheless, from the mid-1920s on, they received support from conservative and right-wing businessmen—a few of them extremely wealthy. Alfred Hugenberg, a film and press magnate who so hated Weimar's republican government that he even called successful negotiations to cut reparation payments ignominious defeats, gave the Nazis massive publicity. His media empire publicized Nazi street brawls with Communists, who were attacking the Weimar Republic as bourgeois and exploitative. Although Communists and Nazis picked fights with each other, Hugenberg's newspapers routinely reported that lawless Communists had attacked law-abiding Nazis, who then restored order while the republic's police stood by helplessly. He helped popularize Nazism among the middle classes, who feared the Communists would take their property. With his aid the Nazis created a cult of sacrifice by celebrating and even occasionally canonizing the many thugs who worked for the party. Pimp and criminal Horst Wessel was killed in a ganglike struggle for turf, but the Nazis' savvy propaganda machine turned his death into the saga of an idealist slain for his beliefs. The "Horst Wessel Song" became a Nazi hymn—a popular song frequently heard on German streets:

> Flag high, ranks closed,
> The S.A. marches with silent solid steps,
> Comrades shot by the red front and reaction
> March in spirit with us in our ranks.
> Gangway for the brown battalions,
> Gangway for the Storm Troopers.
> Millions, full of hope, look up at the swastika;
> The day breaks for freedom and for bread.

The Nazis grew in strength, from a small party receiving 2 percent of the vote in the 1928 Reichstag elections, to a respectable 20 percent showing in 1930, then more than double that in the summer elections of 1932 as the depression tightened its grip.

Many of Hitler's supporters were young, idealistic, and unemployed. In 1930, 70 percent of party members were under age forty. The party capitalized on this youthfulness to highlight the outdated and aging politicians of the parliamentary Weimar regime. As Hitler's paramilitary bands marched through the streets, their vigor and enthusiasm attracted supporters from all segments of German society. The largest absolute number of supporters came from the industrial working class because the Nazis declared themselves the party of workers (45 percent of the population but only 33.5 percent of party members). People from the ruined lower-middle and middle classes constituted a smaller segment of the membership, but they joined in percentages out of proportion to their actual numbers in the population. Employees, businessmen, members of the professions, and government workers were 31 percent of the population but 48.2 percent of party members. They applauded the Nazis' bitter critique of Versailles and its legacy, including the financial costs to respectable people. Unexpectedly, the party roused the enthusiasm of rural folk who had seen their status and prosperity ebb with the collapse of the German monarchy and its base of support in the agrarian upper class. These landed people were further hit with global competition in grain and other produce. Despite the Nazis' lack of polish, aristocrats and army officers found the promise of restored national pride as appealing as did people from the middle and lower classes.

The rising tide of Nazism and communism astonished the conservative ruling elite of the Weimar Republic, who were facing the twin problems of managing the perilous economy and dealing with this populist opposition. As Nazis and Communists—who attracted similarly young, working-class enthusiasts—entered the Reichstag and local councils, their common tactic was to make it impossible for any business to take place. They shouted down speakers, driving them from the podium. Communists and Nazis alike saw their movements as "noble causes" and sneered at parliamentary debate as "mere politics." Both scorned the law, legal processes, judges, and lawyers because they represented the ordinary workings of society not some lofty quasi-religious ideal. Ironically, the elite men in power had also despised the republic from the beginning and hoped to bring about a return to authoritarian, even monarchical rule. Like the former military leader and Weimar president Paul von Hindenburg himself, they were glad to see the Communists and Nazis prevent the Reichstag from doing its work because this disruption would hurry the collapse of the republic and usher in the restoration of the monarchy all the sooner.

After his party's success in the summer elections of 1932, Hitler met with President Hindenburg and demanded to be appointed chancellor of Germany. Hindenburg demurred, telling Hitler that his party was too divisive. In the meantime, the Communists also flexed their muscles by leading the Reichstag to a vote of no confidence in the government. This outcome necessitated additional elections in November, and in those contests the Nazi vote fell by some two million ballots while the Communists gained seats. In local elections in December, support for the Nazis declined by some 35 percent, and Hitler contemplated suicide, thinking his party washed up. Faced with the rising tide of communism, however, Germany's conservative leadership representing the military, business, and the highest reaches of government urged Hindenburg to opt for Hitler, who as chancellor, they believed, would be far preferable and more controllable than the Communists, who might stage a Bolshevik-style revolution. As Hitler took office in

◆ **Hitler Marching in Munich**

In 1938, Nazi officials, with Hitler at their center, marched through the streets of Munich to commemorate Hitler's 1923 Beer Hall Putsch. Their prideful control of the streets stood in marked contrast to the street life of men selling pencils and standing in breadlines in the democracies. © *Bettmann/CORBIS.*

January 1933, tens of thousands of storm troopers (SA), the Nazi Party's paramilitary force, held blazing torches and paraded the streets while millions celebrated. Hitler's reign of terror was about to begin.

Nazi Doctrine and the Regime in Action

The Nazi message, as it developed during the rough-and-tumble of postwar and Great Depression politics, is now so discredited that it is hard to recapture its considerable appeal. It built on the racial antagonisms that had grown in the heated atmosphere of nationalism and imperialism since the late nineteenth century, but the Nazis used the language of science to modernize these hatreds. "National Socialism is a cool and highly reasoned approach to reality based on the greatest of scientific knowledge and its spiritual expression. . . . The National Socialist move-ment . . . aims to cultivate and lead a nation determined by its blood," Hitler ex-plained in a speech in September 1938.[7] Nazis maintained that eternal scientific laws simultaneously showed the inferiority of Jews, Slavs, people with dark skins, and those with physical and mental impairments, and the superiority of so-called Aryan or Germanic peoples. The ordering of races, according to Nazi dogma, was spiritual and sacred, requiring the elite corps of Nazis to mobilize society as a whole to preserve the purity of blood through racially restricted marriage and childbearing. The Nazi elite would rise to the high-minded task of performing what ordinary people would see as cold-hearted: the eradication of "inferior" peoples either by killing them directly as in the case of the mentally or physically disabled or through forced emigration as was first proposed for Jews. The combi-nation of spirituality and science attracted people across classes, political creeds, and educational backgrounds. Hitler did not aim to create his own religion, so he also attracted Catholic, Protestant, and even some Jewish adherents because of the professed high-mindedness of the Nazi cause.

The centerpiece of Nazi racism was anti-Semitism. Hitler held Jews respon-sible for most of Germany's problems, including defeat in World War I and the in-tense suffering caused by the depression. Having spent his formative years in Vienna, where anti-Semitic politics governed at the beginning of the twentieth century, Hitler imbibed its vicious and hateful language. In the rhetoric of Nazism, Jews were "vermin," "abscesses," "parasites," and "Bolsheviks," whom Germany would have to eliminate in order to become a true *Volksgemeinschaft*—a spiritual community of like-minded, Aryan-blooded Germans. By characterizing Jews as dangerous "Bolsheviks" or Communists and as exploitative, wealthy financiers, Hitler created an enemy that many segments of the population could hate. The Nazis' relentless and passionate harping on this theme was so effective that from the 1930s to the very end of World War II many Germans stayed loyal to Hitler's message that superior Aryans were engaged in a life-and-death struggle with the evil forces of worldwide Jewry.

Like Fascism in Italy, Nazism in creed and practice was antifeminist and misogynist, despite women's biological importance to forging a community of pure-blooded Aryans. As early theorists put it: "There is no place for the political woman in the ideological world of National Socialism. The German resurrection is a male event."[8] Nazi propagandist Alfred Rosenberg understood Nazi gender rela-tions in terms of male monopoly of the public sphere and female submission. "There must be clarity on one point," he announced, "only man must be and re-main a judge, a soldier, and ruler of the state." According to Rosenberg, many Nazi women longed for a return to true femininity rooted in their domination by men as part of the creation of the ideal German state: "Emancipation of women from women's emancipation is the first demand of a generation of women who would like to save the Volk and the race . . . from decline and fall."[9] Women, like men, had to serve the race in a way that demanded their submission, but for women this service entailed both subservience to the laws of racial reproduction and acknowl-edgment of the superiority of men.

Upon becoming chancellor, Hitler moved immediately to close down representative government, end liberal freedoms, and deal with his rivals and enemies. Declaring a fire in the Reichstag in February 1933 the work of Communists, he announced that a terrorist menace existed in German society, using this as an excuse for suspending civil rights, censoring the press, and prohibiting meetings of opposition writers. Hitler had made clear throughout his career that *all* political parties except the National Socialists were his enemies. "Our opponents complain that we National Socialists, and I in particular, are intolerant and intractable," he declared. "They are right, we are intolerant! I have set myself one task, namely to sweep those parties out of Germany."[10] Despite the fear of terrorism instilled by Hitler, in the March elections the Nazis won 288 Reichstag seats, but Social Democrats and Communists still retained more than 200 seats, and right and center parties claimed another 158. Storm troopers went on a rampage, beating up opponents and destroying property. They prevented Communist delegates from attending Reichstag sessions and so intimidated other delegates that at the end of March 1933 Hitler was able to secure passage of the Enabling Act, the foundation of Nazi rule, which suspended the Weimar constitution and allowed subsequent Nazi laws to take effect without Reichstag approval. Solid middle-class Germans approved the Enabling Act as providing a way to pull the country out of its economic and political morass, and many across German society agreed that desperate times demanded tough action.

With the Enabling Act in place and the German population if not willing at least acquiescent, institutions of terror quickly took shape under the Nazis. One of the first major acts of murder was directed against the Nazi faithful themselves. When Ernst Roehm, leader of the SA and Hitler's longtime collaborator, called for a "second revolution" to end the corrupt influence of the old business and military elites on the Nazi leadership, Hitler's conservative backers and those in the military became alarmed. Hitler ordered Roehm's assassination. On June 30, 1934, the "Night of the Long Knives," hundreds of SA leaders and innocent civilians were murdered, including a few with whom Hitler wanted to settle old scores. This brutality enhanced Hitler's support among conservatives, who saw that he would deal ruthlessly with those favoring a leveling-out of social privilege.

The Ministry of Propaganda under Joseph Goebbels filled newspapers, radio programs, films, and other media with terrifying material intended to build consensus by describing in frightening detail the enemies—especially agents of "worldwide Jewry"—who menaced Aryans both within and outside of Germany. The presence of such enemies demanded the often distasteful work of terror undertaken by those considered to be among the elite because they would commit cold-blooded murder on behalf of the Aryan people. Heinrich Himmler, who headed the elite SS (*Schutzstaffel*) organization that protected Hitler and other Nazi leaders, commanded the Reich's political police system. The Gestapo, organized by Hermann Goering, and the Order of the Death's Head—both of them brutal police organizations—rooted out individuals who questioned Nazi ideas, helping to enforce obedience in thought and deeds. These organizations had vast powers to arrest, execute, or imprison people in concentration camps, the first of which opened in March 1933 at Dachau, near Munich. The Nazis filled it and later camps with socialists, homosexuals, Jews, and other "antisocial" elements to keep them from polluting and endangering the *Volksgemeinschaft*. Hitler deliberately blurred authority among the agencies of order and terror so that confusion and bitter competition reigned within the government and among the population at large. He thus prevented the emergence of coalitions against him and positioned himself to arbitrate the confusion. Nazism's terroristic politics were the foundation of what was announced as the "Third Reich"—a German empire succeeding the empires of Charlemagne and Kaiser William II. To safeguard the Third Reich, more massive violence was still to come.

Hitler continued his drastic reform of Germany with economic programs that won popular support, strengthened military industries, and provided the basis for German expansion. The Nazi government engaged in what economists call "pump priming"—stimulating the economy through government spending. This policy produced large budget deficits, but Hitler believed the spoils of future conquests would soon refill the nation's treasury. Pretending to make farm equipment, Germany built tanks and airplanes in defiance of the widely hated Versailles Treaty; the Autobahn highway system was developed to serve military as well as civilian ends. Defense spending soared to 50 percent of all government expenditures by 1938. From farms and factories the government demanded high productivity and set goals for national economic independence and self-sufficiency. Skilled workers prospered in the drive to rearm, and unemployment declined from a peak of almost 6 million in 1932 to 1.6 million by 1936. When labor shortages began to appear in certain areas, the government conscripted single women into service as farmworkers and domestics.

Once in power, the Nazis faced the problem of bringing a complex nation of distinctive regions, different social and economic interests, and different beliefs about war, peace, and modernity into line with their goal of making Germany the dominant state in the world. Among the most recalcitrant were workers, especially those committed to socialist internationalism. The Nazi Party reorganized work life to increase efficiency and to curtail labor activism that was often pro-Communist and anti-Nazi. Government officials and industrial managers classified jobs, determined work procedures, and set pay levels, rating women's jobs lower than men's regardless of the level of expertise required. In May 1933, the government closed labor unions and seized their property. All workers, from the lowly unskilled to the top professionals, were compelled to join the Nazi-controlled German Labor Front, which was used to snuff out worker independence. Shifting attention away from politics in the workplace, Nazi initiatives like the "Strength through Joy" program organized working-class leisure. The chance to win vacations or to save enough money for a car replaced politics as the focus of attention: "Save five marks a week and get your own car," one poster read.[11] So, too, initiatives to promote "The Beauty of Labor" by taking pride in the cleanliness of factory floors, or to promote efficiency or identification with Hitler, who had once been a construction worker, served to direct people's aspirations to nonpolitical ends through a unified message. "It is no exaggeration to say that for millions of Germans 'Strength through Joy' has made the world beautiful again and life worth living again," a Nazi official boasted.[12] There was no lack of agreement among the population at large.

Hitler exercised unprecedented power over the details of everyday life, especially gender roles. In June 1933, a law took effect that encouraged Aryans to marry and have children. The law provided for loans to Aryan newlyweds, but only to those couples in which the wife left the workforce. The loans were forgiven on the birth of the pair's fourth child. Nazi marriage programs enforced a nineteenth-century ideal of femininity. Women were supposed to be subordinate so men would feel tough and industrious despite military defeat and economic depression. Although some women complained about having to forfeit their jobs, others, remembering the miserable war and postwar years, believed that Hitler would elevate the Nazi woman who, as a party leader put it, "joyfully sacrifices and fulfills her fate."[13]

Promising to make life better for true German people, Nazism in fact impoverished ordinary social and cultural life. Although Goebbels as minister of propaganda ensured that 70 percent of households had "people's radios" by 1938, the programming was severely censored and listeners often had as their main option Hitler's fiery and hectoring speeches or news and entertainment that focused on the virtues of the Nazi regime. Said to be "degenerate" like the opera *Mahagonny*, modernist paintings in museums and private collections were either destroyed or confiscated. Civil servants, teachers, and other government officials were forced to adhere to Nazism. Another law took jobs from Jews and women and bestowed them on party members as rewards. In 1936, membership in Hitler Youth, an organization that indoctrinated the young, became mandatory for all boys and girls over age ten. These children learned to report the names of adults they suspected of disloyalty to the regime, even their own parents. The presence of informers—more than one hundred thousand were on the Nazi payroll—halted free speech. Ordinary citizens were encouraged to turn in anyone who failed to show sufficient patriotism, and they did so in great numbers. All this helped fulfill Hitler's promise to create a well-ordered national community, as freedom of thought and political debate disappeared. People boasted that they could leave their bicycles out at night without fear of robbery. In general, the improved economy solidified people's belief that Hitler was working an economic miracle while restoring pride in Germany.

Persecution of Jews and the Flight from Terror

For hundreds of thousands if not millions of Germans, however, Nazi rule in the 1930s brought physical and moral suffering. In 1935, the government enacted the Nuremberg Laws, legislation that specifically deprived Jews of citizenship, defined Jewishness according to a person's ancestry (having one Jewish grandparent), ended benefits for Jewish war veterans, and prohibited marriage between Jews and other Germans. To hold jobs, workers had to present their baptismal certificates and other evidence of their Aryan heritage. The Nazis drove Jews from their jobs and housing and reduced the amount of food they were allowed to purchase, much of this to encourage the emigration that Nazis believed would purify the nation. Whereas women defined as Aryan had increasing difficulty obtaining abortions or even birth-control information, both were readily available to the outcast groups, including Jews, Gypsies, Slavs, and mentally or physically disabled people. By 1939, as terror escalated, special courts forced Jews and other so-called inferior groups to undergo sterilization and submit to reproductive experiments performed by Nazi doctors.

In 1938, a Jewish teenager, reacting to the harassment of his parents, killed a German official. In retaliation, Nazis attacked some two hundred synagogues, smashed the windows of Jewish-owned stores, ransacked apartments of known or suspected Jews, and threw more than twenty thousand Jews into prisons and camps. The night of November 9–10 became known as *Kristallnacht*, "Night of Broken Glass." The Nazi rampage stunned not only Jews but many Germans as well. On the eve of World War II the Nazis undertook another action that would have catastrophic consequences not only for Jews but for millions of other Europeans: in the name of improving the Aryan race, doctors helped organize the T4 project, which used carbon monoxide poisoning dispensed in motorized vans and other means to kill large numbers of people—two hundred thousand handicapped and elderly—late in the 1930s, preparing the way for the even larger mass exterminations that would occur later.

Faced with relentless and escalating persecution, which some historians have called a "social death," by the outbreak of World War II in 1939 more than half of Germany's five hundred thousand Jews had left the country. The confiscation of the emigrants' property enriched their former neighbors and individual Nazis; the payment of enormous emigration fees helped finance Germany's economic revival. The Nazi regime also filled its coffers by simply stealing Jewish property, including bank accounts, and forcing Jews themselves to work for practically no wages. Thus, their resources seized by the Nazis, refugees from Nazi totalitarianism sought to eke out a living around the world. Anti-Semitism infected Europe, the United States, and other parts of the globe, and restrictions on Jewish immigration tightened even as news of Nazi persecution spread. Countries like Britain, although they grudgingly admitted them, had laws confining refugees to domestic or other menial service or quotas prohibiting the entry of all but a few. A handful of fortunate refugees found that exceptions could be made. Teams of brilliant scientists—including Nobel laureate Albert Einstein—received a warm welcome and devoted themselves to work advancing war technology. Famous artists and intellectuals, Jewish and non-Jewish, also had a relatively easy time immigrating and finding work, for they added to the luster of their adopted nation. Philosopher Hannah Arendt, architect Ludwig Mies van der Rohe, composer Béla Bartók, and Nobel Prize–winning novelist Thomas Mann were among those who invigorated cultural life in the United States. For most refugees, however, escape brought temporary physical safety but economic misery. The Nazi regime thus accelerated global migration.

Collectivization, Modernization, and Urbanization in Stalin's USSR

A different but equally virulent form of totalitarianism was unfolding in the USSR. Its creator was Joseph Stalin from the Soviet republic of Georgia, who as a young man had studied for the priesthood. Stalin's main assets were political craftiness and ruthlessness, the latter of which he had honed by watching Lenin's violence toward personal and political enemies. Stalin used those qualities to outmaneuver other claimants to leadership, such as Leon Trotsky, whose brilliance and control of the Red Army made him an early and potent rival. Stalin set out to modernize and transform the USSR because neither the goal of industrialization nor the creation of a truly Bolshevik society had been achieved under Lenin. In fact, the chaos of the early 1920s seemed to go hand in hand with the NEP. In the spring of 1929, Stalin presented to the Communist Party congress the first of several five-year plans outlining a program for massive increases in the output of coal, iron ore, steel, and industrial goods. Stalin called the plan, which laid out strict, meticulously calculated production goals, an emergency measure designed to overcome the lead of the advanced industrial countries, who, in his words, had sought to "crush us."

Stalin's state-directed economic plan can be seen as part of a trend. European governments had instituted state direction of the economy during World War I, and even earlier, governmental planning had allowed Japan to industrialize rapidly. After these successes Western economists and industrialists alike increasingly favored some economic planning and state intervention in economic affairs. Indeed, the brutal execution of five-year plans helped make the USSR a leading industrial and modern state. Between 1928 and 1940 the number of Soviet workers in industry, construction, and transport grew from 4.6 million to 12.6 million. From 1927 to 1937, production in metallurgy and machinery rose 1,400 percent, and the USSR exported vast quantities of grain to western Europe in the 1930s—close to three million tons between 1930 and 1933 alone. A modern bureaucracy took shape to execute the plan. For example, the number of managers in heavy industry grew by almost 500 percent between 1928 and 1935. Because of planning, the resettlement of populations, the industrialization of every corner of the USSR, and the organization of a nationwide network of collective farms were also accomplished during these years. Prison camp labor, however, achieved some of the greatest projects, such as the construction of factories in Arctic regions, the building of the Moscow-Volga canals, and the mining of massive quantities of gold and minerals.

Stalin saw the total destruction of the village as essential to industrialization and modernization. He blamed the lack of food in cities during the war years and the 1920s on the small-minded, self-serving greed of the average peasant. In his view this peasant mind-set was not only antisocialist but likely to bring industrialization crashing down for lack of food. Stalin ended the NEP, which he saw as a program benefiting peasants at the expense of proletarian workers, and he sought to collectivize farming by eliminating individual peasant property. He called for liquidation of the kulak—the word literally means "fist" but was applied to prosperous peasants who were said to hold society in their grip. Stalin generated enthusiasm for the attack on the peasantry by presenting it as a revolutionary challenge, and the task he outlined united underfed urban workers to take action. In the winter of 1929–30, party workers armed with quotas scoured villages looking for produce, and party officials encouraged resentful poor villagers to identify the kulaks among them. The so-called kulaks, often turned in because of neighborhood feuds or because they were lucky enough to own a cow or chicken, were evicted from their land and deprived of food or shelter. Some 248,000 families were reportedly shipped to central and East Asia without resources of any kind. Some estimates put the number of evicted families as high as one million. Propaganda units instilled hatred for anyone connected with kulaks. One Russian remembered believing as a teenager that kulaks were "bloodsuckers, cattle, swine, loathsome, repulsive: they had no souls; they stank."[14] One prominent Communist enthused over "the columns of tractors digging the kulaks' graves,"[15] while other party members undertook the difficult job of herding peasants onto the confiscated land where they were supposed to farm in collective units instead of individually.

Stalinist policy reached well beyond the traditional Russian homeland, involving the extension of settlement and industry into the central and East Asian realms of the USSR and requiring enormous effort by Communist Party bureaucrats, scientists, and ordinary people. To lead what the party saw as backward indigenous tribes toward socialism, Russian and other settlers were sent in by the thousands and took over local trade in furs, wood, fish, and other resources. Geologists looking for coal, gold, and oil invaded hunting lands, and state managers took charge of displaced ethnic groups, attempting to transform them into farmers and factory workers. Socialist cadres turned local life upside down, depriving groups of access to fish, reindeer herds, and other animals; they also raped and stole. But the goal—the industrialization of the backward lands and peoples to the north and east—was considered worthwhile: "Sometimes we are asked if it would not be possible to slow down a bit, to reduce the speed," Stalin admitted, then proclaimed: "No, comrades, it would not! We cannot reduce the speed! On the contrary, it should be increased as much as possible."[16]

A watchword under Lenin, modernization because a crusade under Stalin, affecting every part of the realm. From peasants in Ukraine to the hunting populations of the northern tundra, everyone was to be pulled from backwardness. Schools and institutes were established to educate native peoples, eradicating their traditional ways and ignorance of modern life so that they in turn could proselytize among their neighbors. Pamphlets written in the USSR's many languages introduced villagers to the concepts of collective farms and soviets; they also provided simple medical instructions for care of the sick. Tribal customs were made illegal in 1928, and traditional shamans and healers were forced out, to the dismay of many villagers. It was difficult to convince native peoples of the virtues of these drastic changes, but some were caught up in the messianic fervor of the modernizers. "I had always lived in a remote, dark little village," one student testified of the 1930s. "When I first arrived in Leningrad, a new and known world opened before me. . . . I became frightened because I could not understand where all those people were going. . . . All plants grow. We, too, will grow in the direction of the new life—all of us, toilers of the Soviet Union."[17]

Forced industrialization accelerated the already rapid urbanization under way since the late nineteenth century, bringing some ten million new workers to the cities during the first five-year plan alone. Stalin's modernizing drive called for total commitment to socialized production; individual workshops and artisanal occupations were outlawed. Because the state had to provide every necessity of life for urban workers whose numbers were growing by the millions, most goods were scarce. The purge of the kulaks left food in short supply for most of the 1930s. People waited in line to get staples such as bread. Even those lining up at midnight had no guarantee that their patience would be rewarded. The housing situation was also grim, for government resources were used for industrialization and improving showcase cities such as the newly created industrial town of Magnitogorsk and the refurbished capital of Moscow, whose new subway system featured dazzlingly adorned stations. The resulting lack of housing in cities like Moscow, where the population suddenly soared, forced people to live in corridors and sometimes to share a single room with total strangers and their families. Because metal was destined for heavy industry, pots and pans and other basic household items were unobtainable. Because individual enterprise was outlawed, it was impossible to get household goods repaired. Paradoxically, as critics within the Soviet system would later note, communism made people not less but more materialistic because the many shortages turned life's necessities into luxuries to be treasured.

The Purges

The situation in the early 1930s did not live up to official Communist predictions of success, however. Factory workers, many newly arrived from the countryside, were often unable to meet the five-year plans' quotas. In the countryside, party officials' ignorance of agriculture and the lack of equipment and scientific personnel made collectivization an utter disaster. The death or eviction of millions of farmers and their families contributed to the starvation of country people as the grain harvest declined from 83 million tons in 1930 to 67 million in 1934—much of it exported to gain funds for industrial development. Famine became widespread in 1932–1933, and millions of people died. The problems in industrial and agricultural production led to some reining in of Stalin's draconian policies. To boost production, Stalin even allowed people on collective farms temporarily to go back to individual farming.

Communists enlisted youth activism in their cause. Members of the Komsomol youth organization considered themselves an avant-garde that almost single-handedly would usher in a new future, eradicating centuries of Russian "backwardness." These young people viewed the older generation as weak and ineffectual, exhausted by the struggles of World War I and the ensuing revolution and civil war. "I thus came to the conclusion," said one youth, "that success in transforming the country depended entirely on the physical exertions and the will of people like myself." As another put it, "The atmosphere of undaunted struggle in a common cause—the completion of the factory—engaged our imagination, roused our enthusiasm, and drew us into a sort of front-line world where difficulties were overlooked or forgotten."[18] The young son of a kulak who turned in his own family was celebrated with statues across the broad expanse of the Soviet Union. Stalin did not write out commands directly; he generally expressed his orders only vaguely, openly showing his moods when angry or insistent about policies. This style opened the way to improvisation in which local leaders and ordinary people such as youth competed with one another—even in such violent deeds as attacking kulaks—to achieve the goals of communism and to modernize the USSR.

But the Communists also launched a search for political enemies—"wreckers" or saboteurs of communism—to hold responsible for the failures. State violence followed in the form of widespread arrests, imprisonment in labor camps, and executions to purge Soviet society of so-called counterrevolutionaries. In 1934 the gulag system was established, bringing a disjointed array of prison camps under the control of the NKVD, or People's Commissariat for Internal Affairs, which also commanded all police, fire departments, and border guards. The purges continued intermittently as long as Stalin ruled and actually elicited praise of Stalin for using the tough-minded measures needed to protect the infant workers' state.

In 1928, the government tried a group of engineers at the Shakly coal mine for deliberately causing low productivity. Five were shot and others were jailed. Soviet citizens expressed their relief that those wreckers of communism had been punished, and they searched their own workplaces for "concrete bearers of evil, . . . workers guilty of foul-ups, breakdowns, and defects." After a hiatus, the turmoil caused by collectivization and famine was followed in 1934 by a more comprehensive attack on the old Bolshevik leadership.

At the Seventeenth Party Congress, secret balloting gave Stalin 90 percent of the vote for his position as party chairman amid loud acclaim for his leadership. Stalin's paranoia surged when his secret police reported on opposition to him within the Bolshevik elite. Stalin ordered the assassination of Sergei Kirov, one of his best friends and the very popular first secretary of the Leningrad Communist Party. He then used Kirov's death as the pretext to arrest former Bolshevik leaders Grigori Zinoviev and Lev Kamenev and later try them in public spectacles that were ultimately said to unmask a massive conspiracy led by Leon Trotsky to overthrow Soviet rule. At a series of "show trials" held in 1936, 1937, and 1938, the former Bolsheviks were coerced to confess, despite a lack of evidence. In the final purges of the late 1930s Stalin eliminated most of the upper echelons of the military, who were charged as crucial participants in a wide-ranging plot to destroy the new society. Records opened since the fall of the Soviet Union show Stalin intimately involved in these trials, even suggesting the contours of the plots that were supposed to have existed and the words to put in the defendants' mouths.

The trials, public confessions, and executions spread panic everywhere: "Great concert and lecture halls were turned into public confessionals. . . . People did penance for [everything]. . . ," one Soviet citizen recalled.[19] Purges went on in universities and technical schools, and accusations of crimes ranging from treason to industrial sabotage led to the imprisonment or execution of hundreds of thousands of local bureaucrats and their families. Oddly enough, the confessions were sometimes sincere, as victims racked their brains to uncover all the disloyal thoughts and words that might have threatened the revolution. Notable among these sincere penitents was Nikolai Bukharin, editor of *Izvestia*, the government's premier newspaper, and leading Bolshevik intellectual—a potent rival to Stalin at the time. When events had been more fluid in the late 1920s and early 1930s, Bukharin had discussed leadership alternatives to Stalin and like others of the original Bolsheviks remembered a more open political climate. Once caught in the purge, Bukharin confessed—whether freely or not is a subject for debate—suggesting in a letter to Stalin his understanding "that there is some great and bold political idea behind the general purge." It was clearly part of the process toward democracy. "I could not hope to be left out. . . . It would be petty of me to put the fortunes of my own person on the same level as those tasks of world-historical importance, which rest above all on your shoulders."[20] Public and private thinking alike credited Stalin as a visionary, taking the USSR to an entirely new level of socialist perfection and creating the "new" man and woman.

The purges had profound social and political consequences. Those eliminated from the military leadership included heroes from World War I and the civil war as well as brilliant theorists. Weakening the Red Army just as a Nazi invasion of the Soviet Union loomed, the purges rocked the military status quo and allowed younger people with new ideas to emerge. From the lowliest workers and local functionaries to the members of Stalin's own family, no rank of society escaped the purges. Intellectuals such as the writer Osip Mandelstam fell victim, and suffering was widespread and intense not just for those imprisoned and otherwise punished, but for their loved ones, as Anna Akhmatova's poem *Requiem* so movingly shows (see Document 5.2). Like the American slaughter of Native Americans, which opened millions of acres of land to settlers, the massive loss of life in the Soviet Union opened up new jobs and places to live, especially to peasants, workers, and others outside the prewar elites. And like the United States in the nineteenth century, the Soviet Union in the mid-twentieth became a land of opportunity for an entirely new group of people, albeit at a horrifying price for many others.

Cultural Life under Stalin

By 1939 Stalin was viewed by many as "our beloved Leader" and "a god on earth," as two different workers put it.[21] He believed himself to be a modern tsar—the kind of savior people craved and the orderly taskmaster they needed. This is not to say that Soviet people stopped being critical. To the contrary, they wrote millions of letters to local and national officials full of complaints and comments. The party had "got too big for its boots," one writer noted in 1937, "all I hear is cursing Soviet power."[22] Paid official writers, however, produced a godlike portrait of Stalin, approaching in grandeur Lenin himself. Even artists critical of the regime craved Stalin's recognition, showing just how complex the situation was. Mikhail Bulgakov, author of a disrespectful novel, *The Master and the Margarita* (published posthumously) that depicted Stalin as the wily devil Voland, was overwhelmed with joy when Stalin asked him to write a play about his life. Bulgakov collapsed when the offer was withdrawn as the story became too accurate for Stalin's taste. Other artists were similarly manipulated, alternately recipients of privileges or targets of public abuse incited by the government reacting to political whim. The most successful artists contributed not to the glorification of the working classes but to the creation of a "cult of personality" focused on Lenin and Stalin.

Yet Soviet art actually thrived in the 1930s. Modern critics view with distaste the mandated "socialist realist" style, which cast a rosy aura around depictions of loyal workers and party members. But the happiness of characters portrayed in socialist realist art was not false. Socialist realism was a utopian style meant to capture the happiness that socialism ultimately would bring, not to present the bleak, even menacing situation of the present. Writers, visual artists, and filmmakers, such as Sergei Eisenstein, creator of the jump cut and other modern cinematic

◆ **V. I. Lenin on the First Day of Soviet Power**
In the 1930s the Soviet government called for an end to avant-garde experimentation in the arts and its replacement with a style called socialist realism. This style was hardly realistic, as it was intended to portray Soviet life in a positive, even glowing, light. In this example of socialist realism, the painter Babashok aims to show the ethnic and economic solidarity that would be achieved in a communist utopia. How does he attempt to show both diversity and solidarity in this painting? *The Granger Collection, New York.*

techniques, infused their works with spiritual fervor. With the imposition of socialist style much of the early Soviet experimentation ended, but modernists retained their belief in the ability of art to mobilize the masses by appealing to the
unconscious and the emotions. Stalin, who had once written poetry himself, promoted intellectuals' and artists' role in guiding the masses when he called them
"engineers of the soul."

So central were writers that the USSR established the Union of Soviet Writers
to control all matters related to writers' private and professional lives. The union
assigned housing and office space and determined which authors would specialize
in which types of writing—detective novels, essays, or serious fiction. The rewards
could be great: Mikhail Sholokhov received the Nobel Prize for Literature in 1965.
His novel *And Quiet Flows the Don* (1928–1940) focused on the inhumanity of the
revolutionary and civil war periods in the countryside, but his ability to capture the
psychological and inner state of ordinary people during these times so impressed
Stalin and others that he largely escaped harm. By contrast, the gifted composers
Sergei Prokofiev and Dmitri Shostakovich rode the roller coaster of praise and condemnation doled out by Stalin and the party. When to his dismay his ballet *Romeo
and Juliet* was censored, Prokofiev turned to writing music for children's theater,
composing the delightful *Peter and the Wolf* (1936). In addition to symphonies, operas, and chamber music, Shostakovich wrote film scores. His "Song of the
Counterplan," written for a film in which workers come up with strategies to increase productivity, became amazingly popular and was the basis for the anthem of
the United Nations. When Stalin walked out of the performance of one of his
operas in 1936, Shostakovich went from highly regarded composer to nonperson
overnight and continued on that rocky road for as long as Stalin lived.

THE DEMOCRACIES SEARCH FOR SOLUTIONS

During the 1930s, governments across Europe struggled to motivate a mass citizenry in hard times. Schooled in consensus building and believing in debate, democratic politicians increasingly met the crisis with wrangling and even violence as
the depression tightened its grip. Fascist, anti-Semitic, and ganglike factions sprang
up in the democracies, proposing the end of democracy as the only viable solution.
Democracy in France and Great Britain stumbled; both countries were plagued by
riots, governmental instability, and a glaring inability to deal with mounting economic and international crises. As faith in democracy weakened in Britain and
France, Sweden, which lay outside the mainstream struggle for international
power, devised a system that gave government the leading role not only in boosting economic prosperity and population growth but in stabilizing democracy itself. Sweden's system of benefits became the prototype, later followed by governments around the world, of a full-fledged welfare state. Resignation and feistiness
coexisted in these countries. Most people continued to hope that international
peace could be maintained but increasingly feared that it could not. It was cultural
leaders, not dithering politicians, who crafted democracy's strongest defense.

Filmmakers, writers, composers, and other artists tried to revive morale and fight fascism.

Britain and France Defend Democracy

The 1930s saw a political struggle for the allegiance of the masses, and the democracies tried to preserve liberal institutions for citizens experiencing the depths of economic depression. The psychic shock of the Great War remained vivid in Britain and France, and the depression only compounded the trauma. Policies intended to address suffering had the effect of an assault not a remedy. Faced with falling government revenues, Labour Party prime minister Ramsay MacDonald reduced payments to the unemployed. Married women en masse were being laid off from good jobs and were barred from holding many jobs altogether, yet the British parliament in 1931 effectively denied unemployment insurance to such women even though they had paid in to the unemployment fund. The high tariffs imposed on imported goods did nothing to relieve British misery. In the Statute of Westminster of 1931, the government responded to the economic strengthening of Britain's dominions during the war. The statute loosened the political ties of New Zealand, Australia, South Africa, and the Irish Free State to Britain by granting them independence under the crown while linking them and Britain economically as a commonwealth. This linkage gave the British a group of loyal trading partners—the British Commonwealth—until late in the twentieth century.

In 1931 King George V (r. 1910–1936) called for a "National Government"—that is, a coalition of all parties such as had existed during the war—to address the grim economic situation. The coalition was run behind the scenes by the Conservative leadership, which alienated working people with its continuing inattention to their plight. Finally, in 1933, with the economy continuing to worsen, the government began to take effective steps. A massive program of slum clearance and new housing construction provided employment and infused money into the economy. Neville Chamberlain, the Conservative chancellor of the exchequer who as prime minister would soon undertake critical negotiations with Hitler, ably administered this program. The new policy followed in part the emerging ideas of English economist John Maynard Keynes, whose *General Theory of Employment, Interest, and Money* (1936) fully formulated the pump-priming theory for pulling an economy out of recession. It would become an accepted orthodoxy only after World War II. By 1938, an extension of the National Insurance Act was providing minimal health benefits to twenty million workers and their families. In the midst of it all, the British people's faith in their government was severely tested when in 1936 the new king, Edward VIII, demanded to marry a twice-divorced American socialite. When top British politicians refused to change the constitution to allow him to do so, he abdicated, proclaiming, "I cannot govern without the help and support of the woman I love."[23] Although morale sank during the abdication crisis and the mediocre economic revival, Britain maintained its democracy.

The French fared less well, their faith in liberal government and in the rule of law sorely tested during the depression. No strong democratic leader came to the fore during the early 1930s, and deputies with opposing views on the economic crisis frequently came to blows in the Chamber of Deputies. Governments were voted in and out with dizzying rapidity as they refused to put money into economic recovery and modernization. Parisians took to the streets to protest the government's belt-tightening policies, and the press trumpeted the disorderly mass rallies. Right-wing paramilitary groups mushroomed, attracting the unemployed, students, and veterans. They aimed to end representative government, which in their eyes was a "bastion of corruption." In February 1934, the paramilitary groups joined Communists and other outraged citizens in riots around the parliament building in response to a scandal suggesting widespread government corruption. "Let's string up the deputies," chanted the crowd. "And if we can't string them up, let's beat in their faces, let's reduce them to a pulp."[24] Hundreds of demonstrators were wounded and killed; inside the Chamber of Deputies, democratic representatives hurled ink bottles at one another. The antirepublican and anti-Semitic right, however, lacked not only effective leaderhip but also support outside Paris, and for the moment France seemed too well schooled in liberal democracy to dismantle representative government and the rule of law.

As the fascist wave became more menacing, Stalin, in a 1935 policy shift, announced that Communist parties loyal to the Soviets under the Comintern should throw their support to the fight against fascism. In France, this strategy resulted in an alliance of liberals, socialists, and Communists known as the Popular Front. Soon other countries built similar alliances. For just over a year in 1936–1937 and again very briefly in 1938, the French Popular Front had enough electoral support to form a government, with the socialist leader Léon Blum as premier. Instituting long-overdue reforms, Blum extended family subsidies, state services, and welfare benefits, and he appointed women to his government (though French women still were not allowed to vote). In June 1936, the Popular Front government guaranteed workers two-week paid vacations, a forty-hour workweek, and the right to collective bargaining—each of these a linchpin of the European welfare state then in the making.

During its brief life France's Popular Front government made republicanism responsive to the masses by offering a youthful but democratic political culture explicitly meant to challenge Nazism. "In 1936 everyone was twenty years old," one man recalled, evoking the atmosphere of idealism.[25] Local cultural centers sprang up for activities such as popular theater, and Popular Front parades took place in support of representative government. Inspired to express their opposition to fascism, citizens celebrated democratic holidays such as Bastille Day with new enthusiasm. Speakers at these events contrasted their spontaneous solidarity and good humor with the violent fascist style and its programmed abuse of human rights. But although the spirit of democratic resistance to fascism spread in Europe and the Western world in general, Popular Front deeds and style were also controversial. Supported by workers, the Popular Front government in France was hated by the upper classes. Bankers and industrialists greeted Blum's appointment by sending their capital out of the country, leaving France financially strapped. "Better Hitler than Blum" was the slogan of the anti-Semitic upper classes, who despised

Blum's Jewish ancestry. Blum tried to win support from powerful financial interests by holding down taxes on the wealthy, in effect forcing the lower levels of society to pay for Popular Front programs. Blum's government fell when it lost the left by refusing material support in the fight against fascism, most notably in Spain. As in Britain, memories of World War I in France caused leaders to block crucial support to antifascist forces elsewhere. Keeping their military budgets small, they thought, would ensure peace.

Sweden Builds a Welfare State

In Belgium, divided by ethnic and linguistic hatreds, a small but committed core of Nazis arose among the Flemish, a group long dominated by the French-speaking Walloons. Finland also turned toward the right after its struggle against a Bolshevik-inspired coup at the end of World War I. But other small northern countries, held on to their precious rights during these hard times, and politicians turned toward social programs and pump priming for solutions. Committed to democracy, they rejected the attack on human rights that occurred in Germany, Italy, and the USSR. Instead, Sweden along with the Netherlands took concerted action involving cooperation and consensus building to lead their citizenry through the slump.

Nowhere was the response to hard times more effective in boosting population, building the economy, and maintaining democracy than in Sweden. In the 1930s Sweden's ruling Social Democratic coalition enacted a string of laws attacking these problems but without the compulsion and violence found in Germany and Italy. A neutral power that had profited from World War I and then suffered postwar inflation, depression, and population decline, Sweden was able to build a coalition among farmers, workers, and the business community to agree on a basket of economic and social welfare programs. The programs evolved from the 1930s until after the war to include tax and debt relief for farmers and restrictions on lockouts and strikes to benefit both workers and industries. At a time when industrialists were threatening wage cuts, the government negotiated wage stabilization. It increased taxes on the wealthy, but they in turn received guarantees of social peace. The government also devalued the currency to make Swedish exports more attractive on the international market. Using pump-priming programs of public works to maintain consumer spending and to encourage modernization, the Social Democratic leaders saw Swedish productivity rise 20 percent between 1929 and 1935, a time when other democracies were still experiencing decline.

Sweden addressed the problem of declining population with government programs, as did several other Western governments, but without racist and antidemocratic coercion. Alva Myrdal (1902–1986), a social scientist and leading member of the Swedish parliament who believed fertility rates were dependent on the economy and individual well-being, spearheaded the effort. It was undemocratic, she maintained, "that the bearing of a child should mean economic distress to anybody in a country . . . who wants children"[26] (see Document 5.1). Acting on Myrdal's advice to promote "voluntary parenthood," the government started a loan program for married couples in 1937 and introduced prenatal care, free childbirth in a hospital, a food relief program, and subsidized housing for large families. By the end of the decade, almost 50 percent of all mothers in Sweden received government aid. Long a concern of feminists and other social reformers, care of families became integral to the tasks of the modern state, which—as other countries followed Sweden's lead—saw itself as responsible for citizen welfare in hard times.

Cultural Leaders Take Action

Just as Sweden buttressed democracy with some of the same programs the dictators used to crush it, so artists and writers in the democracies employed to different ends the same communications technology as existed in the fascist countries. They filled films, books, and radio with spirited attacks on fascism and programs to revive democratic morale. Modern technology allowed dictators and democrats alike to appeal to a mass community, as loudspeakers and radio reached wide audiences and as automobiles and mass transit took politicians to parades and whistle-stop tours that millions could see. Hitler gave fiery speeches on the radio, but Edward VIII's abdication speech was likewise heard by millions, and in the United States President Franklin D. Roosevelt promoted democratic politics in a series of "fireside chats." In 1930s Europe, however, it was the artistic and literary communities that gave loudest voice to democratic values.

Early in the depression, writers, filmmakers, and artists responded vigorously to counter the hopelessness caused by the economic slump and by the growth of fascism. Many writers exchanged their literary modernism for books and film scripts with a strong antifascist message. In 1938 Virginia Woolf published *Three Guineas,* a searing indictment that linked militarism, imperialism, and the treatment of women. Filmmakers presented historical biographies and thrillers to amuse audiences, but often the latter featured hard-working cops and people of upright values. Other films portrayed the situation of ordinary people such as factory workers, homemakers, and shop girls struggling to support themselves and their families.

In 1931 French director René Clair built on the theme of modern life's degradation when he depicted life in prison as akin to working on an assembly line in *À nous la liberté!* (*Give Us Liberty!*). Other directors caught the feel of life in a mechanized age in films featuring chorus lines and tap dancing in which large groups of women dancers moved with machine-like precision (see the Picture Essay). Like the movements of assembly-line workers, the dancers' movements were disciplined. Assembly lines gripped the imagination. In 1936 Charlie Chaplin released the film *Modern Times,* in which the hero sees even his fellow workers as machines. When he thinks they are malfunctioning, he uses his tools to try to adjust their various body parts.

Contrast in the arts between diversion and critique could not have been starker. George Orwell, an English writer new on the literary scene, wrote about modern-day poverty in *The Road to Wigan Pier* (1937)—a grim portrait of life in the declining industrial communities of northern England that practically begged for attention to these down-and-out citizens as a way to revive democratic citizenship. Films also vividly presented the down-and-out types familiar in everyday life—the tramp, the organ-grinder, and the disillusioned former soldier turned criminal.

Filmmakers used gender stereotypes to explain modern conditions. Made before the Nazi takeover, *The Blue Angel* (1930), a German film starring Marlene Dietrich, showed how a vital and conniving modern woman could destroy men and, by implication, civilization itself. Dietrich plays an attractive, manipulative showgirl who capitvates and completely degrades an impractical and bumbling professor. A different stereotype emerged in musicals and comedies, which aimed to diffuse anger against overpowering women by featuring spunky heroines behaving bravely—pulling their men out of the depths of despair and setting things right. The British comedienne Gracie Fields portrayed lively working-class women who kept on smiling despite hard times. Charlie Chaplin's *The Great Dictator* (1940) showed Hitler as a power-hungry buffoon, not an honorable man.

As in totalitarian countries, films and entertainment in the democracies promoted official social values and political agendas. Popular films about imperialism, however, unwittingly revealed the paradoxes of European democracy. Many Hollywood movies were directed, scripted, or scored by European refugees and were designed to appeal throughout the English-speaking world with thumping tales of imperialism using British, Australian, and Canadian stars as the military heroes. The British produced similar stories of imperial manliness and Western decency struggling with barbaric non-Western foes, most notably in southern and western Asia. *Gunga Din* (1939), a British interpretation of a poem by Rudyard Kipling, was popular on both sides of the Atlantic with its earnest if sometimes raucous comic heroes and its loyal servant Gunga Din, who shows his appreciation of British manly virtues by warning the British forces about an impending ambush. Non-Western peoples also supplied villains, including the South Asian fiend in Gunga Din—a scoundrel with a shaved head and wearing a scanty cotton costume who resembled Mohandas Gandhi.

THE ROAD TO GLOBAL WAR

The Great Depression intensified competition among the major powers, as politicians sought to expand their control of people and resources in hard times. Colonies were more important than ever, continuing to enrich individual investors. "It was impossible not to make money," one British investor claimed of his business in Malaya. Europeans who migrated to the colonies enjoyed living together away from the struggles in Europe: life for them, according to one woman colonist, was full of "sunshine, servants, wonderful memories."[27] New players were determined to get their share of this prosperity, and they joined the race for wealth and prestige by taking land in Asia, the Middle East, Africa, and Europe itself. As a result, tensions mounted, as militarism helped imperialism surge in the 1930s. In bold moves, Japan, Italy, and Germany ran roughshod over people's daily lives. Along with a bitter civil war in Spain, this aggression opened the path to World War II.

◆ **Movie Still from *Gunga Din***
Filmmakers celebrated imperialism in various ways over almost the entire course of the twentieth century. This 1939 film, based on a Rudyard Kipling poem, features witty one-liners, a romance, battles against an evil Indian cult, and a variety of swashbuckling characters, from the noble Gunga Din to bumbling if brave English soldiers on duty in India. In a decade when nations were once again arming themselves to the teeth, how do you imagine European viewers reacted to this film? © *John Springer Collection/CORBIS.*

Surging Global Imperialism: Japan, Italy, and Germany

In the 1930s, the older imperial powers tried to milk their colonies and mandates, and, at the same time, economic and political circumstances in Europe prompted Europeans to relocate to distant regions at a greater pace. For example, European Jews streamed into Palestine, over which Britain held a mandate as a legacy of the Peace of Paris, and claimed the area as theirs. Their numbers rose sharply as Hitler enacted harsh anti-Jewish policies in 1933 and as Jewish people across Europe and Asia felt the impact of the economic slump. Seeking to ward off the migration of Jews to their own countries, the major European states encouraged immigration to Palestine. The Arabs, who even with the rapidly rising numbers of Europeans constituted more than two-thirds of Palestine's population, undertook a general strike in 1936. Nationalist politicians in the Middle East saw evidence of a common threat to Arabs everywhere, and pan-Arabism suddenly intensified. Britain's 1937 proposal to partition Palestine among the Arabs and the Jews turned both sides against the British Empire at a time when it needed all the support it could muster. For the moment, however, most eyes were fixed on Japan, Italy, and Germany, then undertaking a more visible expansion in several different parts of the world.

In the 1920s Japan continued to develop as an industrial power and to see as part of that development the rise of a vocal working and middle class with dreams of political participation and a more just society. The time seemed ripe for more widespread democracy, for Emperor Hirohito was barely of age and was facing a crisis of legitimacy. Japan's military leaders took advantage of the unsettled conditions to declare the military an institution unto itself, an "emperor's army" independent of civilian control. The military said that its well-being was far more important than that of any other group. By the 1930s the young emperor and his advisers had turned popular opinion toward support for the imperial system and military values and away from modern democratic politics. So empowered, military leaders saw China as a storehouse of wealth to which they believed themselves entitled. To them, the future of the superior Japanese race was at stake in the conquest of Asia. They saw their own military success as key to pulling agriculture and small business from the depths of economic depression—"the only way to the eternal growth and development of East Asia," as one policy maker put it[28] (see Document 5.3). Common beliefs in their racial superiority and territorial entitlement to the lands of supposedly inferior people linked Japan with Germany and Italy, setting the stage for a powerful global alliance that unfolded in the 1930s and early 1940s.

The Japanese army swung into action. In September 1931 a railroad train in the Chinese province of Manchuria blew up; bodies of the culprits, dressed as Chinese soldiers, littered the tracks. Japanese officers used the explosion, which they had actually set, as an excuse to invade the territory (Map 5.1). After setting up a puppet government in the renamed state of Manchukuo, the Japanese army pushed farther into China, and Emperor Hirohito's tepid response to this unauthorized military action encouraged expansionists in the army to undertake more extreme initiatives.

During the 1930s, Japan's continuing aggression in China alienated the United States, on whom Japan depended for natural resources and markets, but the military saw itself as fully justified in the face of Anglo-American support of the status quo. As one of the emperor's advisers put it in a well-received and influential public pronouncement, "Unequal distribution of land and natural resources causes war." The British and Americans supported this unequal distribution, the Japanese claimed, because it favored European peoples, harming Asians who had needs and indeed the right to survive. "It is they, not we, who block world peace," one imperial official announced. From the takeover in Manchuria until the end of World War II, the Japanese army waged war, without success, to capture China.

From the late nineteenth century, the Western powers had rolled back the gains made by Japan's victories over China in 1894–1895 and Russia in 1904–1905. The Fourteen Points, the Covenant of the League of Nations, and the other ex-

◆ **Map 5.1 The Expansion of Japan, 1931–1941**
The Japanese conquered lands to make up their
"Greater East Asia Co-Prosperity Sphere." Its stated
aim was "to cause East Asia to return to its original
form of independence and co-prosperity by shaking
off the yoke of Europe and America, and to let its
countries and peoples develop their respective
abilities in peaceful cooperation and secure
livelihood." The Chinese in particular resisted the
Japanese takeover because of the violence the
Japanese inflicted on them during the 1930s.

pressions of human rights for colonial peoples hammered out at the peace conference in Paris suggested that there was even more reason to curb Japan's colonial appetite. It was to that legacy that China appealed when it petitioned the League of
Nations to adjudicate the situation on the basis of the new rules. The European
powers in fact feared the threat to their own economic interests from Japanese expansionism, because the market in Japanese goods had been growing since World
War I and the economic depression made the rise of non-Western competition all
the more aggravating. Sympathetic to China's claims, the League condemned the
invasion of Manchuria but, well aware of the might of Japan, imposed no sanctions
that would have put economic teeth into its condemnation. The government of
Japan considered the condemnation an insult and in 1933 walked out of the League
and huffed its way into an alliance with Hitler's Germany and Mussolini's Italy—
the other have-nots (countries without empires).

Seeing the League's ineffectiveness and the democracies' relative passivity, both
Italy and Germany looked to expand. In the absence of economic or political bite,

moral disapproval meant little to them. Hitler urged businessmen to return in force to Tanzania—a former German colony under British mandate—and start the process of recolonization. In 1935 Mussolini asserted Italy's right to empire by invading Ethiopia, one of few African states to remain independent and thus a beacon of hope to both pan-African and national liberation movements. Like the Japanese attack in Manchuria, the attack on Ethiopia was intended to promote military vigor and to raise the attacker's standing among the colonial powers of Europe. "The Roman legions are again on the march," one Italian soldier boasted.[29] Equipped with spears but incredibly brave in the face of Italian firepower, the Ethiopians resisted but could not withstand the Italian army. Their capital, Addis Ababa, fell in the spring of 1936. As news spread across their continent, Africans were radicalized, outraged at this attack on an important source of African pride. A student in London, Kwame Nkrumah, who would be a leader in the liberation of Ghana after World War II, wept at the tragedy, made all the more humiliating by Italian claims to racial superiority at having conquered "a country without a shadow of civility."[30] A triumph for Italy, the takeover of Ethiopia was a searing moment, unforgivable and unforgettable, leading eventually to the fall of African colonization some two decades later.

The League declared Italy an aggressor state even before the Ethiopian resistance had collapsed, but League action was as counterproductive as its slap on the wrist to Japan. The League imposed economic sanctions on Italy, depriving it of some resources, but Britain and France both backed down when it came to blocking Italy's access to oil. Their own trade interests might suffer, and at least to France, Italy seemed far less menacing than Hitler's Third Reich. The French and British decisions were fatal: Italy became defiant and instead of backing down took part in negotiations that created the Rome-Berlin Axis of 1936–1937—an agreement that brought Italy and Germany formally together as allies.

Hitler was intent on stamping out the legacy of the Versailles settlement, which punished Germany and hemmed it in. In the autumn of 1933, he announced Germany's withdrawal from the League of Nations and from an international disarmament conference then meeting. Portraying himself as a man of peace, he swiftly concluded a Non-Aggression Pact with Poland in January 1934, which reassured Western statesmen that Germany would not threaten Poland's boundaries or the free city of Danzig, a city the victorious Allies jointly held as a mandate under the Peace of Paris even though it was populated by ethnic Germans. European statesmen had yet to learn that such agreements were usually the prelude to German aggression.

Behind the scenes Hitler tried to force the unification of Germany and Austria, but Engelbert Dollfuss, the authoritarian leader of Austria's Catholic political party the Christian Socialists, resisted this attempted *Anschluss* (annexation). As in Germany, the Socialists to the left and the Nazis to the right wanted to overthrow the government. Dollfuss successfully took on the Socialists, sending in the army to put down their resistance to the dictatorship he was undertaking. The Nazis gave way, for Mussolini stood on the Austrian border, not yet ready to let the Nazis have their way, and Hitler himself was still gaining his legs. Instead, in July 1934 Nazis in Austria assassinated Dollfuss for his obstruction and waited for conditions to change.

In 1935, loudly rejecting the clauses of the Versailles Treaty that limited German military strength, Hitler reintroduced military conscription and publicly started rearming, which had been going on in secret almost since the end of World War I. Then, in March 1936, Hitler defiantly sent German troops into the supposedly permanently demilitarized Rhineland, where wildly enthusiastic crowds welcomed them. French protests at this threat to their security were not backed up by the British, who bought the argument that Germany had legitimate grievances left over from Versailles. Soon, statesmen believed, these appetites and just grievances would be satisfied and European tranquillity restored. Meanwhile, as the Rome-Berlin Axis took shape, Hitler prepared for the next steps in his quest for *Lebensraum*—territorial "living space" that would enrich the superior Aryan race and make Germany the most powerful force in the world.

The Spanish Civil War

In 1931 Spanish republicans overthrew Spain's monarchy, which for centuries had fortified the rule of large landowners and the domination of the Catholic clergy. Spain had fitfully developed an industrial capacity in cities such as Barcelona and Bilbao in the early part of the century, but the ruling elites kept an impoverished peasantry in their grip, maintaining Spain as an authoritarian country plagued by extremes of wealth for the few and poverty for the masses. Urban workers and the middle classes enthusiastically supported the end of the dictatorship that ruled in the name of the monarch and began debating the course of change. Constitutionalists, middle-of-the-road liberals, communists, socialists, Trotskyites, and anarchists held widely differing views.

For those committed to a democratic republic, the air was electric with promise. With open public debate now possible, one woman recalled, people sat for hours dreaming dreams: "We saw a backward country suddenly blossoming out into a modern state. We saw peasants living like decent human beings. We saw men allowed freedom of conscience. We saw life, instead of death in Spain."[31] Groups on the center and left were so intent on battling one another to get their way, however, that the government of the Spanish republic had a hard time implementing a political program that would gain it widespread support in the countryside and was forced to resort to symbolic acts such as releasing political prisoners and doling out coveted municipal jobs to the urban unemployed. The Spanish republicans were unable to mount a unified effort to build a modern industrial base or to enact land reform that would have gained them popular support. Instead of undermining the reactionary economic and political forces of the old agrarian economy, antimonarchist factions struggled against one another to dominate the new government. Europe, not surprisingly, was watching this unfolding drama.

Ominously for the fate of democracy in Spain, the forces of the right drew closer together, making use of their considerable wealth to undermine the republican government. In 1936 a group of army officers stationed in Spanish Morocco staged an uprising against the republican government in Madrid, but some army units remained loyal to the government. In the face of this grave threat, the competing pro-republic factions temporarily aligned themselves in a "Popular Front" similar to that in France to fight the forces of the right. The rebellious army officers soon found a determined leader, General Francisco Franco (1892–1975), who was able to unify the right and make use of its greater resources. The rebels—monarchists, landowners, the clergy, and the fascist Falange Party—soon had the help of fascists in other parts of Europe, who saw in Spain a testing ground not only for their beliefs but for new military weapons and tactics. Mussolini's planes transported the Moroccan officers and their colonial troops back to Spain. Soon Hitler was providing weapons and German forces.

On the republican side, citizens supporting democracy—male and female alike—took up arms and formed volunteer units of fighters. In their minds, citizen armies symbolized republicanism, while professional troops followed the aristocratic rebels. As civil war gripped Spain, the republicans generally held Madrid, Barcelona, and other commercial and industrial areas. The rebels found most support in the agricultural west and south (Map 5.2).

The Spanish government appealed everywhere for assistance, but only the Soviet Union answered. Britain and France refused to take effective steps to block aggression despite an outpouring of popular support for the cause of democracy in Spain. Indeed, in August 1936 the French government had released an appeal in all newspapers "for the rapid adoption and rigorous application of the accepted

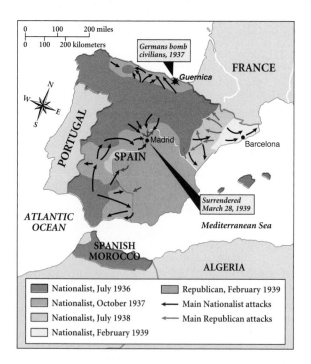

◆ **Map 5.2 The Spanish Civil War, 1936–1939**
The Spanish Civil War was especially bitter, with atrocities committed on both sides. In a war of ever shifting battle lines, republicans held Madrid, Barcelona, and other commercial and industrial areas, whereas the rebels found most support in the agricultural west and south. With Franco's victory and the onset of reprisals against workers and other supporters of the republic, thousands went into exile, crossing into France to find asylum.

♦ **Republican Soldiers during the Spanish Civil War**
Many in Spain's army went over to the rebel side in 1936 when Franco's forces
decided to restore the power of the landowning class and the Catholic Church by
overthrowing the republic. Yet others, like these pro-republican soldiers, remained
to fight, and they were joined by an array of volunteers—constitutionalists,
anarchists, socialists, and thousands of others committed to republican government
based on rights. Supported by Hitler and Mussolini, however, Franco's rebels had
experience, weapons, and financial resources on their side. © *Hulton-Deutsch
Collection/CORBIS.*

rules of non-intervention in regard to Spain."[32] So instead of massive international
support, a few thousand volunteers from a variety of countries—including many
students, journalists, and artists, and the so-called Lincoln Brigade from the United
States—flocked to Spain to fight for the republic and democracy.

The rehearsal for World War II intensified when Hitler and Mussolini sent military personnel to support Franco and the Germans began to practice the terror
bombing of civilians—most tragically in the northern town of Guernica, where on
market day, April 26, 1937, they dropped 40 to 50 tons of bombs. The splinter
groups with which the republic defended itself could not hold. In 1938 Stalin with-

drew his troops and tanks as republican forces floundered. Atrocities were committed by both sides, but the aid Franco received ultimately proved decisive, and his troops defeated the republicans in 1939. Tens of thousands of republicans fled the retribution that followed, and many thousands of others were jailed and executed. The tide of authoritarianism swelled with Franco's victory, appearing unstoppable even to the most committed democrats.

Hitler Conquers Central Europe

Germany was now poised to claim its own empire. The target was central Europe. Austria was to be the first victim. Some Austrians had actually wished for a merger with Germany after the Paris peace settlement stripped them of their empire. In March 1938, Austrian chancellor Kurt von Schuschnigg, an authoritarian who nonetheless hoped to maintain independence, called on Austrians to vote for or against a merger with the Third Reich. Fearing negative results, Hitler ordered an invasion that was so swift and apparently bloodless that it elicited no strong protest either from within or without the country. Hitler built cadres of supporters in every country he coveted, and these people lined the invasion routes to show enthusiasm, making the Anschluss seem like the fulfillment of the Wilsonian idea of self-determination. Moreover, Britain wanted peace with Germany not war, and France, which was more fearful, had no effective leadership that might take strong action.

The annexation of Austria fit Hitler's imperial designs in two ways: it began the unification of "Aryan peoples" into one greater German nation, and it marked the first step toward taking over the resources of central and eastern Europe. The Anschluss netted the Germans hundreds of millions in Austrian gold, a hefty treasure that paid the small costs of the takeover and would help pay for future military action. Within occupied Austria, Nazis generated support not only by unifying Germans across borders but by solving the intractable problem of unemployment—especially among the young and out-of-work rural migrants to the cities. Factories sprang up overnight, mostly to foster rearmament, and new "Hitler housing" was of a quality that suggested the dignity of workers as propounded by the Nazis. "We were given work!" Austrians continued long afterward to exclaim, defending their embrace of the Third Reich. The Anschluss eliminated some of the pain that Austrians suffered when their empire was truncated after World War I.[33] Cautious members of the middle class suddenly became Nazi militants. One novelist described the transformation through one of his fictional characters: "Yes, he Franz Josef Zehetner, was a German, an Aryan, an Austrian, a Christian; he was the prisoner of Versailles and Saint-Germain, he was the victim of Marxist terror and was the oak at whose roots international Jewry gnawed. Even in him most careful of the careful, something at last demanded a great breakthrough." National chauvinism and ethnic hatred, of course, were promoted by the Nazis.[34]

With Austria firmly in his grasp, Hitler turned to Czechoslovakia and its rich resources. To overpower this democracy would be no simple task. Czechoslovakia had a large army, formidable border defenses, and armament factories, and most Czech citizens were prepared to fight for their country. However, betting on democratic yearnings for peace, Hitler gambled correctly that the other Western powers would not interfere. Not only peace-lovers but many others in the West thought that the Czech government, a creation of the Paris settlement, had unjustly denied the right to self-determination to other national minorities living in Czechoslovakia, especially Germans in the mountainous northwestern region known as the Sudetenland. Throughout the spring and summer of 1938, Hitler and his propaganda machine played on these sentiments and poured tremendous abuse on Czechoslovakia for allegedly "persecuting" the German minority. Hitler wooed Czechoslovakia's neighbors into accepting his claims, partly by convincing the Poles and Hungarians that they had something to gain from the country's dismemberment. By October 1, 1938, he warned, Czechoslovakia would have to grant autonomy (amounting to Nazi rule) to the German-populated border region, the Sudetenland, or face German invasion.

As the October deadline approached, British prime minister Neville Chamberlain, determined to avoid another "Great War," met with Hitler. Mussolini and French premier Édouard Daladier joined Hitler and Chamberlain in Munich and agreed not to oppose Germany's claim to the Sudetenland. Hitler topped off the Munich Conference by signing an agreement promising that Germany would never go to war with Great Britain. At the time, what came to be known as "appeasement"—the peacekeeping moves that let Spain, Italy, Japan, and Germany have their way—was widely seen as a positive act, and the agreement between Germany and Great Britain prompted Chamberlain upon arrival home to announce triumphantly that he had secured "peace in our time." Amid great fanfare, crowds lined the streets of European capitals and hailed their returning leaders for averting world war. Not everyone was so confident about appeasement's potential for keeping the peace. Winston Churchill, who as prime minister would lead Britain through World War II, watched those celebrating in the streets of London with a mixture of alarm and sadness: "Those poor people," he commented. "They little know what they will have to face."[35]

Having portrayed himself as a man of peace while seizing part of a sovereign foreign country, Hitler waited another six months, until March 1939, and then sent German troops over the border to take the rest of Czechoslovakia. Britain and France responded by promising military support to Poland, Romania, Greece, and Turkey should they too face Nazi aggression. In May 1939, Hitler and Mussolini countered this agreement by solidifying their alliance in the Pact of Steel—a pledge of mutual offensive and defensive support. An even more momentous alliance was being forged behind the scenes. On August 23, 1939, Germany and the USSR signed a nonaggression agreement. The Nazi-Soviet Nonaggression Pact astonished public opinion in the West, given Hitler's ambition to wipe the Bolsheviks off the face of the earth and official Soviet abhorrence of fascism. The pact provided that if one country became embroiled in war, the other country would remain neutral. The two dictators, each playing for time with the other, secretly agreed to divide Poland and the Baltic states—Latvia, Estonia, and Lithuania—at some future date. Hitler claimed western Poland and Stalin the Baltic states in addition to Finland and eastern Poland.

CONCLUSION

The Nazi-Soviet Pact ensured that if war came, the democracies would be fighting a Germany with no fear of attack on its eastern borders. Believing that Great Britain and perhaps even France would not fight because his aggression had met no resistance from them so far, Hitler next aimed his forces at Poland, another fledgling state established at the end of World War I. Step by step, Hitler was undoing the Peace of Paris and using the context of global depression to build an empire so rapidly and forcefully that it would paralyze the world. In his successes he played on themes from the Great War—the superiority of the nation, the virtues of military strength, and the decadence of democracy and human rights. He was not alone in holding these values, and like other authoritarian and expansionist rulers he had millions of supporters and motivated tens of millions of activists.

Germany, like other totalitarian and authoritarian states, expanded in the 1930s using maximum violence and encountered little resistance. The economic slump had loosened the bonds of both local society and the international order. New political groups preached hatred toward neighbors, while governments waged economic war against one another. The death toll caused by state aggression of the 1930s is now estimated in the millions. Authoritarian slogans and violent politics shaped attitudes toward public life, leading Europeans to a catastrophic war that swept the rest of the world into the whirlwind. The buildup to that war can be charted in the effects of the Great Depression, the individual aggressive acts of the have-not powers, and the failures of democracy in less developed countries such as Spain and in global powers such as France. But though we can map the road to World War II, its horrifying and inhuman course will keep us forever questioning whether it could have been headed off in the 1930s.

DOCUMENTS

Sweden's Battle for Population

HOW DO YOU FORCE PEOPLE TO HAVE CHILDREN? From early in the twentieth century, societies experienced rapidly falling birthrates because millions of couples were using more effective birth control. Many politicians lamented the trend toward smaller families, and some used it to whip up strong emotions against single people and "selfish" new women who were shirking their national duty to procreate. After a short spurt early in the 1920s, the rate kept sliding as the Great Depression deepened. Despite great economic suffering, Hitler railed against Aryans for failing to produce large families and against Jews for polluting the nation by having any children at all. In Germany, heated rhetoric about the decline in family size accompanied bellicose words about conquest and stirring speeches about national destiny.

Alva Myrdal's *Nation and Family: The Swedish Experiment in Democratic Family and Population Policy* was hardly such a tract. Instead, like many democratic pronouncements about population, it was well considered, even dull because so calm. Myrdal wrote *Nation and Family* in the late 1930s to summarize for the rest of the world the way Sweden was addressing its population shortfall. In 1934 Gunnar and Alva Myrdal, social scientists and politicians, had already caught the attention of the Swedish nation with their book *The Population Crisis*. At the time Sweden had the lowest birthrate in the world—thirteen births per thousand population—and in the book the Myrdals discussed the implications of this low rate for the health of Swedish society. They hoped to encourage Swedes to have children but avoided the demagogic, hate-filled language that Hitler used. The response was immediate. Swedes realized that they faced real problems of national survival over the next decades.

As the economic slump drove down birthrates, many countries enacted legislation to keep married women out of the workforce, for two reasons: (1) they took jobs away from men, and (2) relegated to the home, they were more likely to reproduce. Few legislators connected the loss of income generated by women's work with any decline in a family's ability to support its children. In some places, campaigns to provide birth control for the poor and to encourage childbirth among the "pure-blooded" and the upper classes took shape. In Germany Jews and in the United States African Americans were forcibly sterilized. Alva Myrdal saw a different solution and helped lead Sweden toward taking it.

Sweden's program for encouraging fertility, the thinking behind which Myrdal presents in the excerpt from *Nation and Family* reprinted here, became the model for welfare states across Europe after World War II. Sweden's problems with falling rates of fertility, however, diverged from problems elsewhere in Europe. From the end of the nineteenth century, hundreds of thousands of Swedish men had left the country because of rural poverty. Not only did this exodus leave behind many women who would never find a partner, but the shortage of men accounted for high rates of illegitimate pregnancies—some 20 percent of births in the 1920s were illegitimate. The mothers of these children had to work to support their families, and women's right to work no matter what the circumstances became a crucial issue for many women's labor unions and political organizations. By 1938, these groups were so capable politically that they prevented the passing of legislation that would have kept married women out of the workforce. Alva Myrdal summarized their concerns in *Nation and Family* in this way: "The first reform needed is the defense of the right to earn a living both for women in general and for married women in particular."[36]

The population issue and the rights of married women came together during the depression and the rise of fascism. In 1932, taking as his platform his goal to make Sweden "The People's Home," Social Democratic leader Per Albin Hanssen was elected prime minister. Hanssen believed that fascism flourished in places where people were undernourished, underemployed, and anxious about the stability of daily life. Borrowing from the pro-natalist ideas of Swedish reformer Ellen Key, his government allied itself with women activists and allies of the Myrdals. The result was a series of welfare programs targeting a range of social ills, prominent among them the plight of women and children. The preservation of constitutional government was central to the Myrdals' plan.

Alva Myrdal later helped establish the United Nations' program in social welfare and worked in UNESCO on similar issues. As Sweden's ambassador to India, Burma, and Ceylon and as a member of Sweden's parliament, she turned her scholarship to issues of disarmament. She received the Nobel Peace Prize in 1982. But it was the marriage of rights and citizen well-being in *Nation and Family* that caught politicians' attention in the 1930s and made Sweden the model for the welfare state of the future. In the early years of World War II, Britain announced the creation of a welfare state with provisions similar to those in Sweden. In Britain and elsewhere the economic democracy embodied in programs for citizens became a foundation of the fight against fascism. The Swedish welfare state of the 1930s shaped the peacetime welfare state in most of Europe and eventually in much of the world.

Document 5.1

ALVA MYRDAL
Nation and Family: The Swedish Experiment in Democratic Family and Population Policy, 1941

RELIEVING INSECURITY

The causes of the decrease in fertility are varied, and the means to counteract it must also be varied. It is of course not necessary that every cause be counterbalanced by specific means. The remedies have to be affixed to the strategic causes, the ones we want and also are able to influence. However much the decrease in fertility may be due to increasing rationality in human life, few would be willing to try to reduce rationality. Other measures will have to be found which can be reconciled with both growing rationality and increased fertility.

There are three main tendencies working for extreme family limitation: the feeling of insecurity in modern life, particularly with regard to economic support; the cumbersomeness of children and difficulty of fitting their lives into the patterns of adult life in modern civilization, particularly in cities; and the fact that children exert a greater and greater pressure on the family economy. Can any means be found that would tend to counterbalance these tendencies?

A democracy can offer its citizens the fundamental security which is basic to any will to live on in subsequent generations, the possibility of identifying without mental reservation their own interests with the prolonged existence of their children in their culture. Optimism that society is developing in the right direction; confidence in the handling of its joint interests through a government and an administration under one's own control; pride in social development and in economic progress; the identification of individual

interests not only with those of the country in general but also with those of compatriots in other social strata—these are the first prerequisites for people wanting to prolong their interest in society through their children and for awakening an enthusiasm for reforming that society for the children.

It is inherent in such a democracy that reform activities are carried out unceasingly to decrease the impact of all the major insecurities in the lives of its citizens: old age, sickness, invalidism, unemployment, and so on. Unemployment is the main factor in family insecurity. Even when the actual extent of unemployment is small and its worst effects cushioned by some system of public works and by unemployment insurance, the very risk of unemployment acts as a deterrent to childbearing. Therefore, it becomes a general precondition for making any population policy successful under modern conditions that it must be shaped within a progressive economic system operating at near productive capacity and full absorption of labor. There is necessary, too, an effective system of social security for unemployment risks. . . .

MATERNITY BONUS

Even when the birth of a child is made considerably more secure by the state's protective measures as the free right of every woman, there remain other expenses to consider. Some of these are of such a nature that up to a certain minimum they are identical for everybody. They are inevitable in all economic classes. They can be calculated in advance and therefore can easily be transferred to community budgets. They include certain minimum expenses for a layette, bedding for the child, clothes, travel to the hospital or sending for a nurse, and, finally, household help in the home.

SOURCE: Alva Myrdal, *Nation and Family: The Swedish Experiment in Democratic Family and Population Policy* (Cambridge: MIT Press, 1941), 119, 321–324.

Consequently, these must be considered expenses eligible for public grants under a new policy aimed at relieving the individual families of the extra costs of children.

There may, however, in some cases be a more thorough disturbance of the family budget on the occasion of childbirth. A loss of wages may be involved. In earlier legislation this outstanding economic loss, caused by pregnancy and childbearing, was the only one considered for social remuneration. According to a Workers' Protective Law of 1900 mothers in industry were compelled to abstain from work for six weeks after childbirth. Women's organizations were anxious that this negative rule should be recompensed by some social bonus. In Sweden some compensation was provided through the sickness insurance funds. Since 1913 state subsidies have been paid to such funds for benefits to woman members. . . .

A new law was drafted, creating a unified system instead of the old double one. A maternity bonus was proposed for every woman without any income limit. The Population Commission then went on to consider what expenses these benefits were actually to cover.

> Since compulsory maternity insurance would not furnish a satisfactory solution as long as sickness insurance is only voluntary, the Commission has gone no further than to recommend an arrangement whereby childbearers would receive aid in defraying the expenses connected with confinement directly from state funds similar to the procedure in the present maternity aid system. It is here proposed that this be called a "maternity bonus." . . .
>
> After this the Commission wants to consider how much the proposed maternity bonus should amount to. For this purpose the Commission has attempted to estimate the extra expenses connected with childbirth. The Commission desires to detail the steps in this calculation, but feels it necessary to remark that, in the na-

ture of things, any such estimate can to a large extent be only approximate. The Commission concludes that the expenses can be estimated at 100 crs. in round numbers. The Commission has included the following items of expenditure:

> Traveling expenses, either for the childbearer to and from place of confinement or for the midwife to and from the childbearer.
>
> Home assistance, including full-time help during the time the childbearer is absent from home or confined in bed at home—as a rule ten days—and temporary help with heavier household duties two weeks prior to and two weeks after parturition.
>
> Equipment for childbearer, such as proper maternity girdle and dress near the end of pregnancy as well as bedding and layette for the infant. The expenses for bedding and layette for the infant are necessarily higher for a first child than for subsequent children, but this is probably counterbalanced by the fact that help in the home in this case can be arranged at smaller cost.

The final outcome was, however, not a proposal for 100 crs. but for a bonus of 75 crs. This bonus was not to be considered as assistance for those on the margin of poverty but was to be extended to all women without regard to income.

> The Commission is of the opinion that the maternity bonus should in principle be given to all women as an expression of the public appreciation of motherhood.
>
> There are, evidently, some women in such favorable economic circumstances that the maternity subsidy would be no special advantage. But, if the people in the higher income groups are excluded, the diminution of public costs would be so insignificant that such a gain would not counterbalance the loss incurred in the

surrender of the principle. A rough estimate leads to the probable conclusion that at present only about 1 per cent of all births would occur in families with a taxable income in excess of 10,000 crs. . . . It may be expected that childbearers within the highest income groups and prosperous classes will anyway not demand the maternity bonus.

Revolutionary as it may seem to shift over from private to public budgeting of such a personal cost item and to carry it not only for the poor but as an honored gift to all mothers, the scheme met with approval. The government proposed a bill and in 1937 the Riksdag endorsed it. Only one change was made in the original program, slight in effect but important enough in principle. The complete coverage of all mothers was subject to an income limit. This limit, however, was placed above the middle-class group, being fixed at a taxable annual income of 3,000 crs, which often amounts to a net income of 5,000 crs. Not quite 10 per cent of the mothers can by this rule be excluded from the new bonus. No means test is involved, the decision about income

limit being of a strictly formal character. It goes without saying that the bonus is being paid to married and unmarried mothers alike. The law went into effect January 1, 1938.

The change in the reform plan represented by the income restriction is characteristic of a lag in the development of political opinion. The population motivation for the new scheme could not wholly overcome the older philosophy of relief. The fundamental principle of the previous period in social planning was "help to help oneself." Community help should be used only to fill certain gaps in individual incomes. The new outlook contains a much wider recognition of the community as collectively responsible for certain costs of living for the citizens. In actual parliamentary politics these fundamental differences were hard to make clear. The lapse in public generosity was due both to the conservatives arguing that not "everybody ought to be made a reliefer" and to the laboring class's lack of understanding "why rich people should get a bonus." The old clichés have a pernicious longevity. Thus are illustrated some psychological difficulties in making the transition from curative to prophylactic social policy.

QUESTIONS FOR ANALYSIS

1. What specific provisions are outlined in this excerpt, from Sweden's program, and how does the program signal a changing attitude toward parenting?

2. What differences in tone and provisions do you see between Germany's program for encouraging population and Sweden's?

3. What social and political values do you see expressed in the program for the Swedish welfare state?

The Secret Poetry of Stalinism

ONE OF THE FINEST RUSSIAN AVANT-GARDE POETS of the twentieth century was Anna Akhmatova (1889–1966). A great beauty, Akhmatova attracted and was painted by famous artists, especially the Italian modernist Amedeo Modigliani and the Russian N. J. Altman. Before World War I, her poetry contained vivid, condensed word images, and she laced it with references to parasols, chrysanthemums, masks, blue china, and other objects reflecting the powerful influence of Asia on European poets. Akhmatova's first husband, Nicholai Gumilyov (1886–1921), also sparkled in the literary salons of prewar Russia, producing several books of verse that reflected his travels to Africa and his interest in African heroes.

The Bolshevik Revolution changed poets' lives as it changed everyone else's. Gumilyov was arrested for conspiring against the government and shot. In the 1930s their son, Lev Gumilyov, was twice arrested and imprisoned by Stalin's secret police, and Akhmatova became one of tens of thousands of relatives who waited day and night in front of prisons for news of their loved ones. During those years she began secretly writing *Requiem*—a poetic work that she continually revised and that was not published until the 1960s, and then only in western Europe. *Requiem* presents vivid images of individuals whose dear ones were caught in the deadly net of the purges and who themselves stood by, helpless. To remember and bear witness, Soviet citizens recited *Requiem* and passed *samizdat* copies of it from person to person. In the Soviet bloc, because of censorship and the dangers of writing anything at all without the official approval of the Union of Soviet Writers, authors circulated handwritten copies of poetry, short stories, and even novels among themselves and trusted friends. This literature circulated in secret was called *samizdat*.

During World War II Stalin called on Akhmatova, as he called on the censored composer Dmitri Shostakovich, to inspire Russians to patriotism and resistance through art. Akhmatova broadcast her poetry on the radio and became a national hero. Much of her verse from the war is now seen as acceptable but hardly worthy of a poet of her stature. When, after World War II, Stalin resumed the purges of the 1930s, Akhmatova was one of the first to be singled out for disgrace. She was accused of sexual promiscuity and other bad behavior. The official Soviet newspaper *Pravda* in 1946 attacked her as "this representative of a totally empty poetry, stripped of idealism, foreign to our traditions, Akhmatova, a leftover from reactionary literature, neither completely a nun, nor totally a whore, but a demi-nun and a demi-whore."[37] Though disgraced, Akhmatova was not killed but was confined to a hospital where she lived in poor conditions.

After Stalin's death in 1953, Akhmatova's life improved somewhat, and she was allowed to leave the Soviet Union to receive foreign honors before her death in 1966. Her life and her singular poetic accomplishments were varied, spanning the "Silver Age" of Russian arts before World War I and progressing through the trials that most Soviets experienced for almost the rest of the century.

Document 5.2

ANNA AKHMATOVA
Requiem, 1930s–1960s

No, it wasn't under a foreign heaven,
It wasn't under the wing of a foreign power,—
I was there among my countrymen,
I was where my people, unfortunately, were.

1961

INSTEAD OF A PREFACE

In the awful years of Yezhovian° horror, I spent seventeen months standing in line in front of various prisons in Leningrad. One day someone "recognized" me. Then a woman with blue lips, who was standing behind me, and who, of course, had never heard my name, came out of the stupor which typified all of us, and whispered into my ear (everyone there spoke only in whispers):

—Can you describe this?

And I said:

—I can.

Then something like a fleeting smile passed over what once had been her face.

April 1, 1957
Leningrad

DEDICATION

Faced with this grief, mountains sink down,
The great river has to languish,
But the clasps of the prison are made of iron,
And behind them the "concentration den"
And deadly anguish.
Cool winds are stroking someone's hair,

°*N. I. Yezhov:* Head of the NKVD, the Soviet Secret Police from 1936 to 1938, was noted for his ferocity. He presided over the great purges, and the period of 1936–1938 is therefore known as "Yezhovshchina." [Translator's note.]

SOURCE: Anna Akhmatova, *Poems*, ed. and trans. Lyn Coffin (New York: Norton, 1983), 82–87.

And the sun is shining on someone's head—
We don't know, we're the same everywhere,
The gnashing of keys is all we hear
And the soldiers' booted tread.
We get up as if there were priests to assist,
We cross the rebrutalized city squares,
More breathless than the dead, we come to the
     tryst,
The sun is lower and the Neva's all mist,
And far off, the song of hoping flares.
Sentence . . . And at once the tears will start,
How different from the others one's already
     grown,
It's as if they took the life out of the heart,
Like being thrown backwards on a jolting
     cart,
. . . She's coming . . . Staggering . . . Alone . . .
Where now are all the chance-met people,
Friends during those two years in hell?
Of which Siberian storms are they full?
What phantoms do they see in the lunar circle?
It's to them I am sending this farewell.

1940

INTRODUCTION

This happened when only the dead wore
     smiles—
They rejoiced at being safe from harm.
And Leningrad dangled from its jails
Like some unnecessary arm.
And when the hosts of those convicted,
Marched by—mad, tormented throngs,
And train whistles were restricted
To singing separation songs.
The stars of death stood overhead,
And guiltless Russia, that pariah,
Writhed under boots, all blood-bespattered,
And the wheels of many a black maria.

1935

3.

No, this isn't me, someone else suffers,
I couldn't stand it. All that's happened
They should wrap up in black covers,
The streetlights should be taken away . . .
                              Night.

                                                    1939

4.

They should have shown you, girl of the clever
        hello
And the scoffing darling of many a friend,
The happy sinner from Tsarskoe Selo,
What would happen to your life before the
        end—
Carrying bundles, the three-hundredth soul
Waiting at the Cross Prison door,
And your warm tear would burn a hole
In the new year's icy floor.
The prison poplar continues to bend,
There's not a sound to be heard—but how many
Innocent lives are coming to an end . . .

                                                    1939

5.

For months I've filled the air with pleas,
Trying to call you back,
I've thrown myself at the hangman's knees,
You are my son and my rack.
From now on, categories spill,
And I no longer have any solution—
Who's a beast, who's human still,
How long I must wait for the execution.
Besides dusty flowers, there is also
The ringing of censers, and tracks that go
From somewhere into nowhere fast.
And straight ahead, there's this to see:
A gigantic star, threatening me
With death when a day or two have passed.

                                                    1939

EPILOGUE

I

I've seen how a face can fall like a leaf,
How, from under the lids, terror peeks,
I've seen how suffering and grief
Etches hieroglyphs on cheeks,
How ash-blonde hair, from roots to tips,
Turns black and silver overnight.
How smiles wither on submissive lips,
And in a half-smile quivers fright.
Not only for myself do I pray,
But for those who stood in front and behind me,
In the bitter cold, on a hot July day
Under the red wall that stared blindly.

II

Again the memorial hour's drawing near.
You are the one I see and feel and hear:

Who was barely able to come to the window and
        stand,
The one who does not tread her native land.

Who looked at me and tossed her beautiful head,
And "Coming here is coming home," she said.

I'd like to call each one by name, in turn,
But someone took my list away to burn.

For them I've woven a wide shroud today
Of insufficient words I heard them say.

I've thought about them everywhere I've been,
I won't forget them in the new misfortune.

Someone might close my lips, I have no doubt,
Through which a hundred million people shout,

Let them remember me the selfsame way,
On the eve of my memorial day.

And if it ever be this land's intent
To honor me with any monument,

I give permission to that future nation,
With one condition, for the celebration:

Don't put it in my birthplace, ocean-battered,
My last connection with the sea's been shattered,

Nor in the Czar's park by the hallowed tree,°
Where an inconsolable spirit looks for me,

° This tree or stump in Tsarskoe Selo often figures in Akhmatova's poetry. It connects her with Pushkin, symbolizes her
ties to Russian poetic tradition, etc. [Translator's note.]

But here where for three hundred hours I had
    to wait,
And still they didn't open that certain gate.

Because even in blissful death I'd be afraid
To forget the clatter black marias made,

To forget the way the hated door slammed shut
And an old lady wailed like a wounded creature,
    but

Let from the lids of bronze, unmoving eyes
Snow melt and stream like the tears each human
    cries,

And let in the distance the prison pigeons coo,
While along the Neva, ships pass quietly through.

1940

QUESTIONS FOR ANALYSIS

1. What images does this celebrated poem employ, and what do they convey to you about the times in which the author lived?

2. What reactions do the different forms of poetry and the dates attached to each section evoke in you as a reader?

3. Does this poem more vividly convey the personal feelings of the poet or those of the people around her?

4. In what ways does this and other poetry give us some understanding of the past?

Japan on the Move

I N THE 1930s JAPANESE POLITICIANS AND MILITARY LEADERS spoke about "Greater East Asia"—a phrase signaling Japan's interest in unifying the various regions of East Asia, including China and Indochina, into an economic and political whole. These leaders wanted Japan to drive out the Western powers, and the idea appealed not unexpectedly to anti-imperialist activists in the region who wanted national independence. Japanese planners, however, expected to oust the Western powers and unite the region as part of Japan's own empire. The resources needed by the growing Japanese powerhouse would come from countries formerly subordinate to the West.

Japan's vision expanded in the 1930s, and the country came to make fundamental changes in its strategic direction. In the 1920s it had been aligned with the victorious powers of World War I, and its reliance on trade with the United States for raw materials had intensified. This dependency infuriated Japan's leaders. They began to crave the independence implicit in the concept of a "Greater East Asia" and to desire world mastery. Dominating the resources of East, South, and indeed almost all of Asia became central to the Japanese leadership. Only then, they believed, would Japan become sufficiently powerful to defeat the powers that stood in its way: the Soviet Union, Britain, and the United States.

The concept of a "Greater East Asia Co-Prosperity Sphere" evolved over the course of the 1930s, but the idea that Japan's cluster of small islands was too small for its vigorous peoples had a long history that had prompted the country's earlier drive to find living space in Taiwan, Korea, and China. The idea of living space was one Japan shared with the other latecomers to the imperial table—Germany and Italy. In the 1930s, Japanese politicians were increasingly bold in articulating exactly what they believed to be their nation's due. The document excerpted here was produced collectively at the Total War Research Institute in January 1942. It is one draft of the blueprint for a vast Japanese empire, and it summarizes the thinking that emerged among Japan's ultranationalists in the 1930s. The document offers an opportunity to compare Japan's goals as World War II erupted with the goals of Germany and Italy.

Document 5.3

GOVERNMENT DOCUMENT

Draft of Basic Plan for Establishment of Greater East Asia Co-Prosperity Sphere, 1942

PART I. OUTLINE OF CONSTRUCTION

THE PLAN.   The Japanese empire is a manifestation of morality and its social characteristic is the propagation of the Imperial Way. It strives but for the achievement of *Hakkō Ichiu,* the spirit of its founding. . . . It is necessary to foster the increased power of the empire, to cause East Asia to return to its original form of independence and co-prosperity by shaking off the yoke of Europe and America, and to let its countries and peoples develop their respective abilities in peaceful cooperation and secure livelihood.

THE FORM OF EAST ASIATIC INDEPENDENCE AND CO-PROSPERITY.   The states, their citizens, and resources, comprised in those areas pertaining to the Pacific, Central Asia, and the Indian Oceans formed into one general union are to be established as an autonomous zone of peaceful living and common prosperity on behalf of the peoples of the nations of East Asia. The area including Japan, Manchuria, North China, lower Yangtze River, and the Russian Maritime Province, forms the nucleus of the East Asiatic Union. The Japanese empire possesses a duty as the leader of the East Asiatic Union.

The above purpose presupposes the inevitable emancipation or independence of Eastern Siberia, China, Indo-China, the South Seas, Australia, and India.

REGIONAL DIVISION IN THE EAST ASIATIC UNION AND THE NATIONAL DEFENSE SPHERE FOR THE JAPANESE EMPIRE.   In the Union of East Asia, the Japanese empire is at once the stabilizing power and the leading influence. To enable the empire actually to become the central influence in East Asia, the first necessity is the consolidation of the inner belt of East Asia; and the East Asiatic Sphere shall be divided as follows for this purpose:

The Inner Sphere—the vital sphere for the empire—includes Japan, Manchuria, North China, the lower Yangtze Area and the Russian Maritime area.

The Smaller Co-Prosperity Sphere—the smaller self-supplying sphere of East Asia—includes the inner sphere plus Eastern Siberia, China, Indo-China and the South Seas.

The Greater Co-Prosperity Sphere—the larger self-supplying sphere of East Asia—includes the smaller co-prosperity sphere, plus Australia, India, and island groups in the Pacific. . . .

For the present, the smaller co-prosperity sphere shall be the zone in which the construction of East Asia and the stabilization of national defense are to be aimed at. After their completion there shall be a gradual expansion toward the construction of the Greater Co-Prosperity Sphere.

OUTLINE OF EAST ASIATIC ADMINISTRATION.   It is intended that the unification of Japan, Manchoukuo, and China in neighborly friendship be realized by the settlement of the Sino-Japanese problems through the crushing of hostile influences in the Chinese interior, and through the construction of a new China in tune with the rapid construction of the Inner Sphere. Aggressive American and British influences in East Asia shall be driven out of the area of Indo-China and the South Seas, and this area shall be brought into our defense sphere. The war with Britain and America shall be prosecuted for that purpose.

SOURCE: "Draft of Basic Plan for Establishment of Greater East Asia Co-Prosperity Sphere," in *Sources of Japanese Tradition,* ed. Ryusaku Tsunoda et al. (New York: Columbia University Press, 1958), 801–805.

The Russian aggressive influence in East Asia will be driven out. Eastern Siberia shall be cut off from the Soviet regime and included in our defense sphere. For this purpose, a war with the Soviets is expected. It is considered possible that this Northern problem may break out before the general settlement of the present Sino-Japanese and the Southern problems if the situation renders this unavoidable. Next the independence of Australia, India, etc. shall gradually be brought about. For this purpose, a recurrence of war with Britain and her allies is expected. The construction of a Greater Mongolian State is expected during the above phase. The construction of the Smaller Co-Prosperity Sphere is expected to require at least twenty years from the present time.

THE BUILDING OF THE NATIONAL STRENGTH. Since the Japanese empire is the center and pioneer of Oriental moral and cultural reconstruction, the officials and people of this country must return to the spirit of the Orient and acquire a thorough understanding of the spirit of the national moral character.

In the economic construction of the country, Japanese and Manchurian national power shall first be consolidated, then the unification of Japan, Manchoukuo and China, shall be effected. . . . Thus a central industry will be constructed in East Asia, and the necessary relations established with the Southern Seas.

The standard for the construction of the national power and its military force, so as to meet the various situations that might affect the stages of East Asiatic administration and the national defense sphere, shall be so set as to be capable of driving off any British, American, Soviet or Chinese counter-influences in the future. . . .

CHAPTER 3. POLITICAL CONSTRUCTION

BASIC PLAN. The realization of the great ideal of constructing Greater East Asia Co-Prosperity requires not only the complete prosecution of the current Greater East Asia War but also presupposes another great war in the future. Therefore, the following two points must be made the primary starting points for the political construction of East Asia during the course of the next twenty years: (1) Preparation for war with the other spheres of the world; and (2) Unification and construction of the East Asia Smaller Co-Prosperity Sphere.

The following are the basic principles for the political construction of East Asia, when the above two points are taken into consideration:

a. The politically dominant influence of European and American countries in the Smaller Co-Prosperity Sphere shall be gradually driven out and the area shall enjoy its liberation from the shackles hitherto forced upon it.

b. The desires of the peoples in the sphere for their independence shall be respected and endeavors shall be made for their fulfillment, but proper and suitable forms of government shall be decided for them in consideration of military and economic requirements and of the historical, political and cultural elements peculiar to each area.

It must also be noted that the independence of various peoples of East Asia should be based upon the idea of constructing East Asia as "independent countries existing within the New Order of East Asia" and that this conception differs from an independence based on the idea of liberalism and national self-determination.

c. During the course of construction, military unification is deemed particularly important, and the military zones and key points necessary for defense shall be directly or indirectly under the control of our country.

d. The peoples of the sphere shall obtain their proper positions, the unity of the people's minds shall be effected and the unification of the sphere shall be realized with the empire as its center. . . .

CHAPTER 4. THOUGHT AND CULTURAL CONSTRUCTION

GENERAL AIM IN THOUGHT. The ultimate aim in thought construction in East Asia is to make East Asiatic peoples revere the imperial influence by propagating the Imperial Way based on the spirit of construction, and to establish the belief that uniting solely under this influence is the one and only way to the eternal growth and development of East Asia.

And during the next twenty years (the period during which the above ideal is to be reached) it is necessary to make the nations and peoples of East Asia realize the historical significance of the establishment of the New Order in East Asia, and in the common consciousness of East Asiatic unity, to liberate East Asia from the shackles of Europe and America and to establish the common conviction of constructing a New Order based on East Asiatic morality.

Occidental individualism and materialism shall be rejected and a moral world view, the basic principle of whose morality shall be the Imperial Way, shall be established. The ultimate object to be achieved is not exploitation but co-prosperity and mutual help, not competitive conflict but mutual assistance and mild peace, not a formal view of equality but a view of order based on righteous classification, not an idea of rights but an idea of service, and not several world views but one unified world view.

GENERAL AIM IN CULTURE. The essence of the traditional culture of the Orient shall be developed and manifested. And, casting off the negative and conservative cultural characteristics of the continents (India and China) on the one hand, and taking in the good points of Western culture on the other, an Oriental culture and morality, on a grand scale and subtly refined, shall be created.

QUESTIONS FOR ANALYSIS

1. What regions did the planners envision adding to the Japanese empire? What reasons do you discern for conquering each one?

2. What nations did the planners envision defeating militarily in order to annex each region?

3. Some commentators call the plans of the Japanese nationalists who took the country into war "arrogant" and "unrealistic." Do you agree or disagree with this judgment? Why?

PICTURE ESSAY

The Machine, the Military, and the Masses

MILITARY ORDER BECAME A REGULAR PART of life during World War I. From the beginning Europeans became used to the sight of large numbers of soldiers marching off to war, but even after the war these soldiers remained a presence in many societies as some military units refused to disband, transforming themselves into paramilitary groups that shaped politics in the immediate postwar years and thereafter. Demobilized soldiers took over Munich and several other prominent cities. They were active in the revolutionary struggles in Hungary and Poland right after the war. Mussolini's Black Shirts and Nazi Brown Shirts were only the most successful of these groups. Although by later standards somewhat ragtag and hardly precision marchers, men moving in military formation displayed a kind of unity and order that people had become accustomed to during the war and that re-assured them in troubled times.

The war also accustomed Europeans to the regulation of everyday existence in the form of ever more mechanized work. After the war, some European manufacturers adopted Henry Ford's assembly line, routinizing work still more as workers' movements of necessity conformed to the movements and rhythms of machines. The machine enhanced productivity through regulating human movements, and as it put artisanal labor out of business, it flooded the markets with standardized products—from shoes to soap and canned soup. Such results of mechanization became a topic of both horror films and comedies, and social theorists speculated about the effects of the regimentation and standardization of everyday life. However, it was the political dimension of the mechanization and militarization in modern society that attracted the interest of a wide range of people who saw the interwar years as a period in which the masses were coming into their own as a political force. The masses were increasingly fueling the consumer economy and driving its industries. Urban transport, sanitation, public health facilities, and municipal government served their needs. What better representation of that force than in the military marchers who seemed to embody the display of mass might?

As military marches and parades became common public spectacles, other aspects of social and cultural life began to adopt the mass formation as a model. In 1895 the English entrepreneur John Tiller started troupes of dancers—collectively called Tiller Girls—who were sorted into groups according to height. Dancing in formation, the Tiller Girls became increasingly popular in the 1920s and appeared onstage in Europe's premier capital cities and in the United States (Figure 5.1). All of the same race, build, and hairstyle, the girls wore identical costumes and were trained to dance in formations of greater-than-military precision. The choreographed numbers they performed were deliberately mechanical and uniform, eliminating human difference in favor of machine-like movements. They fulfilled the dreams of efficiency experts in showing the mechanized body perfectly attuned to the rhythmic beat of music. The appeal of this kind of chorus-line routine spread to theaters in other countries and eventually to the Hollywood films of Busby Berkeley in synchronization with the spread of mechanized labor. As you look at the Tiller Girls, what features appear most striking?

The appearance of the mechanical and standardized body in mass formation reflected to the masses their own new selves. Chorus-line girls, like factory employees, were interchangeable and indistinguishable. Their faces were often reshaped by a burgeoning plastic surgery industry, which had once remade soldiers' war-torn faces but now created a uniform, glamorous look for chorus girls and movie stars alike. The standardized faces of chorus-line beauties offered mass entertainment for a consumer society, and soon even ordinary women, such as those in England's Women's League of Health and Beauty, appeared in chorus-like formations doing exercises (Figure 5.2). The physical fitness of soldiers, dancers, mountain climbers, athletes, and daredevils, who were increasingly popular after the war, now shaped the aspirations of ordinary men and women. Like these

◆ Figure 5.1 **The Tiller Girls, 1928**
© *Hulton-Deutsch Collection/CORBIS.*

English women, they took up exercise, doing it increasingly in military style, and fitness became a characteristic of the flapper, or 1920s "new woman." In comparing the first two images, we may ask whether the identical uniforms of the amateur women doing exercises and the formations they assumed while doing them were an imitation of the military precision of the Tiller Girls. To what extent do these women look as if they are having a kind of military experience?

People from all walks of life took up mass formations: workers from the labor movement on the left of the political spectrum showed their physical fitness and their ability to follow military drill at the International Worker Olympics in 1931 in the Prater park in Vienna (Figure 5.3). At that event some 77,000 participants from nineteen countries competed in games and gymnastics. There were also mass displays of fitness, similar to that in Figure 5.2, when identically clad sportsmen performed calisthenics. That was not the end of the drills, for there was also a pa-

◆ Figure 5.2 **Members of the Women's League of Health and Beauty Exercise in London, 1935**
© *Topham/The Image Works.*

rade of 100,000 uniformed socialist participants as well as other festivals in which the masses in attendance chanted together an oath of allegiance to socialist principles and then sang the "Internationale"—the working-class anthem. Increasingly, socialists militarized in imitation of the fascists, sporting uniforms and wearing insignia, marching in formation with arms raised, and shouting "Freedom" to drown out "Heil Hitler." As good health was increasingly emphasized to keep nations and political causes fit, these workers acted out an array of values.

Mechanized movement as political spectacle became perfected during the 1930s, and people who might have shunned militarism in the past adopted it for the order it seemed to offer a disordered world mired in depression. When the Nazis came to power in 1933, their gestures became even more regimented, their steps more precise, and their movements more mesmerizing—all displays of confidence at a time when many felt increasingly insecure. Uniforms gained in complexity, with more leather, metal, and other adornments. This evolution was a

◆ **Figure 5.3 International Workers Olympics, 1931**
TASS/Sovofoto.

lesson to political groups like the Popular Front in France, which started holding mass demonstrations featuring regimented crowds. In the photograph of a 1936 Nazi Party rally in Nuremberg (Figure 5.4), a massive crowd of soldiers in full combat regalia listens to Adolf Hitler deliver a speech. What does this image convey about the Nazi regime? Would Germans have found it stirring, frightening, or both? Why? Similarly impressive and impressively regimented, Olympic performances and Nazi Party rallies featured national drill teams making complex geometric formations that could be photographed from above, as in the documentary film *Triumph of the Will* by Hitler's celebrated cineaste Leni Riefenstahl (1902–2003). Riefenstahl excelled in capturing the impressive qualities of militarism on film, especially in *Triumph of the Will* on the newfound unity of Nazi Germany.

Adults also instilled patriotism in children of both sexes by clothing them in military garb, such as sailor suits at the end of the nineteenth century, and making them drill with flags and military music. The Boy Scouts, founded in 1908 by a hero of the South African War, Lord Robert Baden Powell of England, provided a

◆ **Figure 5.4 Soldiers at a Nazi Party Rally in Nuremberg, 1936**
Bettmann/CORBIS.

twentieth-century model for militarization of children in the 1930s. Scouts learned survival skills alongside drills and the building of qualities such as obedience, honesty, and loyalty. Indeed, Mussolini, Stalin, and Hitler all knew the value of reaching children, and they set up many children's and youth organizations. The examples from the 1930s of Christian Boy Scouts in Vienna (Figure 5.5) and Fascist boys in Italy (Figure 5.6) show that militarism knew no age. Nor did it know gender boundaries, as there were also scout troops and Fascist leagues for girls. What role do you see these children playing in the nation as you observe these two images? Are there any ways in which these children's allegiance and militarism differ from those of grownups? Do you get the sense that the activities of these young people are child's play or something more serious?

Several decades later, in the 1960s, protesters would disown the clean, standardized style, opting for one that suited self-styled hippies and flower children. In the 1930s, however, the mechanical and militaristic spirit of the time triumphed in many conceivable venues, from precision dancing in films to amateur fitness clubs,

◆ Figure 5.5 **Christian Boy Scouts in Vienna, 1935**
Hulton Archive/Getty Images.

◆ **Figure 5.6 Young Blackshirts in Italy, 1930s**
© *Mary Evans Picture Library/The Image Works.*

Communist workers' drills, Boy Scouts, and the toy Nazi soldiers with which German children played. As we look ahead to World War II, we can ask ourselves whether these images give us insight into the relationship of military drill, in all its forms, to the outbreak of war itself.

QUESTIONS FOR ANALYSIS

1. When you look at these images, what conclusions can you reach about whether the emphasis on mass formations worked against valuing individual rights and holding differing opinions?

2. Do you think these images of mass formations served to promote conformity and thus dampen creativity? Or do you see them as creative expressions of how humans can arrange themselves aesthetically?

3. Speculate from these images about whether regimentation was likely to make the ordinary person more chauvinistic and less tolerant of difference.

NOTES

1. Quoted in Ross McKibbin, *Classes and Cultures: England, 1918–1951* (Oxford: Oxford University Press, 1998), 154.

2. Quoted in Karin Hausen, "Unemployment Also Hits Women: The New and the Old Woman on the Dark Side of the Golden Twenties in Germany," in *Unemployment and the Great Depression in Weimar Germany,* ed. Peter D. Stachura (New York: St. Martin's Press, 1986), 78.

3. *The Unemployed Man,* quoted in McKibbin, *Class and Culture,* 152.

4. Gaetano Savemini, quoted in Victoria de Grazia, *How Fascism Ruled Women: Italy, 1922–1945* (Berkeley: University of California Press, 1992), 56.

5. Quoted in Anthony Kauders, *German Politics and the Jews: Düsseldorf and Nuremberg, 1910–1933* (Oxford: Clarendon Press, 1996), 164.

6. Quoted in Mabel Berezin, *Making the Fascist Self: The Political Culture of Interwar Italy* (Ithaca: Cornell University Press, 1997), 90.

7. Quoted in Michael Burleigh, *The Third Reich: A New History* (New York: Hill and Wang, 2000), 13.

8. Engelbert Huber, *Das ist Nationalsozialismus* (Stuttgart: Union Deutsche Verlagsgesellschaft, 1931), 121–122, quoted in George L. Mosse, ed., *Nazi Culture* (New York: Grosset and Dunlap, 1966), 47.

9. Alfred Rosenberg, *Der Mythos der XX Jahrhunderts* (Munich: Hoheneichen-Verlag, 1930), 512, quoted ibid., 40.

10. Quoted in Alex de Jonge, *The Weimar Chronicle: Prelude to Hitler* (New York: Meridian, 1979), 216.

11. Quoted in David Welch, "Manufacturing a Consensus: Nazi Propaganda and the Building of a 'National Community' *Volksgemeinschaft,*" *Journal of Contemporary History* 2 (1993), 1:7.

12. Quoted ibid., 8.

13. Quoted in Mosse, *Nazi Culture,* 47.

14. Quoted in Robert Conquest, *The Harvest of Sorrow: Soviet Collectivization and the Terror-Famine* (London: Arrow, 1986), 129.

15. Sergei Kirov, quoted in Edvard Radzinsky, *Stalin: The First In-Depth Biography Based on Explosive New Documents from Russia's Secret Archives,* trans. H. T. Willetts (New York: Doubleday, 1996), 247.

16. Quoted in Yuri Slezkine, *Arctic Mirrors: Russia and the Small Peoples of the North* (Ithaca: Cornell University Press, 1994), 269.

17. Quoted ibid., 222.

18. Quoted in Sheila Fitzpatrick, *Everyday Stalinism: Ordinary Life in Extraordinary Times: Soviet Russia in the 1930s* (New York: Oxford University Press, 1999), 37.

19. Evgenia Ginsburg, quoted in Geoffrey Hosking, *A History of the Soviet Union* (London: Fontana, 1985), 187.

20. Quoted in Radzinsky, *Stalin,* 378.

21. Quoted ibid., 363.

22. Quoted in Fitzpatrick, *Everyday Stalinism,* 177.

23. Edward VIII, radio address following abdication, December 11, 1936, royal.gov.uk.

24. Quoted in David Clay Large, *Between Two Fires: Europe's Path in the 1930s* (New York: Norton, 1990), 45.

25. J. P. Chanois, quoted in Julian Jackson, *The Popular Front in France: Defending Democracy, 1934–38* (Cambridge: Cambridge University Press, 1988), 113.

26. Quoted in Ann-Sofie Kälvemark, *More Children of Better Quality?: Aspects of Swedish Population Policy in the 1930s* (Uppsala: Almquist and Wicksell, 1980), 86.

27. Quoted in Margaret Shennan, *Out in the Midday Sun: The British in Malaya, 1880–1960* (London: John Murray, 2002).

28. "Draft of Basic Plan for Establishment of Greater East Asia Co-Prosperity Sphere," in *Sources of Japanese Tradition,* ed. Ryusaku Tsunoda et al. (New York: Columbia University Press, 1958), 805.

29. Quoted in Large, *Between Two Files,* 162.

30. Quoted in Berezin, *Making the Fascist Self,* 124.

31. Constancia de la Mora, *In Place of Splendor: The Autobiography of a Spanish Woman* (New York: Harcourt Brace, 1939), 140–141.

32. Communiqué of August 3, 1936, quoted in Jean Sagnes and Sylvie Caucanas, eds., *Les Français et la guerre d'Espagne* (Perpignan: C.R.E.P.F., 1990), 33.

33. Quoted in Helmut Konrad, "Support for the Corporate State and National Socialism in the Socially Weaker Groups, 1934–1938," in *Austria in the Thirties: Culture and Politics,* ed. Kenneth Segar and John Warren (Riverside, CA: Ariadne, 1991), 63.

34. Quoted in Horst Jarka, "Everyday Life and Politics in the Literature of the Thirties: Horváth, Kramer, and Soyfer," ibid., 170–171.

35. Quoted in Roy Jenkins, *Churchill* (London: Macmillan, 2001), 527.

36. Alva Myrdal, *Nation and Family: The Swedish Experiment in Democratic Family and Population Policy* (Cambridge: MIT Press, 1941), 120.

37. Lila Lounguina, *Les saisons de Moscou: 1933–1990* (Paris: Plon, 1990), 82, 83, 84 (my translation).

SUGGESTED REFERENCES

Crash and Depression The crash, depression, and population problems intersected to change politics, society, and the everyday life of individuals around the world. The books listed here show not only the worldwide impact of the depression but, as in the work of Wegs, Evans and Geary, and Childers, how people experienced both unemployment and government policies.

Bucur, Maria. *Eugenics and Modernization in Interwar Romania.* 2002.
Chenut, Helen Hardin. *The Fabric of Gender: Working-Class Culture in Third Republic France.* 2005.

Childers, Kristen Stromberg. *Fathers, Families, and the State in France, 1914–1945.* 2003.

Clavin, Patricia. *The Great Depression in Europe, 1929–1939.* 2000.

De Grazia, Victoria. *How Fascism Ruled Women: Italy, 1922–1945.* 1992.

Evans, R. J., and Dick Geary. *The German Unemployed.* 1987.

Hessler, Julie. *A Social History of Soviet Trade: Trade Policy, Retail Practices, and Consumption, 1917–1953.* 2004.

Kindleberger, Charles. *The World in Depression, 1929–1939.* 1986.

McKibbin, Ross. *Classes and Cultures: England, 1918–1951.* 1998.

Rothermund, Dietmar. *The Global Impact of the Great Depression, 1929–1939.* 1996.

Stachura, Peter D., ed. *Unemployment and the Great Depression in Weimar Germany.* 1986.

Wegs, J. Robert. *Growing Up Working Class: Continuity and Change among Viennese Youth, 1890–1938.* 1989.

The Triumph of Dictatorship The 1930s was a decade of dictators. The controversies over Stalinism are reflected in these works. No one denies that he was responsible for the mass murders and deaths from famine of the 1930s, but there are many debates over the levels of support and actual assistance he enjoyed from ordinary Soviets.

Baranowski, Shelley. *Strength through Joy: Consumerism and Mass Tourism in the Third Reich.* 2004.

Browder, George C. *Hitler's Enforcers: The Gestapo and the SS Security Service in the Nazi Revolution.* 1996.

Burleigh, Michael. *The Third Reich: A New History.* 2001.

Fitzpatrick, Sheila. *Everyday Stalinism: Ordinary Life in Extraordinary Times: Soviet Russia in the 1930s.* 1999.

Herzog, Dagmar, ed. *Sexuality and German Fascism.* 2005.

Kauders, Anthony. *German Politics and the Jews: Düsseldorf and Nuremberg, 1910–1933.* 1996.

Kaplan, Marion. *Between Dignity and Despair: Jewish Life in Nazi Germany.* 1998.

Kershaw, Ian. *Hitler, 1889–1936: Hubris.* 1999.

Thurston, Robert W. *Life and Terror in Stalin's Russia, 1934–1941.* 1996.

Tucker, Robert. *Stalin in Power: The Revolution from Above, 1928–1941.* 1992.

Viola, Lynne, ed. *Contending with Stalinism: Soviet Power and Popular Resistance in the 1930s.* 2003.

Weikart, Richard. *From Darwin to Hitler: Evolutionary Ethics, Eugenics, and Racism in Germany.* 2004.

The Democracies Search for Solutions The fight to sustain democracy was widespread, even in Germany, where Nazis had to brutalize many to squelch criticism. In the democracies, writers, filmmakers, and statesmen waged the struggle in a climate of great uncertainty and in the face of great odds, for many in their own societies admired the muscular might of the dictators.

Andrew, Dudley, and Steven Ungar. *Popular Front Paris and the Poetics of Culture.* 2005.

Bok, Sissela. *Alva Myrdal: A Daughter's Memoir.* 1991.

Cook, David A. *A History of Narrative Film.* 2004.

Lebovics, Herman. *True France: The Wars over Cultural Identity, 1900–1945.* 1992.

Pawlowski, Merry M. *Virginia Woolf and Fascism: Resisting the Dictators' Seduction.* 2001.

Rearick, Charles. *The French in Love and War: Popular Culture in the Era of the World Wars.* 1997.

Sternhell, Zeev. *Neither Right nor Left: Fascist Ideology in France.* 1986.

Vernon, James. *Modernity's Hunger: How Imperial Britain Created and Failed to Solve the Problem of Hunger in the Modern World.* 2006.

Wiener, Martin. *English Culture and the Decline of the Industrial Spirit, 1850–1980.* 2004.

The Road to Global War Could Hitler have been stopped? The debate continues, though many historians recognize that there was no single person whose defeat would have blocked the outbreak of war. Communism, fascism, and Nazism, as well as militarism in Japan, had considerable support. We must factor in this support while following through these books the diplomatic and military road to war.

Bix, Herbert. *Hirohito and the Making of Modern Japan.* 2000.

Chickering, Roger, and Stig Förster, eds. *The Shadows of Total War: Europe, East Asia, and the United States, 1919–1939.* 2003.

Imlay, Talbot C. *Facing the Second World War: Strategy, Politics, and Economics in Britain and France, 1938–1940.* 2003.

Jenkins, Roy. *Churchill.* 2001.

Jensen, Geoffrey. *Irrational Triumph: Cultural Despair, Military Nationalism, and the Ideological Origins of Franco's Spain.* 2001.

Martin, Benjamin. *France in 1938.* 2005.

Payne, Stanley G. *The Spanish Civil War, the Soviet Union, and Communism.* 2004.

Peattie, Mark R. *Sunburst: The Rise of Japanese Naval Air Power, 1909–1941.* 2002.

Preston, Paul. *Franco: A Biography.* 1993.

Segar, Kenneth, and John Warren, eds. *Austria in the Thirties: Culture and Politics.* 1991.

Seidman, Michael. *Republic of Egos: A Social History of the Spanish Civil War.* 2002.

Watt, Donald Cameron. *How War Came: The Immediate Origins of the Second World War, 1938–1939.* 1989.

Young, Louise. *Japan's Total Empire: Manchuria and the Culture of Wartime Imperialism.* 1998.

Selected Web Sites

Fordham University's Web site has good material on the depression in Europe and the United States: <**fordham.edu/halsall/mod/modsbook41.html**>. Professor Brad DeLong of the University of California at Berkeley has an ongoing Web site on which he makes many learned comments. This particular part of his site has extensive commentary on the depression of the 1930s: <**econ161.berkeley.edu/ TCEH/Slouch_Crash14.html**>. The University of Toronto has extensive material available thanks to its research project on Stalin: <**utoronto.ca/ceres/serap/**>. The following Web site gives links to much information about Spain's civil war, from major players to important battles: <**www.spartacus.schoolnet.co.uk/Spanish -Civil-War.htm**>. The next site, at University of St. Andrews in Scotland, provides links to sources for the diplomatic history of the origins of World War II: <**www .st-andrews.ac.uk/~pv/courses/prewar/resources.html**>.

6

The Second World War and the Collapse of Europe

1939–1945

IN THE FALL OF 1939 GERMAN TROOPS QUICKLY DEFEATED Poland, starting World War II and beginning the process of turning the country into a death camp for the elimination of Jews and Slavs. Heda Margolius was a young Czech student in 1941 when her family was taken from Prague and moved to a crowded Jewish ghetto in Lodz, Poland. Czechs and other Slavs, especially those with Jewish ancestry, were packed together in the ghetto, deprived of food and access to medicine, and forced to work for the Nazis. Most of those who survived this process of "social death" the Nazis eventually killed outright. Treating people as though they were scarcely human and cutting them off from the normal workings of society made their deaths seem unimportant, even something that could be ignored. Heda Margolius's family and friends died from starvation and illness, and Margolius herself was sent to Auschwitz in Poland to serve as a slave laborer. "Human speech can only express what the mind can hold," she wrote in her spare account of camp life. "You cannot describe hammer blows that crush your brain."[1] In the last months of the war, she escaped from the death march that killed many prisoners from Auschwitz as the Nazis tried to conceal signs of their barbarism from Allied forces liberating central Europe. "The idea of escape began," Margolius

◆ **Jewish Children of the Lodz Ghetto**

The conquering Germans forced Jews into ghettos, like this one in Poland where these children are getting their small ration of food. The Nazis deprived all conquered peoples of some resources but were especially cruel to Jews, Gypsies, and Poles and other Slavs, whom they considered inferior. Their aim was to enrich the "superior" German race while starving or enslaving "inferior" peoples. © *Topham/The Image Works.*

recalled, "back when our guard Franz shot yet another girl."[2] Escape brought her into contact with ordinary people who gave her food, but also with many others who shrank from her gaunt and dirty appearance—the look of a person socially dead. When she finally made her way to Prague, some of her former friends wondered why she had come back to bother them. Such was the destruction wrought by World War II on the moral values of many of the people who survived it.

Civilians did not welcome the outbreak of war in 1939. There were no celebrations or flashy parades to speed

1942	British destruction of shipping in Southeast Asia results in 3 million deaths from famine in Bengal.
1942	U.S. forces defeat Japanese in battles of the Coral Sea and Midway Island.
1942	August: Battle of Stalingrad begins.
1942	Fall: British win battle of El Alamein and invade Morocco and Algeria.
1943	April: Jews stage uprising in Warsaw ghetto against Germans.
1943	July: Allies invade Sicily.
1943	August: Inmates of Treblinka death camp attack Ukrainian guards.
1943	November–December: Big Three meet in Teheran to discuss war strategy.
1944	June 6: D-Day: Allied forces land on Normandy beaches.
1944	July 20: Assassination attempt against Hitler fails.
1945	February: Big Three meet at Yalta.
1945	February: Allied planes firebomb Dresden for two days.
1945	March: Allies firebomb Tokyo.
1945	April: President Roosevelt dies; Harry Truman becomes U.S. president.
1945	May 8: Germany surrenders.
1945	June: United Nations formed.
1945	July 26: Labour Party candidate Clement Attlee becomes prime minister of Britain.
1945	July–August: Allied leaders meet at Potsdam, Germany.
1945	August 6, 9: The United States drops atomic bombs on Hiroshima and Nagasaki.
1945	August 14: Japan surrenders.
1948	More than 50 UN member countries approve the Universal Declaration of Human Rights.

the troops on their way to battle. The wounds of World War I were still raw, even among German citizens. Hitler's invasions of Austria, Czechoslovakia, and finally Poland were explained as necessary because of the dangers to German minority populations living in those countries—an excuse that Germans reluctantly bought.

Initially the Axis—Germany, Italy, and Japan—a coalition formed when Italy in 1940 and then Japan in 1941 declared war, proved militarily dominant. However, the early victories were deceptive, for the countries of northwestern Europe that Hitler so handily defeated in 1939–1940 had global resources on which to draw and kept airplanes and other materiel abroad, in their colonies; both men and ships were stationed far from European shores. Hitler, in contrast, had a concentrated European army. As the war spread, Germany found itself engaged in global warfare from a strictly European base and knowing far less about the world beyond Europe than its enemies. The Axis powers had a poorly calculated, inflated view of their own might.

A war for resources, territory, and plundered wealth, World War II was also a war of ideology. The aggressor states believed themselves not only deprived of their fair share of wealth but also entitled by their ethnic superiority to conquer other lands. Because of the destructive capacity of weaponry, it goes without saying that the conflict was a military nightmare. Racist ideology, however, compounded the grim horrors of the war years. People considered inferior, whether in East Asia or central Europe, were simply eliminated—like the family of Heda Margolius. To an unprecedented extent, this war swept up civilians. They provided the crucial labor needed to manufacture weapons and supplies yet were held in contempt and despised by the leaders of the aggressor states. A legacy of World War I that aimed to resolve its unfinished business, the Second World War brought civilization to a new low. At the war's end in 1945, tens of millions had been killed, entire economies had been crushed, and nation-states, constitutional governments, and institutions of human freedom lay in ruins. World War II was in every sense a total war, whose conduct destroyed lives, resources, empires, and humane values.

RAPID VICTORIES

Unlike the First World War, World War II was a war of movement. Motorized transport, including airplanes, gave armies rapid access both to enemy lines and to urban populations. In the first months of the war, Germany's and Japan's concentrated firepower knocked out resistance with relative ease. The first easy conquests fostered a sense of invincibility among the victors, blinding them to the actual facts. These facts were that Germany had defeated neither Britain nor France's colonial empire and that Japan had not defeated China, its earliest target. Yet despite those failures, each proceeded to take on more powerful foes—the Soviet Union and the United States.

The German Onslaught

On September 1, 1939, Hitler launched an attack on Poland, allegedly to regain the "Polish Corridor," a strip of land separating East Prussia from the rest of Germany that was awarded at Versailles to give Poland access to the Baltic Sea (Map 6.1). Britain and France declared war on Germany in support of their ally Poland, but German ground troops quickly defeated the ill-equipped but valiant Polish troops by launching an overpowering Blitzkrieg ("lightning war"). With overwhelming speed, the Germans concentrated airplanes, tanks, and motorized infantry to encircle Polish defenders and capture the capital, Warsaw. The rapidity of this victory, which allowed German forces to conserve supplies, led many Germans on the home front to believe that the human costs of gaining *Lebensraum*—or living space—for the full flowering of the Aryan race would be low. The quick victories in Austria, Czechoslovakia, and Poland brought in new wealth in the form of gold, natural resources, and industrial capacity to pay for the military campaigns.

On September 17 the Soviets invaded Poland too, expanding the attack to keep up with their Nazi ally. By the end of the month the Polish army was in shambles. Having divvied up the country in accordance with the Nazi-Soviet Nonaggression Pact, Hitler hypocritically made overtures of peace to Britain and France in October so that future clashes could be blamed on the democracies. Britain's and France's refusal to negotiate an immediate end to the conflict allowed Hitler to sell the war within the Reich as one of self-defense, while he simultaneously planned for an attack on France later that fall. Citing Germany's lack of preparedness for such a vast undertaking, German generals persuaded Hitler to postpone the offensive until the spring of 1940. From November 1939 to April 1940, the combatants engaged in a "phony war" to ready themselves rather than engage in direct conflict. Then in April 1940, German forces crushed Denmark and Norway; battles for Belgium, the Netherlands, and France followed in May and June. As German planes strafed them mercilessly, thousands of civilians fled south to escape the invasion. Germany's allies joined in the fray. Mussolini, who envisioned future spoils for Italy, invaded France from the southeast. After consulting with Hitler, Stalin waged war against the vigorously resisting Finns, seized Bessarabia and Bucovina from Romania, and scooped up the Baltic states.

Panic and defeatism infected the French army as it faced the concentrated and terrifying force of Blitzkrieg for the first time. Forward-looking leaders such as (then) Colonel Charles de Gaulle in the French army had predicted the kind of war Hitler was waging and had urged the construction of more planes and tanks, but French military planners had put their faith in the Maginot line—massive fortifications on France's eastern border with Germany—which might have been effective if France were refighting World War I. But that was not the case. Planes and other new technology rendered the Maginot line irrelevant, and new firepower allowed Germany to breach it. Because of falling birthrates and population losses in World War I, France had half as many available recruits in 1939 as it had had in 1914. Moreover, many people in France agreed with German anti-Semitism, and elites in France preferred "Hitler to Blum." In addition, Hitler benefited from France's and Britain's decisions to disperse their military assets abroad to defend their empires instead of their homelands. The French had more airplanes in North Africa than in Europe. The British were actively guarding their possessions in the Middle East and central Asia.

In the spring of 1940, more than 220,000 British troops were in France joining the struggle against Nazism, but they were trapped on the beaches of Dunkirk in northern France. Three hundred fifty thousand Allied soldiers—British, French, Belgian, and Poles—were rescued in a heroic effort by an improvised fleet of naval ships, fishing boats, and pleasure craft that sailed across the English Channel and carried them to the safety of England. France surrendered to the Nazis on June 22, 1940, under an arrangement that let Germany occupy the northern half of the country, including Paris. The Nazis allowed Philippe Pétain, a military hero of World War I who favored Hitler's return to traditional values, to govern the unoccupied south of France, a region named "Vichy France" after the spa town where the collaborationist government sat.

After the fall of France, imperial Britain stood alone against the seemingly invincible Third Reich, intent on creating an empire of its own. Blaming Germany's rapid victories on Prime Minister Chamberlain's policy of appeasement, the British House of Commons had swept Chamberlain out of office as Germany moved westward and on May 10 installed as prime minister Winston Churchill (1874–1965), who early on had come to despise Hitler's ideas. Churchill had been an erratic and often unpopular member of the House of Commons since 1900. In those dark days of 1940, however his energy and eloquence sustained his parliamentary colleagues and the entire British nation. His words still resonate today:

> I have nothing to offer but blood, toil, tears and sweat. You ask what is our policy? I will say: It is to wage war, by sea, land and air, with all our might and with all the strength that God can give us; to wage war against a monstrous tyranny, never surpassed in the dark, lamentable catalogue of human crime. That is our policy. You ask, what is our aim? I can answer in one word: It is victory, victory at all costs, victory in spite of all terror, victory, however long and hard the road may be; for without victory, there is no survival.[3]

▶ Map 6.1 **World War II in Europe and Africa**
Germany's swift victories in Poland, Scandinavia, and western Europe were followed by Hitler's fatal decision to invade the Soviet Union. As ill-equipped German soldiers were subject to punishing battles on the eastern front, the Soviets began inexorably to push Nazi troops westward at enormous cost in lives and property. Britain and the other Allies joined the USSR's offensive against the European Axis powers by invading North Africa, Italy, and finally, in 1944, France, sealing Germany's fate despite Hitler's maniacal refusal to surrender.

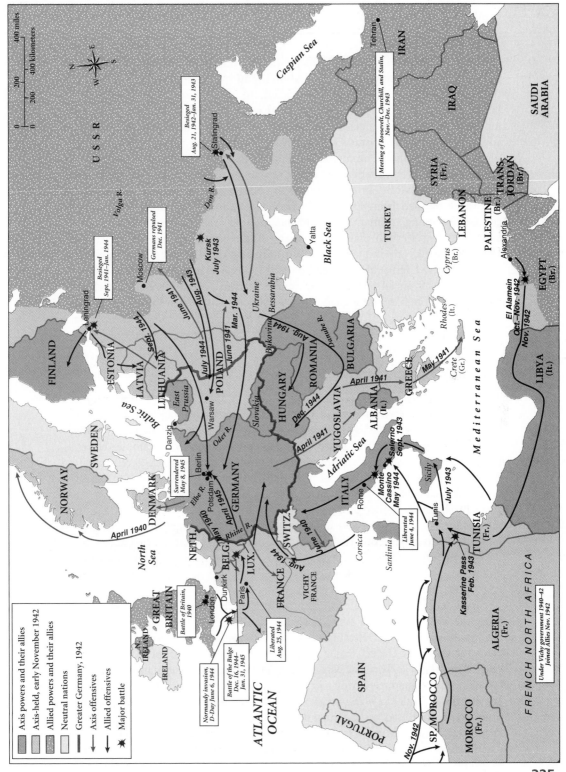

400 miles
400 kilometers
200
200
0
0

N
W S
E
S

U S S R

Caspian Sea

Besieged
Aug. 21, 1942–Jan. 31, 1943

Stalingrad

Volga R.

Besieged
Sept. 1941–Jan. 1944

Germans repulsed
Dec. 1941

Don R.

Moscow

Leningrad

Kursk
July 1943

Aug. 1943

Meeting of Roosevelt, Churchill, and Stalin,
Nov.–Dec. 1943

Tehran

IRAN

IRAQ

**SAUDI
ARABIA**

**SYRIA
(Fr.)**

**TRANS-
JORDAN
(Br.)**

**LEBANON
(Br.)**

**PALESTINE
(Br.)**

Black Sea

Yalta

TURKEY

Alexandria

El Alamein
Oct.–Nov. 1942

Nov. 1942

**EGYPT
(Br.)**

*Rhodes
(It.)*

*Cyprus
(Br.)*

May 1941

*Crete
(Gr.)*

GREECE

**LIBYA
(It.)**

Mediterranean Sea

April 1941

BULGARIA

Danube R.

Aug. 1944

ROMANIA

Ukraine

Bessarabia

Mar. 1944

Bukovina

June 1941

July 1944

Aug. 1943

June 1941

POLAND

Warsaw

Sept. 1941

FINLAND

SWEDEN

NORWAY

Baltic Sea

ESTONIA

LATVIA

LITHUANIA

*East
Prussia*

Danzig

Oder R.

April 1940

DENMARK

Berlin

Surrendered
May 8, 1945

Potsdam
April 1945

Elbe R.

GERMANY

Dec. 1944

HUNGARY

Slovakia

YUGOSLAVIA

**ALBANIA
(It.)**

April 1941

Adriatic Sea

ITALY

Rome

Monte
Cassino
May 1944

Salerno
Sept. 1943

Liberated
June 4, 1944

Sicily

July 1943

Tunis

Kasserine Pass
Feb. 1943

**TUNISIA
(Fr.)**

Sardinia

Corsica

SWITZ.

June 1940

Rhine R.

Aug. 1944

FRANCE

**VICHY
FRANCE**

Liberated
Aug. 25, 1944

Paris

Battle of the Bulge
Dec. 16, 1944–
Jan. 31, 1945

LUX.

BELG.

May 1940

NETH.

Dunkirk

Normandy invasion,
D-Day, June 6, 1944

**GREAT
BRITAIN**

London

Battle of Britain,
1940

**N.
IRELAND**

IRELAND

*North
Sea*

*ATLANTIC
OCEAN*

SPAIN

PORTUGAL

SP. MOROCCO

**MOROCCO
(Fr.)**

Nov. 1942

**ALGERIA
(Fr.)**

FRENCH NORTH AFRICA

Under Vichy government 1940–42
Joined Allies Nov. 1942

Axis powers and their allies
Axis-held, early November 1942
Allied powers and their allies
Neutral nations
Greater Germany, 1942
Axis offensives
Allied offensives
Major battle

In the summer of 1940, Hitler ordered the bombardment of Britain. Churchill used the radio to rally the nation for all-out resistance. In the "Blitz," as the bombardment of British cities was called, the German air force struck at public buildings and monuments, harbors and weapons depots, military bases and industry, and the royal palace. During the Battle of Britain, Churchill kept the country going with his oratory. London was bombed for seventy-eight straight nights, and more than a hundred thousand civilians were killed or wounded (see Document 6.1). The British government developed an effective radar system and decoding tools that began to overcome the Nazi edge by allowing British pilots and those escaped from France, Czechoslovakia, and other allied countries to counter incoming German planes. Money poured into the production of anti-aircraft and artillery airplanes, tanks, and other weaponry, and at the end of 1940, the British air industry was outproducing the Germans by 50 percent. Outmaneuvered, Hitler abandoned his plans for a naval invasion of Britain, effectively called off an all-out air campaign, reallocated some forces to attack the wider British Empire, and looked for new areas to conquer. In little more than a year since the outbreak of World War II, Hitler met his match, but the conflict was far from over.

The Expansion of War and Operation Barbarossa

The war expanded, changing course and becoming more global. In the spring of 1941, Hitler conquered Greece and Yugoslavia. He took advantage of economic relationships that Germany had built in the 1920s with Hungary, Romania, and other eastern European countries to secure their cooperation. For example, Hitler's promise of land was part of the successful wooing of Hungary, embittered at being dismembered in the Peace of Paris. In March 1941, after careful appeals to U.S. officials, Churchill gained important support in the form of the Lend-Lease program, by which the United States provided war materiel to Britain. Encouraged by the conquests of Germany and Italy, in the fall of 1940 the government of Japan joined them in a Tripartite Alliance. At first, officials in Japan worried about how the Soviet Union—Japan's adversary in Asia—would figure in such an alliance, but word that Hitler was planning to wage war against "the center of judeo-bolshevism" reassured them.

In June 1941, having failed to conquer Britain, Hitler attacked the even more powerful Soviet Union—a betrayal of the Nazi-Soviet Nonaggression Pact, then less than two years old. Defeating the USSR, however, was the centerpiece of Nazi plans for the "New Order" that would Germanize eastern Europe. The invasion, called Operation Barbarossa, began when some 3 million German soldiers and 600,000 Axis sympathizers deployed along a two-thousand-mile front crossed the Soviet border. Hitler saw the invasion in apocalyptic terms, predicting that the campaign would lead to the final triumph or the utter defeat of Aryanism. Promising to "raze Moscow and Leningrad to the ground," he approached the campaign believing that if the German people failed, they deserved the harsh fate that would be theirs.[4] Operation Barbarossa was to be a sacred, perhaps sacrificial, test of the bio-religion of terror that the Nazis were waging against Slavs, Jews, Gypsies, and other people whom they considered their inferiors.

Owing to the USSR's lack of preparation, Axis troops quickly penetrated Soviet lines and destroyed massive numbers of planes, tanks, and other machinery. For several months, expert Soviet and even British intelligence had been warning Stalin about an imminent attack and providing precise information about the movements of troops and even the date of the invasion. Stalin, however, treated every new piece of information as evidence of a Nazi disinformation campaign. Newly opened archives show that Stalin—urged on by Churchill, his own ambition, and the advantages of taking the offensive—was at the time hoping to attack the Third Reich and read the signs of the impending invasion from that perspective. Moreover, he believed that Germany would not be ready for such a massive assault for another year. Soon after the invasion began, Stalin disappeared for several days. Some historians interpret his disappearance as a sign of collapse; others see it as a crafty ploy to reawaken in the top Soviet brass a firm commitment to his leadership. In either case, the Soviet leaders ultimately went to Stalin's country estate and begged him to return to the Kremlin.

The German invasion was stunning in its immediate success. Thousands of Soviet tanks and artillery pieces were captured, and almost a million Soviet troops were taken prisoner. "It is probably not too much to assert," German army chief of staff General Franz Halder wrote in his diary on July 3, 1941, "that the campaign against Russia has been won within two weeks."[5] Hitler, who considered himself a military genius, was so confident of a quick victory that he changed the course of military production from manufacturing tanks and artillery to building battleships and planes. Because of this decision, German ground troops lacked the equipment they needed for success in a winter campaign. The German invasion, however, was not just about military success. Hitler wanted to destroy the industrial and agricultural heartland of the Soviet Union. However, he failed to anticipate that resistance by Stalin and Communist officials and by patriotic Soviet citizens would be fierce. Civilians performed superhuman feats, digging antitank trenches and destroying resources to keep them out of German hands. Factories were dismantled and rebuilt farther to the east, beyond the reach of German forces. Moreover, Hitler ordered simultaneous attacks on major Soviet cities including Leningrad and Moscow, on the Baltic states, and on Ukraine, although his generals wanted to concentrate on Moscow. Soviet resistance slowed the accomplishment of Hitler's cumbersome strategy. Then as the autumn rains fell and winter approached, German soldiers and vehicles got bogged down in mud, and the German army was unable to take Moscow and Leningrad, whose citizens continued to endure a devastating seige nonetheless. The Blitzkrieg was over, and the nature of the war changed even though German generals were confident that they would beat the "Reds" in 1942.

Throughout the Russian campaign, Hitler insisted that there would be no turning back—not even a well-considered tactical retreat—from Germany's confrontation with its sacred destiny. For Hitler the war against the USSR was more an ideological conflict than a military one. Because he saw it as a "war of extermination" against "Asiatic" peoples who were enemy "judeobolsheviks," it was waged with even more severity toward civilians and the military than was the case to the west. Literate people were especially vulnerable, because Hitler considered them to be the foundation of the civil society that he was determined to destroy. A ploy of the Nazis was to test the reading skills of captured people, suggesting that those who could read would be given clerical jobs and those who could not would be relegated to hard labor. Those who could read, however, were lined up and shot.

By this time the German army had become so inoculated against objecting to unacceptable treatment of prisoners of war and civilians that many soldiers enthusiastically participated in their murder. In World War I, approximately 5 percent of Russian soldiers had died while being held captive by the Germans. In World War II, by ideological design, close to 60 percent of Soviet soldiers died in German captivity, but only 3 percent of British and American prisoners did. Some 90 percent of French civilians interned in Nazi concentration camps (not including French Jews sent to extermination camps) returned home — many of them damaged psychologically and physically. The Nazis disregarded centuries-old conventions intended to ensure that prisoners of war would receive the same treatment as one's own soldiers. The Nazis' ideas about racial ordering determined their murderous policies toward Soviets, who were systematically shot, starved, or allowed to perish of cold and disease. At least nine million Soviet soldiers and nineteen million civilians died in World War II, and the opening of new archives has caused some historians to revise those figures upwards to over 40 million.

Despite growing resistance, Hitler continued to maintain the siege of Leningrad and simultaneously to turn his armies southward toward the Caucasus and the sources of Soviet grain and oil in 1942 — again overruling his generals' calls to take Moscow, which is where Stalin thought the Germans would strike. Arguing that his generals had no understanding either of the battlefront or of the economic goals of war, in August 1942 Hitler ordered an attack on Stalingrad because of its name and its apparent dedication to Bolshevism. Whenever his generals advocated for the well-being and very lives of their soldiers — to get more food or to undertake a strategic retreat — Hitler responded that he, having served on the front lines during World War I, understood the needs and commitment of soldiers in battle better than they. As a result, German armies bogged down at Stalingrad with no hope of relief, fighting at times house to house against Soviet forces whose access to fresh manpower was far greater than Germany's. The battle for Stalingrad, lasting until January 31, 1943, became emblematic of the way Hitler's ideological and psychological blindspots could turn victory into defeat.

War Opens in the Pacific

The United States and Japan danced around the edges of the European conflict until December 7, 1941, when Japanese planes suddenly attacked American naval bases in the Pacific at Pearl Harbor in Hawaii, seriously damaging or sinking eight U.S. battleships (Map 6.2). The Japanese then decimated a fleet of U.S. airplanes in the Philippines. The attack on Pearl Harbor — "a day that will live in infamy," U.S. president Franklin Delano Roosevelt called it — was the culmination of mounting

Map legend:

- Japanese Empire, 1936
- Japanese-controlled areas, August 1942
- Allied powers
- ← Allied advances
- ← Japanese advances
- ✳ Major battles
- 🍄 Atomic bombs

Map labels:

USSR · Bering Sea · Alaska (U.S.) · Kamchatka · Kiska I. · Attu I. · ALEUTIAN IS. (U.S.) · May 1943 · Sakhalin I. · MONGOLIA · MANCHURIA (MANCHUKUO) · 1945 · Aug. 1945 · 1945 · KURIL IS. · N W E S · KOREA · JAPAN · PACIFIC OCEAN · Hiroshima Aug. 6, 1945 · Tokyo · CHINA · Nanking · Nagasaki Aug. 9, 1945 · 1945 · Okinawa Apr. 1– June 21, 1945 · Iwo Jima Feb. 19–Mar. 16, 1945 · Midway I. June 3–6, 1942 · Midway I. (U.S.) · Wake I. (U.S.) · HAWAIIAN IS. (U.S.) · TIBET · INDIA (Br.) · 1945 · BURMA (Br.) · Formosa (Taiwan) · Apr. 1945 · MARIANA IS. · Nov. 1943 · Pearl Harbor Dec. 7, 1941 · Nov. 1943 · THAILAND · FRENCH INDOCHINA (Vichy) · Hong Kong (Br.) · PHILIPPINE IS. · 1945 · Leyte Gulf Oct. 23–26, 1944 · 1944 · Saipan 1944 · Guam July 21– Aug. 10, 1944 · Eniwetok Feb. 17, 1944 · MARSHALL IS. · MALAYA · Singapore · Sumatra · Borneo · Celebes · NETHERLANDS EAST INDIES · Java · CAROLINE IS. · Tarawa Nov. 29, 1943 · GILBERT IS. (Br.) · 1944 · Apr. 1942 · Rabaul · New Guinea · Lae · SOLOMON IS. · ELLICE IS. (Br.) · Coral Sea May 7–8, 1942 · Guadalcanal Aug. 7, 1942–Feb. 9, 1943 · FIJI IS. (Br.) · INDIAN OCEAN · NEW HEBRIDES (Fr.-Br.) · Aug. 1942 · 1943 · New Caledonia (Fr.) · AUSTRALIA

0 500 1,000 miles
0 500 1,000 kilometers

◆ **Map 6.2 World War II in the Pacific**
As in Europe the Axis powers seized the advantage in the Pacific early in the war. The Allies were slow to mobilize their Asian subjects, whose loyalty to their foreign rulers was always open to question. Although the war in the Pacific was one of movement, it was also one of brutal and lethal battles in which the Japanese government determined that military men should fight to the death. Such a strategy helped determine the policy of massive firebombing of cities and President Truman's decision to drop the atomic bomb in August 1945.

tensions excited by the war in Europe. These tensions were exacerbated by Japan's intervention in parts of the British Empire, bullying of the Dutch in Indonesia, and the invasion of French-controlled Indochina to procure raw materials for its industrial and military expansion.

Rivalry between the United States and Japan, two growing Pacific powers, had accelerated rapidly in the twentieth century. The rivalry reached its breaking point in the summer of 1941 when, in response to Japan's war against China and its moral support for Germany, the United States cut off Japan's access to goods such as scrap metal from the United States and froze Japanese assets in U.S. banks. Also inspiring the attack, from the mid-1930s on, propagandists had reconstructed the image of the imperial ruler. The Meiji emperor who presided over the modernization of Japan served as a Western-style sovereign. Emperor Hirohito (r. 1926–1989), in contrast, had the character of a pan-Asian monarch, ready to lead the liberation and promote the well-being of Asians everywhere. Under Prime Minister Hideki Tojo, the militarist government decided it should settle matters with the West once and for all and forcibly unite Asians in a regional "co-prosperity sphere"—a direct challenge to European empires (see Document 5.3). Such was the context in which the Pearl Harbor attack occurred.

The day after Pearl Harbor, Roosevelt asked Congress for a declaration of war against Japan, which it provided. Hitler faithfully hewed to the Tripartite Pact, declaring war on December 11, 1941, against the United States—a country fit for annihilation, he proclaimed, as it was "half Judaized and the other half Negrified." Mussolini followed suit.

Japan advanced rapidly in the opening months of the war in the Pacific, putting into effect its plan to expand southward as well as to absorb China. By spring 1942, the Japanese had conquered Guam, the Philippines, Malaya, Burma, Indonesia, Singapore, and much of the southwestern Pacific. Japan's military planners counted on Blitzkrieg-like speed and American unpreparedness. Before the United States counterattacked, they reckoned, Japan would have stockpiled massive amounts of resources and expanded its own military capacities still further. Although the assessment of U.S. preparedness turned out to be fairly accurate, the Japanese had entered on a dangerous course. They had not considered the advantages of staying out of the war to profit industrially and commercially from the inability of the European combatants to engage in trade. Warfare was the only option the military-led government put on the table, and there was little concern for Japan's ability to sustain a war against the country on which it depended for trade, technology, raw materials, and loans. Instead, unalloyed confidence in victory encouraged the rapid expansion of Japanese forces in Southeast Asia and the Pacific. As the Japanese foreign minister put it: "In the battle between democracy and totalitarianism the latter adversary will without question win and will control the world. The era of democracy is finished."[6] This confidence produced one of the most dramatic and brutal examples of imperial overreach in modern history.

The globalization of the war gave the Allies several advantages, especially Britain's naval strength and Britain's leaders' and troops' experience in combat around the world. Also, the vast territory that the Allies controlled gave them access to goods from around the world that helped them to survive the war. Given the expanding theater of war, Hitler was not altogether misguided when he shifted manufacturing priorities to battleships. To a certain extent Germany compensated for its deficit in battleships by building submarines, which it used effectively, sometimes destroying as many as two-thirds of the ships in a British convoy. These convoys were lifelines from the United States to Britain and from Britain to the Soviet Union, which was bearing the brunt of the loss in resources. Still, poor coordination among the Axis powers and concentration on conquest in the European theater ultimately constrained Germany and Italy. As the war expanded in scope and duration, the mental limitations and racial ideology of the Axis powers shed a new and deadly light on their inflated global ambitions.

The Grand Alliance

The four members of the Grand Alliance—Great Britain, the Soviet Union, the United States, and the Free French government-in-exile headed by Charles de Gaulle in London—formed to oppose the Axis faced serious challenges in their conduct of the war and in their planning for its aftermath. The alliance evolved slowly over the course of the war through diplomatic negotiations and meetings of its leaders (in contrast, the emperor and the prime minister of Japan never met with their German and Italian partners). The Grand Alliance had much internal strife to overcome. Great Britain and the United States—linked by a common language and economic ties—were wary of the Soviet Union, which likewise mistrusted those two long-standing antagonists of communism. The allocation of resources, the deployment of troops and weaponry, and the postwar settlement were contentious issues throughout the war. Stalin worked hard to ingratiate himself with his allies, exerting his well-developed charm so effectively that in the United States he became known as "Uncle Joe." Some twenty other countries were also part of the alliance, but as junior partners in the stiff negotiations that took place among the "Big Three"—Churchill, Roosevelt, and Stalin.

A driving personality, British prime minister Winston Churchill argued for the use of U.S. and other resources to protect the British Empire. The Soviets desperately wanted their allies to make a more substantial contribution to the war in Europe, which until 1943 they were fighting alone. Stalin argued for the opening of a second, western front against Germany. A second front would force Hitler to remove troops from the USSR and thus lighten Soviet losses. But, acceding to Churchill's demands, the United States agreed to action to shore up Britain's mandates in the Middle East, its control of Egypt, and its position in the eastern Mediterranean that provided critical access to oilfields and the Suez Canal. Although the United States supported the "Europe first" strategy that Stalin wanted, it agreed to military action first in North Africa in 1942 and then in Italy in 1943, with minor deployments in the Balkans. Churchill justified this strategy by claiming that Europe had a "soft underbelly" in these regions and victory would be relatively easy there. Of course he also wanted to protect British interests as well as Mediterranean access to British holdings beyond. To mollify Stalin, President

Roosevelt argued that Allied forces were not yet prepared for the amphibious landing on the heavily fortified French coastline that would be necessary to establish a front in western Europe. His reasoning carried little weight with the Soviets, who were carrying the full weight of brutal fighting against Germany. From the beginning of the Grand Alliance and even on the very eve of the Normandy invasion, which finally opened a second front against Germany, Churchill did not want simply to help the Allies defeat Hitler. His goals reached beyond theirs.

A WAR AGAINST CIVILIANS

Everyone was a target in World War II, and the war killed far more civilians than soldiers, as governments took action against "racial enemies," people with different social, cultural, and religious beliefs, and those who dissented from a particular ideological line. The Axis and the Allies alike bombed cities simply to destroy civilians' will to resist — a tactic that seemed to inspire resistance rather than surrender. The Germans targeted the British people, not British soldiers, in the Blitz, and the Japanese routinely massacred civilians throughout the war. The German army swept through eastern Europe, slaughtering Jews, Communists, Slavs, and others deemed "racial inferiors" as well as intellectual and political leaders. Because many German soldiers initially rebelled at this inhumane mission, special Gestapo forces — the *Einsatzgruppen* (task force) of independent police units — took charge of herding their victims into woods or to the edge of ravines or simply lining them up against town walls and shooting them en masse. Sometimes enthusiastic anti-Semites from the region joined in, or even initiated, the slaughter — a dramatic example of widespread collaboration across Europe with invading and occupying armies. The German military, local collaborators, and ordinary German citizens enlisted from police and other forces were essential to the dramatic numbers — more than a million — deliberately killed in this way. The Japanese did the same in China, in Southeast Asia, and on islands in the Pacific. The number of murdered victims in China alone is said to be at least 2.5 million, with untold millions murdered elsewhere. Estimates of civilians murdered by the Germans exceed twelve million, many of them victims of the Nazis' racial ideology, killed in extermination camps. Along the way, the defeated citizens of Europe often paid the financial costs of their country's occupation, died performing slave labor, and suffered in numerous other ways.

Occupation and Collaboration

The conquered were not all killed, however, for the Axis powers wanted the wealth both from entire nations and from individual citizens to serve their wartime needs. The Nazi government depended on the flow of goods from pillage and thus organized shipments of grain, metals, and other resources from occupied countries to Germany itself. It devalued currency so that the tribute paid to the Reich was more onerous than it superficially appeared. In cash and resources the French paid the most—over 40 percent of what the Germans took in. The tribute supposedly paid for just the army of occupation, but the amount taken from France would have supported an army of 18 million. A small country like Denmark, for example, provided some 15 percent of Germany's food. It should be noted that Britain forced the citizens of India to pay £100 million as a "gift" to help cover its own wartime costs, but it did not confiscate goods to the extent that the Axis powers did. High Nazi officials stole vast quantities of art, silver, cash, housing, luxury automobiles, and jewelry, not to mention the fortune Hitler exacted from supporters and other groups. In Poland, whose people the Nazis considered inferior and subject to extermination, millions were driven from their land so that "true" Germans could repopulate regions that were said to have been Aryan in a distant past. Nazi pillaging thus took many forms, bringing death and destitution.

German police forces composed of ordinary civilians and professional soldiers along with forces specially trained in murder exacted the most horrific costs in eastern Europe. To achieve the goal of Germanizing the east, the underpinnings necessary for the existence of nation-states were eliminated. German forces slaughtered members of the middle and upper classes who might have led a national resistance, and they sent the clergy to concentration camps. At Hitler's order, intellectuals—university professors, writers, artists—who might have been able to mobilize national sentiment were targeted for execution. Soviet troops performed similar massacres in the occupation of Poland, most notably killing fifteen thousand officers and technology specialists at Katyn in 1940 to forestall resistance by eliminating elites. The Germans forbade Poles the accoutrements of culture—such as radios, phonographs, and attendance at concerts and films—and they destroyed Polish churches and schools or closed them down.

The Nazis recognized that by putting the remaining Poles and others to work, they could make up for shortages of German workers. The Nazis thus made the people of eastern and central European countries slave laborers for German industry and agriculture—a policy that seemed justified to the majority of Germans. One young German woman arriving in occupied Poland after the massacres and deportations was utterly shocked at the lack of cultural vitality and agreed that the territory desperately needed foreign rule because the Polish race consisted only of "proletarians, peasants, and the poor." It was obviously "unable to form an enduringly capable ruling class."[7]

Local collaborators aided in the Nazi conquest, plunder, and occupation of their own countries. Many of them believed that they would be rewarded when the Reich triumphed across Europe. Dutch Nazis, for example, believed that because they were Nordic peoples they would receive land to the east and that Hitler would welcome their experience of colonial rule in administering the great empire that Germany would develop across the Eurasian landmass. Collaborators informed on fellow citizens, helped in identifying caches of private resources, and did a lot of brutal dirty work, thus protecting the sensibilities of German soldiers—some of whom led a plush existence in Europe's capitals. Having provided the Nazis with the location of Allied military bases before the attack on Norway, Vidkun Quisling declared himself head of the quasi-fascist Norwegian government upon the Nazi invasion. However, a German regional commander actually ruled, and Quisling himself always promised far more support from the Norwegian people than he ever delivered. Leaders of puppet governments run by the Germans came to be known as Quislings after the Norwegian collaborator.

The French government at Vichy was also a collaborationist government, and its small amount of independence stemmed from the military background of Philippe Pétain. Hitler mightily distrusted collaborators with a fascist background, who often envisioned themselves as soaring to powerful heights during a German occupation. He preferred instead the support of the old ruling classes in the army, industry, and finance, and conservatives in the upper reaches of the bureaucracy. Like Pétain, many of these conservatives endorsed the Hitler program (in France, the slogan "Work, Family, Country" prominently replaced the democratic "Liberty, Equality, Fraternity") and lent a willing hand in turning over dissidents and Jews for execution. Pro-Nazi regimes organized domestic production to benefit the Nazis, while enforcing the onerous taxes and charges that sent most of a country's wealth to support the Germans. Nonetheless, many ordinary French people fervently believed that Pétain had saved them from an even worse fate.

Holocaust

Indeed, far worse fates did exist. Jews in Germany were subjected to reduced food, living quarters, and job opportunities. Upon conquest Polish and other Jews like Heda Margolius were herded into ghettos and camps and stripped of many of their possessions. The idea was that the horrendous conditions would kill people off naturally at low cost: "the more that die, the better," one top German official said in the course of planning for ghettos in the late fall of 1939.[8] Such was the fate of tens of thousands of prisoners in the camp in the Lublin region of Poland that was fully functioning in early 1940. In the Warsaw ghetto, initially some 30 percent of the population occupied 2 percent of the city's space, but more and more people jammed in daily as the Nazis appropriated the land of people living outside the city and sent them to the ghetto. Nazis seized Jewish and Slavic land and housing for the ethnic Germans who were to be resettled on farms and in empty apartments, creating Aryan utopias. Tens of thousands of ethnic Germans from across eastern Europe were transported to these regions and resettled in temporary quarters. The confusion and strain on facilities was massive, and by 1940 the Nazis concluded that they needed a better plan to streamline transportation and confiscate people's property efficiently. In 1942, at a conference in Wannsee, Germany, Nazi leaders drew up plans for a bureaucratically organized, technological system for the extermination of the Jews.

Hitler had long advocated their elimination, and modern acts of mass killing such as that of Native Americans in the United States, the Hereros in Africa, and the Armenians in the Ottoman Empire were well known to him. On the eve of war, in 1939, Hitler had called for "the destruction of the Jewish race in Europe," a marked turn from his 1930s policy of driving Jews to leave Germany.[9] In his oratory, writings, and policies, Hitler inexorably changed the course of anti-Semitism

from expressions of hatred for Jews to a systematic program for their complete extermination as the embodiment of racial evil. In 1941 and 1942, even as the war
turned against the Germans, the "final solution," as the mass murder of the Jews
was called, became a reality.

A technological, bureaucratic, and legalistic system of annihilation in camps
developed alongside the violent but ultimately inefficient rampages against eastern
European Jews, middle-class politicians, intellectuals, and hospitalized citizens. As
millions of Soviet Jews also came under German control, Nazi anti-Semitism
escalated. Six camps were built in Poland specifically for the purposes of mass murder—Auschwitz-Birkenau, Majdanek, Chelmno, Belzec, Sobibor, and Treblinka
(Map 6.3). Some, like Auschwitz-Birkenau, served both as extermination and labor
camps. Others, such as Chelmno, functioned solely as death camps. SS troops
under Reich Commissar Heinrich Himmler supervised the camps and the extermination of victims. Systematic killing had already begun with the Nazi T-4 program that targeted people deemed "racially unsound" (the disabled and terminally
ill) for destruction. The process evolved from the T-4 program's gas-equipped
trucks and temporary killing facilities to a more bureaucratized and solid system
of permanent buildings. These included specially designed gas chambers and crematoria, which replaced the huge open pits in which the Nazis had first burned the
bodies of their victims (see Documents 6.3 and 6.4).

Nazis organized the collection and transport of Jews from all the regions controlled by Germany, using thousands of transit camps across the continent as staging
areas. In the ghettos, councils of Jewish men, chosen by lot or from urban leadership
or appointed by the Nazis, had the grim job of deciding who would be "resettled to
the East." In cities that were less ghettoized, city officials and neighbors provided
names of Jewish residents for deportation. Some Jews were resigned to deportation
in the belief that life elsewhere could not be worse than it was in the ghettos.

As news of gassings spread by "the Jewish mouth-radio", some Jews went into
hiding, forged identity papers, or fought back even in the face of the brutality that
went along with the roundups. Prior isolation and deprivation resulting from Nazi
policies helped reduce opposition, as Jewish populations became weakened by
hunger and disease. Resistance occurred in both ghettos and death camps, however. In April 1943 Jews in the Warsaw ghetto rose up against their Nazi captors in
a show of incredible bravery. Although consuming on average less than 200 calories a day, inhabitants used weapons provided by the Polish resistance to attack
German soldiers entering the ghetto. Outgunned from the start with thousands
mercilessly butchered, survivors nonetheless continued the uprising into the fall,
when the resistance was finally crushed.

To forestall resistance in the camps, new arrivals were greeted with bands, colorful signs of welcome, and even with postcards to inscribe and send back home.
A Jewish opera singer was forced to sing gay arias for newcomers because the
commander of the camp wanted the atmosphere to seem "joyful." However, a dark
reality actually awaited, as families and individuals were triaged for consignment
either to immediate death or to forced labor. Many mothers, unaware that their
children were doomed, refused to be separated from their children and thus went

◆ **Map 6.3 Concentration Camps and Extermination Sites in Europe**
This map shows the major extermination sites and concentration camps in Europe, but
the entire continent contained thousands of lesser camps to which the victims of Nazism
were transported. Some of these lesser camps served as way stations on the path to ultimate
extermination while other camps worked prisoners to exhaustion and often, literally, to death.

directly to the gas chambers. Ordinary citizens simply could not imagine in advance the purpose of the camps; it was so unthinkable. Hungarian Olga Lengyel of
Cluj insisted that her entire family—she, her parents, and her children—accompany her husband, a doctor rounded up for his political beliefs, to a resettlement
location. At Auschwitz she was disabused of all illusions by a surviving inmate:
"You see those flames? That's the crematory oven. . . . Call it by the name we use:

◆ Death Camp Survivors

Many millions of words have been written about concentration camp life during World War II. A prominent theme is the loss of a sense of their own humanity that many captives experienced. This image shows survivors liberated in May 1945 from the camp at Ebensee, Austria, reputedly used for "scientific" experiments. The death and dehumanization of the 1930s and World War II have led some historians to see Europe exclusively as the "dark continent." Recalling the material in this and previous chapters, do you think this categorization is accurate, or should it be qualified? We see in the survivors' faces and bodies the effects of Nazi practices that turned a human into a *Stück,* or thing. What else do you see? © *CORBIS.*

the bakery. Perhaps it is your family that is being burned this moment."[10] Yet even in the camps, where fatalism might have triumphed, uprisings and escapes occasionally occurred. In August 1943, some six hundred inmates of Treblinka attacked their Ukrainian guards. Most were killed, but a few escaped and joined the resistance effort. At Auschwitz in October 1944, male resisters, using explosives smuggled in by women prisoners working nearby, blew up a crematorium and killed several members of the SS. None of these rebels survived, and the women workers were publicly hanged.

Most adults need to consume at least 2,000 calories daily, but hardworking inmates usually took in less than 500. Barracks were grim, with inmates poorly clothed, relegated to sleeping crammed against one another on wooden bunks, and subject to the drunkenness, brutality, or perverse behavior of the guards. Roll calls at odd hours, inspections for tiny or nonexistent infractions, and the unchecked rampage of diseases through the camps also shaped their lives. Many called their experience a "living death." Nazi doctors performed cruel medical experiments and undertook operations without anaesthesia on pregnant women, twins, and other people in the name of racial science. Some prisoners went mad, as did some of the guards. Yet for all those who wanted to commit suicide, few could actually do it. When asked in later life how she managed to survive, Heda Margolius responded, "Everyone assumes it is easy to die but that the struggle to live requires a superhuman effort. Mostly, it is the other way around."[11] Heda Margolius shared one common, but obviously not always successful, survival skill of the camps: she and friends in the camps were not dehumanized but valued one another enough to join forces in a miraculous escape from the death march at the end of the war.

MILITARIZING NATION AND EMPIRE

World War II was like the First World War in depending on nearly total mobilization and militarization of civilians at home and abroad, but it was very different in that civilians were the explicit targets of violence from invasion, bombing, and totalitarian government policies, including those of racial war (Table 6.1). The war against civilians in the form of bombing usually bolstered civilians' resolve to fight, as in Britain, the Soviet Union, and China. Governments also depended on filmmakers, film and radio stars, graphic designers, government censors, and writers to produce propaganda (see the Picture Essay). Governments used available resources and enforcement of sedition laws to take control of the cultural front. To aid the war effort, they produced romantic films about war heroes and horrifying films depicting enemies as perverse, brutal, or culturally backward, or a combination of all three. News was highly censored, featuring in totalitarian countries stories that told of victories while failing to mention defeats. In China, whose fight against the Japanese kept some 40 percent of Japan's armed forces out of the war against the Western allies, mobile troupes of actors performed the news and patriotic stories to inspire rural people in the war effort. Thus, not only soldiers at the front but civilians and civic institutions were militarized mentally and physically, and war planners targeted them for military attack. Whether at home or on the battlefront there grew up in the horrendous conditions of propaganda, battle, deprivation, and slaughter individuals who resisted war and occupation.

Societies in Wartime

Governments built on their experience in the previous world war to militarize the home front. Radio, now two decades old, allowed governments to broadcast information about nutrition, household management, and services available to civilians. Because large numbers of men had been mobilized, imprisoned, or killed, women headed many households, often pooling their resources and sharing housing. Government experts told all these women how to maintain high standards of hygiene and high levels of femininity to help maintain society's morale. On many home fronts conditions were as bad as the conditions experienced by soldiers. Civilians across Europe received poorer rations and were constantly exposed to death from disease, starvation, and direct military attack. Obtaining basic supplies was a daily struggle because of shortages, the more so because civilians generally had to work long hours in order to obtain ration cards and had little time or energy to stand in long lines.

Especially dire conditions existed in besieged cities such as Leningrad, where an estimated one million civilians died (see Document 6.2). The Leningrad siege lasted more than two and a half years, beginning in August 1941 and ending in January 1944. Throughout, there were no heating supplies and—as urgent—no coffins to bury the thousands who died each week and whose bodies piled up around the city. Leningraders ate crows, cats, castor oil, hair oil, and even glue that they scraped from wallpaper and furniture. "But not all people in the enormous city had such supplementary sources of 'food,'" one survivor remarked sarcastically.[12] Civilians behind the lines on the eastern front were even worse off, as the German and Soviet armies alike pursued a scorched-earth policy, burning fields, homes, and entire villages to deprive the enemy of access to any resources. To stiffen the resolve of Leningraders and others, Soviet radio revived nationalism and broadcast the patriotic poetry of Anna Akhmatova—although she was a sharp critic of the regime's brutality (see Document 5.2). It is likely, however, that throughout the war citizens everywhere were too busy providing for themselves to pay full attention to government directives and propaganda.

Once again, the combatants needed every hand to pursue the war, but the revival of the cult of domesticity during the interwar years and legislation against married women working outside the home impeded the mobilization of women. Having been urged to follow a more feminine way of life in order to revive masculinity, many women outside the USSR determined to stay at home in wartime. Men felt the same way—for instance, in Britain, where industrialists refused to consider women as prospective employees when the war first broke out. Nevertheless, in December 1941, as the Blitz took its toll in lives and property, the House of Commons passed the National Service Number 2 Act, which ordered unmarried women between the ages of twenty and thirty to take jobs. Right from the start of their conscription into the war effort, British women fought for benefits and working conditions more nearly equal to men's but avoided the contentious issue of equal pay. Even those modest demands incensed Churchill. He protested that equality might upset men both on the home front and in the army, and he charged that women who wanted equality were unpatriotic.

A greatly exaggerated view of women's duty to stay at home existed in Germany, where Nazi ideology emphasized women's sexual and reproductive nature. By contrast in the United States the civilian war effort that boosted U.S. gross national product 40 percent in less than four years of war relied on the work of stalwart

◆ **Soviet Medics**

These Soviet paramedics were among the millions of women on the Allied side who performed crucial work in factories, agriculture, and the military to bring about victory. Germany and Italy had so masculinized the professions and industrial work that women were declared unwelcome in important service outside the home until almost the end of the war. The USSR, Britain, and the United States, in contrast, had ideologies—no matter how unevenly applied—that stressed the equality of citizens of both sexes. Soviet women were especially prominent as pilots and frontline doctors. © *Topham/The Image Works.*

women. The character "Rosie the Riveter," a woman working on an assembly line, was emblematic of the millions of American women whose blue-collar work was central to the construction of an airplane every five minutes and other incredible feats of wartime production. During the war, Soviet women played an even more active role in the economy than they had done in the early days of Stalinist industrialization. They not only fought in the infantry and served as pilots but also staffed factories, drove tractors, and dug deep antitank trenches around threatened cities. All women who traveled with the armies as soldiers, doctors, and nurses often noticed, as did the men, that life at the front lifted peacetime gender restrictions.

On the home front there were far fewer strikes and uprisings than in World War I. Because of the more successful propaganda effort and the oppressive and threatening conditions, there were fewer civilian rebellions in Europe except for resistance in the occupied countries. In Germany there were mixed reactions to the news that filtered through of the Holocaust: security services of the Third Reich sent in reports of fears that "after the Jews, the sick and the helpless" ordinary citizens would be the next target for extermination. One opponent of the Nazis called it "the greatest shame of mankind of all times," but another felt "We have to thank Hitler for freeing us from this pest."[13] In the democracies, pacifism was weaker than it had been in World War I.

Impact of the War Overseas

In the colonies, a different scenario was unfolding as Japan invaded and successfully drove out the Western powers, imprisoning and executing former officials as well as railroad managers and hospital staff. In some places, the Japanese fortified nationalist movements that they believed would help them drive out the European powers. In other places, they clamped down on independence groups. Later, as a result of fighting the Japanese, as they had fought the Westerners, these groups would expand their organizations and influence. China is a good example, for while struggling against the Japanese, the Chinese Communists led by Mao Zedong built support among ordinary villagers because of the protection they were able to offer and the land reforms they enacted. After the war, the Chinese Communists took political control of the entire country, pitting their newfound strength against any reassertion of European and American influence. In Burma, Indochina, Indonesia, and elsewhere national independence movements intent on blocking both Japan and the Western powers flourished during the turbulent wartime conditions.

The European imperialists did not help their own cause. "The European is my shepherd and I am in want," went one African description of the wartime situation.[14] Britain made great demands in India, Africa, and elsewhere. Taxes were increased on manufacturers and workers, and in populous India citizen activism erupted, led by Gandhi's announcement in 1942 of a "Quit India" movement and by the defection of important leaders such as Subhas Chandra Bose to the Axis. The British bombed merchant ships so that they would not fall into Japanese hands, causing three million deaths from famine in Bengal as food rotted on docks. This callousness intensified the anger felt when swaggering British negotiators stubbornly refused to grant India the political liberties it had been promised. China and India were but two places where the bonds of empire—both formal and informal—loosened on the home front during the war.

Men in Combat

The training and indoctrinating of civilians for combat in this second total war in less than three decades was arduous. The armed forces trained their personnel with extreme discipline to achieve peak performance and make the best use of the available technology. But rational planning and technology were not the only factors affecting the battlefield experience. Soldiers faced the elements, whether fighting in the snows and bitter cold of the Soviet winter or the searing heat of North Africa. The German army fell victim to a process of "demodernization" when production failed to keep up with the demands of modern warfare. As early as the fall of 1941, a German corps commander wrote: "The health of men and horses is deteriorating due to the wretched housing facilities. . . . The men have been lying for weeks in the rain and stand in knee-deep mud. It is impossible to change wet clothing. . . . [The soldiers] are hollow-eyed, pale, many of them are ill."[15] Men suffered frostbite, malnutrition, incapacitating wounds, and, when captured, further deprivation and even torture. Their suffering was alleviated by moments when discipline was relaxed. Some commanders turned their soldiers loose to plunder, maim, and rape.

Many frontline soldiers made sacrifices for the values with which they had been instilled: "Terrible night from the 17th to the 18th," one Italian soldier wrote home in 1941. "In that night, which I will remember for all my life, which I would pass entirely on foot under the snow and rain that soaked my shoes, as if my feet were in a hip bath and froze three toes. The only thing that keeps me always on my feet and always ready: Faith in God and in the Duce." Another saw the home front and battlefront connected as one Italy: "The love of Patria, this sentiment of Italianness, which helps me bear every inconvenience, every sacrifice, for the good, the grandness of Italy, and which ties us like a pure golden thread to you far away, to the family."[16]

Although patriotism and sacrifice were common themes in battlefront writing, soldiers' experience of war, of course, varied a good deal depending on their location and circumstances. The war in the Pacific was especially grim, with rampant disease, short supplies because of the vast distances supply routes covered, and often subhuman conditions of imprisonment. No doubt Japanese soldiers were as much inclined as their German, British, American, or Russian counterparts to complain about the hardships of war, but their culture required a higher degree of sacrifice owing not only to the samurai tradition that death was preferable to surrender but to a generation of propaganda militarizing Japanese society as a whole. Thus, kamikaze pilots sacrificed their lives to ensure they hit their targets by crashing their planes into them, and Japanese soldiers fought to the death to hold their positions even when they had no chance of winning, encouraging civilians to assist them and even to commit suicide.

Some lucky Germans received relatively plush assignments in European capitals such as Amsterdam and Paris. Their wartime experiences starkly contrasted with those of Germans on the eastern front. Some soldiers on the eastern front faced the scorched-earth policies practiced by the Soviets, which left them without food and transport and confronting an increasingly well-equipped enemy. Although some remained inspired by the Nazi ideal of suffering for the fatherland, many became disillusioned and bitter at the bleak and terrifying reality of warfare: "[W]hy is this suffering in itself not great, but so unspeakably common and dirty?" one German soldier asked.[17] Others on the eastern front had to massacre civilians,

◆ **The Walking Wounded**
World War II has the reputation for being highly mechanized and efficient, but on the eastern front chaos, terror, and deprivation reigned. This Soviet soldier rescues a fallen comrade using primitive muscle power. The year is 1941, and Soviets had mustered a strong patriotism that prompted such feats: "We knew our motherland, we knew Stalin, we knew where we were going," one veteran remembered. It would not be long before German soldiers on the Russian front were similarly reduced to abject conditions of cold, illness, and lingering death, and some of them *did* come to question the cause for which they were fighting. *Photo by Keystone/Getty Images.*

including babies and the elderly. For them Nazi doctrine that the weak needed to be eliminated in order for Aryanism to flower may have worked to ward off psychological breakdown.

Literally millions of colonial soldiers fought in the war, often without the commitment that fascist, communist, or democratic ideology provided. The imperial powers used propaganda in the form of films, radio broadcasts, and newspaper articles aimed to encourage colonists to volunteer for the war effort. Among the volunteers were some 100,000 soldiers from French West Africa and 200,000 South Africans, of whom one-third were black. More than 2 million Indian troops fought for the British in the Middle East and in Asia. African troops served in North Africa, the Middle East, Europe, and the Pacific. The imperial powers also drew on the colonies for forced labor as they had in World War I. They pressed local populations into harsh occupations such as mining and forced farmers to produce what the combatants needed.

Many of the colonial soldiers were radicalized as they saw more and more of the world. They fought alongside poor Europeans, and those stationed in Europe saw

Country	Total mobilized	Killed or died of wounds	Civilians killed[1]
Belgium	625,000	8,000	101,000
Britain	5,896,000	265,000[2]	91,000[3]
Bulgaria	450,000	10,000	NA
Czechoslovakia	150,000	10,000	490,000
Denmark	25,000	4,000	NA
Finland	500,000	79,000	NA
France	5,000,000	202,000	108,000
Germany	10,200,000	3,250,000	500,000
Greece	414,000	73,000	400,000
Hungary	350,000	147,000	NA
Italy	3,100,000	149,000	783,000
Netherlands	410,000	7,000	242,000
Norway	75,000	2,000	2,000
Poland	1,000,000	64,000	2,000,000
Romania	1,136,000	520,000	NA
Soviet Union[4]	22,000,000	7,500,000	6-8,000,000
Yugoslavia	3,741,000	410,000	1,275,000

◆ **Table 6.1 World War II Casualties**
Casualty figures for World War II are constantly being revised, especially since the end of the USSR. Russian scholars have used newly opened records and archives to formulate casualty figures for Soviet civilians and soldiers that go as high as 47 million and to revise upward the number killed in other Soviet-bloc states. Notice that these casualties do not include casualties from outside of Europe except for non-Western members of the British military. Non-Western specialists thus put the total deaths in World War II at roughly 100 million.

[1] Includes deaths of Jews in the Holocaust.
[2] Includes overseas troops serving in British forces.
[3] Includes 30,000 merchant seamen.
[4] Approximate figures.
NA Not available.

European poverty up close, unraveling the idea that the West was a land of plenty for all. Those who witnessed the death camps and the destruction wrought by both sides never again believed that the imperial powers were more civilized than they. Caribbean-born Franz Fanon, the future doctor and fighter for colonial independence, could hardly fathom the unequal treatment meted out to dark-skinned soldiers by the very Europeans whose "liberty, equality, and fraternity" had inspired him as a youth. Soldiers had experienced this shattering of their illusions during the Great War, and the same myths were destroyed with even greater force twenty years later.

Resistance

Soldiers were not the only fighters mobilized in this war. The fascist powers faced civilian resistance from the very beginning of their brutal regimes, and this resistance accelerated once war brought much of Europe and Asia under military occupation. For many, resistance was a daily affair. Small acts kept up a fighting spirit even in defeat. For instance, in occupied Paris the recipes for stretching a small amount of food, amusingly described by the famed French writer Colette, cheered citizens whose will Hitler wanted to break. Mimeographed or even handwritten newspapers alerted citizens to the movement of imprisoned family members and warned the young to go into hiding with news of forced labor roundups. Even formal resistance based on widespread networks, one Italian activist declared, was "nested in kitchens," because kitchens not only provided necessary nourishment but also nurturing settings for meetings.[18] All the while, contraband radio broadcasts conveyed uplifting news as well as coded messages that kept morale high.

The brutal fascist regimes also spawned an array of organized opposition, much of it successful even if only in distracting governments from their main goal of conquest. One symbol of resistance in the Allied world was General Charles de Gaulle (1890–1970), who from his haven in London directed the Free French forces—a mixed organization of soldiers who had escaped via Dunkirk, troops from the colonies, and volunteers from other occupied countries. Although the papacy supported Mussolini in Italy, took no stand against the Holocaust, and seemed to many to endorse the Croatian slaughter of some half a million Serbs by the Nazi puppet government, some religious leaders were active in the resistance. Catholic and Protestant clergy and lay parishioners set up resistance networks, often hiding Jews and political suspects. On the left of the political spectrum, Communist parties led highly effective cells, such as those in the Communist-dominated French group Combat. To the right were military people like de Gaulle and the large group of German aristocrats and military men who plotted to overthrow Hitler. The Polish resistance was unified against the Nazis, with no collaborators in sight—and none wanted, so much did the Nazis believe the Poles to be inferior. In Yugoslavia Serbs and Croats attacked each other as much as they attacked the fascists. Resistance leader Colonel Draja Mihailovich, a Serb, wanted Serbian dominance to result from the war and resistance. The Croat leader Ante Pavelich retaliated against brutal Serb treatment with mass slaughter, pleasing the Nazis no end. Across Europe, rural resistance groups known as partisans, or the *maquis,* planned assassinations, disrupted communications, and bombed important war facilities and materiel. After carrying out an act, these people melted away to the mountains, forests, and remote villages.

Individuals across the social and political spectrum with special skills, special daring, or special opportunity became resisters. Hikers and skiers helped escapees cross mountains. Villagers along the Scandinavian coast hid Jews and other refugees brought in fishing boats. In Copenhagen, Ellen Nielsen, a fish-seller, hid as many as thirty refugees at a time in her home while arranging for local boats to transport them safely out of Denmark. Countless thousands took part in local escape networks. In Paris, a woman chemist made explosives for the resistance in her university laboratory. Resisters took advantage of gender stereotypes: "Naturally the Germans didn't think that a woman could have carried a bomb," explained one Italian resister, "so this became the woman's task."[19] Some used lonely German officers' need for female companionship as opportunities for assassination. Unobtrusive laborers such as seamstresses who worked repairing garments for the German army sometimes obtained inside information—about

◆ **Yugoslav Partisans**

Yugoslav partisans, not the Allies, were responsible for driving the Nazis from the region, and their forces grew in number in the face of the harsh and inhuman Nazi rule. As in resistance to Nazism in ghettos and occupied cities, women fought alongside men. These particular partisans are retraining after recovering from their wounds and are not deterred in the slightest from rejoining their comrades in the struggle led by Marshal Tito and his armies. The forces under Tito became dominant as the war proceeded and were soon fighting not only against the Nazis but against other resistance groups that might compete for postwar control of the country. © *Bettmann/CORBIS.*

the concentration of troops, for instance—that they passed along the resistance network to the high reaches of the Allied command.

Resistance produced innumerable heroes and martyrs—some of them still remembered today. French historian Marc Bloch joined the French resistance and was captured and executed by the Gestapo. Swedish diplomat Raoul Wallenberg worked behind the scenes with Nazi officials to save thousands of Hungarian Jews. He disappeared in the Soviet Union after the war. The Hollywood film *Schindler's List* has immortalized the bravery of Oskar Schindler, who at first profited from forced Jewish labor but then changed course and worked to save lives. Many other resisters, active at the grassroots level, proved that voicing opposition worked, although their names have been forgotten. In Bulgaria, public protest against the deportation of Jews forced the government to back down from this cruel program. In 1943 in the Rosenstrasse neighborhood of Berlin itself, Aryan women's sit-in demonstrations over the arrest of their Jewish husbands brought about the men's release.

In Germany groups of conservative army officers, many of them initially eager for the demise of the Weimar Republic, were repulsed by the way Nazism evolved. Destroying religion and social structure, Nazism had created "a welling up of brutish men," one of them wrote in his diary.[20] Although many generals enjoyed the career opportunities that an increasingly expansionist Nazi Germany offered, some became loosely linked in a variety of conspiracies to overthrow the Nazis. Because even their casual questioning of strategy could lead to backdoor murders and because many had been demoted in the 1930s, the cast of upper-class opponents was fluid but resolute. One professed to be "filled with shame" at news of massacred Polish intellectuals, treatment of the Jews, and extermination of the handicapped. Highly connected, they tried to enlist the British against Hitler and passed on news of coming military operations—none of it followed up because the British leadership still believed its own manufactured propaganda from World War I about the "Huns" in the German elite. Then, on July 20, 1944, after many abortive assassination attempts, a bomb exploded close to Hitler but only wounded him. Afterward, hundreds of conspirators and opponents in the German elite were tortured and killed, their family and friends imprisoned.

Many historians question the sincerity of German resistance, citing both the self-serving and the last-minute nature of the July 20 attempt on Hitler's life. Nonetheless, some five million Germans lost their lives in the last nine months of the war, and countless millions more people of other nationalities died. Had Hitler been killed even as late as the summer of 1944, the relief to humanity would have been considerable.

THE WORLD WAR ENDS AND THE COLD WAR BEGINS

From 1943 on, the conduct of the war increasingly reflected the inevitability of Allied victory. Allied resources in men and productive capacity were daunting, far outstripping anything Japan and Germany could muster. Despite astonishing U.S. and Soviet production of weaponry, trucks, airplanes, and other materiel, Hitler and his minions continued to proclaim that the United States was "a big bluff" and the Soviet Union a wasteland filled with inferior Jews and Slavs. Facing enemies who appeared demented in their willingness to fight to total destruction, the Allies met regularly not only to strategize about the war but also, increasingly, to discuss the postwar division of territory. Fighting was fierce and casualties remained enormous. In the midst of carnage, differences over strategic and political expectations increasingly revealed themselves among the Big Three, and these leaders and their advisers feared that the tensions in the Grand Alliance might devolve into outright hostilities. At issue were reparations, resources, and the ultimate postwar disposition of political and strategic power. From 1943 to 1945, however, they worked amid these mounting tensions toward the common goal of beating the Axis forces.

The Axis on the Defensive

Late in 1942 the tide of war shifted on all fronts, as the Allies started tightening the noose around the Axis. Soviet forces led the way, as they held the line against a major German offensive to capture Soviet oil and to bisect the USSR. The German army rapidly took Sevastapol and Rostov and on August 22 began the siege of Stalingrad (see Map 6.1). After months of ferocious fighting, neither side was ready to surrender despite massive casualties. Finally the Soviet army began a pincer movement from the north and south, slowly entrapping and later capturing the ninety thousand German survivors in February 1943. Meanwhile, the British army in North Africa held against German troops under the command of General Erwin Rommel, a skillful practitioner of a new kind of tank warfare. Rommel let his tanks move as far and as fast as they could and improvised in dozens of ways to make up for missing parts and supplies. He was dubbed the "Desert Fox" for his shrewdness and resourcefulness. Yet not even Rommel could overcome the Allies' access to German codes—access that ultimately made possible the British victory at El Alamein and the successful invasion of Morocco and Algeria in the fall of 1942. These crucial successes buoyed Allied spirits and seemed to augur well for a swift defeat of Italy. In July 1943 the Allies invaded Sicily, a landing that sparked the dismissal of Mussolini by King Victor Emmanuel III and an appeal from the new government for a truce. German forces, however, quickly overran northern Italy, putting Mussolini in charge of a puppet government and using precious resources tenaciously to defend the Fascist hold on Italy until April 1945.

After the siege of Stalingrad, Soviet armies began a costly drive through eastern and central Europe. The region's resources and the capture of Berlin were their ultimate goals. There still was no second front in western Europe. Instead, British and U.S. planes bombed German cities to demoralize German civilians and to destroy war industries. But it was an invasion from the west that Stalin needed.

Churchill argued against such an invasion, but to no avail. On June 6, 1944, Allied forces under the command of U.S. general Dwight Eisenhower landed on the heavily fortified French coastline (see Map 6.1). The Nazis had been deceived into concentrating their forces to the north of the actual invasion site in Normandy. After taking the beaches, Allied troops fought their way through the Normandy hedgerows as Allied planes pummeled the cities of western France. In late July, Allied forces—the Free French among them—broke through the German defenses and a month later worked alongside the resistance to liberate Paris, where a rebellion had already erupted against the Nazi occupiers. British, Canadian, U.S., Free French, and other Allied forces then fought their way eastward to join the Soviets in squeezing the Third Reich to its final end.

Several of Hitler's subordinates were secretly trying to negotiate a peace, but Hitler was not about to spare the German people. Hitler believed that if the Germans proved to be unworthy of world rule, they deserved to perish. Despite the crushing defeat, he ordered his troops to burn cities and villages along their path of retreat, and he drafted young teenagers and old men into the German army for a last-ditch stand. He believed to the end that his opponents' racial inferiority would ensure their defeat, and he also had faith that a new secret weapon would bring Germany victory.

◆ Dresden after Firebombing

Some 800 Allied planes dropped tons of combustible material on the German city of Dresden in February 1945, creating a massive firestorm that killed or wounded tens of thousands. A city with countless architectural masterpieces from earlier centuries, Dresden was utterly destroyed by the war's end, even though we see a working tram traveling through the rubble. Goebbels maintained from the outset that the bombing of Dresden was the greatest tragedy of the war, a claim still repeated by some older Germans with vivid memories of the conflict. © *Bettmann/CORBIS.*

German scientists were developing the unmanned V-2 rocket—a prototype of the ballistic missile—to drop bombs on Britain once again. But lacking a system to provide precision guidance to a target, the rocket was not yet effective.

Hitler's refusal to negotiate or surrender led to massive Allied bombing of German cities, including the firebombing of Dresden over two days in mid-February 1945. At the same time, the Soviets engaged in a deadly pursuit of the German army from the east. Tens of thousands of civilians died in this campaign. Soviet armies took the Baltic states, and a small, leading-edge contingent entered Poland, where it paused to wait for critical supplies and reinforcements to catch up.

The Soviet army's temporary weakness allowed the Germans to put down an uprising in Warsaw of the Polish resistance in August 1944. The elimination of the Polish resistance would give the Soviets a freer hand in eastern Europe after the war. At the end of August, facing more than twice as many German troops as were fighting on the western front, the Soviet army took Bulgaria and entered Romania and continued to roll toward Germany. During the winter of 1944–45, Soviet troops overcame fierce German fighting in Hungary.

Allied forces to the west proceeded in a multipronged attack toward Germany. In April 1945, President Franklin Roosevelt died, an event that Hitler, delusional to the end, believed would swing the Americans to his side. As the Allies converged on Berlin and as news reached Germany that Italian partisans had executed Mussolini and displayed his corpse, Hitler married his partner, Eva Braun, and both committed suicide in his bunker. Aides followed his orders to burn their remains. Germany finally surrendered on May 8, 1945.

Surrender in Europe and the Defeat of Japan

Chaos and suffering continued in the midst of the victors' thankfulness for peace. Local and national governments were in shambles, with reprisals against collaborators and struggles for control among a variety of factions. Chaos reigned. Concentration camp victims and slave laborers were sent on forced marches or loaded onto ships without destination as the war ended. One Lithuanian Jewish inmate recalled that the boat he was on pulled up to a dock and the prisoners descended and "Then suddenly, out of nowhere, the guards reappeared. . . . They started shooting at people still on the deck, waiting to go down the makeshift gang plank. Hundreds were killed like that— only a few hours before liberation."[21] At other camps, the guards fled, leaving the inmates alone, but the inmates hardly had the strength or resources to do anything but wait for help. Many were terrified of leaving on their own. Even when help arrived, soldiers were often paralyzed by shock on discovering the situation in the camps. Many young and inexperienced soldiers found themselves without the mental resources, medical knowledge, or supplies to organize relief.

Compounding the chaos was the failure of the news that surrender had taken place to reach all combatants. From Bulgaria to France, fighting continued after Germany's surrender, and Allied soldiers feared snipers, wildcat bombers, and even well-organized attacks. "We had to be extremely vigilant," Major Edmund de Rothschild noted of the war's end in Serbia; "the war was not completely over for our particular group."[22]

The occupying armies caused further distress. Soldiers sometimes evicted civilians from their homes in order to have shelter for themselves. Allied forces from Britain and the United States had food to distribute but sometimes only in exchange for sex. Soviet forces all too frequently raped women along the invasion routes. Women in Germany began asking one another not whether rape had occurred but how often.

Defeated forces also wreaked havoc. Soldiers not captured were often desperate, stealing civilian clothing and food wherever they could find it. German armies retreating from Finland burned every village through which they passed. Literally millions of Europeans had to flee to escape the destructive behavior of the defeated armies. In eastern Europe the situation was particularly acute, as several million Germans sent to resettle conquered areas were massacred by newly liberated locals.

Even as post-surrender anarchy reigned: in Europe, the war in the Pacific extended through the summer of 1945. Although the United States adhered more or less to the "Europe first" strategy formulated by the Grand Alliance, it prosecuted the Pacific war with vigor. In 1942 U.S. forces defeated the Japanese in the battles of the Coral Sea (in May) and Midway Island (in June), relying on aircraft carriers and submarines to pursue the battleships of the vastly overextended Japanese navy (see Map 6.2). While also trying to recoup losses in South, Southeast, and East Asia, the U.S. forces stormed one Pacific island after another, gaining bases from which to cut off Japanese supplies. Island-hopping moved them steadily closer to Japan, enabling American pilots to bomb major cities and industrial sites. Like Hitler, the Japanese military ruled out surrender and used spirited if terrifying propaganda to stiffen public opinion. Unable to compete with U.S. output, the Japanese military increased the use of kamikaze tactics, with pilots deliberately crashing their planes into American ships. For their part the United States stepped up the bombing of major Japanese cities. The firebombing of Tokyo in March 1945 killed more than one hundred thousand civilians—an attack made all the more lethal by the introduction of napalm in 1944.

Meanwhile, an international team of scientists based in the United States succeeded in creating an atom bomb. Working under the code name Manhattan Engineer District—Manhattan Project, for short—the team used a half century's worth of findings by European scientists—many of them refugees from the Nazis—to accomplish its task. The bomb was successfully tested on July 16, 1945, in New Mexico, and after much debate the U.S. government decided that several million lives would actually be saved—given Japan's determination to fight to the death—by deploying it. On August 6, the United States dropped one atomic bomb on the city of Hiroshima. On August 9, it dropped another on the city of Nagasaki. Some two hundred thousand civilians in the two cities were killed, some of them dying from radiation and burns over the course of the next months. The Japanese government surrendered on August 14, 1945.

Like victory in Europe, victory in Asia did not bring a return to the prewar status quo. Even so, for several years Britain, France, and the Dutch mostly believed that things could be as they once were. Heavily in debt and in utter disorder, they briefly deluded themselves into believing that they were still masters of vast empires. The French reentered Vietnam in 1945 and began waging war against the nationalist government there. In Algeria, the French army massacred thousands of activists working for Algerian independence. The British thought they would return to their dominant position in the Middle East, Africa, and Asia as if nothing had happened. Churchill said that he had no qualms about breaking the wartime promises he had made to Indians—"a beastly people with a beastly religion," he had called them during the war—to implement the home rule granted before the conflict broke out.[23] But Prime Minister Clement Attlee, the Labour Party candidate who defeated Churchill in the July 26, 1945, elections, saw that holding India was at best wishful thinking. India, Egypt, and Australia had made so much money selling supplies to Britain during the war that they were able to buy out many British firms, thereby worsening the United Kingdom's already precarious financial well-being after the war. In populous Indonesia, Japanese occupation had destroyed the Dutch stronghold, and it was not to be reestablished. Expectations for a return to empire could not have been more mistaken, as the coming years would amply demonstrate.

The Emergence of the Superpowers

During its conduct of a war in two distant theaters, the United States became unquestionably—and surprisingly to many—the richest and most powerful country in the world. The United States increased its industrial output an incredible 15 percent annually between 1940 and 1944, a growth rate that improved the well-being of the vast majority of American workers. By 1947 the United States controlled almost two-thirds of the world's gold bullion and more than half of its commercial shipping, up from 17 percent only a decade earlier. Postwar spending on industrial goods, military research, and consumer items enhanced the global economic position of the United States still more. The European countries also expanded their technological capacity and production of sophisticated weaponry. But unlike them, the United States emerged from the war with its territory unscathed and its casualties small in comparison with the tens of millions killed elsewhere.

President Harry S. Truman, who succeeded President Roosevelt after his death in April 1945, was emblematic of the new global power. A plain-speaking and inexperienced leader on the world stage, he was less inclined to give Stalin the leeway that Roosevelt accorded him in response to the pressures of a difficult wartime alliance. By the time Truman took office, the war in Europe was winding down, but the war with Japan remained to be won. Everyone was confident, however, that Japan would be defeated. Although Truman shared that confidence, he was not in a conciliatory mood. He became even less so when Stalin entered the war against Japan, as agreed, two days after the atomic bomb was dropped on Hiroshima. The war boosted U.S. morale. Americans believed that they were fighting a "good war," and no one—least of all Truman—wanted to lose the peace as it was believed the peace had been lost to fascism after World War I. In contrast with Americans in 1918, after World War II Americans embraced their global leadership, believing that their second rescue of Europe in less than thirty years testified to American democratic values and national ingenuity and drive. Moreover, since 1933 the storehouse of U.S. talent and cosmopolitanism had swelled with the arrival of some twenty-five thousand scientists, artists, intellectuals, and professionals from Europe. Alongside the U.S. soldiers who had seen the world and the other refugees who had a vast experience of other places, these illustrious Europeans increased America's capacity for global leadership. The United States thus confidently hosted the first meeting of the United Nations and became its home in 1945.

The Soviets also emerged from the war with a well-justified sense of accomplishment. Withstanding horrendous losses, newly estimated at over 40 million dead, they had resisted the most massive onslaught ever launched against a modern nation, and people everywhere almost universally accorded them an important position in world affairs. Instead of the international isolation dealt Russia after World War I, Soviet leadership expected parity in decision making with the United States. More than that, productivity during the war had helped turn the country into the second greatest military power in the world. It was this formidable military strength that backed up Soviet claims to leadership and to reparations and territory as compensation for extensive losses. Unlike the United States, much of the Soviet Union was devastated. Powerful but psychologically fragile, well-armed militarily but worn physically and morally, the Soviet people entered a contest with the United States for which they were only partially prepared. The desperate situation in the Soviet Union, its prior history as an outlaw in world politics, and its demonstrated global might stood behind the Soviet leadership's demands for resources, land, and full recognition of its international stature.

Toward the Cold War

In the immediate postwar years, the United States and the Soviet Union engaged in a *cold war*—the term refers to their mutual animosity manifested not in open warfare but in an unprecedented buildup of deadly weaponry. A battle of ideology, the cold war also played out in the backing of "proxy wars" in Korea, Vietnam, and elsewhere, and these would directly affect the entire world for most of the rest of the twentieth century. The antagonists laid the groundwork for this contest during the difficult days of their military alliance.

Throughout the war, the leaders of these two powers along with Churchill of Great Britain had hammered out the disposition of territories, the principles for peacetime governance, and the future of Germany. With competing agendas but eager to continue to wage war successfully, leaders compromised on divisive issues and left loopholes in agreements to keep the alliance effective. In August 1941 Churchill and Roosevelt laid out important wartime and postwar aims in the Atlantic Charter, in which they said that they had no interest in territorial conquest for themselves and would seek to restore prewar territorial borders and governments chosen by the citizenry. The Atlantic Charter also asked for all nations to abandon the use of force internationally. Once agreed to by the USSR and other allies, it became a foundational document for the establishment of the United Nations. In November–December 1943, meeting in Teheran to discuss the opening of a western front, Roosevelt, Stalin, and Churchill tentatively agreed to divide Europe into two spheres: one in the east under the influence of the Soviet Union and another in the west controlled by an Anglo-American coalition. In 1944, Stalin and Churchill met in Moscow and over dinner informally carved up the Balkans. Britain would exercise power over Greece, the Soviet Union would control Romania and Bulgaria, and Yugoslavia would come under their joint influence. In February 1945, the Big Three met at Yalta. There Roosevelt pushed for the founding of the United Nations and supported future Soviet influence in Korea, Manchuria, Sakhalin, and the Kurile Islands. The postwar disposition of Germany and the postwar Polish government were discussed, but little was resolved. The last meeting of the Allied leaders took place at Potsdam,

◆ The Big Three at Potsdam

These agreeably smiling "Big Three" leaders—Winston Churchill, Harry S. Truman, and
Joseph Stalin—met at Potsdam in July 1945 in yet another wartime meeting to hammer out
a common Allied policy. Even though Clement Attlee replaced Churchill, fateful decisions
made there included the division of Germany into four zones of occupation and the
disarming of the nation. Another portion of the Potsdam protocol called for convincing "the
German people that they have suffered a total military defeat and that they cannot escape
responsibility for what they have brought upon themselves, since their own ruthless warfare
and the fanatical Nazi resistance have destroyed the German economy and made chaos and
suffering inevitable." *© Snark/Art Resource, New York.*

Germany, in July–August 1945 with President Truman representing the United States
and Churchill and Attlee representing Great Britain. At Potsdam the leaders agreed to
give the Soviets control of eastern Poland, to cede a large stretch of eastern Germany
to Poland in exchange for truncating Poland to the east, and to adopt a temporary
four-way occupation of Germany that would include France as one of the supervis-
ing powers. The military scramble for control of Europe in the last weeks of the
Potsdam meetings would spark east-west tensions after the war.

The push for territory turned mutual suspicion into outright antagonism.
Throughout the war, Stalin had felt that Churchill and Roosevelt were deliberately
letting the USSR bear the brunt of Hitler's onslaught on Europe as part of their
long-standing anti-Communist policy. Some Americans believed that dropping
the atomic bomb on Japan would not only bring surrender but serve as a warning
to Stalin not to try any more landgrabs. Stalin, however, seized the opportunity to

declare war on Japan and occupy more of Asia. Even though the western Allies had wanted this intervention earlier in the war, the timing of Soviet entry to occur *after* the detonation of the atom bomb made them suspicious. At war's end Stalin continued to see a world hostile to Soviet security, as many American aid programs to the Soviet people abruptly stopped despite their ongoing intense suffering. In the face of this hostility Stalin believed that the Soviet Union needed not a temporary military occupation of eastern Europe and Germany but a permanent buffer zone of European states loyal to the USSR as a safeguard against a revived Germany in particular and the anti-Soviet western states more generally. Across the Atlantic, Truman saw the initial occupation as heralding an era of permanent Communist expansion, especially since the Soviets were setting up friendly governments in the areas of eastern Europe they liberated. By 1946, members of the U.S. State Department were describing Stalin as the final "neurotic" Asian ruler prepared to continue the centuries-old Russian thirst for "world domination." Stalin similarly announced to his nation that "it was the Soviet army that won" World War II and warned the Anglo-American forces not to continue moving eastward. In March 1946, Churchill countered by warning the world of an "iron curtain" descending across Europe to cut off the east from the west. The cold war was beginning with the future of Europe initially in the balance.

CONCLUSION

World War II spelled the end of Europe's dominance in the world. Its economies were shattered, its population reduced, its colonies on the verge of independence, its peoples starving, and millions uprooted from their homes. Yet Europe's geopolitical importance remained intact because of its high level of technological accomplishment, its urbanized and educated workforce, and its complex institutions of government. The Soviet Union, which had borne far more destruction and loss of life than any other country, oddly enough emerged from the contest technologically strengthened though economically devastated. The large role Soviet forces played in the victory seemed to justify in the eyes of many any seizures of resources from the Axis, most notably the machinery and other equipment of Germany's high-tech industries. The Soviets also simply abducted engineers and other highly skilled workers to help the USSR to rebuild.

From the Soviet Union to Great Britain, civilians wanted a reprieve from the turmoil of war no matter what side they had supported. Exhausted, homeless, starving, and traumatized by the death and suffering around them, many could only hope that the future would be far better. They were not to have a full reprieve, however. The United States and Soviet Union began contesting the postwar disposition of territory and influence under the threat of nuclear arms. Violence continued in the postwar struggle for political control and resources. How Europe—and much of the world—could recover from this long nightmare remained an unanswerable question in 1945.

DOCUMENTS

The War against Civilians

I N THE EIGHTEENTH CENTURY THE WARS OF MONARCHS such as Frederick the Great of Prussia or Louis XV of France were seen as part of power politics and usually had limited goals. Consequently the suffering of ordinary people during wartime was fairly minimal unless they happened to be in the way of the armies, which often lived off the land and seized civilians' dwellings and other property. In the twentieth century and thereafter, warfare came to depend on industrial production and large-scale agriculture, and modern industrial and total wars were spiritualized into a holy struggle against evil—much like the Crusades almost a millennium earlier. Civilians became targets, not only because they produced the goods on which victory depended but also because they represented the evil nature of the enemy. World War II opened an era in which attacks on civilian areas became a staple of warfare. The death of enemy civilians was sometimes hidden behind the term *strategic bombing*, which implied that the targeting was so precise that bombs hit only industrial or political targets without harming civilians. Soldiers, of course, found the idea of strategic bombing ludicrous, for they themselves were often struck by "friendly" bombs gone astray.

Civilians had much to fear in World War II. One hundred thousand Japanese residents died in the firebombing of Tokyo in 1945, an attack that the United States directed specifically against nonmilitary citizens and their wooden, highly flammable homes. Because of persistent German bombing, only six thousand out of ninety-three thousand homes in Hull, England, were not damaged by the end of the war. During the Blitz, hundreds of thousands of Londoners slept in the subways for safety, and parents sent their children out of cities to volunteer families in the countryside. After 1943, German civilians moved often because of the increased Allied bombing of cities. Not only did death haunt civilians and danger cause family breakup, but the level of hard work and stress took its toll on the quality of life. Beyond the reach of the bombers of the time, the United States was the only major combatant power whose civilians were spared direct attacks.

During World War II, civilians learned to sense new dangers and experienced new levels of terror. Their skills changed as they struggled to survive in the face of food and other shortages. As bombs rained from the skies, old landmarks, neighborhoods, and people's homes disappeared, turning overnight into piles of rubble. Bombings caused fire, loss of electricity and water, and disruption of transportation. As the anonymous diarist of Document 6.1 shows, people who survived the Blitz faced nagging, ordinary problems caused by the nightly bombing, and their nerves were on edge from lack of sleep. Although German planes bombed Britain throughout the war, the most sustained campaign—the Battle of Britain—occurred in 1940 to prepare the way for a German invasion of the British Isles. The campaign failed, despite the massive damage and loss of life. Perhaps the one positive outcome of the Blitz was that it actually boosted people's will to survive and resist.

Letter writers and diarists across Europe and around the world described the desperate conditions of civilians. In the Soviet Union, civilians continued to be hunted down in purges, but in addition they faced death at the hands of German soldiers who wantonly killed civilians and captured soldiers alike. The diarist of Document 6.2 conveys the horrendous suffering of residents of Leningrad during the German siege, which lasted nearly nine hundred days. People lost a third to half of their body weight, as their daily food ration fell to somewhere between a quarter and a half pound of bread. When the ration did not materialize, Leningraders learned to eat grass, the bark of trees, pine needles, glue, and anything else they could think of. Winter temperatures fell to twenty degrees below zero. There was no wood or coal for heating, so people tore up cemeteries, taking crosses and unearthing caskets to use for fuel and chopping down every bush and tree. People who dropped dead on the streets often lay there for days, for no one could spare the energy to remove them. Both documents in this section ask us to think deeply about the human costs of war.

Document 6.1

ANONYMOUS
London Diary, 1941

A WEST LONDON OFFICE WORKER kept this diary as she and her family struggled to keep their lives going. She noted the fear and anxiety caused by the bombings and the practical daily problems it brought.

At 6 A.M. bombs dropped.

I awoke to hear a roar and thundering, to feel that horrible "got you" thud of a heavy bomb and the sound of half the world raining down on us. My mother and sister were both giving little screams; I put my arms round my sister and said "It's all right" several times. Mother got off her bed, crying "The house has been hit" as she ran to the stairs. "No it hasn't" I shouted, and then, suddenly felt sorry for her and said "Poor mother." "Get under the bed" said my sister. I didn't want to, because the thought of an iron bedstead falling on me didn't appeal. There was a flash and another came down, and our telephone suddenly started to ring. My sister again told us to get under the bed, so I got under and pulled at her to follow me, but she didn't move. She said afterwards that she *couldn't* move. . . .

SOURCE: Tom Harrisson, *Living through the Blitz* (New York: Schocken, 1989), 88–92.

Daylight had overtaken us and I felt a wreck, still having curlers under my turban. Mother was cooking breakfast and everyone had started to shovel away the mud, so I started on our front path. My sister came back and we had breakfast. Then began a hectic day. First we cleaned up outside, swilling down water, dumping debris into the road for the council to remove. Then we began to sweep away plaster inside. There was another big hole on the landing, a smaller one in my sister's bedroom. Then it began to rain, so I put on old clothes and went into the roof. This was very discouraging. There was a huge hole above the bathroom and quite 20 more small ones; one chimney was off and another had a nasty lean. Everywhere were dripping sounds. I put buckets, tubs, bowls under the worst. I rammed a piece of lino over the landing hole and old mats over the bathroom one. Descended to lunch hungry. . . .

We spent the evening trying to clean ourselves. Afterwards I did a little sewing, and mother knitted but my sister just lay on the bed. I had to do something, although I was so tired, because Jerry was dropping more bombs somewhere. Mother said she would sleep with Dad in the dining-room, so my sister and I tossed for her bed; but I lost! My sister bounced up and down on it and said "The only nice thing that's happened this evening." "To you!" I said gloomily and settled down on our usual mattress. We undressed as usual. When I closed my eyes I could see broken roofs, dust falling in on me, and then tiles would fall away and I would give a little jump. The tick of the clock became the drip of water, but soon after 12 I fell asleep from sheer exhaustion. . . .

I changed into my best frock—tried to do my hair and powder my face and mend stockings—my hands were rough and hard and stiff and just wouldn't do anything—everything fell under chairs or couldn't be found. We were all in a state. So we got tea, *toasted crumpets*. Our decorator came in for a cup, and he and mother started to discuss which of them had been in the district longer. He has been here 31 years—mother 32! We parted the best of friends—we

know for a fact that he skipped one of these upstarts who've only been here about 15 years to come to us! . . .

The council men called as they promised, and told mother they hadn't any slates. She asked them to go up and first aid it—they are *the first aid squad anyway*. They went up, swore at it, and then went away without touching it, or knocking at the door again. When last seen they were mending one of the easy roofs with two or three holes over the road. We have heard of two cases where they have actually removed the lino that owners had laboriously put over their holes, and taken away loose tiles, making the holes bigger. . . .

Had a meal of baked beans on toast, and afterwards we were feeling worn out, but had to start clearing away to make the beds. I made my brother help me with Dad's bed, while Mum and my sister made ours. Then we set Dad and my brother to wash up. Mum went into the front-room to make my brother's bed on the settee, and gave out a cry of horror. There was water dripping from the ceiling. She dashed upstairs and started rolling up the soaked carpets, my sister followed with cloths and basins, I bounded into the roof, seized the tarpaulin lent us by our neighbour, and hauled it through the trap door into the stricken bedroom. We spread it right under the patch, where the paper had stripped off and water was running out of a long crack in the plaster. I tied the strings on the edges to a bed-end, and window knobs, wash-stand, etc., so as to create a puddle; and we set dishes and a bread bin under the actual crack. Then we found there were two holes for tent-poles in the tarpaulin and a small slit, so we had to set bowls underneath the tarpaulin to push it up at those spots. There was a merry sound of dripping into the contrivance when we'd finished. Then we started to readjust the furniture—put them in dry spots, covered them over etc., and spread overcoats and an oilskin cape underneath another suspicious-looking patch.

It was well after midnight before we could drag ourselves into our beds. Slept the sleep of exhaustion.

Document 6.2

V. S. KOSTROVITSKAIA
Diary, January 1942 and April 1943

THIS DIARIST OF THE LENINGRAD SIEGE is Vera Sergeevna Kostrovitskaia, a ballerina who contracted tuberculosis and turned to teaching to earn her living. She notes several not uncommon experiences of famine in Leningrad in the winter and spring of 1942 as well as the behavior of Soviet officials of the ballet, notably Lidiia Semeonova Tager.

L[idiia] S[emeonova] T[ager] called me into her office and tried to persuade me to move to the school to live, but alone, without Mama. Of course I refused. This is her point of view: if a person has a dependent, then the latter has a responsibility to die, and if he doesn't die because you share your ration with him, then that is not only stupid, it is a *superfluous luxury*. The news that your mother *still* has not died she takes as tactlessness and sentimentality inappropriate to wartime conditions, almost as immorality. That an eighteen-year-old girl (a ballet dancer at the Kirov Theater, Tamara Bogdanova) left her dependent mother in an empty apartment for five days and never once brought her anything to eat (the mother died on the fifth day) did not incite L. S. T.'s indignation. She said that Bogdanova acted correctly, since in the first place, one must think about one's own life. For—a young life is needed by the government, but an old one is not.

FEBRUARY

People are worried and always discussing whether they will give us fifteen or twenty grams of herring, ten or twelve grams of sugar. Neither one nor the other will quiet our stomachs. The portions that the blockade has doomed us to are less than what is customarily given to a nursing infant as a "supplement."

[When the ballet school is ordered to help clean up the city in the spring of 1942, Tager threatens the students with the loss of their ration cards.]

"Hypocrites, sluggards, I'll leave everyone without their bread-ration cards." Rosy and chubby-cheeked, she grabs a shovel to give us an example of how to dig, how to throw, and then she stands and watches us for hours.

APRIL

And there, across from the entrance to the Philharmonic, by the square, there is a large lamppost.

With his back to the post, a man sits on the snow, tall, wrapped in rags, over his shoulders a knapsack. He is all huddled up against the post. Apparently he was on his way to the Finland Station, got tired, and sat down. For two weeks while I was going back and forth to the hospital, he "sat"

1. without his knapsack
2. without his rags
3. in his underwear
4. naked
5. a skeleton with ripped-out entrails

They took him away in May.

APRIL

Since in April it became necessary to portray the rebirth of the city at the hands of people half-dead, L. S. T. got the vain idea to give the first public concert on the premises of the Philharmonic through the efforts of our school, or more precisely its remains.

SOURCE: Cynthia Simmons and Nina Perlina, *Leningrad: Women's Diaries, Memoirs, and Documentary Prose* (Pittsburgh: University of Pittsburgh Press, 2002), 50–52.

Some of the girls had maintained relative good health, thanks to a fortunate situation at home, but everyone had scurvy. The most talented, Liusia Alekseeva, couldn't dance the "classics." Her legs, covered with the blue spots of scurvy, gave way and wouldn't obey.

I informed L. S. T. of the situation.

In answer there came a furious shout and threats to deny those who refused to dance their food-ration coupons for the following month. . . .

The concert took place. There was even the "dying swan" and other ballet nonsense. Petia, made by me to look like a living person, "danced" two numbers. The girls, in order to keep him going, brought him bread and a dish of kasha. On stage I led him by the arms as he "danced," I tried not to watch, and during the intervals off-stage, he drooped into my arms and vomited the kasha he had eaten.

There was no public audience at the concert, for there was none in the city. The first two rows were taken by the Council for the Arts [*Upravlenie po delam iskusstv*], representatives from Smolnyi and party organizations. With her hair dyed red and dressed up like a model, L. S. T. shone during the entr'acte, accepting greetings, unnaturally loudly recounting her love for the children and how all winter she had saved their lives.

Just imagine, throughout this terrible period this woman, an official and member of the party, appeared almost daily in expensive new dresses, shoes, and hats. In the course of one winter, four new fur coats and countless pieces of expensive jewelry. They had all been acquired in exchange for food—perhaps that puts Petia's death in a different light. After all, rather than four, wouldn't one fur coat have sufficed? Not twenty dresses, but at most, say, five, and so forth. And Petia, with his forelock and rosy face, would still be among us. Lidiia Semenovna Tager—the wife of the head of provisions for the entire Leningrad front.

Translated by Cynthia Simmons

QUESTIONS FOR ANALYSIS

1. What were these diarists' specific concerns?
2. Referring to these accounts, describe how the war changed public and private life.
3. What values were at play in the brutalization and suffering of ordinary men serving in the military, the annihilation faced by civilians in their homes, and the organized murder of people in the death camps?

Literature of the Holocaust

Survivors and cultural leaders—whether in memoirs, film, literature, poetry, or the visual arts—had to come to terms with experiences of repression, war, and genocide from the time Hitler and Mussolini first came to power. Many were impelled to write about what they witnessed, and firsthand accounts of the Holocaust remain some of the most horrific nonfiction of the human record. Those very few escapees from extermination camps provided some of the first accurate information about the Holocaust, and it was this information that motivated resistance movements and uprisings such as the one in the Warsaw ghetto in 1943. "No illusion greater than that our dear ones are alive," one summons to resistance in the Vilna ghetto went.[24] Accurate reports of mass shootings and eventually of the extermination camps that awaited people who had been told they were being "resettled in the East" swept through the ghettos like wildfire and ultimately coming to the attention of western officials. Document 6.3 is an account of Auschwitz written by two Slovakian Jews after their escape in 1944. When the war was over, their account was more than corroborated by other survivors.

Many novelists and poets also served as witnesses. Novelist Natalia Ginzberg described life under Mussolini's violent rule. Tadeusz Borowski produced the ironic *This Way to the Gas, Ladies and Gentlemen*. Italian author Primo Levi produced many notable works that took his experience of concentration camp life as their horrifying backdrop. The German Jewish poet Nelly Sachs (1891–1970) invoked the Holocaust both as universal loss and as individual suffering—a catastrophe that struck every aspect of existence (Document 6.4). In particular she questioned those who had looked the other way, ignoring suffering or choosing not to intervene.

Poetry does not provide a direct account or a totally realistic vision of an event, an individual, or a moment in time. For the Holocaust many prefer to read the actual experience of the death camps; they feel more comfortable with it, so familiar have the images of death and suffering become in our time. According to some critics, the Holocaust cannot be represented aesthetically and in fact marks the limits of artistic representation. Critics also say that a poetry of the Holocaust is impossible. Sachs's poetry thus raises interesting questions. The documents in this section give us an opportunity to compare two very different types of sources from the Holocaust.

Document 6.3

RUDOLF VRBA AND ALFRED WECZLER
Auschwitz Observed: Reports of Two Escaped Eyewitnesses, 1944

RUDOLF VRBA AND ALFRED WECZLER WERE SLOVAKIAN JEWS deported to Auschwitz in 1942. Because they served on various work crews, they had access to clothing and money, which they hid away to facilitate their escape on April 7, 1944. After leaving the camp, they returned to Slovakia, gave this account to Jewish leaders, and worked in the anti-Nazi resistance. Some say that the community leaders edited the report, but edited or not, its contents were corroborated at the time and subsequently by others. The report was passed along to the United States, where it was reissued as authoritative, eyewitness evidence and played its part in bringing about the trials for "crimes against humanity" at Nuremberg after World War II. Both men have been attacked by Holocaust deniers. Vrba—the more famous of the pair—went on to write many books, including his memoirs of Auschwitz, and to teach pharmacology at the University of British Columbia.

On April 13, 1942, our group of 1,000 men was loaded onto railroad cars at the assembly camp at Sered. The doors were sealed, so that nothing would reveal the direction of the journey. When they were opened after a long while, we realized that we had crossed the Slovak frontier and were in Zwardoń.° Until then the train had been guarded by Hlinka men,° but it was now taken over by SS guards. After a few cars had been uncoupled from our convoy, we continued on our way, arriving at night at Auschwitz, where we stopped at a siding. . . . Upon arrival, we were counted off in rows of five. There were 643 of us. After a walk of about twenty minutes with our heavy packs—we had left Slovakia well equipped—we reached the concentration camp of Auschwitz.

We were led at once into a huge barracks, where we had to deposit all our luggage on one side and on the other undress completely, leaving our clothes and valuables behind. Naked, we then proceeded to an adjoining barracks, where our heads and bodies were shaved and disinfected. At the exit, every man was given a number, beginning with 28,600. With this number in hand, we were then herded to a third barracks, where so-called registration took place. Here the numbers we received in the second barracks were tattooed on the left side of our chests. The extreme brutality with which this was done made many of us faint. The particulars of our identity were also recorded. Then we were led by hundreds into a cellar and later to a barracks, where we were issued striped prisoners' clothes and wooden clogs. This lasted until 10 A.M. In the afternoon our prisoners' outfits were taken away from us and replaced by the ragged and dirty remains of Russian uniforms. Thus equipped, we were marched off to Birkenau.

Auschwitz is a concentration camp for political prisoners under so-called "protective custody." At the time of my arrival, that is, April 1942, about 15,000 prisoners were in the camp, the majority

°Zwardoń: A village on the Polish side of the Polish-Czech frontier.
°Hlinka men: Members of the Hlinka Guard, the paramilitary arm of the Hlinka People's party, a right-wing Catholic nationalist party, the only legal party in Slovakia after March 1939. The Hlinka Guard collaborated with the SS.

SOURCE: Lucy Dawidowicz, ed., *A Holocaust Reader* (New York: Behrman House, 1976), 110–119.

Poles, Germans, and civilian Russians under protective custody. A small number of prisoners came under the categories of criminals and "work-shirkers."

Auschwitz camp headquarters also controls the labor camp of Birkenau as well as the farm-labor camp of Harmense. All the prisoners arrive first at Auschwitz, where they are provided with prisoners' registration numbers and then are kept there, or are sent either to Birkenau or, in very small numbers, to Harmense.

There are several factories on the grounds of the camp of Auschwitz: a war production plant of *Deutsche Ausrüstungswerke* (DAW), a factory belonging to the Krupp works, and one to the Siemens concern. Outside the camp's boundary is a tremendous plant covering several square kilometers named Buna.° The prisoners work in all the aforementioned factories.

The prisoners' actual living quarters, if such a term is at all appropriate, covers an area approximately 500 by 300 meters, surrounded by a double row of concrete posts about three meters high, interconnected, inside and out, by a dense netting of high-tension wires fixed into the posts by insulators. Between these two rows of posts, at intervals of 150 meters, there are five-meter-high watchtowers, equipped with machine guns and searchlights. The inner high-tension ring is encircled by an ordinary wire fence. Merely to touch this fence is to draw a stream of bullets from the watchtowers. This system is called the "small" or "inner ring of sentry posts." . . .

At a radius of some 2,000 meters, the whole camp is encircled by a second ring called the "big" or "outer ring of sentry posts," also with watchtowers every 150 meters. Between the inner- and outer-ring sentry posts are the factories and other

workshops. The towers of the inner ring are manned only at night when the high-tension current is switched into the double row of wires. During the day the garrison of the inner-ring sentry posts is withdrawn, and the men take up duty in the outer ring. Escape—and many attempts have been made—through these sentry posts is practically impossible. Getting through the inner-ring posts at night is completely impossible, and the towers of the outer ring are so close to one another that it is out of the question to pass unnoticed. The guards shoot without warning. The garrison of the outer ring is withdrawn at twilight, but only after all the prisoners have been ascertained to be within the inner ring. If the roll call uncovers a missing prisoner, sirens immediately sound the alarm.

The men in the outer ring remain in their towers on the lookout, the inner ring is manned, and hundreds of SS guards and bloodhounds begin a systematic search. The siren brings the whole surrounding countryside to a state of alarm, so that if by miracle the escaping man has succeeded in getting through the outer ring, he is almost certain to be caught by one of the numerous German police and SS patrols. The escapee is furthermore handicapped by his clean-shaven head, his striped prisoner's outfit or red patches sewn on his clothing, and the passiveness of the thoroughly intimidated population. The mere failure to give information on the whereabouts of a prisoner, not to speak of extending help, is punished by death. If the prisoner has not been caught sooner, the garrison of the outer-ring sentry posts remains on the watch for three days and nights, after which it is presumed that the fugitive succeeded in breaking through the double ring. The following night the outer guard is withdrawn. If the fugitive is caught alive, he is hanged in the presence of the whole camp. If he is found dead, his body—wherever it may have been located—is returned to camp (it is easily identifiable by the tattooed number) and seated at the entrance gate, a small notice clasped in his hands, reading: "Here I am." During our two years' imprisonment, many

---

° *Deutsche Ausrüstungswerke . . . Band:* (German Armament Works) was an SS enterprise founded in 1939. It was administered by the WVHA. Krupp and Siemens were among Germany's largest industrial manufacturers, with plants all over Europe. The Buna plant at Auschwitz, part of the vast network of I. G. Farben industrial enterprises, produced synthetic rubber.

attempts at escape were made, but except for two or three, all were brought back dead or alive. It is not known whether those two or three actually managed to get away. It can, however, be asserted that among the Jews who were deported from Slovakia to Auschwitz or Birkenau, we are the only two who were lucky enough to save ourselves.

As stated previously, we were transferred from Auschwitz to Birkenau on the day of our arrival. Actually there is no such district as Birkenau. Even the word Birkenau is new in that it has been adapted from the nearby Brzezinki. The existing camp center of Birkenau lies four kilometers from Auschwitz, though the outer borders of Birkenau and Auschwitz adjoin. . . .

When we arrived in Birkenau, we found only one huge kitchen there for 15,000 people and three stone buildings, two already completed and one under construction. The buildings were encircled by an ordinary barbed-wire fence. The prisoners were housed in these buildings and in others later constructed. . . . All are built according to a standard model. Each house is about 30 meters long and 8 to 10 meters wide, [divided into tiny cubicles] . . . too narrow for a man to lie stretched out and not high enough for him to sit upright. There is no question of having enough space to stand upright. Thus, some 400–500 people are accommodated in one house or "block." . . .

After three days I was ordered, together with 200 other Slovak Jews, to work in the German armament factories at Auschwitz, but we continued to be housed in Birkenau. We left early in the morning, returning at night, and worked in the carpentry shop as well as on road construction. Our food consisted of one liter of turnip soup at midday and 300 grams of bad bread in the evening. Working conditions were inconceivably hard, so that the majority of us, weakened by starvation and the inedible food, could not endure. The mortality was so high that our group of 200 had 30–35 dead every day. Many were simply beaten to death by the overseers—the *Kapos*—during work, without the slightest provocation. The gaps in our ranks caused by these deaths were

replaced daily by prisoners from Birkenau. Our return at night was extremely painful and dangerous, as we had to drag, over a distance of five kilometers, our tools, firewood, heavy cauldrons, and the bodies of those who had died or had been killed during the working day. With these heavy loads we had to maintain a brisk pace, and anyone incurring the displeasure of one of the Kapos was cruelly knocked down, if not beaten to death. Until the arrival of the second group of Slovak men some fourteen days later, our original number had dwindled to 150. At night we were counted, the bodies of the dead were piled up on flat, narrow-gauge cars or in a truck and brought to Brzezinki, where they were burned in a trench several meters deep and about fifteen meters long. . . .

Until the middle of May 1942, a total of four convoys of Jewish men from Slovakia arrived at Birkenau and all were given treatment similar to ours.

From the first two transports 120 men—90 Slovak and 30 French Jews—were chosen, including myself, and placed at the disposal of the administration of the camp of Auschwitz, which needed doctors, dentists, intellectuals, and clerks. . . . The remaining . . . persons were sent to work in the gravel pits where they all died within a short time.

Shortly thereafter a Krankenbau was set up. It was destined to become the much dreaded Block 7, where I was first chief attendant and later administrator. The "infirmary" chief was a Pole. This building actually was nothing but an assembly center of candidates for death. All prisoners incapable of working were sent there. There was no question of any medical attention or care. We had some 150 dead daily and their bodies were sent for cremation to Auschwitz.

At the same time, the so-called "selections" were introduced. Twice weekly, Mondays and Thursdays, the camp doctor indicated the number of prisoners who were to be gassed and then burned. Those selected were loaded onto trucks and brought to Brzezinki. Those still alive upon arrival were gassed in a big barracks erected near the trench used for burning the bodies. The weekly contingent of dead from Block 7 was about 2,000, 1,200 of whom died a "natural death" and about 800 by "selection." . . .

. . . At the end of February 1943, a new modern crematorium and gassing plant were inaugurated at Birkenau. The gassing and burning of the bodies in Birkenwald were discontinued, the whole job being taken over by the four specially built crematoria. The large ditch was filled in, the ground levelled, and the ashes used, as before, for fertilizer at the farm labor camp of Harmense, so that today it is almost impossible to find traces of the dreadful mass murder which took place.

At present four crematoria are in operation at Birkenau, two large ones, I and II, and two smaller ones, III and IV. Those of type I and II consist of three parts, i.e.: the furnace room, the large hall, and the gas chamber. A huge chimney rises from the furnace room around which are grouped nine furnaces, each having four openings. Each opening can take three normal corpses at once, after an hour and a half the bodies are completely burned. Thus, the daily capacity is about 2,000 bodies. A large "reception hall" adjoins, so as to give the impression of the antechamber of a bathing establishment. It holds 2,000 people and apparently there is a similar waiting room on the floor below. From there, a door and a few stairs down lead into the very long and narrow gas chamber. The walls of this chamber are also camouflaged with simulated entries to shower rooms in order to mislead the victims. The roof is fitted with three traps which can be hermetically closed from the outside. A track leads from the gas chamber to the furnace room.

The gassing takes place as follows: the unfortunate victims are brought into the reception hall where they are told to undress. To complete the fiction that they are going to bathe, each person receives a towel and a small piece of soap issued by two men in white coats. Then they are crowded into the gas chamber in such numbers that there is, of course, only standing room. To compress this crowd into the narrow space, shots are often fired to induce those already at the far end to huddle still closer together. When everybody is inside, the heavy doors are closed. Then there is a short pause, presumably to allow the room temperature to rise to a certain level, after which SS men with gas masks climb on the roof, open the traps, and shake down a preparation in powder form out of tin cans labelled "Zyklon—For use against vermin," manufactured by a Hamburg concern. It is presumed that this is a cyanide mixture of some sort which turns into gas at a certain temperature. After three minutes everyone in the chamber is dead. No one is known to have survived this ordeal, although it was not uncommon to discover signs of life after the primitive measures employed in Birkenwald. The chamber is then opened, aired, and the Sonderkommando carts the bodies on flat trucks to the furnace rooms where the burning takes place. Crematoria III and IV work on nearly the same principle, but their capacity is only half as large. Thus the total capacity of the four gassing and cremating plants at Birkenau amounts to about 6,000 daily.

On principle only Jews are gassed; Aryans very seldom, as they are usually given Sonderbehandlung by shooting. Before the crematoria were put into service, the shooting took place in Birkenwald and the bodies were burned in the long trench; later, however, executions took place in the large hall of one of the crematoria which has been provided with a special installation for this purpose.

Prominent guests from Berlin were present at the inauguration of the first crematorium in March 1943. The "program" consisted of the gassing and burning of 8,000 Cracow Jews. The guests, both officers and civilians, were extremely satisfied with the results and the special peephole fitted into the door of the gas chamber was in constant use. They were lavish in their praise of this newly erected installation. . . .

Document 6.4

NELLY SACHS

Already Embraced by the Arm of Heavenly Solace, 1945

NELLY SACHS (1891–1970) WAS A GERMAN JEWISH POET who like many other German Jews celebrated German culture for its aesthetic beauty and ethical thought. Sachs's parents, again like many other German Jews, were not religiously observant although they donated to their local synagogue. Swedish Nobel Prize–winning novelist Selma Lagerlöf and Viennese writer Stefan Zweig were among Sachs's early literary patrons. When Hitler began menacing Germany's Jews, Lagerlöf encouraged Sachs to leave the country. Escaping Germany with her mother in 1939, Sachs spent the war hiding in Sweden, where she learned Swedish and eked out a living doing translations. After the war she suffered many nervous breakdowns but continued to write poetry. Sachs presents haunting images of the Holocaust. The chimneys of extermination camp ovens, the hands of dying children, the blood of the Nazis' victims, the unending tears of survivors, prisoners, and their relatives are woven together in simple, pointed verse. Sachs received the Nobel Prize for Literature in 1966.

Already embraced by the arm of heavenly solace
The insane mother stands
With the tatters of her torn mind
With the charred tinders of her burnt mind
Burying her dead child,
Burying her lost light,
Twisting her hands into urns,
Filling them with the body of her child from the
     air,
Filling them with his eyes, his hair from the air,
And with his fluttering heart—

Then she kisses the air-born being
And dies!

                                        You onlookers

Whose eyes watched the killing.
As one feels a stare at one's back

You feel on your bodies
The glance of the dead.

How many dying eyes will look at you
When you pluck a violet from its hiding place?
How many hands be raised in supplication
In the twisted martyr-like branches
Of old oaks?
How much memory grows in the blood
Of the evening sun?

O the unsung cradlesongs
In the night cry of the turtledove—
Many a one might have plucked stars from the sky,
Now the old well must do it for them!

You onlookers,
You who raised no hand in murder,
But who did not shake the dust
From your longing,
You who halted there, where dust is changed
To light.

_____
SOURCE: Nelly Sachs, *Selected Poems Including the Verse Play
"Eli,"* trans. Michael Hamburger, Christopher Holme, Ruth
and Matthew Mead, and Michael Roloff (London: Jonathan
Cape, 1968), 15, 19.

QUESTIONS FOR ANALYSIS

1. What differences do you see in these two accounts of the Holocaust?

2. What main points do you take away from each account?

3. Does one kind of source, a factual account by witnesses on a poetic rendering, more effectively convey the horror of the Holocaust than the other? Why?

4. Is it possible that "realistic" accounts are as crafted and artful as poetry and less true to life than they appear?

World War II and Human Rights

Throughout the twentieth century, citizens of a globalized society pushed for peace and respect for human rights. In 1899 the arms race had prompted a meeting in The Hague to address the need for peaceful coexistence. Feminists at the beginning of the century claimed that society was so militaristic because men ran it. In 1915, during World War I, pacifists in the women's movement met at The Hague and then visited heads of state to ask them to stop the war. This effort led to the creation of the Women's International League for Peace and Freedom. Other pacifist groups flourished in the 1920s and 1930s. They were joined in their efforts by other activists interested in human rights, such as the League for the Rights of Man in France—a group founded during the Dreyfus Affair in the 1890s. Efforts to promote human rights gained momentum as a result of the Second World War.

Franklin Roosevelt, president of the United States during most of World War II, coined the term *United Nations* for the alliance of twenty-six countries that on January 1, 1942, declared their intention to fight the Axis. The collapse of the League of Nations after the outbreak of war created a vacuum. In 1944, delegates from the Big Three plus China met at Dumbarton Oaks in Washington, D.C., to draw up plans for a revived League—the United Nations. As a result of this wartime conference, in June 1945, even before the war was over, representatives from fifty countries signed the UN charter, setting the conditions for peaceful international cooperation.

Changing conditions reshaped the original plan for a simple alliance of nations to fight World War II. The issue of human rights emerged in the crucible of war and mass murder. With the opening of the death camps in 1944 and with the shocking news of atrocities in the Pacific, the mandate of the United Nations became more fully developed. It became clear that the Axis powers had disregarded basic standards of humanity, slaughtering millions because of their twisted ideologies and racial hatreds. Genocide and the mind-numbing deaths of tens of millions inspired calls for a bill of rights for humanity as part of the UN mission. U.S. first lady Eleanor Roosevelt headed the commission that drew up the Universal Declaration of Human Rights, approved by more than fifty member countries of the United Nations in 1948. This Declaration has been called a Magna Carta for the human race, countering the horrors of the Holocaust with the noble words of the U.S. Bill of Rights and other fundamental documents ensuring human justice. Although emerging from the suffering of wartime, the UN Declaration of Human Rights and the organization that produced it would become a global political force into the twenty-first century.

Document 6.5

UNITED NATIONS
Universal Declaration of Human Rights, 1948

PREAMBLE

Whereas recognition of the inherent dignity and of the equal and inalienable rights of all members of the human family is the foundation of freedom, justice and peace in the world,

Whereas disregard and contempt for human rights have resulted in barbarous acts which have outraged the conscience of mankind, and the advent of a world in which human beings shall enjoy freedom of speech and belief and freedom from fear and want has been proclaimed as the highest aspiration of the common people,

Whereas it is essential, if man is not to be compelled to have recourse, as a last resort, to rebellion against tyranny and oppression, that human rights should be protected by the rule of law,

Whereas it is essential to promote the development of friendly relations between nations,

Whereas the peoples of the United Nations have in the Charter reaffirmed their faith in fundamental human rights, in the dignity and worth of the human person and in the equal rights of men and women and have determined to promote social progress and better standards of life in larger freedom,

Whereas Member States have pledged themselves to achieve, in co-operation with the United Nations, the promotion of universal respect for and observance of human rights and fundamental freedoms,

Whereas a common understanding of these rights and freedoms is of the greatest importance for the full realization of this pledge.

Now, therefore, The General Assembly *proclaims this universal declaration of human rights* as

a common standard of achievement for all peoples and all nations, to the end that every individual and every organ of society, keeping this Declaration constantly in mind, shall strive by teaching and education to promote respect for these rights and freedoms and by progressive measures, national and international, to secure their universal and effective recognition and observance, both among the peoples of Member States themselves and among the peoples of territories under their jurisdiction.

Article 1

All human beings are born free and equal in dignity and rights. They are endowed with reason and conscience and should act towards one another in a spirit of brotherhood.

Article 2

Everyone is entitled to all the rights and freedoms set forth in this Declaration, without distinction of any kind, such as race, colour, sex, language, religion, political or other opinion, national or social origin, property, birth or other status.

Furthermore, no distinction shall be made on the basis of the political, jurisdictional or international status of the country or territory to which a person belongs, whether it be independent, trust, non-self-governing or under any other limitation of sovereignty.

Article 3

Everyone has the right to life, liberty and security of person.

Article 4

No one shall be held in slavery or servitude; slavery and the slave trade shall be prohibited in all their forms.

SOURCE: Ian Brownlie, ed., *Basic Documents of Human Rights* (Oxford: Clarendon Press, 1981), 21–27.

Article 5

No one shall be subjected to torture or to cruel, inhuman or degrading treatment or punishment.

Article 6

Everyone has the right to recognition everywhere as a person before the law.

Article 7

All are equal before the law and are entitled without any discrimination to equal protection of the law. All are entitled to equal protection against any discrimination in violation of this Declaration and against any incitement to such discrimination.

Article 8

Everyone has the right to an effective remedy by the competent national tribunals for acts violating the fundamental rights granted him by the constitution or by law.

Article 9

No one shall be subjected to arbitrary arrest, detention or exile.

Article 10

Everyone is entitled in full equality to a fair and public hearing by an independent and impartial tribunal, in the determination of his rights and obligations and of any criminal charge against him.

Article 11

1. Everyone charged with a penal offence has the right to be presumed innocent until proved guilty according to law in a public trial at which he has had all the guarantees necessary for his defence.
2. No one shall be held guilty of any penal offence on account of any act or omission which did not constitute a penal offence, under national or international law, at the time when it was committed. Nor shall a heavier penalty be imposed than the one that was applicable at the time the penal offence was committed.

Article 12

No one shall be subjected to arbitrary interference with his privacy, family, home or correspondence, nor to attacks upon his honour and reputation. Everyone has the right to the protection of the law against such interference or attacks.

Article 13

1. Everyone has the right to freedom of movement and residence within the borders of each state.
2. Everyone has the right to leave any country, including his own, and to return to his country.

Article 14

1. Everyone has the right to seek and to enjoy in other countries asylum from persecution.
2. This right may not be invoked in the case of prosecutions genuinely arising from non-political crimes or from acts contrary to the purposes and principles of the United Nations.

Article 15

1. Everyone has the right to a nationality.
2. No one shall be arbitrarily deprived of his nationality nor denied the right to change his nationality.

Article 16

1. Men and women of full age, without any limitation due to race, nationality or religion, have the right to marry and to found a family. They are entitled to equal rights as to marriage, during marriage and at its dissolution.
2. Marriage shall be entered into only with the free and full consent of the intending spouses.
3. The family is the natural and fundamental group unit of society and is entitled to protection by society and the State.

Article 17

1. Everyone has the right to own property alone as well as in association with others.
2. No one shall be arbitrarily deprived of his property.

Article 18
Everyone has the right to freedom of thought, conscience and religion; this right includes freedom to change his religion or belief, and freedom, either alone or in community with others and in public or private, to manifest his religion or belief in teaching, practice, worship and observance.

Article 19
Everyone has the right to freedom of opinion and expression; this right includes freedom to hold opinions without interference and to seek, receive and impart information and ideas through any media and regardless of frontiers.

Article 20
1. Everyone has the right to freedom of peaceful assembly and association.
2. No one may be compelled to belong to an association.

Article 21
1. Everyone has the right to take part in the government of his country, directly or through freely chosen representatives.
2. Everyone has the right of equal access to public service in his country.
3. The will of the people shall be the basis of the authority of government; this will shall be expressed in periodic and genuine elections which shall be by universal and equal suffrage and shall be held by secret vote or by equivalent free voting procedures.

Article 22
Everyone, as a member of society, has the right to social security and is entitled to realization, through national effort and international co-operation and in accordance with the organization and resources of each State, of the economic, social and cultural rights indispensable for his dignity and the free development of his personality.

Article 23
1. Everyone has the right to work, to free choice of employment, to just and favourable conditions of work and to protection against unemployment.

2. Everyone, without any discrimination, has the right to equal pay for equal work.
3. Everyone who works has the right to just and favourable remuneration ensuring for himself and his family an existence worthy of human dignity, and supplemented, if necessary, by other means of social protection.
4. Everyone has the right to form and to join trade unions for the protection of his interests.

Article 24
Everyone has the right to rest and leisure, including reasonable limitation of working hours and periodic holidays with pay.

Article 25
1. Everyone has the right to a standard of living adequate for the health and well-being of himself and of his family, including food, clothing, housing and medical care and necessary social services, and the right to security in the event of unemployment, sickness, disability, widowhood, old age or other lack of livelihood in circumstances beyond his control.
2. Motherhood and childhood are entitled to special care and assistance. All children, whether born in or out of wedlock, shall enjoy the same social protection.

Article 26
1. Everyone has the right to education. Education shall be free, at least in the elementary and fundamental stages. Elementary education shall be compulsory. Technical and professional education shall be made generally available and higher education shall be equally accessible to all on the basis of merit.
2. Education shall be directed to the full development of the human personality and to the strengthening of respect for human rights and fundamental freedoms. It shall promote understanding, tolerance and friendship among all nations, racial or religious groups, and shall further the activities of the United Nations for the maintenance of peace.

3. Parents have a prior right to choose the kind of education that shall be given to their children.

Article 27

1. Everyone has the right freely to participate in the cultural life of the community, to enjoy the arts and to share in scientific advancement and its benefits.
2. Everyone has the right to the protection of the moral and material interests resulting from any scientific, literary or artistic production of which he is the author.

Article 28

Everyone is entitled to a social and international order in which the rights and freedoms set forth in this Declaration can be fully realized.

Article 29

1. Everyone has duties to the community in which alone the free and full development of his personality is possible.

2. In the exercise of his rights and freedoms, everyone shall be subject only to such limitations as are determined by law solely for the purpose of securing due recognition and respect for the rights and freedoms of others and of meeting the just requirements of morality, public order and the general welfare in a democratic society.
3. These rights and freedoms may in no case be exercised contrary to the purposes and principles of the United Nations.

Article 30

Nothing in this Declaration may be interpreted as implying for any State, group or person any right to engage in any activity or to perform any act aimed at the destruction of any of the rights and freedoms set forth herein.

QUESTIONS FOR ANALYSIS

1. What specific policies of the interwar governments does the Universal Declaration of Human Rights aim to correct?

2. Do some of these rights seem more basic or fundamental than others? If so, which ones would you choose and why? How would you make the argument that equal weight needs to be given to each of these rights?

3. Which provisions address the racial thinking demonstrated in the Picture Essay?

World War II
Propaganda and
Modern Racism

LIKE WORLD WAR I, THE SECOND WORLD WAR WAS IDEOLOGICAL, necessitating absolute commitment from all citizens and unwavering obedience to the commands of the state—whether totalitarian or democratic. Such obedience was not to be had by force, because those most adept at using guns and other weapons to exert that force were at the battlefront, not on the home front. Even though people were conscripted into armies, propaganda was the most effective tool for bringing about participation in war, as it had been in World War I, and it thus saturated people's everyday lives. Posters, films, articles in magazines and newspapers, and radio programming all served to motivate people to kill or to perform services such as factory work to create weapons and supplies. In the twentieth century, the most persuasive and often-used theme of propaganda was the racial and ethnic inferiority of the enemy, and propagandists on all sides used race and ethnicity to distinguish the good side from the bad. Images of an evil, inferior enemy had begun to infiltrate people's sensibility in the Great War, and they were meant to inspire people to support the war at home and to fight harder on the battlefront in this war too. In World War I nations on each side considered their opponents atrocious and cruel but did not see them as fully racialized enemies. That situation would change with Hitler.

Hitler chose enemies specifically because of what he considered to be their racial qualities. These enemies included Jews and Slavs, whose features

◆ Figure 6.1 **German Propaganda Poster**
Imperial War Museum.

373

◆ Figure 6.2 **German Poster for the Female Wing of the Hitler Youth**
Bundersarchiv, Koblenz.

were caricatured in German propaganda (Figure 6.1). "Jewish Plot against Europe," the poster blares in huge letters framing Churchill and Stalin shaking hands. The caricature of the menacing Jew looms over the continent. What racial as well as cultural stereotypes do you think were intended to strike viewers of this poster?

In contrast, German racial propaganda glamorized the "Aryan" individual, as in Figure 6.2, a poster promoting the young women's branch of the Hitler Youth organization. People were taught what race was, not only with negative stereotypes but with visual celebrations of an ideal Aryan, Japanese, Caucasian American, and the like. What characteristics of this young woman were meant to appeal to Germans, and what ideas about Germany were viewers of this poster supposed to take away from it? Looking at Figure 6.2, we can imagine that this healthy young woman will become the mother of many Aryan offspring. What features let us draw this conclusion?

From the German point of view, the purpose of World War II was to benefit the superior Aryan race and to conquer, subjugate, and eliminate racially inferior groups. In the fight for democracy, the United States relied heavily on African American troops. Many of these individuals were not allowed to vote in the U.S. South, faced lynching and abuse as civilians, and were strictly segregated in the army. According to a much-repeated story, a black U.S. soldier requested that his tombstone read: "Here lies a black man killed fighting a yellow man for the protection of the white man."[25] The Axis picked up on U.S. racism (Figure 6.3) and throughout the war used American stereotypes of blacks in numerous cartoons and posters. Joseph Goebbels, Hitler's minister of propaganda, saw World War II as a war not only against Jews but against a "negrified" enemy of low culture. In the original caption to this image, one soldier says to the other "We're fighting for culture, Jimmy." "But what is culture?" the other asks stupidly. Once the United States began bombing German cities directly later in the war, Goebbels stepped up the pace of this kind of propaganda to bolster German civilians' resolve. What aspect of Figure 6.3 might make Germans fight harder?

When World War II broke out, the Axis powers were not the only combatants to racialize their enemies in propaganda. The Allies did so too. Soviet posters often depicted Hitler as a lower form of life (Figure 6.4). "The enemy will be mercilessly defeated and annihilated!" exclaims the Russian text as an allied soldier spears a rodent-like, grovelling Hitler with his bayonet. The Russians were eager to dehumanize the German enemy, because the people living in many of the territories they hoped to free from the Nazis were as worried about Communists as they were about Nazis. The Allies portrayed Germans and Japanese as occupants of a low rung on the evolutionary ladder. The Japanese were sometimes represented as beetles and apes. The Germans and Italians appeared as reptiles, apes, and rodents in cartoons, postcards, and posters. Figure 6.5, a U.S. propaganda poster, presents Japan's military leader Hideki Tojo as an apelike monster with blood dripping from his mouth and claws. Can you think of images in today's culture that are similarly effective in degrading and demonizing enemies?

For the Allies, racial representation was a potentially dangerous strategy, given the diversity of Allied armies. Britain, France, the United States, and the Soviet

◆ Figure 6.3 **German Propaganda Cartoon**

Union used soldiers of many races and ethnicities and thus crafted propaganda posters celebrating the contributions of many races, even as they directed racist propaganda against the Axis powers. How does the poster in Figure 6.6 emphasize the unity of the races among British fighting forces? What characteristics distinguish these guardians of the empire and of freedom? How effective do you think such posters were in cementing cross-racial alliances?

Solidarity notwithstanding, there were still other pitfalls for the Allies, as they responded to the global nature of the war and to the complex ethnic composition of global forces. Figure 6.7 is an illustration that appeared in the Australian army's monthly journal *Western Command* and was intended to help soldiers to distinguish the Chinese (friend) from the Japanese (foe). The Australian effort looks scientific in its presentation of racial differences. The figures are plotted on a grid, instead of being portrayed as obvious caricatures. Subtle differences are shown. Such work advanced racial thinking. The British and Americans believed that the Japanese were, in the words of one British army officer, "subhuman," and that defeating them would be "simple," even as the Japanese were scooping up islands in the Pacific and overrunning British possessions.

The viciousness of wartime propaganda would move into the cold war and shape politics to be more accusatory and shrill thereafter. However, some activists—especially soldiers from the colonies and African American troops—recognized the many contradictions in racial propaganda. The awareness of these contradictions, especially whites' reliance on people of color to secure a victory, would promote decolonization movements around the world and civil rights activism in the United States in the years to come.

◆ Figure 6.4 **Russian Propaganda Poster**

◆ Figure 6.5 **Allied Anti-Japanese Cartoon**

QUESTIONS FOR ANALYSIS

1. What visual features of "race" are most emphasized in the seven images in this Picture Essay?
2. Even though all combatants used racial images in their propaganda, do you sense any differences between Axis and Allied images?
3. Why were race and ethnicity such powerful tools for politicians at midcentury?

◆ Figure 6.6 **Allied Propaganda Poster**
National Archives, United Kingdom.

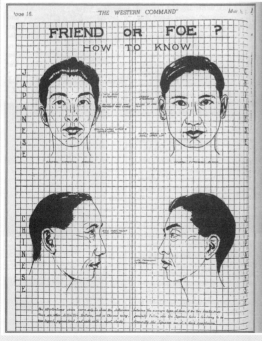

◆ Figure 6.7 **"Friend or Foe? How to Know,"
Australian diagram**

NOTES

1. Heda Margolius Kovály, *Under a Cruel Star: A Life in Prague, 1941–1968* (New York: Holmes and Meier, 1997), 15.

2. Ibid., 16.

3. Randolph Churchill and Martin Gilbert, eds., *The Churchill War Papers*, vol.2 (New York: W.W. Norton, 1993), 22.

4. Quoted in Alan Bullock, *Hitler: A Study in Tyranny* (New York: Harper and Row, 1971), 380.

5. Quoted in Gerhard L. Weinberg, *A World at Arms: A Global History of World War II* (Cambridge: Cambridge University Press, 1994), 266.

6. Matsuoka Yosuke, quoted in Herbert P. Bix, *Hirohito and the Making of Modern Japan* (New York: HarperCollins, 2000), 374.

7. Melitta Maschmann, quoted in Michael Burleigh, *The Third Reich: A New History* (New York: Hill and Wang, 2000), 442.

8. Hans Frank, quoted ibid., 587.

9. Quoted in Lucy S. Dawidowicz, ed., *A Holocaust Reader* (New York: Behrman House, 1976), 33.

10. Olga Lengyel, *Five Chimneys: The Story of Auschwitz* (Chicago: Ziff-Davis, 1947), 31–34.

11. Kovály, *Under a Cruel Star*, 16.

12. Quoted in Alexander Werth, *Russia at War, 1941–1945* (New York: Carroll and Graf, 2000 [1964]), 324.

13. Quoted in David Bankier, *The Germans and the Final Solution: Public Opinion under Nazism* (Oxford: Oxford University Press, 1992), 104, 107, 133.

14. Quoted in Basil Davidson, *Africa in Modern History: The Search for a New Society* (New York: Viking Penguin, 1978), 203.

15. Quoted in Omer Bartov, *Hitler's Army: Soldiers, Nazis, and War in the Third Reich* (New York: Oxford University Press, 1991), 18.

16. Quoted in Mabel Berezin, *Making the Fascist Self: The Political Culture of Interwar Italy* (Ithaca: Cornell University Press, 1997), 224, 226, 227.

17. Bartov, *Hitler's Army*, 24.

18. Giovanna Zangrandi, quoted in Jane Slaughter, *Women and the Italian Resistance, 1943–1945* (Denver: Arden Press, 1997), 1.

19. Carla Capponi, interviewed in Shelley Saywell, *Women in War: From World War II to El Salvador* (New York: Penguin, 1986), 82.

20. Quoted in Burleigh, *The Third Reich*, 691.

21. Quoted in Martin Gilbert, *The Day the War Ended: VE-Day 1945, in Europe and around the World* (New York: HarperCollins, 1995), 58.

22. Quoted ibid., 53.

23. Leo Amery, quoted in Gurcharan Das, *India Unbound: A Personal Account of a Social and Economic Revolution from Independence to the Global Information Age* (New Delhi: Viking, 2000), 6.

24. "Summons to Resistance in the Vilna Ghetto," quoted in Lucy Dawidowicz, ed., *A Holocaust Reader* (New York: Behrman House, 1976), 335.

25. Quoted in John W. Dower, *War without Mercy: Race and Power in the Pacific War* (New York: Pantheon, 1986), 176.

SUGGESTED REFERENCES

General Works
Dear, I. C. B., ed. *The Oxford Companion to the Second World War.* 1995.
Keegan, John. *The Second World War.* 1989.
Weinberg, Gerhard. *A World at Arms: A Global History of World War II.* 2005.

Rapid Victories There are many accounts of Germany's rapid takeover of several European states. A multivolume history of Germany's military activities from the Research Institute for Military History in Germany presents the most detailed information on wartime plans, strategy, capacities, and actual battles.

Beevor, Antony. *Stalingrad: The Fateful Siege, 1942–1943.* 1998.
Burrin, Philippe. *France under the Germans: Collaboration and Compromise.* 1996.
Edmonds, Robin. *The Big Three: Churchill, Roosevelt, and Stalin in Peace and War.* 1991.
Engel, Barbara Alpern, and Anastasia Posadskaya-Vanderbeck, eds. *A Revolution of Their Own: Voices of Women in Soviet History.* 1998.
Gaulle, Charles de. *The Complete War Memoirs.* 1964.
Jong, Louis de. *The Netherlands and Nazi Germany.* 1990.
Maier, Klaus A., et al. *Germany and the Second World War.* 1990.
Murphy, David. *What Stalin Knew: The Enigma of Barbarossa.* 2005.
Overy, Richard. *The Battle of Britain: The Myth and the Reality.* 2000.

A War Against Civilians In a vast literature historians have charted the war's innumerable and global horrors; the Holocaust, industrial killing, and the nature of racial thinking have drawn particular attention. In *Ordinary Men,* Christopher Browning provides an in-depth look at the average German who perpetrated the murders and at the few Germans who refused to participate.

Bankier, David. *The Germans and the Final Solution: Public Opinion under Nazism.* 1992.
Browning, Christopher R. *Ordinary Men: Reserve Police Battalion 101 and the Final Solution in Poland.* 1992.
———. *The Origins of the Final Solution: The Evolution of Nazi Jewish Policy, September 1939–March 1942.* 2004.
Chickering, Roger, et al., eds. *A World at Total War: Global Conflict and the Politics of Destruction, 1937–1945.* 2005.
Dawidowicz, Lucy S., ed. *A Holocaust Reader.* 1976, 2004.
Funck, Marcus, and Roger Chickering, eds. *Endangered Cities: Military Power and Urban Societies in the Era of the World Wars.* 2004.

James, Harold. *The Deutsche Bank and the Nazi Economic War against the Jews: The Expropriation of Jewish-Owned Property*. 2001.

Kovály, Heda Margolius. *Under a Cruel Star: A Life in Prague, 1941–1968*. 1986.

Levi, Primo. *Survival in Auschwitz: The Nazi Assault on Humanity*. 1959.

Slezkine, Yuri. *The Jewish Century*. 2004.

Militarizing Nation and Empire   The works listed here show life on the home front and investigate the ways in which governments mobilized civilians, even when — as in the USSR — there was incredible suffering, including starvation.

Barber, John, and Mark Harrison. *The Soviet Home Front: A Social and Economic History of the USSR in World War II*. 1991.

Berkhoff, Karel C. *Harvest of Despair: Life and Death in Ukraine under Nazi Rule*. 2004.

Glantz, David M. *The Battle for Leningrad, 1941–1944*. 2002.

Hoffman, Peter. *The German Resistance to Hitler, 1933–1945*. 1996.

Miner, Steven Merritt. *Stalin's Holy War: Religion, Nationalism, and Alliance Politics, 1941–1945*. 2003.

Mommsen, Hans. *Alternatives to Hitler: German Resistance under the Third Reich*. 2003.

Rose, Sonya O. *Which People's War? National Identity and Citizenship, 1939–1945*. 2003.

Slaughter, Jane. *Women and the Italian Resistance, 1943–1945*. 1997.

Stoltzfus, Nathan. *Resistance of the Heart: Intermarriage and the Rosenstrasse Protest in Nazi Germany*. 1996.

Vincent, Isabel. *Hitler's Silent Partners: Swiss Banks, Nazi Gold, and the Pursuit of Justice*. 1997.

Welch, David. *Third Reich: Politics and Propaganda*. 1993.

The World War Ends and the Cold War Begins   Historians have charted every aspect of the military victory of the Allies as it unfolded around the world. They have intensely debated the development of the cold war within the "hot war" and in so doing have particularly looked at the way the war ended.

Beevor, Antony. *The Fall of Berlin 1945*. 2002.

Dower, John W. *War without Mercy: Race and Power in the Pacific War*. 1986.

Gardner, Lloyd C. *Spheres of Influence: The Great Powers Partition Europe, from Munich to Yalta*. 1993.

Gilbert, Martin. *The Day the War Ended: VE-Day 1945, in Europe and around the World*. 1995.

Glantz, David M., and Jonathan House. *When Titans Clashed: How the Red Army Stopped Hitler*. 1995.

Grunden, Walter E. *Secret Weapons and World War II: Japan in the Shadow of Big Science*. 2005.

Ishay, Micheline R. *The History of Human Rights: From Ancient Times to the Globalization Era*. 2004.

Overy, Richard. *Russia's War: Blood upon the Snow*. 1997.

Rhodes, Richard. *The Making of the Atomic Bomb*. 1986.

Vassiltchikov, Marie. *Berlin Diaries, 1940–1945*. 1985.

Selected Web Sites

The following is a comprehensive site covering World War II and other historical topics: <**historylearningsite.co.uk/WORLD%20WAR%20TWO.htm**>. Fordham University also has a fine site on World War II: <**fordham.edu/halsall/mod/ modsbook45.html**>. On the Holocaust, go to the U.S. Holocaust Memorial Museum's Web site: <**ushmm.org**>. There are Web sites devoted to the resistance movements in various European countries. For example, the site maintained by Polish resisters contains extensive bibliography and links to other sites on specific acts of resistance such as the Warsaw uprising of 1944: <**polishresistance-ak .org/Main%20Page.htm**>. The U.S. National Park Service maintains a Web site on the war in the Pacific: <**nps.gov/wapa/**>. It covers the military activities of all combatant countries, including the many allies of the United States that committed hundreds of thousands of troops. The Avalon Project of Yale Law School posts many of the key documents of World War II on its Web site, including agreements reached at Yalta and other meetings of the Big Three: <**yale.edu/lawweb/ avalon/wwii/wwii.htm**>.

7

Devastated Europe in an Age of Cold War

1945–1963

O N OCTOBER 16, 1947, A CONVOY OF TRUCKS ENTERED
Warsaw carrying the bodies of around one hundred
American GIs belatedly retrieved from the battlefields of World War II. The next day Stanislaw Mikolajczyk,
respected head of the Polish Peasant Party, entered the U.S.
embassy in Warsaw and asked to be smuggled out of
Poland. The Americans' first thought was to hide him in one
of the coffins intended for the GIs so that he could escape
certain arrest and possible execution at the hands of the increasingly powerful Communists in the Polish government.
While briefly head of the Polish government-in-exile during
the war, Mikolajczyk had clearly stated his principles.
"There is and will be no place in Poland for any kind of totalitarian government in any shape or form," he said in a
1943 radio address. When the war ended in 1945, his
Peasant Party was the most popular political force in the
country and thus a prime target for Soviet leaders increasingly determined to build a buffer of loyal satellite states in
eastern Europe. Polish Communists were gradually putting
the political opposition out of commission, arresting opponents and holding trials reminiscent of the Stalinist purges
of the 1930s. As attacks on his party and his leadership intensified during 1947, Mikolajczyk saw his capture as imminent, and on October 21, after a harrowing truck ride

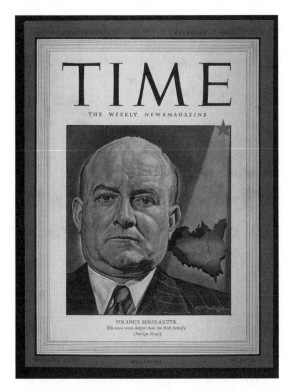

POLAND'S MIKOLAJCZYK
His roots went deeper than the Red Army's.
(Foreign News)

◆ **Stanislaw Mikolajczyk on the Cover of *Time* Magazine**

Stanislaw Mikolajczyk, head of the Polish Peasant Party, tried to ensure a democratic future for his country in the immediate postwar period. But Communists in both Poland and the USSR had other ideas, aiming for a state with allegiance to the Soviet Union, and Mikolajczyk stood in their way. Facing certain arrest, he left Poland aboard a British ship in October 1947. Mikolajczyk became a much-lauded figure in the United States and remained a vocal opponent of communism. He helped create networks of peasants throughout the Soviet bloc as the building blocks of resistance. *Time Life Pictures/ Getty Images.*

during which he was hidden behind baggage and other cargo, he boarded a British ship and sailed to freedom. Poland soon became a Communist state and a linchpin of Soviet domination in eastern Europe.

Mikolajczyk escaped a region that had been devastated by invasions from both east and west and whose civilians had suffered profoundly in World War II. In the midst of death and destruction, leaders like Mikolajczyk and others across eastern and central Europe had worked to keep government structures and resistance groups intact enough to revive their individual nations the minute peace arrived. They undertook this task against all odds. After World War II, Europe was crushed, utterly prostrate, and little able to exercise leadership of any kind. Victorious armies of the Grand Alliance occupied almost the entire continent. Not only were countries economically and physically destroyed, they were often morally bankrupt as well. In a period of oppression and death, the struggle to survive was of higher priority for most people than concern for the greater public good—a concern that those like Mikolajczyk toiled to preserve. People who suffered the insults of the initial defeat, collaboration, and deprivation early in the 1940s wanted revenge; those who were defeated in 1945 felt persecuted by the victors. Cruelty and technological murder had stalked Europe for years, and there seemed to be no basis on which to reestablish social order.

The difference between this postwar period and that following World War I was the collapse of European domination. By 1945 World War II alone had caused the deaths of as many as 100 million people worldwide and uprooted tens of millions more. Europe was a vast highway along which the uprooted millions traveled to find safety and sustenance. But at war's end, Europeans were not necessarily more peaceful, though despite their exhaustion and brutalization many helped one another survive. In striking cases, some were actually more hateful toward one another, the result perhaps not only of wartime propaganda but of postwar uncertainty. Most had hated Jews, Poles, Soviets, Germans, the British, and many others during the war, and tragic violence continued in city and countryside alike as the war ended and the cold war began.

The poisonous atmosphere nurtured the seeds of mutual distrust sown by the two superpowers that came to dominate in Europe's place. This new, bipolar global order emerged slowly because of deteriorating conditions and the great confusion after 1945. The results were increasingly apparent, nonetheless. As the United States and the Soviet Union began to turn their immense power, swollen by increases in wartime productivity, against one another, Mikolajczyk and other leaders with ideas of their own for Europe's rejuvenation and restoration became unwitting victims of the cold war. Not only hate-filled rhetoric but the intensified production of nuclear and other weapons was the legacy the Soviet Union and the United States visited on the rest of the world in the forty-four years of cold war. As communications technology improved, cold war culture flooded people's daily lives through radio, books, newspapers, and eventually television. Stanislaw Mikolajczyk was one of the earliest and most famous victims of a hard and uncertain peacetime that saw the world recover from its wartime trauma but also lurch from one crisis to another.

COLD WAR AND THE NEW WORLD POLITICS

World War II effectively closed the era of Europe's global dominance. From Britain to the Soviet Union, cities lay in ruins, factories and rails were heaps of rubble, and farms had lost their livestock, machinery, and workers. The European population had declined in absolute numbers, but the survivors in Europe were starving. In contrast, the United States, whose territory was nearly untouched by the war, was a healthy economic giant. The Soviet Union had suffered immense destruction— 32,000 factories, 70,000 villages, 1,700 towns, and 40,000 miles of railroad tracks obliterated, and 25 million people homeless. Even so, the USSR had become a formidable military power. The United States and the USSR drew the entire world into the diplomatic battle of nerves known as the cold war. Having occupied Europe as part of the victorious alliance against Nazism and fascism, the two superpowers in a series of moves, countermoves, and improvisations made Germany the pivotal point for dividing Europe into two competing blocs. By the late 1940s, the USSR had imposed Communist rule throughout most of eastern Europe, at the cost of thousands of lives, including the life of Heda Kovály's husband Rudolph Margolius, a fervent believer that communism would bring about a better future (see Chapter 6). In the 1950s the USSR quashed a series of rebellions against its dominance. Western Europeans found themselves partially constricted by the very U.S. economic power that was helping them to rebuild. The trade-off for U.S. aid was the maintenance of U.S. air bases and nuclear weapon sites across western Europe to block the Soviets. Thus Europe's prostrate peoples became unwitting participants in the bipolar superpower contest.

Europe in Ruins

Large stretches of continental Europe and the British Isles in 1945 featured mass graveyards of buildings, transport, and human beings. Bombing had destroyed over half a million houses in France alone, and in Germany the toll was 3 million. In Hungary half the factories had been leveled along with four-fifths of railroad transport. A Polish printer, viewing Wroclaw in 1945, described "Endless ruins, the stink of burning, countless huge flies, the clouded faces of the occasionally encountered Germans, and most important: the emptiness of the desolate streets."[1] Within the devastated physical landscape, the human stock of workers and contributors to society had declined too. Despite continuing advances made during the war in combating disease and infection, the population of Europe had decreased. In 1940, the Soviet population was approximately 193 million; in 1946, 170 million. Inflation was rampant for what goods there were: in France prices rose 600 percent between 1944 and 1948. The result was a barter system for many goods and services, with cigarettes serving as the most common unit of exchange. The biggest problem of all was food.

Peace brought such starvation that the war seemed not to have ended. "Genuine starvation only really began for us in '45," one German woman remembered. "When you see women standing in long lines in front of stores, their faces were all gray, almost black—that's how bad they looked, almost starved to death."[2] Although the average person needs 2,000 calories per day for minimum health, Austrians received only 800 per day after the war. In the Ruhr, the British newsmagazine *The Economist* reported in January 1946, "very few new-born babies are expected to live this winter."[3] In western Europe, Denmark was the only nation that had restored its agricultural output to prewar levels; some four years after the war, the rest of the region was still producing only 91 percent. Needing currency and allies, the Soviet Union sent grain to France and to Bulgaria, Poland, and other eastern European countries even though its own citizens lacked food. In the winter of 1946–47 at least two million people died of starvation in the USSR, while another hundred million suffered severe malnutrition. The government upped its extraction of grain and produce from collective farmers, with the implication that somehow people on the land would find a way to survive. It cut rations for factory and other workers. People poured out their protests. "Our children are living like animals," one Soviet mother wrote the government. "From undernourishment Zhenia has begun to swell up, especially her face, and she is very weak." Thousands of letters arrived: "We have absolutely nothing, we eat only acorns, and we can scarcely drag our feet. We will die from hunger this year," one city dweller predicted.[4] As late as 1947, infant mortality in France and Germany was higher than it had been during the Great Depression.

Governments resorted to rationing to distribute food, but the lack of adequate supply fed social discontent. In France and elsewhere across Europe, production rebounded after the war, but wages did not keep up with the rising prices for food. By 1947, commentators announced a general crisis in Europe as strikes erupted in several countries, slowing the pace of recovery. Although the rebuilding of infrastructure for communications and transport proceeded, housing was generally given low priority despite the destruction caused by wartime bombing and by earlier neglect during the Great Depression. The massive imports of machinery and other goods for rebuilding from the United States adversely affected each European government's balance of payments, which was further worsened by the falloff in European trade with the rest of the world. Citizens expecting rapid recovery and rewards from the state that might have justified their wartime sacrifices were bitterly disappointed. The combination of a rising tide of protest and economic threats to the world financial order posed a problem not only to the superpowers but to the would-be leaders of every European state.

Adding to the chaos were the tens of millions of refugees and migrants, people uprooted, expelled, homeless, or looking for food and work. Millions of defeated veterans and officials made their way home not knowing whether they would arrive safely and what sort of welcome they would receive. Many refugees and migrants were German civilians fleeing the advance of the Russian army and the wrath of the newly liberated peoples whom they had subjugated. They were joined

▶ Map 7.1 **The Postwar Movement of Peoples and Borders**
Postwar Europe was the scene of one of the most massive migrations in human history. Millions of troops and civilians were on the move. Many soldiers were repatriated to their countries; victims of the Axis powers tried to find their homes; civilians—fearing the wrath of Soviet troops or violence within their hometowns—fled westward or even out of Europe altogether. The primary source of humanitarian aid for these migrants was the United States; Europe and much of the rest of the world were so devastated they had nothing to spare.

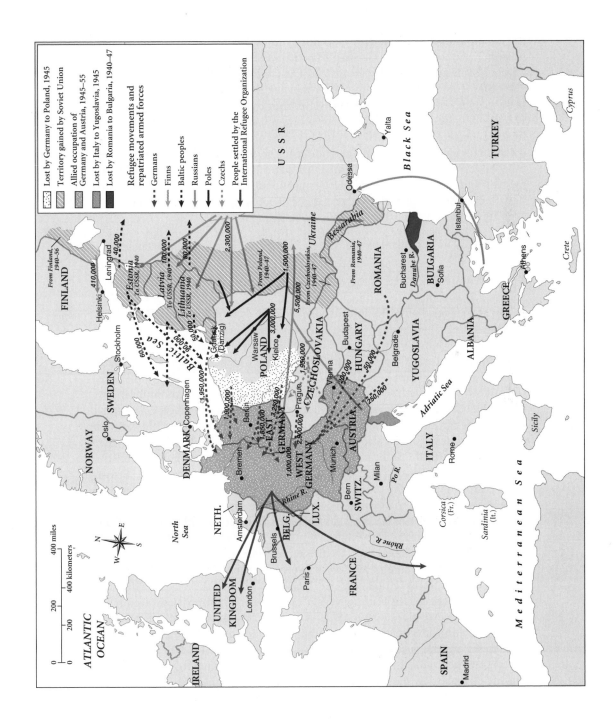

Legend:
- Lost by Germany to Poland, 1945
- Territory gained by Soviet Union
- Allied occupation of Germany and Austria, 1945–55
- Lost by Italy to Yugoslavia, 1945
- Lost by Romania to Bulgaria, 1940–47

Refugee movements and repatriated armed forces
- Germans
- Finns
- Baltic peoples
- Russians
- Poles
- Czechs
- People settled by the International Refugee Organization

ATLANTIC OCEAN

400 miles
400 kilometers
0   200   400

N E W S

North Sea

IRELAND

NORWAY Oslo

SWEDEN Stockholm

Oslo

FINLAND Helsinki Leningrad

From Finland, 1940–56
410,000
40,000

Estonia To USSR, 1940 100,000
Latvia To USSR, 1940 200,000
Lithuania To USSR, 1940 60,000
60,000
36,000
60,000

Baltic Sea

DENMARK Copenhagen
1,950,000

Gdańsk (Danzig)

Warsaw
Kielce 3,000,000
1,500,000
From Poland, 1940–47
2,300,000

POLAND

5,500,000

Ukraine

Bessarabia
From Romania, 1940–47

U S S R

Odessa

Yalta

Black Sea

Istanbul

TURKEY

Cyprus

Crete

Athens

GREECE

Sofia

BULGARIA Bucharest Danube R.
From Romania, 1940–47

ROMANIA

Budapest
HUNGARY 200,000 50,000

Belgrade

YUGOSLAVIA

ALBANIA

Adriatic Sea

Vienna
CZECHOSLOVAKIA Prague 1,950,000
250,000

1,850,000
3,250,000
EAST GERMANY Berlin
900,000
1,000,000

Bremen

WEST GERMANY 2,300,000

Munich

AUSTRIA
1,950,000

Bern
SWITZ.

Milan Po R.

ITALY Rome

Corsica (Fr.)

Sardinia (It.)

Sicily

Mediterranean Sea

Rhine R.

LUX.

BELG. Brussels

NETH. Amsterdam

UNITED KINGDOM London

FRANCE Paris

Rhône R.

SPAIN Madrid

by collaborators with the enemy who hoped to escape punishment. Some thirty million Europeans, many of German ethnicity, were forcibly expelled from Poland, Czechoslovakia, and Hungary (Map 7.1). The Germans had uprooted many Poles and other eastern Europeans to make room for the "master race," and these expellees, along with survivors from the slave labor camps, sought out their original villages and cities, where they were never sure of being welcomed. Hearing of the forced departure of Germans, people flocked to abandoned cities, seizing apartments and supplies and hoping to find jobs. The turmoil intensified as violence over food, housing, and land accompanied a strongly felt desire for revenge. The reestablishment of national and international political order took place against this dismal, even desperate backdrop, and it is estimated that some 1.5 million additional Europeans died in this vast population shift.

The Cold War

No grand peace conference of the victors ended the conflict with Germany, leaving a written record of contest and compromise for historians to analyze what went wrong as happened after the Peace of Paris. There is no disagreement, however, that something went terribly wrong. Some historians point to the U.S. record of antagonism toward the Soviet Union after the Bolshevik Revolution. Others emphasize Stalin's aggressive policies, notably his rapid occupation of the Baltic states and eastern Poland when World War II broke out in 1939. According to the latter view, the United States was a long-standing ideological enemy of communism and feared that Communist influence might expand. Adding to the legacy of mutual mistrust, the agreements that held the Grand Alliance together during the war were never easily reached. Stalin always believed that Churchill and Roosevelt were deliberately letting the USSR bear the brunt of Hitler's onslaught in Europe. His suspicion was justified in the case of Churchill, who hoped to protect the British Empire first and to let the Soviet competitor for influence in central Asia use up some of its strength in the fight against Hitler. Some Americans hoped that dropping the atomic bomb on Japan would frighten the Soviets—and it did, but to opposite effect. Believing the USSR to be threatened by the bomb, Stalin did not back off but rather tried to strengthen the Soviet position by taking more territory to create a buffer against several centuries of Western aggression. He also felt himself in need of a buffer zone of European states linked to the USSR as a safeguard against the Americans, especially given Truman's policies immediately cutting off desperately needed aid to stop the starvation and repair Soviet devastation. Although Stalin's advisers debated the exact intentions of the United States, Stalin came to see a ruthless Western imperialism striking the USSR when it was down and menacing it with the atomic bomb to boot (see Document 7.1). Across the Atlantic, Truman saw the increasingly apparent Soviet grip on eastern Europe as heralding an era in which Stalin like Hitler would seek ever more territory.

In 1945 Communist parties lacked widespread support in eastern and central Europe. Mikolajczyk's Peasant Party and other parties represented local interests and did not seem aligned with the brutal Soviet army. The Communists' initial role in reestablishing governments was as players in a shared effort to revive the major countries of the region. Coalition or popular front-type governments that included liberals, socialists, Communists, and peasant party leaders at first predominated in Hungary, Poland, and Czechoslovakia. But impatient with power sharing, Communists in Poland fixed election results in 1946 and 1947 to create the illusion of approval for communism, though in fact during these years the Communists played second fiddle to the Peasant Party's large constituency of rural workers and peasant landowners and appealing programs for Poland's future. In some cases, peasants took heart that the Communists would redistribute the estates of the largest landowners, but there was also support for a variety of parties and constant resistance to Communist inroads. In Wroclaw, Polish workers protested as Communist leaders forcibly removed Catholic icons and symbols from factories. In a largely peasant country there was simply not a sufficiently urbanized workforce to have prepared the ground for communism; so the Communists pegged Mikolajczyk as the opposition, ultimately forcing him to flee, and then took over the government with backing from the Soviet army.

Between 1945 and 1947, the USSR moved to repress democratic governments elsewhere in eastern and central Europe and install Communist regimes despite resistance. Stalin imposed Communist rule almost immediately in Bulgaria and Romania, which had allied themselves with Hitler. In Romania he cited citizen violence in 1945 as an excuse to oust all non-Communists from the civil service and cabinet. When the Allies protested, a single member of the Peasant Party and another from the Liberal Party were allowed to join eighteen Communists in the government. Party membership in Romania soared from a couple thousand in 1945 to more than 800,000 a year later. People viewed these changes as part of the postwar purge of fascism and the beginning of reform. In Czechoslovakia and Hungary, by contrast, the Communists initially allowed elections that resulted in support for several parties. As the U.S. bloc developed a program of its own, the Soviets and local Communists took increasingly tough countermoves to dominate eastern Europe: the combination of these moves and countermoves propelled the superpowers into the cold war.

Truman Doctrine and Marshall Plan

The United States attempted to influence the hearts and minds of Europeans against the Soviets but took no steps to halt the undermining of democracy in eastern Europe. No effective aid was offered to opponents of communism there, although Americans did help rescue individual leaders such as Mikolajczyk. Instead, the United States blocked the influence of Communists in the region that it considered its own sphere of influence—western Europe, where many citizens held the Communists in real esteem for having led the attack against Hitler. According to one Vienna-born British soldier, the Soviet Union was "a land of heroes,"[5] and Communist parties gained support in postwar French and Italian elections. Starving, ordinary western Europeans hoped that the confiscation and nationalization of fascist and other property would alleviate their misery, and the United

States worried that a communist spirit was infecting its sphere of influence. U.S. concern about the popularity of communism mounted in 1946–1947 when the bankrupt British government could no longer prop up the repressive monarchical regime it had installed in Greece against Communist-led resistance. The Truman administration in Washington feared that all of Europe was on the verge of "going Communist." In addition, western Europe needed to import vast quantities of food, fuel, machinery, and other industrial goods in order to survive and rebuild its shattered industries and transportation networks. But western Europe had nothing to export, and the resulting imbalance threatened the entire economic exchange system. This situation prevented the United States from reverting to isolationism.

In March 1947 President Truman announced the policy that quickly became known as the Truman Doctrine—the willingness of the United States to use economic and military aid to counter political crises in western Europe brought about by support for Communists. The president requested $400 million in military assistance for Greece and Turkey, where the Communists were challenging the government. Fearing that Americans would balk at backing the Greek dictatorship, U.S. congressmen said they would agree to the program only if Truman would "scare the hell out of the country," as one put it. Truman thus promoted the aid program as necessary to fortify the world against a global tide of Soviet conquest. In the fall of 1948, the United States supplied the Greek government with 10,000 transport vehicles, nearly 100,000 rifles, and 140 planes. Stalin, who had agreed to British domination of Greece during the war, did not intervene, although Communist Yugoslavia provided the country with crucial military aid. The show of American support convinced the local Communists and pro-democracy forces to back off. In 1949 the Greek rebels declared a cease-fire.

The United States also devised the Marshall Plan—a program of massive economic aid to western Europe—to counter the impending economic collapse and to offset both the appeal of communism and a rebirth of fascism, which, it was predicted, would accompany economic stress. "The seeds of totalitarian regimes are nurtured by misery and want," Truman had claimed in his justification for aid to Greece.[6] At a Harvard University commencement in 1947, Secretary of State George Marshall announced the plan, citing the deterioration of economic conditions during and after the war as posing a threat to political stability. Congress approved the Marshall Plan in 1948, and by the early 1950s, the United States had sent more than $12 billion in food, equipment, and services to Europe.

U.S. directives for the Marshall Plan stated that it was aimed not "against any country or doctrine but against hunger, poverty, desperation, and chaos."[7] Those horrendous conditions were threatening to overwhelm the restoration of Europeans to civilized life and, implicitly, to prevent their participation in U.S.-dominated international trade. Stalin saw the Marshall Plan as a U.S. political ploy to reduce Soviet appeal, for the USSR lacked resources to offer comparable economic aid, even to its own client countries in eastern Europe. To prevent those states from responding positively to the Marshall Plan, the Soviet Union suppressed the remaining coalition governments and assumed political control in central and eastern Europe. In Poland, where the government found the possibility of

◆ **Marshall Plan Parade in Greece, 1949**
The Marshall Plan blanketed western Europe with much-needed supplies such as basic foodstuffs and material to rebuild industries. In Greece the situation was a little different because the British-imposed monarchy was fighting against popular Communist forces. So Marshall Plan aid to Greece consisted mostly of weaponry and other military equipment until the fighting ended in 1949. At that point goods like wheat—carried in this truck—began arriving to relieve civilian suffering. This parade in December 1949 marks the millionth ton of Marshall Plan aid to Greece. *Library of Congress.*

receiving Marshall Plan aid attractive, the Communists edged out Mikolajczyk in 1947, creating a "people's government"—by which they meant a Communist-controlled state. In Hungary, the prime minister and head of the popular Small-Holders Party was forced out while on a trip to Switzerland in 1947. Czechoslovakia, which by eastern European standards had prospered under a coalition led by Communists, welcomed the Marshall Plan as the beginning of East-West rapprochement. This illusion ended, however, during a purge of non-Communist officials that began in the autumn of 1947. In June 1948, the moderate president, Edouard Beneš, resigned and was replaced by a Communist figurehead. The populace remained passive.

Thus, by 1949, the Soviet Union had successfully created a buffer of satellite states in eastern Europe directed by "people's governments." The United States, in contrast, had tied governments to it through whopping infusions of Marshall Plan cash—"a matter of national self-interest" Secretary of State Dean Acheson called the program. Stalin capped his own victory by organizing the Cominform, a centralized, global association of Communist parties under Moscow's direction. Enthusiastic members of these parties were integral to spreading the cold war to the people of the world.

Only in Yugoslavia did Stalin fail. During World War II, the Communist leader Josip Broz, known as Marshal Tito (1892–1980), had led a powerful coalition of anti-Nazi Yugoslav partisans, perhaps the most successful resistance to the Axis in all of Europe. A Croatian, Tito had fought Nazi sympathizers of all stripes, including Croatians themselves, drawing on vital Allied supplies to mount a successful Communist revolution at the war's end. He crushed nationalist ethnic political groups, and having liberated Yugoslavia without occupation by the Soviet army, Tito was strong enough to resist Stalinization. He sensed that satellites were to serve as servants to Soviet needs: "No matter how much each of us loves the land of Socialism, the USSR, he can in no case love his country less. . . . We study and take as an example the Soviet system but we are developing socialism in our country in somewhat different forms."[8] When Tito's independent brand of socialism became apparent, a furious Stalin ejected Yugoslavia from the Cominform, leaving Tito to forge a different, more prosperous socialist state.

The Battle for Germany

In the escalating postwar struggle, Germany became the focal point of superpower differences, with Berlin an unfortunate symbol of victory or defeat for each side. The Yalta agreements of 1945 provided for Germany's division into four zones of occupation (Map 7.2). The United States, the Soviet Union, Britain, and France each occupied a zone and was determined to control its zone.

The Allies disagreed on fundamental matters regarding Germany's future in the postwar world. Many Americans believed that there was something inherently wrong with the German character, and there was heated debate over Germany's fate. Some U.S. policy makers wanted the country turned into an agricultural backwater, while others proposed even more dire punishment. After the war, the U.S. position softened, even though the occupying forces tried to alter German cultural attitudes by controlling and censoring the press and other media, including film.

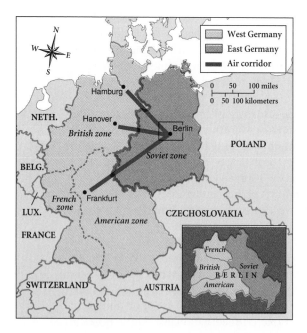

◆ **Map 7.2 Divided Germany and the Berlin Airlift**

Berlin, the once-vibrant cultural and political capital of Germany, was deep inside the Soviet zone of occupation. In 1948, when the western Allies — Britain, France, and the United States — agreed to merge their sectors and create a west German state, the USSR cut off their access to the western part of Berlin. In response, the western Allies organized an airlift of food, coal, and other supplies from Hamburg, Hanover, and Frankfurt, ultimately defeating the blockade and forcing the USSR to end it. Berlin remained divided, a focal point of cold war tensions, until 1989.

Stalin had a different outlook, based on the Communist belief that Nazism was simply an extreme form of capitalism. He looked forward to the confiscation and redistribution of the vast estates and other concentrations of German wealth under Soviet occupation. Thus in the first months after the war, the situation in Germany was as confused as it was elsewhere. Intensifying the chaos was widespread fear of resurgent Nazism. The Allies, however, disagreed about how to prevent the rebirth of Nazism as a menace. They foresaw a potential uprising if the Nazis seemed to be treated too harshly or too leniently.

Another schism arose over goals for the powerful, if temporarily weakened, German economy. The Americans aimed for a revival of German economic strength, intending German output to benefit both the occupying powers and the Germans themselves. The agricultural eastern part of Germany would feed the nation, while the industrial western part would produce manufactured goods to help rebuild the devastated Soviet Union and Germany's own industrial capacity. The Soviets had other ideas. Stalin wanted to see the immediate transfer of any remaining German machine tools and industrial goods to his own battered country. Because the Grand Alliance had agreed to Soviet claims to postwar German manufacturing, the Soviets immediately set to work to transfer machinery, vehicles, and other equipment to the Soviet Union. They transported skilled workers, engineers, and scientists from their sphere of occupation to the USSR to work as virtual slave laborers. The Soviets also manipulated the currency in their zone and were able to buy German goods at unfairly low prices.

The currency situation was one factor that persuaded Britain, France, and the United States to merge their zones in 1948 and establish the separate state of West Germany. The three allies stabilized the German currency by calling in the old marks and issuing new ones, and with this economic foundation laid, German representatives in 1949 drafted the "Basic Law," a constitution creating the Federal Republic of Germany (also known as West Germany). Within the month the Soviets had created a separate East Germany. Instead of curtailing German power as wartime agreements had specified, the three powers used Marshall Plan aid to build up West Germany as a buffer zone against Soviet ambition. To achieve this buffer and solidify the new West German government, the United States enlisted many former Nazi officials as spies and rechanneled into the cold war the hatred of Bolshevism that had been a hallmark of Nazi belief. The West Germans enthusiastically participated in this rehabilitation, coming to see their defeated armies, which had killed tens of millions of Soviet citizens, Jews, and Slavs, as "freedom fighters" against communism. The West German refugee population, whose exodus the Soviet army had overseen, was especially vocal in its support for waging cold war against communism.

Stalin struck back at the Marshall Plan on June 24, 1948. Soviet troops blockaded the western half of Germany's capital, Berlin, which like Germany as a whole had been divided into four occupation zones. Located more than a hundred miles inside the Soviet zone, Berlin was far removed from the West German border (see Map 7.2). The Soviets declared that they now controlled all of Berlin, and they refused to allow cars, trucks, and trains to travel through the Soviet zone of Germany to reach the city. Stalin expected the Western bloc to capitulate to the new situation, as it had done in Hungary, Romania, and elsewhere in eastern Europe.

Instead, the United States responded immediately, flying in 2.3 million tons of provisions to the cutoff city. During the winter of 1948–49 the Berlin airlift— "Operation Vittles," the pilots called it—even funneled coal to the city to warm isolated Berliners. It was an unprecedented effort, given the immense quantities of fuel and food needed to provision the population and the limited number of transport planes. Unloading was designed to take twenty minutes, and pilots left the plane engines running to achieve the rapid turnaround necessary to ensure the needed number of flights each day. Reports of people's suffering, of pilots' valiant deeds, and of Soviet heartlessness transformed the cold war in the popular imagination into a moral crusade (see the Picture Essay). By the time the Soviets ended the blockade on May 12, 1949, divided Berlin had become a symbol of the cold war split. The Soviet Union and the United States drew a line in the sand at Berlin.

◆ **Map 7.3 The Division of Europe in the 1950s**
Nearly all of Europe was drawn into the superpowers' cold war. Two military alliances, NATO and the Warsaw Pact, sealed the division. Both sides engaged in military exercises based on the idea that if a war for superpower domination broke out, it would occur in central Europe. Military spending increased dramatically in the 1950s as Europe became one vast base for both U.S. and Soviet armed personnel and weaponry.

Meanwhile, in April 1949, to counter further threats, the Western-bloc nations had formed the North Atlantic Treaty Organization (NATO). NATO provided a unified military force for the member countries: Britain, France, Belgium, the Netherlands, Luxembourg, Italy, Denmark, Portugal, Iceland, Norway, the United States, and Canada. The membership of the United States and Canada marked the serious involvement of North America in western Europe. It also was a historic outgrowth of a centuries-old North Atlantic community and constituted a formalized and massive regional alliance on which both sides in the cold war were coming to depend. The alliance seemed all the more imperative when the Soviet Union exploded its first atomic bomb at the end of 1949. In 1954, the United States brought West Germany into NATO. In 1955, the Soviet Union responded by starting an alliance of its own client states called the Warsaw Pact (Map 7.3).

BRINGING ORDER TO POSTWAR EUROPE

The chaos after the Second World War differed from the chaos after World War I. Real shortages and physical destruction were more pervasive, and continental Europe was occupied by the victorious armies, not by freelance soldiers like those who had refused to demobilize after World War I. There were more refugees—many millions more—and a greater sense of destabilization and insecurity as people struggled to find shelter and to piece together the means for survival. Local networks built on neighborhood cooperation temporarily replaced central governments, which were generally in disarray. Foraging, procuring abandoned supplies of military food, and finding partners with whom to share housing and goods helped people survive the first few postwar years. In many places people lived under draconian rules enforced by the occupying armies. In the Soviet Union under Stalin, people found to their great surprise that postwar conditions would be even harsher than those before and during the war.

Restoring Government

The presence of occupying armies complicated social and political life, for they formed a competing layer of political authority. Members of governments-in-exile, such as the Free French headed by Charles de Gaulle, returned in force to reconstitute state institutions, but they found themselves confronting not only the armies but entrenched bureaucracies, some of whose members had been Nazis or collaborators. These bureaucracies of experienced officials were highly skilled in administering complex industrial and service-oriented economies, for the war had ratcheted up the numbers of government workers and increased the amount of responsibility bureaucrats exercised. Because essentially *everyone* had worked for the fascists, it would have been difficult entirely to eliminate such a skilled pool of labor. Moreover, in peacetime these bureaucrats were essential to running the country because they were the only people with any remote idea of what to do.

Most Europeans had real grievances against the fascists, except in Germany and Italy, where citizens increasingly came to see themselves as enduring unfair discrimination. The brutality of invasion and occupation were among the burning memories of the war, and these were compounded by the discovery of the death camps' emaciated survivors and the remains of the millions killed in the camps. Anger exploded into revenge as the release of long pent-up rage gave way to swift vigilante justice. Angry mobs punished collaborators and fascist sympathizers for their complicity in the occupation and war crimes, sometimes executing them on the spot. They shaved the heads of French women suspected of willingly associating with the Germans, parading them partially undressed and even naked through local streets. Of some twenty thousand people estimated to have been punished for collaboration by head-shaving, 98 percent were women, 57 percent supposedly for sexual relations. In the face of widespread collaboration by both sexes, the selecting out of women for this kind of punishment papered over men's own lack of heroism but fostered the "remasculinization" of politics after a period in which women had gained so much authority running families and heading households in men's absence. To some, vigilantism was justice; to others, still more barbarism: "I have seen people who seem quite inoffensive turn into beasts, ready to kill," wrote one French observer of postwar mob justice. "I am horrified."[9]

Crowds of men descended on village and town halls to obtain certification that they had worked in the resistance. The celebration of resistance heroes—not a few of them self-proclaimed—influenced the rebirth of politics across Europe. Participation in the resistance, whether invented or real, became the baseline for a political career in postwar Europe.

The victors and their designated officials in national governments undertook a more systematic denazification, often based on intensive investigation of political records in both occupied countries and the Axis powers. At the international level, the Nuremberg trials beginning in the autumn of 1945 provided a horrifying panorama of crimes by Nazi leaders. The Allies contributed their most esteemed legal experts to conduct these unusual proceedings, which were intended to underscore the importance of upholding principles of justice and accountability even in wartime. There was no legal precedent for defining genocide as a crime, but the judges at Nuremberg sentenced twelve of twenty-four defendants to death. Philippe Pétain, who led the Vichy government, escaped a death sentence because of his advanced age and his military leadership during World War I, but other major national-level figures were not so lucky. Belgium investigated seven hundred thousand people (out of a total population of 8 million) suspected of collaboration. Many investigations showed the difficulty of distinguishing collaboration in the name of personal advancement from cooperation in order to survive.

At the local level there were also trials and systematic attempts to denazify people's thinking. The Allies forced citizens of Germany to survey the death camps and undergo denazification by watching films and attending lessons on democratic governance and citizenship. Censors had different standards of what was acceptable literature for citizens in the process of denazification to read. The French were accused of permissiveness, and the Americans provided lectures on democracy to publishers and the press. The Soviets initially wanted an immediate restoration of cultural amenities such as symphonies, theater, and film in Berlin. The British were more concerned that Nazi Party members among the cultural elite not return to their old jobs without some form of punishment. Allied meetings regularly addressed these cultural issues, often heatedly.

A contentious atmosphere shaped the first coalition governments that came to power after the war. Although resistance and old-style politicians with anti-Nazi credentials initially led the provisional postwar governments, some high-ranking Nazi and Fascist officials with expertise kept their posts, and many collaborators gradually worked their way back into the political ranks. Wild fluctuations in the punishments imposed for Fascist crimes marred the public record for fairness. In Italy the artist Cornelia Tanzi, who had been Mussolini's lover in 1936, was sentenced to thirty years in prison, but the head of Naples's Fascist government received only a six-year sentence. Sometimes people charged with relatively minor fascist activities received rapid trials and harsh punishments. Many people who had committed atrocities got away because the Allies either lost interest before they could gather all the evidence or found anti-Communist uses for them.

Allied brutality, especially that of Soviet troops, left Germans skeptical of the highly publicized war crimes trials and the punishment of lower-level Nazi officials. The escape and even promotion of many Nazis also occurred, leading to widespread distrust of the Allies' good intentions. At the local level, people settled old scores, but they also helped one another in what were incredibly tough times. Because resistance leaders had often had a local network of supporters and because local Christian churches and politicians had served as centers of assistance and refuge, they enjoyed moral authority that overrode the legacy of mistrust in the society. But people did not forget the Vatican's constancy in supporting Fascism and the upper clergy's failure to provide leadership against terror and genocide.

Based on coalitions of liberal, socialist, and other resistance parties, the new regimes were completely different from totalitarian regimes based on terrorist single-party rule. In some countries women rose to temporary prominence, their role in postwar politics serving to distinguish these governments from the Nazi *Männerstaat* ("men's government"). A woman served as acting Lord Mayor of Berlin right after the war, and women were elected to the city councils of Munich, Frankfurt, and other German cities. In France, 16 percent of the contenders for government positions in the first three years after the war were women; but after the first flush of enthusiasm for gender democracy, their numbers in the National Assembly declined from forty-two in 1946 to eight in 1968.

Coalitions often favored popular causes such as workers' rights, and they fostered the hope that life would get better. Italians initially chose a resistance-based Socialist government and abolished their monarchy. By late 1945, however, they brought in a more conservative Christian Democratic leadership heading a coalition government that included Communists and Socialists. Democratic reform, including granting the vote to women, and liberal economic programs were at the top of their agenda. The United States encouraged the rise to power of right-of-center Christian Democratic parties generally in western Europe. Charles de Gaulle governed briefly in postwar France in recognition of his leadership of the wartime resistance but soon quit over limitations on the president's power that he judged too confining. The French in 1946 approved a constitution that established the Fourth Republic and finally granted French women the right to vote. In Britain the Labour government of Clement Attlee focused on fulfilling promises that prosperity would be shared more equally among the classes by expanding social welfare programs.

Postwar Society: Women and Refugees

Postwar Europe has been called a continent of women, and this description was especially true from Germany eastward. In 1946 the Soviet Union had 37.6 million women between the ages of twenty and forty-four and 24.8 million men. At the war's close, there were 1.8 million more French women than men and 7.3 million more German women than men. Soviet men had been killed by the millions as they faced the German invasion of 1941 and continued to fight without major intervention in Europe from their English and American allies until 1943. Thus, in the Soviet Union, Germany, and other countries of east and east-central Europe where much of the war had been fought, the surplus of women to men was enormous. As the war ended, some 11 million German soldiers became Allied prisoners of war, leaving households to continue to fend for themselves. In 1944 and 1945 the Soviet army swept through eastern Europe, and women fled westward with their families to head refugee households in uncertain conditions.

Men returned from war—when they returned at all—debilitated as they had done after World War I. Many had been maimed, and for decades buses and subways in London and across the continent saved special seats for those "Mutilated in the War." In the Soviet Union alone, 2 million veterans were invalids, and men missing arms or legs were ubiquitous in the provinces, for the government banished them from the major cities of Moscow and Leningrad. Veterans' immediate health problems arose from the starvation that many had experienced in Soviet and German prisoner-of-war camps, making them prone to infections and other illness. Because these veterans had gone directly into the army after completing school, they had no civilian skills or job experience.

The psychological ravages of war were no less traumatic. Many veterans were haunted by what they had witnessed at the front, and now they had to contend with social change on the home front. Returning to areas of grave devastation, they found that neither they nor their parents had homes. Detention in prison camps left a psychological legacy that was compounded as the postwar divorce rate rose sharply. Whereas in 1939 Germany there had been 8.9 divorces per 10,000 population, in 1946 the figure rose to 11.2 and in 1948 to 18.8. In Britain 1.6 percent of marriages had ended in divorce in 1937, but in 1950 the rate was 6.7 percent. Some couples who had married under the pressure of war discovered in peacetime that they had nothing in common. Many women, thinking their spouses dead, had taken new partners and legalized these relationships once the war was over. Others found the men who returned somehow diminished: "my feeling, the feeling of all women, changed toward men. We felt sorry for them, they appeared so pitiful and weak. The weak sex . . . the male-dominated, man-glorifying Nazi world shook— and with it the myth of man," one German woman wrote. A male therapist noted that "many men, even the young, are prone to increased whining."

Families reintegrated themselves, however, but experiences and family structure varied. "Never have we been so happy and so united," wrote one wife of a French prisoner of war on her husband's return. Others had more trouble because of the intense suffering: "Our characters were embittered. We were run down," another woman noted.[10] Governments recognized that these men needed jobs to resume the role of breadwinner and thus become "men" again. Yet matters were not so simple. Except for a brief period soon after the war when men were demobilized to take over jobs en masse, women were needed in the workforce to rebuild, and they kept working, especially the war widows who had no one to support them. Children rebelled against paternal authority, preferring the simpler family structure of wartime when there was a single authority figure. Although rates of juvenile delinquency seemed to be on the rise, this impression may have been the result of children being forced to forage and steal for their hard-pressed family's survival. Tolerance of unmarried mothers and unmarried cohabitation was high in the immediate postwar period because there were simply not enough men to go around. By giving birth, single women were helping accomplish a major goal of most governments—restocking the human population.

Refugees and the homeless also shaped postwar society. Migration from east to west simply to avoid the Russian army in the last eighteen months of the war had been common, but in the closing days the numbers began to surge. By agreement among the United States, Great Britain, and the Soviet Union, some twelve to fourteen million ethnic Germans were expelled from eastern Europe as a way to make nations such as Poland more ethnically uniform—ethnic cleansing, this was called at the time. Two-thirds of these people settled in West Germany, and most of the rest settled elsewhere in western Europe (see Map 7.1). The conditions of this expulsion were dire: Polish civilians boarded trains at station stops and robbed the expellees of their possessions, even of the clothing they were wearing. Because the boundaries of Poland had been moved 100 miles to the west by an Allied agreement, 1.5 million Poles had been evicted from villages in which their families had lived for centuries. Ukrainians also were driven from Poland, again in support of the Wilsonian (and Hitlerian) view that nations should be ethnically uniform.

Adding to the trauma of everyday life, the Soviet army rampaged through southeastern, eastern, and central Europe during 1945, even after the war's end. Looting and raping occurred everywhere but with particular brutality in Hungary and Germany. Their own country decimated by the German invasion and their own families destroyed, Soviet soldiers raped and gang-raped any females between the ages of ten and eighty. These victims were sometimes killed, and as late as 1950 Soviet occupying forces were not discouraged from rape. "Nothing in Germany is guiltless," went one Soviet army tract, "neither the living nor the yet unborn. . . . Break the racial pride of the German woman. Take her as your legitimate booty.

Kill, you brave soldiers of the Victorious Soviet Army.'[11] Along with the brutalization, abortion rates soared. In Germany, abortion was illegal, and some two million women are estimated to have had abortions annually. In Berlin, six thousand women died each year as a result of botched procedures. Syphilis and other venereal disease spread through the occupied areas; women victims had difficulty getting proper medical treatment. Many eastern European women and their families headed west to avoid rape.[12]

Meanwhile, in western Europe a more subtle kind of postwar sexual dynamic held sway. Since often the surest way to survive was to trade sex for food and other goods, "semi-obligatory prostitution" became common. The U.S. armed forces had the best-provisioned soldiers, and from England to eastern Europe U.S. troops sought out women as lovers, wives, and prostitutes. In exchange for sexual favors, coerced or voluntary, American and British soldiers provided nylon stockings, soap, chocolate, coffee, and cigarettes along with money for food and other necessities. Troops provided companionship and sex to young women for whom a whole cohort of men had either been killed in the war or still remained in prison camps. Marriages and long-term cohabitation resulted in some cases. Once the troops withdrew, many women were left as single parents to raise the children of these relationships—"occupation babies" they were disparagingly called—on their own.

Some women eked out a living by remaining in their jobs. Whereas after World War I women had left the workforce except in the newly socialized Soviet Union, after World War II their numbers in the workforce gradually increased. During the war, Soviet women had comprised 56 percent of the workforce, and afterward their involvement in the monumental task of rebuilding, combined with the loss of men, kept them at more than 50 percent for several years. Like women in Germany, Soviet women dominated farming during the war and remained in agriculture in impressive numbers. In the defeated countries, women ran the black market or worked in the "gray market," where they did odd jobs such as making clothing from used army blankets and trading the garments for food. City dwellers traveled into the countryside, foraging for food, stealing it, or trading for it. Wherever bombing had taken place, women could be found removing rubble. So many did this in Germany that they came to be called *Trümmerfrauen,* women of the rubble. Many of them were relatives of Nazi officials and were conscripted by the victors to do this arduous, menial work. Outsiders may have thought the Nazis as a whole were being punished, but actually only the women were.

Women in Britain and elsewhere in western Europe also remained in the workforce. Some experienced women workers felt that their talent and contributions were unwanted in peacetime. Audrey Russell, the first woman war correspondent for the BBC, sensed distinct animosity toward her among male reporters at the war's end. But the labor shortage persisted, and women stayed on in a range of industries, such as aircraft and synthetic textile manufacturing, that were not dismantled but rather were adapted to civilian consumer needs. In 1950 more than 44 percent of German women and 32.7 percent of British women were still employed. They were not only young unmarried women but also wives and mothers,

◆ **Women Clearing Rubble in Berlin**
Allied troops in Berlin rounded up German women to clear away the rubble. Among the
forced laborers were relatives of Nazi officials, making Germany appear weak and defeated.
Such images conveyed a reassuring message to millions of newspaper readers around the
world. Later, during the cold war, German authorities used such images to argue that the
Germans themselves were the major victims of World War II. *AKG Photo/London.*

many of them stoically surrendering high-paying jobs to the returning men and
taking up low-paying traditional office work. In many countries the percentage of
married women who held jobs was on the rise and would remain so, permanently
changing the character of the European workforce.

The Revival of Stalinism

While Europe as a whole continued to deal with the devastating consequences of
war, Soviet society unexpectedly faced the revival of prewar Stalinist terror. While
toiling to exhaustion during the war, Soviet workers had benefited from greater social freedom and less censorship. Ordinary men in the army had fought their way
westward, seeing a far higher standard of living despite wartime deprivation.
Intellectuals had also expanded their horizons because Stalin gave them a longer
leash in exchange for their participation in advancing technology and science and
promoting cultural cohesion. So optimistic was the climate that peasants on

collective farms believed that these collectives would be disbanded now that they had successfully provisioned a society at war. Land would go to individuals, according to widespread rumors. All these groups expected further relaxation of censorship and improvement in the conditions of everyday life.

The expectation that peace would bring better times was betrayed, however. Conditions only went from bad to worse. The government cut back on allotments of rationed goods, and unpaid peasants on collective farms complained of longer workdays: "We work on the collective farm as we used to work for the landlords in the days of serfdom," one grumbled.[13] Traumatized soldiers returning from the front after years with no leave found themselves unemployed because they lacked training for anything but killing. To pass the time, they sat for days on end in makeshift cafés—"Blue Danubes" they were called owing to the opportunity they provided to air hopes and dreams. As veterans' debate progressed in thousands of these cafés, the government started worrying about "tavern democracy." In the schools teenagers, many of them starving and orphaned, started study groups and clubs apart from the official Komsomol youth groups. They read Marx and Lenin and classic writers such as Tolstoy while mulling over the future. The continuation of wartime conditions and a firm belief that change was just around the corner raised expectations that the government saw as dangerous.

Stalin's reputation had soared because of the Allies' victory. "Turned into a deity," one Communist critic later wrote, "Stalin became so powerful that in time he ceased to pay attention to the changing needs and desires of those who exalted him."[14] Soviet leaders were determined to thwart civilian aspirations for a relaxation of the stringent wartime conditions. Their primary goals were rapid recovery of industrial capacity and military rearmament in the context of the atomic age and achieving parity with the United States in the cold war. This meant more sacrifices and repression, for Stalin needed everyone—from factory workers to scientists—to work harder.

Instead of offering greater social freedom, Stalin instituted a significant crackdown on independent thinking among young people, intellectuals, and cultural leaders, as in the United States, where McCarthyism destroyed the careers of many and sent others to jail for their opinions. Like the American anti-Communist crusaders, Stalin targeted enemies among the elites, citing their so-called crimes as threats to the ordinary citizen because those crimes would bring down the country. A new round of purges began. In 1949 leaders of the Communist establishment in Leningrad were accused of "unhealthy, un-Bolshevik deviation," and the next year six were shot and the others sent to the gulag—the vast prison-camp system. Party members, taking advantage of the atmosphere of repression, accused their rivals of being influenced by "Western ideas" and "cosmopolitanism." Between 1948 and 1952, a top-secret series of executions of leading and lionized Jewish intellectuals and performers took place—the "night of the murdered poets" the attack came to be called. Many had led the Jewish resistance to fascism, and some had also raised support for the Soviets and for Soviet Jews from audiences around the world.

In January 1953, the USSR's official newspaper *Pravda* announced the existence of a "doctors' plot" and claimed that its organizers had long been assassinating Soviet leaders, murdering newborns and patients in hospitals, and plotting to poison water supplies. Doctors were openly accused of being Zionist Jews and thus disloyal because of their alliance with international forces. Hysteria gripped the nation, as people feared for their lives. "I am a simple worker and not an anti-Semite," one Moscow resident wrote, "but I say . . . it's time to clean these people out."[15]

On March 5, 1953, at the height of the doctors' plot hysteria, Stalin died of a stroke. His popularity during and after the war drew the masses to Red Square, where his corpse was put on display. People queued up for hours to pay their respects. At the same time, fear for the future intensified. Ordinary citizens and cultural leaders alike wondered who could ever take Stalin's place. They worried that the leadership might become more violent and that civil war might erupt. Stalin had led ordinary people through the great suffering of the war and before that had overseen the modernization of the Soviet nation. He also had brought prosperity to many, as the need for greater productivity and loyalty in wartime expanded the importance of a middle class of managers, technical workers, and those who could deliver cultural products such as radio and television programs for the masses. In return for their growing prosperity and sense of social importance, the middle classes had given Stalin much-needed support. The immediate postwar period of revived Stalinist repression was over, but a sense of uncertainty, even dread, hovered over the Soviet bloc and, indeed, the whole world.

RESTORING CULTURAL VALUES

Two interrelated views shaped cultural attitudes after 1945. On the one hand, the winning effort in the war was seen as the rescue of a specifically Western civilization from the forces of barbarism represented by the Axis powers. As one British critic put it, the struggle was "a war to defend civilization [from] a conspiracy against man."[16] On the other hand, focusing on the evils perpetrated in the war and on the monstrous harm that had been done, critics wondered whether civilized people had not in fact shown themselves wanting. The victory, however, encouraged many to hope that a better future awaited. "If one could defeat Hitler and hunt down his troops across Europe, one could not but build that ideal society where there was justice and abundance," one Soviet woman believed.[17] Even Holocaust survivors' stories were used to support the cause of humanitarianism and the rebirth of hope. The postwar period was for some a unique moment, full of promise. Momentarily forgotten in this appraisal were the victors' own histories of oppression, racism, and brutality against peoples around the world.

Contested Memories

The landscape of Europe is permanently scarred by World War II, and from the moment the war ended memories of it provoked arguments and debate. Villages and cities still display the war's damage. Empty spaces remain, and bullet holes in surviving buildings are still visible. For decades it was not completely safe to walk on beaches that had once been mined. There was simply more important work to be done than taking the time to tear apart the bunkers and fortifications that had once marked the front lines of fascist expansion. Governments created memorial sites, installing permanent plaques at spots where resisters had been killed and commissioning statues to commemorate the war dead. The number of these memorials increased over time, making the cities of Europe grim and enduring reminders of both inhumanity and resistance.

Because the cause of fascism based on the revival of national might remained a heroic one to many people, memories of the war raised hotly contested issues. For example, the plaques commemorating the death of resistance fighters received pride of place, while the vast number of collaborators who helped the Nazis in ways both large and small disappeared from scrutiny, even in histories of the war. But individuals often did remember: in the early 1960s dog excrement was often placed on the apartment doorstep of a Parisian man said to have been a collaborator. More complex than a simple struggle of good versus evil, the war generated lasting personal vendettas and heated national arguments over how it would be remembered.

Controversy erupted immediately over the nature and accuracy of wartime accounts, particularly of atrocities. As soon as the war ended, survivors set up makeshift memorials to people killed in extermination and concentration camps. Stones, handwritten poems, plaques, flowers, plants, and other objects were left to evoke recollections of what had happened in the camps. Both local and national governments often stepped in to take over these sites, though sometimes waiting years to dispose of the spontaneous memorials and replace them with official monuments and museums. The concentration camp at Dachau near Munich fell into disrepair until a group of survivors, including many Catholic clergy, demanded that it be made into a permanent museum and memorial, with its grisly features preserved. The camp, however, was converted into a museum evoking the extermination camps where Jews died but erasing the fact that it had actually served as a deadly concentration camp for political prisoners, many of them Catholic clergy. Other misremembrances occurred as nationalist and emotional needs displaced historical fact and the experience of survivors.

Contested memories also existed in unexpected places, such as universities, where many professors had endorsed fascism and where the Allied powers wanted to ensure that denazification succeeded. A prominent focus of heated academic debate was the philosopher Martin Heidegger, who as rector of the University of Freiburg had become a Nazi and led the expulsion of Jews from the faculty. In the 1920s and 1930s Heidegger developed ideas that became the basis for literary and philosophical theories of the postwar period, including existentialism, which motivated students and teachers around the world in the 1950s. The question that remains important and contested to this very day is how to reconcile the fact that one of the most important thinkers of the twentieth century was a Nazi and briefly held the belief that he might be the Nazi Party's intellectual leader. Some argue heatedly that we should not read Heidegger at all because of his membership in the Nazi

Party. Others say we should read only Heidegger's philosophy and ignore his complicity in the crimes of the Third Reich. Though begun in the 1940s, the debate rages on.

The controversy over the causes and crimes of Nazism continued in other arenas. After the war, the West German government, while making some restitution to Jews in Israel, shifted its rhetoric to interpret the war and genocide as the work of Hitler and a "handful" of his fanatical followers. In the 1940s and 1950s history was recast to describe the expellees from the east as the war's real victims and their compensation for lost property one of the major undertakings of the West German government. Instead of distinguishing between people of German descent who had lived in the region for centuries and those whom the Nazis had settled in the east to enjoy the plundered wealth of Poles, Czechs, and others, the government equated the dire plight of expellees with the dire plight of all Germans. Focusing on the expellees, government publicists announced that Germans needed to be seen as victims and not as perpetrators of war and genocide. Like the women who worked to clear areas of rubble, they were used to symbolize German innocence and their unfair treatment by the Allies.

As the cold war advanced, the West German government in the 1950s focused on prisoners of war who, it claimed, numbered in the hundreds of thousands and were still being held in the Soviet sector. The Soviet government maintained that most of these prisoners were criminal elements and mass murderers, but the German government and many lobbying organizations countered that they were innocent soldiers. Publicizing the plight of German soldiers held prisoner by the Soviets became a way to shift attention away from German genocide in the east and to transform the prisoners of war into victims of communism toward whom the free world should direct its compassion. Debate over the war's grim legacy shaped politics and individual memories, which kept shifting. The legacy itself remains potent, vital, and contested.

From Holocaust to Hope

Moving documents of the Holocaust and heroism during the war actually filled people with feelings of well-being and hope. Most heartrending was the diary of Anne Frank, a young girl who was hidden away for months in order to escape the roundup of Jews in the Netherlands. Anne Frank's early teens thus took place in the close company of her own and another family, whose struggles and quarrels she recorded in the two years before they were betrayed to the Nazis. Despite her knowledge of the Nazi evil ravaging Europe, Frank maintained her confidence "that people are basically good at heart."[18] Anne and her older sister Margot died in Bergen-Belsen in 1944, tragically only months before the liberation of the camp by the Allies. After the war Frank's father, Otto, censored the passages reflecting her coming of age, sexual awakening, and conflicts with her mother to highlight the noble and touching message. In a culture where good was supposed to triumph no matter what, *The Diary of Anne Frank* (1947) became a best-selling book and a popular theatrical drama (1955).

Searing memoirs slowly appeared from the pens of death camp survivors, and all of them gripped the cultural imagination. Italian chemist Primo Levi had survived the camps because of his scientific background and, he maintained, because of the good luck of being ill when the Nazis forced inmates on a death march to escape Allied detection at the war's close. Levi's moving books, such as *The Monkey Wrench* (1978) and *Survival in Auschwitz* (1947), describe his experiences of humanity and inhumanity. Levi claimed, as later prisoners of the Soviet system would claim, that deep understanding of life was born in conditions of extreme suffering. Simultaneously writers like Levi also faced severe mental suffering as a result of the camps, and some believed that Levi's fall to his death in 1987 was a suicide—the long-term consequence of witnessing Nazi genocide.

From exile, many refugees determined that Nazism resulted from longstanding ingredients of German culture. Secure in the United States, Nobel laureate Thomas Mann wrote *Doktor Faustus* (1947), a dense and erudite rumination on the dark potential in the Western sensibility, especially as it was embodied in philosophy, literature, and the arts. The novel's protagonist, the musician Adrian Leverkühn, is visited by a Satanic figure with whom he engages in speculative discussion of Germany and its culture. The atmosphere in the novel is morbid, tending toward self-destruction and irrationality—qualities that Mann found in the heritage of his native land and its geniuses such as the composer Richard Wagner and the philosopher Friedrich Nietzsche. Yet like other critical novels, this literature served to revitalize the humanistic and Enlightenment belief in the existence of good elements that needed to be restored.

This humanitarian and critical impulse faced many challengers; the war gave inspiration to many "new" literatures. In the opinion of some, the war made the literature emanating from the pens of the aristocracy and leisured classes and intended for them irrelevant. Virginia Woolf, shortly before committing suicide in 1941 in despair at the war's violence and her own ongoing bouts with mental instability, noted her appreciation for the literature of upper-class writers such as Jane Austen and Anthony Trollope: "They gave us comedy, tragedy, and beauty." But, she added, "much of that old-class literature was very pretty; very false; very dull." Woolf hoped for a "stronger, more varied literature in the classless . . . society of the future."[19]

A desire for a more democratized art was in the air as was an intuition that war had utterly transformed art itself. "It was not possible to use the same language as before," the Polish poet Wislawa Szymborska noted after World War II and the Holocaust. "We wanted a poetry without artifice," the Nobel Prize recipient recalled.[20] Dispelling artifice often meant dispelling illusions about truth and goodness. Some artists thought a revival of humanist values unthinkable after World War II and its attendant genocide. In 1952 Irish author Samuel Beckett's play *Waiting for Godot* signaled the arrival of an absurdist school of literature. The play featured two tramps standing around talking nonstop while trusting that something—or someone—good would eventually come along. But nothing other than the tramps' conversation happens.

German artists felt that they were starting from a zero point, reduced to basic material needs and bereft of their cultural heritage:

This is my cap
this is my coat
here is my shaving kit
in a linen bag.

A tin can: my plate, my cup
Into the white tin
I carved my name . . .

Carved here with this
precious nail
which I hide from greedy eyes.

So poet Günther Eich described the spare material and cultural life of postwar Germans, whose simple beauty he sought to contrast with the pomposity of Nazi rule.[21] The Gruppe 47 (Group 47) of young writers to which Eich belonged included novelist Heinrich Böll and poet Ingeborg Bachmann. It emphasized individual morality and simplicity of language and concerns. Eradicated by the Nazis, avant-garde ideas such as psychoanalysis, expressionism, and existentialism had passed young German writers by, and they hoped to recoup these intellectual tools for their public—also deprived of anything but fascist ideology under Hitler. The Frankfurt School of Social Thought tried to use psychoanalysis to explain the Nazi phenomenon. In the opinion of its theorists, Nazism flourished when the ego of any individual collapsed under the weight of modern life. The growing force of state power could make the individual especially pliable, willing to surrender freedom to a strong father figure, no matter how tyrannical.

In the immediate postwar period, cinema emphasized the humanity of poor people. Rejecting either fascist or upper-class privilege, films proposed justice and a fair deal for the ordinary person who had maintained decency despite wartime privations. Italian director Vittorio da Sica's *The Bicycle Thief* (1948), like other neorealist films, avoided the pomp and glitter that characterized films under fascist regimes and instead focused on the aspirations of ordinary people. In *Quai des Orfèvres* (1947), the French director Henri-Georges Clouzot depicted the lives of Parisians living without coal and with few amenities. Scraping by, the characters are always clad in their overcoats whether at work or at home, conveying the reality of postwar discomfort and deprivation. Despite a few bad eggs and some normal human frailties, the protagonists are brave, understanding, and supportive of one another. Roberto Rossellini's *Open City* (1945) similarly stressed values over outward appearances. Its noble working-class characters struggle against the Nazis in grim wartime Rome. In these depictions, filmmakers underscored the message of authors such as Primo Levi and Anne Frank.

Existentialism and the Politics of Commitment

Philosophers and writers in Paris were among the most effective in promoting commitment to a renewed humanism. The situation in France after the war was uneasy: struggles over the meaning of the resistance and collaboration inflamed politics and ruptured relationships. The influence of the Communist Party surged owing to the legacy of Soviet wartime leadership, peacetime deprivation, and the firm belief that the time had come to attend to needs of workers and the poor. In this complex atmosphere attention focused on the philosopher Jean-Paul Sartre (1905–1980), his companion Simone de Beauvoir (1908–1986), his friend Albert Camus (1913–1960), and authors, artists, and thinkers in their orbit. Holding these individuals together was a philosophy called existentialism, especially as it intersected with debates over the future of Europe in a postgenocide, postfascist climate. Specific arguments raged over what had caused the collapse of so powerful a country as France, why so many of the French people had aided Germany by collaborating with the Vichy government, and how the French would rebuild humane institutions.

The answers devised by Sartre emanated from theories that were both philosophical and political in tenor. Sartre's existentialist philosophy explored the meaning (or lack of meaning) of human existence in a world where evil flourished. Borrowing some of the fundamentals of his philosophy from Martin Heidegger, Sartre focused on "being" or "existence"—not on issues of truth and knowledge. In the 1920s Heidegger had rejected concern for the abstract structures of life (metaphysics) in favor of understanding direct experiences of conscience, anxiety, guilt, and even political activism—all of these signaling an intense involvement with the world that went beyond mere philosophizing. Sartre followed this line of thought: existence was not the automatic process found either in the biblical account of God's creation of the world or in scientific theories of the origins of the natural world. Human beings were not *born* with spiritual goodness in the image of a divine Creator, but instead, through action and choice, individuals *created* their own "authentic" existences. Sartre's idea that one could create existence from nothing and actually be "authentic" was a distortion of Heidegger's theory that one was born into a highly determined context of forestructures and already determined horizons of knowledge and insight. Existentialism in Sartre's form was headier, however, for it allowed for freedom, creativity, and a sky's-the-limit approach to life.

There was much more to the cultural sweep of existentialism than one lone philosopher's thought. In 1949, Simone de Beauvoir published the twentieth century's most influential work on the condition of women, *The Second Sex* (see Document 7.2). She believed that most women failed to take the kinds of action essential to leading free and authentic lives, choosing instead to live in the world of nature or "necessity" and following the dictates of biology by devoting themselves exclusively to reproduction and motherhood. Failing to create an authentic self through considered action and accomplishment, they became an object or "Other." Moreover, instead of struggling to define themselves and assert their freedom, women passively accepted their "Otherness" and lived as defined by men. In the 1960s, Beauvoir's elaboration of the concept of "Otherness" would help shape not only the women's movement but various other liberation movements. Beauvoir moved women's activism beyond the push for legal and political reform to investigate the psychological and cultural underpinnings of women's inequality.

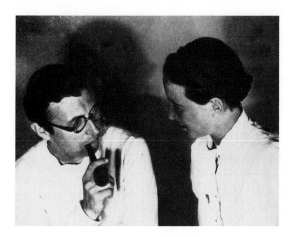

◆ **Jean-Paul Sartre and Simone de Beauvoir**
Even ordinary people in postwar western Europe
recognized this famous couple, both of them well-
known writers of fiction, plays, and philosophy. Their
message emphasized individual responsibility for
creating a meaningful existence, and young people
flocked to universities to discuss their philosophy of
"existentialism." The new glossy media of postwar
Europe and eventually television made not only film
stars but also philosophers like Sartre and Beauvoir
into celebrities. *Editions Gallimard.*

The third towering figure in this existentialist coterie was Albert Camus, an
Algerian-born novelist and theorist who had introduced Sartre to the resistance
and who had first gotten him published in the resistance press. In novels such as
The Stranger (1942), *The Plague* (1947), and *The Rebel* (1951), Camus dissected the
evils of a corrupt political order and pondered human responsibility. Because
Camus shared with other existentialists the idea that life was absurd, he saw freedom as something to be achieved only within oneself, outside the bounds of political activism. Nonetheless, he espoused a political position: The current tyrannical
order was that of the modern state in general and especially the Communist state.
Also, the productivity demands of all modern industrial systems hampered individual freedom, and thus the fundamental Marxist idea of materialism was unfree
at its very core.

Unlike Camus, Sartre supported communism, and a quarrel erupted between
them. Camus questioned his friend's willingness to support the Soviet regime that
had undertaken the purges of the 1930s and 1940s. Sartre replied that the corruption of capitalist and middle-class society was itself a form of violence that could
only be met with violence. In the 1950s, during the Algerian war for independence
(see chapter 9), Camus became an advocate of peaceful settlements among
Algerians and European settlers, but Sartre insisted on the importance of violence
to advance the cause of freedom. According to Sartre, breaking France's grip on
Algeria was the only recourse for Algerians experiencing brutality and exploitation
at the hands of French colonial settlers. Sartre had adopted the pro-violence position of the anti-imperial theorist Frantz Fanon—a position Camus saw as inhumane. Because of their disagreement, Sartre in 1952 declared his friendship with
Camus at an end. Sartre believed that the precondition for freedom in the postwar
world was an alliance between intellectuals and the working classes and masses.
This alliance would allow a merging of the self with the mass, proletarian, communist movement.

Western media snapped up existentialism, marketing it to intellectuals and activists around the world as a sign that European thought still had something to offer. People debated whether Sartre, not Beauvoir, had written *The Second Sex,* and they took a gossipy interest in the couple's failure to marry and in their love affairs with others. The break between Sartre and Camus also drew rapt attention and fostered the taking of sides on cold war issues. Existentialism appealed to young people. Many of them had missed the action of the war and now sought a role in an intellectual struggle if not a physical one. Existentialism provided a role in its core belief that activism must precede the acquisition of freedom and in its insistence that individuals take political sides. Cafés and coffeehouses in Paris and in other cities around the world filled with students debating human values, suicide, and the latest headlines about the cold war and decolonization. Books, newspapers, films, and radio made existentialism a fashionable intellectual movement.

In 1959, the media also brought news of a weighty postwar institutional change that occurred when newly installed Pope John XXIII called for a council of high church officials to consider the role of the Roman Catholic Church in the modern world. "I want to throw open the windows of the Church," he is reported to have said, "so that we can see out and the people can see in." The meeting, known as Vatican II, opened in the fall of 1962. Around twenty-five hundred clergy met in four joint sessions over the course of four years. By the time Vatican II ended in 1965, Pope John XXIII, the leading voice of reform and reflection, had died, but his spirit of deepening pastoral commitment lingered in the council's decrees, some of them revolutionary. The Roman Catholic Church censured "hatred, persecutions, displays of anti-Semitism, directed against Jews at any time and by anyone."[22] Seeking to find common ground with other Christians, such as Eastern Orthodox Catholics and Protestants, Vatican II committed Roman Catholics to reconciliation, tolerance, and an expansion of outreach around the world.

THE DEEPENING COLD WAR

Throughout the 1950s and despite attempts at spiritual renewal, the cold war intensified, then reached a crescendo with the building of the Berlin Wall in 1961 and the Cuban missile crisis in 1962. In China in 1949, soon after the initial showdown in Berlin, Communist armies under the leadership of Mao Zedong defeated Nationalist forces and established the People's Republic of China. The next year Communist North Korean forces invaded the southern part of the Korean peninsula in an attempt to take it over. The United States responded vigorously, sending troops that soon had the backing of the United Nations. A cease-fire finally held in 1953, ending the bloody and costly struggle. The death of Stalin in that same year and successful negotiations to end the Korean War brought some easing of the cold war, but the "thaw" did not last.

Instead, an escalating arms race kept people on the edge of their seats, and so did news of ongoing war games in which Europe was the battleground — only this

time not a battleground of its own making. Continental Europe would remain occupied, although in decreasing numbers until late in the twentieth century, and
both the United States and the USSR would base increasingly powerful nuclear
weapons on European terrain. As culture interpreted and helped perpetuate the
cold war through the media, the hope that many people had felt at the defeat of
Nazism was offset by the superpower conflict, whose potentially deadly consequences became apparent in 1961 and 1962 as the United States and the USSR
pushed the world to the brink of nuclear war.

The Arms Race

The atomic bombs that the United States dropped on Hiroshima and Nagasaki in
August 1945 marked not only a human tragedy but also a deadly advance in the
arms race that had been taking place in the West for more than fifty years. The cold
war accelerated that race. In August 1949, the USSR detonated an atomic bomb;
then in August 1953, it detonated a hydrogen bomb. During World War II,
European and U.S. spies, sympathetic to Soviet leaders' complaints that their exclusion from the atomic bomb project put them at a disadvantage in the fight
against Nazism, had passed atomic secrets to the USSR. After the war, they continued to do so when Stalin made developing a nuclear arsenal a top priority. Under
the direction of Lavrenti Beria, head of the Soviet secret police, teams of scientists
were sent to isolated towns, where they produced first an atom bomb and four
years later a hydrogen bomb.

Led by another team of scientists, many of them refugees from Europe, the
United States had exploded its own hydrogen bomb in the fall of 1952 and proceeded to develop ever more powerful versions—as did the Soviets, whose military
establishment took over Stalin's nuclear crusade after his death. Radiation clouds
circled the earth after each detonation, which destroyed wildlife and even entire islands in the Pacific where the United States and later the French tested their bombs.
Over the course of the nuclear arms race, towering figures in nuclear science such
as Andrei Sakharov (1921–1989), known as the father of the Soviet bomb, became
dissidents and pacifists, warning about the potential annihilation of earth itself.

The political atmosphere was thus supercharged and became more so as the
Soviets and Americans worked on delivery systems. The United States was relying
on heavy bombers based in Europe to deploy its nuclear weapons against the
USSR. In October 1957, the USSR launched Sputnik, the first artificial satellite, into
earth orbit. The successful launch of this spacecraft depended on powerful rocketry. The Soviet spinoff of an intercontinental ballistic missile (ICBM), capable of
delivering a nuclear weapon to a distant continent, imperiled the U.S. lead and
ratcheted up not only the space race but the arms race. By the end of 1957, the
United States had countered with an ICBM of its own. As a result of the cold war
arms race, the U.S. defense budget grew from $10.9 billion in 1948 to $52.2 billion
fifteen years later, while Soviet defense spending increased from $13.1 billion to
$54.7 billion over the same period. As the superpowers shifted their priorities from
manpower to weaponry, they engaged in a costly struggle, which the United States

could afford somewhat more easily than could the USSR. Both countries dragged their European allies into the contest through their domination of NATO and the Warsaw Pact.

Cold War Culture

Europe was enmeshed in the cultural manifestations of the cold war just as it was drawn into cold war alliances that developed around the superpower rivalry. George Orwell's novel *1984*, published in 1949, captured the menacing atmosphere of the times. The English author described a tripartite global contest that kept society on a perpetual wartime footing. In his fictional account citizens were unable to escape messages from their television sets ordering them to increase productivity and to display patriotism in order to win the war. Truth gave way to slogans marketing war, and the standard of living dropped dramatically in order to fund nonstop fighting. In the real world, life seemed to be imitating art, for neither in newspapers nor on radio were Europeans spared the sense of ongoing warfare. Debates among such unlikely people as the existentialists became intertwined with cold war politics. The United States secretly funded European literary journals to shape the cultural cold war, taking up the cause of Camus, for example, while denouncing Sartre. Other U.S.-funded authors, such as the British poet Stephen Spender, produced anti-Communist tracts and secretly helped filter monies from the newly formed U.S. Central Intelligence Agency to found magazines and to buy the services of popular authors who would denounce the Soviet Union and promote the United States among their western European readers. Established in 1947, the CIA secretly financed musicians and art exhibitions it found to represent U.S. values, particularly art whose lack of a social message made it seem neutral. Thus, abstract expressionist artists such as Jackson Pollock mounted shows in major European cities, and modern composers such as the minimalist Pierre Boulez were endorsed and promoted above other contenders no matter what their talent or skill. To extend the influence of pro-U.S. writers, musicians, and social commentators, the U.S. government expanded the Voice of America radio network in the late 1940s to broadcast their work to listeners around the world. Europe was a primary audience, and VOA programs were broadcast in some thirty-eight languages.

The USSR did no less, but it made no secret of its promotion of Communist culture internationally. The Soviet-directed Cominform worked actively and openly to keep Communist propaganda flowing around the world. When a show of abstract art opened in the Soviet Union, Stalin's successor Nikita Khrushchev yelled that it was "dog-shit." Pro-Soviet critics in western Europe saw U.S.-style abstract art as "an infantile sickness" and supported official socialist realist styles with "human content" showing the condition of the workers and the oppressed races in the United States. Even as other loosening of restrictions occurred, the USSR maintained a near total ban on any kind of abstraction that viewers could interpret as they wished, and the government jammed western European and American radio broadcasts aimed at influencing the thinking of people in the Eastern bloc.

Popular culture equally fell under the spell of the cold war. Fiction, films, and radio programs focused on military plots and suspenseful tales of spies and intrigue. The lyrics of popular songs emphasized muscular, sexualized masculinity, and male spies in films and novels were dashing and fearless. In the USSR, the Union of Soviet Writers directed its members to churn out spy stories, and in the West, espionage novels topped the best-seller lists. *Casino Royale* (1953), by the British novelist Ian Fleming (1908–1964), introduced Agent 007, James Bond, who survived tests of wit and physical prowess at the hands of Communist spies and other villains—some of them enticing young women (see Figure 7.4 in the Picture Essay). Traveling to exotic places, Agent 007 brilliantly improvised with sophisticated, futuristic weaponry provided by government scientists hoping to ensure their side's success in the cold war. In the Soviet Union, pilots would delay take off when programs based on the work of Yulian Simyonov, the Russian counterpart of Ian Fleming, were playing on radio or television. Audiences in both the East and the West were riveted by the dangerous suspense of the cold war.

Emphasizing men of prowess and pronounced masculinity, cold war culture also featured attacks on homosexuals as security risks. The French "good morals" law of 1946 forbade their employment in public service. In West Germany from the 1950s to 1965, the incarceration of homosexuals took place at a higher rate than under the Nazis, and those who had survived the concentration camps were imprisoned again as "repeat offenders." The British persecuted gays as unmanly and feminine—characteristics that led to their labeling as "communists." The English mathematician and computer scientist Alan Turing was harassed, convicted of homosexuality, and forced to undergo hormone therapy. In Norway, the Lutheran Church warned of a "world conspiracy of homosexuals," echoing the idea that democratic societies had been infiltrated by forces who were eager to overthrow the government. In France, the Catholic Church expressed similar views of a looming danger, issuing a warning about the "homosexual peril" that menaced free societies. In 1963, an English Sunday paper carried articles titled "How to Spot a Homo" and "The Traitorous Tool of the Russians," referring to gay men.[23]

The cold war influenced every aspect of life—politics, the economy, popular culture, even childbirth. Since the beginning of the twentieth century, doctors in Russia had been working to eliminate the pain of childbirth. Using the Pavlovian method of controlling reflexes, they devised breathing exercises that helped break the connection between contractions and pain. Instead of focusing on their pain, women in labor would concentrate on their breathing; the help of a trained partner or coach would enhance the effectiveness of this strategy. Widespread sympathy in western Europe toward the Communists because of their immense contribution to the Allied victory sparked interest in the Soviets' pain-lessening technique, and the Soviets held many a congress to promote this fresh evidence of Communist superiority. Early in the 1950s, one young French woman, on discovering that she was pregnant, rushed to get information about the new method: "It was a Communist technique and in those days I wanted to do everything in a communist way—even having a baby."[24] Eventually the technique entered the United States, but sanitized of its Soviet origins. It was called "natural childbirth" or the "Lamaze method" after a Parisian obstetrician who in the 1940s had used Soviet techniques in his own practice.

Toward Nuclear Holocaust

The cold war came to a head early in the 1960s, when the Soviet government made some dramatic moves—the first of them in Europe. In the summer of 1961, East German workers, under Communist direction and supervised by the army, stacked bales of barbed wire across miles of the city's east-west border to begin construction of the Berlin Wall. The divided city had served as an escape route by which some three million people had fled to the West. East Germany was hemorrhaging some of its most talented and hardworking citizens, falling to one-third the size of West Germany. As a concrete wall replaced the barbed wire, people resorted to

◆ **Checkpoint Charlie**
Precise points in Berlin marked the division of the city into four sectors, each of which was controlled by one of the four principal Allied victors. As the cold war progressed, getting from the Soviet sector to the other sectors became increasingly difficult. With the construction of the Berlin Wall in 1961, people could only cross from West to East Germany temporarily by presenting identity papers and other credentials at such points as Checkpoint Charlie. The erection of the wall separated families, neighbors, and friends and caused both inconvenience and heartache. *Brown Brothers.*

jumping to freedom through upper-story apartment windows and roofs. As news emerged that would-be escapees were shot and as serious novels and potboiler spy stories provided grim accounts of the divided city, the Berlin Wall became an international symbol of Communist repression.

Cold war tensions increased with the coming to power of two new leaders: John Kennedy and Fidel Castro. John Fitzgerald Kennedy (1917–1963) became U.S. president in 1961. He represented American affluence and youth but also the nation's commitment to cold war. A World War II hero and an early fan of the fictional cold war spy James Bond, Kennedy intensified the arms race and escalated the cold war by falsely charging that the Soviets had far more capacity in missiles than did the United States. A bit earlier, in 1959, Cuban revolutionaries led by Fidel Castro overthrew Cuba's corrupt government, which had close economic and political ties to the United States. After making unsuccessful overtures for support from the United States, Castro became a Communist and allied his government with the Soviet Union. Although Kennedy would eventually visit Berlin, appealing to West Berliners to support freedom, his most dramatic and dangerous cold war role was in Cuba.

In the spring of 1961, Kennedy, assured of success by the Central Intelligence Agency, approved an invasion of Cuba at the Bay of Pigs by U.S.-trained Cuban exiles to overthrow Castro. The invasion failed miserably and humiliated the United States. A few months later, Kennedy had a chilling meeting with Khrushchev in Vienna. The Soviet leader brandished the specter of nuclear holocaust over the continuing U.S. presence in Berlin. "We will bury you," Khrushchev announced. At home, Kennedy responded with a call for more weapons and an enhanced civil defense program.

In October 1962, the CIA reported the installation of launching sites for Soviet medium-range missiles in Cuba, a counter to nuclear weapons aimed at the USSR that the United States had installed in Turkey. Kennedy responded forcefully, calling for a U.S. naval blockade of Soviet ships heading for Cuba and threatening nuclear war if the Soviet missile sites were not removed. For several days the world stood on the brink of nuclear disaster. Some American generals pushed hard for nuclear attacks on the Soviet Union. Then, between October 25 and 27, Khrushchev and Kennedy negotiated an end to the crisis. It was later revealed that the Soviets actually had nuclear weapons aimed at the United States. The Soviets promised to remove the missile installations and weapons, and in secret agreements the United States promised to remove its missiles from Turkey.

Kennedy spent the remainder of his life working to improve nuclear diplomacy; Khrushchev did the same. In August 1963 the USSR and the United States signed the first arms-control agreement banning nuclear tests in the atmosphere. The two leaders had looked deeply into the nuclear future and clearly feared what they saw. Their successors in office were not so prudent and kept the production of new and improved weapons of mass destruction on an upward spiral. The possibility of nuclear annihilation remained the gravest threat to life on the planet into the twenty-first century and was the cold war's grim and enduring legacy.

CONCLUSION

As a result of World War II, the international balance of power shifted dramatically. In the early postwar years much of Europe was too mired in wartime destruction to respond vigorously to the growing Soviet-American breach called the cold war. Unlike the USSR, which despite suffering the greatest wartime losses had achieved colossal military might, the other European Allies were bankrupt and impotent. Continental Europe as a whole was plagued by disorder that was the consequence not only of starvation and the destruction of infrastructure but also of the victorious Allies' political plans. Some thirty million people became refugees, expelled from their homelands so that the nations of eastern Europe would be more ethnically uniform.

The chaos allowed the two superpowers to draw a recovering Europe into their titanic struggle, allotting aid, using force, and stationing troops across the continent. Thus the late 1940s and 1950s echoed the turmoil of the past and set the stage for increased tensions in the future, producing complicated political struggles and a rich cultural outpouring expressing people's hopes and fears. Most eyes were on the United States and the Soviet Union and the increasing danger of war at pivotal moments such as the Berlin blockade, the continuing installation of nuclear devices, the Korean War, the building of the Berlin Wall, and the Cuban missile crisis. Surprisingly, during this period of menace, Europe staged a comeback, rebuilding its economic capacity and creating some dramatically new, supranational institutions.

DOCUMENTS

The Soviet Ambassador
Appraises the United States, 1946

THE IMMEDIATE POSTWAR YEARS WERE FULL OF UNCERTAINTY about the course of global politics. In part this uncertainty resulted from the utter collapse of Britain, Germany, and France—the traditional European leaders of the international order—and the ascent of the United States and the Soviet Union, whose record as international leaders in peacetime was scant. Few knew what further use the United States would make of the atomic bomb. Nor did policy and opinion makers know what the USSR's aims were. Even as the Soviet Union withdrew its troops from Scandinavia, Greece, and the Middle East, it (like the United States) continued to garrison thousands of miles of European territory. Observers around the world wondered what these superpowers would do, and the two military titans speculated anxiously about one another.

The superpowers sought information from all quarters, including spies, the military, and an array of advisers. From Moscow, George Kennan, a high-ranking American diplomat, sent to President Truman an ominous report about Soviet ambitions early in 1946, saying that the Soviets always aimed for "total destruction" of rivals. Newly opened Soviet archives, however, show something else: far from seeking to crush the United States, Stalin was actually trying to figure out how to get on America's good side. As Nikita Khrushchev would later recall, Stalin "lived in terror" of American aggression, especially as Truman seemed willing to use the atomic bomb against the Soviet Union.

Nikolai Novikov was the USSR's ambassador to Washington in 1946 and, like U.S. diplomats in Moscow, was a rich source of information and analysis for policy makers. Document 7.1 is a report that he sent to the Soviet foreign minister, Vyacheslav Molotov (1890–1986). The underlining of the text was done by Molotov.

Document 7.1

NIKOLAI NOVIKOV

Report to Foreign Minister Molotov, September 27, 1946

The foreign policy of the United States, which reflects the imperialist tendencies of American monopolistic capital, is characterized in the postwar period by a striving for world supremacy.° This is the real meaning of the many statements by President Truman and other representatives of American ruling circles: that the United States has the right to lead the world. . . .

The foreign policy of the United States is not determined at present by the circles in the Democratic party that (as was the case during Roosevelt's lifetime) strive to strengthen the cooperation of the three great powers that constituted the basis of the anti-Hitler coalition during the war. The ascendance to power of President Truman, a politically unstable person but with certain conservative tendencies, and the subsequent appointment of [James] Byrnes as Secretary of State meant a strengthening of the influence on U.S. foreign policy of the most reactionary circles of the Democratic party. The constantly increasing reactionary nature of the foreign policy course of the United States . . . laid the groundwork for close cooperation in this field between the far right wing of the Democratic party and the Republican party. This cooperation of the two parties . . . took shape in both houses of Congress in the form of an unofficial bloc of reactionary Southern Democrats and the old guard of the Republicans. . . .

Obvious indications of the U.S. effort to establish world dominance are also to be found in the increase in military potential in peacetime and in the establishment of a large number of naval and air bases both in the United States and beyond its borders. . . .

One of the stages in the achievement of dominance over the world by the United States is its understanding with England concerning the partial division of the world on the basis of mutual concessions. [Those two countries have agreed to include] Japan and China in the sphere of influence of the United States in the Far East, while the United States, for its part, has agreed not to hinder England either in resolving the Indian [demands for independence] or in strengthening its influence in Siam [Thailand] and Indonesia. . . .

In recent years American capital has penetrated very intensively into the economy of the Near Eastern countries, in particular into the oil industry. . . .

In expanding in the Near East, American capital has English capital as its greatest and most stubborn competitor. The fierce competition between them is the chief factor preventing England and the United States from reaching an understanding on the division of spheres of influence in the Near East. . . .

Relations between the United States and England are determined by two basic circumstances. On the one hand, the United States regards England as its greatest potential competitor; on the other hand, England constitutes a possible ally for the United States. Division of certain regions of the globe into spheres of influence of the United States and England would create the opportunity, if not for preventing competition between them, which is impossible, then at least of reducing it. At the same time, such a division fa-

---

°for world supremacy: Molotov marginal query: "A difference from [the] prewar [period]?"

SOURCE: Soviet Foreign Ministry archives. Supplied by Vladimir Shustov and translated by John Glad. Kenneth M. Jensen, ed., *Origins of the Cold War: The Novikov, Kennan, and Roberts "Long Telegrams" of 1946* (Washington, D.C.: United States Institute of Peace, 1991), 3, 5–6, 8, 10–11, 14–16.

cilitates the achievement of economic and political cooperation between them. . . .

The present policy of the American government with regard to the USSR is also directed at limiting or dislodging the influence of the Soviet Union from neighboring countries. In implementing this policy in former enemy or Allied countries adjacent to the USSR, the United States attempts . . . to support reactionary forces with the purpose of creating obstacles to the process of democratization of these countries. In so doing, it also attempts to secure positions for the penetration of American capital into their economies. Such a policy is intended to weaken and overthrow the democratic governments in power there, which are friendly toward the USSR, and replace them in the future with new governments that would obediently carry out a policy dictated from the United States. . . .

. . . [T]he United States is considering the possibility of terminating the Allied occupation of German territory before the main tasks of the occupation—the demilitarization and democratization of Germany—have been implemented. This would create the prerequisites for the revival of an imperialist Germany, which the United

States plans to use in a future war on its side. One cannot help seeing that such a policy has a clearly outlined anti-Soviet edge and constitutes a serious danger to the cause of peace.

The numerous and extremely hostile statements by American government, political, and military figures with regard to the Soviet Union and its foreign policy . . . are echoed in an even more unrestrained tone by the overwhelming majority of the American press organs. Talk about a "third war," meaning a war against the Soviet Union, and even a direct call for this war—with the threat of using the atomic bomb—such is the content of the statements on relations with the Soviet Union by reactionaries at public meetings and in the press. . . .

The basic goal of this anti-Soviet campaign of American "public opinion" is to exert political pressure on the Soviet Union and compel it to make concessions. Another, no less important goal of the campaign is the attempt to create an atmosphere of war psychosis among the masses, who are weary of war, thus making it easier for the U.S. government to carry out measures for the maintenance of high military potential.

QUESTIONS FOR ANALYSIS

1. Which points in Ambassador Novikov's assessment of the international situation seem accurate?
2. What role do the personal characteristics of Americans and U.S. domestic politics play in the ambassador's assessment?
3. What sorts of information and comments did Foreign Minister Molotov underline and why?

"What Is a Woman? . . .
She Is the Other"

PHILOSOPHER AND NOVELIST SIMONE DE BEAUVOIR (1908–1986) was born into a well-to-do professional family. A Parisian for most of her life, she attended exclusive schools where girls received a polished education. World War I started her family—and many other prosperous Europeans—on a downward spiral, ruining their investments and destroying their security. In her teens it became evident that she would need higher education to pursue a career by which she could support herself. Beauvoir was accepted at the most prestigious university in Paris—the École Normale Supérieure—where her classmates included Jean-Paul Sartre and other intellectual stars of her generation.

Sartre had a reputation for brilliance, but he kept flunking the exam that would give him a degree in philosophy. In contrast, Beauvoir not only passed her exam with real distinction but she completed the courses for her philosophy degree in two years rather than the usual three. The examiners, however, felt so sorry for Sartre that they not only passed him but ranked him first in the class, ranking Beauvoir second. Later, Sartre more than once remarked cruelly to friends that Beauvoir was far inferior to him—calling her a plodder and a grind. Beauvoir believed his view of her, and her memoirs are full of tributes to his achievement: "Sartre thought this" and "Sartre claimed that" introduce her retellings of ideas that he may have gotten from her.

The couple's relationship was complicated. Beauvoir was his acknowledged partner, but she willingly found him other women whom he might like. Later in their lives, she also obtained the drugs to which he was increasingly addicted. Beauvoir did her own writing in the morning and then worked on Sartre's from noon until the early evening, while he visited with friends, made public appearances, and conducted other love affairs. This pattern lasted many years and is well documented by their acquaintances and biographers.

That is the background of Simone de Beauvoir's remarkably astute analysis of women's situation in the West. *The Second Sex* (1949) became a best seller in France because of Sartre's fame and then established itself as a classic around the world. Young women like Gloria Steinem and career women like Betty Friedan helped found the women's liberation movement in the United States based on their understanding of women's situation as presented in *The Second Sex*. Translated into dozens of languages, the book inspired millions of women, despite its philosophical rigor. Beauvoir identified a range of women (and men) seen and treated degradingly as "the other," including blacks in the United States. Despite her stirring analysis—which struck readers as providing reasons for discrimination by white men and acquiescence to it by women—Beauvoir did not call for the creation of a women's movement. To the contrary, she saw the problem as purely philosophical and psychological: women simply had to stop seeing themselves as "the other," start behaving authentically, and thereby create equality.

Document 7.2

SIMONE DE BEAUVOIR
The Second Sex, 1949

If her functioning as a female is not enough to define woman, if we decline also to explain her through "the eternal feminine," and if nevertheless we admit, provisionally, that women do exist, then we must face the question: what is a woman?

To state the question is, to me, to suggest, at once, a preliminary answer. The fact that I ask it is in itself significant. A man would never get the notion of writing a book on the peculiar situation of the human male. But if I wish to define myself, I must first of all say: "I am a woman"; on this truth must be based all further discussion. A man never begins by presenting himself as an individual of a certain sex; it goes without saying that he is a man. The terms *masculine* and *feminine* are used symmetrically only as a matter of form, as on legal papers. In actuality the relation of the two sexes is not quite like that of two electrical poles, for man represents both the positive and the neutral, as is indicated by the common use of *man* to designate human beings in general; whereas woman represents only the negative, defined by limiting criteria, without reciprocity. In the midst of an abstract discussion it is vexing to hear a man say: "You think thus and so because you are a woman"; but I know that my only defense is to reply: "I think thus and so because it is true," thereby removing my subjective self from the ar-

gument. It would be out of the question to reply: "And you think the contrary because you are a man," for it is understood that the fact of being a man is no peculiarity. A man is in the right in being a man; it is the woman who is in the wrong. It amounts to this: just as for the ancients there was an absolute vertical with reference to which the oblique was defined, so there is an absolute human type, the masculine. Woman has ovaries, a uterus; these peculiarities imprison her in her subjectivity, circumscribe her within the limits of her own nature. It is often said that she thinks with her glands. Man superbly ignores the fact that his anatomy also includes glands, such as the testicles, and that they secrete hormones. He thinks of his body as a direct and normal connection with the world, which he believes he apprehends objectively, whereas he regards the body of woman as a hindrance, a prison, weighed down by everything peculiar to it. "The female is a female by virtue of a certain *lack* of qualities," said Aristotle; "we should regard the female nature as afflicted with a natural defectiveness." And St. Thomas for his part pronounced woman to be an "imperfect man," an "incidental" being. This is symbolized in Genesis where Eve is depicted as made from what Bossuet called "a supernumerary bone" of Adam.

Thus humanity is male and man defines woman not in herself but as relative to him; she is not regarded as an autonomous being. Michelet writes: "Woman, the relative being. . . ." And Benda is most positive . . . : "The body of man makes

SOURCE: Simone de Beauvoir, *The Second Sex*, ed. and trans. H. M. Parshley (New York: Bantam, 1961 [1949]), xv–xvii, 401, 403–405, 424–425.

sense in itself quite apart from that of woman, whereas the latter seems wanting in significance by itself. . . . Man can think of himself without woman. She cannot think of herself without man." And she is simply what man decrees; thus she is called "the sex," by which is meant that she appears essential to the male as a sexual being. For him she is sex—absolute sex, no less. She is defined and differentiated with reference to man and not he with reference to her; she is the incidental, the inessential as opposed to the essential. He is the Subject, he is the Absolute—she is the Other.

The category of the *Other* is as primordial as consciousness itself. In the most primitive societies, in the most ancient mythologies, one finds the expression of a duality—that of the Self and the Other. This duality was not originally attached to the division of the sexes; it was not dependent on any empirical facts. . . . The feminine element was at first no more involved in such pairs as Varuna-Mitra, Uranus-Zeus, Sun-Moon, and Day-Night than it was in the contrasts between good and evil, lucky and unlucky auspices, right and left, God and Lucifer. Otherness is a fundamental category of human thought.

Thus it is that no group ever sets itself up as the One without at once setting up the Other over against itself. If three travelers chance to occupy the same compartment, that is enough to make vaguely hostile "others" out of all the rest of the passengers on the train. In small-town eyes all persons not belonging to the village are "strangers" and suspect; to the native of a country all who inhabit other countries are "foreigners"; Jews are "different" for the anti-Semite, Negroes are "inferior" for American racists, aborigines are "natives" for colonists, proletarians are the "lower class" for the privileged.

THE MARRIED WOMAN

Marriage has always been a very different thing for man and for woman. The two sexes are necessary to each other, but this necessity has never brought about a condition of reciprocity between them;

women, as we have seen, have never constituted a caste making exchanges and contracts with the male caste upon a footing of equality. A man is socially an independent and complete individual; he is regarded first of all as a producer whose existence is justified by the work he does for the group; we have seen why it is that the reproductive and domestic role to which woman is confined has not guaranteed her an equal dignity. Certainly the male needs her; in some primitive groups it may happen that the bachelor, unable to manage his existence by himself, becomes a kind of outcast; in agricultural societies a woman coworker is essential to the peasant; and for most men it is of advantage to unload certain drudgery upon a mate; the individual wants a regular sexual life and posterity, and the State requires him to contribute to its perpetuation. But man does not make his appeal directly to woman herself; it is the men's group that allows each of its members to find self-fulfillment as husband and father; woman, as slave or vassal, is integrated within families dominated by fathers and brothers, and she has always been given in marriage by certain males to other males.

In such circumstances the girl seems absolutely passive; she *is* married, *given* in marriage by her parents. Boys *get* married, they *take* a wife. They look in marriage for an enlargement, a confirmation of their existence, but not the mere right to exist; it is a charge they assume voluntarily. Thus they can inquire concerning its advantages and disadvantages, as did the Greek and medieval satirists; for them it is one mode of living, not a preordained lot. They have a perfect right to prefer celibate solitude; some marry late, or not at all.

In marrying, woman gets some share in the world as her own; legal guarantees protect her against capricious action by man; but she becomes his vassal. He is the economic head of the joint enterprise, and hence he represents it in the view of society. She takes his name; she belongs to his religion, his class, his circle; she joins his family, she becomes his "half." She follows wherever his work calls him and determines their place of residence; she breaks more or less decisively with her past, becoming attached to her husband's universe; she gives him her person, virginity and a rigorous fidelity being required. She loses some of the rights legally belonging to the unmarried woman.

Since the husband is the productive worker, he is the one who goes beyond family interest to that of society, opening up a future for himself through co-operation in the building of a collective future: he incarnates transcendence. Woman is doomed to the continuation of the species and the care of the home—that is to say, to immanence. The fact is that every human existence involves transcendence and immanence at the same time; to go forward, each existence must be maintained, for it to expand toward the future it must integrate the past, and while intercommunicating with others it should find self-confirmation. These two elements—maintenance and progression—are implied in any living activity, and for *man* marriage permits precisely a happy synthesis of the two. In his occupation and his political life he encounters change and progress, he senses his extension through time and the universe; and when he is tired of such roaming, he gets himself a home, a fixed location, and an anchorage in the world. At evening he restores his soul in the home, where his wife takes care of his furnishings and children and guards the things of the past that she keeps in store. But she has no other job than to maintain and provide for life in pure and unvarying generality; she perpetuates the species without change, she ensures the even rhythm of the days and the continuity of the home, seeing to it that the doors are locked. But she is allowed no direct influence upon the future nor upon the world; she reaches out beyond herself toward the social group only through her husband as intermediary.

Marriage today still retains, for the most part, this traditional form. And, first of all, it is forced much more tyrannically upon the young girl than upon the young man. There are still important social strata in which no other vista opens before her. . . .

We have already considered the many inhibitions and difficulties that the virgin must overcome if she is to accomplish her sexual destiny: her initiation requires a real travail at once physiological and psychic. The attempt to crowd it all into one night is stupid and barbarous; it is absurd to make a duty of such a delicate and difficult matter as the first intercourse. The woman is more frightened because the strange operation she must undergo is sacred, because society, religion, family, and friends have solemnly handed her over to her husband as if to a master; and also because the act seems to her to involve her whole future, marriage being still regarded as a definitive step taken once for all. At this moment she feels herself truly revealed in the absolute: this man to whom she is vowed forever incarnates Man as a whole in her eyes; and now he is revealed to her also as an unknown, but one who is of frightful importance, since he is to be her lifelong companion. Then, too, the man himself is filled with anxiety by the assignment that now weighs upon him; he has his own difficulties, his own complexes, which may make him either timid or clumsy or rough; and sometimes he is rendered impotent on his wedding night by the very solemnity of it all. . . .

The wedding night transforms the erotic act into a test that both parties fear their inability to meet, each being too worried by his or her own problems to be able to think generously of the other. This gives the occasion a formidable air of solemnity, and it is not surprising if it dooms the woman to lasting frigidity. The difficult problem facing the husband is this: if, in Aristotle's phrase, "he titillates his wife too lasciviously," she may be scandalized and outraged; it would appear that the fear of this outcome paralyzes American husbands, for example, especially in couples of college education who have practiced extreme premarital restraint, as the Kinsey Report states, because the women of this group are deeply inhibited and unable to "participate with the abandon which is necessary for the successful consummation of any sexual relation." But if, on the other hand, the husband "respects" his wife, he fails to awaken her sensuality. This dilemma is created by the ambiguity of the feminine attitude: the young woman simultaneously desires and declines sex pleasure; she demands a reserve from which she suffers. Unless exceptionally fortunate, the young husband will of necessity seem either a libertine or a bungler. It is not astonishing, therefore, that "conjugal duties" may often seem boring and repugnant to the wife.

As a matter of fact, many women become mothers and grandmothers without ever having experienced the orgasm or even any sex excitement at all; in some cases they endeavor to escape the demeaning "duty" through a doctor's recommendation or on other pretexts, Kinsey states that there are many wives "who report that they consider their coital frequencies already too high and wish that their husbands did not desire intercourse so often. A very few wives wish for more frequent coitus." But as we have seen, woman's erotic capabilities are almost unlimited. This contradiction clearly indicates that marriage kills feminine eroticism in the effort to regularize it.

But in order to find a hearth and home within oneself, one must first have found self-realization in works or in deeds. Man is but mildly interested in his immediate surroundings because he can find self-expression in projects. Whereas woman is confined within the conjugal sphere; it is for her to change that prison into a realm. Her attitude toward her home is dictated by the same dialectic that defines her situation in general: she takes by becoming prey; she finds freedom by giving it up; by renouncing the world she aims to conquer a world.

It is not without some regret that she shuts behind her the doors of her new home; when she was a girl, the whole countryside was her homeland; the forests were hers. Now she is confined to a restricted space; Nature is reduced to the dimensions of a potted geranium; walls cut off the horizon. But she is going to set about overcoming these limitations. In the form of more or less expensive bric-a-brac she has within her four walls the fauna and flora of the world, she has exotic countries and past times; she has her husband, representing human society, and she has her child, who gives her the entire future in portable form. . . .

Thanks to the velvets and silks and porcelains with which she surrounds herself, woman can in some degree satisfy that tactile sensuality which her erotic life can seldom assuage. These decorations will also provide an expression of her personality; she is the one who has chosen, made, hunted out furnishings and knick-knacks, who has arranged them in accordance with an aesthetic principle in which regard for symmetry is usually an important element; they reflect her individuality while bearing public witness to her standard of living. Her home is thus her earthly lot, the expression of her social value and of her truest self. Because she *does* nothing, she eagerly seeks self-realization in what she *has*.

In domestic work, with or without the aid of servants, woman makes her home her own, finds social justification, and provides herself with an occupation, an activity, that deals usefully and satisfyingly with material objects—shining stoves, fresh, clean clothes, bright copper, polished furniture—but provides no escape from immanence and little affirmation of individuality. . . .

QUESTIONS FOR ANALYSIS

1. In what ways does *The Second Sex* echo themes of postwar moral revival?
2. What aspects of this document would have appealed to reform-minded women?
3. What themes in these passages attack the gender status quo?

The Purges in Czechoslovakia

PURGES CAME TO EASTERN AND CENTRAL EUROPE almost as soon as the Communists took over the region, and like earlier purges in the Soviet Union they targeted sincere party members and committed activists. Communists rooted out their enemies in brutal score-settling and purges of popular political figures or simply by creating a menacing atmosphere such as the one that caused Stanislaw Mikolajczyk to flee Poland. Many purges, such as the trial and execution in 1952 of Rudolf Margolius, husband of Heda Kovály Margolius, followed hard on the heels of Marshal Tito's announcement of the independent Communist course he had in mind for Yugoslavia.

Czechoslovakia had one of the few functioning democracies in eastern Europe before World War II, and right after the war it looked as though democracy there would pick up where it had left off. Political life revived immediately. Many Czechs, however, held that the Slovak population had not developed such a sophisticated political sense as had the Czechs, and this ethnic chauvinism helped poison the political atmosphere. Adding fuel to the political fire, Communist leaders stepped in and brought Slovak political leaders to trial. Having gained some public approval for attacking Slovaks, the Czech Communists proceeded to try resistance leaders. It didn't matter that many of them had a following among the people because of their wartime bravery, and that some of them had worked with the Communists during the war. They were thought to know too much about the workings of the Communist Party's intelligence networks.

In late spring of 1950, Milada Horáková (1901–1950) and twelve other democratic leaders were tried for treason and espionage in the first "show trial" in Czechoslovakia. It was so named because Soviets planned and scripted the prosecution and conduct of the proceedings. Horáková had been a resistance member and an advocate for women's rights; she had been captured and imprisoned by the Nazis. In Czechoslovakia her popularity as a political figure was overwhelming. Historians have compared her with Czech Communist Rudolf Margolius as a person of "clean character" rather than an opportunist or ideologue.[25] Sentenced to death, she was defended by Albert Einstein, who protested her sentence, but by few others.

Document 7.3 contains the official charges against Horáková—the first woman to be executed in this series of purges—and the individuals tried with her. Document 7.4, a letter to her teenage daughter, is one of several letters she wrote in the interval between the time she was condemned to death on June 24 and executed by hanging on June 27. She wrote long letters to her mother-in-law and to her husband, who had fled the country. She thanked her husband for supporting her work and accepting her lack of ability in housewifely tasks: "I was your lover more than your wife, for a wife I lacked the necessary feeling for the exclusiveness of her tasks. I had my wings spread, and you did not keep me from flying even at the expense of your personal happiness. I had in you a perfect husband and pal."[26] These two very different kinds of communications focus our attention on the intersection of public policies and political life with personal and family well-being. In the letter to her sixteen-year-old daughter, Horáková offered not only apologies but advice that was supposed to last a lifetime.

Document 7.3

Official Account of the Trial of Milada Horáková, 1950

The trial of Dr. Milada Horáková and her twelve companions in the state court in Prague. . . .

Here, facing the working people, on the bench of the accused are those who followed the shameful road of the bourgeoisie, of the criminals who joined against the people of this republic in order to thrust a dagger in their back. The traitors of the republic sit here fully unmasked.

The trial of the enemies of the people took place in front of the working people of the whole republic. They were representatives of the class which lost its battles on the open stage, and now it no longer returns as a political force, but as a political underworld. . . .

This trial however is not only ending as the unmasking of those obscure figures but also of the gentlemen whom February blew to the West.

This trial reveals Messers Zenkl and Ripka, Hais and Majer and all the rest . . . as professional agents of the American, English or French imperialists. . . .

After February the rats crawled into their holes, and as a number of trials showed, they continued in the underground dancing according to the American whistle. But the objective situation is not favorable to the gauleiters° and little Hitlers. Our camp, the world camp of peace, democracy and socialism, led by the powerful Soviet Union, grows and becomes more powerful every day. We are fighting, and we are fighting for peace. We are building socialism. The accused want to stand in the way of this building. They are preparing war. . . .

We advise the traitors at home and abroad: keep your hands off the republic. . . . I call on the working people to be ever watchful. May they learn from this case . . . to recognize the enemy, those . . . who prepare the new war, the servants of the aggressors. The people of our republic are not only building paradise on earth; they also will defend this paradise against the forces of the old, mean world which is condemned to destruction.

SOURCE: Karel Beran, *Pred soudem lidu* (Prague, 1950), quoted in Wilma Abeles Iggers, *Women of Prague: Ethnic Diversity and Social Change from the Eighteenth Century to the Present* (Providence: Berghahn Books, 1995), 300–301.

°*gauleiters:* Regional rulers under Hitler.

Document 7.4

MILADA HORÁKOVÁ
Letter to Her Daughter before Execution, 1950

You know that to organize one's scale of values well means to know not only oneself well, to be firm in the analysis of one's character, but mainly to know the others, to know as much of the world as possible, its past, present, and future development. Well, in short, to know, to understand. Not to close one's ears before anything and for no reason—not to shut out the thoughts and opinions of anybody who stepped on my toes, or even wounded me deeply. Examine, think, criticize, yes, mainly criticize yourself, don't be ashamed to admit a truth you have come to realize, even if you proclaimed the opposite a little while ago; don't become obstinate about your opinions, but when you come to consider something right, then be so definite that you can fight and die for it. . . . Death is not bad. Just avoid gradual dying which is what happens when one suddenly finds oneself apart from the real life of others. . . .

Another value is work. I don't know which to assign the first place and which the second. . . . Learn to love work! Any work, but one you have to know really and thoroughly. Then don't be afraid of anything, and things will turn out well for you. . . .

I heard from my legal representative that you are doing well in school, and that you want to continue. . . . I was very pleased. But even if you would one day have to leave school and to work for your livelihood, don't stop learning and studying. If you really want to, you will reach your goal. I would have liked for you to become a medical doctor—you remember that we talked about it. Of course you will decide yourself and circumstances will, too. But if you stand one day in the traditional alma mater and carry home from graduation not only your doctor's diploma, but also the real ability to bring people relief as a doctor—then, my little girl . . . your mother will be immensely pleased. . . .

But your mother would only be . . . truly happy, no matter where you stand, whether at the operating table, . . . at your child's cradle or at the work table in your household, if you will do your work skillfully, honestly, happily, and with your whole being. Then you will be successful in it. Don't be demanding in life, but have high goals. . . .

And now also something for your body. I am glad that you are engaged in sports. Just do it systematically. I think that there should be rhythmic exercises, and if you have time, also some good, systematic gymnastics. And those quarter hours every morning! Believe me finally that it would save you a lot of annoyance about unfavorable proportions of your waist, if you could really do it. It is also good for the training of your will and perseverance. Also take care of your complexion regularly—I do not mean makeup, God forbid, but healthy daily care. And love your neck and feet as you do your face and lips. A brush has to be your good friend, every day, and not only for your hands and feet; use it on every little bit of your skin. Salicyl alcohol and Fennydin, that is enough for beauty, and then air and sun. But about that you will find better advisors than I am.

Your photograph showed me your new hairdo; it looks good, but isn't it a shame [to hide] your nice forehead? And that lady in the ball gown! Really, you looked lovely but your mother's

SOURCE: Wilma Abeles Iggers, *Women of Prague: Ethnic Diversity and Social Change from the Eighteenth Century to the Present* (Providence: Berghahn Books, 1995), 306, 307, 308, 309.

eye noticed one fault, which may be due to the way you were placed on the photograph — wasn't the neck opening a little deep for your sixteen years? I am sorry I did not see the photo of your new winter coat. Did you use the muff from your aunt as a fur collar? Don't primp, but whenever possible, dress carefully and neatly. And don't wear shoes until they are run down at the heel! Are you wearing innersoles? And how is your thyroid gland? These questions don't, of course, require an answer, they are only meant as your mother's reminders.

. . . And so, my only young daughter, little girl Jana, new life, my hope, my future forgiveness, live! Grasp life with both hands! Until my last breath I shall pray for your happiness, my dear child!

I kiss your hair, eyes and mouth, I stroke you and hold you in my arms. (I really held you so little.) I shall always be with you. . . .

QUESTIONS FOR ANALYSIS

1. What values and attitudes are expressed in the official account of the show trial?

2. What values does Horáková express in the advice she gives her daughter?

3. What uses can we make of these two documents in understanding the past? Does one document help us understand the past more than the other? Do they have equal importance as evidence? Why?

PICTURE ESSAY

Cold War Media
and the Struggle
of Good versus Evil

THE COLD WAR WAS AN OMNIPRESENT REALITY in the lives of Europeans, in large part owing to the workings of the media and entertainment industries. Sometimes subtle and sometimes blatant, anti-American and anti-Communist messages pervaded popular culture—turning up in everything from novels and movies to radio plays, television, cartoons, and advertisements. Whatever the medium, the cold war was portrayed less as an international political contest and more as a cosmic drama of good versus evil. Whether moralizing against "godless communism" or attacking fat and decadent "western capitalists," cold war propaganda was ubiquitous in European popular culture.

Of course, demonizing one's enemies was hardly a new phenomenon (think of medieval Christians crusading against Islam and British colonizers inveighing against the barbaric "savages" of North America). But the nature and cost of twentieth-century warfare—with its sophisticated and destructive technology, from machine guns and tanks to nuclear weapons able to annihilate whole populations and habitats—upped the ante considerably. Indeed, the mass mobilization of people needed to produce industrial weaponry and pay the gigantic costs of industrial warfare—not only monetary costs but emotional costs as well—necessitated aggressive marketing on many fronts: the cold war was portrayed as a contest pitting civilization against barbarism, good against evil. As writer George Orwell pointed out, only constant preaching about the morality of one's cause and the tyranny of the other side could keep people riled up enough to work and fight. Mass media—print, radio, television, film—and advertising helped spread the message, making Europeans and their allies more aware of the "enemy" than ever before.

The cast of characters in this cold war drama included military types, picking up on the image of the brave knight or the benevolent superman. Pilots became the heroes of the Berlin story, playing the role of savior by airlifting supplies to Berliners blockaded by the Soviets. Figure 7.1 shows U.S. air force lieutenant Gail S. Halvorsen, "the Candy Bomber," meeting with some of the Berlin children who received the candy he dropped.

The Western media also celebrated the heroism and ingenuity of individuals trying to escape from iron curtain countries. Figure 7.2 shows a little boy trussed up in a harness attached to a pulley that will allow him to slide down a cable to

◆ **Figure 7.1 "The Candy Bomber"**
Brown Brothers.

safety on the western side of the Berlin Wall. What effect do you think this photograph and Figure 7.1 (both published in many Western newspapers) had on their audience? Were people moved by them? Are you? Why? Does it matter that the photograph of the man and child was staged after the fact? Why or why not?

Heroes and heroines took many different forms during this period. When cold war propagandists focused on the space race—which produced rocketry for intercontinental missiles able to deliver nuclear weapons—cosmonauts and astronauts became famous. Their exploits in outer space captured the imagination of people across the world, as the porcelain statuette of Soviet cosmonauts standing in front of a rocket indicates (Figure 7.3). In the USSR, real-live cosmonauts Yuri Gagarin

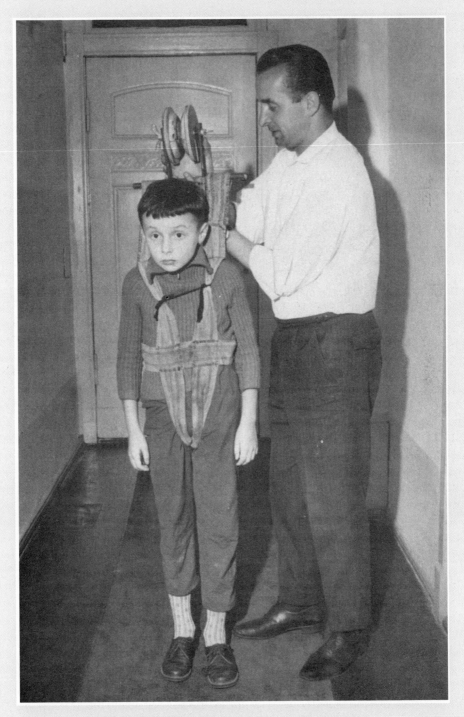

◆ Figure 7.2 **Escapee across the Berlin Wall**

◆ **Figure 7.3 Soviet-era Kitsch**
Cooper Hewitt, National Design Museum, Smithsonian Institute.

and Valentina Tereshkova achieved superstar status. In the United States, the July 1969 moonwalk of astronauts Neil Armstrong and Edwin "Buzz" Aldrin made them popular heroes as well.

Perhaps even more admired were some of the fictional characters featured in the spy literature of British author Ian Fleming and his Soviet counterpart, writer Yulian Simyonov. Fleming's creation, British espionage agent James Bond, also known as "007," became famous for outwitting evil enemies determined to destroy the free world and for seducing the female enemy agents deployed against him, as in Figure 7.4, from the 1964 film *Goldfinger.* What was the cold war message of these espionage thrillers, if any? Think of the early James Bond movies with Sean Connery. What evidence of cold war themes and influence do you see in them? In the original James Bond novels, the standard enemy was an obviously Soviet or Communist intelligence or terrorist organization, such as the evil S.M.E.R.S.H. (the acronym for a real Soviet counterintelligence agency in the 1930s and 1940s). In most of the film adaptations, however, to avoid direct criticism of the Soviet Union, writers and producers substituted an independent criminal organization — S.P.E.C.T.R.E. — that threatened both the U.S. and the Soviet blocs. Why do you think they made that change?

Even as both sides in the cold war celebrated their achievements in the space race and enjoyed the exploits and amorous antics of James Bond and his Soviet counterparts, the looming threat that each side posed to the ideals, way of life, and security of the other remained deadly serious matters to politicians and ordinary people alike. Two cartoons from the period vividly illustrate their fears. The 1962 drawing for the Soviet humor magazine *Krokodil* shows the United States elbowing France and Britain out of any leadership role in NATO rendered in Russian Cyrillic letters as "HATO" (Figure 7.5). *Krokodil's*

◆ Figure 7.4 **Movie Still from *Goldfinger***
The Everett Collection.

circulation reached into the millions and had such influence that even though it lapsed after the fall of the Soviet Union in 1992 it has since been revived to criticize the current Russian leadership. In its early days, however, it was part of a vast publishing system in the Soviet sphere, where some six thousand newspapers, literary and humor magazines, and periodicals addressed to both men and women were printed in sixty languages. What points does this cartoon seek to make to its audience? How does it make them? Four million copies of the comic book cover in Figure 7.6 were published, and similar takeover stories appeared in movies, cartoons, and magazines throughout the era. What will happen to "America under Communism," according to this depiction? This comic book was published by a religious organization in 1947. What effect do the publisher and date have on your analysis of Figure 7.6? Compare the U.S. comic book cover to Figure 7.4. What, if anything, changed in the intervening ten or fifteen years between them that might account for their vast difference in tone?

However seriously people on both sides took the rhetoric and marketing of the cold war, there was one reality that no one could afford to overlook: the potential for nuclear holocaust. With the dropping of atomic bombs on Hiroshima and Nagasaki in 1945, the unthinkable happened, yet by the mid-1950s both the United

◆ **Figure 7.5 Soviet Anti-American Cartoon**
Sovfoto.

States and the USSR had tested hydrogen bombs, and both continued to increase their nuclear arsenals as concern about the intentions of the other mounted. In response, a groundswell of activism began on both sides among those who feared nuclear conflagration more than they feared the enemy. During the Easter weekend of 1958, British protesters from the Campaign for Nuclear Disarmament (CND) marched from London to Aldermaston, where British nuclear weapons were and still are manufactured. Many marchers displayed what we know today as the peace sign, created by British artist Gerald Holtom in that year specifically as a logo for the CND. The logo featured prominently in peace demonstrations thereafter, as is

◆ Figure 7.6 **American Anti-Soviet Cartoon**
From the Collection of Charles Christensen.

◆ **Figure 7.7 Peace March to Aldermaston and Peace Symbol**
Hulton Deutsch/CORBIS.

shown in Figure 7.7 where the eighty-nine-year-old prominent philosopher and peace activist Bertrand Russell appears with his wife. Although thousands of women in many countries mobilized with their neighbors and children to demonstrate, it was Russell who came to serve as a media icon for the campaign. Why do you think that was so? Why do you think this particular logo for peace caught on? What is the logo meant to symbolize? Is the peace sign still popular today?

QUESTIONS FOR ANALYSIS

1. Compare these images to those in the Picture Essays for Chapter 3 ("The Home Front") and Chapter 6 ("World War II Propaganda and Modern Racism"). In what ways are images from the cold war related to the images from World Wars I and II?

2. Do these cold war images play more to reason or to the emotions? Explain your answer. Do you find humor in any of these images? Which ones and why?

3. Consider the different forms—film, cartoons, photographs, a figurine—used to convey cold war messages in this Picture Essay. Which ones seem more likely than others to have effectively conveyed their intended messages? Why?

NOTES

1. Quoted in Padraic Kenney, "Polish Workers and the Stalinist Transformation," in *The Establishment of Communist Regimes in Eastern Europe, 1944–1949*, ed. Norman Naimark and Leonid Gibianskii (Boulder: Westview, 1997), 141–142.

2. Anna Peters, quoted in Robert Moeller, *Protecting Motherhood: Women and the Family in the Politics of Postwar West Germany* (Berkeley: University of California Press, 1993), 20.

3. *The Economist,* January 26, 1946, quoted in Richard Vinen, *A History in Fragments: Europe in the Twentieth Century* (Cambridge: Da Capo, 2001), 239.

4. Quoted in Elena Zubkova, *Russia after the War: Hopes, Illusions, and Disappointments, 1945–1957,* trans. Hugh Ragsdale (Armonk: M. E. Sharpe, 1998), 48–49.

5. George Clare, *Before the Wall: Berlin Days, 1946–1948* (New York: Dutton, 1990), 39.

6. Quoted in Henry Steele Commager, *Documents of American History,* vol. 2, 9th ed. (Englewood Cliffs: Prentice Hall, 1973), 527.

7. Quoted ibid., 533–534.

8. Quoted in Barbara Jelavich, *History of the Balkans* vol. 2, *Twentieth Century* (Cambridge: Cambridge University Press, 1983), 32.

9. Diary of Huguette Robert, August 25, 1944, quoted in Emmanuel d'Astier de la Vigerie, *De la chute á la libération de Paris, 25 août 1944* (Paris: Gallímard, 1965), 215.

10. Quoted in Sarah Fishman, *We Will Wait: Wives of French Prisoners of War, 1940–1945* (New Haven: Yale University Press, 1991), 164.

11. Quoted in Michael Marrus, *The Unwanted: European Refugees in the Twentieth Century* (New York: Oxford University Press, 1985), 325–326.

12. Norman M. Naimark, *The Russians in Germany: A History of the Soviet Zone of Occupation, 1945–1949* (Cambridge: Harvard University Press, 1995), 69–140.

13. Quoted in Zubkova, *Russia after the War,* 60.

14. Milovan Djilas, quoted in Richard Overy, *Russia's War* (London: Penguin, 1997), 290.

15. Quoted in Zubkova, *Russia after the War,* 137.

16. V. S. Pritchett, quoted in Richard Mayne, *Postwar: The Dawn of Today's Europe* (New York: Schocken, 1983), 10.

17. Lila Lounguina, *Les saisons de Moscou, 1933–1990* (Paris: Plon, 1990), 82, 83, 84. My translation.

18. Anne Frank, *Diary of a Young Girl,* trans. B. M. Mooyaart Doubleday (New York: Simon and Schuster, 1953), 237.

19. Virginia Woolf, "The Leaning Tower," in *Collected Essays,* vol. 2 (London: Hogarth, 1966), 179.

20. Wislawa Szymborska, quoted in Edward Hirsch, "A Poetry That Matters," *New York Times Magazine,* December 1, 1996, 50.

21. Quoted in Gerhart Hoffmeister and Frederic C. Tubach, *Germany: 2000 Years,* vol. 3, *From the Nazi Era to the Present* (New York: Ungar, 1986), 89–90.

22. Holy See, II Vatican Council, *Nostra Aetate*. www.vatican.va/archive/hist_councils.

23. Barry D. Adam, *The Rise of a Gay and Lesbian Movement* (Boston: G. K. Hall, 1987), 163.

24. Mme. X, interview by Bonnie G. Smith. Spring 1998, Princeton, N.J.

25. Igor Lukes, "Rudolf Margolius: A Clean Man in a Filthy Time," 2002. Available at http://www.margolius.co.uk/.

26. Wilma Abeles Iggers, *Women of Prague: Ethnic Diversity and Social Change from the Eighteenth Century to the Present* (Providence: Berghahn Books, 1995), 306.

SUGGESTED REFERENCES

General Works

Hitchcock, William. *The Struggle for Europe: The Turbulent History of a Divided Continent, 1945–2002.* 2003.

Hunt, Michael H. *The World Transformed: 1945 to the Present.* 2004.

Judt, Tony. *Postwar: A History of Europe since 1945.* 2006.

Rothschild, Joseph. *Return to Diversity: A Political History of East Central Europe since World War II.* 1993.

Wakeman, Rosemary, ed. *Themes in Modern European History: 1945 to the Present.* 2003.

Cold War and The New World Politics Historians continue to debate the origins and course of the cold war. Some of the most interesting work looks at the creation of Communist rule in eastern Europe.

Cronin, James. *The World the Cold War Made: Order, Chaos, and the Return of History.* 1996.

Eisenberg, Carolyn Woods. *Drawing the Line: The American Decision to Divide Germany, 1944–1949.* 1996.

Gaddis, John. *The Cold War: A New History.* 2006.

Hogan, Michael J. *A Cross of Iron: Harry S. Truman and the Origins of the National Security State.* 1998.

Holloway, David. *Stalin and the Bomb: The Soviet Union and Atomic Energy, 1939–1956.* 1994.

Leffler, Melvyn P., and David S. Painter. *Origins of the Cold War: An International History.* 2005.

Murphy, David E., Sergei A. Kondrashev, and George Bailey. *Battleground Berlin: CIA vs. KGB in the Cold War.* 1997.

Naimark, Norman M. *The Russians in Germany: A History of the Soviet Zone of Occupation, 1945–1949.* 1995.

Naimark, Norman, and Leonid Gibianskii, eds. *The Establishment of Communist Regimes in Eastern Europe, 1944–1949.* 1997.

Wagnleitner, Reinhold. *Coca-Colonization and the Cold War: The Cultural Mission of the United States in Austria after the Second World War*. 1994.

Bringing Order to Postwar Europe   The reconstruction of Europe took place on many fronts, including the diplomatic, social, and cultural realms. Moeller's and Jobs's books show how new stories were told about the war and about the place of soldiers, women, and youth in re-creating peacetime conditions. Courtois, Feinberg, and Frommer paint particularly grim pictures, however.

Brannigan, John. *Literature, Culture and Society in Postwar England, 1945–1965*. 2002.

Courtois, Stéphane, et al. *The Black Book of Communism: Crimes, Terror, Repression*. 1999.

Feinberg, Melissa. *Democracy and Its Limits: Gender and Rights in the Czech Lands, 1918–1950*. 2006.

Frommer, Benjamin. *National Cleansing: Retribution against Nazi Collaborators in Postwar Czechoslovakia*. 2005.

Gross, Jan. *Fear: Anti-Semitism after Auschwitz*. 2006

Hitchcock, William. *France Restored: Cold War Diplomacy and the Quest for Leadership in Europe, 1944–1954*. 1998.

Jobs, Richard I. *Riding the New Wave: Youth and the Rejuvenation of France after World War II*. 2006.

Moeller, Robert. *War Stories: The Search for a Usable Past in the Federal Republic of Germany*. 2001.

———, ed. *West Germany under Construction: Politics, Society and Culture in the Adenauer Era*. 1997.

Trachtenberg, Marc. *A Constructed Peace: The Making of the European Settlement, 1945–1963*. 1999.

Van Hook, James C. *Rebuilding Germany: The Creation of the Social Market Economy, 1945–1957*. 2004.

Zubkova, Elena. *Russia after the War: Hopes, Illusions, and Disappointments, 1945–1957*. 1998.

Restoring Cultural Values   Historians have examined the reestablishment of political institutions, as in the work of Kenney and Wall, and more recently have looked at the way sex and gender worked to reshape the postwar cultural landscape, as in the books of Heineman and Herzog.

Gundle, Stephen. *Between Hollywood and Moscow: The Italian Communists and the Challenge of Mass Culture, 1943–1991*. 2000.

Heineman, Elizabeth D. *What Difference Does a Husband Make? Women and Marital Status in Nazi and Postwar Germany*. 1999.

Herf, Jeffrey. *Divided Memory: The Nazi Past in the Two Germany*. 1997.

Herzog, Dagmar. *Sex after Fascism: Memory and Morality in Twentieth-Century Germany*. 2005.

Hoffmeister, Gerhart, and Frederic C. Tubach. *Germany: 2000 Years.* Vol. 3. *From the Nazi Era to the Present.* 1986.

Judt, Tony. *The Burden of Responsibility: Blum, Camus, Aron, and the French Twentieth Century.* 1998.

Kenney, Padraic. *Rebuilding Poland: Workers and Communists, 1945–1950.* 1997.

Olick, Jeffrey K. *In the House of the Hangman: The Agonies of German Defeat, 1943–1949.* 2005.

Rowley, Hazel. *Tête-à-Tête: Simone de Beauvoir and Jean-Paul Sartre.* 2005.

Wall, Irwin. *The United States and the Making of Postwar France, 1945–1954.* 1991.

The Deepening Cold War   The cold war continued to intensify despite moments of thaw. Both the arms build-up and the Cuban missile crisis were key aspects of that intensification.

Beschloss, Michael R. *The Crisis Years: Kennedy and Khrushchev, 1960–1963.* 1991.

Caute, David. *The Dancer Defects: The Struggle for Cultural Supremacy during the Cold War.* 2003.

Chang, Laurence, and Peter Kornbluh, eds. *The Cuban Missile Crisis, 1962: A National Security Archive Documents Reader.* 1999.

Dickson, Paul. *Sputnik: The Shock of the Century.* 2001.

Gray, William Glenn. *Germany's Cold War: The Global Campaign to Isolate East Germany, 1949–1969.* 2003.

Harrison, Hope. *Driving the Soviets up the Wall: Soviet–East German Relations, 1953–1961.* 2003.

Pasternak, Boris. *Doctor Zhivago.* 1958.

Rhodes, Richard. *Dark Sun: The Making of the Hydrogen Bomb.* 1995.

Saunders, Frances Stonor. *The Cultural Cold War: The CIA and the World of Arts and Letters.* 2000.

Schivelbusch, Wolfgang. *In a Cold Crater: Cultural and Intellectual Life in Berlin, 1945–1948.* 1998.

Solzhenitsyn, Aleksandr. *One Day in the Life of Ivan Denisovich.* 1962.

Selected Web Sites

Web sites abound with information about the many aspects and consequences of the cold war in the immediate postwar years.

Cold war: <**history.sandiego.edu/gen/20th/coldwarO.html**>

Cold war: <**library.thinkquest.org/10826**>

Cold war: <**cnn.com/SPECIALS/cold.war/guides/about.series**>

Cold War Science and Technology Studies Program: <**cmu.edu/coldwar**>

Internet Modern History Sourcebook: A Bipolar World: <**fordham.edu/halsall/mod/modsbook46.html**>

Postwar documents: <**yale.edu/lawweb/avalon/20th.htm**>

8

The Rebirth of Prosperity and the Rise of the Welfare State in the 1950s and Early 1960s

IN THE SUMMER OF 1956 THE AMERICAN FILM *Rock around the Clock,* starring the wildly popular rock 'n' roll band Bill Haley and the Comets, arrived in England. It worked its way across Europe, taking Germany by storm in September and October. Exuberant performances by the Platters, Little Richard, and other celebrated rock figures substituted for a traditional plot. There was a simple message nonetheless: rock 'n' roll music is fun. Teens welcomed the U.S. import by dancing in the theaters, and some were carried away enough to tear up the seats. In Norway and West Germany, youth in several cities got so worked up that they rioted, provoking a huge outcry from journalists, parents, politicians, and educators that this wild new music from the United States endangered civilization itself. German newspapers worried that the film's "sinister power" would produce "degeneration" and "orgies."

Youth in the Communist zone were drawn to rock 'n' roll too and to the American youth culture it celebrated. In East Berlin before the wall was built they headed for theaters to see *Rock around the Clock,* Elvis Presley in *Jailhouse*

◆ **Europe Rocks ('n' Rolls)**
Rock music knew no cold war boundaries and excited fans east
and west. Many young people danced, wore their hair like Elvis,
and sported distinctive clothing. Exuberant, playful, and sexually
expressive, rock 'n' roll was disturbing to the sober adult
generation which had just endured more than a decade of
depression and war. To them, rock 'n' roll and youthful styles
signaled another outbreak of youthful barbarism when what
Europe needed was a return to seriousness and civility.
Bettmann/CORBIS.

Rock, and Marlon Brando in *The Wild One.* They demanded that government stores carry blue jeans and
T-shirts, and they wore their hair slicked back and styled
like Presley's. In the Soviet Union, *stilyagi,* youthful imitators of Western styles, were of perpetual concern to the
government. They were raucous, colorful, and hip—even
the brightly lipsticked young women (see Document 8.3).
Youthful rockers signaled that prosperity was back. Parents
and governments might have been happy for that simple
blessing, but instead many were dismayed by the wild behavior of the young.

The teens who danced to rock 'n' roll were molded by
a new hands-on "welfare state"—one that provided them
with health care, education, school lunches and vitamins,
mass transport, and even gave cash allowances to their
parents to help pay for their upbringing. Politicians recalling Mussolini's and Hitler's popularity among jobless and

1953–1956	Nikita Khrushchev ascends to power in USSR.
1953	Spring: In USSR, government releases over a million prisoners and begins "rehabilitation."
1953	June 17: In East Germany, workers strike to protest cutbacks and increased productivity quotas.
1955	West German chancellor Adenauer restores diplomatic relations with Soviet Union.
1955	USSR legalizes abortion.
1956	Summer: American film *Rock around the Clock* arrives in Europe.
1956	Nikita Khrushchev delivers "Secret Speech" at Twentieth Party Congress.
1956	Summer: In Poland, metal workers strike for better wages.
1956	October–November: Hungarians rebel against Hungary's Communist government; Soviet troops put down the uprising.
1957	EURATOM founded.
1957	Publication of Milovan Djilas's *The New Class* (1955) in west.
1957	European Economic Community (the Common Market) founded.
1958	Boris Pasternak declines Nobel Prize for Literature for *Doctor Zhivago* (1957).
1958	Charles de Gaulle becomes French head of state.
1960s	Spain moves toward democracy in beginning of decade.
1962	Aleksandr Solzhenitsyn publishes *One Day in the Life of Ivan Denisovich.*
1963	Ludwig Erhard succeeds Adenauer as West German chancellor.

445

hopeless people during the Great Depression were determined to convert prewar government programs for piecemeal relief into a full-fledged welfare state. Looking back also laid some of the groundwork for a burst of prosperity in the 1950s, as economic planners and statesmen alike determined to eliminate the competition for resources among states, which they believed had led to war. They began organizing supranational bodies for economic cooperation—institutions that would rise above national interests to arrange for the prosperity of entire regions. The result was what Europeans called "the thirty glorious years," extending well into the 1970s, when a wartorn society developed unprecedented economic capacity that erased the sharp decline brought on by the two world wars. It was this prosperity that allowed teens their foray into the world of rock 'n' roll.

For political leaders prosperity meant rebuilding roads, transport, and housing destroyed by the war; for ordinary adults and teens it meant shopping. In most families there had been precious little surplus money since 1914, as wars and depression plundered household budgets. The 1950s saw the return of prosperity and brought teens buying power—however small—they had not experienced before. Facing rebellion against their rule in East Germany, Poland, and Hungary, the Soviets recognized that citizens needed consumer items, and they diverted scarce resources into producing more food, clothing, and household goods in hopes of gaining political peace. Like many new trends, the burst of prosperity and consumerism was also disturbing. Many of the valued new products came from the United States, and some people wondered whether Europeans would lose their identity, becoming not only materialistic like the Americans but also Americanized by the standardized new products. Even while debate continued, however, consumption brought renewed production of household conveniences and an array of goods that ordinary Europeans soon would not be able to live without. The moment when people could turn their attention to consumer desires has been said to mark the end of the "postwar" period.

THE WELFARE STATE

The transition from wartime to peacetime government saw the disbanding of many military offices, but other features of wartime big government remained. The state's wartime concerns with civilian life remained intact and grew in the postwar period to address the social and economic problems of the late 1940s such as the provisioning of food. People also lacked adequate health care and housing due to the cost and destruction of the war. The urgent need for the welfare state seemed justified in part by the lingering appeal of fascism. As one German sociologist noted in 1947, "A growing number of families are looking backward—the flight into the past and better days, by which they mainly mean the Hitler years." Germans, caught up in their memories of comparative material comfort in the 1930s and early war years, were heard to say, "No one starved, no one froze, and if Hitler were to come back now, everything would fall into place in short order."[1] Fear of a Nazi resurgence and an old-fashioned language of security and state power buttressed a move toward policies that provided government-sponsored health care, family allowances, old-age and workmen's compensation, and unemployment insurance for many in the workforce—especially for men.

The expansion of the welfare state across Europe redefined citizenship. The modern theory of citizenship that had evolved since the seventeenth century considered individuals to have "rights" to claim against the state. On the basis of these rights they participated in the nation. Using these ideas of natural rights—often codified in constitutions or other sets of fundamental laws—women for instance had made their appeal for suffrage in the twentieth century. Since the nineteenth century, the welfare state had evolved piecemeal from legislation providing veterans' pensions and old-age insurance for male workers, which gradually added a sense of social need to the concept of rights-bearing citizenship. As this happened, the function of the state expanded to include not only protection of the nation and the rights of citizens but also protection of society in a wide range of situations, such as economic want. A robust, democratic society, creators of the welfare state like Alva Myrdal (see Document 5.1) and William Beveridge theorized, needed good health, education, and decent housing, and the state needed to use public wealth to ensure that well-being. This new concept, called *social citizenship*, came to be applied broadly across Europe as a distinctive "social" model of what a responsible national community should be.

Enacting Social Programs

In 1942 William Beveridge, former head of the London School of Economics and an official in Winston Churchill's wartime government, produced a report for the British House of Commons on the need for social programs. The report laid the foundation of the British welfare state, constructed within five years of the war's end. It proposed "an attack upon five giant evils: upon the physical Want with which it is directly concerned, upon Disease which often causes Want and brings many other troubles in its train, upon Ignorance which no democracy can afford among its citizens, upon Squalor which arises mainly through the haphazard distribution of industry and population, and upon Idleness which destroys wealth and corrupts men."[2] In Beveridge's broad vision, by improving the quality of life for people through state-sponsored programs, government would improve the quality of citizenship. As in the 1930s, increasing birthrates, given the disastrous loss of life in World War II, was a central goal, but politicians in western Europe had another rationale. They remembered the destitution that followed World War I and that accelerated during the depression of the 1930s, and they judged it to have created conditions favorable for totalitarianism. Thus, the reallocation of government funds to social programs soared. Belgium, for example, which before the war had spent an average of $12 per person annually on civilian well-being, spent $148 per person in 1956. Following the Swedish model, many western European governments hoped to ensure democracy by providing a minimum standard of living. Economic democracy, they believed, would fortify political democracy.

In Britain, Labour candidates campaigned on a platform of integrated welfare-state programs and, despite the wartime record of Conservative prime minister Winston Churchill, handily won the 1945 elections. The new government rapidly introduced legislation providing social security coverage for accident, unemployment, and old-age insurance in 1946. The deplorable shape of housing owing to bombing and lack of investment created support for government-backed programs for rapid rebuilding. Despite intense resistance from the medical profession and hospitals, in 1948 Parliament passed legislation setting up the National Health Service, comprising a network of clinics and nationalized medical care. The British people had a special appreciation for the ways in which socialist institutions seemed to focus on the general good—a remnant of the respect generated by their nation's wartime alliance with the USSR. Seeing what socialism had done for Soviet industrial capacity, the Labour government took over the coal, transport, and several other key industries. It was believed that this action would pull the country out of its deepening economic trough, but such a rescue never took place, and industries such as coal and steel sank still further. The British welfare state was broad in its range of undertakings; its goal was to give ordinary citizens their "fair share" of national resources.

The functioning of the welfare state varied from country to country. In France and elsewhere on the continent the antifascist spirit led to the nationalization of banks and key industries—in some cases because collaborators had run them but in others because it was felt that government involvement would ensure smooth, socially responsible functioning. In Britain and western Europe generally, gendered assumptions also affected the way the welfare state developed. Britain gave fewer benefits to married than to unmarried women in the workforce because policy makers wanted married women to stay at home. The West German government faced the challenge of reconstructing postwar citizenship out of the tatters of Nazism, which had regulated family life and marriage on the basis of belief in women's inequality. Postwar female politicians in Germany scoffed at the notion that men's role was to protect women—the traditional rationale for women's inequality in the law. "There is no aspect of life in which the actions of German men have protected German women from want, misery, and poverty," observed the activist Dorothea Groener-Geyer. "After our men fell victim to the obsession of a man [Hitler] and followed him from Berlin via Paris to Stalingrad and then back again, and did not have the energy to contain the delusion of power of that obsessed individual, thus gambling away the sovereignty of our state, leaving our cities in ruin, destroying our homes, and leaving millions homeless and with no basis for their existence, the equality of women has been accomplished de facto."[3] This argument and others ultimately carried the day, and West Germany's Basic Law (Constitution) of 1949 carried a provision for women's equality.

Nonetheless, the Nazi contention that a woman's main function was to serve as wife and mother, and that the family should be the basis of a reconstructed German nation, shaped welfare-state provisions there. Social critics warned that the standing of men vis-à-vis women needed to be fortified. The gradual erosion of patriarchy in the modern period had made men feel impotent, some argued, leaving them susceptible to the appeal of a militaristic dictator like Hitler, who they hoped would remasculinize them. Thus, the welfare state should aim to buttress the power of fathers and the mental well-being of individual men. The anti-Communist lobby of refugees also opposed women's equality in the workforce as an imitation of Soviet life. German trade unions joined in the fray, many of them opposing women in the workforce as part of their program for economic negotiations with industrial management.

This cluster of sentiments sealed the inequality of West German women in the construction of the welfare state. Benefits to men in the workforce and to veterans improved. The Law for the Protection of Mothers, passed in 1952, authorized employer-paid maternity leaves before and after pregnancy and restricted women from holding certain jobs. The effect was to cause employers to fire single women when they got married and to fire married women in the early months of pregnancy to keep from paying for leaves. Women refused these leaves because the lost pay was far more substantial than the subsidy. A 1953 revision of the Basic Law, the Family Law Reform of 1957, and other legislation in the 1950s restricted the right to divorce, cut married women's access to accident, old-age, and disability insurance, and paid family allowances to "wage-earners," generally defined as fathers.

The differently gendered contours of the welfare state owed much to past history. Both France and West Germany wanted to rebuild population. "The rising generation of a nation . . . must not be endangered," German pronatalists maintained, by giving women the same financial autonomy that men had. They thus continued the Nazi programs for women and the family for decades after the war in order to keep them home having babies. The French had the same goals, but their politicians valued women's participation in the resistance against the Nazis, helping to liberate France and rebuilding wartorn regions. Thus, the postwar French government legislated egalitarian welfare-state programs for pensions, health insurance, and health care. To encourage working women to have children, the French state provided networks of day care, after-school, and early education programs. Unlike stores in West Germany, which were required by the government to close early, making it impossible for married working women to shop for their families, French stores remained open until eight in the evening. Decades later West Germany had the lowest number of women in leadership positions in industry and finance and the highest number of older women living in poverty among the prosperous nations of western Europe.

The Welfare State at Work

Despite such disparities, the welfare state generally brought higher standards of health care and housing and a greater degree of economic security to the population as a whole. Achieving this, however, was a massive undertaking, shifting wartime bureaucracies to peacetime work and establishing new institutions such as public clinics and child-care facilities. Top-ranked wartime officials oversaw the creation of the agencies that would run housing, health, insurance, and other programs. Women had worked in these bureaucracies during the war and continued

◆ **Child Care in Denmark**

Scandinavia pioneered in constructing the postwar welfare state, in which the government provided health care for all citizens, regular medical attention for pregnant women, and preschool programs for small children. In this Danish *crèche,* the common European name for prekindergarten care, children received wholesome meals and regular health checkups. They also played, sang, and learned nursery rhymes. In labor-short Europe the *crèche* made careers for women possible, and most of them needed jobs after the war. *Hulton Archive/Getty Images.*

in them thereafter, advancing the "feminization" of middle-level public sector jobs. In the Soviet Union they served as the health care system's doctors (a lower-status job than elsewhere) and in France as dentists and doctors. They generally filled the ranks of social workers, attendants in public child care and nursery schools, and nurses, nurses' aides, and cleaning staff in public hospitals. The operation of the welfare state was feminized at the bottom to hold down costs. The allocation of jobs in the public sector to women reflected the magnitude of the system. Sweden, for instance, had many programs for women and offered women more job opportunities than did Germany, with the lowest amount of benefits for women and the fewest jobs for them.

Immigrants too played a role in the establishment of the welfare state, taking on menial work such as janitorial and kitchen jobs. They were often recruited from outside of Europe, in particular from colonies or former colonies. There was a flood of Afro-Caribbean migrants into England in the 1950s (some 500,000) and into the Netherlands in the 1950s and 1960s (approximately 250,000). Faced with the sudden creation of public facilities for health care, social security, and other benefits, labor-short European governments made agreements with nations experiencing job shortages.

Even though some of the newcomers might have had prior training qualifying them for skill-based jobs, and they were recruited with promises of opportunities to fill such positions, the reality proved different. Because of labor shortages and the reluctance of white Europeans to do the most menial work, people migrating from the colonies and from southern to northern Europe were with few exceptions shunted into the lowest-paying and most menial work no matter what their qualifications or talents. An immigrant from southern Italy remembered his family's move northward in the 1950s: "people stopped to stare . . . not with sympathy or with indifference but with contempt."[4] As Europe struggled to recover from its violent past, the affordability of the welfare state depended on this low-paid work, often done on a part-time basis without benefits and viewed with scorn. Like women, migrants served to lower the costs of expanding welfare states because they could be paid significantly lower wages than their white male counterparts. Thus, governments achieved their goal in part by segmenting the postwar economy by race and gender.

The welfare state demonstrated concern for the well-being of children and youth by establishing programs to distribute nutritional supplements and to provide regular medical attention in schools (see Document 8.1). Children's health had suffered owing to malnutrition, even bouts of starvation. The majority of Europeans had been deprived of eggs, milk, meat, soap, and other essentials of good health and hygiene during the war, and children experienced an attendant decrease in height and weight as a legacy of war and economic depression. The welfare government provided school lunches and access to vaccines that wiped out such deadly diseases as tuberculosis, diphtheria, measles, and polio. Europe's children became the healthiest in the world. Governments also addressed the teen years. Welfare states set up sports and hiking clubs and other programs intended to engage teenagers in healthy and wholesome activities. Public agencies came into being to deal with "problem" youth, and commissions scrutinized material with which young people might come in contact. American comic books, music, and films were seen as especially pernicious because of their emphasis on sex and violence. One outcome of this concern was editing that flattened the breasts of female characters in imported American comic strips. In the 1950s, however, Sweden and some other countries faced the issue of sexuality differently—by introducing sex education into the primary school curriculum and continuing it through high school.

Ongoing concern for boosting the birthrate and keeping infants healthy led to a striking postwar change: the medicalization of childbirth. At the beginning of the twentieth century, some 90 percent of all births in Europe occurred at home. By the 1970s more than 90 percent took place in hospitals. But, despite widespread publicity campaigns to improve the life of peasant women in the Soviet Union in the 1920s and 1930s, significant change did not reach them until the 1950s. Medical assistance, especially improved conditions for childbirth in state-operated clinics, as well as primary school education, upgraded the conditions of life, and the relegalization of abortion in 1955 in the USSR allowed for a crude form of family planning. It is estimated that because of the lack of reliable means of birth control (resulting from restrictions on consumer needs), the average postwar Soviet woman had more than ten abortions during her lifetime. Attention to the conditions of pregnancy and childbirth occurred amid a strong desire to compensate for the lives lost and the low birthrate of the war years. The attention worked. Like the United States, Europe experienced a "baby boom" from 1948 to the early 1960s, and in western Europe, where maternal care was most advanced, infant mortality rates were the best in the entire world.

ECONOMIC REVIVAL EAST AND WEST

Europe's baby boom helped foster unprecedented economic growth during the 1950s and 1960s. The numbers are staggering: during this period, the rate of growth averaged 5 percent annually in western Europe and was similarly high in the eastern sector. Two interlocking regional economies with global networks took shape in these decades, accomplishing some of the goals of European expansionists. Hitler had envisioned Europe as one vast, interconnected, and efficient regional economy. The economy he established was one of simple plunder without the development of an integrated and pervasive high-tech capability. After World War II, however, such a goal began to be realized under far different conditions. Western European nations collectively implemented transnational planning under the aegis of the Common Market, while in the Soviet sphere a program of rapid industrialization and collectivization of agriculture occurred. In both eastern and western Europe a surge of productivity resulted; cooperation and new technology created conditions for an economic boom that lasted some three decades.

Much of the development in the European economy amounted to a game of catch-up with the United States, which had soared ahead because of the amount of research and development accomplished during World War II while Europe was torn by warfare. Between 1870 and 1913, the rate of growth of gross domestic product in the twelve countries of western Europe averaged 1.3 percent per inhabitant; between l950 and 1973, that rate rose to 3.8 percent, surpassing the 2.4 percent rate per inhabitant in the United States. Most of the increase was due to the rise in individual productivity, though Great Britain remained relatively weak in this regard. Technology transfers under the Marshall Plan account for some of the resurgence in productivity. To be sure, scientific knowledge in Europe during the war years had advanced, but it was not adapted to civilian needs due to the focus on war. Also, with Hitler plundering rather than developing the continent, many scientists had decamped to the United States. Now, with peace and stability reigning in Europe for the first time in decades, there was ample opportunity for the application of science and technology to a broad spectrum of human needs.

The Common Market

Transnational economic cooperation formed the centerpiece for a long-lived revival in western Europe. Although Marshall Plan aid was an important factor in the temporary recovery and in Europe's ability to import new machinery, the creation of strong economic ties, especially between France and Germany, was key. First in 1948 with the development of the Organization for European Economic Cooperation (OEEC) for the joint distribution of Marshall Plan aid, and then in 1952 with formation of the European Coal and Steel Community (ECSC), western European countries that had fought among themselves for centuries put aside age-old differences. The immediate impetus was twofold: France especially needed coal to get its citizens through the difficult winter of 1946–47, and Germany and other European countries needed a tariff-free zone for the exchange of various goods after the destruction of so much industrial capacity. Another spur to cooperation was the Marshall Plan's stipulation that as a condition for receiving funds and technology, European countries would explore the possibility of closer economic and political ties—even a political union. The long-range incentive was articulated by French prime minister Robert Schuman, who in 1950 predicted that the creation of the European Coal and Steel Community would "lay the concrete foundation for a European Federation which is so indispensable for the preservation of peace."[5] From these practical concerns, an "idea of Europe" was born.

Jean Monnet (1888–1979), a French-born international businessman, was instrumental in promoting both specific transnational organizations for economic cooperation such as the ECSC and the broader idea of European unity. He had begun his career in the French cognac business, an enterprise that depended on far-flung global markets and took him to foreign capitals. During World War I, Monnet went to work for the French government, initiating its efforts to coordinate food purchases among the Allies so that they were not competing against one another on the world market. After that war, Monnet served the League of Nations and during World War II helped British and American efforts to devise common procurement policies. A proven facilitator of cooperation, Monnet was familiar with varying cultural practices, adept in multiple languages, and flexible in his dealings with people from different countries. Above all, he believed that the coordination and planning of resources could break down national chauvinism in ways that would benefit Europe as a whole.

Monnet's first post–World War II accomplishment was the establishment of the European Coal and Steel Community, which pooled resources among the six member countries that would later become the Common Market. Coordinating transportation and market conditions for coal and steel, the ECSC became the prototype for further cooperation. Monnet also worked to establish a European Defense Community—a common European army—to offset the fears that arose when the United States suggested rearming Germany, but this project failed. In 1957, he secured agreement to set up the cooperative administration of and research into nuclear energy by the new EURATOM agency; this success foreshadowed the greater success of bringing into being the Common Market.

In 1957 six European countries—France, Germany, Italy, Belgium, Luxembourg, and the Netherlands—signed the Treaty of Rome, creating the European Economic Community (EEC), better known as the Common Market. The treaty lowered tariffs among the six countries by 10 percent, but its ultimate vision was larger. Not only did Common Market participants foresee completely tariff-free trade among the partners, but they also anticipated the free flow of labor and common trade policies among the signatory nations. A commission based in Brussels administered the programs of the Common Market. Experts whose functions transcended those of politicians elected in the individual member nations set common economic policies, issued regulations to implement them, and advised industries, farmers, and financial institutions on economic opportunities and strategy.

The Common Market was an antidote for the situation in Europe at the war's end: destitute, morally defeated, and divided among themselves, the individual countries of Europe were unable to compete as separate states with the superpowers. United, however, they represented formidable economic might based on a citizenry with high levels of education and a concerted determination to restore Europe to its prewar pride and wealth. Not to be overlooked was the presence in the first six Common Market countries of some 200 million consumers and producers whose intertwined economies had drawn them closer together. Trade among the Common Market members grew 400 percent in the first decade of the organization's existence.

The structure of the Common Market was supranational. Although delegates sent by the governments of individual member countries kept their homelands' economic situation in mind, their prime concern was supposed to be the good of the whole. The decision to locate EEC headquarters in Brussels, Belgium's capital, indicated symbolically and practically that the institution would not be the plaything of the two dominant members—Germany and France.

The idea of supranationality was difficult for many Europeans to swallow, accustomed as they were to nationalist ideals and the nation-state as the defining political unit. The EEC often faced opposition from individual leaders, such as

Charles de Gaulle, who became president of France in 1958, advocating a rebirth of French pride and opposing the lure of supranational ideals. Criticizing the Common Market became a way to score political points, but opponents also had a serious objection: Common Market officials were beyond the reach of national parliaments and thus of popular control. A "technocratic body of elders, stateless and irresponsible," de Gaulle called them.[6] Neither the people nor their delegates could rein in the supranational EEC institutions. Despite these drawbacks, the Treaty of Rome provided for increasing the number of member countries and enlarging the powers of the EEC. A bold and unprecedented innovation at the time, the Common Market continues to grow. For its initiator, Jean Monnet, the goal of the Common Market was to make "a genuine step towards a United States of Europe,"[7] and he envisioned—though he did not live long enough to see—the creation of a monetary union as a prelude to the final political unification of the continent.

Not everyone was eager to join the Common Market. Scandinavian countries took years to debate the economic advantages and disadvantages of EEC membership. "No stone was left unturned, no question unanswered," Per Haekkerup, premier of Denmark, recalled, "but while we were discussing and elaborating these problems from every conceivable angle, developments in Europe passed us by."[8] Britain too did not initially join the Common Market, choosing to head off on an independent course despite its ruined finances and outdated industrial infrastructure. British politicians viewed the Common Market as a trap because membership entailed giving up Britain's special trade provisions with the Commonwealth countries, which in 1951 were buying some 55 percent of British exports. Britain was "not a continental nation," former prime minister Lord Salisbury said, "but an island power with a Colonial Empire and unique relations with the independent members of the Commonwealth."[9] So the government distanced itself from the creation of the Common Market, staking its health on continuing brisk trade with the Commonwealth, its closeness with the United States, and its military leadership of non-Soviet Europe. Labor unions supported the government's position, believing that EEC membership might curtail subsidies to ailing industries and thus eliminate jobs. Yet there remained an undercurrent of belief that EEC membership would offer some advantages. The British government tried to set up with the EEC a free-trade policy exclusively on British terms, but the organization did not bite. Britain thus felt some ambivalence when it finally did join the Common Market in 1973, especially given several vetoes of its membership by Gaullist France.[10] Even in the 1990s, it refused to adopt the euro monetary system.

Britain compensated somewhat for its independent status by developing its position in international finance. In the early 1960s, at the height of cold war animosities, the Soviets and their satellites sought to avoid the possibility of the United States freezing their accounts, so they transferred their foreign funds to Great Britain. These funds were to be held in U.S. dollars but in accounts outside the United States, giving rise to the Eurodollar. Using the Eurodollar as a carrot, British banks eventually attracted funds from foreign investors whose investments the United States had decided to tax and from oil-producing countries that wanted the safety of dollars without the disadvantages of keeping funds in the United States. While British industry struggled to revive, the financial sector thrived in part because of this innovative strategy. Despite the surge in this sector, however, Britain's economy grew at a rate of only 2.5 percent per year in the 1950s and 1960s, well below the rate of the Common Market nations. Trying to maintain its nineteenth-century-style position of global leadership, it spent more than it could afford on garrisoning both occupied Europe and its colonies around the world.

The Common Market helped strengthen the panoply of new cooperative agencies. EURATOM, for example, though eventually undermined by de Gaulle's determination that France needed to have a nuclear capacity free from oversight by anyone, allowed Europe to develop alternate energy sources. With the Middle East in turmoil because of the creation of the state of Israel in 1948 and Israel's takeover of Palestinian lands, the move into nuclear energy by the European states helped alleviate pressure on oil supplies. The U.S. government provided low-interest loans to foster adequate energy supplies, whose shortage could promote war. Hoping to monopolize nuclear defense capacity, the United States nonetheless remained suspicious of its allies' pursuit of atomic energy. The discovery of natural gas in Europe opened up another source of fuel on the continent, even as scientists continued to develop nuclear energy despite U.S. objections.

Rebuilding the East European Economy

People in the Soviet sector also achieved a notable recovery in industrial capacity. Hardest hit by the war, the east under Stalin turned its attention to producing capital goods, which would enable the expansion of industry not consumption. Simultaneously under the impetus of the cold war, the USSR advanced its military and scientific capacity, producing atomic and hydrogen bombs and impressive rocket technology that allowed it to take the lead in space exploration. Rates of growth in the USSR between 1945 and 1950 were impressive, and in the 1950s and 1960s the USSR growth rates reached 4.8 percent for gross national product and 3.4 percent for per capita productivity. During these peak years, eastern Europe as a whole conquered the problem of rural underdevelopment and poverty. The forced modernization of the agricultural economy in the new Communist states greatly lessened the peasant character of the region.

The greatest transformations occurred in the Soviet satellites, where as in the USSR in the 1930s, government efforts aimed at rapid industrialization, especially the creation of heavy industry. Bulgaria, Poland, Hungary, and Romania had struggled to shift their economies toward industry in the 1920s and 1930s. Soviet direction in the post–World War II years made that development possible, with the same brutality that had accompanied the industrialization of the USSR. The first move was the collection of enormous reparations from countries that had allied themselves with the Nazis. For example, in 1946 the USSR simply took 65 percent of all Hungarian output—agricultural and industrial. Then, instead of building on the established industrial and entrepreneurial base, Communist governments in eastern Europe nationalized industries and financial and commercial institutions.

The dramatic changes to an older way of life and the confiscation of private property provoked resistance and, occasionally, accommodation to people's demands that their religious beliefs or community traditions be respected. But this was not always the case. Political dissidents and working-class rebels were sent to work in dangerous uranium and other mines, and they provided the labor needed for ambitious projects like the construction of canals. The middle classes of professionals and managers who had survived the wartime policies of the Germans were usually purged. The outcome was the same as in the Soviet Union in the 1930s: the emergence of a "new class" of economic managers loyal to the Communists because of job opportunities and the greater material advantages they enjoyed (see Document 8.2). However, like their Stalinist predecessors, these new cadres were inexperienced and had to resort to a range of deceptive practices to survive the endless demands for increased productivity. The economic results were slightly better than those of the USSR: growth of gross national product at 4.8 percent in the 1950s and 1960s and per capita growth of 3.9 percent.

Simultaneously east European governments undertook collectivization, ruthlessly confiscating peasant farms. After surrendering their prized farmland, peasants were herded onto centrally administered collective farms and became socialist workers. Only in Poland did substantial numbers of individual farms remain. On the collective farms managers assigned work, decided what crops and animals would be raised, and dealt with higher government officials. Productivity increased because of the introduction of machinery and chemicals, but the investment in agriculture was never high enough and the motivation was never strong enough to produce the bountiful harvests of western European farms. In the 1950s and 1960s, productivity generally remained at half the levels of farms in western Europe, and agricultural workers headed to the cities to find opportunity in industry. There was strong economic revival, but shortages of food and housing laid the groundwork for protest.

The Soviet Union bound the satellites to it not only by taking reparations in the form of machinery, rolling stock, and manufactured goods, but by setting up COMECON (Council for Mutual Economic Assistance) in 1949 to match the Marshall Plan and to mirror organization of the EEC. This alliance resembled the Common Market, and it did indeed establish a trading group among Soviet-bloc countries, which now had to abandon economic connections to the West. But unlike the EEC, COMECON was dominated by one country, the USSR, which demanded that satellites trade on unequal terms with the Soviets, though in some instances the Soviets sent lower-cost raw materials to them and received higher-priced manufactured goods. According to some economic historians, the system did not necessarily work to Soviet advantage and, like the stationing of troops and the arms race, ultimately inflicted costs that were beyond Soviet means. Moreover, the violent and extensive political repression that accompanied industrialization in the 1950s did not create the cooperative atmosphere that an advanced, interconnected industrial economy requires.

After Stalin's death in 1953, Soviet economic policy changed in several ways. The overwhelming emphasis on heavy industry was reduced, and somewhat more attention was given to agricultural and consumer output. Coming to power amid protests and uprisings in the satellite countries, Stalin's successor Nikita Khrushchev (1894–1971) listened to popular complaints in both city and country-side about the conditions of agriculture and the scarcity of food. He mandated increased investment in collective farming and turned the bureaucracy to regional planning for agriculture, modifying centralization as was also being done in France and other countries to the west. To meet popular expectations for a better standard of living, Khrushchev diverted greater investment to the manufacture of consumer goods. Nonetheless, the level of compulsion in the economy remained high. Political prisoners still did the most dangerous, onerous work, and a harsh work discipline was applied to farm and factory workers alike. Many ordinary people were sent to work in the Baltic states and satellite countries to advance Russification. The forced labor of German scientists contributed to technological breakthroughs that updated both military and civilian industries. In the end, the increasing prominence of the "new class," combined with the ramped-up exploitation of workers in what was supposed to be a proletarian utopia, worked against the effectiveness of communism. Criticism of privileged elites in a supposedly classless society mounted (see Document 8.2). The joyous workers of socialist theory were in reality often negligent, ill tempered, and alcoholic, undermining the moral and economic health of society.

The Rise of the Technocrats

A new twentieth-century figure—the technocrat or systems planner—directed the post–World War II economic triumph much as the government functionary had worked to achieve military triumph in the two world wars. Planners had been crucial to peacetime economic advances in the Soviet Union and the Third Reich during the 1930s. After the Second World War, Jean Monnet worked with a small group of French economists, politicians, and businessmen to devise a plan for France's postwar recovery. The planners identified the crucial industries that would receive investment, and they plotted the use of resources. This group agreed that it was more important to stimulate transport and industry than to invest in housing—an area that would have to wait until productivity had been restored. Operating outside parliamentary control, the group also negotiated loans from the United States based on the priorities spelled out in the plan. In France and Britain, planners joined with labor reformers and socialists in advocating the nationalization of many services such as transport and banks and, where not already nationalized, radio and television. A wave of nationalization or partial nationalization swept Europe as these many institutions went to the state rather than to their original owners after the war.

In some cases, nationalization was easy to accomplish, for the owners of many enterprises had been Nazi sympathizers and collaborators during the occupation. In other cases, the state held a percentage of the stock in an enterprise, and from that vantage point, government experts directed the functioning of the national-ized assets. The idea was that experts not concerned with generating huge profits for private individuals would create services that were both efficient and beneficial to society. Elite schools for the training of government functionaries sprang up; the French National School for Administration was founded in 1945. Given the un-precedented scale of reconstruction and the complications of postwar economic exchange, such planning seemed imperative to almost everyone. The result of tech-nocratic planning was the "mixed economy" that most advanced capitalist coun-tries adopted after the war, a combination of some nationalized industries such as transportation and privately held firms that profited from the advice of govern-ment and other experts.

Often coming from the same social milieu, industrialists and planners worked well together. Even though the war had seen a number of them on opposite sides, the Nazi or collaborationist past of each easily disappeared into the technocratic state. Planners and industrialists worked together to foster industries that came to be identified with their individual countries. For example, they helped create the image of France as the source of the most up-to-date fashion such as garments de-signed by Dior and Chanel; Italy was seen to provide the best in shoes and other tasteful, elite products. With the help of planners, Germany became the wellspring of high-quality small appliances—coffee grinders, vacuum cleaners, sewing ma-chines—and the small and fuel-efficient Volkswagen car. Planners in western Europe also directed the marketing for export of goods such as French perfume, cheese, and wine, particularly to the United States, cash-rich after the war.

With the aid of modern machinery and the increasing use of chemical fertil-izers and pesticides, agricultural productivity surged under the guidance of the planners. In the Common Market, they brought the agricultural prices of the var-ious countries into line with one another and even subsidized farmers whenever they received lower prices on the international market. EEC bureaucrats provided information on market conditions, allowing farmers to make better decisions about crops and to profit from cooperative purchasing of equipment. Urged on by market studies, many European farmers in the Common Market turned to the pro-duction of luxury goods such as high-quality wines, foie gras, and veal. Efficiency cut the need for farmhands, and individuals expanded their holdings by buying up peasant land, prompting the emigration of the young from the countryside. As farms in Germany, France, and Italy began to look more like the American Midwest, with its vast unbroken miles of agricultural fields, European industry boomed thanks to the influx of inexpensive labor arranged by the technocrats. But the real gain was in agriculture itself, where productivity increased by factors of 500 and 600 percent in breadbaskets such as France and Italy.

Growth was also apparent in smaller nations outside the EEC. The Scandinavian countries in particular executed a smart economic recovery, much of it thanks to technocratic planning. Sweden, for example, continued adapting its welfare state while it succeeded in shipbuilding and in producing desirable auto-mobiles and trucks under the Volvo brand. Aided by natural sources of electricity, iron ore, and timber, the economy depended for its health on cooperation between

◆ **The "New Look"**

Christian Dior launched the "new look" in the late 1940s. His designs for women's clothing called for large amounts of fabric at a time when textiles like other consumer items were scarce, even unobtainable. Dior's new look accentuated a woman's silhouette in ways that brought to mind the tiny waists and flaring skirts of the nineteenth century. Expert at marketing in the United States and elsewhere, Dior made the designer label a coveted possession of middle-class women. *Brown Brothers.*

workers and the state in setting wages and conditions of labor and on high taxation to pay for the welfare state. Women throughout the Scandinavian countries joined the workforce in larger numbers than before the war. The result was greater productivity and the expansion of prosperity. Finland, which had sided with Germany in order to fight off the Russian invasion, had to pay damages to the USSR. This postwar punishment, however, helped the country's industrial sector to expand, as Finland's planners strove to increase efficiencies and growth to meet the reparations demands. Denmark, Finland, and the rest of Scandinavia also advanced general prosperity by a dramatic modernization of farming. At the end of the war close to 50 percent of Finland's workforce were farmers; by the 1960s increased mechanization and the advice of experts had reduced the number to around 10 percent, similar to figures in the rest of the region.

These countries used the resulting increase in tax revenues to promote social welfare, especially by investing in education. Denmark increased the percentage of the national budget spent on schooling from 2.4 percent in 1952 to 7.5 percent in 1974. The public at large—farmers, the middle classes, workers—in these countries welcomed and benefited from the promotion of education, subsidies to injured workers, family allowances, and other social programs. School-leaving ages were raised to the midteens, and officials enforced these laws stringently. The boom in education was just getting started in the 1950s, with the rise of new technical schools, research institutes, and universities. The rapid expansion of postwar prosperity was beginning to make these and other social welfare programs affordable.

THE POLITICS OF PROSPERITY

During the 1950s and early 1960s, European politics edged away from the extremes of the war and prewar years. The death of Stalin brought a mixture of reform and revolt against the Soviet system, as the leadership and ordinary citizens alike looked for an end to the perpetual repression and bloodshed associated with communism. To the west, the popularity of the left waned with the return to prosperity. More conservative politicians shaped national agendas and took credit for the return of economic stability. Many of them were in the forefront of the drive for economic partnerships beyond national borders; they also continued to support the welfare state. Despite the extreme partisanship of the cold war, centrist governments were the order of the day outside the Soviet system; and even within it, with the glaring exception of the bloody repression of Hungary's 1956 uprising, politicians left Stalinist extremism behind.

Revolt and Reform in the Soviet Sphere

Rumblings of discontent could be heard throughout the USSR in Stalin's lifetime, as ordinary people wondered why the end of the war had not made their lives better. The death of their leader in 1953 brought protest immediately to the surface. At several camps in the gulag, uprisings took place after Stalin's death, forcing a rethinking of the system that cost the government more than it would have received had the prisoners been free to work and lead productive lives. Prisoners, both criminal and political, were released in waves, and the system of purges and harsh political repression began to crumble. As over a million found freedom in the spring of 1953, the government began a process of "rehabilitation" by which it declared many sentences to have been unjust, the result of error, jealousy, misguided enthusiasm, or even criminality. This process, however, had a further destabilizing effect, for suddenly everything was open to question and revision. Petty criminals reentered society and caused crime to escalate, and ordinary people no longer had confidence in Communist justice and security. Political prisoners' revealing stories turned the old system of values on its head, as these prisoners suddenly seemed innocent and the officials who had put them in the gulag appeared guilty. Stalinism started to come apart at the seams.

Riots and strikes broke out in the Soviet bloc. In East Germany on June 17, 1953, a labor strike began, prompted by the announcement of cutbacks in food and social services, rising taxes, and increased quotas for worker productivity, in part to pay for policing the East German border. The government had pressed workers into longer shifts to make up for the loss of the hundreds of thousands of people who were leaving for a better life in the West. Rumors that the reunification of Germany was about to take place or that the western Allies were about to invade had fortified the spirit of revolt. Trying to head off trouble, East German officials had retracted the harshest of the new impositions but left in place the new work rules. On June 17, the populace mobilized, chanting "Butter not cannons," and workers congregated in the major cities instead of showing up for work. The East German police failed to quell the protests, and on the afternoon of that same day the Soviet army entered Berlin, eventually putting down an increasingly violent core of protesters.

Opposition to Soviet rule was neither unprecedented nor spontaneous. Communists had come to power using force and violence, but the resistance they met led them to be inventive, diplomatic, and sometimes even accommodating to opposition groups. In East Germany, for instance, the churches constituted the one intact focus of public life after the fall of Hitler. Immediately after the war, Communist authorities noted that the churches saw themselves "as God's appointed opponent" of the new Communist state. Unable to stamp out all believers because they were so numerous, the Communists organized programs to compete with those of the churches. Among them were not only youth groups but also ceremonies similar to the Christian confirmation rite administered to many young people by the clergy. By the late 1960s, some 90 percent of all adolescents were participating in these faux religious ceremonies, yet the churches remained so influential that the East German secret police (the Stasi) resorted to recruiting church officials to report on individuals most adamantly opposed to the regime and to try to influence church policy to be more accepting of communism. For a while, the relationship between the churches and Communist officials worked to the state's advantage, but it ultimately undermined the long-term survival of communism.

The churches remained intact and offered people an alternative view of the world. Always preaching faith in God and denigrating the "useful knowledge," "internationalism," and "scientific worldview" celebrated in Communist schools, the churches attracted eager audiences of believers and were often the major force behind public protest.[11]

In the midst of uprisings across eastern Europe, the post-Stalin government and then Nikita Khrushchev, who by 1956 was the top leader in the USSR, worked to fortify the political allegiance of the Soviet people. Options were limited, however, by the restricted—almost nonexistent—space for public debate, because it always spelled trouble for the regime, as the cases of East Germany, Poland, and Hungary showed. The Soviet leadership condemned harsh policies and advised rapprochement and social peace. It lowered food prices, but this action had the effect of increasing pressure on the government when citizens proceeded to ask for even more improvements in the quality of life. For the first time since the Bolshevik Revolution, the drivers of public policy were personal and family well-being instead of broad public goals such as the triumph of socialism, the modernization of the USSR, or victory over the Nazis.

By curtailing public debate as an outlet for dissent, the Communists had signaled that public issues and politics were not open to reform, leaving only the private and cultural realm such as consumer issues. Faced with a single alternative, the post-Stalinist government sought to regain stability by bumping up the production of household goods, most notably food. New lands were opened to cultivation, and the state took less of the harvest from collective farms in hopes that liberal treatment would encourage farmers to produce more and to sell on the open market. More grain for fodder would also enhance the production of meat.

At the Twentieth Party Congress in 1956 Stalinism unraveled even more. Toward the end of the Congress, Nikita Khrushchev presented a list of criticisms against Stalin in an elaborate accusation of mistakes and even crimes. The audience was riveted, though a warning was issued that the text of the speech should not be revealed. In this "Secret Speech," Khrushchev continued the strategy that had been unfolding since 1953—making Stalin, not communism itself, the focus of criticism and debate. Khrushchev leveled two serious charges against the former Soviet leader: first, his "cult of personality" was at odds with the goals of a workers' state; second, he had destroyed the lives and careers of many loyal Communists. Having been responsible for purges and brutality in the past, Khrushchev was careful to soften his denunciation with praise for Stalin's early accomplishments, but the floodgates of debate opened nonetheless. Workers, minor officials, university students, and party intellectuals were thrown off guard; many of them refused to believe the charges: "it is difficult, very difficult to extinguish in the heart that great love that was so strongly rooted in our whole organism," one of them mournfully reported.[12] For some the revelations were more crushing than the Nazi invasion. Others wondered why the top party brass had allowed such things to happen. Debate and uncertainty replaced the firm convictions that many had held, and today many attribute to Khrushchev's remarks the gradual undoing of the Soviet system.

Cultural Thaw Leads to Further Revolt

The freer discussion that took place after the Twentieth Party Congress has been called the "thaw," implying a release from the glacial and deadly censorship under Stalin. Khrushchev's speech gave writers "a holiday of the soul," as one of them put it, and heartened and inspired cultural leaders.[13] They gained confidence that there would be no further attacks on writers and artists who wanted to innovate. In fact a shift was already under way in Soviet cultural life, brought on by postwar concerns for personal well-being and the publication of popular fiction that examined people's relationships beyond the world of work and productivity. Characters in novels sought intimacy and love, and in magazine articles women workers, despite their arduous factory routines, described their struggle to achieve romantic happiness with their mates. Like other changes, this one in popular culture provoked intense debate about the value of personal well-being as a component of socialism. Such works quietly undermined the utopianism of socialist realism by concentrating on the emotions and feelings of individuals. The publication in 1956 of Vladimir Dudintsev's novel *Not By Bread Alone* caused a public outburst around such issues, since it focused on a lone factory laborer caught in and crushed by the bureaucratized world of Soviet industry. Lopatkin, the novel's hero, has invented a new machine, whose development is blocked by the apparatchik Drozdov, the ultra-loyal Communist agent. The inventor's battles against the factory bureaucracy get him sentenced to a prison camp.

What bound the worlds of dissidents and writers like Dudintsev was an affirmation of the worth of the individual. People stood outside overflowing buildings to witness the spectacle of intellectual forums on the questions of power, the bureaucracy, and personal autonomy. The thaw was threatening to produce a civil society of questioning, public discussion, and the open expression of opinion. As this movement gained followers, the term *Drozdovism* was widely applied to the entrenched Communist bureaucracy, and critics announced that *Not by Bread Alone* captured the "spirit of 1956"—that is, the spirit of Khrushchev's speech against Stalin. Khrushchev, however, was not sure of himself when it came to cultural matters and feared that the thaw might get out of control. Because of his vacillation, writers in the Soviet sphere endured a series of thaws and freezes throughout his period of leadership.

Indeed, in some cases the thaw provoked more resistance to the Soviet system, not less, especially as word of the "Secret Speech" spread in eastern Europe. Anti-Russian demonstrations broke out when the speech was read at party meetings. It was, said one Polish Communist leader, "like being hit over the head with a hammer."[14] In the early summer of 1956, Polish metal workers struck for better wages. Popular support for their cause and against Soviet domination forced the return of Wladislaw Gomulka, a Communist imprisoned during a Stalinist purge. Gomulka initiated a more liberal and deft Communist program. Soviet leadership turned its attention to an increasingly restive eastern Europe.

Inspired by the Polish example, Hungarians rebelled against forced collectivization in October 1956—"the golden October," some would later call their

◆ The Hungarian Uprising of 1956
By the fall of 1956 word of Khrushchev's speech denouncing Stalin had reached Hungary and, as in Poland, sparked anti-Communist outrage. Hungarians took to the streets demanding change. They attacked Communist and Soviet domination from every angle, including the symbolic one. Soviets used symbols to help them rule, changing flags, ceremonies, and public monuments to reflect Soviet or Communist political values. Hungarian opponents of communism toppled a giant statue of Stalin to reflect their rage at the takeover of their country. *Hulton Archive/Getty Images.*

uprising. As in Poland, economic issues, especially announcements of reduced wages, sparked some of the first outbreaks of violence in Hungary, but the protest soon targeted the entire Communist system. Intellectuals and students turned universities into major political centers and attacked Communist Party headquarters. Residents of Budapest filled the streets and toppled a huge statue of the recently denounced Stalin. Crowds of demonstrators convinced the Hungarian army, sent to disperse them, to join the rebellion and succeeded in returning a popular hero, Imre Nagy, to power. As the Soviet government debated its response, Nagy, a less adept politician than Gomulka, announced that Hungary might leave the Warsaw Pact. Khrushchev decided to send in Soviet troops: "We have no other choice," he told the Soviet Presidium.[15] The Soviet army killed tens of thousands and caused hundreds of thousands more to flee to western Europe. Nagy appealed to the United States for help, but President Eisenhower refused to intervene, showing that despite a rhetoric of freedom, the United States was unwilling to risk World War III by militarily challenging the Soviet sphere of influence. Nagy was arrested, tried, and hanged.

The Hungarian uprising clarified the cultural issues on the table, if only temporarily. Dudintsev was denounced, and another "freeze" set in. Among the victims was Boris Pasternak, poet and author of the novel *Doctor Zhivago* (1957), which became a best seller when it appeared in English in 1958. When the Nobel Prize committee selected Pasternak to receive the coveted award in literature, the Soviet government made clear that accepting it would mean permanent exile for Pasternak. *Doctor Zhivago* proclaimed in its lyrical story a message that was unacceptable to the Communist Party: the intertwined lives of idealistic revolutionaries went tragically awry because these enthusiasts for socialism did not critically examine their idealism. Pasternak, his heart in Russia, refused the Nobel Prize and died in 1960.

Then, dizzyingly, another change of policy occurred. The appearance of Aleksandr Solzhenitsyn's *One Day in the Life of Ivan Denisovich* in 1962 marked the beginning of another brief thaw. The book describes the horrifying struggle to survive hard labor, cold, and inhumane treatment—even at the hands of the hero himself—in a prison camp. Soon thereafter Khrushchev changed his mind again, denouncing modern art and sending dissident writers to the gulag. But socialist realism and Communist orthodoxy never regained their complete domination. Dissidence expanded across the arts, as artists devised new styles that, while steering clear of forbidden techniques such as abstract expressionism, nonetheless provided critical glimpses of Soviet life.

Conservative Politics in Western Europe in the 1950s

In western Europe the postwar economic boom drove socialist and working-class parties into the wings, and conservative governments gained support during the return to prosperity. In West Germany, with the Soviets hovering on their borders, communism had not appealed to the electorate at all in the postwar period, though the Social Democrats were initially strong. In 1949, centrist politicians—many of them scarred from standing up to the Nazis—built the capacious Christian Democratic Party from the prewar remnants of smaller parties with particularist interests. It was pivotal to making the Federal Republic of Germany viable after its creation in 1949.

The first chancellor of West Germany was the seventy-three-year-old Catholic, anti-Communist, and Christian Democrat Konrad Adenauer, who was so strong a leader that people generally called West Germany a "chancellor democracy." Working with other democrats, Adenauer drafted a constitution that would prevent the emergence of a dictator and guarantee individual rights, all the while accepting the popular belief that Nazis had been few and most Germans had been victims of the war. Adenauer allied himself with Ludwig Erhard, an economist who had stabilized the postwar German currency so that commerce could thrive and the welfare state operate smoothly. Erhard used his academic expertise and commitment to the free market to "turn a lunar landscape into a flourishing beehive," in the words of one German commentator.[16]

The economist and the politician successfully guided Germany away from both fascism and communism and restored the representative system that Hitler had overthrown. The war itself had obliterated militarism and the authoritarian and monarchical bureaucracy—another obstacle to democratic rule under Weimar. The reward was steadily mounting support for the Christian Democrats. Adenauer restored diplomatic relations with the Soviet Union, visiting Moscow in 1955 and negotiating the release of some ten thousand German prisoners of war. The Christian Democrats were so powerful that opposition parties, notably the Social Democrats, could do little more than criticize everything the Christian Democrats did, gaining for themselves a reputation for being obstructionists rather than creative politicians. Eventually, however, Adenauer's control began to slip. With attacks on his policies and authoritarian ways mounting in the press, he directed the police to invade the offices of *Der Spiegel*—West Germany's upscale version of *Time*. His party felt the effects of the resulting scandal over an act that recalled the Nazi abuse of power, and as the Christian Democrats' majority faded, the aging Adenauer was effectively forced to resign in 1963, succeeded by Erhard.

Germany's successful conservative coalition under the Christian Democrats was matched in Britain by the return of Conservative Party leader Winston Churchill to power in 1951. Neither he nor his successors Anthony Eden and Harold Macmillan diverged from the commitment to the welfare state, although Churchill began the process of halting nationalization. The Conservatives preserved Britain's "mixed economy" of private and public enterprise, and they worked to keep down costs. By the late 1950s it was becoming abundantly clear that the country was no longer a great world power—despite Lord Salisbury's beliefs—and that Common Market countries, most notably West Germany, were surpassing it. The Labour Party was embroiled in its own disputes over values and goals, leaving the Conservatives victorious in elections but also responsible for handling the mounting crises of decolonization and state programs that seemed too expensive in light of the shift of global power.

The Christian Democrats of Italy under the leadership of Alcide de Gaspari were likewise able to build an increasingly strong base of support among the people. As in Germany and Britain, growing prosperity in the 1950s and early 1960s dulled the appeal of left-of-center parties. News of purges, Soviet army brutality, and other Stalinist excesses sent the Communists' popularity—based on their wartime resistance record—plummeting even though hard-pressed factory workers struck from time to time under the Communist banner.

The ineffectiveness of Communist politics was especially apparent in Italy and France. In both nations, centrist programs supporting private property and social reforms including subsidies to restore family life that the war had badly damaged enjoyed cross-class appeal. In Italy, landless people in the south aimed to drive the wealthy landowners who had prospered under Mussolini from their vast estates. Christian Democrats seized control of this issue. The Communist Party helped peasants in Italy organize dramatic occupations of major estates in 1949 and 1950, but these same peasants had no truck with collectivization, preferring their individual plots of land. When the Christian Democrats offered a half-hearted plan to redistribute land and when the Common Market later added subsidies for some farmers, the Communists lost ground along with right-wing social movements. Although many found new displays of wealth vulgar coming so hard on the heels of unspeakable suffering, and although Marxism remained alive among intellectuals as an analytical tool, the frightful Stalinist legacy and the desire for social peace were powerful forces allowing centrists to appeal across the political spectrum. In France, there was one major obstacle to social peace. The unfolding violence of decolonization in France's overseas possessions, especially Algeria, was a wild card, but the authoritarian resistance hero Charles de Gaulle stood waiting in the wings to usher in real political change (see Chapter 9).

In a climate of international balance of nuclear terror, even the most reactionary dictators survived because of their promise to maintain political and social calm. Francisco Franco in Spain and Antonio Salazar in Portugal set their countries on a course of virtual military rule that lasted into the 1970s. However, they kept their positions not because they represented the conservative mood of a prospering people but because they supported the traditional ruling forces in society—the Catholic Church, the military, and the agrarian aristocracy. Instead of pushing for economic modernization, Salazar and Franco let their resources languish. Farming deteriorated under a landed elite that feared change, and manufacturing capacity was left to stagnate. Modern problems crept in nonetheless. Improved life expectancy and high birthrates swelled the population of both countries, and without a modern industrial economy hundreds of thousands were forced to migrate to find work. In Spain strikes broke out in the aging industries of Barcelona, and the breakaway Basque movement began its campaign of violence against the central government. Those responsible for the outbursts might have expected swift and merciless punishment, for Franco was not a believer in individual rights and free speech. He had executed, thrown into prison, and driven into exile tens of thousands of republican loyalists after his victory in the Spanish civil war. But in this instance, though protests were suppressed, the government showed more restraint than it had in the past. By the early 1960s Spain was witnessing movement—no matter how faint—toward democracy.

THE REBIRTH OF CONSUMERISM

Robust consumerism was the big surprise of the 1950s. The immediate postwar period had seen rationing extended and scarcity even of basic foodstuffs and items like soap. Because of the need to rebuild major industries, transportation, and other infrastructure, consumer contentment was a low priority. That situation began to change early in the 1950s, and by the middle of the decade a consumer boom was taking shape thanks to the "golden age" of European productivity. The restoration of consumer capacity and the availability of goods helpful in everyday life signaled the end of the postwar period and the beginning of a new age. Consumerism brought anxiety as well as the rebirth of Western abundance, however, for many of the most desired goods, from Coca-Cola to appliances, came from the United States. There was concern that materialistic values from American culture would infect the younger generation of Europeans as they watched films, bought motorbikes, and listened to the newly fashionable rock 'n' roll music performed by stars such as Elvis Presley and Bill Haley and the Comets. Consumerism also shaped gender identity by offering not only goods but a whole marketplace of ideas that both challenged and reinforced traditional notions of masculinity and femininity. Overlaying the range of concerns was the simple enjoyment of comforts that had disappeared for many over the course of thirty years of European intramural warfare.

Europe Goes Shopping

The desire to replace material possessions lost during the war partially fueled the consumer boom, and consumption also increased in the 1950s because of the ongoing baby boom, which began after the war and extended into the 1960s. The postwar recovery of consumption in part addressed the labor that women did to perform ordinary household tasks such as laundry and housecleaning and to find scarce resources to support their families. Their behavior as postwar consumers focused on alleviating those burdens. Women's first consumer purchases in the late 1940s and early 1950s were vacuum cleaners and sewing machines—not the newest of inventions but ones that performed necessary jobs, formerly done by hand, more rapidly and with better results. Secondary purchases included more expensive but equally useful items such as refrigerators, which reduced the need for shopping on a daily basis, and washing machines, which cut the time—often as much as a day—demanded for washing done by hand. In Austria between 1953 and 1962, the number of washing machines rose from 8,000 to 28,000, and the number of refrigerators went from 30,000 to 591,000. In the Soviet bloc, appliances were not readily available, and women consumers were urged to cut housekeeping time with simple furniture. As the popular Soviet newspaper *Ogonek* put it in 1959, "the interior organizes everyday life." Streamlining the interior would make household tasks easier.

Across Europe, advertising and film media played on women's obligations as consumers. The heroine in the West German film *Without You All Is Darkness* (1956) sports luxurious clothes and jewelry, until she marries and becomes a proper housewife simply dressed and surrounded by the modern appliances that indicate her growing consumer maturity. The focus on women as consumers came from the recognition that, since the immediate postwar days when men were participating in consumption, the new domesticity meant that women were doing most of the purchasing: "Women's decisions on the allocation of disposable income exert a decisive upward or downward pressure on company turnover," as one businessman put it.[17] Advertisers also played the cold war card—for example, depicting West German women living in cozy, well-appointed homes in contrast to the reportedly grim daily life led by women in East Germany. The implication was that women allied with Americans enjoyed not only a higher standard of living but

◆ **The Kitchen Debate**

In Moscow on July 22, 1959, Soviet premier Nikita Khrushchev and U.S. vice president Richard Nixon faced off in a modern American kitchen displayed at the American National Exhibition. America held a clear advantage in the production of consumer items, not having suffered massive losses of population and industrial capacity as the Soviets had. After the war, Europeans yearned for some of the conveniences that were available, and Nixon pointed to the abundance of consumer items in the United States as a mark of capitalist superiority. *Photo by AP.*

freedom to buy a broader range of goods and to provide their families with luxuries.

Consumption was also on the rise in the Soviet bloc. With the end of Stalin's era, consumer fantasies in Communist countries heated up. Governments allowed a network of free stores to operate outside the system of state institutions. Goods such as the fine wines and imported clothing available in many of these stores were beyond the means of ordinary people, but their very existence (like the existence of wildly expensive luxury goods in the U.S. sphere) provoked consumer interest. Communists countered U.S.-bloc claims to superior consumer goods. A renowned East German plastics designer explained in 1959 that capitalist products were nothing but "cheap and shockingly kitschy mass wares." Unlike the "Woolworth goods" designed to sell in great numbers to make huge profits, Communist items, he said, were based on "industrial refinement" that sought nothing but beauty and utility in products.[18] Communist advertising in official magazines appealed to women as consumers to perpetuate socialist taste: "We women value the ability to set a nice table and present our families with varied, good, and tasty fare. In a friendly, comfortable environment we feel well: nice, fashionable clothes give us new productive energy. We also know, however, that this can only be achieved when we actively support our socialist trade."[19] Soviet women had their own "socialist" fashions consisting of more practical clothing than that shown in western Europe. Smocks, aprons, jumpers, and other amply cut garments were the norm instead of the increasingly revealing clothing in the west (see the Picture Essay).

A whole way of life developed around the practices of Communist consumerism. With everyday goods in short supply and stylish clothing at a premium, Soviet women put energy into their hair, and regular sessions at the beauty salon became a popular way of socializing. Working women in offices and factories kept each other abreast of the arrival of goods in any particular store. One designated person would leave work during the day to do the shopping for her colleagues, so that only one woman had to stand long hours in a shopping queue. Once acquired, goods such as yogurt, honey, oil, and eggs not only enlivened meals but were also whipped up into beauty concoctions according to recipes found in magazines.

The Perils and Possibilities of Americanization

Consumerism meant the influx of American goods, sometimes seen as threatening to overwhelm European culture. In American-occupied Austria the goods ranged from films featuring Marilyn Monroe, James Dean, and Judy Garland to flannel shirts, aftershave lotion, and chewing gum. "It did not help our elders to warn us that if we chewed gum we would look like Americans," one Austrian remembered of the 1950s; "that was exactly what we wanted to look like!"[20] As European television developed, it featured American-style quiz shows, while radio adopted the American format of hourly newscasts. Slogans like "All for Hoover, a Hoover for all" touted vacuum cleaners, and American words—*hello, darling, baby, okay*—crept into the language.[21] Because of censorship and military occupation, American record and film companies dominated what most western Europeans were allowed to see and hear. Initially Coca-Cola was imported only for U.S. occupation forces, but gradually Coke became emblematic for Europeans of their growing servitude to American culture and the economic forces behind it. Communists in France took the lead in asserting that France, even the whole of Europe, was being drained of its identity, and they tried unsuccessfully to get the French parliament to ban the sale of Coke altogether.

Young people were on the cutting edge of consumerism and other aspects of Americanization and postwar revival as they rushed to acquire American goods and styles: "I bought myself records, American blues and jazz, Benny Goodman and Louis Armstrong. I was happy dancing the boogie-woogie," a young Austrian woman wrote of spending her first earnings early in the 1950s.[22] Jazz and rock 'n' roll recordings were special favorites of the young, even across the Soviet-U.S. divide. Although adults often disapproved of the "low" American culture, the U.S. culture industry overpowered the opposition. Interestingly in the case of music, what passed for "American" contained vast quantities of non-Western material. Rumba, jitterbug, samba, cha-cha, calypso, and jazz took their rhythms, harmonies, and lyrics from Latin American, Caribbean, and African music.

Americanized consumption and loss of national identity by the young became a focus of concern. There was a sense that delinquency was sweeping youth, a portent of national decline into crime and degeneracy. In the late 1940s a Berlin-based gang had rampaged in the city, robbing and wounding citizens both in their homes and in public. The teenage leader of the gang was executed, but the trial and newspaper stories centered on the condition of youth. It was a combination of the "Wild West and Gestapo," wrote one journalist, focusing on two looming enemies: the pernicious influence of American culture as exemplified by the westerns playing at local cinemas, and the resurgence of Nazi thuggery.[23] One evening in 1959 students flocked en masse through the streets of East Berlin shouting, "We want our old Kaiser Wilhelm . . . we want Rock 'n' Roll."[24] From Spain to the Soviet bloc, rampaging youth beset cities, modeling themselves on characters in American films and comics. Facing the unexpected flood of American goods that accompanied the Marshall Plan and postwar prosperity, parents and politicians in Europe saw the transformation of young people into crude materialists and, paradoxically, the promise of a better life that Americanization seemed to offer.

Cultural Consumption

With more and more disposable income, Europeans began to purchase an array of cultural items. Slick weekly newsmagazines inspired by the success of *Time* appeared across western Europe. Becoming informed like Americans was part of changing the old patterns of government that had brought about a half century of total war. "The mission of *L'Express* [a French counterpart to *Time*] was to support and advance political reform based on accurate information for the French," wrote one of the publication's founders of her journalistic adventure in 1952.[25] "It was normal that the new public wanted a new press," one like the American press, which informed the public with statistics, news about business, and commentary on political events. Both West Germany's *Der Spiegel* and Britain's *The Economist* emerged during this period to meet this need. Such magazines, not incidentally, were filled with advertisements for the latest products, highlighting the freedom of choice available to western Europeans.

High-end cultural consumption increased. By the late 1950s new literary styles were emerging that ran counter to the trend of engagement that had shaped fiction since the Great Depression. Distancing themselves from existentialism and earnest socialist fiction, writers and filmmakers created both New Wave cinema and the New Wave novel. New Wave films and novels were elite consumer items that conspicuously lacked the easy accessibility of mass culture, especially anything smacking of American influence. French New Wave cinema developed in reaction to mass-market Hollywood films. Aiming to attract a higher-class audience and thus have avant-garde cachet, François Truffaut, Jean-Luc Godard, and other French directors focused on the maker, or *auteur,* of a film to contrast their work with movies concocted by anonymous studio executives. French writers pioneered the New Wave novel as an antidote to the best sellers that pumped up the U.S.-style mass market. The model for this genre, Nathalie Sarraute's *Tropismes,* was written in 1939, but the majority of New Wave novels appeared in the 1950s and thereafter. Sarraute wrote *Tropismes* and subsequent works in terms of human "gestures," "subconversations," and fleeting glimpses of the interior of the human psyche; her aim was to produce a disjointed, interior reality. Alain Resnais adapted a Marguerite Duras story into the grainy film *Hiroshima Mon Amour* (1959), in which the two characters—a French woman and a Japanese man—stumble through fragmented, even incomprehensible accounts of their horrifying experience of the war. The effect of this kind of fictional rendering was to distance the story from the world of the average person and to create a commodity with snob appeal.

German authors took a different route to restoring the arts in an era of renewed prosperity. In 1959 Gruppe 47 novelist Günter Grass published *The Tin Drum*, the story of a boy, Oskar Mazerath, whose brief experience of the adult world makes him decide to stop growing. The motif of stunted growth flies in the face of the entire German middle-class tradition of self-development through cultural exchange and thought. Instead of communicating through the richness of the German language, Mazerath drums incessantly to make himself heard, and his piercing voice, which can smash glass, stands in contrast to the well-modulated rationality of German philosophy and its fictional conventions. The works of Thomas Mann and others had included bulky and intense debates among protagonists, many of them members of high society and the intelligentsia, about life's meaning and deep theoretical issues. Grass debunked that tradition, charting Mazerath's more appropriate if bizarre response to the horrors of life under Nazism and portraying an absurdly and cruelly irrational world.

Grass's compatriot Heinrich Böll wrote *The Clown* (1963), a novel whose hero from a respectable family takes to performing as a clown and begging in a railroad station. The story to some extent recapitulated the lives of some Gruppe 47 members, who were themselves living as vagrants in order to reject the rebirth of German respectability. In their eyes the restoration of middle-class norms and prosperity was obscene when genocide and other wartime horrors were still so fresh.

Many culture makers, however, reacted not to the war but to the needs of the postwar period. Some films and magazines worked to reinvigorate and resexualize the population after the spartan regimen of the war years. Some French films featured sexy teenage women such as Brigitte Bardot clad in alluring, skimpy clothing. Promoters of consumer demand targeted young couples as part of the effort to rebuild and to repopulate Europe. Tracts with prefabricated bungalows arranged in suburban "subdivisions" sprang up overnight across western Europe to provide an intimate setting for young couples, while in the Soviet bloc modern apartment buildings went up once the thaw began. One sensational piece of thaw literature was Marek Hlasko's *The Eighth Day of the Week* (1956), a novel describing a Warsaw couple's attempt to find privacy for lovemaking when housing was in short supply.

This resexualization entailed clearly distinguishing between masculinity and femininity to give society a heterosexual look. Here again consumerism played an important role. Consumer society's intellectuals rebelled against some social and cultural trends and in so doing updated the image of artistic creativity as masculine and consumerism as feminine. Male poets, artists, and performers created a non-conformist image of bad boys, gangsters, pornographers, and addicts. They were the Beat poets and angry young men who refused to dress nicely or buy proper consumer goods. They became "pop artists" who simultaneously replicated and mocked consumer goods such as vacuum cleaners, lipstick, and ketchup. Others turned to abstract expressionism, rejecting even the hint of realism in their representations of objects or people.

CONCLUSION

The rebirth of consumption in an expanded, exuberant form was an emphatic sign that the war was over. It was time for people to get on with their lives, especially by having more children and buying more goods. They could afford to do both because of the productivity made possible by the "economic miracle" of the 1950s. Catching up with the new technology, Europe as a whole became more prosperous. In western Europe, economic cooperation facilitated by the Common Market spurred the revival—which lasted well into the 1970s—and government planners replaced wrangling politicians as policy leaders in the economic arena. Prosperity cost leftist parties much of their appeal. Although cold war politics persisted, the Common Market was laying the groundwork for even greater unity among nations in the future. On the other side of the so-called iron curtain, the Soviets were also trying to reform their image, shedding some of the most brutal aspects of Stalinism and shifting economic priorities to please consumers.

In the midst of this striking postwar restoration, momentous changes were occurring around the world. As the European economy prospered, European imperial leadership collapsed, altering global politics and bringing real change to Europe itself. Europe's imperial age ended, and it remained to be seen what the significance of such a dramatic shift would be.

D O C U M E N T S

Childhood in the British Welfare State

T̲HE GROWTH OF THE WELFARE STATE shaped people's sense of themselves as employees, workers, and citizens. Organizing a range of programs, governments ensured that no stigma was attached to receiving benefits such as public schooling, veterans' pensions, old-age insurance, and school lunches. The welfare state changed people's experience of citizenship. Government help in obtaining housing and good health care was sometimes interpreted as payment for the wartime sacrifices of loved ones, homes, and the right to lead a normal life. The experience of "using" or "interacting" with one's own state was an active form of civic participation involving legitimation of one's status as a worthy citizen.

Society devoted a lot of attention to ordinary citizens during the postwar period. The author of this autobiographical excerpt describes an impoverished, working-class child's feelings about the British welfare state in the 1950s and describes family life in a heart-wrenching, if detached way. Children are usually not featured in history books, and children's and young people's experiences are a neglected part of the past. For some of these reasons, this autobiography has become a well-read classic.

The British child in this passage was born to a mother who was unhappy with her lot in life and to whom everything that happened seemed unfair. The girl and her sister hardly ever saw their relatives, and no friends came to their house because their poverty was an embarrassment. As for children, they were "burdens, expensive, never grateful enough." The writer's mother did not know how to affirm her own children's existence: "Never have children dear," she said; "they ruin your life."[26] Instead of finding this attitude abnormal, however, the author found it the normal attitude of many working-class families. Also normal was that her mother did not feel the solidarity attributed to the working class by socialists and union members. Rather she was envious and wanted the latest and most fashionable clothes, often complaining bitterly about her fate to the author's father. To some extent, the state stepped in to provide schooling and the affirmation that parents failed to give. With the help of her teachers the author received much-needed eyeglasses and encouragement to use her talents—her parents failed to provide either. Some have said that the welfare state became like a comforting parent to people who had experienced war and emotional deprivation for practically their entire existence.

Document 8.1

CAROLYN KAY STEEDMAN
Landscape for a Good Woman, 1986

... My teacher was worried at my failing sight, I couldn't see the board by the spring of 1957 and read a book under my desk during arithmetic lessons. Did he send a note to my mother? Surely he must have done; what else could have shaken her conviction that glasses would be bad for me? ... I think they must have used the eleven-plus and the amount of blackboard work it involved as a lever, because I got a pair of glasses before the exam.

... The next year, standing by my new teacher's desk, now in the eleven-plus class, he showed my book to what must have been a student on teaching practice. "This one," he said, "has an inferiority complex." I didn't understand, had no dictionary in which to look up the words, but preserved them by my own invented syllabary, rehearsing them, to bring out for much later scrutiny. ... By the time I was fifteen we'd all three of us given up, huddled with tiredness and irritation in the house where my father was only now an intermittent presence. The house was a tip; none of us did any housework any more; broken china wasn't replaced; at meal times my mother, my sister and I shared the last knife between us. Responsible now for my own washing, I scarcely did any, spent the winter changing about the layers of five petticoats I wore to keep warm, top to bottom through the cold months. One morning, asked by the games mistress why I wasn't wearing my school blouse, I said I hadn't been able to find it in the place I'd put it down the night before (not true; I hadn't a clean one), presenting thus a scene of baroque household disorganization, daring her to disapprove, hoping she would.

Ten years before this, school had taught me to read, and I found out for myself how to do it fast.

By the time I was six I read all the time, rapidly and voraciously. You couldn't join the library until you were seven, and before that I read my Hans Christian Andersen from back to front when I'd read it from start to finish. ... Not being hungry and having a warm bed to lie in at night, I had a good childhood, was better than other people; was a *lucky* little girl.

My mother had wanted to marry a king. That was the best of my father's stories, told in the pub in the 1960s, of how difficult it had been to live with her in 1937, during the Abdication months. Mrs Simpson was no prettier than her, no more clever than her, no better than her. It wasn't fair that a king should give up his throne for her, and not for the weaver's daughter. From a traditional Labour background, my mother rejected the politics of solidarity and communality, always voted Conservative, for the left could not embody her desire for things to be *really* fair, for a full skirt that took twenty yards of cloth, for a half-timbered cottage in the country, for the prince who did not come. For my mother, the time of my childhood was the place where the fairy-tales failed. ...

The 1950s was a time when state intervention in children's lives was highly visible, and experienced, by me at least, as entirely beneficent. The calculated, dictated fairness of the ration book went on into the new decade, and we spent a lot of time after we moved from Hammersmith to Streatham Hill, picking up medicine bottles of orange juice and jars of Virol from the baby clinic for my sister. I think I would be a very different person now if orange juice and milk and dinners at school hadn't told me, in a covert way, that I had a right to exist, was worth something. My inheritance from those years is the belief (maintained always with some difficulty) that I do have a right to the earth. I think that had I grown up with my

SOURCE: Carolyn Kay Steedman, *Landscape for a Good Woman: A Story of Two Lives* (New Brunswick: Rutgers University Press, 1986), 44–47, 121–123.

parents only twenty years before, I would not now believe this, for children are always episodes in someone else's narrative, not their own people, but rather brought into being for particular purposes. Being a child when the state was practically engaged in making children healthy and literate was a support against my own circumstances, so I find it difficult to match an account of the welfare policies of the late 1940s, which calls the "post-War Labour government . . . the last and most glorious flowering of late Victorian liberal philanthropy," which I know to be historically correct, with the sense of self that those policies imparted. If it had been only philanthropy, would it have felt like it did? Psychic structures are shaped by these huge historical labels: "charity," "philanthropy," "state intervention."

It was a considerable achievement for a society to pour so much milk and so much orange juice, so many vitamins, down the throats of its children, and for the height and weight of those children to outstrip the measurements of only a decade before; and this remains an achievement in spite of the fact that the statistics of healthy and intelligent childhood were stretched along the curve of achievement, and only a few were allowed to travel through the narrow gate at the age of eleven, towards the golden city. Nevertheless, within that period of time more children were provided with the goods of the earth than had any generation been before. What my mother lacked, I was given; and though vast inequalities remained between me and others of my generation, the sense that a benevolent state bestowed on me, that of my own existence and the worth of that existence—attenuated, but still there—demonstrates in some degree what a fully material culture might offer in terms of physical comfort and the structures of care and affection that it symbolizes, to all its children.

QUESTIONS FOR ANALYSIS

1. In what ways did the welfare state serve this child?
2. What is the author's attitude toward the world around her in the 1940s and 1950s?
3. What historic insights do we gain from this autobiography?

The Myth of Classlessness

MILOVAN DJILAS (1911–1995) WAS AN EARLY BELIEVER IN COMMUNISM, studying it from his youth at the University of Belgrade; he also was a Yugoslav patriot. An ally of the Yugoslav Communist leader Marshal Tito from 1932 on, Djilas fought the Nazis during World War II and then royalists who wanted to return Yugoslavia to a monarchy. When Tito took power, Djilas became one of his trusted officials, supporting his nationalist brand of socialism and equally criticizing of Stalin's attempts to dictate policies to Yugoslavia. Djilas was outspoken and impolitic, however, and soon became an outcast for his vocal protest against Soviet imperialism. At considerable risk to himself, Djilas forthrightly expressed support for the Hungarian uprising and was imprisoned in its aftermath. Media attention protected him from worse. His book *The New Class: An Analysis of the Communist System* (1955) was published in western Europe and the United States in 1957, and his use of the Western media was a tactic that other well-known dissidents soon adopted.

The *New class* was Djilas's term for the bureaucracy that became entrenched in the Soviet Union and other Communist states. Instead of becoming classless, as Marx had predicted, Communist society gave birth to a powerful set of managers and officials who controlled the Communist state. A devoted student of Marxist and Leninist texts, Djilas pointed out that the very existence of a centralized government flew in the face of Marx's writing. Marx had interpreted the nineteenth-century state as the protector of upper-class interests. Once the oppressive class structure and the private property on which power depended gave way to classlessness under socialism, Marx said, there would be no reason for the state to exist; the state would "wither away." Djilas blamed not only the Soviets but also the tsarist tradition of large bureaucracy for the emergence of the "new class." He also criticized Lenin and the Bolsheviks for their belief that the proletariat, or workers, needed an elite group to lead them to true socialism. Lenin's theories about the backwardness of ordinary Russian people and his faith in the superior Bolshevik understanding of communism became justifications, Djilas charged, for the development of the "new class."

Djilas may have drawn his analysis not only from Stalin's USSR but also from the situation in Yugoslavia, as the committed freedom fighters of World War II began to change once in power. Even Tito, it is said, made peace with the Soviet bosses and came to lavish more attention on developing his own privileges and enjoying luxuries than he did on public affairs.

Document 8.2

MILOVAN DJILAS
The New Class, 1957

. . . The greatest illusion was that industrialization and collectivization in the U.S.S.R., and destruction of capitalist ownership, would result in a classless society. In 1936, when the new Constitution was promulgated, Stalin announced that the "exploiting class" had ceased to exist. The capitalist and other classes of ancient origin had in fact been destroyed, but a new class, previously unknown to history, had been formed.

It is understandable that this class, like those before it, should believe that the establishment of its power would result in happiness and freedom for all men. The only difference between this and other classes was that it treated the delay in the realization of its illusions more crudely. It thus affirmed that its power was more complete than the power of any other class before in history, and its class illusions and prejudices were proportionally greater.

. . . The initiators of the new class are not found in the party of the Bolshevik type as a whole but in that stratum of professional revolutionaries who made up its core even before it attained power. It was not by accident that Lenin asserted after the failure of the 1905 revolution that only professional revolutionaries—men whose sole profession was revolutionary work—could build a new party of the Bolshevik type. It was still less accidental that even Stalin, the future creator of a new class, was the most outstanding example of such a professional revolutionary. The new ruling class has been gradually developing from this very narrow stratum of revolutionaries. These revolutionaries composed its core for a long period. Trotsky noted that in pre-revolutionary professional revolutionaries was the origin of the future Stalinist bureaucrat. What he did not detect was the beginning of a new class of owners and exploiters.

This is not to say that the new party and the new class are identical. The party, however, is the core of that class, and its base. It is very difficult, perhaps impossible, to define the limits of the new class and to identify its members. The new class may be said to be made up of those who have special privileges and economic preference because of the administrative monopoly they hold. . . .

Since administration is unavoidable in society, necessary administrative functions may be co-existent with parasitic functions in the same person. Not every member of the party is a member of the new class, any more than every artisan or member of the city party was a bourgeois.

In loose terms, as the new class becomes stronger and attains a more perceptible physiognomy, the role of the party diminishes. The core and the basis of the new class is created in the party and at its top, as well as in the state political organs. The once live, compact party, full of initiative, is disappearing to become transformed into the traditional oligarchy of the new class, irresistibly drawing into its ranks those who aspire to join the new class and repressing those who have any ideals.

The party makes the class, but the class grows as a result and uses the party as a basis. The class grows stronger, while the party grows weaker; this is the inescapable fate of every Communist party in power.

If it were not materially interested in production or if it did not have within itself the potentialities for the creation of a new class, no party could act in so morally and ideologically foolhardy a fashion, let alone stay in power for long. Stalin declared, after the end of the First Five-Year Plan: "If we had not created the apparatus, we

SOURCE: Milovan Djilas, *The New Class: An Analysis of the Communist System* (New York: Harcourt Brace Jovanovich, 1985 [reprint of 1957 edition]), 37–40, 65–71.

would have failed!" He should have substituted "new class" for the word "apparatus," and everything would have been clearer. . . .

The new class is most sensitive to demands on the part of the people for a special kind of freedom, not for freedom in general or political freedom. It is especially sensitive to demands for freedom of thought and criticism, within the limits of present conditions and within the limits of "socialism"; not for demands for a return to previous social and ownership relations. This sensitivity originates from the class's special position.

The new class instinctively feels that national goods are, in fact, its property, and that even the terms "socialist," "social," and "state" property denote a general legal fiction. The new class also thinks that any breach of its totalitarian authority might imperil its ownership. Consequently, the new class opposes *any* type of freedom, ostensibly for the purpose of preserving "socialist" ownership. Criticism of the new class's monopolistic administration of property generates the fear of a possible loss of power. The new class is sensitive to these criticisms and demands depending on the extent to which they expose the manner in which it rules and holds power.

This is an important contradiction. Property is legally considered social and national property. But, in actuality, a single group manages it in its own interest. The discrepancy between legal and actual conditions continuously results in obscure and abnormal social and economic relationships. It also means that the words of the leading group do not correspond to its actions; and that all actions result in strengthening its property holdings and its political position.

This contradiction cannot be resolved without jeopardizing the class's position. Other ruling, property-owning classes could not resolve this contradiction either, unless forcefully deprived of monopoly of power and ownership. Wherever there has been a higher degree of freedom for society as a whole, the ruling classes have been forced, in one way or another, to renounce monopoly of ownership. The reverse is true also: wherever monopoly of ownership has been impossible, freedom, to some degree, has become inevitable.

In Communism, power and ownership are almost always in the same hands, but this fact is concealed under a legal guise. In classical capitalism, the worker had equality with the capitalist before the law, even though the worker was being exploited and the capitalist was doing the exploiting. In Communism, legally, all are equal with respect to material goods. The formal owner is the nation. In reality, because of monopolistic administration, only the narrowest stratum of administrators enjoys the rights of ownership. . . .

This makes the legal position of the new class uncertain and is also the source of the new class's biggest internal difficulties. The contradiction discloses the disharmony between words and actions: While promising to abolish social differences, it must always increase them by acquiring the products of the nation's workshops and granting privileges to its adherents. It must proclaim loudly its dogma that it is fulfilling its historical mission of "final" liberation of mankind from every misery and calamity while it acts in exactly the opposite way.

The contradiction between the new class's real ownership position and its legal position can furnish the basic reason for criticism. This contradiction has within it the ability not only to incite others but also to corrode the class's own ranks, since privileges are actually being enjoyed by only a few. This contradiction, when intensified, holds prospects of real changes in the Communist system, whether the ruling class is in favor of the change or not. The fact that this contradiction is so obvious has been the reason for the changes made by the new class, especially in so-called liberalization and decentralization.

Forced to withdraw and surrender to individual strata, the new class aims at concealing this contradiction and strengthening its own position. Since ownership and authority continue intact, all measures taken by the new class—even those democratically inspired—show a tendency toward strengthening the management of the political bureaucracy. The system turns democratic measures into positive methods for consolidating the position of the ruling classes. Slavery in ancient times in the East inevitably permeated all of society's activities and components, including the family. In the same way, the monopolism and totalitarianism of the ruling class in the Communist system are imposed on all the aspects of social life, even though the political heads are not aiming at this.

Yugoslavia's so-called workers' management and autonomy, conceived at the time of the struggle against Soviet imperialism as a far-reaching democratic measure to deprive the party of the monopoly of administration, has been increasingly relegated to one of the areas of party work. Thus, it is hardly possible to change the present system. The aim of creating a new democracy through this type of administration will not be achieved. Besides, freedom cannot be extended to the largest piece of the pie. Workers' management has not brought about a sharing in profits by those who produce, either on a national level or in local enterprises. This type of administration has increasingly turned into a safe type for the regime. Through various taxes and other means, the regime has appropriated even the share of the profits which the workers believed would be given to them. Only crumbs from the tables and illusions have been left to the workers. Without universal freedom not even workers' management can become free. Clearly, in an unfree society nobody can freely decide anything. The givers have somehow obtained the most value from the gift of freedom they supposedly handed the workers.

This does not mean that the new class cannot make concessions to the people, even though it only considers its own interests. Workers' management, or decentralization, is a concession to the masses. Circumstances may drive the new class, no matter how monopolistic and totalitarian it may be, to retreat before the masses. In 1948, when the conflict took place between Yugoslavia and the U.S.S.R., the Yugoslav leaders were forced to execute some reforms. Even though it might mean a backward step, they set up reforms as soon as they saw themselves in jeopardy. Something similar is happening today in the eastern European countries.

In defending its authority, the ruling class must execute reforms every time it becomes obvious to the people that the class is treating national property as its own. Such reforms are not proclaimed as being what they really are, but rather as part of the "further development of socialism" and "socialist democracy." The groundwork for reforms is laid when the discrepancy mentioned above becomes public. From the historical point of view the new class is forced to fortify its authority and ownership constantly, even though it is running away from the truth. It must constantly demonstrate how it is successfully creating a society of happy people, all of whom enjoy equal rights and have been freed of every type of exploitation. The new class cannot avoid falling continuously into profound internal contradictions; for in spite of its historical origin it is not able to make its ownership lawful, and it cannot renounce ownership without undermining itself. Consequently, it is forced to try to justify its increasing authority, invoking abstract and unreal purposes.

This is a class whose power over men is the most complete known to history. For this reason it is a class with very limited views, views which are false and unsafe. Closely ingrown, and a complete authority, the new class must unrealistically evaluate its own role and that of the people around it.

Having achieved industrialization, the new class can now do nothing more than strengthen its brute force and pillage the people. It ceases to create. Its spiritual heritage is overtaken by darkness.

While the new class accomplished one of its greatest successes in the revolution, its method of control is one of the most shameful pages in human history. Men will marvel at the grandiose ventures it accomplished, and will be ashamed of the means it used to accomplish them.

When the new class leaves the historical scene—and this must happen—there will be less sorrow over its passing than there was for any other class before it. Smothering everything except what suited its ego, it has condemned itself to failure and shameful ruin.

QUESTIONS FOR ANALYSIS

1. To what does Djilas attribute the power of the "new class"?
2. What policy results of the presence of the new class explain the ups and downs of the thaw in the USSR?
3. How does Djilas's critique of the Soviet system parallel the critique of the rise of technocrats in western Europe? In what ways is it different?

Teen Culture in the Soviet Union

In March 1946 in a speech delivered in Fulton, Missouri, former British prime minister Winston Churchill declared that an "iron curtain" had fallen across Europe, dividing Germany and closing off eastern from western Europe. Even the iron curtain, however, did not completely halt the flow of products, styles, and ideas from the West. These imports did not always receive official approval, but the "new class" of managers and top political figures themselves enjoyed a wide range of goods from beyond Soviet borders. Foreign food, fashion, appliances, and entertainment came their way; so did teen culture.

A phenomenon especially disturbing to right-thinking socialists was the mimicking of teen culture from the United States and western Europe. In the 1950s this culture entered easily through the porous borders in Berlin, and teens from East Berlin crossed into the western zone to attend films and concerts. Radio Luxembourg and American radio stations operating across Europe broadcast jazz and pop music, including rock 'n' roll. Communist officialdom tried to match the appeal of this imported youth culture with locally produced films and radio broadcasts.

The Soviet literary establishment—the massive stable of writers of all kinds of works—resorted to satirizing Western ways. The satire reprinted here, most likely written by a party writer, effectively conveys what avant-garde teen culture was like in the Soviet Union. It also expresses the official attitude toward it. We are likely to think that cold war propaganda was heavy-handed and not amusing, but this piece lets us see why many readers enjoyed such works. First published in the humor magazine *Krokodil,* this document is part of a rich treasure trove of Soviet humor that comes down to us not only in official magazines but also in the oral tradition of anti-Soviet jokes and satirical dissident stories and art.

Document 8.3

D. BELYAEV
Stilyaga, 1949

Last summer, an agronomist friend and I were wandering across a field of rye.

Suddenly I noticed an ear of rye that stuck out sharply from the masses of grain. It was taller and swayed proudly above them.

"Look," I said to the agronomist, "what a strong and beautiful ear. Maybe it's a special variety?"

The agronomist pitilessly tore off the ear and handed it to me. "Feel it: this beautiful ear won't yield a single grain. It's a parasite ear; it sucks moisture and every thing else from nature, but doesn't give grain. The common folk call it an empty-head. There are also flowers like that in nature—degenerate mutants. They often look very pretty, but they're empty and barren inside. Just like the ear of rye."

"A stilyaga ear," I exclaimed.

It was the agronomist's turn to be surprised: "What was that?"

"Stilyaga," I repeated and told the agronomist the following story.

A literary evening was going on in the student club. After business had been taken care of and the dance was beginning, a young man appeared in the doorway. He looked incredibly absurd: the back of his jacket was bright orange, while the sleeves and lapels were green; I hadn't seen such broad canary-green trousers since the days of the renowned bell-bottoms;° his boots were a clever combination of black varnish and red suede.

The young man leaned against the doorway and with a uniquely casual motion put his right foot on the left, revealing his socks, which looked as though they were stitched together from an American flag—that's how bright they were.

He stood and surveyed the room with a scornful squint. Then the young man walked over in our direction. When he reached us, we were enveloped by such a strong smell of perfume that I involuntarily thought: "He must be a walking signboard for Tezhe."°

"Aha, stilyaga, you've graced us with your presence! And why did you miss the report?" asked one of my companions.

"Give me five!" answered the youth. "I was consciously late: I was scared the yawning and boredom would bust my jaws. Have you seen Mumochka?"

"No, she hasn't appeared yet."

"That's a shame, there's no one to dance with."

He sat down. But how he sat down! He turned the back of the chair forward, wrapped his legs around it, stuck his boots between the legs, and in some improbable manner turned his heels out with the clear intent of showing off his socks. His lips, eyebrows, and thin mustache were made up, and the most fashionable lady in Paris would have envied his perm and manicure.

"How'ya doing, stilyaga? Spending all your time in the ballet studio?"

"The ballet's a thing of the past. I cast off. I'm stuck on the circus now."

"The circus? And what will Princess Maria Alekseevna say?"°

"Princess? Maria Alekseevna? And what sort of bird is that?" asked the young man in stupefaction.

Everyone laughed.

"Oh, stilyaga, stilyaga! You don't even know Griboyedov."

About that time a girl appeared in the room who looked as if she had fluttered straight off the

---

° *bell bottoms:* Popular in the 1920s and early 1930s.

SOURCE: D. Belyaev, "Stilyaga" (1949), in James von Geldern and Richard Stites, eds., *Mass Culture in Soviet Russia: Tales, Poems, Songs, Movies, Plays and Folklore, 1917–1953* (Bloomington: Indiana University Press, 1995), 450–453.

° *Tezhe:* A Soviet perfume maker.
° *"The circus? . . . Alekseevna say?"* From Griboyedov's classic comedy *Woe from Wit* (1824).

cover of a fashion magazine. The young man howled out for everyone to hear: "Muma! Mumochka! Here, kitty, kitty!"

He crooked a finger at her. Not at all offended by his conduct, she fluttered over to him.

"Shall we stomp one out, Muma?"

"With pleasure, stilyaga!"

They went to dance.

"What a strange young man," I turned to my neighbor, a student. "And a strange last name: Stilyaga. This is the first time I've heard it."

My neighbor laughed.

"That's not a last name. That's what such types call themselves, in their own birdy-words. As you can see, they've worked out their own style of clothing, speech, and manners. The most important part of their style is not to resemble normal people. And as you see, their efforts take them to absurd extremes. The stilyaga knows the fashions all over the world, but he doesn't know Griboyedov, as you've discovered yourself. He's studied all the fox trots, tangos, rumbas, and lindy hops in detail, but he confuses Michurin with Mendeleev, and astronomy with gastronomy. He's memorized all the arias from *Sylvia* and *Maritza*,° but doesn't know who wrote the operas *Ivan Susanin* and *Prince Igor*. Stilyagas aren't alive as we understand the word, but they flutter above life's surface, so to speak. Take a look for yourself."

I had long ago noticed that, whatever ordinary dance music—a waltz or krakowiak—was playing, the stilyaga and Mumochka were doing some sort of horribly complicated and absurd movements, something in between a can-can and the dance of the savages from the Land of Fire.° Their ecstatic exertions had them twisting around in the very center of the circle.

The band fell silent. Stilyaga and Mumochka came over. The scent of perfume was mixed with the bitter smell of sweat.

"Tell me, young man, what is the dance you're dancing called?"

"Oh, Mumochka and I worked on that dance for half a year," the youth explained with self-satisfaction. "It chicly harmonizes body rhythm with eye expression. Take note that we—me and Muma—were the first to heed the fact that not only foot movement but facial expression is the most important part of dancing. Our dance consists of 177 vertical leaps and 192 horizontal pirouettes. Each leap and pirouette is accompanied by a distinct smile unique to that leap or pirouette. Our dance is called the 'stilyaga de dri.' Do you like it?"

"And how," I answered in the same tone. "Even Terpsichore° will faint from ecstasy when she sees your 177 leaps and 192 pirouettes."

"Terpsichore? Is that what you said? What a chic name! Who is she?"

"Terpsichore is my wife."

"Does she dance?"

"It stands to reason. And how! In St. Vitus' Dance° she used 334 leaps and 479 pirouettes."

"St. Vitus' Dance? Wow! Even I never heard of that dance."

"You're kidding. But it's the most popular dance in the court of the French king, Heinrich Heine."°

"But I heard somewhere that France doesn't have a king," Mumochka timidly objected.

"Muma, clam up!" remarked the stilyaga with an air of superiority. "Don't manifest your bad upbringing. Everyone knows that Heinrich Heine isn't only a king, he's a French poet."

The group's Homeric laughter drowned out his words. The stilyaga thought it was meant for Mumochka and laughed loudest of all. Muma was embarrassed, blushed, and got angry.

"Mumochka, don't get all puffed up. Wipe that frown off and let's go stomp out a stilyaga de dri."

Muma smiled, and they resumed their twisting.

° *Sylvia and Martiza:* Operettas of the Hungarian composer Imre Kálmán (1882–1953). Very popular and watchable (*Silva* was made into a film during the war), to some in postwar Russia they were ideologically suspect because of their foreign origin and lightness of genre. The following two operas, by Glinka and Borodin, respectively, are commendable for their high tone and their Russian origin.

° *Land of Fire:* From Stravinsky's *The Firebird* (1910), disdained for its "decadent" modernism.

° *Terpsichore:* The muse of dance.

° *St. Vitus' Dance:* A disease.

° *Heinrich Heine:* German poet of the nineteenth century.

"Now do you know what a stilyaga is?" the student asked. "As you see, it's a fairly rare type, in this case the only one in the room. But would you believe there are guys and girls who envy the stilyagas and mumochkas?"

"Envy? That abomination?" exclaimed one of the girls with indignation. "Personally, I'd like to spit."

I also wanted to spit, and walked over to the smoking room.

QUESTIONS FOR ANALYSIS

1. What are the narrator's views of stilyaga?
2. What characterizes Soviet youth culture in the story? In what ways is Soviet youth culture part of the new consumerism?
3. Do you see a gap between the generations in this story? Is the stilyaga out of bounds even in his own generation?

P I C T U R E   E S S A Y

European Consumerism
in the 1950s and 1960s

T HE REBIRTH OF CONSUMERISM IN EUROPE was an outcome of the new prosperity of the 1950s. Factors that contributed to this orgy of buying included economic recovery, the advertising industry, the influence of the United States and its powerful economy, and Europe's own baby boom. At long last emerging from extreme wartime privation people across Europe went on a shopping spree. They purchased products such as shaving cream and hand lotion as well as to big-ticket items like cars and appliances, the latter purchases made affordable by an expanding system of consumer credit. The availability of goods exploded when military industries were converted to consumer ones and wartime inventions, such as the synthetic material used to make parachutes, found peacetime uses, such as nylon stockings. Targeting the entire population, not just the middle and upper classes, consumerism became a mass phenomenon from the 1950s onward.

Many of the large consumer items that Europeans purchased were sewing machines, washing machines, vacuum cleaners, and other labor-saving devices for women. Advertising for these items targeted women specifically. Their growing importance as consumers—a function of the "new domesticity"—gave them power over buying decisions. Advertisers tried to curry their favor, and women themselves could initiate boycotts and undertake other types of consumer activism. The Frenchwoman showing off her new refrigerator in Figure 8.1, a 1957 magazine advertisement, presides

◆ **Figure 8.1** **French Refrigerator Advertisement, 1957**

The Granger Collection.

proudly and confidently over her domestic domain. "Never unprepared," she exclaims to her friend. "A few friends over for dinner—no big deal!"

Men were not immune to consumerist desires. Just as women eagerly purchased much-coveted home appliances, many men were captivated by the speed and freedom afforded by all manner of personal transportation, including motorbikes, cars, buses, and trucks. During the 1950s, Europeans—mostly male—took to the road in some forty million motorized vehicles, and not surprisingly, the automotive industry became a leading economic sector. How might the purchase of a motorbike have affected the social life of the average young and single European male? What impact do you suppose it had on the lives of the Italian family shown in Figure 8.2? What factors, historical and social, do you think made these and other Europeans eager to purchase their own vehicles?

Men also tended to be the primary buyers of radios and eventually televisions. The number of radios in homes grew steadily—for example, by 10 percent a year in Italy between 1945 and 1950—and the 1950s marked the high tide of radio influence. The development of television in the 1920s and 1930s was interrupted

◆ **Figure 8.2 Family on Motorbike**
Bruno Barby/Magnum Photos.

by the war, but peacetime saw its rapid spread in the United States. By 1953, Americans owned twenty million sets. In Britain, only 20 percent of the population purchased TVs in the early 1950s, but 75 percent of all households owned one by 1961. The acquisition of televisions increased more slowly in France and Italy, but by the mid-1960s, the majority of western European households boasted television sets. The woman shown in Figure 8.3 demonstrates the "Knightsbridge Projection Television" whose console also contained "an 8 wave band radio receiver and a dual turntable radio gramophone." What impact do you think televisions and multipurpose entertainment appliances such as this had on the lives of European families in the 1950s and 1960s?

Consumerism was not without its critics. According to some Europeans, all this acquiring of goods promoted superficial values and conformity, making people, especially youth, more materialistic, like Americans. To the enemies of consumerism, Coca-Cola perfectly symbolized the menace of Americanization and its insidious displacement of traditional European culture. Critics worried that, instead of thinking for themselves in the European tradition of Enlightenment and reason, Europeans were succumbing to the lure of marketers and advertisers, even

◆ Figure 8.3 **Big TV Console with Built-in Hi-fi**
Topham/The Image Works.

to the point of turning from traditional beverages such as wine and beer in favor of Coke and consuming a host of other American products (see Figure 8.4). As one reporter in the French daily *Le Monde* complained, "Chryslers and Buicks speed down our roads; American tractors furrow our fields; Frigidaires keep our food cold; stockings 'made by Du Pont' sheathe the legs of our stylish women."[27] What European beverages does the Coca-Cola ad compete with in the shop window in Figure 8.4? Why might Coke have been appealing to European youths like the one who sits in the background?

◆ **Figure 8.4 French Coca-Cola Ad in a Shop Window**
Topham/The Image Works.

Others defended consumerism, insisting that the products available testified to human ingenuity. Far from promoting conformity and Americanization, they argued, consumerism was both a manifestation of and a contribution to human creativity, as people used the things they bought in a rich variety of ways. People as "users" of commodities often diverged from the original intent of a given product's promoters. Television viewers, for example, processed the messages in TV dramas in many different ways, often taking away from a program a lesson completely the opposite of the one intended. European consumers favored a range of characters, products, and forms of programming.

Consumerism in its amazing variety also had the subversive potential to break down barriers in Europeans' lives. In Franco's Spain, the conservative ideology aimed to instill Catholic values. The ideal Spanish woman devoted herself to raising a Christian family and to following religious precepts in her daily activities. But the appearance of a wide array of consumer goods in the 1950s and 1960s provided distinct alternatives, as this Spanish advertisement for Dermilux makes clear (Figure 8.5). How might the message in this ad have conflicted with Franco's calls for modesty and chastity among Spanish girls and women? What values does the consumer shown in the ad seem to convey?

"Youth and beauty is marvelous" declares the Spanish caption in Figure 8.5. Youth was an important theme in advertising, and young people themselves were a crucial segment of the market. Coca-Cola was not the only popular item targeted to the young, as Figure 8.6 indicates. Teens and young adults had money to spend and advertisers appealed to their urge to try new luxury products such as fancy makeup and rich chocolates. What message do the image and text in this advertisement send about the product, and what is the appeal of that message? Are the words as important as the pictures? Why or why not?

East and West were equally affected by the postwar burst of consumerism, and appeals to shopping took on a cold war flavor. At times, shopping was presented as a form of anti-Communist patriotism in western Europe and the United States because it boosted capitalism and carried messages of free choice—even freedom. As

◆ Figure 8.5 **Dermilux advertisement, "Youth and beauty is marvelous"**

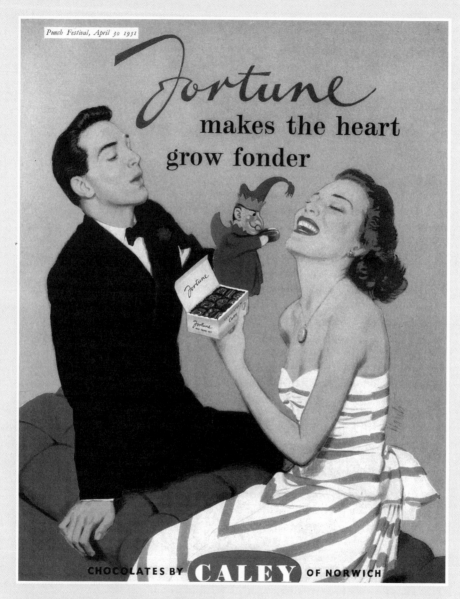

◆ **Figure 8.6 Chocolates by Caley of Norwich**
Mary Evans Picture Library/The Image Works.

one U.S. newspaper editorial proudly stated, "You can't spread the doctrines of Marx among people who drink Coca-Cola."[28] Consumerism also flourished in the Soviet bloc, and socialist values of simplicity and utility were often stressed, albeit with some flair (Figure 8.7). Compare these Soviet dresses with the clothes women

◆ **Figure 8.7 Soviet Fashions in Retail Shop**
Henri Cartier-Bresson/Magnum Photos.

sport in the Western advertisements. What differences do you see? What similarities? How do you account for them?

Whatever the differences, inhabitants of the Soviet bloc prized possessions as much as, and perhaps more than, their Western counterparts, owing to the widespread scarcity not only of consumer goods but also of basic necessities. And as it became more difficult to voice opposition to the status quo and to be active in public, people responded by turning inward and focusing on personal matters. For their part, men in the Soviet sphere found comfort and "a kind of moral satisfaction," as one St. Petersburg man put it, from finding materials to build themselves tiny dachas—country cottages—to provide relief from the cramped conditions and chaos of city life.[29] Clearly, whichever side of the iron curtain one happened to live on, a motorbike, a house in the country, or a television of one's own simply made life better.

QUESTIONS FOR ANALYSIS

1. What arguments for and against consumerism do you find in these images? Was consumerism a force for good or ill in postwar Europe? Give reasons for your opinion.

2. How did consumer images mold postwar gender roles?

3. In what ways do these consumer images reflect both wartime and cold war concerns in the lives of ordinary people?

NOTES

1. Hilde Thurnwald, *Gegenwartsprobleme Berliner Familien: Eine soziologische Untersuchung an 498 Familien*, quoted in Robert Moeller, *Protecting Motherhood: Women and the Family in the Politics of Postwar West Germany* (Berkeley: University of California Press, 1993), 14, 23.

2. William Beveridge, *Social Insurance and Allied Services* (London: HMSO, 1942), 170.

3. Dorothea Groener-Geyer, quoted in Moeller, *Protecting Motherhood*, 55.

4. Antonio Antonuzzo, quoted in Paul Ginsborg, *A History of Contemporary Italy: Society and Politics, 1943–1988* (London: Penguin, 1990), 217.

5. Robert Schuman, "The Schuman Declaration," in *Documents on European Union*, ed. A. G. Harryvan and J. van der Harst (New York: St. Martin's Press, 1997), 62.

6. Quoted in Derek W. Urwin, *The Community of Europe: A History of European Integration since 1945*, 2nd ed. (London: Longman, 1995), 111.

7. Jean Monnet, *Memoirs* (New York: Doubleday, 1978), 414.

8. Quoted in Urwin, *The Community of Europe*, 90.

9. Quoted in Kenneth O. Morgan, *The People's Peace: British History, 1945–1989* (Oxford: Oxford University Press, 1990), 134.

10. Alan S. Milward, *The United Kingdom and the European Community*, vol. 1 passim. (London: Cass, 2002).

11. Quoted in Mary Fulbrook, *Anatomy of a Dictatorship: Inside the GDR, 1949–1989* (Oxford: Oxford University Press, 1995), 93, 95.

12. Quoted in Elena Zubkova, *Russia after the War: Hopes, Illusions, and Disappointments, 1945–1957*, trans. Hugh Ragsdale (Armonk: M. E. Sharpe, 1998), 185.

13. Maya Turovskaya, quoted in William Taubman, *Khrushchev: The Man and His Era* (New York: Norton, 2003), 306.

14. Quoted ibid., 290.

15. Quoted ibid., 297.

16. Quoted in Gerhart Hoffmeister and Frederic C. Tubach, *Germany: 2000 Years*, vol. 3, *From the Nazi Era to the Present* (New York: Ungar, 1986), 102.

17. Franz Greiser, "Der Kaufeinfluss der Frau und die Begeutung der Zeitungsanzeigen," *ZV & ZV*, 18 (September 1958), 730, quoted in Erica Carter, *How German Is She? Postwar West German Reconstruction and the Consuming Woman* (Ann Arbor: University of Michigan Press, 1997), 66.

18. Horst Redeker, *Chemistry Gives Beauty*, quoted in Raymond G. Stokes, "Plastics and the New Society," in *Style and Socialism: Modernity and Material Culture in Post-war Eastern Europe*, ed. David Crowley and Susan E. Reid, (Oxford: Berg, 2000), 74, 75.

19. *Demokratischer Frauenbund Deutschlands* (1956), quoted in Katherine Pence, "Labours of Consumption: Gendered Consumers in Post-war East and West German Reconstruction," in *Gender Relations in German History: Power, Agency and Experience from the Sixteenth to the Twentieth Century*, ed. Lynn Abrams and Elizabeth Harvey (Durham: Duke University Press, 1997), 234.

20. Reinhold Wagnleitner, *Coca-Colonization and the Cold War: The Cultural Mission of the United States in Austria after the Second World War,* trans. Diana M. Wolf (Chapel Hill: University of North Carolina Press, 1994), 279.

21. Quoted ibid., 280.

22. Quoted ibid., 287.

23. Quoted in Uta G. Poiger, *Jazz, Rock, and Rebels: Cold War Politics and American Culture in a Divided Germany* (Berkeley: University of California Press, 2000), 49.

24. Fulbrook, *Anatomy of a Dictatorship,* 164.

25. Francoise giroud *si je mens _ _ _ _ Conversations avec Claude Glayman* (Paris: Stock, 1972), 158.

26. Carolyn Kay Steedman, *Landscape for a Good Woman: A Story of Two Lives* (New Brunswick: Rutgers University Press, 1986), 17.

27. Richard Kuisel, *Seducing the French: The Dilemma of Americanization* (Berkeley: University of California Press, 1993), 52.

28. Ibid., 65.

29. Quoted in Stephen Lovell, "Soviet Exurbia: Dachas in Postwar Russia," in *Socialist Spaces: Sites of Everyday Life in the Eastern Bloc,* ed. David Crowley and Susan E. Reid (Oxford: Berg, 2002), 114.

SUGGESTED REFERENCES

The Welfare State Scholarship on the welfare state looks at the variety of particular national settings in which politicians crafted programs for welfare benefits. Voter, class, and gender interests come to the fore in these discussions.

Baldwin, Peter. *The Politics of Social Solidarity: Class Bases of the European Welfare State, 1875–1975.* 1990.

Bock, Gisela, and Pat Thane, eds. *Maternity and Gender Policies: Women and the Rise of the European Welfare States, 1880s–1950s.* 1991.

Canning, Kathleen, and Sonya O. Rose. *Gender, Citizenships, and Subjectivities.* 2002.

Carter, Erica. *How German Is She? Postwar West German Reconstruction and the Consuming Woman.* 1997.

Fulbrook, Mary. *The People's State: East German Society from Hitler to Honecker.* 2005.

Koven, Seth, and Sonya Michel, eds. *Mothers of a New World: Maternalist Politics and the Origins of Welfare States.* 1993.

Mazower, Mark. *After the War Was Over: Reconstructing the Family, Nation, and State in Greece, 1943–1960.* 2000.

Moeller, Robert. *Protecting Motherhood: Women and the Family in the Politics of Postwar West Germany.* 1993.

Sullivan, Michael. *The Development of the British Welfare State.* 1996.

Economic Revival East and West   Scholars, like people alive at the time, marvel at the revival of European economies and particularly look at the role of interstate cooperation as key to three decades of mounting prosperity. They also explore the turn to provisioning consumers under communism.

Berend, Ivan. *The Hungarian Economic Reforms, 1953–1988*. 1990.

Crowley, David, and Susan E. Reid, eds. *Socialist Spaces: Sites of Everyday Life in the Eastern Bloc*. 2002.

Crowley, David, and Susan E. Reid, eds. *Style and Socialism: Modernity and Material Culture in Post-war Eastern Europe*. 2000.

Fontaine, Pascal. *A New Idea for Europe: The Schuman Declaration, 1950–2000*. 2000.

Gillingham, John. *Coal, Steel, and the Rebirth of Europe, 1945–1955: The Germans and French from Ruhr Conflict to Economic Community*. 1991.

Harrison, Hope M. *Driving the Soviets up the Wall: Soviet–East German Relations, 1953–1961*. 2003.

Kerr, Peter. *Postwar British Politics: From Conflict to Consensus*. 2001.

Rioux, Jean-Pierre. *The Fourth Republic, 1944–1958*. 1988.

Schissler, Hanna, ed. *The Miracle Years: A Cultural History of West Germany, 1949–1968*. 2001.

Urwin, Derek W. *The Community of Europe: A History of European Integration since 1945*. 1995.

The Politics of Prosperity   The 1950s and early 1960s resonated with national and international political change, bringing reform in the Soviet bloc and the consolidation of conservative political control to the West. Historians have richly explored these divergences, especially since the opening of Soviet archives.

Berend, Ivan. *Central and Eastern Europe, 1944–1993: Detour from the Periphery to the Periphery*. 1996.

Dobrynin, Anatoly. *In Confidence*. 1995.

Frost, Robert. *Alternating Currents: Nationalized Power in France, 1946–1970*. 1991.

Landsman, Mark. *Dictatorship and Demand: The Politics of Consumerism in East Germany*. 2005.

Milward, Alan S. *The United Kingdom and the European Community*. 2002.

Monnet, Jean. *Memoirs*. 1978.

Moravcsik, Andrew. *The Choice for Europe: Social Purpose and State Power from Messina to Maastricht*. 1998.

Ransel, David L. *Village Mothers: Three Generations of Change in Russia and Tataria*. 2000.

Richmond, Yale. *Cultural Exchange and the Cold War: Raising the Iron Curtain*. 2003.

Taubman, William. *Khrushchev: The Man and His Era*. 2003.

Toker, Leona. *Return from the Archipelago: Narratives of Gulag Survivors*. 2000.

The Rebirth of Consumerism Consumerism took many forms, including the consumption of popular culture, fashion in clothing, and heavy appliances. The role of Americanization is a topic of special scholarly interest.

Cross, Gary, and John K. Walton. *The Playful Crowd: Pleasure Places in the Twentieth Century.* 2005.

De Grazia, Victoria. *Irresistible Empire: America's Advance through Twentieth-Century Europe.* 2005.

Endy, Christopher. *Cold War Holidays: American Tourism in France.* 2004.

Furlough, Ellen, and Shelley Baranowski. *Being Elsewhere: Tourism, Consumer Culture, and Identity in Modern Europe and North America.* 2001.

Kuisel, Richard. *Seducing the French: The Dilemma of Americanization.* 1993.

Marwick, Arthur. *British Society since 1945.* 1996.

Ramet, Sabrina P., and Gordana P. Crnković, *Kazaaam! Splat! Ploof! The American Impact on European Popular Culture since 1945.* 2003.

Ruff, Mark Edward. *The Wayward Flock: Catholic Youth in Postwar West Germany, 1945–1965.* 2005.

Strasser, Susan, et al., eds. *Getting and Spending: European and American Consumer Societies in the Twentieth Century.* 1998.

Varnedoe, Kirk, and Adam Gopnik. *High and Low: Modern Art and Popular Culture.* 1991.

Selected Web Sites

Open Society Archives provides many resources on the cold war, the gulag, and events in the Soviet bloc after the death of Stalin: <**www.osa.ceu.hu.**> In addition, explore the following Web sites: Europa: Gateway to the European Union: <**europa.eu**> European Union: Delegation of the European Commission to the USA: <**eurunion.org**> Fondation Robert Schuman: <**robert-schuman.org**> The History of Rock 'n' Roll: <**history-of-rock.com/index.html**>

9

Postimperial Europe
c. 1947–1980

I N 1961 BUCHI EMECHETA (B. 1944) LEFT HER HOME IN Nigeria, where she worked in a government office, to follow her husband to a new life in England. Emecheta, who became a successful novelist, was part of a swelling migration from former colonies that gained their independence in the postwar years. While her husband pursued a Western education in London, Emecheta herself continued supporting the family—as she had done in Nigeria with the skills she had learned in high school. Conditions in London did not provide immigrants—especially those of color—with the opportunities Emecheta expected. Instead, she found discrimination in housing and in hiring: "Nearly all the notices had 'Sorry, no coloureds' on them." Emecheta later wrote, "She was beginning to learn that her colour was something she was supposed to be ashamed of."[1] Emecheta also faced difficulties obtaining health care for herself and her five children, and her husband became involved with other women and left her without any support. She came to the realization that in England as in Nigeria she was a "second-class citizen."

Perseverance and luck brought her a good job in a library at the British Museum and lifted her *Head above Water*, as she titled her 1986 autobiography. In the 1970s, Emecheta began writing fiction about the African past and

◆ **Algerian Workers in France**

Foreign workers were a familiar sight in Europe after World War II. War had depleted the population, and enormous amounts of work needed to be done to repair the damage inflicted on the continent. For the most part it was northern European governments that made agreements with states in southern Europe and Africa for "guest workers." Immigrants arrived in search of jobs came from the Caribbean, South Asia, and other areas colonized by Europe, as the war and decolonization had upset their economies too. *Peter Turnley/CORBIS.*

about women migrants in Europe, and novels such as *In the Ditch* (1972) and *Second Class Citizen* (1974) brought her international success. The poor immigrant from Nigeria became a literary star, even though bad feelings toward immigrants increased during the years when Europe's empire ended and formerly colonized subjects became free.

Buchi Emecheta migrated to a dramatically changed Europe—one that in the first three postwar decades lost nearly its entire empire. World War II had so weakened the great imperial powers of Britain and France and the smaller ones of the Netherlands, Belgium, and Portugal that their empires began to disappear almost as soon as the war ended. Beyond bankrupting Europe, the war had given birth to a new generation of leaders in the colonies, and they were determined to gain independence. To a large extent the imperial nations had not ever fully controlled areas outside of Europe. Resistance was constant, and the European powers always had to struggle to maintain their grip on foreign peoples. This meant that the process of decolonization evolved even as empires were being acquired,

1961	Frantz Fanon's *The Wretched of the Earth* published.
1960s	In Britain, arrival of migrants from West Indies, India, and Pakistan sparks racist riots.
1960s	Europe becomes home to hundreds of thousands of Southeast Asian refugees.
1960s	Viet Minh efforts to unite North and South Vietnam prompt the United States to send in troops.
1962	Evian accords make Algeria independent from France; influx of refugees to France.
1964	British East Africa gains independence (as Kenya).
1965– 1968	House of Commons passes bills mandating equal treatment for immigrants in housing, jobs, and services.
Late 1960s	Illegal workers constitute 88 percent of Europe's non-European workforce.
1970– 1980s	In Germany number of foreign residents increases by 50 percent and includes many dependent children.
1970s	In France, workers from North Africa become politically active.
1972– 1973	Thousands of Ugandans of Asian lineage, expelled from Uganda, flee to Britain.
Mid- 1970s	Economic downturn prompts Germany and France to end programs for migrant workers.
1970s– 1980s	European governments set up programs to repatriate foreign workers.
1980	Bonnet Law drastically limits immigration and immigration rights in France.
1980s	8 percent of the European population is foreign-born.

499

and liberation movements kept Europeans alert throughout the twentieth century. Moreover, persistent European violence against colonized peoples, necessary, it was believed, to keep order, fueled anger all the more. In the colonies there was rarely a peaceful status quo or contentment with imperial rule, as Emecheta's fiction showed, except among those individuals who made fortunes dealing with the colonizers.

Like Emecheta, those who lived under colonial rule took seriously the doctrine of equality and opportunity preached by the West, and tens of thousands headed to the European capital cities from which these promises had emanated. Europe needed workers to rebuild prosperity, and along with decolonization the labor shortage led to the region's dramatic reshaping. A flood of migrants from the former colonies came in search of political asylum, a safe harbor from civil turmoil, and economic opportunity. Many were Anglophiles or Francophiles, eager to taste firsthand the much-touted culture of their former European masters. Buchi Emecheta arrived in England full of hope, as did her fellow migrants.

With the end of empire Europeans were forced to readjust their vision of themselves, jettisoning the idea that they were citizens of dominant imperial powers. Instead they became dependent on the cheap labor that flocked to the continent and British Isles. Former colonial administrators and soldiers returned; neighborhoods changed into immigrant enclaves whose inhabitants — Pakistanis, Indonesians, Sri Lankans, Bangladeshis, Cameroonians, and countless other groups — went out every day to perform the menial jobs that Europeans did not want. Artists wrestled with depicting the end of empire, producing a wave of nostalgic films and bitter memoirs of racism, violence, and white supremacy lost. "New Europeans" like Buchi Emecheta added their voices to the discussion, bringing to public attention issues of multiculturalism and citizenship. The end of empire transformed Europe as it transformed the world.

DECOLONIZATION

Europeans wanted and expected to keep their empires at the war's end, but their own weakness and the unstoppable mobilization of opposition brought an end to more than a century of political domination. Decolonization — that is, the lifting of imperial rule — occurred in two waves (Map 9.1). The first took place right after the war when India, Burma, Sri Lanka, and Palestine became independent, as Britain's capacity to maintain colonies simply collapsed, especially in the face of

▶ **Map 9.1 The Decolonizing World**
Independence movements were especially vigorous during the war and in the years thereafter. Local entrepreneurs and politicians took advantage of European vulnerabilities to build financial strength, and many colonies were populated with skilled, experienced veterans. As a result, many countries in Africa and Asia gained their independence in the postwar period, sometimes after military struggle, civil wars, and other bloodshed.

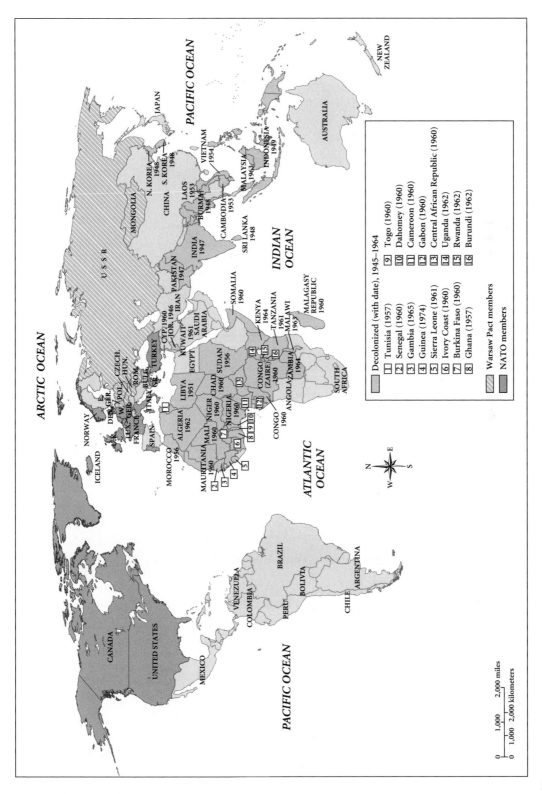

ARCTIC OCEAN

PACIFIC OCEAN

PACIFIC OCEAN

INDIAN OCEAN

ATLANTIC OCEAN

Decolonized (with date), 1945–1964

1	Tunisia (1957)	9	Togo (1960)
2	Senegal (1960)	10	Dahomey (1960)
3	Gambia (1965)	11	Cameroon (1960)
4	Guinea (1974)	12	Gabon (1960)
5	Sierra Leone (1961)	13	Central African Republic (1960)
6	Ivory Coast (1960)	14	Uganda (1962)
7	Burkina Faso (1960)	15	Rwanda (1962)
8	Ghana (1957)	16	Burundi (1962)

Warsaw Pact members

NATO members

USSR

MONGOLIA

JAPAN

N. KOREA 1948
S. KOREA 1948
CHINA
VIETNAM 1954
LAOS 1953
BURMA 1948
CAMBODIA 1953
INDONESIA 1949
MALAYSIA 1963
SRI LANKA 1948
INDIA 1947
PAKISTAN 1947

IRAN 1946
JOR. 1946
KUWAIT 1961
SAUDI ARABIA
EGYPT
SUDAN 1956
SOMALIA 1960
KENYA 1964
TANZANIA 1961
MALAWI 1963
MALAGASY REPUBLIC 1960
ZAMBIA 1964
ANGOLA
CONGO (ZAIRE) 1960
CONGO 1960
SOUTH AFRICA

CYP. 1960
TURKEY
GR.
BULG.
ROM.
HUN.
CZECH.
POL.
W. GER.
E. GER.
DEN.
NORWAY
ICELAND

SPAIN
ITALY
FRANCE
LUX.
BEL.
U.K.
NETH.

MOROCCO 1956
ALGERIA 1962
LIBYA 1951
MALI 1960
NIGER 1960
CHAD 1960
NIGERIA 1960
MAURITANIA 1960

AUSTRALIA

NEW ZEALAND

CANADA

UNITED STATES

MEXICO

VENEZUELA
COLOMBIA
PERU
BRAZIL
BOLIVIA
CHILE
ARGENTINA

N
E
S
W

0   1,000   2,000 miles
0 1,000 2,000 kilometers

massive resistance from both the colonized leadership and the masses. During these years France immediately gave up Lebanon and Syria and lost Vietnam and Algeria in bloody defeats. A second wave began in Ghana in 1957 and spread throughout sub-Saharan Africa, with the same uneven mixture of quietly achieved independence in some states and violent resistance from whites in others. By the 1980s European political empire was almost over. Britain—once again a small island nation—was the greatest loser. Economic, social, and cultural ties remained strong, however, providing both Europe and its former Asian and African colonies a partnership that in some respects sheltered both sides from the demands of cold war. Those ties permitted the development of neo-imperialism—that is, a client relationship in which industrialized Western nations were still able to exploit the newly liberated countries economically even if they no longer controlled them politically.

The Legacy of War

British strategy during World War II was shaped to achieve Winston Churchill's major wartime goal: to protect if not strengthen the British Empire. The effect of the war for every imperial power was exactly the opposite. Asian and African soldiers' experience of World War II once again pulled back the mask of European supremacy. The slaughter those soldiers witnessed was even more massive than in World War I and the depraved behavior more extreme. Several opportunities came their way to reinforce discontent. Mingling with an array of forces in the Allied armies, African troops had come in contact with highly politicized Indian and African American forces, and many had met soldiers from other parts of the African continent, swelling pan-African ideology. "We are unwilling to starve any longer while doing the world's drudgery," announced a communiqué from the Pan-African Congress in 1945, "in order to support by our poverty and ignorance a false aristocracy and a discredited imperialism."[2] In many cases soldiers from the colonies learned about highly complex technology that imperialists otherwise might have tried to keep out of their hands, and they improved their reading and writing. At the same time instances of discrimination were glaring. Although African conscripts had constituted some 20 percent of Free French forces and had fully participated on the front lines of the war, they were pushed to the rear and made invisible in ceremonies celebrating the liberation of French cities. No African troops, for instance, were apparent in the company of troops commemorating the liberation of Paris. Indian soldiers, active in the defeat of Japan, had to look on as the Allied powers returned Indonesia to the Dutch and Vietnam to the French colonial administrations. Like many African American soldiers in the postwar United States, these returning veterans joined civil rights and liberation movements.

The progress of war in the colonies further weakened the already fragile colonial grip on power. At the height of combat against Hitler, the imperial nations could not exercise the political oversight they had wielded before the war, leaving colonies to run themselves. Forced conscription and forced labor by millions of colonized civilians aggravated all the political and social tensions of imperialism.

Of all the ills of imperialism, forced labor during the war aroused the most enduring hatred toward the imperialists and became a rallying cry for independence. Pay differentials among Indian and British sailors sparked riots at the end of the war, and forced labor itself served as the basis for films and novels remembering the war and preparing the way for rebellion. "When white men kill each other," one high school teacher in the Caribbean informed his students, "it is a blessing for blacks."[3]

All sides had plundered the colonies, but the desperate needs of the Allies allowed local entrepreneurs to flourish while the imperial powers were too preoccupied with war to offer competition or to prohibit colonized people's initiatives. It was also cheaper and more certain to have raw materials converted into finished goods in the colonies than to waste money by shipping natural resources to already hard-pressed powers like Britain for manufacturing. India thus developed an aircraft industry during the war. Oil, steel, iron, and other enterprises flourished along with increased capabilities in banking, finance, and trade outside Europe's own entrepreneurial system. Wealthy manufacturers, traders, and large landowners joined other pro-liberation forces to preserve the business independence they had achieved.

The problems that the war brought the lower classes of colonized peoples only piqued their anger. The pursuit of war impoverished European civilians, but it selectively impoverished local people in the colonies even more. The colonies, whose well-being in terms of supplies, economic development, or even basic necessities like food was not a high priority for the imperial powers during wartime, experienced famine, rapid urbanization, and social upheaval between 1939 and 1945. Grave conditions of urban poverty struck Africa and other parts of the colonized world as trade was disrupted. Rural people, their livelihoods on plantations threatened by uncertainty, flocked to cities in hopes of finding jobs. Thus, while the war primed distress and anger, conditions favorable for revolt—urbanization, advanced industrialization, and the uneven increase in individual wealth and development—ripened, creating a potentially explosive situation. As World War II ended, there was widespread rebellion in Algeria, Vietnam, Indonesia, and other colonies, much of it reflecting colonized leaders' assumption that the end of empire was at hand. It sometimes took several decades of war and negotiation, however, before liberation from Europe was fully realized.

Ending the Empire in Asia

South Asia was the first major region to achieve independence, but the process was fraught with bloodshed and shaped by British interference. In 1945 and 1946 an array of protests erupted, the first expressing outrage because the British prosecuted Indian soldiers who had not supported the Allies. Other protests addressed issues of landowning and the conditions of work. The British had proposed several self-serving plans for South Asian self-governance. One plan called for the creation of separate nations based on religion—a proposal hardly suited to the mixture of religions existing throughout the region. Spurred by that plan, Mohammed Ali Jinnah of the Muslim League incited his followers to agitate for an independent

Muslim nation. The result was massacres of Hindu and Sikh shopkeepers in north-west India and elsewhere.

The British also proposed a system of small, loosely confederated independent states. This plan inspired the hopes of regional leaders, who mobilized their supporters, among them wealthy landowners. The British would have benefited from a subcontinent composed of small and weak nations dependent on British economic and political power. The response to this plan was months of chaos — violence, a rising toll of murders, and a flood of millions of refugees trying to find safe haven among people of a similar religion. Amid it all Gandhi and other politicians traveled from city to city and region to region, trying to calm tensions and to promote harmony among different religious groups and economic classes.

The chaos led the British to announce that they were leaving, and in 1947 an independent Pakistan was created for Muslims and an independent India for Hindus, despite the considerable intermingling of religions across South Asia. On January 30, 1948, a radical Hindu assassinated Gandhi as he continued to work for religious reconciliation. India itself remained within the British Commonwealth, although its own trading reach was vast. Ongoing violence and disputes over religious jurisdiction and the relationship of small states to the central Indian government contributed to the increasing flow of emigration.

The withdrawal of Britain from direct rule encouraged the superpowers to engage in a contest for influence in India, Pakistan, and smaller states in the region that also became independent as Britain relinquished control. Britain's dominion over half a billion Asians thousands of miles away came to an end. The British political grip on Asia (except in Hong Kong) was replaced by crucial economic connections that sustained an increasingly wealthy cohort of international financiers and businessmen who worked to reestablish the globally based prosperity of the prewar period.

In 1949, Communists under the leadership of Mao Zedong (1893–1976) defeated a corrupt Nationalist government under Jiang Jieshi, whose unpopular regime the United States had bankrolled. Gaining support for its attention to the plight of peasants, Communist rule brought to an abrupt end the interference of Europe and the United States in the government and economy of China. With an undeveloped industrial proletariat, Mao emphasized his differences with Stalin's and Lenin's versions of Marxism, yet he too collectivized agriculture, instituted a crash program for industrialization, and brutally repressed the privileged classes. Until the 1970s China's ties with the West were limited, and hundreds of millions of Chinese people experienced decades of social and political turmoil as Mao and his government subjected them to one brutal scheme after another. Perceiving Mao to be identical to Stalin, the Western powers in NATO saw only monolithic red extending from Leningrad to Beijing.

The Chinese Revolution spurred both superpowers to increase their involvement in Asian politics, and for decades to come the cold war complicated the course of decolonization both for the Europeans and for their former colonies. The USSR and the United States faced off indirectly in Korea, which had been split in two at the thirty-eighth parallel as the country was liberated from the Japanese. In 1950 the North Koreans, supported by the Soviet Union, invaded U.S.-backed South Korea. The United States maneuvered the United Nations Security Council into approval of a "police action" against North Korea—a maneuver that would set a precedent for intervention in Europe itself in the 1990s. Eventually, the United States deployed 400,000 troops to help the South Korean army repel the invaders. The combined military forces quickly pushed far into North Korean territory— almost to China's border—where they were met by the Chinese army rather than the Soviet army. After two and a half years of stalemate, the opposing sides agreed to a settlement in 1953: Korea would remain divided at its prewar border, the thirty-eighth parallel.

The Korean War affected the push for independence in Southeast Asia, raising the cold war stakes and thus the number of deaths. The French surrendered control of Indochina (modern-day Vietnam, Cambodia, and Laos) after a devastating defeat at the hands of peasant armies under the Communist leadership of Ho Chi Minh. As in China and other parts of Asia, peasant agriculture had produced bountiful crops, but Indochina had suffered both from the steep fall in agricultural prices in the 1920s and 1930s and from the turmoil of war that followed hard on the heels of the global economic depression. Ho had his own brand of nationalist socialism, and his main goal was liberation from the colonial French. He advocated the redistribution of land held by big landowners, especially in the rich agricultural area in southern Indochina where some six thousand local and French owners possessed more than 60 percent of the land. The French army fought Ho's efforts for independence with the help of the big landlords in the south, but Ho's Viet Minh soldiers surprised the French with their tenacious resistance. Because of the Viet Minh's Communist connections, the United States started funneling money and supplies to the French side despite its official anti-imperial position. Even so, the Viet Minh forces, using guerrilla tactics, forced the technologically advanced French army to withdraw after the bloody battle of Dien Bien Phu in 1954.

The Geneva Accords of 1954 carved out an independent Laos and Cambodia and divided Vietnam into North and South, each free from French control. French influence in the region, however, remained strong, because of the presence of French architecture, schools, and cultural institutions. Also, many inhabitants had adopted the French language. French businessmen maintained their contacts in Indochina, and the French government continued to support *Francophonie*—the promotion of French language speaking, which promoted business and financial connections with France in place of political ones. Viet Minh efforts to unite North and South Vietnam prompted the United States to send troops to the region in the 1960s to keep it from going Communist. Economic and political connections with Europe diminished temporarily during the Vietnam War as American bombs and other weaponry battered Southeast Asians and the Viet Minh fought to establish a Communist nation-state. However, from the 1960s on, Europe became home to hundreds of thousands of Southeast Asian refugees from what seemed like never-ending violence.

The Quest for Autonomy in North Africa and the Middle East

North Africa and the Middle East experienced both fairly smooth transitions to in-dependence and violent wars for liberation. France—although eager to regain its great-power status after its humiliating defeat and occupation in World War II—easily granted certain demands for independence in the 1950s, such as those of Tunisia, Morocco, and West Africa, where there were fewer settlers, more limited economic stakes, and less military involvement. Stakes were higher in Algeria, how-ever, where France conducted a bitter war against Algerian independence.

When Algerian nationalists, many of them former soldiers and French-educated young people, resisted the restoration of French rule in the final days of World War II, the French army, determined to recoup its reputation after its quick defeat at the hands of Hitler, massacred tens of thousands. The Algerian liberation movement regrouped, surfacing in 1954 as the National Liberation Front to attack French settlers and their Arab allies. Ten percent of the Algerian population was of French ancestry, and the region had been declared officially part of France and its inhabitants French citizens. However, the rights of citizenship were limited, in par-ticular for Muslims, segregation existed; and Arabs and Berbers held menial jobs after being dispossessed of their lands. Algerians of French, Spanish, and Italian descent were more privileged, owning prosperous vineyards and holding good jobs administering Algeria's thriving cities. Elites claiming European heritage led the brutal, military opposition to Algerian independence. "The only negotiation," de-clared French minister of the interior François Mitterrand, later president of France, "is war!"[4]

Mindful of Algeria's large European settlement and Algeria's legal status as part of France, the French government sent hundreds of thousands of troops to the re-gion. Some 200,000 soldiers from North and West Africa served in the French army. In 1954 they comprised 43.5 percent of France's forces in Algeria. One of the most bitter contests for liberation, the war featured the torture and murder of civil-ians by both sides. Algerian women used the tactics of French women under Nazi occupation: shielded by gender stereotypes, they planted bombs in European clubs and cafés and carried weapons to assassination sites. The French were fiercely de-termined to hold on to Algeria. Its loss, one official stated, "would be an unprece-dented national disaster." European Algerians took the war to Paris, hoping to in-timidate politicians who doubted the wisdom of the war with bombings and as-sassinations in the name of "Algérie française"—French Algeria.

Ruling cabinets collapsed with dizzying rapidity. Then in 1958, General Charles de Gaulle emerged from retirement. As his price for heading the govern-ment, he demanded that the impotent Fourth Republic give way to a new "Fifth Republic," and he received plentiful backing. The French military believed de Gaulle was a hawk on the war—"I have understood you," he announced reas-suringly to the leadership. He then revised France's constitution to centralize power in the executive office of a president, chosen by popular mandate and joined by a prime minister responsible to the National Assembly of popularly elected representatives.

◆ **De Gaulle in Algeria, 1961**
When Charles de Gaulle became president of France, many Algerians of European descent
were under the impression that France would retain possession of Algeria. De Gaulle even
visited Algeria, fortifying belief in his imperial ambitions for France. As shown here, both
protesters and supporters turned out for his visit. De Gaulle, however, was determined to
release Algeria to become an independent state, and in 1962 he agreed to the Evian accords,
which formalized the separation. Assassination attempts and bloodshed plagued him,
and the chaos of an unexpectedly massive immigration into France followed Algerian
independence. *Topham/The Image Works.*

The conservative de Gaulle negotiated Algerian independence—an independence that seemed at odds with his stated belief in the grandeur of French destiny. Vastly outnumbered and militarily weak, Algerian nationalists publicized French atrocities worldwide and appealed to the postwar affirmation of human rights. The campaign led the United Nations, the United States, and other powers to withdraw support from their former ally. The nationalist publicity campaign tore the population in metropolitan France apart; civil war threatened to erupt with each new revelation of torture and increased casualties. After four years of cryptic maneuvering, in 1962 French president Charles de Gaulle signed the Evian accords, which separated Algeria from France and made Algeria an independent country.

As Algerian nationalists demonstrated how to conduct war by publicity, the Middle East heated up because oil fueled superpower interests there. The potential resources had in part drawn them to intervene in Algeria. The success of the Algerian nationalists showed smaller countries how to navigate global politics successfully. There was thus new impetus to take an independent path in the Middle

East, though the British, Americans, and French had other agendas. Weakened by the war, British oil companies wanted to tighten their grip on profits, as the value of petroleum soared. The cold war gave Middle Eastern leaders an opening to play the superpowers against one another.

The Holocaust had fortified the Western powers' commitment to secure a Jewish homeland, but this goal complicated politics in the Middle East, further stirring up Arab determination to regain economic and political control of the region. When World War II broke out, 600,000 European Jewish settlers and twice as many Arabs were living in British-controlled Palestine. In 1947, an exhausted Britain ceded the area to the United Nations to work out a settlement between the Jews and the Arabs. The United Nations voted to partition Palestine into an Arab region and a Jewish one. Conflicting land claims, however, led to war, and Jewish military forces prevailed. On May 14, 1948, the victorious settlers declared the state of Israel. "The dream had come true," future Israeli prime minister Golda Meir remembered, but "too late to save those who had perished in the Holocaust." Israel opened its gates to more European Jewish immigrants, pitting its ambitions against those of its Arab neighbors.

European governments were happy to welcome the Jewish state of Israel because the European origin of most of the settlers promised a potentially secure exit route for Middle Eastern oil should the need arise. Toward the end of World War II an eminent American geologist, surveying the oil fields of the Middle East, had predicted a shift in natural resource power from the Gulf-Caribbean region to the Middle East, then supplying only 5 to 6 percent of the world's oil. "The oil in this region is the greatest single prize in all history," he wrote.[5] As the war was winding down, Western leaders realized the industrial societies' boundless dependence on oil, perhaps the most essential natural resource after food. For Europe the need was particularly acute. It was predicted that by the early 1950s Europe would depend on the Middle East for 80 percent of its oil. Britain and the United States thus were eager to extend their business alliances in the Middle East, and Saudi Arabia became the prime focus of their attention.

Britain, however, faced a towering legacy of bitterness. But despite the need for respectful diplomacy in the mid-1950s, Prime Minister Churchill compounded Saudi anger by insisting that he be provided with plenty of alcohol and tobacco during his meetings with Saudi royalty—an offense to devout Muslims. At the height of British power, Churchill's haughty disrespect would have been bad enough. At a time when Britain's dependence on the Middle East was so overwhelming, his behavior was disastrous. Saudi king Faisal struck back, showing himself eager to negotiate for expanded drilling in his country, provided that the British be excluded. Simultaneously the Saudis successfully demanded the revision of the existing division of revenues. The Western oil companies agreed to increase the percentage that Saudi Arabia would receive for its oil to 50 percent. These companies, primarily of Dutch and U.S. origin, with British firms as secret partners, essentially acknowledged that the oil was not theirs but belonged to the country from whose territory it was extracted. These agreements were important to the survival of Europe, for Europe's and indeed the world's reliance on Middle Eastern oil sky-rocketed in the postwar period to fuel the economic boom then underway.

The Saudi victory had a snowball effect, pushing the insecure shah of Iran to demand the same revision in the percentage his country received from foreign oil companies. Burgeoning nationalist and Islamic movements in Iran challenged the participation of the British in oil extraction from Iranian territory at any price and threatened to topple the shah's shaky regime and boot Britain out. Intransigent, leaders of British petroleum firms reacted violently because they saw the oil as theirs. The United States, however, feared that the Iranians would nationalize the oil industry, turn away from the West, and bring in the Soviets to run the industry. These fears led to a CIA-directed coup against Iran's secular but nationalist prime minister Mohammad Mosaddeq in 1953 and to an agreement among the oil companies, with British financial interests once again hidden in a U.S.-government-backed cartel.

The success of Saudi Arabia and Iran prompted further action against European colonial interests, as news of Britain's collapse spread. Egypt, which had gained its independence from Britain at the end of the war, sought to end British dominance of Asian shipping through the Suez Canal, which was owned by a British-run company. In 1952, Colonel Gamal Abdel Nasser became Egypt's president after the ousting of its king. Nasser's dreams for Egypt included economic modernization and true national independence. As he watched the Saudis, Iranians, and Kuwaitis gain greater control of their own oil, his prime goal was similarly to reclaim the Suez Canal, "where 120,000 of our sons had lost their lives in digging it [by force]," he stated. In July 1956, Nasser nationalized the canal after the United States, prodded by the British government, blocked loans for the building of the crucial Aswan High Dam (see Document 9.1).

Conservative British prime minister Anthony Eden was determined that Britain should not lose ground in Egypt and immediately demanded the canal's return, claiming that the Egyptians were not up to running this critical shipping channel on their own (they actually had been expertly running it from the outset). To back down to Nasser, British politicians screamed, would be "appeasement" and "another Munich." As public outraged soared, Israel and France opportunistically joined Britain in concocting a secret plot whereby Israel would attack Egypt and thus open the door for all of them to make gains in the region. The French and British would then offer their "disinterested" services as arbiters. France hoped as a result to curtail Egypt's support for the Algerian liberation movement.

In October 1956, with the United States preoccupied with the upcoming presidential election, Israel attacked Egypt, bringing the Suez crisis to a head while the Hungarian revolt (see Chapter 8) was in full swing. When Egypt would not agree to stop fighting the invasion, the British bombed the suburbs of Cairo, branded Nasser another Hitler, and called on the United States to help defeat this friend of the USSR. The United States, however, responded with fury at the independent action by its allies that had turned the spotlight from Soviet repression in eastern Europe and shone it on Western repression in the developing world. For its part, the Soviet Union threatened the British, French, and Israelis if they chose not to withdraw.

A UN General Assembly resolution condemned the invasion with only five negative votes. Scolding its allies for their imperialistic behavior, the United States struck an anticolonial posture for the benefit of the developing nations whose economic and political partnership it sought. Vice President Richard Nixon himself declared that the U.S. refusal to intervene was a "declaration of independence" from Europe's colonial ambitions. Firm American opposition and U.S. manipulations of the financial markets to hurt British currency brought an end to what one British diplomat called "a squalid and most humiliating episode," and the hawkish Eden, who had set the escapade in motion, resigned. Nasser's triumph inspired confidence that the Middle East could assert its interests and win, and it signaled to other developing nations that they could act independently even in a world run by superpowers.

Decolonization in Sub-Saharan Africa

In sub-Saharan Africa, nationalist leaders roused their people to challenge Europeans' increasing demand for resources and labor, which often resulted in poverty for African peoples. "The European Merchant is my shepherd, and I am in want," went one African version of the Twenty-third Psalm. Even though African products had been crucial to winning the war, Europeans treated Africans with racist contempt despite their hard-fought war against Nazi racism—the irony was not lost on Africans. Disrupted in their traditional agricultural patterns, many Africans had flocked to shantytowns in cities during the war, where they kept themselves alive through scavenging, craft work, and menial labor for whites. Protests that had begun during the depression of the 1930s multiplied, and underemployed city dwellers and landless rural people formed one power base for local politicians committed to decolonization.

Shaken by the defection of India from the British Empire, the British wanted to control as much of Africa and the Middle East as possible. Africans, however, had other ideas, having vowed at the 1945 Pan-African Congress that "if the Western world is still determined to rule mankind by force, then Africans, as a last resort, may have to use force to achieve freedom." The first blow to Britain's control of Africa came in 1957 when crowds of veterans in the British West African colony of Gold Coast protested their lack of promised pay. After years of arresting and jailing the protesters, British policemen fired on the group and killed several demonstrators. At the head of the elites backing the protesters, Kwame Nkrumah led the diverse inhabitants of the relatively prosperous colony to passive resistance, in imitation of Gandhi's methods. The British withdrew, and the state of Ghana came into being soon after in 1957. Nigeria, the most populous African region and home to author Buchi Emecheta, became independent in 1960 after the leaders of its many regional groups and political organizations reached agreement on a federal-style government. Despite factionalism, in these and other African states where the population was mostly black, independence came less violently than in territories with a higher percentage of white settlers.

European settlers living along the eastern coast and in the southern and central areas of Africa violently resisted independence movements. In the colony of British East Africa, where white settlers ruled in splendor and blacks lacked both land and economic opportunity, violence erupted in the 1950s. African men, almost all of whom had fought for the British as soldiers in World War II, formed rebel groups calling themselves the Land and Freedom Army but called "Mau Mau" by the British. They maintained their solidarity through ceremonies, oaths, and rigid discipline. Aided by women serving as provisioners, messengers, and weapon-stealers, Mau Mau bands formed from the Kikuyu ethnic group tried to recover land by force from whites. In 1964, after the British, by their own count, had slaughtered some ten to fifteen thousand Kikuyus—today historians estimate the dead to number far more—British East Africa finally gained formal independence as the nation of Kenya under the leadership of Europeanized elites.

South Africa was another site of strife after World War II. In 1948, Afrikaners took control of the South African government and formalized white supremacy in the brutal system of *apartheid* ("apartness"), which would last until the 1990s. Among the most urbanized and wealthiest of African nations, South Africa also had the most numerous Western-educated black elites, many of whom formed the leadership of an ongoing and increasingly powerful resistance movement. Some of these movements coalesced around influential Xhosa and Zulu chiefs; others, such as the African National Congress (ANC), cut across ethnicity and class. The apartheid government repressed these groups through murder, imprisonment, and other forms of intimidation.

After three decades of war and depression during which the imperial powers stripped African colonies of as much wealth as possible, the postwar years proved a grim time for fledgling states to strike out on their own. Many countries in Africa had witnessed intensified surveillance and plunder by the Europeans during the war even as some local planters and businessmen prospered. In many of these cases, the Europeans, while resisting independence, had entrenched themselves in other ways in the country, ensuring, in the words of one Colonial Office memo, "that British standards and methods of business and administration permeate the whole life of the territory," in order to keep informal control after formal rule had ended.[6]

Independence leaders relied on long-standing cartels such as the cocoa and coffee businessmen and traditional sources of income from taxing exports and imports. The rulers of new states such as Ghana, Nigeria, and Ivory Coast, however, had to provide jobs and prosperity for a wider constituency, build national institutions and national loyalty, initiate smooth political procedures, and generally foster economic growth. For ideas and know-how, many of them turned to traditional elites and to European theorists and experts, who were maintaining colonial networks by creating the field of "economic development." Students of economic development lumped the new states together as "developing" or "third world" nations, and the ongoing reliance of the new states on colonial institutions for economic support caused critics to issue warnings about "neocolonialism."

EUROPE'S EMPIRE COMES HOME

The politics of decolonization were as tumultuous in Europe as in the colonies, though the outcomes in Europe were far less lethal. Europeans were used to ruling people of other races and ethnicities at great distance, but as decolonization accelerated, formerly subject people like Buchi Emecheta left their homelands to seek for themselves all the promised benefits of Western civilization. Especially in areas where there was European and American resistance to liberation movements, warfare made colonial subjects flee for their lives. Newcomers, however, did not always find the freedom and rights that were said to shape the West.

As great numbers of immigrants from former colonies arrived, European nations wrote laws to disqualify them from citizenship and equal treatment. Many immigrants entered countries whose governments sought them because of a scarcity of native-born workers, but as one German critic put it, "We wanted workers and we got human beings." Turks flooded into Germany in fulfillment of international agreements that they would help rebuild in the face of labor shortages, and a host of other countries experienced similar waves of immigration. The new policy of encouraging labor immigration, however, called for complex planning and perhaps more resources than European countries had foreseen. Immigrants needed housing, a place in society, education, civil rights, and ultimately families and human relationships. Their children demanded the rights of citizens. All of these human necessities shaped political debate and provided new concern for policy makers.

Refugees and Guest Workers

New immigrants entered a battered continent. The atmosphere in Europe was shrouded with a sense of decline and loss that citizens of former colonial domains felt. Their European homelands had been reduced to bankruptcy. The effort to maintain even a few colonies such as Kenya or Algeria was a budget- and morale-breaker. Former colonial officials, army officers, and plantation owners returned to France, Britain, the Netherlands, and Belgium angered, even embittered, and often unemployed. A returning Dutch official remembered Indonesia as a "paradise lost" and as Holland's "valuable creation, which represented the work of three-and-a-half centuries . . . its tropical treasure trove."[7] Because of their administrative skills, some found government jobs, becoming administrators in the homeland as they had been in the colonies. An estimated 5.5 million to 8.5 million people of European origin returned to Europe during decolonization. A number of them kept their contacts in the former colonies and succeeded in trade, banking, and consulting with the new leaders.

Between 1947 and 1954 a million North Africans entered France. In 1962 Algerian independence brought an enormous new influx of refugees to the French mainland—a veritable flood of people of European, Arab, and Berber descent, most of them believing that their fortunes would be better served in France. The hundreds of thousands who fled in what came to be known as the "exodus" surprised French officials, who had no inkling of the vast numbers that would want to settle in the metropole. Whatever their background, all of these people were legally French citizens because Algeria had been declared a legal part of France. However, to their hosts, they were *pieds noirs*—"black feet"—a common nickname for Algerians of French descent, or they were *harkis,* Muslims who had served in the French army in Algeria and who emigrated to escape retribution. Whatever the new settlers' origins, decolonization opened the gates to a search for new policies and sparked heated debate over citizenship—a debate that became more explicitly about race and ethnicity than at almost any other time in the past except for the Nazi years and that continues to this day.

Immigrants of a different sort came from Britain's Caribbean possessions right after the war. These people—many of them World War II veterans—sought jobs and opportunity in the United Kingdom. Scandinavia received immigrants from around the world, who flocked there because of how effectively the social safety net of programs integrated newcomers. Immigrants from the former Dutch territory of Surinam and Indonesia headed toward the Netherlands to an uncertain welcome. In West Germany, the labor situation was particularly dire. In 1950, the German working-age population (between ages fifteen and sixty-four) consisted of 15.5 million men and 18 million women. In an ideological climate keeping women out of the workforce, the government resorted to immigration to make up for the shortfall of men. After southern European workers' reserves proved insufficient in number, Germany and France both turned to North African and then to sub-Saharan countries in the 1960s. In the late 1970s, clandestine workers from Africa and Asia began entering formerly labor-exporting countries like Italy. By the 1980s approximately 8 percent of the European population was foreign-born, compared to only 6 percent in the United States.

During the cold war, countries in the Soviet bloc welcomed refugees from war-torn Korea and Southeast Asia and integrated numerous people from central Asia into their armies and bureaucracies. In this way, leaders of future independence movements, such as in Chechnya, received training not only in politics but in technology and military tactics. The Soviet Union also recruited African and Asian youth to attend its engineering schools and universities. Migration thus became part of the war for hearts and minds occurring at the time, but in general migration into the Soviet bloc was miniscule compared to the influx occurring in western Europe. There was simultaneously a small number of defectors from the Soviet bloc—a movement that practically stopped after the building of the Berlin Wall. Migration from socialist Yugoslavia was large, however. Greater ease of movement allowed some 850,000 Yugoslavians to enter other parts of Europe by 1970.

The first immigration negotiated by governmental agreement was for temporary male workers and allowed for a regular process of emigration back to the workers' homelands. In Germany the Turks or in France the North Africans would arrive to work for a set period as "guest workers," return home temporarily to see their families, then go back to Europe for another stint. At first these male workers were housed in barrack-like dormitories, and their host governments paid relatively little attention to their quality of life. They did not assimilate into communities around them but rather created their own enclaves. Governments and businesses alike welcomed them because as primarily adult men they utilized few social services, needing neither education nor family subsidies. Employing temporary workers made economic sense. They were ineligible for nearly all of the welfare state benefits. "As they are young," one French business publication explained in 1970, "the immigrants often pay more in taxes than they receive in allowances."[8]

Immigrants saw Europe as a land of relatively good government, wealth, and opportunity. Some simply appreciated the conditions of everyday existence. As one Chinese immigrant put it: "If you want to be a millionaire, you must go to Singapore; if you want to be rich, you must go to Germany; but if you want good weather and an easy life, go to Spain."[9] Immigrants recognized both the advantages and disadvantages of life in their adoptive countries: "The good thing about Germany is the cleanness of the cities and the discipline of the German people, but their faces are without smiles and they look coldly on children and Asian people," one Thai woman reported in the 1970s. "I miss Thai food and the Thai way of life, Thai hospitality and people helping each other. I don't miss the bureaucracy in Thailand or the transportation system." Because the first groups of workers lived together, networks of immigrants were in place to initiate later arrivals into the system, alleviate homesickness, and provide support.

The advantages of living in Europe, especially the plentiful jobs and higher wages, attracted undocumented workers; by the late 1980s, legal laborers formed only 12 percent of the non-European workforce, illegal workers some 88 percent. Then, during an economic downturn in the mid-1970s, Germany and France put an end to their programs for migrant workers because of soaring unemployment. "Guest workers" already in Europe, fearing that they would not be allowed to return on the regular cycle, began demanding the right to settle permanently. Governments set up programs for repatriation in the 1970s and 1980s, paying for return tickets and even a bonus for staying in their homeland. Some guest workers eagerly accepted the offer; far more did not, either because they did not want to return to unemployment or because they had become used to their new country. These workers mobilized to change the guest worker policy altogether so that it would allow for the immigration of a resident worker's family.

Civil Rights and Ethnic Politics

The arrival of large numbers of people of non-European lineage prompted European politicians to start focusing for the first time on race and immigration. In Britain, still reeling from the war, its loss of empire, and the continuing relative

On the signs in the image:

SOUTHALL
3,250000 COLOURED
POPULATION IN BRITAIN.
POP. SOUTHALL 58,000
COLOURED POP 30,000.
WITH NEARLY 1 MILLION
UNEMPLOYED URGENT
ACTION IS NEEDED NOW.
STOP — IMMIGRATION.
MASS—REPATRIATION.
CLEAR THE GHETTO'S
AND CLEAN THE ROADS
OF FILTH & HOUSES OF
VERMIN.

NO MORE ASIANS

SOUTHALL
POWELL FOR PREMIER

◆ **British Protest Immigration**

As immigration changed the face of Europe, many Europeans demonstrated their dislike for the change. The presence of immigrants in construction, sanitation, and hospital jobs was a vivid reminder of the loss of empire and loss of status in the world. In Britain, Enoch Powell used Hitlerian rhetoric to whip up racist opposition to immigration. He warned Britons that "rivers of blood" would flow because of immigration. The demonstrators in this picture testify to the enormous appeal of Powell and politicians like him. *Hulton Deutsch/CORBIS.*

decline of the economy, panic broke out over immigration. In addition, Britain still maintained a high level of military expenditures in comparison with Common Market countries, in order to defend its Commonwealth partners, and it could no longer afford these expenditures. But anxious political leaders focused on immigration, especially early in the 1960s after a surging tide of new arrivals from the West Indies, India, and Pakistan met with racist riots.

In 1956 a high British government official had pronounced immigrants not essential workers but "a headache."[10] In 1961 the number of newcomers reached 115,000, and in 1962 parliament legislated that would-be Commonwealth immigrants who lacked a skill that Britain could use or who did not have a secure job would have to be chosen as part of a quota. Also in 1962, the right to Commonwealth immigration was legally separated from the right to British citizenship. A few years later, the imminent arrival of more holders of British passports prompted another push to restrict the number of newcomers. Because these potential immigrants held British passports, they were entitled to enter Great Britain. The parliament headed them off in 1968 by passing the second in a series of bills limiting entry even of British passport-holders. The newly formed National

Front, bringing together holdovers from the prewar fascist leagues and other racist groups, helped anti-immigration politicians launch a fiery campaign in favor of restrictions: Conservative Party member Enoch Powell gave speeches predicting rivers "foaming with much blood" if Asians were allowed to enter.[11] Powell's allies argued that humans were "immutably programmed" with instincts of "territorial defense, racial prejudice, [and] identification with one's group," and that keeping Europe "white" was not only natural but healthy.[12]

Popular opposition to the restrictive legislation arose as a countercurrent to the racism of Powell and his allies. As each anti-immigration bill received approval, the Labour Party in the 1960s ran pro-integration campaigns advocating toleration and integration. England did not have an immigrant problem, one social worker in Liverpool maintained: "What it has is a race problem."[13] Bills mandating equal treatment in housing, jobs, and advertising, and providing services such as medical care, financial services, and education, passed in 1965 and 1968. In 1971, however, a Conservative government passed legislation ending the priority Commonwealth citizens had in immigration, putting them in a pool of applicants from all foreign countries.

In the 1970s, as the economy worsened, Britain was not alone in hardening its attitude toward immigration and foreign residents. Conditions outside Europe worsened too, increasing pressure on the comparatively peaceful and secure European nations to accept more immigrants from endangered regions despite legislation and the objections of racists. In 1973, for example, after the dictator Idi Amin of Uganda expelled all Ugandans of Asian lineage to make Uganda "a black man's country" (Uganda had a long-standing and substantial Indian and Pakistani minority), restrictions were loosened and these refugees came pouring into Britain. Some thirty thousand arrived in Britain; tens of thousands of others were diverted to different parts of the world.

The political climate in Europe was prominently shaped by racist rhetoric combined with very real economic and social concerns about accepting so many new people in tough economic times. Sociological studies from the late 1960s showed that despite official denials of any discriminatory practice—it happened only in the United States, Europeans maintained—racism was widespread in every sphere of society. For example, in the Netherlands researchers sent out identical job applications with different signatures to employers, and they found that the letters with identifiable Surinamese or Antillean names received a negative response 20 to 50 percent more frequently than the letters with a Dutch name. The same test was employed in requests to rent apartments, with similar results. Other studies showed that managers of companies expected newcomers to fit into "company culture." This meant tolerating racist and sexist language and jokes and sometimes more blatant discrimination in the workplace. Anyone who could not accept hate speech was a bad sport and therefore not really suitable for a managerial position. In addition, studies found that many employers expected minorities and women to fail at anything but menial work.

Politicians and company managers did not generally see antidiscrimination legislation as having a positive value, especially if they meant adding immigrants or their children to the ranks of higher-paid workers. Efforts to integrate new Europeans into the workforce to make things fairer and more representative of the population often provoked outcries of "reverse discrimination." As one Dutch manager put it: "Before we start talking about equal representation, we had better start worrying about where all the Amsterdammers have gone to. Nice talk when you first do nothing but chase Amsterdammers out of Amsterdam. And once they have been pushed out you suddenly want the company to reflect the composition of the population of Amsterdam."[14] This man and other white male leaders claimed to be protecting European standards from invasions by uncivilized "others," while workers simply wanted protection from the competition they believed low-paid newcomers represented on the job front.

These attitudes and the growing array of legislation promoted the development of immigrants' own political activism. In the first years of foreign immigration in the mid-1960s, guest workers had focused their energy on improving the conditions in factories or in the dormitories where they were housed. As the doors to immigration began to close and as governments worked to repatriate temporary workers, immigrant politicians became more visible. Guest workers forged alliances with settled immigrant residents and citizens of non-European origin. The foreign workers in particular changed their platforms and political claims, demanding that their relatives be allowed to join them in Europe.

In France, workers from North Africa, among the first non-Europeans entering in the 1950s and 1960s, became politically active in the 1970s, pushing for family reunification and better living conditions. In 1980 the National Assembly passed the Bonnet Law, drastically limiting immigration and the rights of immigrants. Second-generation North Africans moved into leadership positions during debates on these immigrant issues, tipping the focus of French immigrant activism toward civil rights within their homeland. The early 1980s in France witnessed marches against racism. Elsewhere, in Sweden, coalitions such as Stop Racism and Hasan's Friends were formed to eliminate the disadvantages faced not only by immigrant-citizens but also by their offspring. The new Europeans also agitated for toleration of their customs and beliefs. Muslims, for example, sought the right to worship and dress in accordance with their religious principles.

Activists also homed in on foreigners' rights to citizenship. Since the French Revolution, France had had procedures for naturalization, believing itself to be a country grounded in principles of universal rights—including the right to citizenship. Few countries actually embraced immigrants of non-Caucasian origin, however, and Germany, in particular, insisted that it was "not a country of immigration." Instead, the Germans considered themselves citizens exclusively on the basis of German blood (see Document 9.2). Thus, Turkish immigrants and their descendants, no matter how acculturated, civic-minded, wealthy, or educated, and no matter how "German" they might feel themselves to be, could never become citizens. They would remain legal immigrants with a resident status for as many generations as their family existed. This German policy was not changed until late in the 1990s.

A NEW SOCIETY

The wave of non-European immigration altered not only European politics but society as well. Social policy, once directed toward a group of homogeneous poor and working-class people, began to center on whether and how to integrate those of non-European ethnicity. From being minimally concerned with insulated clusters of single men, governments started to concern themselves with entire families. Meanwhile, immigrants organized their own communities within European society, setting themselves apart in the first generation. All that changed with the second generation—the children of the newcomers who took part in politics and adopted a mixed identity. As their schooling in European skills advanced, they took on higher-paying jobs, moved into the middle and upper classes, and even gained high positions in government. All of these achievements reshaped the composition and outlook of European societies.

Social Policy for Migrants

Sweden made a determined effort to provide the same kind of housing for immigrant workers as for citizens. In Sweden social policy allowed migrants to choose to live in integrated neighborhoods, neighborhoods composed of those with a similar ethnic lineage, or neighborhoods of some other ethnicity. In France, activism in the 1970s helped immigrants secure better housing for their families, usually in publicly financed high-rise apartments, replacing the shantytown barracks in which foreign workers had previously been lodged. But generally, immigrants across Europe had trouble finding decent accommodations.

Many policies for immigrants from the former colonies seemed to repeat the policies of the colonial period, when forced labor and few amenities were standard. Migrants were crammed into workshops, and governments housed them in crowded dormitories, often lacking sanitary facilities. One woman from the Caribbean described her search for housing in 1970s Britain: "The front doors were broken, the gas heaters had been pulled out and just thrown on the floor, the inside doors weren't on their hinges, there was rubbish all over the passageway, and all the wiring had been pulled out to prevent squatters from using the place."[15] Urban housing was often hard to find because many immigrants preferred life in big cities where people were more cosmopolitan and where there was more diversity. A teenager, settled in the rural French countryside after migrating from Algeria after the war, recounted the difficulties of country life in the mid-1970s: "When I came here, I tried. I wanted to be friends. But the children here avoided me. They treated me as if I were a sort of germ—a dangerous germ to be avoided. I felt it. So I fought, and I tried, and then I fought again. The outlook is small here. My teacher—she was small because I was a *pied noir,* and so she said to my mother that I was an imbecile. She said that sending me to school was just a waste of time. That is the French spirit. It is not politics or pride that makes them hate us—it is the peasant mind."[16]

Failures in social policy were also legion, especially efforts to protect would-be immigrants from unscrupulous or dangerous people—even their spouses. A

Caribbean woman in Britain reported that even the police station could not provide inadequate protection. "Yes, I've been in there with black eyes and blood trickling down my face all over my white t-shirt. I mean Mike followed me one day into the police station and told the policeman he'd done it. He said, 'Yeah, I did it. She wouldn't cook my dinner so yeah—I licked her round the head with it.' And the blood was trickling down my back." The response of the police was that she should "kiss and make up."[17] Perhaps such a reaction would have occurred no matter what the ethnicity, but these kinds of situations were often compounded by the authorities' racism and by immigrants' inadequate language skills and insufficient understanding of European procedures and rights. Entitled to government benefits including health care, many did not know the means for obtaining them.

Providers of educational and other social services were hard-pressed to meet the influx of newcomer families, many of whom prized education and sought to have their children receive the best schooling possible. This new burden on educational systems meant a changing situation for parents of German origin, for example, who in the late 1970s were upset as class sizes increased dramatically and as overcrowding occurred in school and social facilities. This growth occurred because, although the working population of foreign residents remained the same between 1970 and 1981, the absolute number of foreign residents increased 50 percent and the majority of these newcomers were dependent children. Among the Turkish population, the number of workers increased by close to 40 percent while the number of nonworkers increased by 300 percent as male guest workers brought in wives and children. Simultaneously, hard economic times put pressure on budgets for social services, often causing the native-born to resent the newcomers as the source of all their ills. Nonetheless, public sentiment was always mixed: in an anonymous opinion poll conducted in the late 1970s, some 69 percent of Germans responded that German children were not innately more intelligent than immigrant children.

Immigrant Communities

Community life sustained many new migrants facing the hardships associated with relocating. Many initially moved in family groups or in clusters of male relatives. In Britain, spouses, in-laws, uncles, aunts, and cousins were already present in the 1950s and early 1960s. In Germany and France, entire families were not generally present until the 1970s and 1980s. First-generation families supported each other, setting up babysitting and other cooperative groups. They endeavored to sustain their children, whose experiences at school were often harsh: "My memories of school are of being really laughed at and being called a golliwog," reported one young woman from the Caribbean. Another recalled that "this teacher pulled me up in front of the class and said that I was dirty. . . . My father is usually a quiet man, but he went up there with a machete." Parents did their best in the face of harsh odds, helping their children advance if possible through a system that generally found them "not clever enough" and "better off cleaning the streets"—as one teacher told an immigrant pupil.[18] Overcoming a system that disproportionately classified them as "Educationally Sub-Normal," immigrants often hungered

◆ **Immigrant Children in Paris**
Immigrants often faced difficult conditions unless they were able to join the professional classes. As the novels of Buchi Emecheta testified, housing and health care were often substandard. These four children from West Africa shared a single bed, and their parents probably paid more in rent than did the European-born, for whom a wider choice of housing was available. As the twenty-first century opened, immigrants continue to protest their situation in an effort to bring about change. *Roger Violett/The Image Works.*

for higher education and funded their own education and their children's through university even if doing so meant having to hold many jobs at once.

Governments and social practices also forced segregated community life on migrants in the same ways they had forced ethnic segregation on colonized peoples. One way was to stereotype them, as the example of education shows. In the Ruhr coal area, workers' councils that assigned housing in the late 1970s and early 1980s usually gave Turkish workers the worst housing in segregated areas of the coal residential area. These were the same sections that Poles had occupied in the 1920s as the least favored workers of that generation. Buchi Emecheta described her life in segregated housing as a nightmare. Quarters were cramped, and the community life was oppressive. Instead of finding freedom, she found the same narrow-mindedness she had disliked in Nigeria.

In this complex amalgam of old and new social settings, migrants often had to refashion themselves: older women who remained at home might maintain a traditional way of life almost entirely in keeping with that of their country of origin, but immigrant men might switch back and forth from the public persona of their adopted country to the persona of their country of origin. Issues of identity were more complicated for the second generation (see Document 9.2.). Educated in schools of their new country and either permanent residents or citizens, they often found their relationship to their origins outside of Europe puzzling. One young German woman with an African grandfather recalled that her fellow students thought she was an American black and people often asked her if she knew German even though she had been born and always lived in Germany. When she visited Africa, however, her sense of belonging did not improve: "When I went there I thought that people would be darker, but I wasn't prepared to have them shout 'white people' after us. They said: 'Toubab,' which means stranger. It was meant to be friendly and kids would laugh and wave. I had thought they would take me for one of their own. Here they shout 'black girl' and there they shout 'white girl' — Where does one really belong?"[19] Yet some second-generation children chose to hang on to their non-European identities. For example, many children of Turkish guest workers in Germany would not surrender their Turkish passports and took frequent trips back to their parents' place of origin.

Domestic Life and Gender Roles

The first waves of migration involved large groups of single men, admitted to do construction and other manual labor. Wives sometimes followed, and then entire families left their home countries. This was the case, for example, of Ugandans arriving in London in the 1970s. Although they came in stages, individual family members ultimately reunited. As quotas for migrants went into effect, single women sometimes received slight preference because they could serve as domestic servants — positions for which there were shortages among the European working population. Other single women came as mail-order brides or were smuggled in as sex workers. Many of the women who arrived in families, however, had the responsibility for maintaining customs of the country of origin, and many did not work outside the home. Those who did want employment found it most easily in sweatshops, working off the books in jobs without benefits. People of non-European ethnicities walked the wholesale districts of big cities with enormous sacks of outwork — purses, hair decorations, artificial flowers, and other small items — made at home. In Britain, where the waves of women's migration occurred as early as the postwar years, the harsh conditions of work and daily life led many into the activism that would soon erupt around the world.

Aisha (a pseudonym), who arrived in France in the mid-1960s with her construction-worker husband, brought many aspects of North African life with her, passing them on to her children. Housing three generations by the 1980s, her apartment outside Lyons, France, was divided into men's and women's quarters for the more than twenty people who inhabited it. In this observant Muslim household, only Aisha and the younger children and grandchildren could cross the divide. In the common room where meals were served, the walls were lined with benches and a few low tripods for holding serving dishes. Family members sat on the benches and ate from common trays of food. Much of that food was prepared in a traditional way; couscous, for instance, was not bought prepackaged but rather pounded out by hand from semolina flour. Aisha returned to North Africa each summer to get a year's supply of provisions such as spices because the quality and types that she wanted were not available in France. She also found Algerian brides for her eldest sons, who had been born in Algeria. Children born in France were provided spouses from neighboring Algerian immigrants.

Aisha made some concessions to European mores and interacted with government and local institutions. For instance, the common room in her apartment had European-style tables, which were used only for the children to do their homework. Like the husbands of many early migrants to France, Aisha's husband had to retire early because of injuries on the job and utter exhaustion from backbreaking work. This retirement entailed negotiating between French and Algerian welfare services. Because Aisha's grown children drove cars, they would take her to government offices; thus the seclusion in which she lived most of the time and in which she would have lived in the home country was only partial. Like other North African women she could and did return home to enjoy the company of those family members who remained.

While women like Aishe could only imperfectly re-create their culture in a new country, the immigration of extended family networks did allow women a rich social life in their adoptive homelands. North African women reported that their first menstruations sometimes occurred while visiting an aunt or other female relative. The occasion was one for celebration, new clothes, special food, and the hennaing of hands. Women enjoyed festive dancing parties together, full of laughter and games. Pregnant women at these parties received special attention, as older women taught them undulating dancing movements that were their customary ways to prepare the body for childbirth and to help reduce labor pains. These occasions along with the meeting of women at bathhouses allowed the unmarried to bring themselves to the attention of the female relatives of someone they might have met at school and with whom they might want a marriage arranged.

As they migrated, men kept many of their masculine prerogatives, because Europe had similar and in some cases even more restrictions on women, including lower salaries and government benefits. Men socialized in public places more often than did women. Men young and old belonged to cricket clubs and soccer leagues which provided companionship, exercise, and perhaps even some degree of social mobility if they excelled at these sports. Yet migrant men also lost privileges, especially their patriarchal authority which usually had been stronger in their countries of origin. As their children were absorbed into public schooling, government regulation of children began to compete with parental authority. At the same time wives and daughters sometimes grew less deferential or subservient after having been exposed to Europe's more liberal social climate.

Single women arriving on their own were in a weaker position than either married women or men. Thai women emigrating to Germany, for example, often came without their families through marriage agencies or sex traffickers. Mail-order brides married German partners after brief or even no acquaintance; other women were forced into prostitution. Some mail-order brides, however, saw their experience of migration in a nuanced light. Forced to leave their country to help families or because emigration was simply a more realistic survival strategy than any other, they found both advantages and disadvantages in their situation. "I like the order and the system of Germany," one reported; "the laws are good here; security, quality of life, society, and the future of people, all is very good here." Another complained about German racism: "I don't like the locals in the countryside who love to put down foreigners; they are stupid."[20] This single woman migrating to a variety of European countries as domestic and other menial workers felt the benefits of their new situation because of improved finances and personal security even though they might reject European manners and culture.

CULTURE AFTER COLONIZATION

Decolonization and increased global migration had dramatic effects on many aspects of European culture. New perspectives from people who had been colonized suddenly joined the old imperial culture of Europe, and people immigrating from around the world were often shocking in their complete and utter rejection of white values. An entire world of criticism opened up, as theorists came to see the importance of non-Western societies and even to find deep commonalities—finding that undermined white claims to superiority. As in earlier decades, the rich contributions from outside Europe continued to benefit life in general, as music, art, and everyday life absorbed these new influences. Immigrants helped European culture thrive in the postwar era.

Decolonizing the Mind

The most influential theorist of decolonization was Frantz Fanon (1925–1961), a black psychiatrist from the French colony of Martinique who began analyzing liberation movements while serving in a French-run North African hospital. He argued that the psyche of the colonized individual had been traumatized by the violence and brutal imposition of foreign values and rules in economic and social life. People emerging from colonization faced the enormous task of re-creating a "national culture," by which Fanon meant not a reversion to some romanticized past but rather the "whole body of efforts made by a people in the sphere of thought to describe, justify, and praise the action through which that people has created it-self."[21] Fanon developed his activist opinions as he imbibed the brisk critique of Western institutions that local North African intellectuals had been developing over the course of colonial rule. What Europeans described as the colonized person's madness was only the double bind Europeans imposed when they professed to want to civilize the "native" but then said that the native was too backwards to attain European culture fully and properly. Fanon believed that the nationalist leaders who had staked their leadership of liberation movements on their ability to imitate the Europeans by mastering European culture were misguided. Once co-opted by European values, these leaders, Fanon believed, ended up betraying their followers by becoming "the general president of that company of profiteers" that like the Europeans exploited the common people.[22]

Quitting his post in the French government hospital, Fanon advanced explanations for the turn to violence of liberation movements like the one in Algeria: The colonized person often adopted the identity imposed by Europeans who wanted to rule him. He was characterized as a madman, liar, thief, and ne'er-do-well, and eventually he turned the full brutality of that characterization on his oppressor. Ruled by guns, the colonized person only knew the politics of violence and naturally sought independence by means of violence. Translated into many languages, Fanon's *Black Skin, White Masks* (1952) and *The Wretched of the Earth* (1961) posed the question of how a colonized individual, filled with the rules and values of the colonizer, could establish an authentic identity—how, in effect, one could "decolonize" the mind (see Document 9.3). "In the period of decolonization, the colonized masses mock at these very values [the white man's values], insult them, and vomit them up."[23] Fanon did not live to see the many attempts to resolve these issues in the postcolonial world, for he died of leukemia at the age of thirty-six.

Novelist V. S. Naipaul (b. 1932) migrated from Trinidad in the Caribbean to London in 1950 as part of the first postwar wave of newcomers to Europe. Of Indian heritage, Naipaul explored the condition of global migrants, the meaning of cultural mixture, and the impact of European domination on those living under imperialism. Naipaul's novel *A House for Mr. Biswas* (1961) was a meditation on the life of his father in Trinidad as he struggled to understand his Indian heritage and his social ascent into the colonial administration of the island. Mr. Biswas at the end of his life still feels a longing to have made it to England, for there "was surely where life was to be found."[24]

Naipaul's work offended many of South Asian origin. *India: A Wounded Civilization* (1977) called attention to the violence underlying the accomplishment of independence and dismissed the celebration of Gandhi's movement as a romantic national myth. In other works Naipaul characterized the behavior of South Asians as mimicry of imperialist overlords. Admiring neither their own culture nor their values, these "mimic men" in business, the bureaucracy, and the army acted out their fantasy of English behavior. In *The Mimic Men* (1967) Naipaul portrays a Caribbean politician who finds that imitation of an imagined European culture has left him and his contemporaries essentially hollow.

Naipaul's portrait of South Asians and peoples of the Caribbean was hardly flattering, but it created a terminology of mimicry on which later theorists would build. Additionally, in the 1950s a more positive attitude toward mimicry was being constructed. In 1957 the Tunisian-born author Albert Memmi, writing from his own experience, captured the rage the well-educated and upwardly mobile colonized person could provoke in the imperialist: "The shrewder the ape, the better he imitates, and the more the colonizer becomes irritated."[25]

Literature by whites also contributed to debates over decolonization, articulating a complexity of feeling. Written before World War II, George Orwell's *Burmese Days* (1935) foregrounded the unabashed racism of most of the major characters, exposing the claims to a civilizing mission as "the lie that we're here to uplift our poor black brothers instead of to rob them."[26] In fact, Orwell showed that most colonizers did not want Africans and Asians to have access to European culture or even to speak grammatical English. After the war, many prominent writers took up similar themes. British intellectual Anthony Burgess (1917–1993) in his *Malayan Trilogy* (1956–1959) portrays the unfolding realization of an English teacher that the Asians really have no use for Europe and, astonishingly to the Englishman, want all Europeans to be gone. South African–born Bessie Head (1937–1986), in *When Rain Clouds Gather* (1968), showed the ambiguous value of an English agricultural expert in postliberation Botswana. This agent represented one type in a wide-ranging cast of white postcolonial characters, some of them well-meaning but others simply ne'er-do-wells who remained in formerly colonized areas "develop" the economy long after imperialism had collapsed.

In the context of decolonization, much literary and social scientific attention focused on furthering themes found in Darwin, Freud, and writers of an earlier period suggesting that all humans, even "civilized" Europeans, had a "savage" core, especially in the tendencies to murder and irrational behavior. The core of savagery, invoked in postwar considerations of the Holocaust, was similar whether one was outside of the West or inside it. In 1962 French anthropologist Claude Lévi-Strauss (b. 1908) published *The Savage Mind,* in which he contrasted human behavior in Western and non-Western cultures. He found that people in both cultures engaged in purposive behavior to achieve distinct ends, but that non-Westerners tended more toward improvisation than toward the rational planning and engineering favored by Westerners. In *The Elementary Structures of Kinship* (1949), Lévi-Strauss examined peoples and cultures under the analytic umbrella of "structuralism." Societies, posited the anthropologist, function within controlling structures—kinship and exchange, for example—that operate according to inflexible rules similar to those of language. These structures, at work in societies globally, are based on binaries or oppositions—such as *raw* and *cooked, male* and *female, pure* and *impure*—that create hierarchies of value. Thus, *cooked, male,* and *pure* are more highly valued than *raw, female,* and *impure.*

As Lévi-Strauss and other anthropologists added Western cultures to their lists of cultures to be studied, the idea that the West might be as primitive as the non-West did not seem far-fetched to many in the aftermath of World War II and the Holocaust. Indeed, some intellectuals argued, the barbarity of European imperialism, total warfare, and genocide seemed explicable only if one acknowledged that Germans and French, Italians and Poles, Belgians and Dutch and British were as capable as any other people of savagery. In 1954 William Golding (1911–1993) wrote *Lord of the Flies*. The novel is about a group of English schoolboys, stranded on an island, who set up a vicious social order. The youths descend into savagery, killing one of their own in the process. The message of Golding's story was that without due vigilance Europeans could become like savages elsewhere, falling from a civilizational high to an innate state of barbarism. As nations emerged from the grip of imperialism, these speculations about a core identity among all humans cast doubt on the supposed superiority of Westerners and fostered the belief that the potential to be civilized and savage was evenly distributed around the world.

A New Burst of Cultural Mixture

Europeans had long been importers of non-European ideas, products, and cultural forms. This period of decolonization saw a continuation of that trend, which shifted to new areas and accelerated. Cultural practices brought by immigrants to Europe influenced nearly every facet of culture from fine arts and literature to popular music and cuisine. In this period of cultural mixing, Europeans for the first time began to acknowledge that their society and customs were becoming increasingly multicultural. Many saw the change as a positive development. In Britain, Sweden, and the Netherlands, to name a few countries, cultural differences among nationality groups were openly recognized in the form of concern for special housing needs, traditions, and training. In France, by contrast, there was a tendency to speak of "universal citizens," each of them having the same rights and needs and sharing the same language and customs. However, even the French early in the 1980s developed a slogan exhorting people to honor each other's "differences and our resemblances."

European citizens of immigrant backgrounds integrated elements from their native cultures into their new lives. In Britain, migrants of African descent incorporated elements of reggae from Jamaica, jazz and soul from the United States, samba from Brazil, and highlife from Nigeria in their music, while those in France added aspects of the griot tradition. A group of eight youths from Cameroon, Angola, Benin, the United States, and France formed the rock group Ghetto Blaster, combining a variety of musical traditions to bring listeners "le black feeling." Europeans soaked up this music but also gravitated toward the evolving rock tradition, which was adding new international dimensions to its songs. In 1957 four working-class youths from Liverpool formed a rock 'n' roll band that gave energetic, even violent performances across Europe and later became globally celebrated as the Beatles. In 1965, while based in India to film *Help*, the group began developing an interest in Asian music, musical instruments, and religious and philosophical thought. In the course of recording "Norwegian Wood," George Harrison began using the sitar and later wrote songs, as did rock musicians who

◆ **Turkish Restaurant in Britain**
Immigrants often had a difficult time adjusting to the food of the countries in which they
worked. To make familiar food available, entrepreneurs with the right contacts back home set
up grocery stores, wholesale supply businesses, and restaurants. The most successful of these
entrepreneurs became millionaires, eventually supplying native as well as new Europeans.
Inexpensive and flavorful, ethnic cuisine appealed to Europeans both new and old, and it
eventually fundamentally changed the European palate. *Maurice Hibberd/Evening Standard.*

followed the Beatles, with Asian musical patterns and with lyrics such as "Within
You, Without You" that deliberately echoed Asian themes.

Cultural mixture extended into the most everyday aspects of life when
European eating habits were revolutionized during decolonization. Taste in food
became even more polymorphous and hybrid than it had been in the early modern
period when chocolate, coffee, tea, the tomato, and other products were introduced. Chinese food had the first culinary impact in this period with restaurants
cropping up in the 1940s and 1950s. Chinese food was tasty and inexpensive, making it appealing to the masses and creating the first wave of restaurants that lured
people out of the home. Soon, restaurants in Amsterdam featured Indonesian,
Indian, and Caribbean foods, and housewives knew how to prepare Indonesian

dishes such as *gado gado* and many curries. The best restaurants in Germany were Italian and Turkish, reflecting the early presence of foreign workers from these countries.

English food was said to be notoriously bad in the post–World War II decades. Yet as the quality of English food plummeted, flavorful Indian cuisine was introduced, boosting the appeal of non-European cooking still more. The expanding popularity of "ethnic" food provided opportunities for migrants to open restaurants and grocery stores. As large grocery chains came into being, they carried popular Indian items. Many migrants from Asia were able to enter the food business whether they had had experience or not, and they helped Europeans become more knowledgeable about the world. As Meena Pathek, owner of the highly successful global food brand Patel, put it, "I have to educate people in the West that Indian food is not all hot—that there is tremendous variety in India."[27] In England suppliers of Indian food to chains became among the wealthiest newcomers to the country, some of them eventually establishing global empires.

The French flocked to North African restaurants, and entire neighborhoods in Paris were devoted to establishments offering Vietnamese and Thai food. At home even the least adept French housewife knew how to make couscous and often served it as a celebratory meal. As migration and travel continued, nearly every European city's restaurants and grocery stores mirrored the world's cuisines—a cornucopia that had not existed fifty years earlier.

In high culture, artists such as Louise Bourgeois (b. 1911) and Niki de Saint Phalle (1930–2002) integrated non-Western forms into their sculpture. Bourgeois's statues in the late 1940s and early 1950s looked like slim, colorful totem poles. Saint Phalle created huge papier-mâché statues of women, brightly garbed and called "Nanas," after the powerful Caribbean women they were meant to celebrate. The composer György Ligeti (b. 1923–2006), a refugee to Germany from Communist Hungary, studied the music of African Pygmies and modeled some of his compositions on it. German composer Karlheinz Stockhausen (b. 1928), who traveled widely, incorporated musical sounds from beyond Europe into his music in such pieces as *Ceylon*. Gongs, chimes, and other percussive instruments from outside Europe along with Western electronic music became standard tools of these composers.

The colonial past and the multicultural present reached Europeans in the many public exhibitions and popular films that stressed a global heritage. Governments converted their "colonial" museums into collections with different names: the colonial museum in Amsterdam became the Tropical Museum, for example. The government in Paris united its non-Western holdings into a collection called "first arts" as opposed to the old titles of "colonial" and "primitive arts." In the 1980s and thereafter French and British films like *The Far Pavilions, A Passage to India,* and *Gandhi* provided scenes of a lush but decaying imperial past peopled by Europeans both corrupt and noble, the latter sometimes aiding their colonial brethren in their fight against injustice. Some critics accused these films of indulging in a faddish nostalgia for imperialism, and of sentimentalizing a past that was supposed to hold useful lessons for behavior in the multicultural present. In the 1990s filmmakers with a colonial heritage would begin making alternative versions of these global relationships—witty, disturbing, and tragic.

CONCLUSION

The transformation of Europe from an imperial to a postimperial cluster of states marked a profound and historic transition. The world as a whole saw the birth of dozens of independent nations from the remnants of empire, many of them keeping their close ties with European businesses. These new states wielded influence by contesting the domination that European nations still hoped to exercise. As both the USSR and the United States lured students from the new nations and as they intervened in places such as Iran and Vietnam, decolonization became intertwined with the course of the cold war. Despite losing their empires, many European states were booming economically and needed more workers. From the 1950s on, millions immigrated from the former colonial empires to Britain and the European continent. By the 1970s the need for workers had diminished as baby boomers reached working age and as economic growth stalled, but immigration continued despite attempts to stop the influx of newcomers. Social services and education changed to reflect the new composition of Europe, and novels and critical writing infused its culture with new perspectives. As European culture advanced and as the immigrants and migrants helped rebuild the continent, many Europeans became furious at the presence of these newcomers, and politics became infused with racism and even violence against them. Soon, however, reform movements of the late 1960s and 1970s were finding inspiration in the writings of non-Westerners and building new programs for reform and social justice.

D O C U M E N T S

Nasser Faces Off with
Imperial Europe

IN 1952, GAMAL ABDEL NASSER (1918–1970) took part in the military overthrow of the Egyptian king, a puppet of the English government, which had granted Egypt its independence but stayed on to rule behind the scenes. The son of a postal inspector, Nasser quickly rose from being an army officer to president of Egypt—a position he used to improve the economic well-being of his people by redistributing land from the wealthiest estates. Most notably, he faced off with European powers that wanted to keep their hands on Egyptian resources. His particular nemesis was Conservative prime minister Anthony Eden, who sought unsuccessfully to reassert Britain's prewar influence. Failing to charm Nasser, Eden waged a publicity campaign against him, calling him among other things a "Muslim Mussolini." More ominously the British secret service began working on various assassination scenarios.

In 1956, the British persuaded the United States not to provide Egypt with loans to build the Aswan High Dam, which would create vast hydroelectrical resources. In response, Nasser nationalized the Suez Canal in order to return its income to Egypt. The British stormed that the Egyptians were hardly advanced enough as a people to run so complex an operation as the Suez Canal and proposed that they themselves head a consortium to run it.

On September 15, 1956, Nasser responded to that proposal in the speech excerpted here. He articulated the attitude of many in the Middle East toward the Western powers. At the time, Nasser already was a hero in the Middle East for his strong stand against continued Western domination. With the nationalization of the canal, his reputation soared. The Egyptian leader became the politician most respected by Middle Eastern people and by those in other regions emerging from colonial rule.

Document 9.1

GAMAL ABDEL NASSER

*Speech on the Nationalization
of the Suez Canal, September 15, 1956*

In these decisive days in the history of mankind, these days in which truth struggles to have itself recognized in international chaos where powers of evil domination and imperialism have prevailed, Egypt stands firmly to preserve her sovereignty. Your country stands solidly and staunchly to preserve her dignity against imperialistic schemes of a number of nations who have uncovered their desires for domination and supremacy.

In these days and in such circumstances Egypt has resolved to show the world that when small nations decide to preserve their sovereignty, they will do that all right and that when these small nations are fully determined to defend their rights and maintain their dignity, they will undoubtedly succeed in achieving their ends. . . .

I am speaking in the name of every Egyptian Arab and in the name of all free countries and of all those who believe in liberty and are ready to defend it. I am speaking in the name of principles proclaimed by these countries in the Atlantic Charter. But they are now violating these principles and it has become our lot to shoulder the responsibility of reaffirming and establishing them anew. . . .

We have tried by all possible means to cooperate with those countries which claim to assist smaller nations and which promised to collaborate with us but they demanded their fees in advance. This we refused so they started to fight with us. They said they will pay toward building the High Dam and then they withdrew their offer and cast doubts on the Egyptian economy. Are we to disclaim our sovereign right? Egypt insists her

SOURCE: Speech of Gamal Abdel Nasser, in *The Suez Canal Problem, 26 July–22 September 1956*, U.S. Department of State Publication No. 6392 (Washington, D.C.: G.P.O., 1956), pp. 345–351.

sovereignty must remain intact and refuses to give up any part of that sovereignty for the sake of money.

Egypt nationalized the Egyptian Suez Canal company. When Egypt granted the concession to de Lesseps it was stated in the concession between the Egyptian Government and the Egyptian company that the company of the Suez Canal is an Egyptian company subject to Egyptian authority. Egypt nationalized this Egyptian company and declared freedom of navigation will be preserved.

But the imperialists became angry. Britain and France said Egypt grabbed the Suez Canal as if it were part of France or Britain. The British Foreign Secretary forgot that only two years ago he signed an agreement stating the Suez Canal is an integral part of Egypt.

Egypt declared she was ready to negotiate. But as soon as negotiations began threats and intimidations started. . . .

Eden stated in the House of Commons there shall be no discrimination between states using the canal. We on our part reaffirm that and declare there is no discrimination between canal users. He also said Egypt shall not be allowed to succeed because that would spell success for Arab nationalism and would be against their policy, which aims at the protection of Israel.

Today they are speaking of a new association whose main objective would be to rob Egypt of the canal and deprive her of rightful canal dues. Suggestions made by Eden in the House of Commons which have been backed by France and the United States are a clear violation of the 1888 convention, since it is impossible to have two bodies organizing navigation in the canal. . . .

By stating that by succeeding, Abdel Nasser would weaken Britain's stand against Arab nationalism, Eden is in fact admitting his real objective is not Abdel Nasser as such but rather to defeat Arab nationalism and crush its cause. Eden speaks and finds his own answer. A month ago he let out the cry that he was after Abdel Nasser. Today the Egyptian people are fully conscious of their sovereign rights and Arab nationalism is fully awakened to its new destiny. . . .

Those who attack Egypt will never leave Egypt alive. We shall fight a regular war, a total war, a guerrilla war. Those who attack Egypt will soon realize they brought disaster upon themselves. He who attacks Egypt attacks the whole Arab world. They say in their papers the whole thing will be over in forty-eight hours. They do not know how strong we really are.

We believe in international law. But we will never submit. We shall show the world how a small country can stand in the face of great powers threatening with armed might. Egypt might be a small power but she is great inasmuch as she has faith in her power and convictions. I feel quite certain every Egyptian shares the same convictions as I do and believes in everything I am stressing now.

We shall defend our freedom and independence to the last drop of our blood. This is the staunch feeling of every Egyptian. The whole Arab nation will stand by us in our common fight against aggression and domination. Free peoples, too, people who are really free will stand by us and support us against the forces of tyranny. . . .

QUESTIONS FOR ANALYSIS

1. What is Nasser's view of the imperial powers?
2. How does Nasser defend nationalization of the canal?
3. What aspects of the speech would most appeal to other peoples striking out for independence?

Racial Differences in
Postwar Germany

GERMAN POLITICIANS HAVE MAINTAINED THAT all Germans are white by definition and that Germany is not a country of immigrants, no matter how many
foreigners reside there. This view is not particularly unusual in Europe, and it has
widely influenced European attitudes toward people of other races. Among the foreign residents in Germany were African soldiers who fought with the Allies in
World War I and remained in Germany when the war was over, African American
soldiers who were part of the post–World War II occupation, and African immigrants from Germany's colonies. Many of these people had relationships with
white Germans, sometimes marrying them and having children. Abena Adomako,
the author of Document 9.2, born in 1963, was from one of these families. Her
mother and grandmother were Afro-Germans, and her father was an immigrant
from Ghana. Even though she was born in Germany and her family was partly of
German descent, she felt herself an outsider.

During the Third Reich, people with African blood were among those sterilized and also among those later exterminated in the death camps, although some
served in the German army. Because of this injustice, postwar West Germany tried
to compensate for the past with scrupulous attention to equal treatment of people
of all ethnicities and races. But the idea that Germany had no immigrants and that
Germans were white made their lives often difficult and confusing, as Abena
Adomako describes. Children born to African American fathers and German
mothers after World War II were particularly singled out by everyone—from
classmates to neighbors—and even given the collective name "occupation babies,"
as all Afro-German children came to be so identified.

The growth of the civil rights and immigrant rights movements in the
European Union and in global organizations protecting foreigners encouraged
these "new Germans" to speak out about how racial and ethnic difference affected
their lives. Women's and immigrant groups collected and published testimonials,
and ethnographers made films about immigrant workers. An anthology called
Showing Our Colors: Afro-German Women Speak Out, published in 1986, featured
the stories of German women of color in what was to many people's minds an all-
white Germany. In this document, first published in that collection, the twenty-
three-year-old author describes what it was like to not look German but be
German nonetheless.

Document 9.2

ABENA ADOMAKO

Mother: Afro-German, Father: Ghanaian, 1986

My skin is black. As a result I am seen as a foreigner—African or American. I am always asked why my German is so good, where I come from, etc. These questions are irritating. Mostly I answer provocatively that I am German. Even then the questions don't stop—Why, how come, how so?

I am African but I am also German. My appearance makes me African, my thoughts and my behaviour are German, the way I move is European.

Africans are described as lovable, dumb, stupid and dirty. My mother and grandmother grew up as Afro-Germans in Germany. To avoid prejudice they brought me up to be particularly neat and clean and to perform well in school and in my profession. I had to be better than the others, or at least among the best.

Whenever I go to Ghana to see my relatives it's always a big adjustment for me at first. Then I just mix with all the Africans, even though my European manner makes me stand out. Ghana! I'm at home, but it's not my home. Yet I feel comfortable there.

I used to be jealous whenever I saw lighter coloured Afro-Germans. I thought their skin colour was more beautiful, like a suntan, and that they would have fewer problems and would be sooner accepted by society. I never recognized that they had problems simply because their colour was visible.

As a child I knew very few other Afro-German children. There was one boy in my class with whom I didn't really have much contact. I'd

have been interested to find out what he thought and felt. There was another girl in our neighbourhood and I started to wonder about things when she was going with a friend of mine. Was I too dark to be someone's girlfriend? I can't blame everything on the colour of my skin. Maybe I just wasn't the right type. I still wonder about that today.

At that age I really didn't have any opportunities at all to go out with boys. Some of my girlfriends already had boyfriends and I felt excluded not being able to discuss boys with them. One even said that I was too dark to have a boyfriend. I kept hearing this until I actually had my first boyfriend. I still think that, while I was liked and accepted, the boys were afraid to show too much affection for me or to be too friendly towards me in case obligations and complications arose, such as my bringing a really Black girlfriend along.

I also suffered through not being able to take part in pranks since I would have been too easily recognized if a group of us played at ringing doorbells and running. I'd always been told to be careful, to behave. That's the way I was until I was 17.

All families aim at good behaviour in their children to give them a good upbringing. Our parents had the additional burden of prejudice. Don't draw attention to yourself in any negative way, no matter the cost. Always be polite and nice to everyone. That's what was expected from "decent" Africans. That's how one had to be and what was expected.

When contact games between boys and girls began at the onset of puberty, I felt excluded. I was usually made the custodian of coats and bags on those occasions. Up to today I react badly whenever anyone tries to give me chores like that.

. . . I started to look for a job. I had trained as a foreign-language secretary, and I began making applications in writing and by phone. They asked

SOURCE: Margaret Busby, ed., *Daughters of Africa: An International Anthology of Words and Writings by Women of African Descent from the Ancient Egyptian to the Present* (New York: Ballantine, 1992), 961–962.

for information: age, nationality. My mind began to work. Could I go for a job with my Berlin accent and colour? Was I asked about my nationality because of my surname Adomako? I go for interviews. Amazing performances take place to conceal xenophobia and prejudice from me. So I write and phone endlessly in the search for a halfway neutral person who will employ me. Even once I'm employed, it all continues; I sense the prejudices of colleagues and superiors. "You wrote that wrong." Doubts about my ability. Africans just aren't supposed to be able to do this. But I trained for this job. Then I'm not so sure who is right. It's a spiral and I continue to fight my battle.

In recent years in Germany I've lost some of my strength and confidence. The desire and wish to leave for a place where people can move free of prejudice, where I can cross the street without being seen as a foreign object, begins to grow. People always say, "If you leave, you'll miss your homeland." That may be true, but rather a little homesickness than unhappiness "at home."

When it's time for discos, pubs and relationships—to dress up, to go out and go dancing—this means stress for me from start to finish.

(1) Getting ready. I must appear clean and well groomed. Why? There are prejudices against grubby, poor-looking African girls, or those just the opposite—too chic and she can almost certainly be bought. So what to wear? I choose something neutral if possible, so as not to appear sexy. . . .

(2) At the disco. The stares and whispers of men and women and the pressure of my escort at being observed too. Or maybe enjoying being the centre of attention.

(3) Dancing. Generally it is assumed that people of African descent can dance better. So I go on to the dancefloor with special attention being paid to "little old me." It doesn't matter whether I think I danced well or if I don't really feel up to it—I am always congratulated.

(4) Flirting. All women are flirted with. With me there's absolutely no restraint shown. I find the way it's done degrading and clumsy. "Everyone knows what a Black woman can offer a man." First, she is a sexually attractive woman, secondly, a woman without character. I like to be complimented on looking good, but the question is whether it's an insult. Wherever I go, I get a lot of reaction but I would prefer not to stand out all the time. I'm not the type who likes to put on a show in the way that is often expected of me. To protect myself from undesirable suitors it was necessary for me to erect a wall around myself. I have no desire to be chatted up by pimps and horny old goats. That's not how I want to live. Being full of mistrust and caution all the time, I appear to be hard, rejecting, quiet and try to hide any possible attraction. That's when I am left in peace.

This hardness carries over into my normal daily life. It's difficult for a really nice guy to get to me and I can hardly recognize his honesty. At this point I begin unconsciously to set tests. It's hard to explain why it's like this. Maybe it's because I want to know whether he's able to stick to me in spite of the prejudice and opposition from outside. But all this only makes me sad.

Even when it sounds as if some of my experiences have been harsh, I have learned to stand by myself and to find a way to be myself and to develop myself. I am finding more and more courage to stand out, and the courage to show my body without hiding in buttoned-up blouses and loose skirts and feeling ashamed. That's important for me.

I have to establish myself in a society which may appear to be neutral but which is not so in fact. I can appear self-assured, but I'm only strengthened by the thought: *You must or you'll go under.* Why can't I simply be the way I want to be, without taking up a fighting stance?

[Translated by George Busby.]

QUESTIONS FOR ANALYSIS

1. What range of feelings about her identity did Abena Adomako hold as a child?

2. What were the attitudes of others toward her as seen through her eyes?

3. In what ways did race affect the author's development as a citizen, family member, and worker?

A Powerful Voice of Decolonization

FRANTZ FANON WAS BORN ON THE CARIBBEAN ISLAND OF MARTINIQUE in 1925, the son of middle-class parents and the descendant of slaves. By the time he finished high school, World War II had broken out, and Martinique, a possession of France, was caught in the middle of the struggle between the forces of the government at Vichy and the Free French government in England. At the age of seventeen Fanon tried to escape the Vichy-controlled island to join up with the Free French, who came to control Martinique in the summer of 1943. A year later, he joined the Free French army, shipping out in March 1944 and fighting in Europe until the war's end.

A decorated soldier, Fanon was among those colonized young men whom the war radicalized. He experienced the way the French segregated their troops, privileging the Caribbean blacks over the North Africans and the North Africans over the sub-Saharan Africans. This policy pitted the troops against one another rather than against their common oppressor the French. When packages arrived for the soldiers from the Red Cross and other volunteer organizations, the officers divided them so that each white soldier received an individual package while groups of three black soldiers had to share a package. Fanon learned in the war that the cause of universal freedom for which he was supposedly fighting was a sham because it applied only to whites. It was, he said, an "obsolete ideal."[28]

After the war, Fanon took up medical studies in France. It was there that he came to understand how deep racism ran, even against individuals steeped in French culture. Like many of his peers in Martinique, Fanon had soaked up his French education, working hard because he believed that knowledge of French culture and facility in speaking French would open all the privileges of French citizenship to him. He became "more French than the French."[29] He confronted a bitter reality, however: to the French he was simply a negro, a black man. While training in psychiatry, he wrote his first book, *Black Skin, White Masks* (1952), exposing as a delusion the belief held by colonized peoples that education could trump racism and bring equality with whites.

Having established himself as a psychiatrist, Fanon accepted a post in Blida, Algeria, in the fall of 1953. His assignment took him to one of the premier institutions of France's "civilizing mission." Psychiatrists there used cutting-edge techniques such as electric shock therapy on mentally ill patients, a practice Fanon himself had used in France. The general situation in Algeria, however, was not what he expected. In less than a year, full-scale war for liberation from the French erupted, and Fanon soon found himself in the middle of it.

Fanon's now-classic text *The Wretched of the Earth*, published in 1961, took its title from the socialist anthem "The International," whose first words summon poor workers to action: "Arise ye wretched of the earth." In the war for Algerian independence, Fanon—who had grown up under colonialism and experienced its racism throughout his adult life—was on the side of freedom. However, in his book he emphasized the obstacles that colonialism had laid in the path to freedom. Colonized people had to be violent in their struggles, he warned, because violence was the only political action the whites had ever used on them. Violence would decolonize the minds of the oppressed.

Working on a daily basis with Algerians, Fanon became an honored soldier of the liberation movement. He died at age thirty-six of leukemia, but his books remained influential around the world, changing the attitudes of everyone from civil rights activists in the United States to philosophers in Europe itself. Fanon's picture of the colonizer and the colonized was shocking in its honest, brutal description of malignant social and psychological conditioning, and many could see their own situation in his words.

Document 9.3

FRANTZ FANON
The Wretched of the Earth, 1961

. . . The colonized man will first manifest this aggressiveness which has been deposited in his bones against his own people. This is the period when the niggers beat each other up, and the police and magistrates do not know which way to turn when faced with the astonishing waves of crime in North Africa. . . . When the native is confronted with the colonial order of things, he finds he is in a state of permanent tension. The settler's world is a hostile world, which spurns the native, but at the same time it is a world of which he is envious. We have seen that the native never ceases to dream of putting himself in the place of the settler—not of becoming the settler but of substituting himself for the settler. This hostile world, ponderous and aggressive because it fends off the colonized masses with all the harshness it is capable of, represents not merely a hell from which the swiftest flight possible is desirable, but also a paradise close at hand which is guarded by terrible watchdogs.

The native is always on the alert, for since he can only make out with difficulty the many symbols of the colonial world, he is never sure whether or not he has crossed the frontier. Confronted with a world ruled by the settler, the native is always presumed guilty. But the native's guilt is never a guilt which he accepts; it is rather a kind of curse, a sort of sword of Damocles, for, in his innermost spirit, the native admits no accusation. He is overpowered but not tamed; he is treated as an inferior but he is not convinced of his inferiority. He is patiently waiting until the settler is off his guard to fly at him. The native's muscles are always tensed. You can't say that he is terrorized, or even apprehensive. He is in fact ready at a moment's notice to exchange the role of the quarry for that of the hunter. The native is an oppressed person whose permanent dream is to become the persecutor. The symbols of social order—the police, the bugle calls in the barracks, military parades and the waving flags—are at one and the same time inhibitory and stimulating: for

SOURCE: Frantz Fanon, *The Wretched of the Earth*, trans. Constance Farrington (New York: Grove Press, 1963), 52–53, 93–95.

they do not convey the message "Don't dare to budge"; rather, they cry out "Get ready to attack." And, in fact, if the native had any tendency to fall asleep and to forget, the settler's hauteur and the settler's anxiety to test the strength of the colonial system would remind him at every turn that the great showdown cannot be put off indefinitely. That impulse to take the settler's place implies a tonicity of muscles the whole time. . . .

. . . The settler's work is to make even dreams of liberty impossible for the native. The native's work is to imagine all possible methods for destroying the settler. . . .

. . . For the native, life can only spring up again out of the rotting corpse of the settler. . . .

But it so happens that for the colonized people this violence, because it constitutes their only work, invests their characters with positive and creative qualities. The practice of violence binds them together as a whole, since each individual forms a violent link in the great chain, a part of the great organism of violence which has surged upward in reaction to the settler's violence in the beginning. . . .

The mobilization of the masses, when it arises out of the war of liberation, introduces into each man's consciousness the ideas of a common cause, of a national destiny, and of a collective history. . . . During the colonial period the people are called upon to fight against oppression; after national liberation, they are called upon to fight against poverty, illiteracy, and underdevelopment. The struggle, they say, goes on. The people realize that life is an unending contest.

We have said that the native's violence unifies the people. By its very structure, colonialism is separatist and regionalist. Colonialism does not simply state the existence of tribes; it also reinforces it and separates them. The colonial system encourages chieftaincies and keeps alive the old Marabout° confraternities. Violence is in action all-inclusive and national. It follows that it is closely involved in the liquidation of regionalism and of tribalism. Thus the national parties show no pity at all toward the caids° and the customary chiefs. Their destruction is the preliminary to the unification of the people.

At the level of individuals, violence is a cleansing force. It frees the native from his inferiority complex and from his despair and inaction; it makes him fearless and restores his self-respect. . . . When the people have taken violent part in the national liberation they will allow no one to set themselves up as "liberators." They show themselves to be jealous of the results of their action and take good care not to place their future, their destiny, or the fate of their country in the hands of a living god. Yesterday they were completely irresponsible; today they mean to understand everything and make all decisions. . . . From now on the demagogues, the opportunists, and the magicians have a difficult task. The action which has thrown them into a hand-to-hand struggle confers upon the masses a voracious taste for the concrete. The attempt at mystification becomes, in the long run, practically impossible.

° *Marabout:* A spiritual leader in the Islamic faith.

° *caids:* Group leaders.

QUESTIONS FOR ANALYSIS

1. What justification does Fanon provide for violence by the colonized?
2. How does he describe that violence?
3. How will violence shape the future once the nation is liberated?

The Changing
Face of Europe

FOR BOTH THE IMMIGRANTS AND THE COMMUNITIES THAT RECEIVED THEM, the experience of immigration in Europe over the last half century and more has been difficult, conflict-ridden, surprising, and enriching—usually all at once. Newcomers who settled into neighborhoods and jobs, bringing their own distinct cultural traditions, had both an exciting and sometimes unsettling effect on their host countries. The resulting issues of contact and conflict, assimilation and segregation, provoked and continue to provoke debate over what it means to be "European." No matter how Europe's peoples—old and new—have framed that debate and attempted to answer that question, all would agree that immigrants have changed and will continue to change the face of Europe in ways both small and profound.

The first postwar immigrants were primarily men—many from the Caribbean and from South Asia—staying only temporarily to earn money to bring back home to their families. As time went on, many brought their families over to settle permanently and partake of the benefits of living in western Europe. People from countries across the globe—Nigeria, Algeria, Vietnam, Pakistan, Bangladesh, Sri Lanka, Turkey, and a host of other nations—established permanent communities in Europe's cities and towns.

Not all immigrants, however, aspired to or had the opportunity to take up permanent residence in Europe. The political turmoil wrought by decolonization often forced into exile groups and factions who were unwelcome in the postcolonial power structure. The Moluccans, inhabitants of a group of islands in formerly Dutch-controlled Indonesia, are a case in point. When their own attempt at independence ran afoul of the Javanese forces that controlled newly independent Indonesia, 12,500 Moluccans went into "temporary" exile in Holland in the years after 1949. Many were housed in former German concentration camps, and they were discouraged from looking for work because of the fear that they would drive down Dutch wages. At any rate, both the Dutch and the Moluccans themselves considered the situation only temporary. "Forced to idleness, isolated in their camps, robbed from their military status, confronted with another climate and struggling with their language problems there was nothing left for them then but to drift on their hope," as one Dutch account put it.[30] There they waited, eagerly anticipating the chance to return to Indonesia once the political climate at home improved in their favor. That never happened, and a substantial population of second- and third-generation Moluccans resides in the Netherlands today. Some remain committed to gaining a political foothold in Indonesia, but others are reconciled to the Netherlands as their permanent residence. Figure 9.1 shows members of an exiled Moluccan family in 1955 outside their temporary home in a Dutch camp. What impact do you think living in limbo had on these parents? On their children?

Immigrants who came to Europe to stay tended to settle in communities where people from their home country or ethnic group were already clustered. Thus, certain neighborhoods took on a predominately Turkish, Algerian, Vietnamese, Moroccan, or other ethnic character, bringing social change and cultural mixture to cities across Europe. Grocery and clothing stores with familiar goods from their homelands, cinemas showing movies from their cultures, ethnic

◆ Figure 9.1 **Exiled Moluccans**
Hulton Archive/Getty Images.

restaurants, and storefront mosques and temples sprang up in these neighbor-hoods (Figures 9.2 and 9.3). These cultural institutions helped newcomers to keep their bearings in strange and sometimes hostile environments, where they often experienced prejudice or were otherwise singled out because of their skin color, foreign accents, and "exotic" dress, including women's saris and headscarves.

The southwest London suburb of Brixton became an enclave of immigrants from the West Indies. Figure 9.3, a 1973 photograph, shows a woman and her son

◆ Figure 9.2 **Indian Man at Cinema Showing Indian film**

◆ Figure 9.3 **Woman in Brixton Market**

buying manioc and bananas at an outdoor market stall in Brixton. What clues, if any, do Figures 9.2 and 9.3 provide about the degree to which these people became assimilated in Britain? Brixton later became infamous for violent clashes between blacks and police in 1981 and again in 1985, sparked in some measure by the wretched living conditions, crime, and poverty of the neighborhood. During the same period in Germany, punks and terrorists blew up migrant housing and harassed and even killed immigrants, while France's large North African populations clashed with police when protesting their lack of basic services. Given the images in this Picture Essay, what cultural differences might have become flashpoints for conflict?

Another source of tension was competition for jobs among the working poor. Many poor native-born whites attributed their own unemployment to the newcomers' willingness to work for very low wages. Indeed, immigrants performed a variety of low-paying, backbreaking jobs—working as everything from street cleaners and construction workers to hospital orderlies and fruit pickers. Women in immigrant families could sometimes earn a living by producing local products at home. Leatherwork, lace (Figure 9.4), and other needlework brought in much-needed cash, and handmade products for the family, including specially made traditional food for holidays, maintained cultural patterns even as these became interwoven with the culture of Europe.

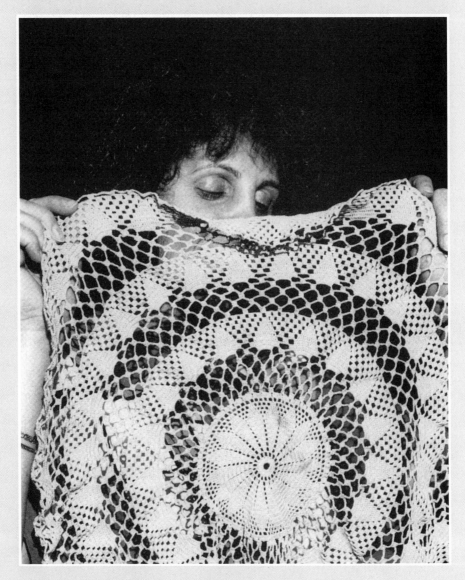

◆ **Figure 9.4 Turkish Émigré to Germany Showing Her Handmade Lace**

The visibility of immigrants was one factor increasingly changing the face of postwar Europe and transforming politics. Many governments tried to promote tolerance through posters and meetings, but, at least at first, these efforts amounted to little more than lip service and rarely resulted in better circumstances for immigrants. Some political parties and organizations, either out of a genuine commitment to tolerance or as a strategy for attracting voters, emphasized that their programs welcomed and benefited ethnic and racial minorities. In 1983, the Greater London Council, a coordinating body for London's thirty-three districts and dozens of governing boards, issued a poster announcing "London against Racism." "If you're not part of the solution, you're part of the problem," it proclaimed. "You've got the power to challenge the damaging effects of racism. Use it!" As shown in Figure 9.5, Britain's Conservative Party, the Tories, produced an

With the Conservatives, there are no 'blacks', no 'whites', just people.

Conservatives believe that treating minorities as equals encourages the majority to treat them as equals.

Yet the Labour Party aim to treat you as a 'special case', as a group all on your own.

Is setting you apart from the rest of society a sensible way to overcome racial prejudice and social inequality?

The question is, should we really divide the British people instead of uniting them?

WHOSE PROMISES ARE YOU TO BELIEVE?

When Labour were in government, they promised to repeal Immigration Acts passed in 1962 and 1971. Both promises were broken.

This time, they are promising to throw out the British Nationality Act, which gives full and equal citizenship to everyone permanently settled in Britain.

But how do the Conservatives' promises compare?

We said that we'd abolish the 'SUS' law.

We kept our promise.

We said we'd recruit more coloured policemen, get the police back into the community, and train them for a better understanding of your needs.

We kept our promise.

PUTTING THE ECONOMY BACK ON ITS FEET.

The Conservatives have always said that the only long term answer to our economic problems was to conquer inflation.

Inflation is now lower than it's been for over a decade, keeping all prices stable, with the price of food now hardly rising at all.

Meanwhile, many businesses throughout Britain are recovering, leading to thousands of new jobs.

Firstly, in our traditional industries, but just as importantly in new technology areas such as microelectronics.

In other words, the medicine is working.

Yet Labour want to change everything, and put us back to square one.

They intend to increase taxation. They intend to increase the National Debt.

They promise import and export controls.

Cast your mind back to the last Labour government. Labour's methods didn't work then.

They won't work now.

A BETTER BRITAIN FOR ALL OF US.

The Conservatives believe that everyone wants to work hard and be rewarded for it.

Those rewards will only come about by creating a mood of equal opportunity for everyone in Britain, regardless of their race, creed or colour.

The difference you're voting for is this:

To the Labour Party, you're a black person.

To the Conservatives, you're a British Citizen.

Vote Conservative, and you vote for a more equal, more prosperous Britain.

LABOUR SAYS HE'S BLACK. TORIES SAY HE'S BRITISH.

CONSERVATIVE ☒

◆ Figure 9.5 **Conservative Party Election Poster**
Conservative Party Election Poster.

election poster directly challenging the Labour Party's position on minorities. "Is setting you apart from the rest of society a sensible way to overcome racial prejudice and social inequality?" the Tories asked. Their answer to this question was an emphatic "no." What arguments does their poster make to persuade immigrants to vote Conservative? How effective do you think it was? What other constituents and concerns, aside from immigrant communities, does this poster address? What role does the image of the fine-looking black man in a business suit play in making the argument?

As Europe became ever more ethnically and racially diverse with increasing immigration during the 1980s and 1990s, debates continued over issues of European identity, cultural values, the rights of European citizens, and especially the role of religion as it related to all three. Figure 9.6 shows Muslims in the port city of Marseille, France, at prayer. What, if anything, does this picture tell you about the religious comfort level of some "new Europeans"? How might Marseille's non-Muslim residents react to this open display of religious faith?

In a sometimes strained social and political climate, one group of "new Europeans" received consistently enthusiastic acceptance: the many talented athletes who played on soccer and other sports teams across Europe. In Figure 9.7, soccer players Selim Teber and Herve Nzelo-Lembi flank their teammates Christian Timm and Markus Anfang. All four play or played for the German

◆ Figure 9.6 **Muslims at Prayer in Marseille, France**
Steve McCurry/Magnum Photos.

◆ Figure 9.7 **Kaiserslautern Soccer Stars**
Landov.

"football" club FC Kaiserslautern. Teber, of Turkish background, lists his nationality as German/Turkish on his Web site for fans. Nzelo-Lembi, from Congo, who has played defense for Kaiserslautern since 2002, was born in Kinshasa and holds dual Congolese and Belgian citizenship. Sports fans across Europe enthusiastically cheered on these players and others from a wide array of non-European backgrounds. Many believe that multiethnic sports teams, which emerged as early as the late 1940s, have helped to break down racial barriers and prejudices. Does the participation of diverse athletes suggest that there is a fuller integration of people of non-European origin and a greater acceptance of diversity in the modern European nation-state? Why or why not?

QUESTIONS FOR ANALYSIS

1. What do these images indicate about the public impact of immigration? What aspects of the new Europeans' presence seem to be most prominent?

2. What arguments for and against immigration can you find in these images?

3. What do think it meant to be "European" in 1950? Given these images and what you know about immigration to Europe, has that definition changed over the intervening decades? If so, how? Does it matter? To whom?

NOTES

1. Buchi Emecheta, *In the Ditch* (Oxford: Heinemann, 1979 [1972]).

2. Quoted in H. S. Wilson, *African Decolonization* (London: Edward Arnold, 1994), 101–102.

3. Joseph Henri, quoted in David Macey, *Frantz Fanon: A Biography* (New York: Picador, 2000), 88.

4. Quoted in Wilson, *African Decolonization*, 128.

5. Everette Lee DeGolyer, quoted in Daniel Yergin, *The Prize: The Epic Quest for Oil, Money, and Power* (New York: Simon and Schuster, 1991), 393.

6. Memo quoted in Frederick Cooper, *Africa since 1940: The Past of the Present* (Cambridge: Cambridge University Press, 2002), 76.

7. Quoted in Frances Gouda, *Dutch Culture Overseas: Colonial Practice in the Netherlands Indies, 1900–1942* (Amsterdam: University of Amsterdam Press, 1995), 237–238.

8. Quoted in Maxim Silverman, *Deconstructing the Nation: Immigration, Racism, and Citizenship in Modern France* (London: Routledge, 1992), 47–48.

9. Quoted in Gregor Benton and Frank Pieke, *The Chinese in Europe* (New York: St. Martin's, 1998), 223.

10. Quoted in Keith Robbins, *The Eclipse of a Great Power: Modern Britain, 1870–1975* (Essex: Longman, 1983), 285.

11. Quoted in Alan Sked and Chris Cook, *Postwar Britain: A Political History* (London: Penguin, 1990), 232.

12. Richard Verrall, quoted in Martin Barker, *The New Racism* (London: Junction Books, 1981), 100.

13. Quoted in Jacqueline Nassy Brown, *Dropping Anchor, Setting Sail: Geographies of Race in Black Liverpool* (Princeton: Princeton University Press, 2005), 109.

14. Quoted in Philomena Essed, "The Politics of Marginal Inclusion: Racism in an Organizational Context," in *Racism and Migration in Western Europe,* ed. John Solomos and John Wrench (Oxford: Berg, 1993), 151.

15. Beverley Bryan et al., *The Heart of the Race: Black Women's Lives in Britain* (London: Virago, 1985), 96.

16. Quoted in Jane Kramer, *Unsettling Europe* (New York: Penguin, 1990), 209.

17. Amina Mama, "Black Women and the Police: A Place Where the Law Is Not Upheld," in *Inside Babylon: The Caribbean Diaspora in Britain,* ed. Winston James and Clive Harris (London: Verso, 1993), 144–145.

18. Bryan et al., *The Heart of the Race,* 63, 67, 69.

19. Julia Berger, in May Opitz, Katharina Oguntoye, and Dagmar Schultz, eds., *Showing Our Colors: Afro-German Women Speak Out,* trans. Anne V. Adams (Amherst: University of Massachusetts Press, 1992), 196–198.

20. Quoted in Eva Humbeck, "The Politics of Cultural Identity: Thai Women in Germany," in *Women of the European Union: The Politics of Work and Daily Life,* ed. Maria Dolors García-Ramon and Janice J. Monk (London; New York: Routledge, 1996), 198.

21. Frantz Fanon, *The Wretched of the Earth,* trans. Constance Farrington (New York: Grove Press, 1963), 233.

22. Ibid., 166.

23. Ibid.

24. V. S. Naipaul, *A House for Mr. Biswas* (London: Penguin, 1961), 540.

25. Albert Memmi, *The Colonizer and the Colonized,* trans. Howard Greenfield (New York: Orion, 1965 [1957]), 124.

26. George Orwell, *Burmese Days* (London: Penguin, 1967 [1935]), 37.

27. Quoted in Shrabani Basu, *Curry: The Story of the Nation's Favourite Dish* (London: Sutton, 2003), 77.

28. Quoted in Macey, *Frantz Fanon: A Biography,* 87.

29. Quoted ibid., 114.

30. Quoted in Ben Allen and Aart Loubert, "History and Identity: Moluccans in the Netherlands," The Hague Justice Portal, http://thehaguelegalcapital.nl/lc/publications/articles/HistoryandIdentity.doc (document no longer available).

SUGGESTED REFERENCES

General Works Keylor, William. A World of Nations: The International Order since 1945. 2003.

Reynolds, David. *One World Divisible: A Global History since 1945.* 2000.

Vadney, Thomas E. *The World since 1945.* 1992.

Westad, Odd Arne. *The Global Cold War: Third World Interventions and the Making of Our Times.* 2005.

Decolonization Sometimes decolonization was a peaceful process, but as Elkins's work shows, decolonization could be inhumane and violent in the extreme. Shepard's account of the end of the Algerian War shows how this event and by implication all of decolonization made race central to European politics thereafter.

Aldous, Richard, and Sabine Lee, eds. *Harold Macmillan and Britain's World Role.* 1996.

Connelly, Matthew. *A Diplomatic Revolution: Algeria's Fight for Independence and the Origins of the Post–Cold War Era.* 2002.

Duara, Prasenjit, ed. *Decolonization: Perspectives from Now and Then.* 2004.

Elkins, Caroline. *Imperial Reckoning: The Untold Story of Britain's Gulag in Kenya.* 2005.

Ferguson, Niall. *Empire: The Rise and Demise of the British World Order and the Lessons for Global Order.* 2003.

Hargreaves, John D. *Decolonization in Africa.* 1996.

Kunz, Diane B. *The Economic Diplomacy of the Suez Crisis.* 1991.

Marsh, Steve. *Anglo-American Relations and Cold War Oil.* 2003.

McIntyre, W. David. *British Decolonization, 1946–1997: When, Why, and How Did the British Empire Fall?* 1999.

Shepard, Todd. *The Invention of Decolonization: The Algerian War and the Remaking of France.* 2006.

Spruyt, Hendrik. *Ending Empire: Contested Sovereignty and Territorial Partition.* 2005.

Wilson, H. S. *African Decolonization.* 1994.

Decolonizing Europe It was difficult for Europeans to adjust to loss of empire, and racism—a prominent feature of wartime thinking—soared even as the number of citizens of color increased. The books listed here demonstrate that many had difficulty seeing people of color as citizens with rights. More often they were merely menial workers to be exploited or competitors for services and jobs.

Behdad, Ali. *Belated Travelers: Orientalism in the Age of Colonial Dissolution.* 1994.

Bleich, Erik. *Race Politics in Britain and France: Ideas and Policymaking since the 1960s.* 2003.

Brubaker, Rogers. *Citizenship and Nationhood in France and Germany.* 1992.

Collings, Rex, ed. *Reflections of a Statesman: The Writings and Speeches of Enoch Powell.* 1991.

Dummett, Ann, and Andrew Nicol. *Subjects, Citizens, Aliens, and Others: Nationality and Immigration Law.* 1990.

Herbert, Ulrich. *A History of Foreign Labor in Germany, 1880–1980: Seasonal Workers, Forced Laborers, Guest Workers.* 1993.

Kramer, Jane. *Unsettling Europe.* 1980.

Peabody, Sue, and Tyler Stovall, eds. *The Color of Liberty: Histories of Race in France.* 2003.

Ross, Kristin. *Fast Cars, Clean Bodies: Decolonization and the Reordering of French Culture.* 1995.

Silverman, Maxim. *Deconstructing the Nation: Immigration, Racism, and Citizenship in Modern France.* 1992.

Spencer, Ian R. G. *British Immigration Policy since 1939: The Making of Multi-Racial Britain.* 1997.

A New Society Newcomers to Europe found conditions difficult, for although laws promised equality, society did not generally provide equality. The anthology on black women working in Britain's welfare state is but one that shows these conditions. Second and third generations, most of them legal citizens, were especially angered by discrimination and took action.

Adi, Hakim. *West Africans in Britain.* 1998.

Anthias, Floya, and Gabriella Lazaridis, eds. *Gender and Migration in Southern Europe: Women on the Move.* 2000.

Benton, Gregor, and Frank Pieke. *The Chinese in Europe.* 1998.

Brown, Jacqueline Nassy. *Dropping Anchor, Setting Sail: Geographies of Race in Black Liverpool.* 2005.

Bryan, Beverley, et al. *The Heart of the Race: Black Women's Lives in Britain.* 1985.

Chapman, Herrick, and Laura Frader, eds. *Race in France: Interdisciplinary Perspectives on the Politics of Difference.* 2004.

James, Winston, and Clive Harris, eds. *Inside Babylon: The Caribbean Diaspora in Britain.* 1993.

King, Russell, and Richard Black, eds. *Southern Europe and the New Immigrations.* 1997.

Opitz, May, Katharina Oguntoye, and Dagmar Schultz, eds. *Showing Our Colors: Afro-German Women Speak Out.* 1992.

Solomos, John, and John Wrench, eds. *Racism and Migration in Western Europe.* 1993.

Webster, Wendy. *Imagining Home: Gender, "Race" and National Identity, 1945–1964.* 1998.

Culture After Colonization Music, literature, food, and culture generally reflected the increasing diversity of European society, while leading thinkers proposed an array of ideas of what this diversity meant, both for old but especially for new Europeans. These books provide a sampling.

Baker, Houston A., Jr., Manthia Diawara, and Ruth H. Lindeborg, eds. *Black British Cultural Studies.* 1998.

Basu, Shrabani. *Curry: The Story of the Nation's Favourite Dish.* 2003.

Blackshire-Belay, Carol Aisha, ed. *The African-German Experience: Critical Essays.* 1996.

Edwards, Brent Hayes. *The Practice of Diaspora: Literature, Translation, and the Rise of Black Internationalism.* 2003.

Fanon, Frantz. *The Wretched of the Earth.* 1961.

Gilroy, Paul. *"There Ain't No Black in the Union Jack": The Cultural Politics of Race and Nation.* 1991.

Keller, Richard. *Colonial Madness: Psychiatry in North Africa.* 2007.

Macey, David. *Frantz Fanon: A Biography.* 2000.

Oliver, Paul, ed. *Black Music in Britain.* 1990.

Tignor, Robert. *W. Arthur Lewis and the Birth of Development Economics.* 2006.

Wright, Michelle M. *Becoming Black: Creating Identity in the African Diaspora.* 2004.

Selected Web Sites

The Web site maintained by the National University of Singapore provides information on a wide variety of postcolonial writers (including Buchi Emecheta), while there are several sites with reliable information on migration and immigration. Those of the United Nations and the University of California at San Diego are particularly good.

Decolonization African biography: <**www.fordham.edu/halsa/mod/modsbook .html**>

National University of Singapore, Buchi Emecheta: <**www.thecore.nus.edu.sg/ post/nigeria/emecheta/emechetaov.html**>

National University of Singapore, Postcolonial Writers: <**postcolonialweb .org**>

United Nations, Global Commission on International Migration: <**gcim.org**>

University of California, San Diego, Center for Comparative Immigration Studies: <**www.ccis-ucsd.org**>

10

Postindustrial Europe and Its Critics

1965–1979

IN MARCH 1978, ALDO MORO, FORMER PRIME MINISTER of Italy and the country's most prominent political figure, was kidnapped in downtown Rome. A terrorist group, the Red Brigades, claimed responsibility. Moro had helped forge the postwar political consensus that contrasted so sharply with the brutal politics of the fascist period. A seasoned politician, he had even helped Italian Communists to reject Stalinism in favor of participating in consensus politics. He also had endorsed the economic growth and consumer abundance that made life more comfortable for the average citizen, and this abundance helped make political militancy less attractive than it had been before World War II. The Red Brigades wanted old-style, fisticuff politics and at first demanded that Moro be exchanged for political prisoners, eventually asking for the release of one ill inmate. The Italian government refused, claiming that such bargaining would open the door to more terrorism. The kidnappers allowed Moro to send heart-wrenching letters to his wife and friends in politics. In them he asked why his former comrades bore such malice toward him that they would not communicate with the kidnappers and afford them the recognition as political actors that they craved. On May 9, authorities found Moro's lifeless body in the back of a car, directed there by the Red Brigades. To Italians and

◆ Aldo Moro in Captivity

In March 1978, the Red Brigades, a radical rebel group in Italy, kidnapped former prime minister Aldo Moro. This was one among many acts of terrorism committed by disaffected young people in the 1970s and early 1980s. The most powerful Italian politician at the time, Moro listened to his captors and wrote heart-wrenching letters to his colleagues in government begging them to give the Red Brigades a hearing. The government turned a deaf ear to the kidnappers' desire for an airing of their grievances. On May 9, the Red Brigades directed the authorities to the backseat of a car, where they found Moro's murdered body. *Bettmann/CORBIS.*

many other Europeans the kidnapping and murder of Moro was the most shocking event on their soil in decades.

The Red Brigades aimed to overturn the status quo, and in this aim they were part of an outpouring of grass-roots activism—some peaceful and some violent. An uprising of students, antiwar protesters, feminists, and gays in

1968 featured an array of tactics ranging from public demonstrations in support of civil rights to the destruction of property and even murder. From Czechoslovakia to the United States and around the world, protests arose against the direction in which industrial nations in general and the superpowers in particular were moving. The murder of Aldo Moro had the same ends as more peaceful protest in targeting political repression, postwar consensus politics, and the human consequences of technology's dizzying pace. Technological advances, reformers believed, had given enormous power to a handful of financiers, managers, and bureaucrats—the new (but unelected) leaders of "postindustrial society." The term *postindustrial* pointed to the emergence of the service sector—including finance, engineering, and health care—as the dominant force in the economy in the West, replacing heavy industry. Many of the protesters were being educated to enter this service elite. As critics, however, they saw mindless bondage resulting from work in which the majority of people merely tended an ever growing number of machines.

Amid these critiques, Europe seemed to sink from its postwar optimism into a less confident mood. While reformers questioned the values of technological society, whole nations challenged the superpowers' monopoly of international power. An agonizing war in Vietnam sapped the resources of the United States, and the People's Republic of China confronted the Soviet Union with increasing confidence. The oil-producing states of the Middle East formed a cartel and reduced the flow of oil to the leading industrial nations in the 1970s. The resulting price increases helped bring on a biting recession that was especially harsh in Europe. Other third world countries resorted to terrorism to achieve their ends, and all the wealth and military might of Europe and the superpowers could not guarantee that they would emerge victorious in this period of increasingly global competition. Nor during these decades could governments prevent the erosion of their legitimacy—an erosion often brought on by ordinary citizens in their acts of brave resistance, terrorism, and the turn to grassroots politics. Along the way there were many victims: in Europe the most famous was Aldo Moro.

THE TECHNOLOGY REVOLUTION

Three decades after World War II, technological advances continually boosted prosperity and changed daily life in industrial countries. In Europe and the United States, people awoke to instantaneous radio and television news, worked with computers, and used revolutionary contraceptives to control reproduction. Satellites orbiting the earth reported weather conditions, relayed telephone signals, and collected military intelligence. Europeans moved from buying necessities like washing machines to purchasing innovative smaller gadgets—electric popcorn poppers, portable radios and tape players, automatic garage door openers—that simply made life more pleasant. The reliance of humans on machines led one scientist and philosopher, Donna Haraway, to insist that people were no longer self-sufficient individuals but rather *cyborgs*—that is, humans who needed machines to sustain ordinary life processes. These machines, Haraway wrote, "have made thoroughly ambiguous the difference between natural and artificial, mind and body."[1]

The Information Age: Television and Computers

Information technology catalyzed social change in these postindustrial decades just as innovations in textile making and the spread of railroads had in the nineteenth century. Its ability to convey knowledge, culture, and politics globally appeared even more revolutionary. In the first half of the twentieth century, mass journalism, film, and radio had begun to forge a more homogeneous society based on shared information and images. In the last third of the century, television, computers, and telecommunications made information more accessible and, some critics said, culture more standardized. These cultural developments signaled, one British commentator complained, the "rapid assimilation of this country to America."[2]

Yet there were differences in European and U.S. television at least. Between the mid-1950s and the mid-1970s, Europeans rapidly adopted television as a major entertainment and communications medium. In 1954, only 1 percent of French households had television; by 1974, almost 80 percent did. With the average viewer tuning in about four and a half hours a day, the audience for newspapers and theater declined. "We devote more . . . hours per year to television than [to] any other single artifact," one sociologist commented in 1969.[3] As with radio, European governments funded television broadcasting with tax dollars and controlled TV programming to avoid what they perceived as the substandard fare offered by American commercial TV; instead they featured drama, ballet, concerts, variety shows, and news. Complex political debate and discussion of serious books were regular highlights: the philosopher Jean-Paul Sartre, like other intellectuals, often discussed his work at length on television. Thus the European welfare state assumed a new obligation to fill its citizens' leisure time with elevating programs — and also gained more power to shape daily life.

With the emergence of communications satellites and video recorders in the 1960s, state-sponsored television encountered competition, however, and became more American in western Europe. Satellite technology allowed for the transmission of sports broadcasts and other programming to a worldwide audience. Feature films on videotape became readily available to television stations, and competition only increased in 1969 when the Sony Corporation introduced the first affordable color videocassette recorder to the consumer market. What statesmen and intellectuals considered the junk programming of the United States — soap operas like *Dallas*, westerns like *Gunsmoke*, and a variety of game shows — arrived dubbed in the local language, amusing vast audiences with the joys, sorrows, tensions, and aspirations of daily life. Critics acknowledged that TV provided more information than had ever been available before, but they complained that the transnational fare represented the lowest common denominator of "moderate" opinions in the news and "bland" entertainment.

East and west, television exercised a powerful political and cultural influence. In one rural area of the Soviet Union, over 70 percent of the inhabitants watched television regularly in the late 1970s; the rest continued to prefer radio. Educational programming of classical literature and drama united the far-flung population of the USSR by broadcasting shows designed to advance Soviet culture. At the same time, with travel impossible or forbidden to many, shows about foreign lands were among the most popular, and these joined the postcards that adorned many homes in expanding the horizons of many Soviet families.

Television also superseded radio as the primary vehicle for politicians to reach out to their constituents. A successful media image became crucial to advancing or maintaining a political career, and those who mastered the medium of TV wielded more power. Heads of state could usually preempt regular programming. In the 1960s, French president Charles de Gaulle addressed his fellow citizens frequently over television, employing the grandiose gestures of an imperial ruler to stir patriotism. As electoral success in western Europe increasingly depended on cultivating a successful media image, political staffs came to rely on media experts as much as they did on policy experts.

Just as revolutionary, the computer reshaped work in science, defense, and ultimately industry. Computers had evolved dramatically since the first electronic computer, Colossus, which, aided by technological information on computing from refugee eastern European scientists, the British used in 1943 to decode Nazi military and diplomatic messages. Awesome in its day, Colossus was primitive by later standards—gigantic, slow, able only to decode, and noisy. With growing use in civilian industry and business after the war, computing machines shrank from the size of a gymnasium in the 1940s to that of an attaché case in the mid-1980s. They also became far less expensive and fantastically more powerful, thanks to the development of sophisticated digital electronic circuitry implanted on tiny silicon chips, which replaced the clumsy radio tubes used in the 1940s and 1950s. Within a few decades the computer could perform hundreds of millions of operations per second, and the price of the integrated circuit at the heart of computer technology would fall to less than a dollar, allowing businesses and households access to computers at a reasonable cost.

Computers changed the pace and patterns of work not only by speeding up and easing tasks but also by performing many operations that workers had once done themselves. In garment making, for example, experienced workers no longer painstakingly figured out how to arrange patterns on cloth for maximum efficiency and economy. Instead a computer figured out the optimal positioning of pattern pieces, and trained operators simply followed the machine's directions as it both placed and ordered the mechanical cutting of the fabric. Women experts in placement and skilled male cutters of fabric lost out. By the end of the 1970s, the miniaturization of the computer had made possible a renewal of the eighteenth-century-style "cottage industry." As in earlier times, people could work in the physical isolation of their homes, but they were connected to a central mainframe. The French Minitel, an online service available through telephone lines, was developed in

1981. It first made Internet-style communication available to the general public and opened the way to still faster and more abundant interaction in both work and leisure.

Did computers transform society for the better? Whereas the Industrial Revolution had seen physical power replaced by machine capabilities, the information revolution witnessed brainpower augmented by computer technology. Many believed computers would profoundly expand mental life, providing, in the words of one scientist, "boundless opportunities . . . to resolve the puzzles of cosmology, of life, and of the society of man."[4] Others maintained that computers programmed people, reducing human capacity for inventiveness, problem solving, and initiative. Such predictions had not been fully tested even as the information revolution moved toward a more dramatic unfolding in the 1980s and 1990s.

The Space Age

When the Soviets launched the satellite *Sputnik* in 1957, they ignited competition with the United States that was quickly labeled the "space race." After the founding of the National Aeronautics and Space Administration (NASA) in 1958, President John F. Kennedy became determined to beat the Soviets into space by putting a man on the moon by the end of the 1960s. The French founded their center for space research in 1962, and the European Space Research Organization (ESRO) went into operation in 1964. Throughout the decade, increasingly complex space flights tested humans' ability to survive the rigors of space exploration, including weightlessness. Astronauts walked in space, endured weeks (and, later, months) in orbit, docked with other craft, fixed satellites, and carried out experiments for the military and private industry. Meanwhile a series of unmanned rockets filled the earth's gravitational sphere with weather, television, intelligence, and other communications satellites. In July 1969, a worldwide television audience watched as U.S. astronauts walked on the moon's surface—the climactic moment in the space race. As Neil Armstrong stepped out of Apollo II's lunar module, he remarked, "That's one small step for man, one giant leap for mankind."

The space race also drove Western cultural developments. U.S. astronauts and Soviet cosmonauts were perhaps the era's most admired heroes: Soviets Yuri Gagarin and Valentina Tereshkova—the first woman in space—and American John Glenn topped the list. A whole new fantasy world developed. Children's toys and games revolved increasingly around space. Films such as *2001: A Space Odyssey* (1968) portrayed space explorers answering questions about life that were formerly the domain of church leaders. Likewise, in the internationally popular television series *Star Trek*, members of the starship *Enterprise*'s diverse crew wrestled with the problems of maintaining humane values against less-developed, often menacing civilizations. In the Eastern bloc, Polish author Stanislaw Lem's novel *Solaris* (1961) similarly portrayed space-age individuals engaged in personal quests and likewise drew readers and, in 1972, moviegoers into a futuristic fantasy.

The space age grew out of cold war concerns, but it also offered the possibility of more global political cooperation: the diffusion of rocket technology, for

◆ **Hungarians Watching Television**
In this photo from March 1975, a group of pedestrians gathers in front of an
electronics shop window to watch a television broadcast by the Hungarian Socialist
Workers Party. Do you think they are more interested in the broadcast or what it is
being shown? Why? *Hadas/Keystone/Getty.*

example, resulted from international efforts. Many European countries cooperated
as part of the European Space Agency, which evolved from ESRO and came to include scientists and astronauts from fifteen nations. From the 1960s on, U.S. space-
flights often involved the participation of other countries such as Great Britain
and the Netherlands. Thanks to international cooperation, Telstar was launched
in 1962, Intelsat I in 1965. A consortium of nineteen countries first ran these

communications satellites, led by the United States, France, Great Britain, and Germany. By the 1970s more than four hundred stations worldwide and some 150 countries were working together to maintain global satellite communications. Transmitting signals for both telephone and television, the communications satellites opened the door to improved access for citizens of every nation. Joint ventures also allowed unmanned spacecraft to land on Mars, and in 2005 the Huygens probe developed by the European Space Agency explored the surface of Titan, Saturn's largest moon—a cooperative undertaking of three space agencies and seventeen nations.

Revolutions in Biology, Reproductive Technologies, and Sexual Behavior

Sophisticated technologies extended to the life sciences, bringing dramatic new health benefits and ultimately changing reproduction itself. In 1952, scientists Francis Crick, an Englishman, and James Watson, an American working in a British lab, discovered the configuration of DNA, the material in a cell's chromosomes that carries hereditary information. Apparently solving the mystery of the gene and thus of biological inheritance, they showed how the "double helix" of the DNA molecule splits in cellular reproduction to form the basis of each new cell. This genetic material, biologists concluded, provides a chemical pattern for an individual organism's life. Beginning in the 1960s, genetics and the new field of molecular biology progressed rapidly, advancing knowledge of viruses and bacteria. As a result, dangerous diseases such as polio, tetanus, syphilis, and tuberculosis were effectively cured or controlled in the West.

This biological revolution raised questions about the ethics of tampering with the natural processes of life. For example, understanding how DNA works allowed scientists to bypass natural animal reproduction by a process called *cloning*—obtaining the cells of an organism and dividing or reproducing them (in an exact copy) in a laboratory. In 1967, Dr. Christiaan Barnard of South Africa performed the first successful heart transplant, and U.S. doctors later developed an artificial heart. These medical miracles, however, prompted questions about the criteria doctors should use in selecting recipients of scarce reusable organs. Commentators also debated whether the enormous cost of new medical technology to save a few people would be better spent on helping the many who lacked basic health care.

Technology also influenced the most intimate areas of human relations—sexuality and procreation. In traditional societies, community and family norms dictated marital arrangements and sexual practices, in large part because too many or too few children threatened the crucial balance between population size and agricultural productivity. As Western societies industrialized and urbanized, however, not only did these considerations become less urgent but the growing availability of reliable birth-control devices permitted young people to begin sexual relations earlier, with less risk of pregnancy. In the 1960s these trends accelerated, as the birth-control pill came on the Western market. By 1970, its use was spreading around the world, though some European women reported being humiliated by disapproving pharmacists. The pharmacist "boomed the directions for use of the contraceptive pills I had gone to collect right across his dispensary, so that the entire village might know what to think of me," one woman remembered of her first purchase of "the pill" in the 1960s.[5] Doctors also developed an intrauterine device for preventing contraception.

In eastern and central Europe abortion was the most common form of birth control in the postwar period. The number of legal abortions peaked in the late 1960s when there were 130 abortions per 100 live births. But as oral contraceptives, the IUD, and voluntary surgical sterilization became more widely available in the 1970s, the number of abortions fell. In eastern Europe people obtained contraceptives without a prescription, helping the number of abortions to fall to a historic low at the beginning of the 1980s. New techniques brought abortion, traditionally performed by amateurs, into the hands of medical professionals, making it a safe procedure for the first time. Only later, after campaigns by women in western Europe, did abortion become legal there.

Childbirth and conception itself were medicalized beyond the move to hospital rather than home births. Obstetricians now performed much of the work midwives had once done. As pregnancy and birth became a medical process, innovative new procedures and equipment made it possible to monitor women and fetuses throughout pregnancy, labor, and delivery. The number of medical interventions rose: cesarean births increased 400 percent in the United States in the 1960s and 1970s, and the number of prenatal visits per patient in Czechoslovakia, for example, rose 300 percent between 1957 and 1976. Europe pioneered another new process when, in 1978, the first "test-tube baby," Louise Brown, was born to an English couple. She had been conceived when her mother's eggs were fertilized with her father's sperm in a laboratory dish and then implanted in her mother's uterus—a complex process called *in vitro fertilization*. If a woman could not carry a child to term, the laboratory-fertilized embryo could be implanted in the uterus of a surrogate, or substitute, mother. After the birth of Brown, more than a million babies (including her younger sister) were conceived in this way. These procedures allowed childless spouses, single individuals, and homosexual couples to become parents of children who had a biological link to them.

All these procedures stirred controversy. The Catholic Church firmly opposed abortion and mechanical or chemical means of contraception. Vatican II charged that "married love is too often profaned by . . . the worship of pleasure and illicit practices against human generation."[6] Thus, as rapid technological and social changes were occurring, Pope Paul VI reiterated the ban on artificial birth control in the 1968 encyclical *Humanae Vitae*. Other conservative Christians and even some ardent postwar nationalists shared the Vatican's belief that women using birth control were evading their biblically mandated duty to reproduce and endure pain in childbirth and that nonreproductive and nonheterosexual sexual activity was sinful. Socialists and communists often joined devout Christians in opposing birth control during these years, seeing in it a program to limit the size of the poor and working classes.

POSTINDUSTRIAL ECONOMY AND SOCIETY

Reshaped by soaring investments in science and the spread of technology, Europe in the 1960s progressed on what social scientists labeled a postindustrial course that would change the day-to-day lives and material conditions of millions of working people and their families. Instead of being centered on manufacturing and heavy industry, postindustrial society involved the distribution of such services as health care and education. Tourism was also a growing service field in Europe, where four of the world's five top tourist destinations lay (France, Britain, Spain, and Italy).° The service sector was the leading force in the economy, and this meant that intellectual work, not industrial or manufacturing work, had become primary. The number employed in agriculture declined even more dramatically than manufacturing workers, though western Europe remained fully self-sufficient in food. Moreover, all parts of society and industry interlocked, forming a system constantly in need of complex analysis. Thus, unlike the preindustrial age dominated by agrarian landlords or the industrial age dominated by manufacturers, postindustrial society brought to the fore highly educated professionals such as analysts and engineers who could calculate needs, gather information, and make predictions for sectors of the economy. These characteristics of postindustrial society would carry over into the twenty-first century.

Multinational Corporations

A major innovation in the postindustrial era was the rise of multinational corporations. These multinationals in turn led the way in business innovation and the transfer of technology around the world, producing for a global market and conducting business worldwide. Unlike older kinds of international firms with limited business outposts, they established many of their major factories in countries abroad. The Swiss multinational Nestlé had begun as a small company selling infant formula locally and then in Europe more generally. Before World War I it had established an office in Japan, and by World War II it had branched out into chocolate and instant coffee, setting up factories globally but especially in Latin America. By 2000, Nestlé had over five hundred factories on five continents employing a quarter of a million workers who manufactured some three thousand products. Of the 500 largest businesses in the United States in 1970, more than 100 did over a quarter of their business abroad. IBM operated in more than one hundred countries. Although U.S.-based corporations initially led the way, European and Japanese multinationals like Volkswagen, Shell, and Sony also had a broad global scope. By 1973, Britain, West Germany, France, the Netherlands, and Switzerland had some 49 percent of the world's total multinational corporations. By 1997, 44 of the world's 100 largest firms were controlled by countries of the European

° By the twenty-first century, the top tourist destinations were France, Spain, the United States, Italy, and China, in that order.

◆ **Philips Electronics in Africa**
Multinational corporations thrived from the 1960s on, among them the Dutch firm of
Philips Electronics, which had plants in Africa and around the world in the 1960s.
Multinational corporations globalized the workforce by moving some of their manufacturing operations beyond the company's home base. By the late twentieth century,
multinational corporations were moving many service jobs to locations around the world
where wages and the costs of doing business were lower. The improved job opportunities
for people outside the West made the rest of the world more active consumers of European
goods. *Hulton Archive/Getty Images.*

Union (the former Common Market) and Switzerland, and 30 were controlled by
the United States.

The revenues of some multinational corporations exceeded the revenues of
entire nations. Indeed, many multinationals appeared to burst the bounds of the
nation-state, setting up shop in whatever part of the world offered cheap labor.
Their interests differed starkly from those of ordinary people with a local or national outlook. In the first years after World War II, multinationals preferred
European employees, who constituted a highly educated labor pool, had a strong
consumer tradition, eagerly sought secure work, and would accept low wages.
Then, beginning in the 1960s, as labor costs or taxes and regulations increased at

home, multinationals gradually moved more of their operations to the emerging economies of formerly colonized states. Although multinational corporations provided jobs in developing areas, profits usually enriched foreign stockholders. Some thus saw multinationalism as a form of economic imperialism, one that perpetuated colonial relationships between Europe and its former colonies.

European firms were leaders in staying competitive by expanding, forming mergers, or becoming business partners with the government. In France, for example, Saint-Gobain, a massive glass conglomerate, merged with a metallurgical company to form a new group specializing in all phases of construction—a wise move given the postwar building boom. Governments encouraged the concentration of production in larger and larger firms. The aim, as a French plan outlined in 1964, was to create businesses of an "international size built on the commercial and financial concentration of business." Germany, Great Britain, and France in particular aimed to generate ever larger firms. In France, the number of mergers rose from an average of 59 a year between 1959 and 1965 to an average of 103 a year between 1966 and 1974. In Great Britain, the value of mergers increased from £1507 million between 1950 and 1959 to £4906 million between 1960 and 1969. In the Common Market the largest 50 firms produced 35 percent of the gross domestic product of member countries in 1960 and 46 percent in 1970.

European firms increased their investment in research and used international and governmental cooperation to produce major new products from clothes dryers and microwave ovens to nuclear reactors. This emphasis on research was a crucial ingredient in postindustrial society. Ventures such as the British-French Concorde, a supersonic passenger airliner that from 1976 to 2003 crossed the Atlantic from London to New York in under four hours, and the formation in 1970–1971 of Airbus Industries, a consortium of French, German, and Spanish aerospace firms, attested to the strong relationship among government, business, and science. The relationship allowed for successful competition with U.S.-based multinational giants such as Boeing. Within ten years, for example, Airbus became a major player in the aircraft market. Whereas U.S. production had surpassed the combined output of West Germany, Great Britain, France, Italy, and Japan in the immediate postwar years, by the mid-1970s the situation was reversed.

The firms with the largest reach faced the temptation to cut back their investment in research and development and instead introduce their already established products into new international markets. In addition, the availability of cheap labor lured some European businesses into remaining labor-intensive rather than becoming more mechanized and efficient. The outcome of innovation and research, however, was not always positive. A product had to be not only cutting-edge but also interesting and useful to consumers. An example of a technologically advanced product that failed to catch on is provided by a French automobile, the Citroën. Despite its comfortable suspension, which cushioned a ride beyond the capability of any other car, the Citroën's innovative engineering did not capture the interest of the mass market. Disappointing sales indicated that the car maker's skills in product development and marketing lagged behind its technical expertise. At the opposite extreme, some firms substituted marketing for research. For example, the U.S. auto industry in the 1960s began to reduce its investment in research, concentrating mostly on flashy models such as the Corvette that might appeal to consumers and on blocking improvements in public transportation to keep demand for automobiles high. As a result, fuel-efficient European and Japanese automobiles began making inroads into the U.S. market, especially after the first oil crisis of the 1970s.

Innovation by the multinationals created real advances in public life and human amenities. Following the lead of the Japanese, who opened the Tokyo-Osaka high-speed "bullet" train line in 1964, the French began constructing a high-speed rail system in the 1970s, which eventually allowed for trains traveling some 200 miles per hour. By 1994 the UK and France were linked by trains running under the English Channel through a tunnel—known as the "Chunnel." The French also significantly improved their subway system, producing smoother, faster rides and eventually driverless lines throughout Paris. European multinationals were also leaders in developing drugs for diabetes and other conditions that significantly increased longevity in western and northern Europe.

The New Worker: The Rise of the Service Sector

Early industrial production depended on workers who labored to exhaustion, endured malnourishment, and lived in a state of poverty that sometimes led to violence. This scenario changed fundamentally in postwar Europe with the reduction of the blue-collar workforce, resource depletion in coal mines, the substitution of oil for coal and of plastics for steel, the growth of manufacturing overseas, and the automation of industrial processes. Within firms, the relationship of workers to bosses shifted, as employers started grouping workers into teams that set their own production quotas and organized and assigned tasks. At Volvo automobile factories in Sweden, and even in service departments, red and blue teams competed to see who could produce more or provide better service. As workers adopted attitudes and gained responsibilities that had once been managerial prerogatives, union membership declined and unions became fully integrated into the service economy.

In both U.S.-led and Soviet-bloc countries, a new working class consisting of white-collar service personnel emerged. Its rise undermined long-standing social distinctions based on what type of work a person did. Service workers and individuals with managerial responsibility were not necessarily better paid than blue-collar workers. The ranks of service workers swelled with researchers, health-care and medical workers, technicians, planners, and government functionaries. Employment in traditional parts of the service sector—banks, insurance companies, and other financial institutions—also surged because of the vast sums of money needed to finance technology, in research. The consumer economy provided additional service-sector jobs in restaurants, in personal health, fitness, and grooming, and in hotels and tourism. Managers at large hotel and restaurant chains such as Mövenpick and Club Med devised strategies both to standardize service and to make niche hotels for singles, families, and more staid seniors and couples. By 1969, the percentage of service-sector employees had passed that of manufacturing workers in several industrial countries — for example, 61.1 versus 33.7 percent in the United States, and 48.8 versus 41.1 percent in Sweden (Chart 10.1).

Postindustrial work life had some different ingredients in the Soviet bloc. Late in the 1960s, Communist leaders announced a program of "advanced socialism" — more social leveling, greater equality of salaries, and the nearly complete absence of private production. But this program did not really dent the privileges of the new class of upper-echelon bureaucrats or make their privileges less apparent to

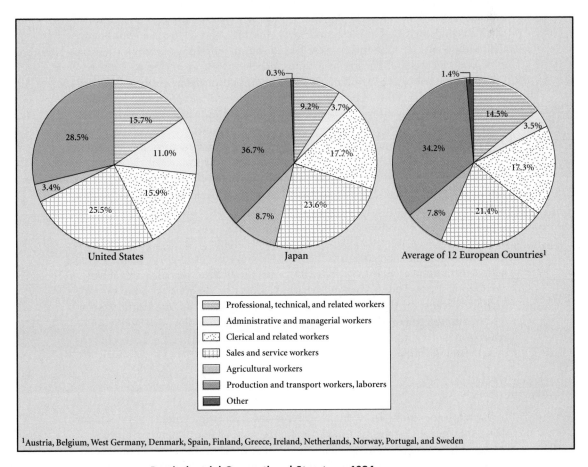

¹Austria, Belgium, West Germany, Denmark, Spain, Finland, Greece, Ireland, Netherlands, Norway, Portugal, and Sweden

◆ Chart 10.1 **Postindustrial Occupational Structure, 1984**
The most striking change in the composition of the workforce in the postwar period was the expansion of the service sector, which came to employ more than half of all workers. The percentage of population engaged in agriculture in advanced industrial countries continued its decline and by the 1980s had dropped well below 10 percent in Europe, the United States, and Japan.

the population at large. The percentage of farmers remained higher in the Soviet bloc than in western Europe. A huge difference between professional occupations such as doctors and jobs involving physical work remained as well in socialist countries. Less mobility existed between the two broad classes of work. Much as in the U.S.-led bloc, sexism also shaped the workforce into two groups. Men generally earned higher pay and held better jobs, and women generally were relegated to lower pay and inferior jobs. Somewhere between 80 and 95 percent of women worked in socialist countries, but they generally held the most menial and worst-paying jobs such as sanitation worker.

Across Europe, the coming of the postindustrial economy brought hard times to workers employed in "outmoded" jobs. Because of the expansion of oil and natural gas extraction, for example, coal mines in western Europe were routinely closed. Deindustrialized workers and their children, who in the past would have followed parents into the mines, were forced into the service economy—the parents going on welfare, finding part-time unskilled work, or trying to learn new skills, and the young ones training for work in offices, tourism, health care, or personal service. Behind these changes were the long arms of planners who helped direct investment away from outmoded and inefficient industries and toward new enterprises including training centers and technical schools.

The reach of the modern economy, spurred by government policy, extended into the remote countryside, increasing the presence of industrial development and bringing significant social and environmental change. Hard-pressed to rebuild and expand, the Soviet Union intensified geological exploration and economic penetration of the north Asian tundra, the source of the bulk of Soviet tin, tungsten, gold, nickel, and other resources. Loggers stripped the region's forests to feed the vast mills that produced paper and lumber. Holding on to traditional local livelihoods became increasingly difficult as the Soviet central government forced native northern peoples into supposedly more "productive" work as menial workers in domestic and other kinds of service. Reindeer herding, fishing, and hunting declined because of the oil rigs erected on hunting grounds, the decimation of forests, and the poisoning of fishing grounds by toxic dumping. Advancing modernization had a similarly destructive impact on many other northern and mountainous regions of Europe.

Women in the Postindustrial Economy

In Eastern-bloc countries women experienced full employment, although for many this meant low-paying, make-work jobs such as floor attendants in hotels, who simply sat and observed the hallways most of the time. In western Europe conditions varied. Job opportunities were greatest in the Scandinavian countries, especially Sweden and Denmark. They were scant in West Germany, Spain, Italy, and the Netherlands. Women who found work in these low-employment countries were hindered by the lack of child-care facilities and by laws that kept stores closed on weekends, during the lunch hour, and after five or six in the afternoon. The double job of working and caring for the family was almost impossible to fulfill (see Document 10.1). Most women in the Eastern bloc did all the housework, with few modern appliances; in Great Britain some three-quarters of those surveyed in 1980 indicated that they did too. Throughout Europe, women dominated the part-time workforce. For example, half of all women working in Great Britain did so on a part-time basis. Part-time work lowered wages, benefits, and opportunities to advance in a career.

As women's paid employment edged up in postindustrial society, reaching the top levels of management remained an elusive goal. A few women succeeded in doing so, however. "Even when we got managerial status," one top female executive at a major French bank reported, "we were really considered as high-level personal assistants. I officially obtained managerial status in 1956, but up until 1977 I was working as a personal assistant." As a survey of women in French banking showed, many women who reached the managerial level in these institutions often did not have personal lives similar to those of their male counterparts or those of women in lower positions in the bank. For instance, this manager was neither married nor had children. As another bank employee commented: "I don't think I would be able to aspire to the highest positions if I had a child. . . . I see successful high-level women with a child but . . . we are strongly advised not to take advantage of these possibilities (i.e., of maternity and further leave). Let's say that it wouldn't be looked on very favourably . . . it would be taken as proof of the lack of commitment of the individual to the bank." Even striving for managerial positions under a mandated equal opportunity policy women met with bias: "The senior director at the time, who interviewed me when I came up for the job, told me quite clearly that, as far as he's concerned a woman's place is in the home having children and house-keeping."[7]

Women's postindustrial work often had a large component of smoothing over the tensions brought about by rapid technological and social change calling for the same kind of wide-ranging skills that mothers and wives brought to caring for their families. Service jobs often involved direct contact with clients, who were sometimes in a bad or abusive mood, and women were given these jobs. Many thrived in these positions, which demanded self-discipline and solic-itude—both seen as "feminine characteristics." Some service jobs required considerable skill in "emotional management." Airline stewardesses, for example, were responsible for the safety of growing numbers of passengers squeezed into small spaces, simultaneously having to serve them food and drinks and to cater to an array of psychological needs. Flight attendants had to be pert, happy, and flirtatious, or firm and commanding when passengers were inquisitive, complaining, frightened, abusive, drunk, or violent. This was seen as a low-skill job meriting low pay, even though sociologists pointed to the complex skills needed to deal with difficult human situations at the core of the service sector. "Now don't think that it's easy," one Dutch stewardess maintained of her job. "Before you can do it well, you ought to have imagined yourself in the shoes of a lot of people and have analyzed an awful lot."[8]

Despite the fact that postindustrialization drew many to jobs in banks, hospitals, schools, and factory offices, some women continued to engage in highly traditional kinds of outwork from their homes. They stitched leather purses, decorated articles of apparel with beads, sequins, and other small items, painted pottery, and did other kinds of work by hand. Such work often demanded great skill, but these laborers received far less pay than unionized workers in factories. Both their isolation at home and their less valued female status kept their pay low, and lower still if they were immigrants. The benefits of outwork included being able to tend to household chores such as child care at the same time. Also, a woman working at home could enlist small children or underemployed males in these activities, improving the family economy still more.

Both urban and rural women performed outwork. Immigrant urban families undertook outwork as a stepping-stone to full integration into the new culture, first working through a "jobber" of their own national origin who found them the work and interacted with the boss. In rural areas outwork supplemented male income at a time when self-sufficiency on farms was disappearing because of the rapid modernization and consolidation of farming. For instance, in rural Spain under dictator Francisco Franco there was a demand for traditionally embroidered household linen and clothing worn on special occasions. Franco emphasized a domestic role for women, but most families could not survive without their income, especially in rural areas. Urban linen factories were thus able to contract out to women in the countryside the much sought after embroidery. Because this embroidery required great skill, some women were able to make a good though still supplementary living. Their underemployed male relatives contributed to the enterprise by laundering and ironing the finished linen. Although cooking a meal would have undermined male identity, the new circumstances shifted gender expectations and roles enough to make laundry and ironing acceptable male practices among Spanish families who engaged in this outwork. In fact fancy hand ironing came to be seen as requiring male skill and machine ironing as calling for male strength.[9]

The Boom in Research and Education

Education and research were key to running postindustrial society and the means by which nations maintained their economic and military might. In the West, common sense, hard work, and creativity had launched the earliest successes of the Industrial Revolution. By the late twentieth century, success in business or government demanded humanistic or technological expertise and growing staffs of researchers. As one French official put it, "the accumulation of knowledge, not of wealth, . . . makes the difference" in the quest for power. To accomplish this end, a system of new schools and research centers promoted large-scale science involving massive research teams. The Soviets built huge complexes for their scientists, offering such amenities as theaters and quality shopping. In the 1960s, the French government expanded towns and built entirely new cities—*technopoles*—intended to advance science and technology. It was hoped that the technopoles would lure graduates of the top schools to live in Grenoble and other regions distant from Paris. The French government made sure the technopoles contained amenities such as theaters, cinemas, museums, and other recreational facilities that members of the intellectual elite saw as central to their quality of life. Only in that way would the technopoles attract a "New Man with a taste for risk, proficiency, and the belief that anything is possible," as one government official put it.[10] The mystique of the isolated scientific genius endured, but it was diminished as large teams of scientists advanced knowledge in pivotal fields such as nuclear energy, space technology, the life sciences, and communications.

Investment in research was key to military and industrial leadership. The United States funneled more than 20 percent of its gross national product into research in the 1960s, in the process siphoning off many of Europe's leading intellectuals and technicians in a so-called brain drain. Complex systems—for example, nuclear power generation with its many components, from scientific conceptualization to plant construction to disposal of radioactive waste—required intricate professional oversight. Thus, scientists and bureaucrats frequently made more crucial decisions than did elected politicians in the realm of space programs, weapons development, and economic policy. Soviet-bloc nations proved less adept at linking their considerable achievements in science to actual applications because of bureaucratic red tape. In the 1960s, some 40 percent of Soviet-bloc scientific findings became obsolete before the government approved them for application to technology.

The new criteria for success—research and a well-educated workforce—fostered unprecedented growth in education, especially in universities, scientific institutes, and other postsecondary institutions. The number of university students in Sweden rose by about 580 percent and in West Germany by 250 percent between 1950 and 1969. In Italy the number doubled during the 1960s, and in 1967 French universities grew by 62,000 students. Great Britain established a new network of polytechnic universities around the country to encourage the technical research that elite universities like Oxford and Cambridge often scorned. France set up administrative schools for future high-level bureaucrats. Old universities such as the University of Paris added campuses, and entirely new universities appeared in Germany and the Soviet Union. Technical schools opened too, offering training in engineering, health care, hotel services, and eventually computer studies. By the late 1970s, the Soviet Union had built its scientific establishment so rapidly that the number of its advanced researchers in the natural sciences and engineering surpassed that of the United States. Meanwhile, even the oldest and most revered institutions of higher learning in western Europe added courses in business and management, information technology, and systems analysis. The University of Edinburgh added a business school in 1978; Oxford University added one in 1996.

In principle, education democratized the avenues to success by providing the knowledge necessary in postindustrial society to all students—whether rich or poor, male or female. Although this principle was true for many young people in the Soviet bloc, western European universities remained the preserve of white males from wealthy families. As the number of students rose in the 1960s and 1970s, women students became far more common, but generally in declining fields such as the humanities and at the low end of new fields such as health care. In the latter they were trained as technicians, social workers, and reproductive counselors. Instruction often remained rigid. Although eighteenth-century Europeans had pioneered educational reform, students in the 1960s reported depressing scenarios in which teachers discouraged independent thinking in the classroom, lecturing at students—even young children—who spoke in class only to echo the teacher or to recite homework memorized the night before. At the university level, as one angry student put it, the professor was "a petty, threatened god" who puffed himself up "on the passivity and dependence of students."[11] Such judgments would provoke young people to rebel late in the 1960s against the traditional authority not only of parents and bureaucratic officials but of teachers as well.

The Redefined Family

Just as education changed dramatically to meet the needs of postindustrial society, the contours of the family and the nature of parent-child relationships shifted from what they had been a century earlier. Family roles were transformed, and the relationship between parents and children—long thought to be natural and fixed—looked to some alarmingly different. Even though television and media commentators often delivered messages about what the family should be, technology, consumer goods, and a constant flow of guest laborers and migrants from the former colonies made for enormous variety among households. Single-parent families became more common as did families with stepchildren as a result of parents remarrying. Couples increasingly lived together before marriage or continued their cohabitation without ever tying the knot, and households of same-sex partners also became more common. At the end of the 1970s, the marriage rate had fallen 30 percent in the West from its 1960s level and divorce was on the rise. People were also having fewer children. After almost two decades of baby boom, the birthrate dropped significantly. The average Belgian woman, for example, bore 2.6 children in 1960 but only 1.8 by the end of the 1970s. Although the birthrate fell, the percentage of children born outside of marriage soared.

Daily life within European families was also different. Technology became more readily available as consumer items saturated domestic space. Radio and television filled a family's leisure time and often formed the basis of its common social life. Machines such as dishwashers, washing machines, and clothes dryers became more affordable and more widespread, reducing the time women had to devote to household work and raising standards of cleanliness. More women worked outside the home during these years to pay for the prolonged economic dependence of children, who entered the workforce later as mandatory schooling was extended to build postindustrial skills. Whereas the early modern family organized labor, taught craft skills, and monitored reproductive behavior, the modern family seemed to have a primarily psychological or postindustrial mission as parents and scores of counselors and social workers provided emotional nurture to the young.

Postindustrial society thus transformed teenagers' lives. A century earlier, teens had been full-time wage earners; now most were students, financially dependent on their parents into their twenties. Commentators noticed a growing "generation gap" based on sexual freedom and liberated forms of expression, and teens simultaneously gained new roles as a special cohort of consumers. Advertisers and industrialists saw the baby boomers as a multibillion-dollar market and wooed them with consumer items associated with rock music—records, portable radios, stereos. Replacing romantic ballads, rock music celebrated youthful rebellion against adult culture in biting and often explicitly sexual lyrics. Explicit sexuality in the music industry did not necessarily translate into sexual equality. Despite the popularity of a few individual women rockers, promoters focused on men, whom they depicted as surrounded by worshipful female "groupies." The new models for youth such as the Beatles and the Rolling Stones were themselves the products of advanced technology and savvy marketing for mass consumption.

AN AGE OF PROTEST AND REFORM

Even as rebellious youth were featured in films, on records, and on radio during this period, tens of thousands of real life students, racial minorities, women, antiwar protesters, environmentalists, and gays and lesbians raised their voices to demand that Western reality match the lofty postwar idealism. Small groups of activists, some of them steeped in existentialist philosophy, challenged consumer society and the injustices growing up around them; behind the scenes some homosexuals were lobbying for an end to discriminatory legislation (see Document 10.2.); women were organizing for better jobs and better pay. Simultaneously, revolutions and national liberation struggles—most notably in Vietnam—provided further inspiration for Japanese and European activists. The civil rights movement in the United States ignited huge and fiery protests in the streets, in universities, and in the halls of government, and news of these events helped fuel activism from Europe to Turkey, Egypt, Mexico, Japan, and India. In the Soviet bloc dissident movements demanded political democratization and social change, and in Czechoslovakia they nearly succeeded in sweeping away the Communist system. Activists vociferously and often violently condemned superpower domination and their own governments, and they contested the values of the new technological order.

Student Protest

Students and others in the European population felt the rush of reform and revolution sweeping the globe. Heroes of decolonization such as Mao Zedong of China, Che Guevara of Cuba, and Ho Chi Minh of Vietnam inspired students across Europe to conclude that they too should take a stand against imperialism—Soviet, U.S., and European. Europeans also watched the bold activism of the U.S. civil rights movement and the 1965 strike of Mexican American migrant workers in California for better working conditions and for an end to deportation, inferior schooling, and discrimination. They saw the way all these movements ultimately

◆ **Gay Activists in London**
Homosexuals suffered widespread and persistent abuse in Western societies, including legal discrimination and violent personal attacks. During a wave of reform in the 1960s, gays and lesbians increased their efforts to right the wrongs committed against them. In 1969 gays in New York fought back when police attacked them for frequenting Greenwich Village bars, and after the "Stonewall Riots" gays began holding regular parades in June to assert their solidarity and pride—not shame—in their sexuality. By the twenty-first century, citizens in cities across Europe were attending such parades in the tens of thousands. *Hulton Archive/Getty Images.*

resorted to violence, and some took up the call of Che to be guerrillas (see the Picture Essay)—in their case, "urban guerrillas." Inspired by Frantz Fanon and other third world writers (see Document 9.3), black activists transformed their struggle into a militant affirmation of racial differences. They urged blacks to push not for mere equality but for a celebration of their race under the banners "Black Is Beautiful" and "Black Power" by reclaiming rights instead of begging for them nonviolently.

European youth caught the fever of these global events. In the mid-1960s, university students in Rome occupied an administration building after right-wing opponents assassinated one of their number during a protest against the 200-to-1 student-teacher ratio. Polish high school and university students created Michnik Clubs, named for the outspoken dissident Adam Michnik, to study Western political theory, science, and economics but faced constant harassment by the secret police. In Prague in 1965, students held a carnival-like procession celebrating the American Beat poet Allen Ginsberg as their May King, and on May Day in 1966 they chanted, "The only good Communist is a dead one." In commemorating the tenth anniversary of the 1956 uprisings in the Eastern bloc, some Czech students were arrested and expelled from their universities. The Federation of [West] German Socialist Students (SDS), led by Rudi Dutschke, and the "situationists" in Strasbourg, France, called on students to wake up from the slumbering pace of student life and reform the world. Dutschke, who had left East Germany after his refusal to serve in the army prevented his attending university, emphasized practice in politics and an alliance of European students with anticolonial freedom fighters from emerging countries. Situationists believed that bureaucratic, mass society numbed people, and they watched for opportunities to create "situations"—emblazoning university walls with challenging slogans, for example—to jolt individuals to action.

Students attacked the traditional university curriculum as irrelevant to postindustrial society. On these grounds, they tried to exclude from the curriculum required humanities courses in the arts, philosophy, and literature, questioning how the study of Plato or Dante would help them after graduation. Students turned the defiant rebelliousness of 1950s youth culture into a political style by mocking education: "How to Train Stuffed Geese," French students called the way universities taught them. "No professors over forty" and "Don't trust anyone over thirty" were powerful slogans of the day. Students with long hair and blue jeans announced their rejection of middle-class values and their scorn for sexual chastity by bathing infrequently and living communally. With widespread use of the pill reducing the risk of pregnancy, some students made the sexual revolution explicit and public with open promiscuity and experimentation.

This youth counterculture was nourished with heavy doses of sex, rock and folk music, and drugs. Electronic rock music and mind-altering chemicals like LSD—produced by the very technology that youth culture scorned—induced new sensations, created a sense of personal creativity, and restored a belief in the individual experience. Businesses made billions of dollars selling blue jeans, dolls dressed as "hippies," natural foods, and drugs such as amphetamines and barbiturates to these young consumers. Certain leaders goaded the young with their disapproval: in West Germany influential publisher Axel Springer likened the activists to the young Nazis who had brought down Weimar democracy. Springer's readers responded with letters asking: "When will this communist pig Dutschke finally croak?" even though Dutschke had escaped the Soviet bloc and like other rebels agitated against both sides in the cold war.[12]

Feminism

Students were far from the only force for change: across western Europe and even into the Soviet bloc feminism erupted as a social and cultural force. In Germany young women students hurled tomatoes at the student leaders who refused to let them speak. In Italy they took to the streets, even seeming to dominate student demonstrations, and they were angry, not ladylike: "Tremble! Tremble! the witches have returned" ran one Italian slogan. These new feminists challenged both the

sexism of the universities and the masculine privilege of the student movement—
a movement that was supposed to be about society's inequities but that had as a
side effect the self-promotion of male leaders and the relegation of women to service jobs in the movement. They were the secretaries, the cleaners and cooks, and
the adoring sexual partners of men who fashioned themselves as political rock stars
or tough, virile he-men. "It was a guy's game," one woman activist reported.[13]
While to male activists it seemed natural that women would play a supportive, behind-the-scenes role in protest movements, many women soon rebelled against the
injustice and hypocrisy of their lowly status in movements urging reform for every
oppressed group but their own. Like blacks, they called for equality.

Women's groups split off from student and antiwar protesters, labeling the
sum of their efforts the "women's liberation movement." A number drifted away
from the Communist Party with the realization that communism had paid only lip
service to women's well-being. Many groups assumed a "collective" organization in
which consensus replaced hierarchy and individual leadership—both of them seen
as oppressive, male institutions. The movement attracted housewives and women
who worked outside the home. Their sense of injustice was different, comprising
issues of housework, child rearing, unequal pay, segmentation of the labor force,
and the "second shift"—that is, their responsibility for both household chores and
child-care duties after a full day's work.

The feminist movement that emerged in the 1960s and 1970s thus revived issues from the beginning of the century. These included societal expectations about
appropriate clothing and grooming, the problems of health and health care that
were ignored by professionals, the mystification of women's bodies, and the ignorance of bodily functioning that was supposed to be the mark of a "lady." Feminists
maintained that these issues were unique to women and—echoing Simone de
Beauvoir's *Second Sex* (see Document 7.2), which only gained in appeal—that they
constituted the ground of women's serving as the inferior "other" to men's norma-
tive and privileged role. In addition, almost every country had some variant of the
slogan "If men could get pregnant, abortion would be a sacrament" (see the Picture
Essay).

Like the students, many feminists looked beyond Europe for revolutionary
models. Many adopted a technique called consciousness-raising, which stemmed
from Maoist, collectivist practices called "speaking bitterness." Speaking bitterness
in the case of women's activism was meant to correct the traditional ladylike behavior in which women suffered abuse in silence, blaming themselves. Women
testified publicly to their feelings and their oppression even when doing so
was dangerous. In Portugal, for example, three women met weekly to rewrite the
Letters of a Portuguese Nun, a classic work of a young woman confined to a convent
by her parents on the heels of an unrequited love. In this work the "Three Marias,"
as the authors were known, used the convent to symbolize women's domestic,
religious, and legal confinement. So shocking was the depiction of the nuns'
eroticism that the Portuguese government banned the book and pressed legal
charges—unsuccessfully—against its authors. A still different form of dangerous
activism occurred in 1979 when, after the contract killing of a judge, women held

a mass rally in the Sicilian capital Palermo denouncing the Mafia as an example of the vicious effects of masculinity.

In the Soviet bloc, feminism was similarly full of risk. According to official Communist ideology, the triumph of the people in the Revolution of 1917 had automatically liberated Soviet women, and this liberation had spread across the Eastern bloc. The reality on the ground did not reflect this, and in 1969 a heavily censored novella, *A Week like Any Other* by Natalya Baranskaya, was an immediate sensation for its depiction of the harried life of a woman scientist. Forced to attend political meetings at work while attempting to do her job, rushing to tend her home and family with no help from her husband, and always worried about becoming pregnant, she wonders "what is a 'real Soviet woman' anyway?"

In the 1970s Tatyana Mamonova, following Baranskaya's lead, gathered writings from Russian women in all walks of life and packaged their testimony initially as a *samizdat* work—that is, one copied by hand and circulated among trusted friends and acquaintances. In the spirit of consciousness-raising, the authors reported on job inequity and the terribly difficult conditions of most women's lives. As one scientist reported of her communal apartment where families lived in a single room, "I see a father slowly and monotonously beating the children, punishing them repeatedly, and they don't even cry anymore."[14] Alcoholic neighbors, difficulties provisioning their families, abusive salesclerks, and crowded living conditions tore at the fabric of life, revealing that many aspects of Soviet equality were not afforded women—and many others for that matter. Mamonova was sent into exile, but women continued to agitate, some working within Russian Orthodox networks to block their sons from serving in the Soviet war in Afghanistan.

In western Europe, where public protest carried much less risk, women took to the streets in large groups to support reform in divorce, marriage, and anti–birth control legislation. In Catholic countries they launched two-pronged assaults to overcome both church and governmental prohibitions on abortion and restrictions on divorce. These mass demonstrations helped Simona Mafai shepherd an abortion bill through a recalcitrant Italian parliament in 1978, as Simone Veil had done in 1974 in France. But every sphere of public life felt women's presence. Artists and performers mounted all-women performances and exhibitions, justifying them by pointing to the privileging of male artists and intellectuals just because they were men.

The positive results of feminist activism were palpable, with Britain providing but one example. The number of women in British universities rose from 15,000 in 1965–1966 to 33,000 in 1981–1982. The British passed an equal pay act in 1970 to take effect in 1975; it provided not only that women receive equal pay for the same job but, by a 1983 amendment, that they could receive the same pay for a job of comparable worth. This stopped employers from circumventing equal pay by such practices as naming a woman's job as making "boxes" and a man's as making "cartons," thus permitting the employer to pay the woman lower wages. Women's pay in Britain rose from 54 percent of men's earnings in the 1950s and 1960s to 74 percent in the 1970s. With the decline in feminist activism, European women's pay dropped in the 1980s but then rose to 80 percent in the 1990s.

1968: Year of Crisis in Western and Eastern Europe

Student protest came to a head in 1968, propelled by grievances building in the university and by events on the other side of the world. In January, on the first day of Tet, the Vietnamese New Year, the Vietcong and the North Vietnamese attacked more than one hundred South Vietnamese towns and American bases, inflicting heavy casualties. The U.S. antiwar movement of students, clergy, and pacifists suddenly gained crucial momentum from a disillusioned public, while tens of thousands burst into violence over the assassination of civil rights leader Martin Luther King Jr. in April. They torched U.S. cities, bombed university buildings, and generally let loose an orgy of sorrow and rage.

At the same time, student protest was escalating in Italy, France, and other countries over the pitiful intellectual and physical conditions on university campuses and the general shape of life in prosperous, postwar Europe. Banners proclaiming "I want to be an orphan" were common in Italian universities, where students protested the stodgy and materialistic face of family life.[15] In January, students at Nanterre in the suburbs of Paris went on strike, invading administrative offices and demanding a say in university governance. They called themselves a "proletariat"—an exploited working class—and considered themselves part of a New Left. When students at the more prestigious Sorbonne in Paris showed solidarity with students of Nanterre in street demonstrations, the police arrested and assaulted hundreds of them. Some in the Parisian middle classes reacted with unexpected sympathy to the student uprising because of their own resentment of bureaucracy. They were also horrified at seeing the elite and brutal police force, the CRS, beating middle-class students and passersby who expressed their support (see the Picture Essay).

By May the violence had accelerated into outright revolt in many European cities. French students handed out advice for evading tear gas and fragmentation grenades used by the CRS:

VARIOUS PROTECTIVE MEASURES

Garbage can cover as a shield. . . . Lemon—wet a handkerchief with it, suck on it. Bicarbonate of soda around the eyes, in diluted form on a handkerchief. Goggles, motorcycle or ski, or a swimming mask.[16]

French workers joined in: some nine million went on strike, occupying factories and calling not only for higher wages but also for "la participation" in everyday decision making. Rebelling against unequal wages and work speedups caused by new technology, women workers staged a takeover of the Lip factory in France and the Ford factory in England. Prostitutes across Europe also protested their circumstances, while simultaneously asserting that they were not so different from married women in that their bodies were not necessarily their own. Italian students and workers also joined forces from 1967 on, as young workers from rural areas took the side of semiskilled workers to protest assembly-line speedups and then joined students in the streets—all of them protesting not only the high-tech status quo but also the stultifying control of Communist leaders on the shop floor.

The worst revolts—in Paris—were eventually put down. The normally decisive president Charles de Gaulle seemed paralyzed at first, but he soon took steps to undermine support for the students with a divide-and-conquer strategy. In June he announced a raise for workers, and businesses offered them a strengthened voice in decision making. Many citizens, tired of the street violence, the destruction of private property, and the breakdown of social services (for example, garbage was not collected for weeks), were ready to dissociate themselves from the student protesters. After skillfully using the media to solidify the separation of students from the wider population, de Gaulle sent tanks into Paris.

Meanwhile, in Czechoslovakia, a quieter movement against Soviet cold war domination had sprung up, but a wider range of people shaped its strategy and goals. The revolt began within the Czechoslovak Communist Party. In the autumn of 1967 at a party congress, Alexander Dubček (1921–1992), head of the Slovak branch of the party, called for more social and political openness. First Party Secretary Antonín Novotný, who had ruined the Czech economy, responded with ridicule: "We've had more than enough of democracy."[17] In a culture where, despite Communist rhetoric of worker solidarity and brotherhood, anti-Semitism and ethnic prejudice remained formidable political weapons, Novotný taunted Dubček as an inferior Slovak. Yet the call for reform struck a chord among frustrated party officials, technocrats, and intellectuals. Czechoslovaks began to dream of creating a new society—one based on "socialism with a human face." Novotný was ousted and replaced by Dubček in January 1968.

Dubček changed the Communist style of government, ending censorship, instituting the secret ballot for party elections, and allowing competing political groups to form. The public mood changed abruptly: "Look! Everyone's smiling today!" one little girl remarked as the new government took power.[18] The "Prague Spring" had begun—"an orgy of free expression," one Czech journalist called it (see the Picture Essay). People bought uncensored publications, packed uncensored theater productions, and engaged in almost nonstop political debate. They crammed into cafés and wine bars, creating overnight a public sphere of free political debate. "Nobody talks about football [soccer] . . . anymore," one taxi driver complained.[19] Meanwhile, Dubček 's new government faced the enormous problem of negotiating policies acceptable to entrenched party functionaries and to the USSR, which threatened to intervene if the liberalization continued. Radicals pressed for fundamental change, but those with a vested interest in the Communist system wanted more limited reform. Announcing new recognition of civil rights and the separation of the Communist Party from the government, Dubček warned that democracy demanded "a conscious civic discipline" and "statesmanlike wisdom of all citizens."[20]

Poland and East Germany were foremost among Warsaw Pact members fearful that such a "deviation" would spread, and on the night of August 20–21, 1968, Soviet tanks rolled into Prague in a massive show of force. Citizens resisted by painting graffiti on tanks and by removing street signs to confuse the invaders. Illegal radio stations broadcast accounts of Soviet brutality and warnings to people about to be arrested. Store owners refused to sell food or other commodities to Soviet troops.

Filled with despair, having watched as the Soviets gradually removed reformers from power, in January 1969, Jan Palach, a twenty-one-year-old philosophy student, drove to a main square in Prague, doused his body with gasoline, and set himself ablaze. In his coat—deliberately put to one side—was a paper demanding an end to Soviet-style repression in Czechoslovakia and promising more such suicides. The manifesto was signed: "Torch No. 1." Across a stunned nation black flags were flown, close to a million people flocked to Palach's funeral, and shrines to his memory sprang up overnight. For the next few months, as repression continued, more Czech youth followed Palach's grim example and became torches for freedom.

ATTACKING AND DEFENDING AN ERODING STATUS QUO

By the early 1970s, much student and other protest had evolved into ongoing re-form movements. Yet some groups, such as the Basque independence movement in Spain, the Catholic civil rights movement in Northern Ireland, and a variety of "Red Brigades," turned to violent action including terrorism and murder. It was in this climate that Aldo Moro was murdered. Distress was compounded by the eco-nomic uncertainty that replaced the buoyant postwar boom. Middle Eastern governments' assertion of control over their oil worsened the downturn. Neither superpower had leaders wholly competent to face these challenges and to offer the security and prosperity they had promised their allies in Europe. To calm the situ-ation at home, they undertook détente and lowered international tensions with a series of international agreements. As U.S. president Richard Nixon was forced to resign because of his tampering with free elections—the linchpin of democracy—and the United States continued its losing war in Vietnam, repression in the Soviet bloc increasingly alienated the citizenry there. Political, social, and economic in-stability confronted Europeans in the 1970s.

Oil Crisis and Stagflation

While the superpowers wrestled with internal political embarrassments and the intricacies of nuclear diplomacy, the European nations were developing new eco-nomic muscle. Since 1960, the six Common Market countries, led by West Germany, had surpassed the United States in percentage of gross world product. This achievement made the Common Market a countervailing economic power to the Soviet Union and the United States. Backed by big businesses, the West German chancellor Willy Brandt formalized agreements with the Soviet bloc for improved relationships—a policy known as *Ostpolitik*. The opening of eastern European markets helped bolster western European prosperity, so that by the end of the decade, western European exports to the Soviet bloc totaled some $45 bil-lion annually, producing a burden of debt that Communist countries could ill af-ford. In 1973, Britain joined the Common Market, followed by Ireland and Denmark. Common Market exports now amounted to almost three times U.S. exports.

In 1973–1974, the European economy, like the American economy, suddenly stalled. Although the Common Market maintained the lead, its economic ascent was slowing as early as the mid-1960s; by 1965, the rate of West German economic growth had fallen from a high of 9.4 percent between 1951 and 1955 to less than 5 percent—still a substantial rate. As the downturn caused rising unemployment in the early 1970s, politicians used pump-priming techniques to stimulate industrial investment and also put foreign "guest" laborers and married women out of work in favor of native-born men. But it was the entire global system that was coming unglued.

The United States, trying to pay for social programs, the space race, the cold war, and the war in Vietnam, was becoming a huge debtor nation. In 1971 the debt forced Nixon to announce the end of the convertibility of U.S. dollars to gold and to put a 10 percent tax on all imports into the United States. Awash in dollars, the Bretton Woods currency system, created during World War II to maintain stable international markets, collapsed. The international monetary crisis actually strengthened European integration as Common Market countries agreed to cooperate to prevent financial chaos. Economic clout allowed the Common Market to force the United States to relinquish its single-handed direction of Western economic strategy.

While the European economy grew closer together and moderated its growth, economic and geopolitical power spread not only beyond the United States but also beyond the West. Japan emerged from its postwar reconstruction to challenge western Europe and the United States as manufacturing and exporting giants. In the 1960s, its rate of growth accelerated from an annual average of 9 percent in the 1950s to more than 11 percent, thanks in part to heavy buying by the United States for the wars in Korea and Vietnam. Even without oil and other key natural resources, Japan had become the world's largest shipbuilder by the 1970s, and only the United States and the Soviet Union surpassed it in iron and steel production.

It was the Middle East's oil-producing nations, however, that dealt Western dominance a critical blow and threatened to topple the European economy altogether. Tensions between Israel and the Arab world provided the catalyst. Between June 5 and June 10, 1967, Israeli forces, responding to Palestinian guerrilla attacks, seized Gaza and the Sinai Peninsula from Egypt, the Golan Heights from Syria, and the West Bank from Jordan. Humiliation in this "Six-Day War" led the Arab states to try to forge a common political and economic strategy. This strategy ranged from the populist militancy of the defeated Egyptian leader Gamal Abdel Nasser to the more conservative and somewhat more pro-Western leadership in Saudi Arabia to the radical factions of the Palestine Liberation Organization (PLO), which used terrorism against Israel. In October 1973, Egypt and Syria attacked Israel on Yom Kippur, the most holy day in the Jewish calendar. Egypt initially made headway, but Israel, with material assistance from the United States, stopped the assault and counterattacked.

Having failed militarily against Israel and the United States, the Arab nations turned decisively to economic clout. Some members of the Organization of Petroleum Exporting Countries (OPEC) quadrupled the price of their oil and imposed an embargo, cutting off all exports of oil to the United States and its allies in retaliation for support of Israel. For the first time since imperialism's heyday, the *producers* of raw materials—not the industrial powers—controlled the flow of commodities and set prices to their own advantage. Europe was now mired in an oil crisis.

Throughout the 1970s, oil-dependent Europeans watched in astonishment as OPEC upset the balance of economic power. No longer dictated to by the Western powers, the oil-producing nations helped provoke an economic recession by restricting the flow of oil and raising prices. Unemployment surged by more than 50 percent in Europe and the United States. Economic policy makers found old economic theories ineffective. In the past, recessions had brought falling prices as goods went unsold, but this recession resulted in soaring inflation. By the end of 1973, the inflation rate was over 8 percent in West Germany, 12 percent in France, and 20 percent in Portugal. In 1974, it reached 13 percent in Britain and Italy and 8 percent in the United States. Eastern-bloc countries, dependent on Soviet oil, fared little better. Formally outside the Soviet bloc, Yugoslavia felt the effects, with 40 percent inflation by the end of the decade. Skyrocketing interest rates in the U.S.-led bloc discouraged both industrial investment and consumer buying. With prices, unemployment, and interest rates soaring—the unusual combination of economic conditions was dubbed *stagflation*—a sense of discouragement took hold with the realization that not only were energy resources finite but also economic prosperity had limits.

Troubled U.S. Leadership

As growth slowed, western Europe found its chief ally floundering too. Amid a host of international and domestic troubles, in November 1968, the conservative Richard Nixon (1913–1994) was elected president of the United States. Nixon claimed to have a "secret plan" to bring peace to Southeast Asia, but warfare continued to ravage Vietnam and to mount up debt in the United States. Campuses erupted in protest in the spring of 1970 when Nixon ordered an "incursion" into Cambodia. There were countermoves to stabilize these domestic upheavals partly by taming the cold war. Henry Kissinger, Nixon's secretary of state, decided to take advantage of the ongoing conflict between China and the USSR. In February 1972, Kissinger's efforts to bring the United States and the People's Republic of China closer resulted in Nixon's visiting the *other* Communist power, an act that undermined Soviet claims to supremacy. The mainland Chinese had their own domestic difficulties—not to mention difficulties with the USSR—and this state of affairs gradually led to Chinese pragmatists interested in technology, trade, and relations with the West replacing hard-line ideologues, and to further lessening of cold war tensions.

Putting his own house in order as the USSR worked its way through continuing resistance, Soviet leader Leonid Brezhnev made overtures to the U.S.-led bloc. In 1972, the superpowers signed the Strategic Arms Limitation Treaty (SALT I), which set a cap on the number of antimissile defenses each country could have. In 1975, in the Helsinki accords on human rights, the Western bloc officially acknowledged Soviet territorial gains in World War II in exchange for the Soviet bloc's guarantee of basic human rights. Détente—the policy of lessening global tensions between the two superpowers—lightened the load of fear that the nuclear rivalry of the superpowers had dealt ordinary people. Today historians claim that global leaders negotiated détente during the explosive years of decolonization and rebellion in order to lessen the issues around which youthful rebels could coalesce.

Nixon resigned in disgrace in 1974, leaving his successors to deal with the stagnating U.S. economy and the ongoing war in Vietnam, which finally ended with U.S. withdrawal in defeat in 1975. The Vietnam War cost the United States billions of dollars, more than fifty thousand lives, and its moral authority. Although often admiring democracy, many countries now viewed the United States not as a defender of liberty but as an oppressor of third world people. Its European allies faced the problem of adjusting to this situation as they strove to maintain their markets and to forge more independent diplomatic ties.

Repression and Dissent in the Soviet Bloc

The Soviet leadership tried conservative solutions to meet mounting criticism within the Soviet bloc. In November 1968, hard-liner Leonid Brezhnev announced what would be called the "Brezhnev Doctrine," maintaining that reform in Soviet satellites was not merely a domestic matter. "A common problem and concern of all socialist countries," moves toward change would meet repression similar to what had occurred in Czechoslovakia. As Brezhnev clamped down on critics, the Soviet dissident movement was at a low ebb. "The shock of our tanks crushing the Prague Spring . . . convinced us that the Soviet colossus was invincible," explained one pessimistic liberal.[21] Dissent persisted, however. In 1974, Brezhnev expelled Aleksandr Solzhenitsyn (b. 1918) from the USSR after the publication of the first volume of *The Gulag Archipelago* (1973–1978) in the West. Composed from myriad biographies, firsthand reports, and other sources of information about prison camp life— including his own experiences—Solzhenitsyn's account of the gulag (the Soviet system of internment and forced-labor camps) documented the brutal conditions Soviet prisoners endured under Stalin and his successors. The book appeared at a time when western European Ostpolitik was spreading dissatisfaction with the economy and the repression of free speech in the Eastern bloc. It further exposed people outside the Soviet bloc to the grim reality of the Communist system, draining, like repression of the Prague Spring, support among left-leaning Europeans.

The Kremlin persecuted many ordinary people who did not have Solzhenitsyn's international reputation along with additional luminaries. Soviet psychologists, complying with the government, certified the "mental illness" of people who did not play by the rules; thus some dissidents wound up as virtual prisoners in mental institutions. Andrei Sakharov (1921–1989), towering scientist and the first Russian to win the Nobel Peace Prize (1975), was not only smeared in a vicious campaign against his advocacy of human rights and world peace but after 1979 held in confinement and not allowed to talk with his children or grandchildren.

◆ Aleksandr Solzhenitsyn

The publication of the first volume of Aleksandr Solzhenitsyn's *The Gulag Archipelago* (1973–1978) in Paris in 1973 was a momentous event in European history. It documented the experiences of thousands of prisoners in the notorious camps of the gulag from firsthand reports that Solzhenitsyn had committed to memory and then recorded in his work. The publication so weakened the faith of Communist Party members elsewhere in Europe and so exposed the USSR's harsh treatment of its own citizens that Brezhnev's government expelled Solzhenitsyn in 1974. *Bettmann/CORBIS.*

The crudest Soviet persecutions, however, involved anti-Semitism. Jews were subject to educational restrictions (especially in university admissions), severe job discrimination, and constant assault on their religious practice. It was "not dramatic" persecution, as one Jewish writer put it, "but daily . . . always present." A commonplace accusation by Soviet officials was that Jews were "unreliable, they think only of emigrating. . . . [T]heir allegiance is elsewhere. It's madness to give them an education, because it's state money wasted."[22] As attacks intensified in the 1970s, Soviet Jews protested and sought to emigrate to Israel or the United States, but the Soviet government severely restricted emigration, often claiming that Jews who had finished their compulsory military service could not leave because they knew "state secrets."

The post-1968 period was bleak across the Soviet empire. People endured deprivation and repression, and even some of the most ardent supporters of the "socialist experiment" became disillusioned. In Poland and Czechoslovakia intellectuals felt utterly defeated after the arrest of so many of their numbers. The manipulation of wages and food prices entailed for all citizens "the permanent humiliation of their human dignity," playwright Václav Havel commented.[23] Many notable intellectuals were forced into exile or went voluntarily as the regime cracked down. Writer and former Communist Milan Kundera (b. 1929) left Czechoslovakia for Paris, where he published best sellers such as *The Book of Laughter and Forgetting* (1979) and *The Unbearable Lightness of Being* (1984). These books chronicled his own descent from enthusiasm for communism to despair, leavened by bitter humor. In Kundera's interpretation, the Soviet regime in Czechoslovakia depended on forgetting, from the bitter erasure of fallen leaders to individuals' papering over of grim reality in futile behavior such as sexual promiscuity.

Emigrating eastern European intellectuals strengthened western European culture and attitudes. Two Nobel Prize laureates in literature, Czeslaw Milosz (1911–2004) from Poland and Joseph Brodsky (1940–1996) from the Soviet Union, enriched the English language as they moved from their homelands to western Europe and then to the United States. Brodsky, exiled from the USSR just before Solzhenitsyn, maintained his bitter running critique of the Soviet regime in widely read essays. The political influence of the exiles matched their literary mastery. In France, for example, a group of "new philosophers" loudly demanded that leftists justify their commitment to Soviet communism in light of the brutal practices that Solzhenitsyn, Brodsky, and others revealed. Communist parties in the West broke their last remaining ties to the Soviet Union, but even after declaring an independent path, their success at the polls dwindled.

Despite ongoing repression throughout the 1970s, workers and intellectuals generated protest writing and formed activist groups. In an open letter to the Czechoslovak Communist Party leadership in 1975, playwright Václav Havel (b. 1936) accused Marxist-Leninist rule of making people materialistic, not socialist, and indifferent to civic life. The only viable conduct under Communist repression, Havel wrote, was either to disengage from public life or to work for the special privileges awarded to successful technocrats. In 1977, Havel, along with a secret group of fellow intellectuals and workers, signed Charter 77, a public protest against the Communist regime and its harassment of the rock music group The Plastic People of the Universe. The police imprisoned and tortured many of the charter's signatories, including Havel; philosopher Jan Patocka died after his "interrogation." But in Havel and other dissidents, repression could produce a kind of quiet resolve.

Charter 77 was an open statement proclaiming support for human rights, notably those articulated in the Helsinki accords of 1975. After the signing of Charter 77, issues of human rights became a rallying point for anti-Soviet resistance.

Protest differed from place to place but never died. In Poland strikes broke out in factories over demands for increased productivity despite the use of outmoded equipment and machinery that constantly broke down. When propaganda was broadcast over factory loudspeakers, Polish workers sang or whistled in chorus and women wrapped scarves around their heads. Schoolchildren caught the spirit and drew swastikas in protest, while teens sported fascist insignias as a sign of discontent — conveying their opinion that things had been far better under Nazism than under communism. As the inferior conditions of everyday life in East Germany became more apparent in the 1970s with satellite television and Ostpolitik, officials surveyed public opinion for signs of what needed to be changed. In a 1977 poll roughly one-third of East German adults surveyed said that their access to shopping was good. In a 1969 survey of young people only 40 percent believed that they received honest information from the media. Two-thirds said that they preferred media coming from outside the Soviet bloc. Never having known or visited any other place than the GDR and Poland, one woman claimed, she had thought the gray and crumbling buildings and the pollution a normal part of life around the world.

ALTERNATIVE POLITICS

In the 1970s, the unprecedented economic situation and the changing global balance of power inspired waves of activism — ranging from peaceful to violent. Feminists continued to lobby for causes connected with equality, and gay politics became more visible in the 1970s and thereafter. Several other political movements in these years also profoundly altered the social and political landscape: environmental parties and political groups seeking fundamental ethnic, religious, and political change.

Environmentalism and the Green Party

A sense of limits to global resources encouraged the formation of an environmental movement and later political parties committed to ecology. An escapee from Nazi Germany, E. F. "Fritz" Schumacher (1911–1977), produced one of the bibles of the environmental movement, *Small Is Beautiful: A Study of Economics As If People Mattered* (1973), a collection of essays spelling out how technology and industrialization threatened the earth and its inhabitants. In an essay titled "Buddhist Economics," he castigated modern economists who "assume[ed] all the time that a man who consumes more is 'better off' than a man who consumes less." Schumacher pointed to the Buddhist "middle way" — consuming only what was necessary for life — which he believed would allow people to "live without great pressure and strain and to fulfill the primary injunction of Buddhist teaching:

'Cease to do evil; try to do good.'" The result would be less bloodshed over resources.[24] Other environmentalists, many of them equally inspired by pantheist ideas coming from Asian philosophy, advocated the immediate rescue of rivers, forests, and the soil from the ravages of chemical farming and factories (see Document 10.3). Instead of massive agribusiness, which required huge doses of chemical fertilizers and produced single crops for the market, they pleaded for small-scale, diverse, organic (pesticide-free) farming. They demanded that factories be scaled back and made more environmentally responsible. These attitudes challenged almost two centuries of faith in industrial growth and in the limitless resources of the natural world.

Initially the environmental movement had its greatest political effect in West Germany. As student protest subsided in the 1970s, environmentalism united members of older and younger generations. Using a 1960s political tactic called citizen initiatives, groups of Germans organized against public transportation fare increases and plans for urban expansion, and they targeted nuclear power and nuclear installations. Demonstrations against nuclear power stations drew crowds in the tens of thousands, often armed with wirecutters to enter fenced-in areas. The tactic spread beyond Germany, and women in England stationed themselves at Greenham Common—an airbase said to house cruise missiles with nuclear warheads.

In 1979, West German environmental activists put issues such as nuclear waste, air pollution, and deforestation at the top of the political agenda when they founded the Green Party and then launched candidates for political office. The vote-getting power of the West German Greens encouraged the founding of Green parties in other countries, including the United States, forced mainstream politicians to voice their concern for the environment, and eventually led governments to establish ministries for the environment.

Not all European governments turned their attention toward the environment. In the Soviet bloc, commitment to industrial development blinded political leaders to environmental destruction and to the effects of pollution on people. As for ordinary people, they focused primarily on meeting basic needs and securing individual freedom.

Political, Ethnic, and Religious Violence

Some Europeans seeking reform and individual rights resorted to violence—sometimes out of principle, at other times out of desperation. Terrorist bands like the Red Brigades responded to the conservative political climate and worsening economic conditions with kidnappings, bank robberies, bombings, and assassinations. Disaffected and well-to-do youth, steeped in the most extreme theories of society's decay, often joined these groups. As one theorist, experienced with the Cuban revolution and with Che Guevara's tactics, wrote of the Europeans' task: "the principle stress must be laid on guerrilla warfare and not on the strengthening of existing parties or the creation of new parties."[25] They saw the violence of Mao's revolutionary youth and Che Guevara's peasant guerrillas as their model, and these tactics often became ends in themselves without clear programmatic goals. Eager to bring down the Social Democratic coalition that governed West Germany throughout the 1970s, the Baader-Meinhof gang assassinated prominent businessmen, judges, and other public officials. Italy's Red Brigades murdered public figures and randomly shot pedestrians. Murders and kidnapping grew in number in many countries. Joining the chorus against centralized governments and feeding the stirrings for ethnic rights, advocates of independence for the Basques in northern Spain turned to violence. They assassinated Spanish politicians and police and attacked tourist destinations, causing terror in the region for decades.

In Northern Ireland, nationalist and religious violence in the 1970s pitted Catholics against Protestants, who had dominated politics and the economy since the partition of Ireland in the 1920s (see Chapter 4). Catholics experienced job discrimination and a lack of civil rights. In 1969, Catholic student protest turned into demonstrations on behalf of union with the Irish Republic, as a twenty-two-year-old Catholic student activist, Bernadette Devlin, was elected to the House of Commons. Despite this modest electoral success, violence escalated in Northern

◆ **Conflict in Northern Ireland**
Long-standing grievances erupted into sustained violence in Northern Ireland in the 1970s.
The Catholic minority opposed the economic and political discrimination handed out
by the dominant Protestants. Members of the Irish Republican Army (IRA) had long
campaigned against the 1922 partition of Ireland, and in the 1970s, the IRA targeted British
soldiers, civilians, and the royal family. British soldiers, meanwhile, took prisoner suspected
IRA members and activists wanting to improve the situation of Catholics. Only late in the
1990s was there a serious move toward reconciliation and an end to violence in Northern
Ireland. *Brian Aris/Camera Press London.*

Ireland, and the British government sent in troops. On January 30, 1972 — "Bloody Sunday" — British troops fired on demonstrators and killed thirteen, setting off a cycle of bloodshed that left five hundred dead in that single year. Protestants fearful of losing their dominant position combated the reinvigorated Irish Republican Army. The IRA escalated the bombings and assassinations in the 1980s and 1990s toward the end of uniting the two Irelands and ending the oppression of Catholics.

Terrorists failed to overturn existing political structures even though murder and other violence dominated the political news. In Italy, Christian Democrats and Communists managed to govern together throughout the terrorist crisis. In West Germany, Chancellor Willy Brandt resigned in 1974 amid a spy scandal, economic downturn, and ongoing terrorism. But his successors continued his policies of rapprochement with East Germany and the Soviet Union. Sorely tried as it was, parliamentary government across western Europe did not merely hold steady; it scored important successes in the 1970s. Suffering under the dictatorship of Antonio Salazar since the 1930s, Portugal gradually regained its freedom as the military leadership recognized the devastation caused by Salazar's authoritarianism and negligence. After Salazar's stroke in 1968 and death in 1970, modernizers in the military worked to end Portugal's backwardness and ongoing, costly war to hold on to its colony Angola. In Spain, the death of Francisco Franco in 1975 ended more than three decades of dictatorial rule and brought rapid improvement. Franco's handpicked successor, King Juan Carlos (b. 1938), surprisingly steered his nation to Western-style constitutional monarchy, facing down threatened military coups. Investment in economic modernization picked up, as Spain became one of the fastest growing economies in all of Europe. In 1974, Greece also ousted a right-wing dictatorship and thus paved the way for its integration into western Europe and for substantial economic growth.

Simultaneously, political change emanating from outside Europe had consequences within. Late in the 1970s, students, clerics, shopkeepers, and unemployed men in Iran — a U.S. ally and client — began a religious agitation that forced the repressive Shah Mohammad Reza Pahlavi (1919–1980) into exile in January 1979. Brutally ruled by the U.S.-backed shah, Iran had enormous but unevenly distributed wealth and a large population of discontented, poor Shi'ite Muslims. The militants installed a fundamentalist Muslim leader, the ayatollah Ruhollah Khomeini (1900?–1989), who had been living in forced exile since 1964 because of his criticisms of the shah's government. From exile Khomeini had sent taped messages to his supporters in Iran and in this way had consolidated opposition to the shah. Khomeini called for a transformation of the region into a truly Islamic society awaiting the coming of the Mahdi, or Messiah. Iran, he believed, could lead this transformation if it renounced the Western ways advocated by the shah and followed the strict rule of Islam. On November 4, 1979, student supporters of Khomeini seized the U.S. embassy in Teheran and took sixty-three Americans hostage because the United States had allowed the shah to receive treatment for cancer in America. Some of the hostages were freed, but fifty-two were held for 444 days. The impotence of the United States in the face of Islamic militancy, soaring inflation, and further OPEC price hikes suggested the presence of new global forces. Those forces, along with homegrown terrorists, would deal deadly blows to Europe in the 1980s and ultimately throw Western nations into an unprecedented state of confusion and fear.

CONCLUSION

Protest in 1968 altered the style and direction of politics in Europe. It challenged superpower dominance on which the cold war was based. Whether demonstrating against war and repression or scribbling graffiti on public buildings, activists in Europe made all government open to question. But change did not necessarily occur in the way reformers hoped. Governments turned to conservative solutions in the 1980s, as disappointed activists considered more radical avenues—namely terror and violence. Despite protest, the advance of technology accelerated. From space and biotechnology to electronic gadgets for consumers, postindustrial, high-tech developments became increasingly influential.

From a certain vantage point, however, it looked as if drastic changes had occurred in the political landscape. The linchpin of the capitalist West—the United States—appeared to falter under the weight not only of protest but also of its own corruption, defeat in Vietnam, and Islamic militancy. The oil crisis all but paralyzed U.S. allies in western Europe, and the future turned frightening as terrorism made inroads into everyday life. By contrast, the USSR appeared strong, its supplies of oil ensuring its economic health and its defeat of protest in Czechoslovakia demonstrating its political will. The view from outside was deceptive, however, and the future would utterly reverse that picture, as strong leaders took power in western Europe and the United States and as, almost overnight, the Soviet bloc collapsed.

DOCUMENTS

The Postindustrial Worker and Family Life

How much did postindustrial conditions affect ordinary people? The following description of a typical workday of a woman in Hungary—an "architectural drafter"—gives us one set of clues. Wherever it took hold, postindustrial work in the service sector was cleaner and less physically demanding than blue-collar jobs in manufacturing. The phenomenon was so novel that researchers undertook studies to see how postindustrial organization affected life both inside and outside of work. Had life become easier in postindustrial society? researchers asked.

It was not only work life but household life that changed. The burst of consumerism in the 1950s gave some people mechanized help at home, but many in eastern Europe could not afford or obtain appliances such as washing machines. In addition, in the 1960s and 1970s women performed all household and child-care tasks. Even though society came to see women as important to the workforce in the same way that men were, social norms everywhere required women to continue to do all the housework and wait on their menfolk.

In eastern Europe, with very few conveniences and consumer goods and with nearly full female employment, women led especially busy lives, as the architectural draftsman's schedule reprinted here shows. In the West, feminists demanded that men share child care and domestic tasks with their wives. In contrast, magazines and other state propaganda in the Soviet bloc emphasized women's roles as both workers and household servants. Sociological studies of the use of time, like this one from the 1970s, indicate how tasks in everyday life affected a typical service worker on a daily basis.

Document 10.1

A Day in the Life of a White-Collar Worker in Budapest, 1970s

M.K.: architectural drafter, age twenty-seven. Education: Architectural College, Budapest (*Foiskola*). Married: husband is an architect. Two children: boy, age two, girl, age seven. The family has a nice two-room apartment and a Fiat. Both parents work in Budapest. The husband frequently works late at his job.

5:45 M.K. wakes up, turns off the alarm clock quietly so as not to disturb her husband. She goes to the bathroom, takes a quick shower.

6:00 M.K. wakes her husband and while he's shaving, she puts on the coffeepot and spreads two pieces of butter on his bread.

6:10 M.K. unmakes their two beds. (Bedding is always put away during the day in Hungarian apartments to convert beds to sofas for daytime use.)

6:15 M.K. wakes up the two children, bathes her son, supervises the dressing of the two children, and puts away their bedding.

6:55 M.K.'s husband leaves: officially he works from 7:30 to 4:30 five or six days a week.

7:00 M.K. prepares the children's breakfast, feeds them, eats a slice of bread herself, washes the dishes, makes a sandwich for her daughter, and at 7:45 sends her off to school.

7:50 M.K. presses her blouse, puts on her make-up, bundles up her son, and leaves the apartment.

8:00 The nursery is luckily only ten minutes away by bus. At 8:00 she is waiting for the crowded bus;

son in arms, she pushes her way up the steps (luckily again, an old man offers her a seat). At 8:15 M.K. drops her son off at the nursery and rushes on foot in another direction toward her office.

8:30 M.K. starts work.

12:15–12:45 Lunch. (During the day there are two coffee breaks.)

5:00 M.K. finishes work. Twice in the afternoon she called her daughter to make sure she got home all right and is doing her homework alone as she is supposed to.

5:15 M.K. picks up her son at the nursery.

5:20 M.K. shops at a big food store with son in one arm, handbag and food basket on the other. She buys a few items for dinner (2 liters of milk, butter, frozen meat patties, green beans, bread for breakfast, cooking oil, and orange juice for the children). She leaves the store at 5:55. Meanwhile a defectively sealed plastic bag of milk has spilled on her coat and her son has dropped and broken open a box of chocolates. She pays for everything without a word. She's used to it.

6:20 M.K. arrives home with her son. Her husband telephoned that he'll be home by 7:30. It's a rare occasion when he finds both an unoccupied and a functioning phone.

6:30 After changing clothes, straightening out the mess her daughter has made in her absence while fixing a snack, M.K. begins to fix supper. The milk is boiled, the beans are thawed, onions chopped, and table set. Dinner is ready at 7:20.

7:25 M.K.'s husband arrives home dead-tired. He gulps down a shot of brandy, and they sit down to supper.

SOURCE: Iván Völgyes and Nancy Völgyes, *The Liberated Female: Life, Work, and Sex in Socialist Hungary* (Boulder: Westview Press, 1977), 161–163.

7:50 After supper, the two children and their father watch the nightly *Bedtime Story* program on TV. M.K. opens her second pack of cigarettes.

8:00 Table-clearing, dishwashing, floor-mopping.

8:30 M.K. starts the children's bathing routine.

9:00 M.K. reads the children their bedtime story, making sure that the door to the other room is carefully closed so as not to disturb her husband who is studying for a language exam that will mean a 15 percent increase in salary.

9:15 Lights out for the children.

9:20 M.K. begins to wash by hand clothes to wear the next day. Clothes are washed and hung up by 10:05.

10:10 M.K. begins to iron her husband's shirts and her own clothes for the next few days.

11:00 M.K. makes up their beds and goes to the bathroom to get ready for bed. She also does her nails.

11:20 M.K.'s husband goes to bed.

11:40 M.K. collapses in bed, sets the alarm clock, smokes her last cigarette, and tries to mumble a few coherent sentences to her husband before dropping off to sleep.

2:00 M.K.'s son throws up. Pajama, bed-linen change. Tucks him back in bed.

3:08 M.K. falls asleep the second time. Getting-up time is two hours and thirty-seven minutes away. . . .

QUESTIONS FOR ANALYSIS

1. Which aspects of M.K.'s life appear postindustrial, and which appear to be traditional?

2. What consumer items does M.K. use in her household work?

3. Whose career seems more important in the family? Why is this so? Does the gender division of labor in this family fit with socialist theories?

Gay Liberation

IN THE TWENTIETH CENTURY, homosexuals across Europe continued developing rituals and a subculture of their own. The wealthy elite formed literary circles and clubs. Working-class homosexuals frequented their own cafés, boarding-houses, and clubs and lived together in working-class neighborhoods. During these years, homosexuals were pursued by police and still stigmatized and even arrested for breaking society's moral codes. The work of scientists and theorists such as Havelock Ellis and Sigmund Freud had some effect in "normalizing" the activities of homosexuals but wrought little change in public attitudes. By the 1930s Hitler was actively pursuing homosexuals, rounding them up, and confining them in concentration camps. During the cold war, capitalist countries in particular hunted down homosexuals out of the belief that they were likely to be Communist spies, and they made laws excluding homosexuals from certain kinds of employment. Thus it long seemed prudent for homosexuals to be "invisible" in twentieth-century life, unless they were in private places such as homes or in secure ones such as clubs. They simultaneously worked to gain political allies in the 1950s and 1960s to help overturn some of the most oppressive legislation.

The visible politics of the 1960s changed all that, and homosexuals decided to make their cause public. As they put it, the 1970s was a time when many came "out of the closet" and into public view, proud and sparring against those who opposed their civil rights. The 1969 Stonewall riots in New York were a prime inspiration for this public activism, as gays across Europe decided that it was time to take a stand. Like many other minority groups, gays continued to work for the same rights and opportunities as other people, but they added a measure of affirmation of their identity. They also expressed the range of gay identities in mocking, exuberant, and circuslike performances, most notably in "Gay Pride" parades.

In addition to parades, demonstrations, and active public resistance, gay people organized strong gay rights associations, issuing sober proclamations of their rights and analyses of the discrimination they faced in all aspects of their lives. Gays increased their activism to gain political representation as well as to improve the lives of individuals such as teens and gays in the workforce. In 1971 the Gay Liberation Front of London—notice the third-world term *liberation front* used by activists in decolonizing nations—issued a widely distributed public manifesto on the situation of gays.

Document 10.2

GAY LIBERATION FRONT
Manifesto, 1971, revised 1979

INTRODUCTION

Throughout recorded history, oppressed groups have organised to claim their rights and obtain their needs. Homosexuals, who have been oppressed by physical violence and by ideological and psychological attacks at every level of social interaction, are at last becoming angry.

To you, our gay sisters and brothers, we say that you are oppressed; we intend to show you examples of the hatred and fear with which straight society relegates us to the position and treatment of sub-humans, and to explain their basis. We will show you how we can use our righteous anger to uproot the present oppressive system with its decaying and constricting ideology, and how we, together with other oppressed groups, can start to form a new order, and a liberated lifestyle, from the alternatives which we offer.

HOW WE ARE OPPRESSED
Family

The oppression of gay people starts in the most basic unit of society, the family, consisting of the man in charge, a slave as his wife, and their children on whom they force themselves as the ideal models. The very form of the family works against homosexuality.

At some point nearly all gay people have found it difficult to cope with having the restricting images of man or woman pushed on them by their parents. It may have been from very early on, when the pressures to play with the "right" toys, and thus prove boyishness or girlishness, drove against the child's inclinations. But for all of us

this is certainly a problem by the time of adolescence, when we are expected to prove ourselves socially to our parents as members of the right sex (to bring home a boy/girl friend) and to start being a "real" (oppressive) young man or a "real" (oppressed) young woman. The tensions can be very destructive.

The fact that gay people notice they are different from other men and women in the family situation causes them to feel ashamed, guilty and like failures. How many of us have really dared be honest with our parents? How many of us have been thrown out of home? How many of us have been pressured into marriage, sent to psychiatrists, frightened into sexual inertia, ostracised, banned, emotionally destroyed—all by our parents?

School

Family experiences may differ widely, but in their education all children confront a common situation. Schools reflect the values of society in their formal academic curriculum, and reinforce them in their morality and discipline. Boys learn competitive ego-building sports, and have more opportunity in science, whereas girls are given emphasis on domestic subjects, needlework, etc. Again, we gays were all forced into a rigid sex role which we did not want or need. It is quite common to discipline children for behaving in any way like the opposite sex; degrading titles like "sissy" and "tomboy" are widely used.

In the content of education, homosexuality is generally ignored, even where we know it exists, as in history and literature. Even sex education, which has been considered a new liberal dynamic of secondary schooling, proves to be little more than an extension of Christian morality. Homosexuality is again either ignored or attacked with moralistic warnings and condemnations. The

SOURCE: Printed by the Russell Press Ltd., 45 Gamble Street, Nottingham NG7 4ET and revised 1979 and reprinted by Gay Liberation Information Service, 5 Caledonian Road. London N1.

adolescent recognising his or her homosexuality might feel totally alone in the world, or a pathologically sick wreck.

Church

Formal religious education is still part of everyone's schooling, and our whole legal structure is supposedly based on Christianity whose archaic and irrational teachings support the family and marriage as the only permitted condition for sex. Gay people have been attacked as abominable and sinful since the beginning of both Judaism and Christianity, and even if today the Church is playing down these strictures on homosexuality, its new ideology is that gay people are pathetic objects for sympathy.

The Media

The press, radio, television, and advertising are used as reinforcements against us, and make possible the control of people's thoughts on an unprecedented scale. Entering everyone's home, affecting everyone's life, the media controllers, all representatives of the rich, male-controlled world, can exaggerate or suppress whatever information suits them.

Under different circumstances, the media might not be the weapon of a small minority. The present controllers are therefore dedicated defenders of things as they stand. Accordingly, the images of people which they transmit in their pictures and words do not subvert, but support society's image of "normal" man and woman. It follows that we are characterised as scandalous, obscene perverts; as rampant, wild sex-monsters; as pathetic, doomed and compulsive degenerates; while the truth is blanketed under a conspiracy of silence.

Words

Anti-homosexual morality and ideology, at every level of society, manifest themselves in a special vocabulary for denigrating gay people. There is abuse like "pansy," "fairy," "lesbo" to hurl at men and women who can't or won't fit stereotyped preconceptions. There are words like "sick," "bent" and "neurotic" for destroying the credence of gay people. But there are no positive words. The ideological intent of our language makes it very clear that the generation of words and meanings is, at the moment, in the hands of the enemy. And that so many gay people pretend to be straight, and call each other "butch dykes" or "screaming queens" only makes that fact the more real.

The verbal attack on men and women who do not behave as they are supposed to reflects the ideology of masculine superiority. A man who behaves like a woman is seen as losing something, and a woman who behaves like a man is put down for threatening men's environment or their privileges.

Employment

If our upbringing so often produces guilt and shame, the experience of an adult gay person is oppressive in every aspect. In their work situation, gay people face the ordeal of spending up to fifty years of their lives confronted with the anti-homosexual hostility of their fellow employees.

A direct consequence of the fact that virtually all employers are highly privileged heterosexual men, is that there are some fields of work which are closed to gay people, and others which they feel some compulsion to enter. A result of this control for gay women is that they are perceived as a threat in the man's world. They have none of the sexual ties of dependence to men which make most women accept men as their "superiors." They are less likely to have the bind of children, and so there is nothing to stop them from showing that they are as capable as any man, and thus deflating the man's ego, and exposing the myth that only men can cope with important jobs.

We are excluded from many jobs in high places where being married is the respectable guarantee, but being homosexual apparently makes us unstable, unreliable security risks. Neither, for example, are we allowed the job of teaching children, because we are all reckoned to be compulsive, child molesting maniacs.

There are thousands of examples of people having lost their jobs due to it becoming known that they were gay, though employers usually contrive all manner of spurious reasons. . . .

The Law

The practice of the police in "enforcing" the law makes sure that cottagers° and cruisers will be zealously hunted, while queer-bashers may be apprehended, half-heartedly after the event.

Physical Violence

On 25 September 1969 a man walked onto Wimbledon Common. We know the common to be a popular cruising ground, and believe the man to have been one of our gay brothers. Whether or not this is the case, the man was set upon by a group of youths from a nearby housing estate, and literally battered to death with clubs and boots. Afterwards, a boy from the same estate said: "When you're hitting a queer, you don't think you're doing wrong. You think you're doing good. If you want money off a queer, you can get it off him—there's nothing to be scared of from the law, cause you know they won't go to the law" (*Sunday Times*, 7/21/1971).

Since that time, another man has been similarly murdered on Hampstead Heath. But murder is only the most extreme form of violence to which we are exposed, not having the effective rights of protection. Most frequently we are "rolled" for our money, or just beaten up: and this happens to butch-looking women in some districts.

Psychiatry

One way of oppressing people and preventing them getting too angry about it, is to convince them, and everyone else, that they are sick. There has hence arisen a body of psychiatric "theory" and "therapy" to deal with the "problems" and "treatment" of homosexuality.

Bearing in mind what we have so far described, it is quite understandable that gay people get depressed and paranoid; but it is also, of course, part of the scheme that gay people should retreat to psychiatrists in times of troubles.

Operating as they do on the basis of social convention and prejudice, NOT scientific truth, mainstream psychiatrists accept society's prevailing view that the male and female sex roles are "good" and "normal," and try to adjust people to them. If that fails, patients are told to "accept themselves" as "deviant." For the psychiatrist to state that homosexuality was perfectly valid and satisfying, and that the hang-up was society's inability to accept that fact, would result in the loss of a large proportion of his patients. . . .

WHY WE'RE OPPRESSED

Gay people are oppressed. As we've just shown, we face the prejudice, hostility, and violence of straight society, and the opportunities open to us in work and leisure are restricted, compared with those of straight people. Shouldn't we demand reforms that will give us tolerance and equality? Certainly we should—in a liberal-democratic society, legal equality and protection from attack are the very least we should ask for. They are our civil rights.

But gay liberation does not just mean reforms. It means a revolutionary change in our whole society. Is this really necessary? Isn't it hard enough for us to win reforms within the present society, and how will we engage the support of straight people if we get ourselves branded as revolutionaries?

Reforms may make things better for a while; changes in the law can make straight people a little less hostile, a little more tolerant—but reform cannot change the deep-down attitude of straight people that homosexuality is at best inferior to their own way of life, at worst a sickening perversion. It will take more than reforms to change attitude, because it is rooted in our society's basic institution—the Patriarchal Family.

We've all been brought up to believe family is the source of our happiness and

---

° *Cottagers:* People who go to public restrooms for sex.

But look at the family more closely. Within the small family unit, in which the dominant man and submissive woman bring up their children in their own image, all our attitudes towards sexuality are learned at a very early age. Almost before we can talk, certainly before we can think for ourselves, we are taught that there are certain attributes that are "feminine" and other that are "masculine," and that they are God-given and unchangeable. Beliefs learned so young are very hard to change; but in fact these are false beliefs. What we are taught about the differences between man and woman is propaganda, not truth.

The truth is that there are no proven systematic differences between male and female, apart from the obvious biological ones. Male and female genitals and reproductive systems are different, and so are certain other physical characteristics, but all differences of temperament, aptitudes and so on are the result of upbringing and social pressures. They are not inborn.

Human beings could be much more various than our constricted patterns of "masculine" and "feminine" permit—we should be free to develop with greater individuality. But as things are at present, there are only these two stereotyped roles into which everyone is supposed to fit, and most people—including gay people too—are apt to be alarmed when they hear these stereotypes or *gender roles* attacked, fearing that children "won't know how to grow up if they have no one to identify with," or that "everyone will be the same"; i.e., that there will be either utter chaos or total conformity. here would in fact be a greater variety of models more freedom for experimentation, but there reason to suppose this will lead to chaos.

our very existence as gay people, we chale roles. It can easily be seen that homo-'t fit into the stereotypes of masculine and this is one of the main reasons he the object of suspicion, since 't that these and only these two e.

ty is built around the patri- shrinement of these mas-

culine and feminine roles. Religion, popular morality art, literature and sport all reinforce these stereotypes. In other words, this society is a sexist society, in which one's biological sex determines almost all of what one does and how one does it; a situation in which men are privileged, and women are mere adjuncts of men and objects for their use, both sexually and otherwise.

Since all children are taught so young that boys should be aggressive and adventurous, girls passive and pliant, most children do tend to behave in these ways as they get older, and to believe that other people should do so too.

So sexism does not just oppose gay people, but all women as well. It is assumed that because women bear children they should and must rear them, and be simultaneously excluded from all other spheres of achievement. . . .

But why can't we just change the way in which children are brought up without attempting to transform the whole fabric of society?

Because sexism is not just an accident—it is an essential part of our present society, and cannot be changed without the whole society changing with it. In the first place, our society is dominated at every level by men, who have an interest in preserving the status quo; secondly, the present system of work and production depends on the existence of the patriarchal family. Conservative sociologists have pointed out that the small family unit of two parents and their children is essential in our contemporary advanced industrial family where work is minutely subdivided and highly regulated—in other words, for the majority very boring. A man would not work at the assembly line if he had no wife and family to support; he would not give himself fully to his work without the supportive and reassuring little group ready to follow him about and gear itself to his needs, to put up with his ill temper when he is frustrated or put down by the boss at work.

Were it not also for the captive wife, educated by advertising and everything she reads into believing that she needs ever more new goodies for the home, for her own beautification and for the children's well-being, our economic system could not function properly, depending as it does on people buying far more manufactured goods than they need. The housewife, obsessed with the ownership of as many material goods as possible, is the agent of this high level of spending. None of these goods will ever satisfy her, since there is always something better to be had, and the surplus of these pseudo "necessities" goes hand in hand with the absence of genuinely necessary goods and services, such as adequate housing and schools.

The ethic and ideology of our culture has been conveniently summed up by the enemy. Here is a quotation, intended quite seriously, from an American psychiatric primer. The author, Dr. Fred Brown, states:

> Our values in Western civilisation are founded upon the sancity of the family, the right to property, and the worthwhileness of "getting ahead." The family can be established only through heterosexual intercourse, and this gives the woman a high value. [Note the way in which woman is appraised as a form of property.] Property acquisition and worldly success are viewed as distinctly masculine aims. The individual who is outwardly masculine but appears to fall into the feminine class by reason . . . of his preference for other men denies these values of our civilisation. In denying them he belittles those goals which carry weight and much emotional colouring in our society and thereby earns the hostility of those to whom these values are of great importance.

We agree with his description of our society and its values—but we reach a different conclusion. We gay men and women *do* deny these values of our civilisation. We believe that the society Dr. Brown describes is an evil society. We believe that work in an advanced industrial society could be organised on more humane lines, with each job

more varied and more pleasurable, and that the way society is at present organised operates in the interests of a small ruling group of straight men who claim most of the status and money, and not in the interests of the people as a whole. We also believe that our economic resources could be used in a much more valuable and constructive way than they are at the moment—but that will not happen until the present pattern of male dominance in our society changes too.

That is why any reforms we might painfully exact from our rulers would only be fragile and vulnerable; that is why we, along with the women's movement, must fight for something more than reform. We must aim at the abolition of the family, so that the sexist, male supremacist system can no longer be nurtured there.

We Can Do It

Yet although this struggle will be hard, and our victories not easily won, we are not in fact being idealistic to aim at abolishing the family and the cultural distinctions between men and women. True, these have been with us throughout history, yet humanity is at last in a position where we can progress beyond this. . . .

The present gender-role system of "masculine" and "feminine" is based on the way that reproduction was originally organised. Men's freedom from the prolonged physical burden of bearing children gave them a privileged position which was then reinforced by an ideology of male superiority. But technology has now advanced to a stage at which the gender-role system is no longer necessary.

However, social evolution does not automatically take place with the steady advance of technology. The gender-role system and the family unit built around it will not disappear just because they have ceased to be necessary. The sexist culture gives straight men privileges which, like those of any privileged class, will not be surrendered without a struggle, so that all of us who are oppressed by this culture (women and gay people), must band together to fight it. The end of the sexist culture and of the family will benefit all women, and gay people. We must work together with women, since their oppression is our oppression, and by working together we can advance the day of our common liberation. . . .

Aims

The long-term goal of Gay Liberation, which inevitably brings us into conflict with the institutionalised sexism of this society, is to rid society of the gender-role system which is at the root of our oppression. This can only be achieved by eliminating the social pressures on men and women to conform to narrowly defined gender roles. It is particularly important that children and young people be encouraged to develop their own talents and interests and to express their own individuality rather than act out stereotyped parts alien to their nature.

As we cannot carry out this revolutionary change alone, and as the abolition of gender roles is also a necessary condition of women's liberation, we will work to form a strategic alliance with the women's liberation movement, aiming to develop our ideas and our practice in close interrelation. In order to build this alliance, the brothers in gay liberation will have to be prepared to sacrifice that degree of male chauvinism and male privilege that they still all possess.

To achieve our long-term goal will take many years, perhaps decades. But attitudes to the appropriate place of men and women in our society are changing rapidly, particularly the belief in the subordinate place for women. Modern conditions are placing increasing strain on the small nuclear family containing one adult male and one adult female with narrowly defined roles and bound together for life.

THE WAY FORWARD

Free Our Heads

The starting point of our liberation must be to rid ourselves of the oppression which lies in the head of every one of us. This means freeing our heads from self oppression and male chauvinism, and

no longer organising our lives according to the patterns with which we are indoctrinated by straight society. It means that we must *root out* the idea that homosexuality is bad, sick or immoral, and develop a gay *pride*. In order to survive, most of us have either knuckled under to pretend that no oppression exists, and the result of this has been further to distort our heads. Within gay liberation, a number of consciousness-raising groups have already developed, in which we try to understand our oppression and learn new ways of thinking and behaving. The aim is to step outside the experience permitted by straight society, and to learn to love and trust one another. This is the precondition for acting and struggling together.

By freeing our heads we get the confidence to come out publicly and proudly as gay people, and to win over our gay brothers and sisters to the ideas of gay liberation.

Campaign

Before we can create the new society of the future, we have to defend our interests as gay people here and now against all forms of oppression and victimisation. We have therefore drawn up the following list of immediate demands.

- that all discrimination against gay people, male and female, by the law, by employers, and by society at large, should end.
- that all people who feel attracted to a member of their own sex be taught that such feelings are perfectly valid.
- that sex education in schools stop being exclusively heterosexual.
- that psychiatrists stop treating homosexuality as though it were a sickness, thereby giving gay people senseless guilt complexes.
- that gay people be as legally free to contact other gay people, through newspaper ads, on the streets and by any other means they may want, as are heterosexuals, and that police harassment should cease right now.
- that employers should no longer be allowed to discriminate against anyone on account of their sexual preferences.

- that the age of consent for gay males be reduced to the same as for straight.
- that gay people be free to hold hands and kiss in public, as are heterosexuals.

Those who believe in gay liberation need to support actively their local gay group. With the rapid spread of the ideas of gay liberation, it is inevitable that many members of such groups have only partially come to terms with their homosexuality. The degree of self-oppression is often such that it is difficult to respect individuals in the group, and activists frequently feel tempted to despair. But if we are to succeed in transforming our society, we must persuade others of the merits of our ideas, and there is no way we can achieve this if we cannot even persuade those most affected by our oppression to join us in fighting for justice.

We do not intend to ask for anything. *We intend to stand firm and assert our basic rights.* If this involves violence, it will not be we who initiate this, but those who attempt to stand in our way to freedom.

QUESTIONS FOR ANALYSIS

1. What kind of discrimination seems most prominent in this manifesto?
2. What particular solutions does the manifesto emphasize?
3. How do the arguments and aims of this manifesto relate to those of the other activist movements of the late 1960s and early 1970s? How are they different?

The "Green" Analysis

T‌HE GERMAN GREEN PARTY ACTIVIST PETRA KELLY (1947–1992) had watched her young sister die from cancer, and the experience changed her life and her politics. In the 1970s the Greens attacked industrial practices and urban waste and pollution in order to improve both the natural and the lived environment. They wanted emissions controls, green areas in cities, and a certain number of carless streets in major urban areas. Recycling and the conservation of resources were important to them. Formerly a supporter of mainstream politician Willy Brandt, Kelly became an early Green Party leader. Taking on nuclear energy, chemicals in the environment, and the production of poison gasses, she quickly became a spokesperson for the green movement. Her heartfelt commitment came through because of the tragedy of her sister's death.

Many women were attracted to the ecology movement, arguing that their concern was life, while men's was industrial and military production, much of it causing destruction and death. Women argued that men had set priorities such as sending men to the moon instead of focusing on the good of society, especially the future of their own children. Caring for children and for all people's everyday needs, women, some people argued, were more in touch than men with the vital forces of the universe. By the end of the twentieth century there were also "deep ecologists," and these thinkers were different from environmentalists. Instead of protecting nature and righting the wrongs committed against the environment, deep ecologists sought to understand the fundamental processes of the natural world and to let them be. Deep ecologists wanted people to stand aside, ending their struggle to conquer an unconquerable force.

Petra Kelly in her early years favored the practical work of environmentalists and lobbied against the chemical and other industries. She too maintained that environmentalism had a special appeal to women, who had to be concerned for the fate of their children and were naturally drawn to issues that aimed at the preservation of the human race. "Countless children are condemned to illiteracy, disease, starvation and death by the massive diversion of resources (natural and human) to the arms race," she wrote in 1983.[26] However, her work contained a mix of environmental and ecological ideals.

Petra Kelly's partner was Gert Bastian, another well-known activist. In 1992, Kelly was found murdered, with Bastian also dead nearby. The deaths have never been fully explained. Were they a murder-suicide, as most people believe? Or did opponents of environmentally sound policies murder the pair, as some claim? Kelly's ideas about environmentalism are captured in her collections of essays—many of which began as speeches. Two of them are excerpted here.

Document 10.3

PETRA KELLY
Fighting for Hope, 1984

THE CHEMICAL INDUSTRY AND POLLUTION

According to the OECD (Organization of Economic Cooperation and Development) report, there are more than 70,000 chemicals on the market today, and 1,000 new chemicals a year are introduced into the twenty-four OECD states. Where chemicals are concerned, there are two things to be borne in mind: (a) the effects of a massive dose of chemicals; and (b) the effects of constant exposure to a small amount of any one substance over a period of time. After all, the effect of a small but constantly active dose could well be fatal, whereas the short-term effect of a massive dose of the same substance need not necessarily be so. In the field of radiation risk especially, the evaluation of data about atomic bomb victims, workers in the nuclear industry, and patients who have received clinical radiation treatment has shown that radiation has a cumulative effect, several small doses together having the same effect as one large one.

Almost all countries have inadequate legislation where chemical toxins are concerned. It will be the developing countries which will have to bear the brunt of any chemical catastrophes in the future. Products which are banned in their country of origin, in Europe, say, find lucrative markets in the developing countries.

We, the Greens, are deeply concerned about the increasing danger to babies and children of toxins in the environment. Their concentration in breast milk, in particular, can no longer be accepted. To be breastfed is one of the most basic human rights and it must not be jeopardised by the creeping contamination of mothers' milk.

Politicians say a great deal about protecting children, but in practice they do very little about it. Our environment is already stacked to the hilt with chemical substances and toxins, quite aside from the radioactivity from nuclear bombs and power stations. An adult's daily life is already characterized by waste-gas clouds, radioactive substances, and contaminated foodstuffs, but a child is exposed to a much greater degree. Children absorb chemical toxins and radioactivity into their bodies while they are still in the womb. They are born contaminated. Children are the first to be affected by environmental disasters, such as those in Japan or Seveso, and they suffer the greatest damage. We must wake up to the fact that the legacy we are leaving to future generations is a highly contaminated environment.

In this connection, I would like to quote Jörg Zink, a Green clergymen, because he puts it very clearly. "We usually regard violence by one person against another as a crime, but an act of violence by a group of people or an individual against the lives of an unspecified number of others is not termed a crime. We must rethink our ideas on what constitutes a crime." He goes on to say, "Measured against an ordinary crime, what a small debt is owed, in contrast to the industrial concern which buries its toxic waste under the green grass by the wagonload, or which travels the world's oceans in a tanker ready for the scrapheap. How much guilt does a man incur when he is responsible for burdening our successors with hundreds of generators and the job of looking after our nuclear waste?"

We put this question to chemists, physicists, nuclear technicians, town planners, politicians, and technocrats: what does it take to make you act as responsible people? How much longer can the principle of profit maximisation, and an economy that is preoccupied with minimizing costs, go on enslaving and deceiving us in a contaminated world?

SOURCE: Petra Kelly, *Fighting for Hope*, trans. Marianne Howarth (Boston: South End Press, 1984), 84–86.

A few months ago, I invited the Jesuit fathers, Philip and Daniel Berrigan, to West Germany. Daniel Berrigan, working in a hospital for terminal cancer patients at the time, said, "What cancer patients are suffering is a rehearsal for the future that is being planned now. Being with people who are dying of cancer means being with people on whom the bomb has already dropped." . . .

THE GOALS OF THE GREEN PARTY

The Green Party must remain a movement for non-violent change, and, at the same time, it must use parliament to make the case for non-violence to the electorate. One of the most important tasks for a parliamentary, extra-parliamentary party is to campaign for the recognition and protection of human rights. Food, health care, work, housing, freedom of religion and belief, freedom of assembly, freedom of expression, humane treatment of prisoners—all these human rights have been formally recognized by the member states of the United Nations, and all of them continue to be abused. These rights derive from a human being's right to life. Abuse of human rights can lead to the outbreak of war. Respect for human rights can help to build peace.

The Greens demand the unconditional abolition of all weapons of mass destruction. This demand is addressed to everybody, immediately and without exception, regardless of whether or when others make the same move. The destruction of mankind is the most heinous crime against humanity imaginable. There can be no justification for it or for any action which might cause such destruction.

The Greens seek a new life-style for the Western world, as well as in their own personal lives. They would like to see an alternative way of life without exploitation, and they aim for non-violent relationships with others and with themselves. . . . We should muster some solidarity, some friendship, in the face of our throw-away life-style. More important than material goods, is enhancing the quality of life and living in harmony with the need for the preservation of nature and cyclical renewal. This is one of the most important objectives that the Greens are working for in the new political culture.

However, there can be no future for the Greens if they go in for gaining power in the same way as the established parties. The Greens are ready to work with others if the demand that parliament should speak the language of the people is finally met. So far, parliaments have acted simply as the executive body of the bureaucracy in the ministries, especially where important proposals such as airports or nuclear power stations are concerned. . . .

We are, and I hope we will remain, half party and half local action group—we shall go on being an anti-party party. The learning process that takes place on the streets, on construction sites, at nuclear bases, must be carried into parliament.

QUESTIONS FOR ANALYSIS

1. What are Petra Kelly's various ideas about nature?
2. What specific action does Kelly suggest in her essays?
3. To what extent does Kelly seek social and political change?

PICTURE ESSAY

Politics in the Streets

POLITICS HAS OCCURRED in the streets for centuries—in the form of food riots, labor strikes, demonstrations in support of religious causes, and more recently feminist and gay pride parades and antiwar protests. Both monarchical rule and representative government, however, are supposed to substitute for politics in the streets, because kings, parliaments, and national assemblies have indicated that the interests of all people are theoretically represented in these institutions. People can simply protest policies by appealing peacefully to officials and representatives. In both communist and democratic systems, governmental institutions and the citizenry are supposed to be one.

In the mid-1960s, however, activists in capitalist and communist countries began protest the failure of representative government to enact meaningful reform on a number of fronts. Maintaining that too many people were unaware of this fact, they used the streets to call attention to issues such as racism and sexism, the Vietnam War, and environmental pollution. Bringing politics to the streets by means of public oratory, highly visible graffiti, parades, and demonstrations, protesters in the 1960s and 1970s caught the public's eye—and especially the eye of the media.

One of the most effective ways to bring an issue to the public's attention was to march, preferably in large numbers, and make good use of signs and chants. The

◆ Figure 10.1 **Anti-Vietnam War Demonstrator, London**
Photograph by Henri Bureau/Sygma/CORBIS.

◆ Figure 10.2 **Demonstration for Abortion Rights, New York**

Elliot Landy/Magnum Photos.

British youth shown in Figure 10.1 is marching in a demonstration against the Vietnam War. Although it was not a war involving British troops, the conflict was seen by people across the world (not just Americans) as emblematic of the kind of great-power colonial and cold war overreach and intervention that stymied the development of Vietnam and other third world nations. What might this young man be chanting? In Figure 10.2, women in New York City demonstrate for abortion rights in 1968, carrying makeshift signs with a frightening message. What is that message, and what impact do you think the marchers and their message had on passersby? This picture was taken by Elliott Landy, a photographer who attempted to document and support social movements through his photojournalism. Do you think the juxtaposition of the marchers with the billboard for the movie *Gone With the Wind* was intentional? Why or why not?

Another effective way to get a message out was through slogans and images on posters and murals. Activists covered building exteriors and telephone poles and bulletin boards and university hallways with eye-catching and often very professional posters as well as hastily scrawled graffiti. Slogans that were easy to remember and easy to repeat were important to movements as was the vivid art that illustrated them. "Don't be sheep" urges a poster directed at Parisians during the heady and chaotic days of uprising of French university students and workers in 1968. The body of the sheep depicted in that poster is cleverly composed of initials for different unions and government agencies. "Back to Normal" reads the Paris 1968 silk-screen poster (Figure 10.3) that features sheep, mocking the French government's ultimately successful efforts to end the chaos wrought by the uprising.

◆ Figure 10.3 **Student poster, France**

Here the stylized sheep all face in the same direction, heads bent submissively. How might this poster's message and image have persuaded passive or indifferent Parisians to join the student/worker cause? Could its message have backfired? Why?

    Brightly colored clothing, goofy styles, and mischievous behavior also characterized public activism during this period. Infractions to the rules of dress and deportment are often called "carnivalesque" — invoking the gay and transgressive spirit of carnival, a traditional pre-Lenten celebration in Christian countries. Carnival was a time when the world was turned upside down and when poor and ordinary people mocked the sober, highfalutin' airs of society's leaders. In support of numerous causes, and sometimes just for the fun of disturbing the status quo, hippies, braless women, and eccentric cross-dressers celebrated their differences with outlandish demonstrations, mocking the suit-wearing, briefcase-carrying technocrats, bureaucrats, and business leaders who were in power. Figure 10.4 shows women daubed in colorful paint and bedecked with flowers marching in Prague's May Day parade in 1968, at the high point of Czechoslovakia's "Prague Spring." What effect might such transgressive behavior have had on hard-line Czech Communist officials and their superiors watching from Moscow?

◆ Figure 10.4 **May Day Parade in Prague**
JK/Magnum Photos.

In the same spirit of gaiety and impetuousness, demonstrators sometimes called their gatherings "happenings" and did incongruous things. An antiwar protester in the United States stuck a flower in the barrel of the gun a soldier was pointing at him. The protesters dancing on silos housing nuclear weapons in 1983 (Figure 10.5) are also engaging in the time-honored practice of putting the forces of oppression off their guard by indulging in humane, humorous, and even ridiculous behavior to make their case. What is important symbolically about this act? How did the dancers get into the facility, do you think? What is the significance of their holding hands in a circle?

The impact of politics in the streets was increased by the novelty of live television coverage. Whereas earlier in the century street politics aroused the participants and drew in passersby, television extended the influence of protest movements, gaining adherents for causes but also making enemies. What might television viewers have thought about Figure 10.6, a shot of a French student being beaten up by a *flic* (French slang for "policeman")? Not only carnival but violence shaped politics in the streets, as this image vividly portrays, as citizens confronted and clashed with the very forces of democratic power that were supposed to represent them.

Although television and other media coverage had the beneficial effect of carrying news and images of protests far beyond their immediate location, it is important to keep in mind that camera operators and the TV networks could focus on whatever aspect of a demonstration or movement they wanted and thus skew the representative nature of politics in the streets. Media coverage could make a

◆ **Figure 10.5 Dancing on the Silos**

◆ **Figure 10.6 A Student Felled by a *Flic* Paris**
Henri Bureau/CORBIS.

movement appear to be something that it was not. During coverage of demonstrations by feminists, for example, cameras focused on certain leaders, making stars of the most glamorous or the most outrageous, and overlooked the crucial participation and contributions of ordinary women in feminist politics. The movement was often portrayed on television, in magazines, and in other media as one composed of glamorous socialites or shrill extremists. Civil rights, pacifist, and student movements faced a similar, novel challenge due to the small eye of the camera and the media's desire to keep the newspaper-buying and television-watching public entertained. The numerous images of famous 1960s leaders like Paris student Daniel Cohn-Bendit (known to the French simply as "Dany" and around the world as "Dany the Red"), U.S. civil rights leader Martin Luther King Jr., and popular revolutionary Che Guevara, indicate just how much the media fixated on certain figures. Some leaders, like Che, who died in their prime were romanticized, even almost deified, by their followers and the media. In the years following Che's death in 1967 at the hands of right-wing militias while he was fomenting revolution in Bolivia, Guevara was lionized by socialist revolutionary movements worldwide and continues to be up to this day. Figure 10.7 shows a billboard in Cuba in 1988 based on the iconic portrait of Che by Alberto Korda, called by some the most famous photograph in the world. The portrait circulated worldwide on t-shirts and posters. What do you suppose accounts for Che's enduring popularity?

However much the media shaped or distorted the public's view of activists, in the 1960s and 1970s simply being out in public demonstrating, in whatever way, shape, or form, was an important gesture. It pulled politics out of the massive and ornate state buildings and reclaimed the political process for women and men often denied access to that power.

◆ **Figure 10.7 Che Guevara**
Tim Page/CORBIS.

QUESTIONS FOR ANALYSIS

1. What impressions do these images convey to you?
2. In what ways do the images convey a sense of power? In what ways a lack of power?
3. What effect did politics in the street have on the course of history in the 1960s and 1970s?

NOTES

1. Donna Haraway, "A Cyborg Manifesto: Science, Technology, and Socialist-Feminism in the Late Twentieth Century," in *Simians, Cyborgs, and Women: The Reinvention of Nature* (New York: Routledge, 1991), 152.

2. F. R. Leavis, *English Literature in Our Time and the University* (London: Chatto, 1969), 33.

3. Ray Brown, ed., *Children and Television* (1976), quoted in Panos Bardis, *Dictionary of Quotations in Sociology* (Westport: Greenwood, 1985), 283.

4. W. O. Baker, "Computers as Information-Processing Machines in Modern Science," *Daedalus* (Fall 1970), 99:1120.

5. Michèle Le Doueff, *Hipparchia's Choice: An Essay Concerning Women, Philosophy, Etc.,* trans. Trista Selous (London: Blackwell, 1991), 256.

6. Second Vatican Council, "Pastoral Constitution on the Church in the Modern World/*Gaudium et spes*," http://www.ewtn.com/library/COUNCILS/VZmodwor.htm.

7. Rosemary Crompton and Nicola LeFeuvre, quoted in "Gender and Bureaucracy: Women in Finance in Britain and France," in *Gender and Bureaucracy,* ed. Mike Savage and Anne Witz (London: Blackwell, 1992), 111–113 passim.

8. Quoted in Cas Wouters, "The Sociology of Emotions and Flight Attendants: Hochschild's *Managed Heart*," *Theory, Culture and Society,* vol. 6 (February 1989), 117.

9. Alison Lever, "Capital, Gender and Skill: Women Homeworkers in Rural Spain," *Feminist Review,* no. 30 (Autumn 1988), 3–24.

10. Rosemary Wakeman, *Modernizing the Provincial City: Toulouse, 1945–1975* (Cambridge: Harvard University Press, 1997), 171.

11. Quoted in Alain Schnapp and Pierre Vidal-Naquet, *The French Student Uprising, November 1967–June 1968,* trans. Maria Jolas (Boston: Beacon Press, 1971), 10–11.

12. Quoted in Stuart J. Hilwig, "The Revolt against the Establishment: Students versus the Press in West Germany and Italy," in *1968: The World Transformed,* ed. Carole Fink et al. (Cambridge: Cambridge University Press, 1998), 333.

13. Quoted in Christine Bard, *Les femmes dans la société française au 20e siècle* (Paris: Armand Colin, 2001), 171.

14. "Interview with a Career Woman," in *Women and Russia: Feminist Writings from the Soviet Union,* ed. Tatyana Mamonova (Boston: Beacon Press, 1984), 18.

15. Quoted in Paul Ginsborg, *A History of Contemporary Italy: Society and Politics, 1943–1988* (London: Penguin, 1990), 305.

16. Quoted in Schnapp and Vidal-Naquet, *French Student Uprising,* 1650.

17. Quoted in David Caute, *Sixty-Eight* (London: Hamilton, 1988), 162.

18. Quoted in Heda Margolius Kovály, *Under a Cruel Star: A Life in Prague, 1941–1968* (New York: Holmes and Meier, 1997), 181.

19. Quoted in Caute, *Sixty-Eight,* 165, 168.

20. Quoted in Philip Windsor and Adam Roberts, *Czechoslovakia, 1968* (New York: Columbia University Press, 1969), 169–173.

21. Lila Lounguina, *Les saisons de Moscou, 1933–1990* (Paris: Plon, 1990), 183.

22. Ibid., 193.

23. Quoted in Gale Stokes, *The Walls Came Tumbling Down: The Collapse of Communism in Eastern Europe* (New York: Oxford University Press, 1993), 20.

24. E. F. Schumacher, "Buddhist Economics," first appeared in *Asia: A Handbook,* ed. Guy Wint (London: Anthony Blond, 1966). 695–703.

25. Régis Debray, *Revolution in the Revolution?* (New York: Monthly Review Press, 1967), 116.

26. Petra Kelly, *Fighting for Hope,* trans. Marianne Howarth (Boston: South End Press, 1984), 103.

SUGGESTED REFERENCES

The Technology Revolution Scholars and popular commentators have examined the boom in technological innovation from a variety of perspectives, especially historical, sociological, and economic. They also focus on controversies that have arisen around technology's impact on European lives.

Bauer, Martin W., and George Gaskell, eds. *Biotechnology: The Making of a Global Controversy.* 2002.

Boym, Svetlana. *Common Places: Mythologies of Everyday Life in Russia.* 1994.

Brock, Gerald W. *The Second Information Revolution.* 2003.

Edwards, Jeannette. *Born and Bred: Idioms of Kinship and New Reproductive Technologies in England.* 2000.

Frachon, Claire, et al. *European Television: Immigrants and Ethnic Minorities.* 1995.

Harvey, Brian. *Europe's Space Programme: To Ariane and Beyond.* 2003.

Hecht, Gabrielle. *The Radiance of France: Nuclear Power and National Identity after World War II.* 1998.

Launius, Roger D., et al., eds. *Reconsidering Sputnik: Forty Years since the Soviet Satellite.* 2000.

Natalicchi, Giorgio. *Wiring Europe: Reshaping the European Telecommunications Regime.* 2001.

Siddiqi, Asif A. *The Soviet Space Race with Apollo.* 2003.

Webb, R. C. *Tele-Visionaries: The People behind the Invention of Television.* 2005.

Postindustrial Economy and Society There is no doubt that technology changed patterns of work and living dramatically from the 1960s on. Commentators debate the fairness of multinational corporations and wonder about their effect on communities in the face of growing global prosperity.

Audretsch, David B., and Paul J. J. Welfens, eds. *The New Economy and Economic Growth in Europe and the U.S.* 2002.

Bell, Daniel. *The Coming of Post-Industrial Society.* 1973.

Boyd, Carolyn. *Historia Patria: Politics, History, and National Identity in Spain, 1875–1975.* 1997.

Chandler, Alfred D., Jr., and Bruce Mazlish, eds. *Leviathans: Multinational Corporations and the New Global History.* 2005.

Clark, Terry Nichols, and Michael Rempel. *Citizen Politics in Post-Industrial Societies.* 2001.

Cook, Hera. *The Long Sexual Revolution: English Women, Sex, and Contraception, 1800–1975.* 2004.

Coopey, Richard, et al. *Mail Order Retailing in Britain: A Business and Social History.* 2005.

Jones, Geoffrey, and Harm Schroter. *The Rise of Multinationals in Continental Europe.* 1993.

Meyrowitz, Joshua. *No Sense of Place: The Impact of Electronic Media on Social Behavior.* 1985.

Wakeman, Rosemary. *Modernizing the Provincial City: Toulouse, 1945–1975.* 1997.

An Age of Protest and Reform Were the protests of the 1960s important, influential, or principally young people letting off steam? These works present different pictures of the protests of the 1960s and most notably provide an array of voices from the uprisings and reform movements.

Ahonen, Pertti. *After the Expulsion: West Germany and Eastern Europe, 1945–1990.* 2003.

Bono, Paola, and Sandra Kemp, eds. *Italian Feminist Thought: A Reader.* 1991.

Branch, Taylor. *America in the King Years.* 3 vols. 1988–2006.

Dominick, Raymond H. *The Environmental Movement in Germany: Prophets and Pioneers.* 1992.

Dubček , Alexander. *Hope Dies Last: The Autobiography of Alexander Dubček.* 1993.

Fink, Carole, et al., eds. *1968: The World Transformed.* 1998.

Lawrence, Mark Atwood. *Assuming the Burden: Europe and the American Commitment to War in Vietnam.* 2005.

Mirza, Heidi, ed. *Black British Feminism: A Reader.* 1997.

Seidman, Michael. *Imaginary Revolution: Parisian Students and Workers in 1968.* 2004.

Varon, Jeremy. *Bringing the War Home: The Weather Underground, the Red Army Faction, and Revolutionary Violence in the Sixties and Seventies.* 2004.

Williams, Kieran. *The Prague Spring and Its Aftermath: Czechoslovak Politics, 1968–1970.* 1997.

Attacking and Defending An Eroding Status Quo The uprisings took place at a time when the cold war antagonists were challenged in foreign policy and domestically. Jeremy Suri's book brings the domestic and the foreign challenges together in his analysis.

Christofferson, Michael Scott. *French Intellectuals against the Left: The Anti-totalitarian Moment of the 1970s.* 2004.

Coopey, Richard, and Nicholas Woodward, eds. *Britain in the 1970s: The Troubled Economy.* 1995.

Olson, James S., and Randy Roberts. *Where the Domino Fell: America and Vietnam, 1945–1995.* 1996.

Ouimet, Matthew J. *The Rise and Fall of the Brezhnev Doctrine in Soviet Foreign Policy.* 2003.

Rosenfeld, Alla, and Norton T. Dodge. *From Gulag to Glasnost: Nonconformist Art from the Soviet Union.* 1995.

Sarotte, M. E. *Dealing with the Devil: East Germany, Détente, and Ostpolitik, 1969–1973.* 2001.

Suri, Jeremi. *Power and Protest: Global Revolution and the Rise of Détente.* 2003.

Yergin, Daniel. *The Prize: The Epic Quest for Oil, Money and Power.* 1991.

Alternative Politics   Domestic politics following on the heels of 1968 often brought conflict, much of it related to the aspirations of people for a different kind of society. Bess's study of environmental politics in France shows how conflicted and even contradictory such movements could be.

Bess, Michael. *The Light-Green Society: Ecology and Technological Modernity in France.* 2003.

Coopey, Richard and Nicholas Woodward, eds. *Britain in the 1970s: The Troubled Economy.* 1995.

Engene, Jan Oskar. *Terrorism in Western Europe: Explaining the Trends since 1950.* 2004.

Harford, Barbara and Sarah Hopkins. *Greenham Common: Women at the Wire.* 1984.

Hayes, Patrick, and Jim Campbell. *Bloody Sunday: Trauma, Pain and Politics.* 2005.

Jackson, Alvin. *Home Rule: An Irish History, 1800–2000.* 2003.

Laqueur, Walter. *The Age of Terrorism.* 1987.

Nic Craith, Máiréad. *Plural Identities—Singular Narratives: The Case of Northern Ireland.* 2002.

Sarkar, Saral. *Green-Alternative Politics in West Germany.* 1993.

Talshir, Gayil. *The Political Ideology of Green Parties: From the Politics of Nature to Redefining the Nature of Politics* 2002.

Zirakzadeh, Cyrus Ernesto. *Social Movements in Politics: A Comparative Study.* 1997.

Selected Web Sites

The following sites provide a good range of sources and resources on the events of the 1960s and 1970s. Brown University's oral history project offers a particularly interesting time line on events around the world in 1968.

Battlefield Vietnam: <**pbs.org/battlefieldvietnam/index.html**>

Brown University, The Whole World Was Watching: An Oral History of 1968: <**www.stg.brown.edu/projects/1968/reference/timeline.html**>

European Space Agency: <**esa.int/esaCP/index.html**>

Holy See, Documents of the Vatican Council II: **vatican.va/archive/hist _councils/ii_vatican_council/**>

Satellite Communications Systems and Technology: <**wtec.org/loyola/satcom/ toc.htm**>

World Oil Market and Oil Price Chronologies: <**strata.geol.sc.edu/petroleum/ Chronology%20of%20World%20Oil%20Market%20Events%201970% 20-%202000.htm**>

11

Europe Changes Course

The 1980s and Beyond

IN THE EARLY 1980s, CITIZENS IN LEIPZIG, EAST GERMANY, started to gather weekly in St. Nikolai Church to pray for world peace. Only occasionally were the police bold enough to arrest any of these steadfast activists. The prayer services continued throughout the 1980s, growing more popular when Mikhail Gorbachev, a reformer, came to power in the Soviet Union in 1985. Gorbachev initiated a freer press, encouraged economic change, and generally made people across the Soviet bloc hopeful once more. On the eve of Gorbachev's visit to East Germany in October 1989, the throng of demonstrators in Leipzig swelled, growing from 15,000 to 300,000. They sang "We Shall Overcome" and chanted "Gorbi, Gorbi," signaling their approval of Gorbachev's loosening of Communist rule. "The people of Leipzig," wrote one observer, "were on the brink of reclaiming their city."[1]

People in other East German cities followed their example until in November 1989 a half million massed in East Berlin. "We can't beat up hundreds of thousands of people," a senior East German official advised, sparking rumors of free passage to western Europe, which would spell the end of the Berlin Wall.[2] When guards at the Wall heard the story, they reacted by spontaneously letting hundreds of thousands of elated demonstrators pass through to the

◆ **Mass Demonstrations in Leipzig, 1989**
Leipzig, in the Soviet-bloc state of East Germany, was one of many centers of popular protest in the 1980s. Protests in Leipzig began as activism on behalf of world peace, then in 1989 evolved into massive outpourings to end Communist repression in East Germany. In October 1989 the number of demonstrators reached 300,000, and they chanted "Gorbi, Gorbi, come help us," appealing to the leader of the Soviet Union who had opened the USSR to greater political freedom and economic reform. Across the Soviet bloc, crowds in the hundreds of thousands gathered, swarming around cars, buses, and trams halted on their tracks. Eventually they brought the Soviet system crashing down, ending the cold war. *AP Photo.*

other side, where they bought bananas and other scarce goods and celebrated with West Berliners, hugging and fraternizing with total strangers. November 9, 1989, when the Berlin Wall opened, stands as the date of the collapse of the Soviet empire. It happened because Leipzigers holding prayer vigils week after week and year after year, and other ordinary people, kept alive a commitment to change.

The 1980s had begun with far less hope. Economic crisis had hit the capitalist countries hard, and although the Soviets seemed strong, they had just embarked on what turned out to be a disastrous war in Afghanistan. The Communist economies of eastern Europe were drowning in inefficiency and corruption. Making matters worse, demoralized workers were awash in vodka, as Russian critics were quick to point out, and life expectancy was plummeting. These problems did not necessarily add up to collapse, and in 1985 the outlook brightened when the

1989	November 9: Berlin Wall opens; comes down by the end of 1990.
1989	November: "Velvet Revolution" leads to the downfall of communism in Czechoslovakia; activist playwright Václav Havel elected president.
1989	December: Widespread resistance to Nicolae Ceaușescu's regime ends with the execution of the Communist dictator and his wife.
1989	December: Slobodan Milosevic elected president of Serbia.
1990	Reunification of Germany.
1991	June: Republics of Slovenia and Croatia secede from Yugoslavia.
1991–1995:	Civil war engulfs Croatia and Bosnia-Herzegovina.
1991	August: Russian president Boris Yeltsin thwarts coup attempt against Gorbachev by antireform hard-liners.
1991	September: Lithuania, Latvia, and Estonia declare independence from USSR.
1992	January 1: USSR legally dissolved; twelve of the fifteen former Soviet republics band together as the Commonwealth of Independent States.
1993	January: Democrat Bill Clinton becomes U.S. president.
1994	Russia invades independent republic of Chechnya.
1997	Andreï Makine publishes *Dreams of My Russian Summers.*
1997–1999	Serb militias and Yugoslav army slaughter civilians in Kosovo.
1999	Irish Catholics and Protestants agree to end violence in Northern Ireland.
1999	December 31: Yeltsin resigns and appoints Vladimir Putin as his successor.
2001	July: Serb government turns Milosevic over to a war crimes tribunal in the Netherlands.

energetic Mikhail Gorbachev came to the fore, promising new freedoms and modern economic reforms. To the west, Margaret Thatcher took charge in Britain, and she too promised drastic changes to draw her people out of the economic morass. Her strategy was to attack the very welfare state that Gorbachev was trying to revive, even to the point of alienating powerful vested interests such as labor unions. In the 1980s strong domestic winds forced nearly all of Europe to seek a new course as Gorbachev and Thatcher were doing.

The impetus for change came from many directions. Around the world economic forces emerged to contest Western industrial and financial domination. Not only did the Middle East's control of oil dictate change, but countries of the Pacific Rim were developing into powerful economic competitors. These countries were producing automobiles, televisions, video recorders, and many other consumer goods popular in the West more efficiently and less expensively than manufacturers in Europe and the United States. At the other extreme, the continuing spirit of revolt at the grassroots level, coming from 1960s and 1970s activists such as the Greens and women, was now taken up by millions of protesters in the Soviet bloc. Despite governments' attempts at reform in eastern Europe, ordinary citizens like the hundreds of thousands in Leipzig brought the Soviet system crashing down. The story of that crash, including the transition from communist to capitalist economies and from satellites to independent states, unfolded in a climate of rapid transformation. That crash would reverberate in aftershocks throughout the coming decades, from civil war and crisis in Yugoslavia to the faraway former Soviet republic of Chechnya. The uncertainty in everyday life brought about by this transformation has lasted down to the present.

EUROPE FACES THE GLOBAL ECONOMIC CHALLENGE

Stagflation remained a powerful economic threat to western Europe and the United States as the 1980s opened, and the pillar of the capitalist alliance—the United States—staggered additionally under the weight of its Vietnam war debt. Europe's thirty golden years of prosperity ended abruptly with the oil crisis of the 1970s and with increasing global competition, which forced these nations to put their economic houses in order. In this endeavor Margaret Thatcher of Great Britain led the way by reversing the Keynesian practice of pump priming through government spending to recharge a flagging economy. This time the problem was not one of a simple downturn. Instead, inflation, not the rapidly dropping prices that usually accompanied unemployment, cut the amount of money available to save and thus invest in new businesses. The problems were compounded by the growing economic competitiveness of the Pacific Rim, which made European goods less appealing. The political result was that European voters, frustrated by a declining standard of living, elected conservative politicians, who maintained that decades of support for the welfare state were at the heart of economic problems. Tough times intensified feelings that the unemployed and new immigrants were responsible for the downturn. Broad segments of the public looked to nineteenth-century values of competitiveness, individualism, and revival of privilege for the "best circles" and questioned the postwar emphasis on economic democracy embodied in welfare-state programs.

The Rise of the Pacific Economy

From the last third of the twentieth century on, an incredible rise in industrial entrepreneurship and development of technology took place outside the West, especially in Asia and some countries in Latin America such as Chile. Just as economic change in the early modern period had redirected European affairs from the Mediterranean to the Atlantic, so explosive productivity from Japan to Singapore in the 1980s began to spread economic power from the Atlantic region to the Pacific. In 1982, the Asian Pacific nations accounted for 16.4 percent of global gross domestic product, a figure that had doubled since the 1960s. More surprising, by the mid-1990s China was achieving economic growth rates of 8 percent and more, while Japan had developed the second-largest national economy after the United States—displacing any single European country.

During this period, South Korea, Taiwan, Singapore, Hong Kong, and China were called "Asian Tigers" for the ferocity of their growth, but it was Japan that led the charge. Investment in high-tech consumer industries drove the Japanese economy. In 1982, Japan had 32,000 industrial robots in operation, western Europe 9,000, the United States 7,000. In 1989, the Japanese government and private businesses invested $549 billion to modernize industrial capacity, a full $36 billion more than American public and private investment combined. Such spending paid off substantially, as buyers around the world snapped up automobiles, televisions, videocassette recorders, and computers from Japanese and other Asian Pacific companies such as Sony, Toyota, and Mitsubishi. By the end of the 1980s, Japan was home to the world's eight largest banks and to a brokerage house twenty times larger than its nearest American competitor. As the United States poured vast sums into its cold war military budget, Asian Pacific funds purchased U.S. government bonds, thus financing America's ballooning national debt. Forty years after its total defeat in World War II, Japan was bankrolling its former conqueror and offering tough competition everywhere. Europe faced an additional challenge to its competitiveness in world markets.

Thatcher Reshapes Political Culture

More than anyone else, Margaret Thatcher (b. 1925), the outspoken leader of Britain's Conservative Party who served as prime minister from 1979 to 1990, reshaped the West's political and economic ideas to address the challenging new conditions. Unfazed by continuing economic decline, revolt in Northern Ireland, and labor unrest, the combative Thatcher eschewed the strategy of consensus building that postwar politicians had carefully used to prevent any drift toward totalitarianism. With that danger seemingly over and a larger economic one looming, Thatcher felt it was time to be bold. "I don't spend a lifetime watching which way the cat jumps," she announced. "I know really which way I want the cats to go."[3] In parliamentary speeches, Thatcher lashed out at union leaders, Labour politicians, and people who received welfare-state benefits as enemies of British prosperity. In 1978, on the eve of being selected prime minister, she invoked the menace of Britain being "swamped" by immigrants.

Thatcher believed that only a resurgence of private enterprise could revive the sluggish British economy, and her anti-welfare-state attitudes were welcomed (see Document 11.1). The daughter of a hardworking grocer, Thatcher had worked as a chemist and then studied law, specializing in tax law. She called herself "a nineteenth-century liberal," alluding to the economic individualism of that age. In her view, business leaders and entrepreneurs were the key members of society—a point she hammered home in speech after speech. Although immigrants often worked for the lowest wages, which in fact boosted profits, she claimed that they made no contribution at all to national wealth. As former secretary of state for education and science, she had ended programs giving milk to schoolchildren and had cut subsidies for school lunches. According to her calculations those programs wasted money that could be used more wisely by giving tax cuts to the wealthy, who would then invest the money. "I have changed everything," Thatcher exulted, and indeed, these beliefs marked a profound shift from those that underlay the welfare state.[4] Her policies, she claimed, represented a much-hoped-for return to "Victorian values."[5]

The policies of "Thatcherism" were based on monetarist or supply-side theories associated most prominently with U.S. economist Milton Friedman. Monetarists contend that inflation results when government pumps money into the economy at a rate higher than a nation's economic growth rate. They advocate a tight rein on the money supply to keep prices from rising rapidly. Supply-side economists maintain that the economy as a whole flourishes when business prosperity "trickles down" throughout the society. To implement these theories, the British government under Thatcher cut income tax rates on the wealthy by more than 50 percent to spur new investment and, to compensate for the lost revenue, pushed up sales taxes on items that ordinary people needed. The result was an increased burden on working people, who bore the brunt of the sales tax. The goal was to tax consumption, not income, and thereby create wealth. Thatcher also vigorously pruned government intervention in the economy: she sold publicly owned businesses and utilities such as Britoil, British Airways, and Rolls-Royce; refused to prop up outmoded industries such as coal mining; and slashed education and health programs. As the influence of these economic policies spread through the West and the world, they became known as neoliberalism.

In the first three years of Thatcher's prime ministership, the British economy did not respond well to her shock treatment. The quality of universities, public transportation, highways, and hospitals deteriorated, and leading scholars and scientists left the country in a renewal of the brain drain. In the 1990s, longevity in Britain sank to thirty-eighth among the world's nations. In addition, social unity fragmented: in 1981, blacks and Asians rioted in major cities, and urban strife increased thereafter. Thatcher's popularity sagged. A turning point came in March

1982, when Argentina invaded the British Falkland Islands in the South Atlantic. Thatcher invoked patriotism to unify the nation and refused to surrender the islands without a fight, even though they were thousands of miles away. The war paid off politically, as public support for the prime minister soared. The appeal to nationalism replaced economic democratization as a unifying social force. In the long run, however, many parts of the British welfare state, such as the national health service, survived, though at reduced levels of service. It was the ethos that had been transformed.

By the early 1990s, inflation and unemployment in Britain had fallen sharply, and business was on a decided upswing. Historians and economists debate whether the change resulted from Thatcher's policies or stemmed from a normal swing of the business cycle. The government saved vast quantities of money formerly used to subsidize a range of nationalized and failing industries, and Britain's economy became one of the most competitive in Europe. Thatcher's program set the standard, especially the turn to privatization of industry. When the Labour Party regained power in 1997, it did so under the banner of competitiveness and "workfare" (a term suggesting that people receiving government benefits should work for them) instead of welfare. As enacted by Labour (and by Democrats in the United States), the cutbacks traditionally associated with the right came to be called the "Third Way," a merging of conservative and liberal programs into an alternative policy. Formerly one of the pioneers of the welfare state, Britain pioneered in rethinking that course.

The Reagan Revolution's Global Impact

In a world of multinational corporations and global trade, the lagging health of the world's largest economy impinged on the economic health of Europe, creating a drag on its industry and trade. Moved by the same social and political vision as Thatcher, Ronald Reagan (1911–2004; president 1981–1989) worked to revive the business climate for the Western alliance. The former actor used Thatcher's idea that immoral, spendthrift forces in the nation were destroying a more moral majority; his policies ended the sense of national community that undergirded programs such as the Great Society of Lyndon Johnson. Reagan vowed to promote the values of the "moral majority"—among them commitment to Bible-based religion, dedication to work, sexual restraint, and unquestioning patriotism.

In domestic affairs, Reagan pursued a radical course on a par with Thatcher's. His program—known as "Reaganomics"—produced a whopping income tax cut of 25 percent between 1981 and 1983, combined with massive reductions in federal spending for student loans, school lunch programs, and mass transit. Like Thatcher, Reagan believed that tax cuts would lead to investment and a reinvigorated economy and that federal outlays for welfare programs, which he felt only encouraged sloth, would generally become unnecessary. Government investment would shift to the military budget to counter the Soviet arms buildup of the 1970s. In March 1983, Reagan announced the Strategic Defense Initiative (SDI), known popularly as "Star Wars," which was a plan to put lasers in space to defend the

United States against a nuclear attack. The combination of tax cuts and military expansion had pushed the federal budget deficit to $200 billion by 1986. Yet European leaders like Thatcher saw deficits as a godsend, reducing their need to defend social programs and thus further trimming their budgets.

The election of Democrat Bill Clinton (b. 1946) as U.S. president in 1992 did not fundamentally change the move away from the welfare-state ethos. As in Britain, an ethic of workfare continued in the United States, and the goal of competitiveness in an increasingly global economy justified crumbling urban schools, the decline in literacy, and the United States' position as forty-eight on longevity charts. In fact, the economy soared in the 1990s, lifting people in the professions and top management to ever greater wealth, while real wages continued the slight decline that had begun in the 1970s. Thus from the vantage point of growth, cuts in social programs in the United Kingdom and the United States were a real success. Backed by their financial and military power, these two countries were able to press neoliberal economic policies on other states, which began to increase their productivity, output, and levels of consumption.

◆ **Ronald Reagan and Margaret Thatcher, 1982**
Margaret Thatcher taught heads of state how to cut back the welfare state by slashing government programs of support for universities, schools, and health care. Ronald Reagan, one of her best pupils, enacted cuts similar to hers in the United States. Nonetheless, the idea that the state should use some public monies for the good of its citizens did not completely die as an ideal, though it was tested by the need to fight stagflation and the desire to boost the profitability of businesses. *Hulton Archive/Getty Images.*

ALTERNATIVES TO THATCHERISM

Other western European leaders found retrenchment of social programs necessary as well, but unlike Thatcher they aimed to maintain the welfare-state rhetoric of social cohesion. This policy ultimately translated into fewer cuts in expenditures and in the exceptional case of France to deliberate increases to pump-prime recovery. In western Europe generally, the retirement age dropped — to age fifty-two on average in Italy — because of generously funded pensions. The cost of these pensions and other social spending increased taxes paid by businesses. As a result, even as economic growth resumed in western Europe, unemployment remained high, businesses invested less, and recovery was muted.

Germany Turns to the Right

In West Germany unions and managers cooperated to fight inflation by keeping prices and wages down. However, during 1981 and 1982 the West German economy succumbed to forces plaguing other Western-bloc states: consumption and trade dropped as the cost of energy skyrocketed. Facing unemployment, rising costs for basic commodities, and persistent terrorism by radicals, voters elected a center-right coalition headed by Helmut Kohl (b. 1930), who took power as chancellor in October 1982. Far less outspoken and ideological than Thatcher, Kohl reduced welfare spending, froze government wages, and cut corporate taxes. By 1984, the inflation rate was only 2 percent, and West Germany had acquired a 10 percent share of world trade. Kohl claimed that his curbing of the welfare state brought about a *Wende* ("turning") of the economy.

Unlike Thatcher, Kohl did not fan class and racial hatreds for political purposes, and he presided over the relatively peaceful incorporation of an outspoken opposition — the Green Party — into the German parliament. Early in the 1980s the Greens garnered from 5 to 10 (and eventually higher) percentages of the votes in some elections, and their concerns started to shape governmental programs. The politics of divisiveness was particularly unwise in Germany, where terrorism on the left and on the right continued to flourish. Fearful businessmen hired bodyguards to avoid kidnapping and assassination and refused to travel by air because of frequent bomb threats. The government responded by making it a crime to "defame the state," curtailing the civil rights of suspected terrorists, and imprisoning their lawyers. The legacy of Nazism also loomed menacingly, but this time threats were used against foreign workers. "Let's gas 'em," said unemployed German youth of immigrant Turkish workers. The revival of Nazi tough talk appalled many in Germany's middle class rather than winning their support for discrimination.

Across the West, tensions arising from economic and political shifts often played out in other arenas. Not only were youth reviving Nazi rhetoric in their protests against unemployment, but intellectuals launched a bitter public debate about the origins and significance of the Nazi years and the mass annihilation of Jews and others. The basic issue of this *Historikerstreit* or "Historians' Quarrel" was whether the Third Reich and its deeds were a product of or a deviation from the main thrust of German history under Bismarck and Prussian rule. In the midst of revived and public anti-Semitism among the young, historians wrote of the "past that would not disappear." Many felt that historical scholarship was not up to absorbing the lessons of Nazism. Others felt that Nazism was a taboo subject—one beyond human inquiry and judgment—and warned that if people inserted Nazism into the normal historical narrative, they might seem to be normalizing and even legitimizing Hitler's racist ideas and the Nazis' murderous policies. By writing about these topics analytically, wouldn't they be legitimizing the "state murder" of millions of Jews? Journalists and filmmakers joined the fray. Some argued that Nazism was a necessary defense against—and indeed a lesser evil than—the "asiatic threat" of Stalinism. Others noted that the twentieth century had seen and continued to witness mass murderers as bad as Hitler—Cambodia's Pol Pot and the Turkish perpetrators of the 1915 Armenian genocide, for example—and complained that Germans should not have to live forever "in the shadow of Hitler."[6]

The controversy intensified when U.S. president Ronald Reagan on a visit to West Germany in 1985 paid respects to German soldiers buried in a cemetery in the town of Bitburg, among them members of the Waffen-SS, which had been pivotal in perpetrating Nazi violence and genocide. "Victims of Nazism" Reagan called them, leaving observers to brand the entire ceremony "a callous offense for the Jewish people," as one rabbi put it. West German–U.S. relations became strained, and unresolved social enmities made it difficult for the West German government to address tough issues such as the costs of social services. These issues would resurface after the mid-1990s as budget spending outpaced revenues. For the moment, a full-scale attack on welfare-state spending was blocked by the need to maintain social peace.

France Charts a Different Course

France's political path through the 1980s differed from both Germany's and Britain's. In 1981, French citizens elected a leftist president—François Mitterrand. At the time stagflation had put more than 1.5 million people out of work and reduced France's economic growth rate to an anemic 1.2 percent. Mitterrand (1916–1996), who had served both the Vichy government and the revived postwar French republic, nationalized banks and certain industries and stimulated the economy by wage increases and social spending—the opposite of Thatcherism. A consensus politician, he tried to find common ground with both the extreme left and the right. He ordered the construction of new public buildings such as museums and libraries along with new subway lines and improved public transport. French financial leaders reacted by sending capital abroad rather than investing it at home, thereby curtailing growth. Even so, many ordinary citizens continued to favor the protections offered by government programs, and good health care and cultural amenities for everyone made the French public supportive and proud.

Then in the spring elections of 1986, during Mitterrand's second term as president, conservatives captured the majority of seats in the assembly and were able to choose the prime minister. Mitterrand lived with this "cohabitation," as it was called, and until the end of the century, conservatives and socialists continued to share power. Thus French policy swung between the conservatives' efforts to encourage investment by cutting the costs of social programs and the left's commitment to social security programs and to subsidies for culture in public life. By 2000, the economy of France was among the most prosperous in Europe, except for Britain's, but it was hardly matching the growth rate of the Asian Tigers.

At the same time, France like Germany suffered from continuing high unemployment as businesspeople refused to create new jobs because of the high costs of social programs. As elsewhere, changing social and economic conditions had political repercussions, and racism emerged as an expression of discontent. Beginning with the June 1984 elections for the European parliament, Jean-Marie Le Pen's National Front Party, which promised to deport African and Muslim immigrants and cut French ties with nonwhite nations, won 10 percent or more of the vote, and in 2002 Le Pen was runner-up for the presidency, edging out the left-of-center candidate. Le Pen declared himself to be for "multiculturalism" as long as each culture was kept distinct and separate from each other in different countries. Whereas once the French had pioneered the idea of nationhood based on common beliefs in such institutions as constitutions and parliamentary government, after decolonization and the flood of immigrants there was a shift in rhetoric to perceiving citizenship as racial. The class antagonisms that had once shaped politics changed to expressions of racial prejudice and ethnic purity as the economic golden age became a thing of the past.

Smaller States Pursue Prosperity

Meanwhile, a cluster of smaller states in the Western bloc without heavy defense commitments enjoyed increasing prosperity after the recession of the early 1980s ended. In Spain, tourist dollars helped rebuild the southern cities of Granada and Córdoba, and Spanish per capita income rose from $300 in 1957 to $3,000 in 1987 because of industrial expansion. Under a moderate socialist prime minister, Felipe González—who, like Mitterrand and other socialist leaders, supported the aspirations of the middle class—the country joined the Common Market in January 1986. The economy of Italy grew slowly amid pervasive political corruption. In Ireland a surge of investment in education for high-tech jobs combined with low wages to attract new business. While Ireland began to enjoy its newfound prosperity, the Irish people as a whole began to find the death toll among Catholics and Protestants in Northern Ireland increasingly unacceptable. Leaders agreed to a political rapprochement between the two factions in 1999. Unionists in Northern Ireland would accord Catholics their rights, while Catholics, including those in Ireland, would lay down their arms and curtail their support for violence.

Austria prospered, too, in part by reducing government pensions and aid to industry and agriculture. Austria's chancellor Franz Vranitzky summed up the changed focus of government in the 1980s and 1990s: "In Austria, the shelter that the state has given to almost everyone—employee as well as entrepreneur—has led . . . a lot of people [to] think not only what they can do to solve a problem but what the state can do. . . . This needs to change."[7] The case of Austria further illustrates that the century-long growth of the welfare state was ending in small and large states alike, and there was general retrenchment or at least steps toward it. And here too divisive language of race and ethnicity replaced the rhetoric of healing and inclusion on which the welfare state had flourished after World War II.

Maintaining a broad array of social programs despite the prevailing mood, Sweden stood out as an exception. But even there, the government's panoply of choices for immigrants began to seem overly expensive: the tax rate on income over $46,000 was 80 percent. As productivity flagged, the government took stern measures, denying benefits to unemployed workers who refused retraining or a job offer. The Swedes also reduced their costly dependence on foreign oil by cutting consumption in half between 1976 and 1986. Despite anti-inflationary success and a highly skilled workforce, Sweden dropped from fourth to fourteenth place among nations in per capita income by 1998 as other countries invested more. "Sweden is no longer the good solidarity-committed country it once was, but a hard-pressed country . . . with 12 percent unemployment," the regional director of the UN High Commission for Refugees noted in the 1990s.[8] Businesspeople looked to invest in countries where taxation for such programs as unemployment insurance was far lower. With Soviet communism all but dead, Sweden's "middle way" (between communism and capitalism) had come to seem extreme. Like other Europeans, Swedes stopped seeing naturalized immigrants as fellow citizens: "How long will it be before our Swedish children will have to turn their faces toward Mecca?" asked one member of the Swedish parliament in 1993, echoing the racist backlash in France and other European countries.[9]

REFORMERS CHANGE THE SOVIET BLOC

Ongoing dissident activism and persistent criticism of Communist rule stealthily weakened the grip of Communist governments by throwing their legitimacy into doubt. They also exposed the economic woes of people living in the Soviet bloc. Although perhaps insulating their citizens from the extreme ups and downs of capitalism, Soviet-style economies left people vulnerable to the bitter consequences of the rampant decay in the system. Spending on resources to meet the ever-rising military needs of the cold war intensified the deprivation felt in everyday life. A legacy of resentment built as the decades of dreary and degrading Communist rule accumulated.

Gorbachev Comes to Power

Soviet citizens experienced a deteriorating standard of living as years of economic stagnation and then declining productivity took their toll. After working a full day, Soviet homemakers had to stand in long lines to obtain basic commodities.

Housing shortages and straitened family budgets often necessitated a three-generation household, in which grandparents took over tedious homemaking tasks from their working children and grandchildren. "There is no special skill to this," a seventy-three-year-old grandmother and former garbage collector remarked of the chore of shopping. "You just stand in line and wait."[10] Even so, would-be consumers often left empty-handed, and more than one foreign visitor complained that she had never eaten so many varieties of cabbage salad. Soap and other basic household supplies disappeared instantly from stores, and the quality of medical care varied according to social status. One cheap and readily available product was vodka, and alcoholism reached crisis levels, diminishing productivity and sapping the nation's morale. In 1978, Soviet leader Leonid Brezhnev had warned the party faithful of the costs to productivity of "drunkenness . . . violation of work discipline, indifference, parasitism, and the claim to reap more from society than one gives."[11]

Economic stagnation had many other ramifications. Many ordinary people decided not to have children, and fertility fell below replacement levels throughout the Soviet bloc, except in Muslim areas of Soviet Central Asia. The country was forced to import massive amounts of grain because 20 to 30 percent of the grain produced in the USSR rotted before it could be harvested or shipped to market, so great was the inefficiency of the state-directed economy. Industrial pollution, spewed out by enterprises responsible only for meeting production quotas, reached scandalous dimensions. The massive and privileged Communist Party bureaucracy hobbled industrial innovation and failed to achieve socialism's professed goal of a decent standard of living for working people. To match American military growth, the Soviet Union diverted 15 to 20 percent of its gross national product (more than double the U.S. proportion) to armaments. As this combustible mixture of problems heated up, a new generation was coming of age that had no memory of World War II or Stalin's purges. One Russian observer found members of the younger generation "cynical, but less afraid." "They believe in nothing," a mother said of Soviet youth in 1984. "They won't be pushed around," added another.[12]

In 1985, Mikhail Gorbachev (b. 1931) opened an era of unexpected change. Gorbachev was part of the new Soviet world of opportunity and mobility, studying law and gaining an advanced degree in agriculture. Although he was a son of the poor peasantry, he worked his way up through the Communist Party ranks, gaining power at the local level and then entering the central government as an economic expert. In 1956, Gorbachev, then only twenty-five, attended the party congress at which Nikita Khrushchev first condemned Stalin's excesses. Later, as a trusted party official, he traveled widely in the Soviet bloc and got a firsthand glimpse of life in the West during trips to France, Italy, and West Germany.

Gorbachev had risen through the party ranks as an agricultural specialist, and when he became head of the party in March 1985, he quickly proposed broad plans to reinvigorate the Soviet economy. His program of *perestroika* ("restructuring") aimed to streamline production and management. The economy depended not on innovation but on labor-intensive production, and outmoded machinery was hampering Soviet industrial output. Against the wishes of managers who were benefiting from the status quo, Gorbachev set out to reverse economic decay by improving productivity, increasing the rate of capital investment, encouraging the use of up-to-date technology, and gradually introducing market features such as prices and profits. Doubters remarked that these were hardly new ideas.

Along with perestroika, Gorbachev proclaimed a policy of *glasnost* (usually translated as "openness" or "publicity"). To the Soviet leader, glasnost meant speaking "the language of truth," disseminating "wide, prompt, and frank information," and allowing Soviet citizens new measures of free speech.[13] When party officials complained that glasnost threatened their status, Gorbachev replaced more than a third of the party's leadership in the first months of his administration. Free speech started to surface.

In the mid-1980s, the Soviet magazine *Ogonyok* ("Small Fires"), instead of making up patriotic "letters to the editor" as was the custom, began printing actual mail from readers. A woman identifying herself as a "mother of two" protested that the cost-cutting policy of reusing syringes in hospitals was spreading AIDS. "Why should little kids have to pay for the criminal actions of our Ministry of Health?" she asked. Other readers complained of corrupt factory managers, of "the radioactive sausages" foisted on the public after the explosion of a reactor at the Chernobyl nuclear power plant on April 26, 1986, and of endless lines at grocery stores and the lack of food. Sales of *Ogonyok* soared from a few hundred thousand copies to four million, and the experiment in printing real letters flooded the offices with hundreds of thousands of them. The *Ogonyok* example was not unique: all across the Soviet bloc, people were tentatively exploring political participation and resistance.

The pressing need for glasnost became most evident after the Chernobyl catastrophe, when bureaucratic cover-ups of the explosion at the nuclear plant delayed the spread of information about the accident, with lethal consequences for people living nearby. After Chernobyl, even the Communist Party and Marxism-Leninism itself were subjected to public criticism as people openly took to the streets to commemorate those who had lost their lives. Attendees at party meetings suddenly heard complaints about the highest leaders and their policies. Even the state-run media were not immune. Television shows such as *The Fifth Wheel* adopted the outspoken methods of American investigative reporting. One program showed an interview with an executioner of political prisoners and exposed the plight of Leningrad's homeless children. "Work is getting pretty easy around here," remarked TV censor Natalya Strepetova, who had less and less to do at her job.[14]

Political factions arose, not only for and against Gorbachev but across the political spectrum. Many people welcomed Gorbachev as a breath of fresh air, but they simultaneously saw in his regime the kind of class privilege that communism was supposed to eliminate. Gorbachev's wife Raisa was an educated and very public figure—quite different from the retiring spouses of earlier Soviet leaders. Her sophisticated dress and polished image aroused the people's wrath. "Her well-manicured fingers [are] decorated with diamonds bought with our money," one critic said.[15] Raisa Gorbachev became the most visible sign of the great difference in lifestyle between the "new class" and everyone else.

Dissent appeared in the heart of the government too. In the fall of 1987, one of Gorbachev's erstwhile allies, Boris Yeltsin, quit the governing Politburo after denouncing perestroika as inadequate for real reform. Yeltsin's political daring, which in the past would have consigned him to oblivion or Siberia, inspired others to organize in opposition to the crumbling ruling orthodoxy. By the spring of 1989, in remarkably free balloting, not a single Communist was chosen for office in Moscow's local elections.

Glasnost and perestroika dramatically affected superpower relations as well. Recognizing how severely the cold war arms race was draining Soviet resources, Gorbachev almost immediately began scaling back missile production. His unilateral actions gradually won over Ronald Reagan. The two leaders met at Geneva, Switzerland, in the autumn of 1985 and then in Reykjavik, Iceland, in October 1986 to begin defusing the cold war. "I bet the hard-liners in both our countries are bleeding when we shake hands," said the jovial Reagan at the Reykjavik summit's conclusion.[16] Although meetings did not always go smoothly, a major breakthrough from the U.S. point of view occurred in February 1989, when Gorbachev at last withdrew his country's forces from the debilitating war in Afghanistan. By the end of the year, the United States was beginning to cut back its own vast military buildup.

Poland and the Birth of Solidarity

Poland was energized by the changes taking place in the USSR, but its economic situation had been dire since the 1970s and remained so. Poland lagged behind other Eastern-bloc countries in provisioning consumers. Food, clothing, and other necessities of life often were in short supply. This situation heightened people's dissatisfaction with the government and increased workers' willingness to organize over issues of pay, working conditions, and the availability and cost of basic necessities—all of them tightly controlled by the Communist government.

In 1970 the government had introduced a wage freeze and an increase in food prices. Coming at Christmas—food was an important part of the holiday festivities—the measures seemed especially harsh. Workers were outraged. Strikes and violence in the Polish shipyards eventually caused the government to collapse. The new head of state, Edward Gierek, appealed to the strikers' pride as workers and Polish citizens. "I am a worker just like you," he announced as he implored the shipyard workers to think of Poland and its economic future. "We will help," they shouted, affirming their identities as patriotic Poles and workers by ending their protests.

In February 1971, as the winter advanced, the government's policies met an entirely different reception from women workers. In strikes continuing into the 1980s and ultimately toppling the Polish regime, one government after another faced strong female opposition. In the city of Lodz, a textile center with a workforce dominated by women, strikers sang protest songs, harassed high officials with accusations that each one's wife "loads ham on her sandwiches while my children eat dry bread," and sat crying en masse. When asked as the men had been "Will you help us?" the women shouted a resounding "No." Within days the government rolled back price increases on food, as women maintained a united front on not only workplace issues but also their families' well-being.

Hoping to maintain peace, Gierek decided to increase supplies of food and other consumer necessities and to promote civic unity through appeals to Polish nationalism and devotion to the Catholic Church. Each part of this plan faced intractable problems, however. Increasing both productivity and the supply of goods was accomplished, but it meant borrowing funds and purchasing supplies from western Europe and the United States, and Poland quickly amassed a large foreign debt. As for the government's endorsement of nationalism and Catholicism, both isms won the allegiance of Poles at the expense of whatever allegiance they felt for Soviet-led communism. When in 1978 the archbishop of Krakow, Cardinal Karol Wojtyla, was elected pope, Catholicism's potential for subversion became explosive. The new pope, John Paul II, had never concealed his anticommunism, and he supported all Catholic initiatives, such as forming groups to combat poverty, to bring people together in a common cause against communism.

In 1980, economic issues resurfaced when Gierek's government again began curbing supplies of goods by raising prices in order to pay interest on the burgeoning foreign debt. Strikes and demonstrations erupted across the country, resulting once more in the gendered partitioning of demands and demonstrations. Shipyard workers in Gdańsk on the Baltic coast took the lead in demanding economic reform, the legalization of workers' organizations independent of Communist control, and greater freedom of speech. They organized a national political and worker group to institutionalize their political power. They called their group Solidarity, and at its head was the wily, politically savvy Lech Walesa (b. 1944), recently fired from his job as an electrician in the Gdańsk shipyards. A devout Catholic and, like Gorbachev, a son of peasants, Walesa had slipped into the shipyards as the strikes erupted and quickly rose to head the movement. Although women were involved in Solidarity and brought food and other supplies to the strikers, Solidarity members saw their organization as a masculine one. "Women, don't interfere with us—we are fighting for Poland," they chanted.[17]

In the summer of 1981, as protest kept pace with the dwindling of supplies, women workers in Lodz once again took to the streets in a huge demonstration. This time they brought their children and pushed baby carriages. Their fierce slogan "Hungry people of the world, unite" once again made the individual human right to food and shelter the crux of the protest. The leaders of Solidarity came to believe that such actions by consumers to gain basic goods like food threatened their union's control. The government agreed, but it targeted both consumers and Solidarity, declaring martial law and outlawing Solidarity in December 1981. By then, consumer issues were intractable problems, and the government lacked a way to talk about basic social needs, policies to address them, and the supplies to meet them. Appeals to patriotism and to workers' loyalty no longer worked. Martial law seemed the only solution.

Members of Solidarity saw their movement as not only economic and political but also cultural and social. Living in a country that for two centuries had been

◆ **Solidarity in Poland, 1987**
Striking workers in the Gdansk shipyards organized the trade union Solidarity in 1980. It mustered hundreds of thousands of supporters and remained an underground political force even after it was outlawed in 1981. Solidarity was committed to freedom to organize and strike, and its members objected to cutbacks in wages while prices for food and other essentials were being raised. Many members announced their allegiance to the Roman Catholic Church, and in this photo they are shown parading with their banner aloft during a visit by the Polish pontiff, John Paul II. Solidarity came to stand for courage in the face of oppression, for at the time of this demonstration the union remained illegal. *Peter Turnley/CORBIS.*

dominated culturally by outsiders, Solidarity workers flocked by the tens of thousands to hear history lectures on the Polish resistance in World War II. Their banners, waving across the shipyards and universities, carried poetry—both traditional and written on the spot to express feelings of patriotism and resistance. Posters visible to spouses and lovers waiting outside the gates of strikebound factories carried this sentimental verse: "Oh why beats your heart, why tears in your eye? / I owe you my Love, owe my country, my Life. / Think who you are, and think of our Duty. / Your rival, my girl, is Poland's Liberty." Poetry readings from the works of famed dissidents of the past, such as Polish nationalist Adam Mickiewicz, who in the nineteenth century had opposed Russian domination, were filled with overflow crowds. "People openly wept. . . . We were begged for encores. . . . I talked to the workers myself, and it appeared that they really needed great literature and poetry," recalled the director of one such event. Having little access to anything but Sovietized culture and propaganda, Polish workers were both awed and spurred to action by the restoration of cultural freedoms.[18]

Poland's Communist Party teetered on the brink of collapse, until hard-liners in the Polish police and army, pressured by the USSR and other states in the Warsaw Pact, imposed martial law in December 1981 and outlawed Solidarity. Nevertheless, continued efforts by reporters and dissidents—using phones, fax machines, newspapers, and radio—kept Solidarity alive as a force both inside and outside of Poland. Stern and puritanical, General Wojciech Jaruzelski had taken over as the head of Poland's government in October 1981 and soon thereafter in an open letter thanked Soviet leader Leonid Brezhnev for Soviet "economic aid which allowed us to resolve the difficulties we have had to face."[19] The military government rounded up many Solidarity leaders. Blinded by its "juvenile emotional dynamism," Jaruzelski charged, the union had "trodden on the law, ruined the economy, [and] waged a struggle against the party and the Government."[20] The general, however, could not push repression too far: he needed loans from the U.S.-led bloc to keep the sinking Polish economy afloat. Under Jaruzelski the first socialist military regime came into being, with worrisome implications for communism's commitment to a people's or workers' state. In the midst of this tense situation, a high-ranking military official made this damning statement in a secretly taped speech: "I have serious doubts if the working class's wishes would be compatible with the proper functioning of the state."[21] The implication was that the state took precedence over the working class.

THE END OF THE SOVIET SYSTEM

Despite the situation in Poland in 1981, reform could not be suppressed once Gorbachev came to power in 1985, especially when he made it clear that changes needed to occur throughout the Soviet bloc. In the midst of Gorbachev's initiatives, tremors shook the Communist Chinese world in the spring of 1989. Inspired by Gorbachev's May 15 visit to China's capital, Beijing, thousands of students massed in Tiananmen Square to demand democracy. They used telex machines and electronic mail to rush their messages to the international community, and they effectively conveyed their goals in front of the cameras that Western television reporters trained on them. China's aged Communist leaders, while pushing economic modernization and even allowing market operations, refused to consider the introduction of democracy. As workers began joining the "Democracy" forces, as the activists called themselves, the government quickly crushed the movement in early June, executing as many as a thousand rebels. Nonetheless, there was an expectant air in the Communist world—a sense that something monumental was about to happen.

The spirit of revolt, growing in Poland, advanced across eastern Europe in 1989 and brought decades of Communist rule to an end (Map 11.1). Indeed, Europeans designated 1989 the twentieth century's *annus mirabilis* ("year of miracles") because of the sudden and unexpected disintegration of Communist power throughout the region. Events in Poland took a dramatic turn first, as Solidarity's strength persisted and as grassroots supporters remained active and committed. In direct confrontation with Soviet dogma, Poles flocked to Catholic churches across the country, and volunteers worked to help alcoholics, holding up signs warning that people would "turn red" if they drank. Large sums of money circulated from city to city to provide a defense for dissidents rounded up and prosecuted by the government, and Catholics held prayer vigils. The goal was simply "to ensure there is a gathering," in the words of one organizer.[22] In the spring of 1989, Jaruzelski's government, weakened by its mishandling of the economy and lacking Soviet support for further repression, again legalized Solidarity and promised free elections. In parliamentary elections in June, Solidarity candidates drove out the Communists. "Our defeat," Jaruzelski admitted, "is total."[23] By early 1990, Jaruzelski had been replaced as president by Solidarity spokesman Lech Walesa, who began Poland's rocky transition to a full-blown market economy.

Hungary

Soviet leaders from Khrushchev to Gorbachev paid lip service to the independence of Soviet-bloc nations, but when it became apparent that Gorbachev was serious and that the Soviet Union would not intervene in Poland, the fall of communism repeated itself in one country after another. Hungary was next. In Poland, workers and housewives had spearheaded protests for change. While in Hungary, it was party officials who played the key role in communism's collapse. Having experimented with "market socialism" since the 1960s, government planners were able to work for economic reform from within. Though politically repressive, János Kádár, who took over after the failed 1956 uprising, directed government planners to divert some segments of the economy toward market-based activity. Artisans and restaurateurs set up businesses outside the state-controlled system. Architects, engineers, and mechanics contracted out their services after putting in their hours for state-owned companies. Because the government moved to solidify its credibility with international lending institutions by raising state-controlled prices, many Hungarians worked overtime to keep up with the rising cost of living, often competing for extra work. These workers actually generated one-third of Hungary's income in their activities outside the Communist system. Their extra work, much of it for free enterprise businesses, made the Hungarian economy more robust than other Soviet-bloc economics, where workers and innovators lacked free market outlets for their productivity.

At the beginning of 1989, demands for liberalization spread from economics to politics, and government planners actually joined ordinary people in insisting

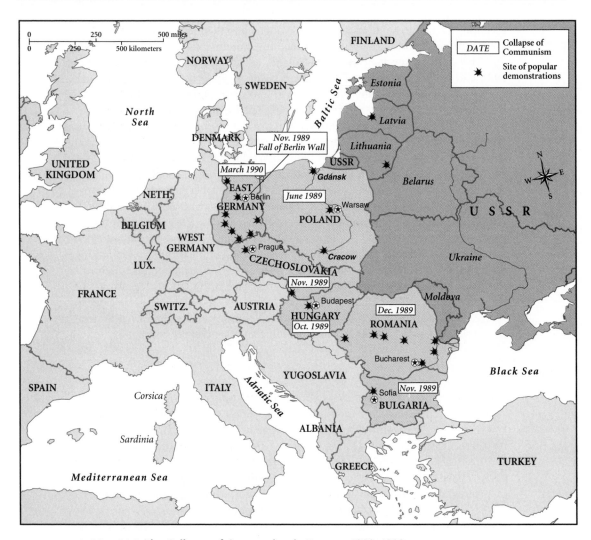

◆ **Map 11.1 The Collapse of Communism in Europe, 1989–1990**

In 1989 resistance to communism spilled out into the streets of many cities within the
Soviet bloc. Throughout the decade Polish workers were in the vanguard of activism. As
Gorbachev's reforms became a reality after his rise to power in 1985, opposition began to
snowball even further. This led to the relatively bloodless overthrow of the Soviet system and
then of the USSR itself from 1989 into the early 1990s.

that political democracy accompany economic freedom. Organized opposition had taken shape, using environmental, cultural, and ethnic issues to garner support. Since the mid-1980s individuals had been protesting the construction of a dam that would upset the local ecology, encouraging a boycott of Communist holidays in favor of traditional Hungarian ones, and holding public demonstrations on behalf of ethnic Hungarians living in Romania who were persecuted by Romanian dictator Nicolae Ceauşescu's. But it was less the causes than the growing crowds that emboldened reform-minded Communist leaders. In 1988 they eased out the senile Kádár and looked the other way as Hungarians began to form new political associations with names such as Democratic Forum, Young Democrats, and Free Democrats that announced an alternative politics in the making. By 1989 the Hungarian Communist leadership was endorsing what it called "socialist pluralism," as hundreds of thousands of Hungarians celebrated on March 15 to commemorate the 1956 Hungarian uprising and on June 16 to reinter the remains of Imre Nagy, martyred leader during the 1956 uprising. They also boycotted the official May Day parade sponsored by Hungary's Communist regime. This "battle of the holidays" was successful. In the fall of 1989, Hungary's parliament dismissed the Communist Party as the official ruling institution, and people tore down Communist symbols throughout the country. The Soviet system, a top Communist stated, "was wrong in its entirety."[24]

Post-Communist Hungary still faced huge challenges, many of them reflecting the complicated modern history of central, eastern, and southeastern Europe. The end of the Soviet empire meant that Hungary had not only to rebuild political institutions but also to select the cultural symbols that would unify the nation around the new government. October 23 became a national holiday, commemorating not only the day in 1989 on which the new Hungarian Republic was proclaimed but also the day in 1956 on which students had made their first mass demonstrations. In order to erase the Communist past, streets were renamed to honor important political figures from the nineteenth century. When it came to a flag and other national symbols, the question was whether to devise new ones or to draw from the Hungarian past. But from which past—imperial, republican, or the period of resistance to Soviet rule in 1956? Ultimately Hungary chose to use a crown on its coat of arms because so many of the republican symbols had been tainted by use under communism. Such complicated cultural and economic questions would continue to plague Hungary and other former Communist countries in the years to come.

The Reunification of Germany

The most potent symbol of a divided Europe—the Berlin Wall—stood in the midst of a divided Germany. East Germans had attempted to escape over the wall for more than two decades, despite their country's reputation as having the most dynamic economy in the socialist world. To compound the sense of things going wrong, opposition groups like those in Leipzig and other East German cities grew in size over the course of the 1980s. As communism unwound in Hungary, Austria and Hungary opened their common border in August 1989, and thousands of East Germans turned what looked like vacation travel to Hungary into escape. From Hungary they passed to Austria and on to West Germany, where the government had long promised citizenship to *all* Germans. In the elections of March 1990 the voters of East Germany handed the Allianz party, which favored a market economy and reunification, a stunning victory over Communists. But it was ever mounting protest at home that ultimately toppled the regime, no longer able to count on backup from Soviet tanks. As thousands of East Berliners flooded through the wall on November 9, protest turned to festive holiday: "We are one people," chanted the crowds. West Berliners handed out bananas, a consumer good in short supply in the Communist zone, and that fruit became the unofficial symbol of reunion, even though some West Berliners scorned the "banana gobblers" from the east. Berliners released years of frustration at their division by assaulting the wall with sledge-hammers and bringing home chunks as souvenirs. The government completed its destruction in the fall of 1990.

The official reunification of Germany occurred on October 3, 1990, faster than anyone expected. Many in the east were eager for the prosperity and democracy that they believed such a merger would ensure. Helmut Kohl, with supreme political skill, negotiated the reunification on those terms. He promised "a flourishing industrial landscape"—a far cry from the dysfunctional East German economy—and was confident that the West German model of democracy would prevent any resurgence of Communist rule. He had the support of the East German people, and he used that support against the entrenched Communist bureaucrats in East Germany—most of them opposed to the end of the state that had given them their jobs.

In fact, economic integration turned out to be less successful than anticipated. Planners underestimated the number of jobs that would be lost, especially in the east. As West German industrialists bought up East German assets, the balance in the east tipped toward the new owners. Everyone in the east, from day laborers to university professors—said to lack modern skills—faced job loss, and unemployment reached 18 to 20 percent in Rostock and other cities. The planners' goal, however, was to improve the industrial productivity and capacity of the east, not to dismantle East German industry and turn the region into an economic backwater. Facing a globalizing economy and the high price of the welfare state like the rest of industrialized Europe, German planners also had to figure out how to integrate the decaying eastern economy into the newly expanded national economy.

With much in the east discredited as unworkable and undesirable, the merger took place on West German terms but its monetary and human costs were far greater than expected. Social services such as day care were eliminated in the east to bring the region into alignment with West Germany, whose laws and institutions discouraged women from entering the workforce. Unemployment soared, and in many other ways the quality of life in the east deteriorated. These developments spurred intense political debate and produced a sense of helplessness. Marion Doenhoff, editor of the influential newsmagazine *Die Zeit,* and former West German chancellor Helmut Schmidt lamented in a jointly authored article, "It is as if history gushes by us like an unchanneled white-water river, while we, standing on the riverbank, raise the alarmed question as to where all this should lead."[25] A form of cultural prejudice emerged as West Germans began noting with distaste the differences between themselves and Germans from the east. As suffering increased and tensions mounted, Doenhoff and Schmidt were part of a swelling cry among intellectuals and union leaders for government intervention against the powerful forces of globalization that they also blamed for making reunification so painful.

Czechoslovakia

In Czechoslovakia, which after 1968 was firmly restored to Soviet-style rule, people watched the progress of glasnost expectantly. They saw Gorbachev on television calling for free speech, but he never mentioned reform in Czechoslovakia. Moreover, the government of Gustav Husak was immovable; no reforming party bureaucrats were encouraging change of any kind. Dissenters met instant arrest and imprisonment, and no mass demonstrations or large-scale opposition groups protested. Among the few signs of opposition was persistent dissent by grassroots activists and intellectuals, among them playwright Václav Havel. Then in the winter of 1989, crowds began to face down the police and never more so than at the commemoration of anti-Soviet protester Jan Palach's suicide on January 16, 1969, which resonated ever more loudly as glasnost proceeded elsewhere. In the usual post-1968 reaction, the government arrested and imprisoned Havel and several other leading intellectuals. In the spring of 1989, a petition campaign secured Havel's release. Despite ferment elsewhere, the situation in Czechoslovakia appeared hopeless to some. "Communism will prevail," party chairman Jan Fojtik told a visiting American in the fall of 1989.[26]

Demonstrators continued to protest sporadically in the streets for democracy, and the government cracked down by turning the police on them. On November 17, a student commemoration of the victims of Nazi atrocities once again brought out the police. This time, police brutality fueled popular anger to the boiling point. Students circulated a video of police violence from neighborhood to neighborhood and city to city. With anger rising, the break came on November 24. Flanked by Havel, Alexander Dubček, leader of the "Prague Spring" of 1968, addressed a crowd of 50,000 in Prague's Wenceslas Square with a call for the ouster of Stalinists from the government. The crowd responded, shaking its keys to signal the Communists that it was time for them to go. Almost immediately, the Communist leadership resigned. Capping the country's "Velvet Revolution," as this change of direction became known because of its lack of bloodshed, the formerly Communist-dominated parliament elected Havel president.

Romania

As the Berlin Wall tumbled and the repressive Communist regime in Czechoslovakia collapsed, the world's attention fastened on the political drama unfolding in Romania. Since the mid-1960s, Nicolae Ceaușescu had ruled as the harshest dictator in Communist Europe since Stalin. In the name of modernization he destroyed whole villages and to pay for this modernization exacted a heavy toll of deprivation on Romanians. To cut back on the use of power, heat was turned off and no room could have more than one 40-watt light bulb. To save on food, he launched a countrywide program of fitness and weight reduction for Romanians. Like many European countries Romania suffered labor shortages, which increased as couples had fewer children because of the difficult conditions of everyday life. Ceauşescu's solution to this problem was characteristically fierce: to increase the population, he outlawed contraceptives and abortions, a restriction that led to the abandonment of tens of thousands of children. While most Romanians lived in utter poverty, Ceauşescu and his wife Elena, behaving like absolute monarchs from centuries earlier, channeled almost all the country's resources into elegant residences for themselves, the ultimate project being a massive palace and state building in Bucharest. After working-class housing and dozens of other buildings, including historic ones, were razed to the ground, the palace was constructed of the most luxurious materials and still stands today, unfinished and grotesque.

Despite the brutality and censorship of Ceauşescu's regime, in early December 1989, a Reformed Church opposition movement coalesced around the refusal of a Protestant minister to leave his parish as decreed by Ceauşescu's "modernization" program for the countryside. Crowds gathered in cities and towns throughout Romania in support of the pastor and in defiance of the government. "Down with Ceauşescu" and other antiregime slogans filled banners hanging from monuments and walls of buildings. Ceauşescu left the country for a state visit to the Middle East, leaving orders for the army to gun the demonstrators down. On his return he improvised a huge rally, but instead of wild applause the crowds met him with jeers and shouts of "Ceauşescu dictator!"[27] The spirit of resistance spread to the population at large and to the army, which crushed the forces loyal to Ceauşescu and his wife Elena.

The consequences were dire and singular, for this revolution against communism ended differently from all the others. On Christmas Day, 1989, viewers watched on television as a military court tried the dictator and his wife and then had them shot. Soon after, Western photographers displayed a sampling of the horrors Ceauşescu had wrought, from orphanages packed with thousands of unwanted, uncared-for children to the mass graves of men and women who had dared to dissent.

YUGOSLAVIA AND THE USSR DISINTEGRATE

By 1989, the need for economic reform had already brought attempts to right the economy in both Yugoslavia and the Soviet Union and to implement a measure of political change. Other issues boiled over. Like Hungarians and Czechs in the early-twentieth-century Habsburg Empire, nationality groups in the USSR began to demand political and cultural autonomy in the 1980s. The Soviet empire held together more than one hundred ethnic groups, and the five republics of Soviet

Central Asia were home to fifty million Muslims. Sometimes the government attempted to instill Russian and Soviet culture into the communities; at other times it encouraged cultural autonomy. Neither policy produced genuine allegiance to the Soviet Union. Similarly in Yugoslavia, Communist rulers enforced unity among religious and ethnic groups, and intermarriage among them occurred regularly; but gradually the republics and autonomous provinces of which Yugoslavia was composed gained more autonomy. In both the Soviet Union and Yugoslavia, politicians within the various republics turned events in ever more revolutionary or violent directions. During the unstable years of the early 1990s, ethnicity and ethnic violence emerged as effective political tools for ambitious politicians. First Yugoslavia and then the Soviet Union itself fell apart, and ethnicity continued to shape politics in those regions into the new millennium.

The Breakup of Yugoslavia

Slobodan Milosevic (1941–2006) was one of those politicians who fanned ethnic tensions. In 1987, a time of deepening economic crisis in Yugoslavia, he discovered his issue, invoking Serbian nationalism and claiming that Serbs were being oppressed by other groups in the country. Ethnic claims resonated because Yugoslavia was so ethnically diverse. Unlike Hungary and Poland, which had been "ethnically cleansed" earlier, Yugoslavia was ripe for politicians whose only issue was ethnic nationalism. A Communist opportunist, Milosevic turned his energies to removing competitors and having opponents thrown in jail, ultimately winning the presidency of the republic of Serbia in 1989 on a platform promoting Serb ethnicity. Seeing the handwriting on the wall, leaders of the other Yugoslav republics called for secession (Map 11.2).

More prosperous than the other republics because of greater economic development, and resentful of subsidizing the rest of the country, Slovenia led the way: "Slovenians . . . have one more reason to say they are in favor of independence," announced one leader as Serb claims to dominate the other republics and create a Serb-run centralized state mounted. In the spring of 1991, first Slovenia and then Croatia seceded, depriving Yugoslavia of its most literate and wealthiest citizens. Eager to enforce Serbian supremacy in the region, the Serb-dominated Yugoslav army successfully took more than a quarter of Croatia's land but was swiftly defeated in Slovenia. An even more devastating civil war engulfed Bosnia-Herzegovina, which seceded from Yugoslavia in March 1992. The republic's Muslim majority tried unsuccessfully to create a multicultural and multiethnic state. Backed by covert support from Milosevic's government, Bosnian Serbs formed a guerrilla army and gained the upper hand. A UN arms embargo prevented the Bosnian Muslims from equipping their forces adequately to defend themselves even when the Serbs took to massacring them. Political leaders in Europe and the United States sought to remain aloof from the deepening conflict.

The consequences, however, were relentless and visible to everyone. Some three million Yugoslavs fled, most to Germany, Austria, and Scandinavia, which unlike Britain agreed to harbor the refugees. During the 1990s, civilians died by the

◆ **Muslim Refugees in Croatia, 1992**
The division of Yugoslavia after the fall of communism brought misery to its many ethnic and religious groups. Serbia was determined to keep the other states from seceding in hopes of dominating a large union. At the same time, the different ethnic groups took their ambitions out on one another so that every group suffered from ethnic strife. This image shows hungry Muslim refugees from Bosnia-Herzegovina hoping to get bread. They are at a refugee station in Croatia before being transported by the Red Cross to Germany. Western Europe became crowded not only with migrants from beyond the continent but also with those from former Communist states seeking safety and opportunity. *AFP/Getty Images.*

tens of thousands as Serbs under Milosevic's leadership, and to a lesser extent Croats and Muslims, pursued a policy of "ethnic cleansing"—genocide. Serb militias raped Muslim and Croat women to leave them pregnant with Serb babies. They rounded up Muslim men and boys, murdered them, and dumped the bodies in mass graves. A 1995 Croatian massacre of Serbs who had helped seized land from Croatia was followed at Srebrenica by the Serb slaughter of 8,000 Muslim boys and men. "Kill the lot," the commander of the Serb forces ordered at Srebrenica. Some months later, given the lack of any international response, the Serbs gunned down civilians in the marketplace of Sarajevo.

Each competing force also took aim at the cultural heritage of its opponents. Military units damaged and destroyed libraries and museums and attacked Dubrovnik and other Yugoslav cities rich in medieval history. In 1993, Croats, having taken over part of Bosnia, blew up the Mostar Bridge, built in 1566, eradicating a treasure dating from a time when ethnic pluralism reigned under the Ottomans. Ethnic cleansing brought destruction not only to actual people but to all traces of their rich and complex past.

Many observers in the West dismissed the violence in the Balkans as another in a series of "age-old" blood feuds manifesting the backwardness of a quasi-"Asian" society. Others warned that ethnic cleansing was destroying the complex, intertwined pasts of people who spoke many languages and shared many customs—in order to revive a mythical national unity that had never existed. Still others saw ethnic rivals resorting to genocide simply to gain power for themselves and their friends.

Most European governments refused to help end the violence. Then after the slaughter at Srebrenica and Sarajevo, U.S. president Bill Clinton directed NATO forces to bomb Serb positions in Bosnia. Facing no long-term sanctions, however, Serb forces attacked again late in the 1990s, this time targeting people of Albanian ethnicity living in the Yugoslav province of Kosovo (Map 11.2). Milosevic explained the aggression as part of an attempt to right an injustice done to the Serbian people

◆ **Map 11.2 The Former Yugoslavia, c. 2000**
Communist leader Marshal Josip Broz Tito had held the six republics and two autonomous provinces of Yugoslavia together as a unified state from 1945 until his death in 1980. After that, a variety of political and ethnic tensions mounted, until 1991 when Slovenia and Croatia declared their independence. Bloodshed and genocide followed; the final remnants of the once-united Yugoslavia—Montenegro and Serbia—declared their independence from one another in 2006.

in the Middle Ages. From 1997 to 1999, Serb militias and the Yugoslav army murdered the civilian population. NATO pilots bombed Kosovo in an attempt to drive back the army and militias. The Serbs ultimately gave up their positions but not before driving close to a million Albanian Kosovars into a crude exile in neighboring countries. Finally, amid incredible suffering, UN peacekeeping forces stepped in to enforce an interethnic truce. People throughout the world felt that this intervention came far too late and reflected great-power self-interest rather than any true commitment to maintaining peace and protecting human rights.

Alongside the decimated republics of Bosnia and Croatia, a new regime emerged in Serbia. After international threats to withhold economic aid of any kind, the government of Serbia in July 2001 turned Milosevic over to a war crimes tribunal in the Netherlands to be tried for crimes against humanity. In 2003, Milosevic loyalists, many of them in line to be rounded up for trial in the world court, assassinated the new reform-minded prime minister Zoran Djindjic. When the imprisoned Milosevic died of natural causes in 2006, some of the most culpable military leaders remained at large, and Milosevic's message remained a potent one. Across both western and eastern Europe, racial, ethnic, and religious differences shaped the political landscape, perhaps most violently in the former Communist states.

The Soviet Union Comes Apart

While genocide was unfolding in the former Yugoslavia, political stability crumbled in the Soviet Union in 1990 and 1991, and a string of secessions ensued, threatening regional and global politics. Perestroika had failed to revitalize the Soviet economy. People confronted soaring prices, the specter of unemployment, and even greater scarcity of goods than they had endured in the past. Although Gorbachev announced late in 1990 that there was "no alternative to the transition to the market," his plan was too little, too late and satisfied no one.[28] The Russian parliament's election of Boris Yeltsin as president of the Russian Republic over a Communist candidate provoked a coup against Gorbachev in August 1991 by a group of eight antireform hard-liners, including the Soviet vice president and the head of the Soviet secret police, the KGB. Holding Gorbachev under house arrest, coup leaders claimed to be rescuing the Soviet Union from the "mortal danger" posed by "extremist forces."[29] Yeltsin, however, standing atop a tank outside the Russian Republic's parliament building, called for mass resistance. Thousands of residents of Moscow surrounded the parliament to protect it, the heads of the other republics declared their support for Yeltsin and Gorbachev, and units of the army defected to protect Yeltsin's headquarters. People used fax machines and computers to coordinate internal resistance and send messages to the rest of the world. The coup fell into complete disarray in the face of citizens' determination not to allow a return of Stalinism or indeed any form of Soviet orthodoxy.

The Soviet Union disintegrated. People tore down statues of Soviet heroes. Yeltsin outlawed the party newspaper, *Pravda,* and sealed the KGB files. At the end of August the Soviet parliament suspended operations of the Communist Party itself. One republic after another followed the lead of the Baltic states of Lithuania, Latvia, and Estonia, which declared their independence in September 1991. Blood was spilled throughout the disintegrating Communist world in a variety of ethnic conflicts. In the Soviet republic of Tajikistan, native Tajiks rioted against Armenians living there; in Azerbaijan, Azeris and Armenians continued to clash over contested territory as they had since the winter of 1987–88. Churches, which had been active in focusing opposition, revived. In the Baltic states, anti-Semitism resurfaced as a political tool. The USSR legally dissolved on January 1, 1992. Twelve of the fifteen former Soviet republics banded together as the Commonwealth of Independent States (Map 11.3).

The coup and dissolution of the USSR so weakened Gorbachev that he ceded power to Yeltsin. Increasingly plagued by corruption, the Russian economy went into an ever-deepening crisis. Yeltsin's political allies bought up or simply seized national resources, stripped them of their value, and sent billions of dollars out of the country. By 1999, Yeltsin's own family appeared deeply implicated in stealing the wealth once seen as belonging to all the people. Managers, military officers, and bureaucrats took whatever they could lay their hands on, including weaponry, and sold it, often to make money simply to survive. Ethnic and religious battles continued throughout the 1990s as the government undertook disastrous policies. Military action against the Muslim province of Chechnya after it declared its independence in 1991 inflicted destruction and massive casualties on both sides, and Russian troops were forced to withdraw. In June 1992, after the demise of the Soviet Union, Chechen rebels gained control of massive numbers of Russian airplanes, tanks, and some 40,000 automatic weapons and machine guns. On December 10, 1994, the Russian government sealed the Chechen borders, then invaded the next day. In January 1995, a high Russian official defended a war in Chechnya as crucial to bolstering Yeltsin's position: "We now need a small victorious war, as in Haiti. We must raise the President's rating."[30] In 1996 the KGB assassinated the Chechen head of state with a rocket as he spoke on his cell phone, but the war persisted and criminal gangs gained control of the country and its precious supplies of oil.

Mindful of distress over the war and the uncertain economy, the political right in Russia appealed to nationalist sentiments, to Orthodox Christianity, and to ethnic hatred and won increasing support. Political disorder was accompanied by social disarray: members of organized crime, many of them unemployed veterans of the Soviet army, interfered with the distribution of goods and services and assassinated legitimate entrepreneurs, legislators, and anyone who criticized them. The chronic instability discouraged potential investors, and as a result, the Western powers drastically reduced their aid to rebuild Russian infrastructure. In 1998 the Russian government devalued its currency and defaulted on its loans, bringing temporary chaos to world markets. As the Russian parliament pursued an investigation into the business dealings of Yeltsin, his family, and allies and threatened to try him on charges of corruption and theft, Yeltsin resigned. On December 31, 1999, he appointed a new protégé, Vladimir Putin, as interim president.

Putin was the little-known head of the new security police, which had replaced the old KGB but provided employment to many former KGB operatives. He was so

◆ **Map 11.3 Countries of the Former USSR, c. 2000**

The final dissolution of the Soviet bloc occurred when the USSR itself fractured into many successor states in the early 1990s. Some of these states allied themselves as the Commonwealth of Independent States in 1992, but others went their own way and some eventually joined the European Union in 2004. The control of and access to the immense natural wealth of the region was a bone of contention into the twenty-first century, leading to diplomatic tensions and even violence among and within the new nations.

◆ **Chechen Separatists, 1995**
Among the many horrifying stories from the post-Communist world was that of Chechnya, whose predominantly Muslim population sought independence from Russia in the 1990s. Russia aimed to keep the oil-rich territory and invaded the country in 1991 and 1994. As the Russian army pounded Chechen cities to bits and executed citizens, Chechen rebels took the war to the heart of Russia, blowing up airplanes, apartment buildings, and buses. They took hostages and killed Russian schoolchildren and theatergoers, without hesitation. *Peter Turnley/CORBIS.*

unknown that some predicted he would garner only about 1 percent of the vote in the spring elections of 2000. Putin, however, surprised everyone. Although he was associated with the Yeltsin family corruption, he showed himself to be a leader committed to legality. "Democracy," he announced, "is the dictatorship of law," and the electorate voted him in, abandoning the old Communist bosses and the new robber barons. With a solid mandate, Putin proceeded to drive the biggest figures in regional government, usually the henchmen of the robber barons, from power, and he fired Yeltsin protégés who had high positions in the central government. He sent into exile Boris Berezovsky, Russia's first billionaire, who gained his fortune by wresting control of the Russian media and oil resources from the former Soviet government. Berezovsky had exercised power as an entity unto himself from the heart of the Russian parliament. Faced with a desperate situation, Putin aimed to restore "strong government" and end the influence of a "handful of billionaires with only egotistical concerns." In 2005, another political opponent, Mikhail Khodorkovsky, CEO of highly prosperous Yukos Oil, was convicted of fraud and tax evasion. Putin sold off the company to his own allies.

While appearing to reform the government and the economy, Putin continued the war in Chechnya, where the casualties, atrocities, disease, and physical devastation of the cities plagued soldiers and civilians alike. The war inflicted great suffering on the Chechens. The sister-in-law of a Chechen woman killed by a mortar shell while she slept held up her orphaned nephew and screamed, "They are killing us like sheep."[31] As the war dragged on, the Chechen city of Groszny was pounded to bits, but Russian casualties mounted too. The Chechens brought terrorism to Russia itself in a string of urban bombings of apartment buildings. In 2002, dozens of Chechen loyalists took hundreds of hostages in a Moscow theater but were killed by nerve gas in a liberation attempt that also killed some 130 of the hostages. In 2004 two women suicide bombers blew up two Russian passenger jets. As the Chechen war continued to unfold across the region, it merged with a crescendo of global terrorism, compounding the problems of establishing a sound economy and a credible post-Communist government.

THE BIRTH PAINS OF A NEW EASTERN EUROPE

The development of free markets and republican government brought suffering to Russia and other countries of central, eastern, and southeastern Europe, just as the much earlier transition to free markets and democratic government had brought revolutions, wars, and civil wars to Western nations. The conditions of everyday life grew increasingly dire as salaries went unpaid, food remained in short supply, and essential services disintegrated across the region. In Russia inflation soared to a rate of 14 percent a month in 1994, while in Ukraine it was over 800 percent and in Romania 135 percent. Industrial production in Russia dropped by 15 percent. People took drastic steps to stay alive. Hotel lobbies in capital cities became clogged with women turning to prostitution because they were the first employees fired as industry privatized and service jobs were cut back. Ordinary citizens stood on the sidewalks of cities and towns alike selling their household possessions. Simultaneously there was pent-up demand for items never before available. An enormous underground economy existed in goods such as automobiles stolen from people in other countries and then driven or shipped to Russia and other places for sale.

There were, of course, many plusses. People were able to travel freely for the first time, and the media were more open than ever before in Communist history. Both young and highly educated people profited from access to new technology and up-to-date business contacts while professional schools sprouted in Warsaw, Budapest, and Prague. However, frequent emigration to more prosperous parts of the world further depleted the human resources of former Soviet-bloc countries. At the same time, as the different republics formerly comprising the Soviet Union became independent, the hundreds of thousands of Russians sent by Soviet officials to colonize those outlying regions returned to Russia as refugees, putting further stress on the chaotic Russian economy. Some 900,000 returned in 1993 alone.

The dismantling of communism was more complicated and painful than anyone anticipated. "I knew in my heart that communism would collapse," said one ex-dissident Romanian, commenting sadly on the exodus of youth from his country, "but it never crossed my mind that the future would look like this." Alongside such human costs lay the question of who would control the massive Communist arsenal of weapons, including nuclear ones, and how global politics would shape up without cold war guidelines.

An Elusive Market Economy

For many, the first priority was getting economies running again but on new terms. Replacing a command economy with a market one took government planning, for the transformation was not one that would happen naturally or automatically. Given the spiraling misery, however, many opposed the introduction of new measures. In Russia many members of collective farms fought to preserve them because they represented at least some security in a rapidly changing world. With the farms up for sale, most collective farmers faced landlessness and starvation. The countries that experienced the most success were those like Hungary and Slovenia, where administrators had gradually been introducing aspects of free trade such as allowing farmers to sell their produce on the open market or encouraging independent entrepreneurs or even government factories to participate in international trade. Countries had to recognize that the emergence of a free market would take time and require governmental support. Hungary and Poland emerged from the transition with the least pain because of previously established markets and the hiring of experienced advisers to speed the transformation of the economy.

Elsewhere, things happened differently. In countries where Communist managers and administrators remained in charge of production and trade, they often sold goods and entire industries for their own personal benefit. In the 1990s, the former Soviet Union itself, in the words of one critic, was one vast "kleptocracy"; high officials and their allies simply took the country's resources—theoretically the property of all the people—for their individual gain. In this regard, one Polish adviser noted, democracy and a successful transition went hand in hand, for unless the people were represented and institutionally powerful enough to prevent criminal behavior, former dictatorial leaders and administrators would operate in this unlawful way. In the long run, in the worst-case scenarios, post-Communist countries had to deal with the cancerous inheritance of corruption, tax evasion, and off-the-books dealing. Moreover, because the socialist leaders had removed their nations' economies from global developments, the fast pace of technological change abroad had left their plants and personnel hopelessly out of date.

A final element in post-Soviet economic difficulties stemmed from the drain of a talented workforce that plagued the region. The fall of the Soviet empire and the economic hardship that followed brought a new rush of migration from east to west. Many people with marketable skills headed to Austria and Germany because they bordered the Soviet bloc. Individuals emigrated to find jobs, or to benefit from the higher pay offered to well-educated workers, and to escape the rising tide of ethnic hatred and anti-Semitism. Some post-Communist politicians used anti-Semitism to build a following as Hitler and others had done so effectively in the past. Western Europe also offered everyday amenities such as safe water, better housing, and better roads. Some migrants from the east, fearful of reprisals, sought political asylum. Banditry and violence inflicted by organized crime also prompted people to leave eastern Europe.

Post-Communist Culture

Many things stayed the same in the aftermath of the Communist collapse: inferior public services, a deteriorating standard of living, and declining longevity. The world of the arts, however, received a real jolt. First came the shock of discovery that many noted intellectuals, such as East German celebrity author Christa Wolf, had in a variety of ways collaborated with the secret police of their respective regimes. Equally damaging to the arts was the loss experienced by literary and artistic dissidents who had helped bring down the regime: they had lost their subject matter—that is, the critique of what had been a tyrannical system (see the Picture Essay). Tied as it was to the drama of the Soviet empire, their work had no drama left. Moreover, the lack of state support meant that writers faced the challenge of selling their work in countries where economic conditions were so harsh that books were an unaffordable luxury. In addition, there was no consensus about what post-Communist art should be. Was everything that had appeared under the Soviets utterly worthless because it was produced by a corrupt system? Some seemed to think so, for novels shortlisted for the Russian Booker Prize in the 1990s included works shaped by the authors' engagement with Buddhism or strongly influenced by German authors Hermann Hesse and Thomas Mann. The post-Soviet legacy induced artists to look beyond the region for subject matter and inspiration.

There were exceptions. Andreï Makine (b. 1957), an expatriate Russian author, became popular worldwide for his poignant yet disturbing novels of the collapse of communism, many of them ruminating on the cultural power of western Europe, the war, and the gulag. Both *Dreams of My Russian Summers* (1997) and *Once upon the River Love* (1996) showed young people raised on fantasies about the wealth and material goods of western Europe and America. Victor Pelevin (b. 1962) wrote more satirically and bitingly. Although indebted to Franz Kafka's short story "Metamorphosis," written some eighty years earlier, Pelevin's *The Life of Insects* (1993) shows insect-humans buzzing around Russia trying to discover who they are in the post-Soviet world. Pelevin, a Buddhist and former engineer, wrote hilarious send-ups of the almost sacred Soviet space program in *Omon Ra* (1991), depicting it as a ruse run from the depths of the Moscow subway system in which hundreds of cosmonaut-celebrities are killed to prevent the fiction from getting out. Its would-be space hero has been named by his father "Omon" after the acronym for the Soviet riot police, while he himself chooses the surname "Ra" after the Egyptian sun-god. Because the Russian people in the post-Soviet world in particular and Westerners in general watched so much television, Pelevin labeled them "techno-modified." For him "any politician is a TV program, and this doesn't change from one government to another." So one simply judged politicans by their haircuts, ties, and other aspects of personal style, as he showed in his novel *Homo Zapiens* (1999), in which politicians are all "virtual"—that is, produced by technical effects and scriptwriters.[32]

The situation was similarly complex across the arts. Music had flourished under the repressive Soviet regime, not only bringing to the fore geniuses like Dmitri Shostakovich, whose works were sometimes in and sometimes out of favor, but also provoking others to extreme creativity. Literally dozens of first-rate composers had written classical works in private for fear that they might contain phrasings, sounds, and rhythms that would be called subversive. They had earned a living writing for films—even the most famous of them, like Sofia Gubaidulina (b. 1931) and Giya Kancheli (b. 1935), who wrote immensely popular music for more than forty films. The composer Alfred Schnittke (1934–1998) had produced rich compositions—dozens of operas, symphonies, chamber music pieces, concertos, and other works—that were extremely sad, punctuated with anger in loud bursts of dissonance, and full of deep bass notes. All of these composers had become world celebrities and, like the Estonian composer Arvo Pärt (b. 1935), conveyed a sense of decline, much like the grinding demise of the Soviet bloc itself. Pärt had written religious works and "starvation music" in the 1970s and 1980s, emphasizing the scarcity of goods and emotional constraint in eastern-bloc life. But once the Soviet empire crashed, the composers who followed Shostakovich and Schnittke found themselves without the political and artistic spark of resistance that had so motivated their predecessors. Nevertheless, because so much of this music had gone unperformed, the opportunity to hear these lost works filled the cultural sphere with excitement.

The public also discovered hitherto unknown composers, such as Galina Ustvolskaya (b. 1919), a protégé and lover of Shostakovich. Enduring utter poverty because she shunned the Communist cultural system, Ustvolskaya had lived in obscurity, writing music that surfaced for the global public only after the USSR collapsed. Evident in her music and in the music of many others was respect for the work of Shostakovich. It was this respect that unified the underground music of the Stalinist and post-Stalinist years.

As entirely new authors and artists surfaced and as unknown works by classical writers such as Mikhail Bulgakov (1891–1940), author of *The Master and Margarita,* appeared, other challenging debates began. Classical ballet and music—which had flourished under communism—could be sold globally; but this marketability was often jarring to artists who thought it important to catch up with challenging new trends in modern art—trends emphasizing the low and common stripped of the socialist realist glow. These cultural reappraisals produced tense moments of introspection that helped the entire intellectual world get its bearings in a new situation — that of artistic freedom.

CONCLUSION

Linking events in eastern and western Europe was the desire to advance liberal market economies by cutting back on social services provided by the welfare state. Political leaders throughout Europe tried to curtail social programs in the belief that they cost too much. If businesses paid lower taxes to fund reduced benefits, they could divert more resources into economic growth, the argument went. In eastern Europe, where there was a shortage of funds to begin with, the demands of creating a market economy left no money for veterans' and others' pensions, for health care, or for day care and, instead of creating jobs, brought unemployment and other hardships. In more prosperous western Europe, however, neoliberal economic policies lifted a few countries out of the mire of stagflation.

The economic situation in eastern Europe was but one aspect of the greater difficulties faced by the millions of Soviet-bloc citizens who brought the Communist system crashing down. The initial euphoria was succeeded by the sometimes harsh realities of attempting to install democratic governments and to build a culture of civic participation. Although some countries achieved success, there was also violence, most notably ethnic cleansing in the former Yugoslavia, followed by the politics of anti-Semitism in some of the republics spinning off from the USSR. The gravest problem in the early twenty-first century was the brutal struggle between Russia and Chechnya.

In the long run, however, although the end of the Soviet system fractured a large regional economy and brought considerable political instability in its wake, it gave further impetus to the expansion of the European Community and to the achievement of European unification. The nations of eastern Europe struggled to put their economic houses in order and to ensure democratic government in the face of the persistent legacy of Communist rule: corruption, banditry, and violence in everyday life. Simultaneously the end of the cold war rivalry between the superpowers and their allies allowed nations in Europe and around the world more freedom and opportunity to trade and interact with each other. Further advances in communication added to the potential for global relationships, and spurred by the fall of the Soviet realm, these advances paved the way for Europe fully to enter the global age.

Thatcher and Neoliberalism

TIME MAGAZINE NAMED MARGARET THATCHER (b. 1925), the first woman prime minister in English history, to its list of the one hundred most important people of the twentieth century. Thatcher was a notable revolutionary in many ways—and not just because she held such high office. She won successive uphill battles and advanced in the Conservative Party hierarchy. In 1970, she received the cabinet post designated for the ruling party's token woman—secretary of state for education and science. Six years later, she became head of the Conservative Party and led it to victory in the 1979 elections, catapulting herself to power as prime minister.

As prime minister, Thatcher wrought a policy revolution. Britain's stagnating industries supported by the government and its soaring inflation caused not only by the oil crisis but by budget deficits that financed the welfare state appalled her, and she attributed both problems to bad economic programs. Government spending was a tax on business, she believed, and support for failing industries made bad economic sense. Thatcher determined to set things right by eliminating the costs of the welfare state—though she never succeeded entirely in this goal.

Thatcher often referred to her humble origins—her father was a small-town grocer—to gain support for her "common-sensical" approach to policy making. Her ideas became the foundation of "Reaganomics" in the United States and shaped the policy of international organizations such as the World Bank and the International Monetary Fund. Before lending money to poor countries, these organizations demanded cuts in social services to bring down government spending and thus reduce budget deficits. Without such cuts, they maintained, loans could not be put to good use because no one could do business in countries that taxed and spent beyond their means. The European Union also demanded as a condition for admission and for continued membership that governments reduce budget deficits that financed services and keep them below 3 percent of gross domestic product.

Because of the political fallout from such a drastic policy move, Thatcher made many strong speeches outlining her program and describing its successes. The following speeches were made at Conservative Party conferences: the first in 1981 at a high point of stagflation in most advanced countries soon after she came to power; the second in 1988 to explain her neoliberal policy in greater detail.

Document 11.1

MARGARET THATCHER
Speeches to the Conservative Party Conference, 1981 and 1988

[*Speech delivered October 16, 1981*] . . . Once more the Conservative Party has demonstrated that it is the party of all the people. We are not here to manipulate millions of block votes in some travesty of democracy;[1] nor were we drawn here by the tinsel glamour of a marriage of convenience.[2] We are here as representatives of a myriad of different interests from every constituency in the land. We are here because we share a deep and abiding concern for the future of our country and our Party. . . .

The concern of this Conference is focused on the plight of the unemployed. But we seek not only to display and demonstrate that concern, but to find and pursue those policies which offer the best hope of more lasting jobs in future years.

To do that, we must learn the lessons of the past in order to avoid the mistakes that led to the increase in inflation and unemployment in the first place. Today's unemployment is partly due to the sharp increase in oil prices;[3] it absorbed money that might otherwise have gone to increased investment or to buying the things which British factories produce. But that is not all. Too much of our present unemployment is due to enormous past wage increases unmatched by higher output, to union restrictive practices, to overmanning, to strikes, to indifferent management, and to the mistaken belief that, come what may, the Government would always step in to bail out companies in difficulty. No policy can succeed that shirks those basic issues. . . .

There have been many voices in the past few weeks calling on us to spend our way back towards a higher level of employment, and to cut interest rates at the same time. It is a familiar treatment, and it has been tried by many different Governments these past thirty years.

In the early days it worked well enough. In the 1950s a few million pounds of what we learned to call reflation earned a swift reward in jobs and output. But, as time went on, the dose required grew larger and the stimulus achieved grew less. By the 1960s it was needing hundreds of millions of extra spending to lift some hundreds of thousands of our people back into employment. By the 1970s we found that after thousands of extra millions had been spent we still had unemployment at levels which ten or twenty years before would have been unthinkable. The trick had been tried too often. The people, as earners and consumers, had rumbled° what the Government was doing to their money. They knew the Government was creating inflation and they took that into account in their wage demands. So all the extra money went into wages and prices and not into more jobs.

So today, if we were to heed the calls to add another thousand million pounds to our plans for spending, we might thereby create an extra fifty thousand jobs in two years' time; and even those would be all too swiftly cancelled out by the loss of other jobs in private industry as the result of what we had done. The fact is that a good chunk of the higher taxes and the higher interest rates needed to find the money for the extra spending would come from the tills of every business in the land.

---

[1] A reference to the trade-union block votes which were decisive at Labour Party conferences.

[2] A reference to the Liberal-SDP "Alliance."

[3] Oil prices doubled in 1979–1980 under the impact of the Iranian Revolution.

SOURCE: *The Collected Speeches of Margaret Thatcher*, ed. Robin Harris (New York: HarperCollins, 1997), 136–141, 338–339.

° *rumbled:* To discover, to find out.

"Ah," but we are told, "don't put up the taxes or the interest rates—put them down instead." In other words, "Print the money." That way, I must tell you, lies a collapse of trust in sterling both at home and abroad, lies the destruction of the savings of every family. It would lead to suitcase money and penury as the sole reward for thrift. That is not what this Government was elected to do. . . .

That is why it is not a question of choosing between the conquest of inflation and the conquest of unemployment. Indeed, as one of our speakers reminded us yesterday, we are fighting unemployment by fighting inflation. Of course, there are those who promise success without tears. I wish they were right. Who more than the Prime Minister would benefit from an easy answer to our troubles? But they would not benefit, because there is no easy answer. . . .

[*Speech delivered October 14, 1988*]. . . .When we were returned at that historic election in 1979 we were faced with the overriding threat of inflation. It was inflation that had redistributed wealth from the thrifty to the fly-by-night. It was inflation that had undermined confidence first in the currency, then in savings, then in investment, and finally in the country's future. To salvage our economy, we had first to defeat inflation, and only then could the great revival of the British economy begin.

Today we are in our eighth year of growth. Our unemployment figures are below the Community average. We have created more jobs than they have. Other countries come to our shores to see what we do and go home to copy.

Since we took office, we have handed eighteen state enterprises back to the British people—so far. We have encouraged ownership at home and ownership at work. We have turned small business from an endangered species to a vital and rapidly growing part of our economy. The habits of hard work, enterprise and inventiveness that made us great are with us again.

But however firmly rooted our new-found strength, you can't steer an economy on automatic pilot. Success doesn't look after itself. You have to work at it. In economics, there are no final victories.

At home, the fast pace of economic growth has put more money into people's pockets and more money into industry's profits. Some has been invested, but with rapid growth in consumption, imports have grown faster than exports, leaving us with a substantial trade deficit. And too much buying has been paid for by too much borrowing.

To encourage people to spend less and save more, the Chancellor has to raise interest rates. It's never popular to push them up—except perhaps with savers—but, popular or not, the Chancellor has done the right thing. And the right thing is to make sure that we continue to grow steadily, if less fast than in recent months.

Too much borrowing has also meant that inflation today is too high. Make no mistake: we intend to bring inflation down again. That's not an expression of hope. It's a statement of intent. I think the country knows us well enough by now to recognize that we say what we mean and mean what we say.

There are always pressures on Government to spend more than the country can afford. We're not going down that road. Not this year. Not next year. Not any year. We will continue to keep a firm grip on public spending. And I look forward to those who so roundly condemn extravagance with private money giving their wholehearted support to our prudence in handling the public's money. . . .

QUESTIONS FOR ANALYSIS

1. What were the main challenges facing Britain, according to Thatcher?
2. What did she think government should do to find solutions?
3. In what ways did Thatcher set Britain on a new course? What were the limits to her program?

Gorbachev on Glasnost and Perestroika

MIKHAIL GORBACHEV, LIKE MARGARET THATCHER, worked a revolution in his country, although as he proceeded to change Soviet policy he was perhaps less aware than she of what the consequences were likely to be. Also one of *Time* magazine's one hundred most important people of the twentieth century, Gorbachev was born in 1931 as Stalin set the USSR on the course of drastic industrialization. Some biographers trace Gorbachev's fervor for reform to his own family's experience of Stalinist brutality. His grandfather Andrei was hauled off in the middle of the night and sent to the gulag, his only crime being that he was an independent peasant farming his own land. Thus the great discrepancy between the noble aspirations of many Communists and the harsh reality of Communist rule was brought home in a very personal way to young Mikhail.

When Gorbachev came to power in the Soviet Union in 1985, one of his first acts was to go after the "new class"—striking out at a group rooted in privilege, exploitation of ordinary people, and lies. Gorbachev was a committed reformer to undertake so bold a stroke against the Communist power structure, because he undermined entrenched interests and not so subtly began the transformation of the USSR. In this speech to the Communist Party Congress in 1987, he presents and elaborates on his program.

Document 11.2

MIKHAIL GORBACHEV
Speech to the Communist Party Congress, January 1987

. . . The April plenary meeting and the 27th Party Congress prepared the ground for an objective critical analysis of the situation in society and took decisions of historic importance for the country's future. We have begun reorganisation and will not look back. The first steps on that road have been taken.

SOURCE: Mikhail S. Gorbachev, "Report and Concluding Speech at the Plenary Meeting of the CPSU Central Committee 27–28 January 1987," *Socialism, Peace and Democracy: Writings, Speeches and Reports* (London: Zwan, 1987) 113, 136–140, 162–167.

Drawing an overall political conclusion, we can say with confidence that major changes are taking place in the life of Soviet society and that positive tendencies are gaining momentum.

Before the plenary meeting I myself and other Political Bureau members and central committee secretaries had many meetings and conversations with members of the Central Committee, public figures, workers, collective farmers, intellectuals, veterans and young people. The overall tenor and meaning of what they had to say was unambiguous: the policies for renovating our society should be firmly pursued and effort redoubled in every area. . . .

While normalising the atmosphere in society it is essential to further encourage openness. This is a powerful lever for improving work in all sectors of our development and an effective form of control by the whole people. The experience which has been gained since the April plenary meeting of the Central Committee is good proof of this.

Obviously the time has come to begin elaborating legal acts guaranteeing the openness. These should ensure maximum openness in the activities of state and public organisations and give the working people a real opportunity to express their opinions on any question of social life.

Criticism and self-criticism are a tested instrument of socialist democracy. There seems to be no open objection to this. However in real life we encounter situations indicating that by no means everyone has become aware of the need to support critical-mindedness in society. Matters at times go so far that some officials regard even the slightest remark as an encroachment upon their prestige and defend it in any way they can. Then there are those officials, the more experienced ones, who admit the justness of criticism and even thank you for it, but are in no hurry to eliminate drawbacks, expecting to get away with things as usual.

Such an attitude to criticism has nothing in common with our principles and ethics. At the present stage, when we are asserting new approaches in sociopolitical life, in the cultural and intellectual sphere, the importance of criticism and self-criticism grows immeasurably. People's attitude to criticism is an important criterion of their attitude to reorganisation, to everything new that is taking place in our society.

And here I cannot but say regretfully that we continue to encounter not only cases of non-acceptance of criticism but also facts of persecution for it, of direct suppression of criticism. Not infrequently this assumes such proportions and takes such forms that the Central Committee has to intervene in order to re-establish the truth and justice and to support honest people who take the interests of work close to heart. I have already spoken of this matter, but things are improving only slowly. Take, for instance, the central press reports for January and you'll see that the persecution of people for criticism is far from a rare thing.

In this connection we must support the efforts of the mass media to develop criticism and self-criticism in our society. Their position in the struggle for reorganisation has been appreciated by the Soviet people.

The readership of central newspapers and magazines has increased by over 14 million and Central TV programmes on topical subjects are attracting audiences of many millions. People are impressed by the bold and profound treatment of urgent problems which are involved in the acceleration of the country's socioeconomic development and which cover all aspects of life in our society. The Party believes that the programmes of the mass media will continue to be marked by depth and objectivity and a high degree of civic responsibility.

Many things can be said about the positive changes taking place in the republican and local press. Far from all of them have joined in the work of restructuring. Some lack firmness of principle and boldness in raising questions, and a critical attitude to shortcomings. Many Party Committees sometimes fail to use properly the mass media, a powerful lever in the restructuring process. In some places they continue to restrain mass media activity.

While continuing to count on principled and constructive criticism of shortcomings and omissions, the Party expects the mass media to publicise more widely the experience gained by work collectives, Party, local government and economic bodies, public organisations and top officials in conditions of reorganisation. We badly need answers to many of the burning problems reorganisation has raised or will raise. We must all help in changing our ways more quickly and in the spirit of the time. As V. I. Lenin said, this organising function of the press should be strengthened from day to day and it should learn in practice to be a collective agitator, propagandist and organiser of the masses.

There is one more question that must be made clear. In Soviet society there should be no zones closed to criticism. This refers in full measure to the mass media. . . .

Speaking of democratisation of Soviet society—which is a matter of principle to us—it is important to underline once more the main, distinguishing feature of socialist democracy—an organic combination of democracy and discipline, of independence and responsibility, of the rights and duties of officials and of every citizen.

Socialist democracy has nothing in common with permissiveness, irresponsibility, and anarchy. Real democracy serves every person. It protects his political and social rights and simultaneously serves every collective and the whole of society, upholding their interests.

Democratisation in all spheres of Soviet society is important first of all because we link it with the further development of working people's initiative and the use of the entire potential of the socialist system. We need democratisation in order to move ahead, to ensure that legality grows stronger, that justice triumphs in our society and that a moral atmosphere in which man can freely live and fruitfully work is asserted in it.

Comrades, it is well known that the effectiveness of real democracy depends on how far it reflects the interests of broad numbers of people, how it relies on them and is supported by all segments and groups of society. In this respect, too, the tasks of reorganisation make it necessary for us to analyse again our resources and possibilities for further expanding the social base of democracy. The pertinence of such an approach is obvious. . . .

Open selection of workers to be promoted—from among both Communists and non-Party people—will accord with the aims of democratisation and will help involve large numbers of working people in management.

There is also the question of promoting more women to leading positions. There are many women holding Party and state posts and working successfully in science, health care, education, culture, light industry, trade, and public services. In order to meet our country's needs today we must more actively involve women in running the economy and culture on an All-Union or republican scale. We have such possibilities. All we have to do is trust and support women.

Comrades, there isn't one single fundamental issue that we could resolve, now as in the past, without taking into account the fact that we live in a multinational country. There is no need to prove the importance of socialist principles in the development of relations between the nationalities. It is socialism that did away with national oppression, inequality, and infringements upon the rights of people on grounds of nationality. It ensured the economic and cultural progress of all nationalities and ethnic groups. In short, the successes of our Party's nationalities policy are beyond any doubt and we can justly take pride in them.

But we must also see the real picture of the relations between nationalities and the prospects for their development. Now that democracy and self-government are expanding, that there is rapid growth of national awareness of all nationalities and ethnic groups, and the processes of internationalisation are developing in depth, it is especially important to settle promptly and fairly outstanding questions in the only possible way—in the interest of the progress of each nationality and ethnic group, in the interest of their further drawing closer together, and in the interest of society as a whole. . . .

We wish to turn our country into a model highly developed state, into a society with the most advanced economy, the broadest democracy, the most humane and lofty ethics; where the working man feels he is real master, enjoys all the benefits of material and intellectual culture, where the future of his children is secure, where he has everything that is necessary for a full and interesting life. And even sceptics will be forced to say: yes, the Bolsheviks can accomplish anything. Yes, the truth is on their side. Yes, socialism is a system serving man, working for his benefit, in his social and economic interests, for his cultural elevation. . . .

Certainly, reorganisation is already a reality. Today we realise ever more clearly and profoundly that from the standpoint of both internal development and external conditions, the international situation, we must ensure the country's more rapid social and economic progress. But there will be no acceleration without society's renovation. Nor will there be any change in all spheres of its life without its renovation. The new tasks cannot be tackled by taking the old approaches, especially the historic tasks facing us today.

Reorganisation is not strolling along a well-beaten path. It is going uphill, often by untrodden ways. As the Central Committee's plenary meeting has shown once again, quite a few problems have accumulated in our society. Immense creative efforts and a long, selfless stuggle are needed to carry out the great cause of reorganisation as our people and the time demand. . . .

Today at the plenary meeting of the Central Committee we must express the Party's immense gratitude to our people for realising and feeling that they are called for a difficult struggle for such changes and such goals which will bear fine fruit to our entire society, to every family and every person.

The Soviet people have believed us and supported the Party. This is why the good changes achieved in 1986 are so important to us. They are of importance because they reflect our people's powerful support for the Party's policy and for its course for acceleration.

I want to emphasise some other points mentioned at the plenary meeting. To my mind it is quite legitimate that the subject of serious in-depth democratisation of Soviet society has been put as the major one in the Report of the Political Bureau.

This is, comrades, the lever which will make it possible to draw into the reorganisation its decisive force—the people. If we do not do this we will never accomplish the tasks of acceleration, nor achieve reorganisation. There will be just no reorganisation at all.

On the other hand, while developing and furthering socialist democracy and bringing its potential into play we must create most reliable guarantees that will prevent a repetition of the errors of the past. But the point is not only in that.

We need democracy like air. If we fail to realise this or if we do realise it but make no real serious steps to broaden it, to promote it and draw the country's working people extensively into the reorganisation process, our policy will get choked, and reorganisation will fail, comrades. . . .

The Communist Party is firmly of the opinion that the people should know everything. Openness, criticism and self-criticism, and control exercised by the masses are the guarantees for Soviet society's healthy development. . . .

Today we all are arriving at the same conclusion: we need openness, criticism and self-criticism as effective forms of socialist democracy. In our state, a state of workers and peasants, everything concerns the people, because it is a state of the people. They should know everything and be able to consciously judge everything. These words, as you know, were said by Lenin. . . .

It is the openness and democracy that have allowed the working class, the peasantry, our intelligentsia and all healthy forces to hold up their heads. Once a demagogue appears, they put him down. I have seen this dozens of times. People will always see which is which.

Openness, criticism and self-criticism are vital for us. These are major requisites of the socialist way of life. If someone believes that we need these only for criticising past drawbacks he is making a big mistake. The main point is that openness, criticism and self-criticism, democracy, are necessary for our advance, for accomplishing immense tasks. We shall not be able to accomplish these tasks without the people's active involvement. . . .

Reorganisation, comrades, is a great school. It sets formidable tasks and we must pass through this school with flying colours. I would like to repeat once again: we must act, act and act—energetically, boldly, creatively and competently! This is, if you will, the principal task of the moment. Everybody, all Party organisations, all Party committees, all leaders, all Communists should regard this task as their own.

On behalf of the Central Committee of the CPSU I would like to address all comrades in the Party and all Soviet people: the cause of reorganisation, the cause of the revolutionary revitalisation of society, and the country's future, are in the hands of the people. The future will be what we make it, by our common labour, our intellect, and our conscience.

Reorganisation is the frontline for every honest person, for every patriot. There is enough work for everyone and the road ahead is long. . . .

QUESTIONS FOR ANALYSIS

1. What changes does Gorbachev propose for the USSR?
2. What are his criticisms of past policies?
3. Is Gorbachev more accurately described as a reformer or as a revolutionary? Why?

Days of Confusion and Turmoil in Yugoslavia

Even as Yugoslavia began to disintegrate from the weight of the ethnic conflict stirred by ambitious politicians and even before deadly hostilities erupted in full, individuals and families of mixed ethnicities were under intense pressure to define themselves. People in the Balkans had intermarried for centuries; but as communism broke down, politicians focused the post-Communist political climate on ethnic identity. Those aspiring to political leadership gained adherents not by calling for a free market or for political democracy or by promising to bring about social reform. Instead, they whipped up concern among a populace with multiple heritages around a single issue: to which ethnic identity did any individual belong?

In this heated, hate-filled, and increasingly violent atmosphere people identified with minority ethnicities sought safe havens. By the mid-1990s the European refugee population contained tens of thousands escaping from rapidly disintegrating Yugoslavia. Although the rest of Europe was a first option for sanctuary, it was often a temporary one. There were also false starts, leading to return and then a second departure. Confusion reigned. In this document, a Croatian lawyer married to a Serbian psychotherapist describes eighteen months of wandering with her husband and two children that began when they left their home in Osijek for Vienna and that ended up in Canada.

Women and children dominated many of the refugee camps that rose across Europe, both within and outside the former Yugoslavia, as many of their male relatives had been killed, imprisoned, or drafted into militias and armies. Jelena, a nine-year-old refugee from Sarajevo, gave a worker for the International Red Cross this account of her thoughts about being a refugee in Serbia. Scholars have gathered the many poems, interviews, and short stories of these refugees into chilling anthologies of the Yugoslav wars.

Document 11.3

Sara Bafo

Between Despair and Hope: A Belgrade Diary, 1991–1992

SEPTEMBER 7, 1991. We are setting off from Vienna to the south, still not knowing exactly which direction to go. Before the last crossroad for Bratislava and Budapest, Milosh stops the car several times and urges me to go to Czechoslovakia, but I am too stubborn to agree to that. After the Austrian-Hungarian border, we have a new dilemma: Croatia or Serbia? Belgrade or Zagreb? Dozens of times I have measured and scaled the good and bad sides of both decisions, my first consideration being the security of my family. And finally, after we have covered more than half the distance through Hungary, and after a really hard internal fight with myself, I decide to return to Belgrade. . . .

SEPTEMBER 11, 1991. The school year has already started and we have decided to send our children to the nearest school. Before that we have to go to the Red Cross to be officially registered as refugees. Until now, we have been refugees only in our souls and hearts; officialdom hasn't yet recognized us as refugees. While we stand in line in the hall of a drab building in Studentski Square, I watch the river of people who are waiting to obtain their refugee status. After registration we become 10927, 10928, 10929, 10930. These numbers tell us that in the last few months, perhaps since May, more than 10,000 people from Croatia have escaped to Belgrade. They are the ones who are registered. How many of them are not?

ON THE WAY TO OSIJEK FROM BELGRADE, SEPTEMBER 13, 1991. At the Belgrade bus station I buy a ticket, and on platform 28 I recognize the people who wait with me, people I know from the bank and post offices, different stores, schools, restaurants, or just from the streets. The bus is full and we leave Belgrade in a relaxed atmosphere, listening to a Belgrade radio station and talking to each other. This atmosphere lasts only until we reach Shid. When we pass this last place in Serbia, the driver turns off the radio, the passengers stop talking, and those who were having a nap wake up. A ghostly silence falls. Only a hundred meters past Shid, although there are still a few kilometers to the Croatian border, the highway is absolutely abandoned. Our bus is the only vehicle going either direction on what was, not so long ago, one of the busiest Yugoslav roads. We are approaching the Serbo-Croatian border. The very dense Spachvanske forests are in front of us. Almost all the passengers expect something horrible to happen. The tension in the bus is unbearable. I can't explain it, but I, too, begin to feel frightened. All of us are staring at the deserted highway around us and listening to the silence.

SEPTEMBER 21, 1991. Both of us are looking for jobs everywhere, but without success. The official pressure on men who escaped or were exiled from Croatia grows bigger and bigger. These men are more desirable as soldiers, dead somewhere on the numerous battlefields as proof that they are not cowards and traitors to their nation, than they are alive, choosing not to participate and use weapons to kill people on the other side of the war. Commit yourself! Commit yourself! Everyone around us says just that, but we can't share ourselves in so many pieces and we don't want to either.

OCTOBER 10, 1991. Every day we learn to live in this new town. It's hard and laborious. Above all, we are absolutely alone, very lonely, without any

SOURCE: Sara Bafo, "Between Despair and Hope: A Belgrade Diary," *Canadian Woman Studies/Les Cahiers de la Femme* 16 (Winter 1995), 6–8.

real help and moral support which is even more important now for us. The children are also very lonely. Our whole world is, at the moment, in this room, four by five meters; only here can we feel secure and protected. This is our territory, without borders or any danger or threat.

OCTOBER 19, 1991. I remember just half a year ago I was at Milosh's uncle's funeral with my mother-in-law and brother-in-law. It was a strange time, a period of no war, no peace. We were travelling by car with license plates from Zagreb. According to the circumstances of that time, we had two kinds of newspapers with us, Croatian one called *Vjesnik*. While passing Serbian villages we put *Politika* out to be seen and while passing through Croatian villages we put out *Vjesnik*. . . . A woman who was also at the funeral came to me and said that she would like to burn all the cars with Zagreb license plates if she could. I didn't understand why she would tell me something like this. After she came to apologize, saying she heard that terrible things are happening to Serbs there. I tried

to tell her it wasn't true, but I think she didn't believe me. Now I can say we were blind, we didn't notice, we didn't care or we didn't want to see, where all these "little" things, events from everyday life, have led our country.

ON THE WAY TO PRAGUE, NOVEMBER 13, 1992. I admit that we set off full of hope and expectations, enthusiasm, and a wish to start from the beginning, this time not as refugees, but as immigrants with a huge life experience. I believe that material things are nothing in comparison to the beauty of living, peace, and fundamental human values; those things that have remained with us along with the knowledge that just a moment of evil and impetuousness is sufficient for humans to lose everything, even their souls and their humanity. We leave with an enormous pain in our hearts. It is eight o'clock in the evening. Through the darkness and silence, and without a hitch at the Yugoslavian-Hungarian checkpoint, we leave our former country Yugoslavia, leaving everything and bringing everything with us.

Document 11.4

JELENA
Untitled, 1994

I lived in Sarajevo. Our house was a big one. The upper story was in red brick and the lower in stone. My mother used to work as a medical doctor. She wore a nice dress and walked around the hospital.

I am here with Nikola, Nemanja and Mummy and that's all. My daddy was killed there. I don't know how. Grandpa came and told us that Daddy was in prison. He told us to leave. We went by bus at about five o'clock. Then the shooting started again. I

don't know how it happened, but they told me that I don't have a father anymore. My mummy cried, together with our neighbor Milena and my brothers.

In the beginning, I dreamt that I was playing with him. Last night, I dreamt that I was on a sleigh and that an old woman was hugging me around the neck and that I pushed her over the balcony. She was the sort of old person who wears strange dresses. I looked for a hole in the dress but there wasn't one. There wasn't even a dress or a head. She didn't have any teeth.

Belgrade, Serbia, 1994

SOURCE: Julie Mertus et al., eds., *The Suitcase: Refugee Voices from Bosnia and Croatia* (Berkeley: University of California Press, 1997), 150–151.

QUESTIONS FOR ANALYSIS

1. What sense of "home" and "family" do you derive from these accounts?
2. What sense of geography and location do these accounts give?
3. What are the main concerns of the authors of these accounts? What are their hopes and dreams, if any?

PICTURE ESSAY

Dissident Art in the Soviet Bloc

Tʜʀᴏᴜɢʜᴏᴜᴛ ᴛʜᴇ ᴘᴀsᴛ ᴄᴇɴᴛᴜʀʏ, there were moments when artists overtly or subtly commented on their times through their work. But beginning in the 1960s, perhaps not coincidentally given that era's penchant for social protest, and continuing on to the present, art has tended to be highly critical of political, social, and cultural values. We think of the ways in which artists mocked mass consumption and advertising by depicting cans of Campbell's tomato soup or by making soft sculptures of vacuum cleaners and telephones. West German artist Sigmar Polke (whose family left East Germany in 1953 when he was a boy) captured the critical spirit in childlike sketches of faddish clothing and in bold representations of glamorous women whose bodies enticed people to buy alcohol, cars, and cosmetics. Polke also used the techniques of newsprint advertisements (as did Andy Warhol and Roy Lichtenstein in the United States) to raise critical and often political awareness. His newsprint-like image (Figure 11.1) shows jelly doughnuts, called in German "Berliner," and a baker who is also supposedly a Berliner. The political commentary addresses President John F. Kennedy's 1963 statement at the Berlin Wall, "I am a Berliner," ("Ich Bin Ein Berliner") which could also be interpreted to mean "I am a jelly doughnut." How might a German have reacted to this image? Do you find it playful and humorous or more pointed?

Culture in western Europe was critical and occasionally revolutionary. In the Soviet bloc it paved the way for the political collapse of communism. Nonconformist visual artists deviating from the official socialist realist style, used religious motifs, abstract forms, or subtly altered socialist realism to convey subversive messages. Socialist realism was a style intended to build loyalty to the regime by depicting heroic workers or exemplary political leaders such as Lenin. It showed people what to think and encouraged them to feel joy in the message of socialism. By contrast, non-conformist art, including outlawed abstract art, forced people to think for themselves. Abstract art could also provide purely visual pleasure without any message at all. Like erotic art, which Communist authorities also forbade, abstract art was considered "decadent."

Since the government was acutely aware of the dangers posed by dissident painters and treated them harshly, these artists tried to circumvent the censors in clever ways. "A fish could be perceived as a religious propaganda since it symbolized Christ," explained Elena Figurina, a dissident painter. People "could see in the smallest star or abstract shape or title of a painting an anti-Soviet message," she reported.

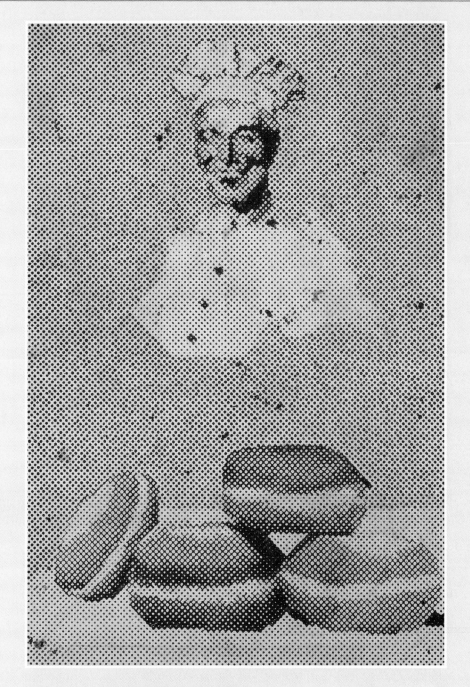

◆ Figure 11.1 **Sigmar Polke, *Berliner, 1965***

Sigmar Polke, Berliner (Bächerblume), *1965, Städtische Galerie Karlsruhe, Sammlung Garnatz.*

◆ **Figure 11.2** **Erik Bulatov, *Danger, 1972–73***

Erik Bulatov, Danger, 1972–1973. Oil on canvas, 108.6 × 110 cm. Jane Voorhees Zimmerli Art Museum, Rutgers, The State University of New Jersey. On loan from the collection of Norton and Nancy Dodge. Photograph by Jack Abraham 06181.

Some artists used the rosy style of socialist realist art but incorporated in their work small signs and hints that something was amiss. In Figure 11.2, a Moscow artist shows a picnic in a lush natural setting posted with danger signs. The artist alerts people across the Soviet bloc to the pollution that is all around them and thereby captures the reality of their lives. Why would images of pollution be more politically damaging in a socialist country than in a capitalist one? Although presented in a realistic way, the passengers on the subway train in Aleksei Sundukov's painting *Endless Train* hardly look like the joyful workers of socialist realism (Figure 11.3). The subway was a source of pride to Soviet officials, signaling the ways in which communism had modernized life in all parts of the USSR. We can't see the colors in this image, but Soviet viewers could see that the passengers are all

◆ Figure 11.3 **Aleksei Sundukov, *Endless Train, 1983–84***

Aleksei Sundukov, The Endless Train, *d. 1983–1984. Oil on canvas, 160 × 201.5 cm, Jane Voorhees Zimmerli Art Museum, Rutgers, The State University of New Jersey. On loan from the collection of Norton and Nancy Dodge. Photograph by Jack Abraham 07774.*

dressed in monochromatic gray. What might these colors have signaled to viewers of the painting? Would they have considered the passengers' expressions realistic? How might the Soviet government have viewed such an image?

The depiction of drunkards was also a common subject for dissident artists. Alcoholism was a sad reality of life across the Soviet bloc. Ukrainian and Russian artists, in particular, called attention to the unhappiness of the ordinary person under communism and the refuge many took in alcohol suggested the falsity of claims to having achieved a workers' paradise. Figure 11.4 is a painting by Ukrainian artist David Miretsky titled *Russian Trinity*. What is he depicting? Why do you think he gave his painting this title? Other paintings, such as Figure 11.5, (*Untitled*) by the Armenian artist Suren Arutiunian, invoked the religious tradition that Communists hoped to supplant with a secular culture. Arutiunian surrounds the mother and child with Soviet icons—a male and a female worker bearing a hammer and sickle—and modernist buildings serve as background. Yet there seems to be something amiss in the Armenian artist's depiction of the mother and child. What are the major distortions in the central figures, and what do these distortions seem to symbolize?

◆ **Figure 11.4 David Miretsky, *Russian Trinity*, 1976**
David Miretsky, Russian Trinity, *d. 1976. Oil on canvas, 123.8 cm (diameter). Jane Voorhees Zimmerli Art Museum, Rutgers, The State University of New Jersey. The Norton and Nancy Dodge Collection of Nonconformist Art from the Soviet Union. Photograph by Jack Abraham 06229.*

◆ **Figure 11.5 Suren Arutiunian, *(Untitled), 1977***

Suren Arutiunian, (Untitled), d. 1977. Gouache, 35.4 × 25.1 cm. Jane Voorhees Zimmerli Art Museum,
Rutgers, The State University of New Jersey. The Norton and Nancy Dodge Collection of Nonconformist
Art from the Soviet Union. Photograph by Jack Abraham 03992.

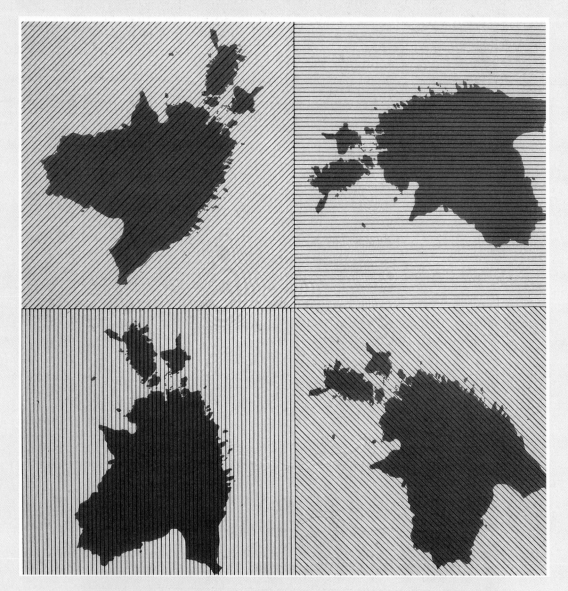

◆ Figure 11.6 Raul Meel, *This Beautiful Land is My Home No. 15, 1980*

Raul Meel, This Beautiful Land is My Home No. 15, *d. 1980. Screenprint, 59.7 × 49.1 cm. Jane Voorhees Zimmerli Art Museum, Rutgers, The State University of New Jersey. On loan from the collection of Norton and Nancy Dodge. Photograph by Jack Abraham 07065.*

In all parts of the Eastern bloc, dissident art flourished and sometimes carried nationalistic messages even though, according to Marxist-Leninist theory, communism eradicated the need for nationalism. In Figure 11.6 internationally known Estonian artist Raul Meel presented outlines of his homeland in four different positions. Harmless-looking enough, a viewer might conclude. But how might we interpret the lines that crisscross these maps? How might Communist officials interpret them? What makes Meel's maps subversive?

In 1974, Moscow artists held what came to be known as the Bulldozer Show, an open-air exhibit of their works. Some depicted men in varying stages of drunkenness as a commentary on the way many citizens escaped the hardships of their lives. Others painted in monochromatic grays to indicate the drabness of existence under socialism. The KGB broke up the exhibition by using heavy machinery to destroy the art and to obliterate all traces of the show. The KGB made some art dealers from the West who were dealing with the dissidents to disappear from sight—apparently kidnapped and murdered—causing the artists to fear for their own lives. But they persisted, holding exhibitions in a variety of cities. To avoid the secret police, artists would change the site of exhibits at the last minute and announce them by word of mouth the day before they were to take place. Alerted by "the human radio," thousands of people attended displays of contemporary art held in parks, studios, and apartments. For many, these shows provided their first glimpse of abstract art, collages, and other forms of avant-gardism. Though constantly harassed by the KGB because of the subversive nature of their art and having their works confiscated and the electricity to their studios and exhibitions cut, dissident artists undermined the state's claims to a monopoly on all that was valuable in thought and creativity.

QUESTIONS FOR ANALYSIS

1. What ills do dissident artists highlight in their work? What values do they express?

2. How do you explain the official and often violent suppression of this art?

3. Do official actions in regard to culture seem especially characteristic of totalitarian government, or do they seem rather a standard feature of the cold war? Explain your answer.

4. Why did dissident art play such a revolutionary role in the USSR, while in the West critical art like that of Sigmar Polke became a highly prized and expensive commodity?

NOTES

1. Christian Joppke, quoted in Padraic Kenney, *A Carnival of Revolution: Central Europe 1989* (Princeton: Princeton University Press, 2002), 279.

2. Quoted ibid., 279.

3. Quoted in Dennis Kavanagh, *Thatcherism and British Politics: The End of Consensus?* (Oxford: Oxford University Press, 1987), 252.

4. Quoted in Kenneth O. Morgan, *The People's Peace: British History, 1945–1989* (Oxford: Oxford University Press, 1990), 438.

5. Quoted ibid., 442.

6. Quoted from *Forever in the Shadow of Hitler? Original Documents of the Historikerstreit, the Controversy concerning the Singularity of the Holocaust,* trans. James Knowlton and Truett Cates (Atlantic Highlands: Humanities Press, 1993).

7. Quoted in Wayne C. Thompson, *Western Europe 1987* (Washington, D.C.: Skye, 1987), 105.

8. Quoted in Allan Pred, *Even in Sweden: Racisms, Racialized Spaces, and the Popular Geographical Imagination* (Berkeley: University of California Press, 2000), 51.

9. Quoted ibid., 50.

10. "The Old Soldiers of Moscow's Shopping Wars," *New York Times,* December 12, 1990.

11. Quoted in Gisèle Bernstein et al., *Histoire du 20e siècle de 1953 à nos jours: la croissance et la crise* (Paris: Hatier, 1990), 457.

12. Quoted in Robert Kaiser, *Why Gorbachev Happened: His Triumphs and His Failures* (New York: Simon and Schuster, 1991), 70–71.

13. Ibid., 78.

14. Quoted in David Remnick, "Leningrad TV: On the Cutting Edge," *International Herald Tribune,* July 8–9, 1989.

15. Tatyana Tolstaya, *Pushkin's Children: Writings on Russia and Russians,* trans. Jamey Grambrell (Boston: Houghton Mifflin, 2003), 35.

16. Quoted in Kaiser, *Why Gorbachev Happened,* 119.

17. Quoted in Padraic Kenney, "The Gender of Resistance in Communist Poland," *American Historical Review* 104 (April 1999), 2:400.

18. Quoted in Norman Davies, *Heart of Europe: A Short History of Poland* (Oxford: Oxford University Press, 1986), 383.

19. Quoted in *Le Monde,* December 20–21, 1981.

20. Quoted in Gale Stokes, *The Walls Came Tumbling Down: The Collapse of Communism in Eastern Europe* (New York: Oxford University Press, 1993), 103.

21. Colonel Wislicki, quoted in Davies, *Heart of Europe,* 390.

22. Quoted in Kenney, *Carnival of Revolution,* 40.

23. Quoted in *Newsweek,* December 25, 1989.

24. Quoted in Stokes, *Walls Came Tumbling Down,* 100.

25. Michael Geyer, "The Long Goodbye: German Culture Wars in the Nineties," in *The Power of Intellectuals in Contemporary Germany,* ed. Michael Geyer (Chicago: University of Chicago Press, 2001), 364.

26. Quoted in Stokes, *Walls Came Tumbling Down,* 154.

27. Quoted ibid., 165.

28. "Gorbachev's Economic Program," quoted in *New York Times,* October 17, 1990.

29. Quoted in "State of Emergency Committee's Statement: 'A Mortal Danger Has Come,'" *New York Times,* August 20, 1991.

30. Oleg Lobov, quoted in Valery Tishkov, *Ethnicity, Nationalism and Conflict in and after the Soviet Union: The Mind Aflame* (London: Sage, 1997), 218.

31. "Chechens Resigned to More Slaughter," *GW,* November 14–20, 2002, p. 32.

32. Leo Kropywiansky, "Victor Pelevin," *Bomb Magazine,* http://www.bombsite.com/pelevin/pelevin3.html.

SUGGESTED REFERENCES

Europe Faces Global Economic Challenge In the face of global competition, Margaret Thatcher set the trend for downsizing commitments to social citizenship and for turning one group of citizens into internal enemies. Both her programs and rhetorical style influenced politics outside her nation and outside her party, as Reiton's book shows.

Kingston, Jeff. *Japan in Transformation 1952–2000.* 2001.
Nakayama, Shigeru. *A Social History of Science and Technology in Contemporary Japan.* 2001.
Reitan, Earl A. *The Thatcher Revolution: Margaret Thatcher, John Major, Tony Blair, and the Transformation of Modern Britain.* 2002.
Schoenwald, Jonathan M. *A Time for Choosing: The Rise of Modern American Conservatism.* 2001.
Sheridan, Greg. *Tigers: Leaders of the New Asia-Pacific.* 1997.
Sloan, John. *The Reagan Effect: Economics and Presidential Leadership.* 1999.

Alternatives to Thatcherism Europeans were inventive in facing the trials of the late-twentieth-century economy. The books below provide examples of different policies and attitudes toward the welfare state and democracy.

Bell, David S. *François Mitterrand: A Political Biography.* 2005.
Cox, Robert H. *The Development of the Dutch Welfare State: From Workers' Insurance to Universal Entitlement. 1993.*
Dahl, Hanne Marlene and Tine Rask Eriksen, eds. *Dilemmas of Care in the Nordic Welfare State: Continuity and Change.* 2005.

Keating, Michael. *Culture, Institutions, and Economic Development: A Study of Eight European Regions.* 2003.

Lewis, Flora. *Europe: A Tapestry of Nations.* 1987.

Pruys, Karl Hugo. *Kohl: Genius of the Present: A Biography of Helmut Kohl.* 1996.

Taylor-Gooby, Peter. *New Risks, New Welfare: The Transformation of the European Welfare State.* 2004.

Reformers Change the Soviet Bloc   The "Gorbachev phenomenon," as it has been called, was popularized by many U.S. observers. Read Tatyana Tolstaya's journalism for a different account.

Cerf, Christopher, et al., eds. *Small Fires: Letters from the Soviet People to* Ogonyuk *Magazine 1987–1990.* 1990.

Davies, Norman. *Heart of Europe: The Past in Poland's Present.* 2001.

Lewin, Moshe. *The Gorbachev Phenomenon: A Historical Interpretation.* 1991.

Merridale, Catherine. *Night of Stone: Death and Memory in Twentieth-Century Russia.* 2000.

Sternthal, Susanne. *Gorbachev's Reforms: De-Stalinization through Demilitarization.* 1997.

Thomas, Daniel C. *The Helsinki Effect: International Norms, Human Rights, and the Demise of Communism.* 2001.

Tolstaya, Tatyana. *Pushkin's Children: Writings on Russia and Russians.* 2003.

Weigel, George. *Witness to Hope: The Biography of Pope John Paul II.* 1999.

The End of the Soviet System   Kenney, Kotkin, and Stokes provide differing and lively accounts of what went right in the people's uprising against the Soviet system.

Kenney, Padraic. *A Carnival of Revolution: Central Europe 1989.* 2002.

Kligman, Gail. *The Politics of Duplicity: Controlling Reproduction in Ceauşescu's Romania.* 1998.

Kotkin, Stephen. *Armageddon Averted: The Soviet Collapse, 1970–2000.* 2001.

Nelson, Arvid. *Cold War Ecology: Forests, Farms, and People in the East German Landscape, 1945–1989.* 2005.

Paczkowski, Andrzej. *The Spring Will Be Ours: Poland and the Poles from Occupation to Freedom.* 2004.

Siani-Davies, Peter. *The Romanian Revolution of December 1989.* 2005.

Stokes, Gale. *The Walls Came Tumbling Down: The Collapse of Communism in Eastern Europe.* 1993.

Tismaneanu, Vladimir. *Stalinism for All Seasons: A Political History of Romanian Communism.* 2003.

Yugoslavia and the USSR Disintegrate   Because the remaking of both regions continues, many of these studies are necessarily tentative, but they present a vivid story of the real pain and trauma involved in the collapse of communism.

Fink, Sheri. *War Hospital: A True Story of Surgery and Survival.* 2003.

Finkielkraut, Alain. *Dispatches from the Balkan War and Other Writings.* 1999.

Fitzpatrick, Sheila. *Tear Off the Masks! Identity and Imposture in Twentieth-Century Russia.* 2005.

Glenny, Misha. *The Fall of Yugoslavia: The Third Balkan War.* 1996.

Mertus, Julie, et al., eds. *The Suitcase: Refugee Voices from Bosnia and Croatia.* 1997.

Naimark, Norman. *Fires of Hatred: Ethnic Cleansing in Twentieth-Century Europe.* 2001.

Suny, Ronald Grigor. *The Soviet Experiment: Russia, the USSR, and the Successor States.* 1997.

Birth Pains of a New Eastern Europe Both journalists and scholars investigate the new eastern Europe. Humphrey looks at what has happened to ordinary people in the transition.

Brudny, Yitzhak, et al., eds. *Restructuring Post-Communist Russia.* 2004.

Goldman, Marshall. *Lost Opportunity: What Has Made Economic Reform in Russia So Difficult?* 1996.

Humphrey, Caroline. *The Unmaking of Soviet Life: Everyday Economies after Socialism.* 2002.

Khazanov, Anatoly M. *After the USSR: Ethnicity, Nationalism, and Politics in the Commonwealth of Independent States.* 1996.

Rothschild, Joseph, and Nancy M. Wingfield. *Return to Diversity: A Political History of East Central Europe.* 2000.

Service, Robert. *Russia: Experiment with a People.* 2003.

Steen, Anton. *Political Elites and the New Russia: The Power Basis of Yeltsin's and Putin's Regimes.* 2003.

Selected Web Sites

The Margaret Thatcher Web site <**margaretthatcher.org**> contains not only biographical and career information but also a listing of some 8,000 speeches Thatcher made over the course of her political life. CNN <**cnn.com/SPECIALS/cold.war/**> provides documents from all stages of the cold war, including its demise in the 1980s. Also check the Balkan Pages to read about the former Socialist Federal Republic of Yugoslavia as well as the plight of Srebrenica at <**balkansnet.org/srebrenica.html**>.

12

Europe in the Global Age

I N EARLY SPRING OF 2004, JUST AS TEN ADDITIONAL NATIONS were about the join the European Union, the Roma in one of them, the newly independent state of Slovakia, rioted angrily in cities and villages, battling the police and other officials. Enraged by the Slovakian government's plan to cut their welfare payments in half to about $50 per family, they looted stores for supplies. For the six million European Roma—also known as Gypsies—life in the twenty-first century was becoming increasingly difficult. Modern society demanded higher education and skills for employment, but many of the Roma were illiterate and in ill health, living in strong family units but isolated in some of Europe's worst slums. "We see hungry people who are afraid that their children will die," one Roma rights official said; "it's somehow an overflowing of anger." Because membership in the European Union required the curtailing of public expenditures to balance budgets, governments hoping to join the EU slashed benefits and services—among them payments to the Roma of eastern Europe, where the majority of them lived. Despite these stringencies, many Roma had high hopes for EU membership, believing that the EU would enforce tolerance as much as it enforced financial stringency. It might even be that the EU would help the Roma develop political leader-

◆ **Young Czechoslovakian Men of Roma Descent, 1990**
These Roma youth posed for the camera before the breakup of Czechoslovakia into the Czech Republic and Slovakia in 1993. All over Europe, majority ethnic groups have long discriminated against people of Roma descent in housing, social services, and employment. Today the Roma of Slovakia are fighting this injustice with the help of both local and international nongovernmental organizations. *Shepherd Sherbell/CORBIS.*

ship to lobby for the education, services, and jobs they needed.

The Roma exemplify the complexities of European citizenship in the global age. Despite having lived in Europe for centuries after their migration from Asia, they had little civic connection with any nation-state. They had settled in clans in relative isolation, remaining stateless. In the late twentieth and early twenty-first centuries the number of at least temporarily stateless peoples in Europe would swell as tens of thousands of asylum seekers and political refugees from around the world fled difficult living conditions in their countries of origin. Globalization weakened national borders as did the European Union, and continuing migration made populations in every nation more varied, creating mixtures of peoples from around the world with various degrees of interest in assimilation to a single national culture. The situation of the Roma in eastern Europe, and indeed the deepening diversity of European populations, reflected a new stage in the globalization not simply of Europe but of every portion of the world. Issues of political inclusion, social and educational standards, and general

2002	Residents of Poland, Slovenia, and Estonia achieve purchasing power some 40 percent higher than in 1989.
2002	February: Slobodan Milosevic goes on trial for crimes against humanity committed against Bosnian Serbs in the former Yugoslavia.
2002	Avian flu virus first appears in Asian chickens.
2003	March: United States leads a small coalition, including Great Britain and Spain, in an invasion of Iraq.
2004	EU admits Estonia, Latvia, Lithuania, Poland, Czech Republic, Slovakia, Hungary, Malta, Cyprus, and Slovenia.
2004	Seven eastern European countries join NATO, increasing the alliance to twenty-six members.
2004	Spring: Roma in Slovakia riot in response to social welfare cuts.
2004	Bombings in Madrid and Indonesia.
2004	17.1 million individuals around the world are living in refugee camps.
2004	December: Viktor Yushchenko, despite poisoning attempt, wins election in Ukraine.
2005	February: Kyoto Protocol goes into effect but without U.S. participation.
2005	July: Terrorist bombings on London transport.
2005	Youths in Muslim suburbs of Paris riot to protest police harassment and discrimination.
2005	Europe consists of 45 nations, more than double those existing in 1945.
2006	March: ETA, a Basque separatist group in Spain, announces complete cessation of violence.
2006	French youths protest unemployment and government policies.

679

economic and cultural fairness resonated across an expanding European Union and across Europe as a whole. Like the Roma, many Europeans hoped that the tighter integration of nation-states in an age of global prosperity would inspire a spirit of cooperation and lead to human betterment.

There was every reason for optimism. Technological advances such as the Internet effectively eliminated political obstacles to the exchange of ideas and made censorship of opinions increasingly difficult. Satellite communications and the Internet allowed supranational organizations—whether economic, political, or humanitarian—to function more efficiently, if not as efficiently as those of a single nation. People's allegiances broadened, and many were pulled from poverty by increasing global prosperity and from disease by the biological breakthroughs that scientists continued to make. As countries such as India and China unleashed their productive power, abundance seemed attainable for ever larger numbers of people no matter where they might be living. Global investors came to see the economic promise of central and eastern Europe, and as countries there prospered at the beginning of the twenty-first century, Europe as a whole seemed a highly desirable location in a rapidly modernizing world.

Nevertheless, despite all the improvements brought by transnational communication and cooperation, the global age opened up intractable problems. Mass communication and rapid transportation helped diseases, disasters, and political violence cross oceans and other natural boundaries with lightning speed. The natural environment continued to deteriorate. The global AIDS epidemic afflicted more than 40 million people as the twenty-first century began. Despite the efforts of international organizations, global terrorism escalated throughout the 1980s and 1990s and into the next century. As nations became more ethnically diverse, the popularity of violent political opposition groups grew, and newcomers to European nation-states suffered attacks and worse. The global age—so ripe with possibilities—was fraught with dangers and new challenges.

THE PERILS AND POSSIBILITIES OF GLOBALIZATION

Made possible by the end of the cold war and improving technology, the global age was one of movement in every realm of experience. No superpower rivalry stood in the way of technology transfers, nor did national borders impede the flow of information by means of the Internet, satellites, faxes, and other telecommunications systems. Access to entertainment and consumer goods from around the world increased. As global flows of people, goods, and ideas accelerated, some saw a reason to fortify the nation-state against things foreign—be they immigrant populations, diseases, or pollutants from abroad. Others worried that supranational organizations, whether massive corporations or governmental bodies, would undermine individual rights and freedoms. To still others the global age seemed to offer an opportunity for profit, escape, and the dizzying exploration of all that globalization had to offer. It was an age of opportunity and of disturbing new realities in almost every sphere of endeavor. People had to—and did—rethink citizenship and careers, health and global politics.

Europe and the Environment

Even as the ecology movement gained political clout and as general environmental awareness grew, threats to the global environment accelerated. These threats emanated from both local and global conditions. The danger was laid bare starkly in 1986, when a reactor at the nuclear plant at Chernobyl in the USSR republic of Ukraine exploded and spewed radioactive dust into the atmosphere. The reactor, like most in the USSR, had been constructed with only minimal safety features, and its workers were poorly trained. Thirty-one people died instantly; some fifteen thousand more perished slowly from the effects of radiation. Soviet officials tried to hush up this local event; but when Scandinavian agencies revealed rising levels of radioactivity hundreds of miles from the disaster site, it was clear that environmental disaster had crossed national boundaries. By the 1990s cancer rates in affected regions were ten times higher than elsewhere, particularly among children. In a vast region of the Soviet Union, stretching for thousands of miles, toxic waste polluted lakes and rivers, used nuclear fuel had been dumped into neighboring seas, and many parts of Soviet Central Asia were so contaminated by nuclear and other testing that entire regions were unfit for human and other life.

More widespread, the use of fossil fuels created a less dramatic but no less toxic environmental hazard. Pollutants from the burning of oil, natural gas, and coal mixed with atmospheric moisture to produce acid rain, a poisonous brew that destroyed forests. Acid rain damaged more than 70 percent of Europe's Norway spruce trees. In eastern Europe, where people burned fossil fuels with practically no safeguards, forests looked as if they had been ravaged by fire, and children suffered from chronic bronchial disease and other ailments. In less industrialized areas, rain forests were hacked down at an alarming rate, as people sought to open land for cattle grazing or for growing cash crops. Clearing the forests depleted the global oxygen supply, promoted desertification, and threatened the biodiversity of the entire planet.

Global warming and the greenhouse effect also affected Europe and the rest of the world. By the late 1980s scientists had determined that the public's use of chlorofluorocarbons (CFCs), chemicals found in aerosol and refrigeration products, had blown a hole in the ozone layer. Part of the blanket of gases surrounding the earth, the ozone layer prevents harmful ultraviolet rays from reaching the planet. Simultaneously, automobile and industrial emissions of chemicals were adding to the thermal blanket of which ozone was a part. The result is global warming, an increase in the temperature of the earth's lower atmosphere. Changes in temperature and dramatic weather cycles of drought, then drenching rain, indicated that a greenhouse effect might be permanently warming the earth. Some scientists predicted dire consequences for the planet. In the 1990s one worrisome effect was apparent: the breaking up of Arctic pack ice began to open a new trade route for northern countries such as Finland, Russia, and Canada. There were predictions that regular summer traffic through the new "Northwest passage" would be possible by 2010, and scientists warned that by 2080 the ice would completely disappear during the summer. Reality, however, exceeded even these dire predictions. As early as 2002, Finland was shipping oil along the route. Both Canada and Russia claimed the passage as their national waters, and security issues such as piracy and safety needed to be addressed by international bodies. Scientists forecast additional, more dire, environmental changes: the rate of global ice melting, which had more than doubled since 1988, would raise sea levels 27 centimeters (about 10½ inches) by the year 2100.

Europeans proposed to attack environmental problems on both the local and the global levels. Frankfurt, Germany, developed car-free zones. Venice operated completely without the use of automobiles. In Paris, when emissions levels reached a certain point, the use of automobiles was restricted, and when pollution reached dangerous levels, cars were banned altogether. Paris and Amsterdam had well-developed bicycle lanes on major city streets. Very small cars, using minute amounts of fuel, became a fashionable way to reduce dependence on fossil fuels, the consumption of which was at the heart of global warming and the greenhouse effect. To reduce dependence on fossil fuels, the Netherlands and Germany harnessed wind power to such an extent that 20 percent of their electricity was generated by wind. To reduce pollution, Denmark banned the use of aluminum cans in favor of glass containers. By 2000, the Netherlands had reached a recycling level of 90 percent for automobiles.

Those successes, the results of changing habits and dependencies, were achieved by some of the most industrialized countries in the world. By 1999, some eighty-four countries including European Union members had signed the Kyoto Protocol, an international treaty fashioned to reduce emissions of greenhouse gases and other pollutants around the world. The Kyoto program received a blow, however, when President George W. Bush of the United States—the world's top polluting nation—refused to sign the international agreement. There was progress nonetheless: the Kyoto emissions reductions finally went into effect in February 2005, and by then the Russian government had agreed to join the effort.

The Global Spread of Disease

From the early 1980s on, both Western values and Western technological expertise were challenged by the global spread of an epidemic disease: acquired immune deficiency syndrome (AIDS). An incurable, highly virulent killer, AIDS initially afflicted heterosexual people in central Africa. Its first European victim, Danish physician Grethe Rask, died in 1977 after working among the sick in that region. The disease later turned up in Haitian immigrants to the United States and in homosexual men worldwide. In 1983 researchers at the Pasteur Institute in France isolated the virus that causes AIDS, discovering that the mysterious ailment effectively shuts down the body's immune system. For a time AIDS in Europe and the United States was a crisis of huge proportions. By the late 1990s people recognized that an even greater AIDS crisis existed outside the West, where social and political factors hindered both discussion of the illness and preventive measures. In the early twenty-first century, no cure had yet been discovered, though protease-inhibiting drugs helped alleviate symptoms and were beginning to prolong the lives of those infected.

The mounting death toll from AIDS prompted some to view this disease as the Black Death of the twentieth century, reinforcing prejudices and stereotypes about some of its most vulnerable victims. As millions in Africa contracted the disease, treatment was not forthcoming because the ill were so poor. African nations called upon wealthy governments and pharmaceutical firms to provide drugs to control the disease, but to small effect. In addition, the Ebola virus and dozens of other deadly organisms lay in waiting.

Dangerous diseases were not limited to humans, and the threat they posed was global because of worldwide trade. For instance, fear of hoof-and-mouth disease and especially of mad-cow disease periodically shut down Britain's cattle-raising industry in the 1980s and 1990s, and millions of animals were slaughtered for fear that herds and people worldwide would be infected. Europeans boycotted beef on an individual basis for a time. In 2002, avian flu virus—potentially deadly to humans—appeared in Asian chickens. Isolated cases of the flu also appeared in countries closer to Europe like Egypt and Turkey and even reached Romania—that is Europe itself.

Corporate and government "megasystems" failed to address adequately the important challenges faced by society such as the spread of AIDS. The failure showed that although global forces could promote technological advance, they did not necessarily supersede nation-states' abilities to safeguard citizens' well-being. There was greater success in Europe's handling of the threat of mad-cow contamination than there was in preventing and treating AIDS.

Migration Continues

In the late twentieth century, global migration accelerated, swelling the numbers of people arriving in Europe as it continued to develop industrial capacity and a service economy. Fleeing wars in parts of the Middle East, Africa, and Asia, many entered Europe as refugees, and applications for political asylum ballooned in the 1990s and early twenty-first century. Of the 551,000 asylum seekers applying for admission to industrial nations in 2000, some 391,000 applied to the fifteen member countries of the European Union. In 2004, 17.1 million refugees were living in camps around the world, many of them hoping to reach Europe (see Document 12.1). The breakup of the Soviet Union and wars in the Balkans (see Chapter 11) raised the numbers of those seeking physical and economic security. In fact, the fall of the Berlin Wall was the first blow to cold war–era migration restrictions. The movement of people from eastern Europe westward assumed huge proportions, including some five million into Germany alone between 1989 and 1996. Not every newcomer was willing to serve in the lowest ranks of the economy. Well-educated migrants arrived to take advantage of openings in technical fields like computers and telecommunications and in the sciences. Europe increasingly meant opportunity and a new way of life: "I do not want to go back to China," said a woman restaurant owner in Hungary in the 1990s. "It is not only the hard work. . . . I have relatives in the restaurant business and they have to have good relations with the officials, local authorities, tax collectors, even the police. They have to make everyone happy and sometimes they have to bribe somebody to help them. I would not be happy living like that."[1]

Migration from eastern to western Europe slowed by the late 1990s, but migration from North Africa, Latin America, and Southeast Asia continued, as civil wars and natural catastrophes prompted many people to move. The profile of host countries differed somewhat from that before 1980. Italy, Spain, Greece, Cyprus, and Ireland reversed the earlier trend of exporting their labor and became destinations for immigrants. These countries had experienced net losses of population and needed new, unskilled workers. By the mid-1990s, an estimated 10 percent of the Greek labor force was foreign, and in Italy some 5 percent of the population was legal immigrants—a lower percentage than in other western European countries, but a dramatic change, nonetheless.

Among the immigrants were significantly more women than in previous decades. Many of them were destined for the informal economy of household work, domestic service, and the sex trade. Large numbers of the migrants from eastern Europe were women lured to work in the sex industry, conceding that it was the only job from which they could earn a livelihood, given the firing of women after the fall of communism. In the new climate in which imitation of the U.S. "free market" was equated with eliminating women from good jobs or from the workforce altogether, sex work in western and southern Europe was often the *only* work they could find. Some who applied for secretarial positions had their passports confiscated at the hiring interview and found themselves being shipped from eastern Europe to destinations abroad to work as sex slaves. In addition, the countries of southern Europe had less munificent welfare states, and cheap female labor took up the slack in child care and care of the incapacitated and elderly.

European doors were open to migrants in the 1980s and early 1990s because of the indisputable advantages migrants continued to bring. Policy makers had long recognized that there were many jobs that Europeans were unwilling to do in a labor-short economy—jobs in sanitation, heavy construction, and domestic service. As in decades past, migrants did manual labor in sweatshops and outwork such as making toys and trinkets at home. The migration of elites also flourished because in order to maintain high standards of industrial and scientific development Europe needed the very best brains the world had to offer. Moreover, in a global economy transnational workers provided links to the diverse economies in the system and enhanced their adopted country's well-being with their multicultural skills. "We are becoming more and more dependent upon contacts and impulses that transcend borders," Swedish prime minister Olof Palme announced in addressing the nation in 1985. "We can't build walls facing the surrounding world: walls mean isolation and retrogression."[2] Palme's reference to retrogression and isolation had both economic and political meanings, for many in Europe believed that it was part of their "civilized" duty to admit people in need of refuge and opportunity.

As the twenty-first century began and many European countries faced the prospect of supporting aging populations at a time of fertility decline, politicians saw another practical reason for migration. In 2001 a UN report pointed out that "replacement migration" to Europe would enhance the number of young workers whose contributions to social security funds would serve to alleviate the looming shortfall in pension money. "If retirement ages remain essentially where they are today . . . international migration is the only option."[3]

Immigrants tended to be segregated in entire cities, such as Leicester, England, or in the suburbs and separate neighborhoods of major cities such as Paris. Segregation often allowed immigrants to keep their extended families together and to develop community networks of support. Cultural centers, temples and mosques, and ethnic food stores and restaurants mushroomed: the rue de Belleville in Paris saw adjacent Arab, African, Jewish, Thai, and other ethnic grocery stores and small eateries. Immigrants who became citizens of the host countries and those who migrated to support the prosperity of businesses back home made these institutions flourish. The success of karaoke bars around the world testified to the global importance of Japanese businesspeople.

Sometimes segregated conditions arose rapidly. In Sweden, as soon as immigrants moved in, native-born Swedes moved out. The Swedes who remained, the newcomers complained, were alcoholics and petty criminals who made neighborhoods insecure. Police harassment plagued some immigrant neighborhoods, individual immigrants, and even citizens of immigrant extraction. In times of trouble police were nowhere to be found. Nevertheless, Europe maintained its reputation for being a refuge and a source of jobs and was thus the principal destination of the world's migrants.

Neoliberal skepticism about government-provided social services and the heightened insecurities spawned by global competition intensified the animus toward immigrants. Native-born residents sometimes blamed the newcomers for all the problems facing modern society. An unemployed youth in Palermo, Sicily, complained in the 1990s that Asian and African newcomers were "taking our bread." Even while admitting that the newcomers did menial jobs that Sicilians would no longer perform, this young man said, "They're infecting our city, we must ship them back home."[4] In 2002 a conservative candidate for the chancellorship of Germany, where unemployment was high, argued that "With 4.3 million unemployed, we can't have more foreign workers coming to Germany."[5] On the eve of EU enlargement in 2004, the highly respected weekly *The Economist* whipped up anti-Roma sentiment with an article titled "The Coming Hordes," which warned of Britain's being overrun by Gypsies from eastern Europe.[6]

After the 1980s, anti-immigrant and racist parties flourished, spurred by global communications. As the Soviet Union disintegrated, its traditional minorities were cast as "dirty Ukrainians," "whores" (of whatever ethnicity), and "yid face."[7] Language and ideology drawn from the Nazi past resurfaced in many parts of Europe: "let's gas 'em," German youth chanted of immigrants in street demonstrations. In Austria the Austrian Freedom Party of Jörg Haider came to power in 2000 on a platform that denounced racial mixing and multiculturalism, claiming that immigrants did not value human rights and democracy. A charismatic campaigner, Haider demanded a constitutional amendment that would express antagonism to immigrants, the segregation into special schools of students whose mother tongue was not German, and the expansion of a police force devoted to monitoring immigrants. Opponents publicized Haider's Nazi connections. His parents had been members of the Nazi Party; he had inherited a large and valuable estate seized from its Jewish owners during the war and bought at a bargain-basement price by his uncle; he openly praised Third Reich social and political policies. International condemnation swelled to force Haider to work from behind the scenes in a coalition government.

Globalization of culture also produced strange hybrids. The Moscow rock band Corroded Metals campaigned for right-wing candidates. Its songs were anti-Semitic and full of hatred for the many ethnic minorities in Russia, with chants in English of "Kill, kill, kill, kill the bloody foreigners" running in the background.[8] In an age of global communications Europe's radical right maintained close ties with right-wing extremists in the United States, who sometimes provided financial support.

Many immigrants had a sophisticated understanding of what was happening. Those whose parents and grandparents had migrated for jobs were now maturing, continuing the process of making Europe more cosmopolitan and multicultural. Second- and third-generation migrants entered the professions and civil service; they became noted filmmakers, artists, and intellectuals. From these positions they influenced politics, developing "rainbow coalitions" to protect both the European tradition of multiculturalism and their own rights as citizens and ethnic minorities. Immigrants created mixed art forms such as Afro-Caribbean music and multicultural forms of rap, often conveying a message of tolerance, as in this song by a Swedish multicultural hip-hop band:

> Me say me come to Sweden and me get treated like dirt
> Not by everyone but at least me got hurt
> Come now red man, black man and also white
> No time for prejudice just time to unite. . . .[9]

Yet despite these cultural ways of dealing with discrimination, explosions of anger continued to occur. In the fall of 2005, after the deaths of two young men hiding from police, youth in the mostly Muslim suburbs of Paris mounted protests not only over the deaths but over joblessness and police harassment. The spread of protest to other cities led to the burning of thousands of cars, numerous injuries, and the continuation of violence for a month. In the spring of 2006 young people in Paris again took to the streets to protest unemployment and new government policies that seemed to discriminate against them. Issues of ethnicity, religious discrimination, and lack of economic opportunity were high on the European agenda early in the twenty-first century.

World Networks and Organizations

The Internet in particular linked organizations and enterprises around the world, globalizing postindustrial society and expanding economic connections. By the early twenty-first century, as postindustrial skills spread, the Internet brought service jobs to countries that previously had suffered unemployment and severe poverty. One of the first to recognize the possibilities of computing and call-desk services was Ireland, which pushed computer literacy and worked to attract business. In 2003 U.S. firms spent $8.3 billion outsourcing to Ireland, as well as $7.7 billion outsourcing to India. The Internet allowed for some work to be done anywhere. Moroccans could do help-desk work for French- or Spanish-speakers, and by the end of the twentieth century, customer service jobs had moved from western Europe and the United States to Estonia, Hungary, and the Czech Republic.

Accounting, credit checks, and legal services became global by the end of the twentieth century. Not only India and China, both of them having good systems of education, but also the well-educated workforce of eastern Europe profited from the Internet revolution. Three percent of India's gross domestic product came from outsourced work done for English-speaking governments and private industries based in Europe, the United States, and Austronesia. Indians developed computer software to handle accounts and provide customer and payroll services.

The people who worked in these outsourcing enterprises were increasingly likely to participate in the global consumer economy as buyers of Western goods. A twenty-one-year-old Indian woman, working for a service provider in Bangalore under the English name "Sharon," was able to buy a cell phone from the Finnish company Nokia and other consumer items with her salary. "As a teenager I wished for so many things," she said. "Now I'm my own Santa Claus."[10] Once lagging behind economically, the Irish and eastern Europeans had access to automobiles, CD players, and personal computers, items that would have been far beyond their means before the 1990s.

Globalization led to the proliferation of supranational organizations, many of them regulating economies and exchange but others addressing social issues. The World Trade Organization, the World Bank, and the International Monetary Fund had been in existence for several decades, but as national economies interacted more closely, these supranational organizations gained in power. Raising money from individual governments, the International Monetary Fund made loans to developing countries but on the condition that they restructure their economies according to neoliberal principles. Other supranational organizations took the form of charitable foundations, many of them in Europe and the United States. Because they controlled so much money, many of these nongovernmental organizations (NGOs) wielded considerable international power.

After the fall of the Soviet bloc, NGOs used their resources to shape economic and social policy and the course of political reform in the region. In countries where Communist policy had always aimed to prevent the creation of independent organizations, clubs, and journalism that might push for reform, the presence of NGOs helped school locals in how to be active rather than passive citizens and how to work for the public benefit.

Some NGOs operated on a vast scale. The French-based Doctors without Borders (Médecins sans Frontières), for example, gained money through global contributions and used it to provide medical care in the former Yugoslavia, the Democratic Republic of Congo, and other places where people were facing war without benefit of medical help except whatever Doctors without Borders could provide.

Critics castigated the neoliberal bias of some global organizations—whether powerful organizations like the World Bank or smaller individual foundations like the British world charity Oxfam—for ignoring the will of the local communities they were trying to help with their bureaucratically oriented policy making. Even as the World Bank, World Trade Organization, and International Monetary Fund forced poor nations to adopt free trade, the European Union and the United States imposed huge tariffs to prevent cheap goods from competing with their own products. In 2002 the U.S. government under George W. Bush, a staunch advocate of free trade, levied large tariffs on imported steel in order to win the votes of steelworkers in this declining U.S. industry. The European Union threatened retaliation with its own list of U.S. goods to be taxed. The biggest threat to free trade, however, came from government subsidies to European and U.S. agribusiness that amounted to a tariff on goods from poor countries, for the subsidies allowed agribusinesses to lower their prices and depend on government for their profits. Tariffs and subsidized profits, it was estimated, diverted $100 billion worth of business away from poor nations even though their goods offered consumers better bargains.

Globalization gave rise to global activism, some of it directed against globalization itself. In 1998 Bernard Cassen of France founded ATTAC, a French acronym for Association for Taxation of Financial Transactions. The organization, which soon had adherents in forty countries, stood against the control of globalization by the forces of high finance: "Commercial totalitarianism is not free trade," Cassen commented. "The globalizers want to streamline the art of living, but to live is much more fulfilling than to shop." ATTAC took its major policy goal from U.S. economist and Nobel Prize winner James Tobin: it aimed to tax financial transactions (just as the purchase of household necessities was taxed) and to create with the tax revenue a fund for people living in underdeveloped countries. Cassen was in favor of European integration and opposed the "balkanization" of regions and countries, but he professed not to be left-wing: "Behind every left-winger," he claimed, "I smell a bourgeois." Thus, ATTAC distanced itself from many organizers who simply demonstrated against international meetings and visiting political leaders in order to cause an antiglobalization ruckus.

Even though ATTAC did support some protests, such as French farmers' boycott of McDonald's, it refused to sponsor candidates in elections: "Just let the heads of political parties not become overconfident, for we intend to play a permanent role to stimulate democracy in every party." That role became quickly apparent in the winter of 2002 when ATTAC held a conference at Porto Allegro, Brazil, to compete with the annual conference at Davos, Switzerland, attended by leaders of multinational corporations and globally active politicians and economists (see Document 12.2). Indicating the success of the strategy to offer policy alternatives, political leaders flocked to Porto Allegro as well as to the Davos forum.[11]

◆ **José Bové Protests Globalization, 2000**

French activist farmer José Bové is an outspoken critic of the effects of globalization on food. Here he is shown protesting the closed and well-policed meetings of the World Economic Forum in Davos, Switzerland—a gathering of the world's top business leaders and most powerful economic officials. The poster shows these leaders as both elegantly attired and deathlike in contrast to those ordinary people who put the rights of ordinary people first. French authorities sent Bové to jail for leading an attack on a McDonald's restaurant, and at the Davos forum in 2000 some of his supporters again damaged a McDonald's outlet. *AP Photo.*

BEYOND THE NATION-STATE: INTEGRATION AND FRAGMENTATION

In the 1990s the peoples of Europe took immense strides to strengthen transnational organizations and allegiances that operated beyond the traditional nation-state. NATO expanded dramatically after the collapse of the Soviet bloc to include many of the post-Communist countries formerly part of the Warsaw Pact. In 1999 Hungary, the Czech Republic, and Poland became members, and in 2004 seven other eastern European countries joined. In addition, NATO reached formal agreements on European security with Russia in 1997 and 2002. By 2004 NATO had twenty-six member countries, all of them contributing financially to support the institutions of the transnational military alliance based in Brussels.

Like NATO, the Common Market had begun to take shape in the 1940s. Its formal founding in 1957 had opened the pathway to a supranational, unified policy in economic matters, and its evolution into the European Union extended that cooperation to political and cultural matters. The nationalist function of capital cities—where wide boulevards and massive public buildings, such as parliaments, showed off the splendor of the state—diminished as London, Paris, and other major urban areas became packed with people from other countries who introduced new ideas and attractive new customs. These developments, however, aroused resistance from those who wanted to preserve their familiar ways of life and mourned the loss of what they felt to be local traditions. For many, globalization posed the problem of preserving the best of global, national, and local relationships, which might be in conflict. When all was said and done, however, the expansion of the European Union marked a historic step beyond national rivalries and the cold war rupture of the twentieth century.

From Common Market to European Union

In 1992, the twelve countries of the Common Market ended national distinctions in the spheres of business activity, border controls, and transportation, effectively halting passport inspection at their mutual borders. Citizens of European Community member countries were issued a common burgundy-colored passport, and governments, whether municipal or national, had to treat all member nations' firms the same. In 1993 by the terms of the Maastricht Treaty, the EC became the European Union (EU). Austria, Finland, and Sweden joined the EU in 1995 and adopted the common policies that governed everything from the number of American soap operas aired on television to pollution controls on automobiles to standardized health warnings on cigarette packages. In 1999 a common currency, the European Currency Unit, or euro, came into being, though Britain, Sweden, and Denmark did not adopt it. "People with the same money don't go to war with one another," a French nuclear scientist remarked. An Italian student enthused that the euro provided "a sense of belonging to a European Union and I think it's beautiful that there's this big European country."[12] The EU Parliament convened regularly in Strasbourg, France, and subgroups met to negotiate additional cultural, economic, and social policies. With the adoption of the euro, the European Central Bank gained more control over economic policy.

The EU also played a pacifying role in Europe. It was Greece that pushed for the admission of its traditional enemy Turkey in 2002 and 2003, despite warnings from former French president Valérie Giscard d'Estaing that a predominantly Muslim country could never fit in with the Christian traditions of EU members. Many in the population of Europe at large agreed, but EU member states fought Giscard d'Estaing, with Greece taking the lead as a result of its hard-won diplomatic ties with Turkey. "Turkey has been a great European power since the sixteenth century," Greek prime minister Costas Simitis maintained in 2003. Rejecting religious criteria to resolve political issues, Simitis pointed to the common desire of Turks and other Europeans for "democratization and economic stability"—both of them fundamental tenets of the European Union.[13] Both Greece and Turkey stood to benefit by having their disputes adjudicated by the larger body of European members. Both would be able to cut their defense spending—most of it used for weaponry against the other country. It was hoped that the rivalry between Turkey and Greece, like the rivalry between Germany and France, would dissolve if the strong economic and political ties of the EU linked the two countries. Gradually an EU identity might soften nationalist antagonisms across the region.

Drawbacks to EU membership remained, however. The EU enforced few common regulatory practices, and economic policies calling for cooperation among members were sometimes ignored. Individual governments set up hurdles and barriers for businesses—for instance, to thwart transnational mergers that they did not like. One government might secretly block the acquisition of a company based on its soil no matter what the advantages to shareholders, the economy, the workforce, or consumers. Nonetheless, countries of eastern and east-central Europe clamored to join and worked hard to meet not only the EU's fiscal requirements but also requirements pertaining to human rights and social policy.

Problems affecting individuals tainted the EU in popular opinion across Europe. For example, in 2002, reacting to the depletion of fish in European coastal waters, the European Union ordered a 40 percent reduction in ocean fishing. This decision hit the Spanish particularly hard because they constituted the largest cohort of fishermen in the EU, and it indicated how easily the interests of any single occupational group and the technocrats in Brussels could diverge. A Spanish fisherman from Vigo near the Portuguese border put it this way: "The bureaucrats in Brussels have signed my death warrant and that of all the other people you see here in the port. The worst thing is that these gentlemen in their suits have never been on a boat and know nothing about the ocean."[14] Rodrigo Duran used a boat that had cost him $2 million, and he supported a crew of seventeen and their families, often remaining at sea for a month at a time to obtain his catch. Each person going to sea created jobs for five persons on land in conserving, shipbuilding, and other occupations. In order to join the European Union, Spain had earlier cut its fleet of fishermen by 50 percent, leaving a legacy of bitterness among those whose jobs and way of life had revolved around the fishing industry.

As the EU expanded in power and reach (Map 12.1), anti–European Union sentiment provided fodder for right-wing, nationalist parties. In 2004, representatives of the individual governments approved an EU constitution. In order for it to take effect, it had to be ratified within the member states, either by parliaments or by referendum. While parliaments across Europe were ratifying the constitution, Spain held an election in which voters also ratified the constitution. Referenda in France and the Netherlands, however, produced majorities against ratification. Anger directed at the EU bureaucracy headquartered in Brussels and against foreigners swirled around the ratification debate. By late spring 2006 some fifteen countries had ratified the EU constitution, but the convergence of citizen unease with immigrants and anger at high-handed EU officials blocked full ratification for the time being.

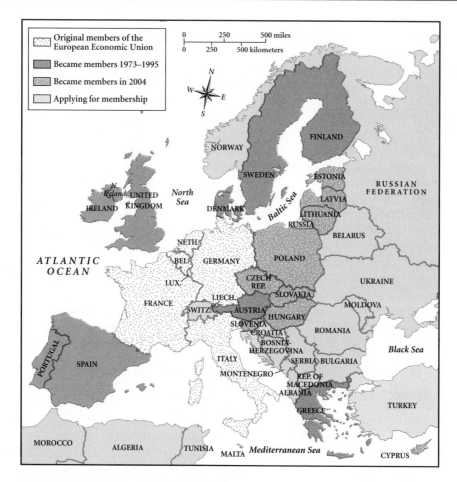

Legend:
- Original members of the European Economic Union
- Became members 1973–1995
- Became members in 2004
- Applying for membership

◆ **Map 12.1 The European Union, 2006**
The European Union continued to expand, adding ten new members in May 2004. What the addition of these new members would mean remained unclear, with many commentators pointing to a future in which eastern European states might meaningfully tip the balance of power away from the West. Bureaucratic domination of the organization, the admission of Turkey, and issues of immigration policy continued to trouble the EU early in the twenty-first century even as the addition of more states loomed on the EU's agenda.

East Joins West

As the European Union grew more powerful, nations once committed to remaining outside the euro zone or the EU itself scheduled referenda to rethink membership. Post-Communist countries almost immediately sensed the European Union's attractions. The case of Greece, which had long been considered the poor relative of the other member countries, showed the advantages clearly to them. Greece joined the Common Market in 1981. After its per capita gross domestic product fell from 64 percent of the European average in 1985 to 58.5 percent in 1990, a real effort took place in the 1990s to bring the country closer to EU norms. By the early twenty-first century, thanks to advice from the EU and an infusion of funds— 8.3 percent of the total EU budget—Greece reached 80 percent of the EU per capita gross domestic product and achieved the presidency of the EU in 2003. It also aimed to develop economic relations in the Balkans and eastern Mediterranean. Like most countries in the EU, Greece was a pro-federalist nation: "The new European aedifice that Greece wants is not a centralized superstate but a federation of national states united as a supranational and decentralized entity," a Greek economist maintained in 2003. Moreover, new economic conditions made the EU more important than ever "to palliate some of the more unfortunate effects of globalization," he said.[15]

Throughout the 1990s the countries to the east moved toward EU membership. The collapse of the Soviet system advanced privatization of industry. Governments late in the twentieth century sold off publicly owned industrial assets and natural resources to the highest bidders. Often this privatization worked to the advantage of the wealthy members of the EU, which alone could afford to purchase eastern European assets. For example, the Czech Republic in 2001 sold its major energy distributor Transgaz and eight other regional distributors for 4.1 billion euros to a German firm. Lower wages and costs of doing business attracted foreign investment to the Czech Republic, which reached a peak of $20 billion in 2000. The most attractive countries for investment had a history of a market and industrial economy—Poland, the Czech Republic, Hungary, and Slovenia. Although their economies grew at a faster rate than national economies elsewhere in Europe, unemployment remained high and the former socialist countries still had little margin if their economies slowed. Nevertheless, seeing the advantages of EU membership, most governments in east, east-central, and southeast Europe applied for membership despite the real disadvantages that might be waiting if their economies prematurely entered fully into competition with long-standing and more prosperous members.

In 2004 the EU admitted ten new members, mostly from central and eastern Europe: Estonia, Latvia, Lithuania, Poland, the Czech Republic, Slovakia, Hungary, Malta, Cyprus, and Slovenia. These countries entered as poor cousins. On the eve of admission to the European Union, the standard of living in Poland was 39 percent of EU standards, up from 33 percent in 1995. The Czech Republic and Hungary enjoyed 55 and 50 percent respectively, but these figures masked the discrepancy between the ailing countryside and thriving cities. In all these countries a far larger proportion of income went for food purchases rather than for leisure and other nonessentials, and on the cusp of entering the European Union, citizens of eastern Europe were fearful at the prospect. "It's bad," a farmer in the Czech Republic maintained, "the European Union is already imposing various quotas and regulations on us." A retiree foresaw the cost of beer going up: "If I wanted to join anything in the West, I would have defected," he groused.[16] Still others felt that because their countries had established an independent national identity so recently, it was premature to join a body that might swallow them up or exploit them as the Communist system had done.

Despite these concerns, the economic life of eastern Europe had picked up considerably by the early twenty-first century. In contrast to the first bleak years of massive layoffs, soaring inflation, and unpaid salaries, in 2002 residents of Poland, Slovenia, and Estonia had purchasing power around 40 percent higher than in 1989. Even in Latvia, Romania, and Bulgaria—among the poorest post-Communist states—a greater number of residents enjoyed freezers, computers, and portable telephones. Automobile purchases were increasing 10 to 12 percent a year, but these purchases showed the great disparity between the country and the city. Moreover, 30 to 40 percent of the people, many in rural areas, were automatically excluded from the consuming public because they simply lacked the means to make what in western Europe would be considered basic purchases. Located around capital cities for the most part, the new shopping malls that sprang up testified simultaneously to the urban nature of the benefits of the free economy and to the fact that eastern Europe was seen as a great new market consisting of 100 million customers for superstores such as IKEA and Electroworld. "When Electroworld opened in Budapest (April 2002), it provoked a riot. Two hundred thousand people crowded to get in the doors," reported one observer.[17] A French entrepreneur, calling the rapid development of the superstore in the Czech Republic a marvel, said, "In France it took thirty years to build a network of stores . . . but in the east we only needed three years to provision the entire country with them." Critics called the phenomenon "Consumania."[18]

Consumption evolved over the first decades of the free market. At first, people spent money on any available product; such spending was, according to one eastern European businessperson, "a social act, indicating that one had joined consumer society." Later, people learned to read labels and to shop at superstores where prices were lower. Because of relentless housing shortages, many young adults with adult incomes lived with their parents. Their purchasing power made them the targets of eager advertisers. Italian fashions, fast cars, and exotic products sold especially well among the young. Regions also manifested special tastes: northern consumers fancied French, German, and Dutch products; southerners craved those from the Mediterranean. New configurations of regions, nations, and cultures emerged with EU enlargement, which many observers consider the most important institutional change of recent decades.

Global Cities

Questions of traditional national and local identity were most apparent in the changes experienced by the largest European cities. Many of them lost their exclusive function as national capitals and became pivotal centers of global economics, politics, and communications. These cities' institutions, functions, and vision were overwhelmingly shaped by activities beyond any single region or even beyond the concerns of the nation-state in which they were located. Global cities such as London, Paris, and Moscow contained stock markets, legal firms, insurance companies, financial service organizations, and other enterprises that operated across local and national borders to provide links to similar enterprises in other global cities. Within these cities high-level decision makers came together to set global economic policy and to transact global business.

The high-powered and high-priced nature of these global business operations made life in global cities extremely costly, driving middle managers and engineers to lower-priced living quarters in suburbs that nonetheless provided these well-educated white-collar earners with good schools and other amenities. Remaining behind and living in squalid conditions in the global cities were the lowest-paid service providers—maintenance, domestic, and other workers. So unconcerned were policy makers about the lives of these people—many of them immigrants— that one theorist used the term "lumpentrash" to indicate how those at the top viewed them.

As centers of international business and with huge infrastructures to support, global cities attracted immigrants ranging from highly skilled to more modest workers. As a result, global cities were seen as cosmopolitan centers and often were contrasted with cities that saw themselves as maintaining a distinctive national culture or way of life (see the Picture Essay). Paris, London, Tokyo, Hong Kong, and New York—the five quintessentially global cities—located mostly in the north, drew criticism for their concentrations of wealth, amassed, in the opinion of critics, at the expense of poorer people in southern countries, through sophisticated financial and other deals.

In some cases, however, globalization produced intentional diasporas of willing migrants to the five leading cities and to the secondary global cities such as Frankfurt and Amsterdam. In the mid-1990s, for example, an estimated 90,000 Japanese lived in London specifically to support Japan's global enterprises such as Sony and Toyota. Because such migrants did not aim to become citizens, they made no economic or political claims on their country of residence and were thus sometimes said to be invisible migrants. These global citizens tended not to suffer from the trauma of exile because most of them lived in communities of like-minded wanderers and because of the multiculturalism of the cities themselves. Transnational people who lived in global cities often benefited from "advantages" such as tax exemptions and generous employer-provided "hardship" allowances that the locals didn't enjoy and perhaps resented. Global cities were said to produce a "deterritorialization of identities"—meaning that many urbanites could be said to lack both a national and a local sense of themselves, so much did they travel the world.

National Divisions and Movements for Local Autonomy

By 2005, there were twice as many nations in Europe as there had been in 1945, for even as Europe as a whole was coming together in the EU, individual nation-states were fragmenting under the rising tide of ethnic distinctiveness. Despite two centuries aimed at building Slavic nationalism and the trend toward larger nation-states, ethnic groups separated in the 1990s (in Yugoslavia and the Soviet Union;

◆ **Basque Demonstrators, 2002**

These Basque nationalists demonstrating in the French coastal town of Saint-Jean de Luz insist that "Basque Country," straddling the borders of Spain and France, constitutes a nation. They celebrate their national holiday—"Day of the Basques' Fatherland"—and hold pictures of Basque activists held prisoner by Spain and France. Basque terrorists also acted for independence by assassinating officials and by setting bombs in tourist towns of northern Spain and southern France. After killing more than 800 people, the Basque separatist group ETA called a cease-fire in 2006, believing it would better serve their cause. *AFP/Getty Images.*

see Chapter 11) and early twenty-first century. In 1993 Czechoslovakia split into the Czech Republic, with Václav Havel holding the presidency, and Slovakia, with Vladimir Meciar as prime minister. Meciar served from 1993 to 1998, during which time the government sold the country's industrial and financial assets to his political allies. During his tenure the secret police fueled tensions against the Roma, although Czechs also attacked the Roma, and widespread corruption tainted the political atmosphere. As in Yugoslavia, the idea was that the existence of the fused entity—Czechoslovakia—during the interwar years was a travesty of ethnic distinctiveness and led to oppression. For their part, new states such as Slovenia, Croatia, and Bosnia, continued to stress their ethnic autonomy, hastened to apply for membership in the EU and NATO.

Ethnic and regional autonomy were not limited to southeastern Europe. In 1998 the United Kingdom devolved many functions of government to Scotland, Wales, and Northern Ireland—including independent parliamentary control of education, health, roads, and tourism—to address long-standing grievances within those countries. Across western Europe, local activists also worked to assert regional autonomy, fostering movements for the independence of Brittany in France and of northern Italy. The push for an independent northern Italy began somewhat halfheartedly, but when politicians saw its attractiveness to voters, they formed a political party—the Northern League—and even elected a separate parliament, which ultimately had no power. The growth of the movement led to the creation of a terrorist wing, the Padanian Armed Separatist Phalanx, which advertised its frightening attacks as the work of "fanatic Kamikaze northerners."

From the 1980s, Corsicans demanded their independence from France, publicizing their cause through violent attacks on national officials and hundreds of bombings. The government of France offered the island a measure of autonomy but would not permit classes in school to be conducted in Corsican and did not relent on attempts to get to the bottom of the corruption behind several factions in the independence movement.

The Corsicans acted in imitation of Basque nationalists in northern Spain, who assassinated tourist, police, and other public officials to advance their goal of creating an independent state for the Basque people. The ETA group (Basque Fatherland and Liberty) observed a cease-fire in 1998 and 1999, then resumed its campaigns in the twenty-first century. In March 2006, however, it announced a complete cessation of violence because the public had come to equate ETA with the more lethal global terrorist groups then active. All these violent groups took a grim toll in death and destruction, while the questioning of the nation-state grew more complex. Historic forces produced both huge transnational organizations and ever smaller political entities at the same time.

THE FUTURE OF EUROPEAN SOCIETY

By the end of the twentieth century Europeans appeared to have put many of the worst problems of that disastrous century behind them. One overriding question loomed, however: shorn of empires, could the nations of Europe keep up with the pace of global change? Pessimists feared that the rapid decline in fertility would deprive national economies of the effervescence that typically accompanied population growth. It also was clear that some European countries were refusing to cut social services because their citizens valued the benefits of social citizenship such as good roads and public transportation more than they desired rapid economic growth. Less physically apparent benefits such as the safeguarding of human rights and the promotion of equality also were high on the agenda in both eastern and western Europe. Would all of these, it was asked, weigh Europe down?

Population and Prosperity

Early in the twenty-first century, Europe faced the problem of thirty years of low productivity. In the developed countries, including the United States, the high rate of economic growth lasting from the end of World War II until 1973 declined by half or more between 1973 and the mid-1990s. Then, in the second half of the 1990s, the United States began to achieve higher employment and rapidly to increase productivity again. By contrast, in 1994 the average rate of unemployment was a staggering 12 percent in the European Union, and it remained in the high single digits even after 2000. Economists attributed this decline to a lack of investment in research and development, which hurt both job growth and productivity.[19] In addition, many believed that the lack of a burgeoning population and the corresponding lack of stimulation and ferment of ideas also would undermine economic growth.

According to some analysts, Europe faced a demographic situation that worked against economic well-being as levels of fertility dropped. In many countries, the population was aging, and there was a shortage of young people to come up with new ideas and promote change. Europe as a region had the lowest fertility levels in the world. Severe shortages of the young occurred not only in the countries of eastern Europe as they faced the challenges of entering a market economy without the safety net once offered by socialism, but also in the countries of western Europe. The lowest levels of fertility in 2003 were in the Czech Republic and Ukraine with a rate of 1.1 children, and in Italy and Spain the rate was 1.3 children—all far below the replacement level of 2.1.[20] According to some predictions, by 2050 the population of Europe would fall from 725 million to 600 million, and too few young workers would be paying into the social security system to fund retirees' pensions.

The implications for gender and family roles were still unfolding as the twentieth century drew to an end. Women on average had their first child at age twenty-eight, and in countries such as Iceland and Sweden some 50 percent of those births were outside of marriage. In the 1990s, high percentages of births outside marriage were also found in Denmark, Norway, and East Germany. Single-parent households were becoming more common, as were households in which unmarried parents cohabited. Cohabitation was rarer in Ireland, Spain, and Italy, perhaps because they were heavily Catholic countries. The most prevalent kind of cohabitation was among young people, and these relationships also tended to be the shortest-lived. Yet unmarried couples with children were one of the fastest-growing family types, rising in Norway from 61,000 in the mid-1980s to 100,000 in 2004. In the 1980s in Denmark some 15 percent and in the United Kingdom 17 percent of all families with children were headed by a single parent, and women headed 80 to 90 percent of all such European families. These families were also among the poorest. But the trend to long-term cohabitation by both homosexual and heterosexual couples grew to such proportions that France, Portugal, Denmark, Germany, and the Netherlands had all legislated a variety of legal rights for partners in such relationships.

With globalization and restructuring, patterns of work and family life varied across Europe and were often more alike in different parts of the world than in Europe as a whole. Traditions of women not working or working in the most menial jobs were common only in Germany and Japan. The Netherlands, a northern European country that had scant numbers of women in the workforce, was more similar to Spain than it was to neighboring France or the Scandinavian countries.

Lower fertility also meant that more women were in the workforce, but it was not necessarily true that the countries with the lowest fertility had the largest percentage in the workforce. The southern European countries had among the lowest fertility levels and the lowest percentages of women in the workforce.

The trend toward very low fertility was accompanied by new attitudes toward male and female roles. A survey taken in the late 1980s showed that Europeans favored an egalitarian partnership in which both men and women had interesting jobs and both members of a couple took equal responsibility for the household. Men in the survey, especially younger men, were not especially keen to take on *all* household chores. They preferred shopping, doing dishes after dinner, and child care to cooking and housecleaning, which they favored women retaining as part of their responsibilities. People's attitudes toward equal partnerships in personal life also depended on their nationality. West Germans, Luxembourgers, and the Irish tended to prefer a family in which the wife did not work and roles were not equal.

Among the most shocking demographic changes in Europe from the 1980s to the early twenty-first century was the decline in well-being in eastern Europe. From the postwar period until the late 1970s, regions such as southern Europe, where life expectancy traditionally had been lower than in the north, began to catch up because of the spread of public health, medicine, and improved nutrition. Simultaneously, from late in the 1970s the general improvement in life expectancy either stopped or began to drop among people in the USSR and its allies. Between 1992 and 2002 the Russian population declined from 149 million to 144 million, as the average life expectancy of Russian men fell to 56 in 1994. A child in eastern Europe lived an average of twelve years less than her western European counterpart. Whereas the French and Swedish enjoyed a life expectancy of 79 years in 1998, people in Commonwealth of Independent States countries could expect to live about 65 years. Czechoslovakia, relatively prosperous before World War II, was the first country to experience this deterioration. There the life expectancy for men dropped from 67.8 years in 1960 to 67.3 years in 1990, though by 1998 there was an upsurge to 74. Male life expectancy in Russia had climbed only to 60.25 in 2000. With heart disease and cancer the leading cause of male death, these stark death rates were generally attributed to increased drinking (one in seven men was an alcoholic in Russia), smoking (two-thirds of all men and one-third of all women in Russia), drug use, bad diet, accidents, and general stress. In the mid-1990s formerly Communist governments, eager to adapt to the free market, did not have the resources or inclination to improve this situation.

Neoliberalism and the Crisis of Social Citizenship

Whether post-Communist or not, all European states faced challenges to their economic future. In the 1990s neoliberalism became the cutting-edge economic model, and one with wide-ranging political and social consequences. Under neoliberalism, the most important aim was to increase profit and investment by cutting benefits to workers, reducing the number of jobs by streamlining the workforce (a process known as downsizing), and enhancing the productivity of any individual worker. The resulting growth would eventually produce more jobs that would in turn employ those who were put out of work by downsizing. Another focus of neoliberalism was further reducing the services and costs of the welfare state. Although Europeans still believed in social services, the tightening of budgetary rules by the EU meant that social services had to constitute a smaller part of the budget. Because employers matched many contributions to social services, any reduction in benefits advanced neoliberalism. Lowering employer contributions freed up money for investment.

Neoliberalism produced economic and social challenges. In 1992, the British government under Conservative prime minister John Major undertook to privatize British Rail, the publicly owned railroad system. The rationale for this decision was that the profit motive ensured the best service and that administration by government experts in railroad administration was inherently inefficient. The result of the sale, however, was not what was expected. Investors made a great deal of money from buying individual pieces of the system and selling them to other investors, and British Rail became the worst rail service in western Europe. Disastrous accidents occurred after the new owners decided to reduce operating costs by eliminating safety procedures recommended by rail-safety experts. Commuters could no longer depend on the trains. The government had to pay more to the private owners in subsidies than the old system of public administration of the rails had cost at its height. The public protested that some services were so important to the functioning of a modern, complex society and so demanding of expertise that they simply should not have been entrusted to investors whose first motive was making money.

Despite the disaster of rail privatization, in the late 1990s Labour Party leader Tony Blair announced the sale of the London subway system. Critics said that Blair had sold out the interests of the ordinary people whom the Labour Party claimed to represent. His supporters insisted that Blair was modernizing Labour and making the party more adept at dealing with the needs of a global economy. Blair himself called Labour's new approach the "third way."

Neoliberalism intensified the debate over the capacity and indeed the desirability of government support for social citizenship programs, especially costly social security systems. The primary candidates for reform were pension systems. As people retired earlier and lived longer, financing pensions from the contributions of current workers became increasingly difficult. These retirement systems were complex and sometimes allowed retirement even before the onset of middle age. In Italy, for example, certain categories of public workers could retire at age 35. The average age at retirement in Luxembourg was 56.8 years in 2002, and in the European Union as a whole it was 59.7 years. Italy had the lowest average retirement age at 52.

Though often criticized for having the most permissive and costly pension system, Sweden was the first to attempt reform, transferring some funds to investments in the private sector and raising the age for full benefits to 65. Cautiously, other countries also began raising the retirement age and looked anxiously over their shoulders to see how other governments were handling what promised to be a looming crisis. Neoliberal arguments for reform were legion. Foremost among them was that businesses would simply move elsewhere, as in the case of German companies, to cut back on the increasing costs of their pension contributions. To ordinary people, the proposed reforms looked grim. As one worker complained of the reformed Swedish system: "It means that we have to work our entire life."[21]

The many piecemeal compromises and experiments caused concern across Europe, as unemployment generally remained higher than it was in the United States. As life became harder, center-left parties found themselves accused of being out of touch with their core constituencies—the working classes. In France, the socialist government attempted to cut double-digit unemployment by mandating a thirty-five-hour workweek beginning in 2000, and many workers suddenly found themselves unable to make ends meet because overtime was forbidden. "How can I prepare my children for a knowledge-based society when I can't even put food on the table," one complained.[22] Despite the decree, unemployment remained stubbornly high in France. Continuing the trend since the mid-1980s of shifts in government leadership between the center left and center right, in 2005 a center-right government voted to keep the thirty-five-hour week but allow up to thirteen hours of overtime. In times of compromise and ongoing social unease, parties of the right became attractive because they blamed bad conditions on immigrants. Analyzing the situation, a young Algerian woman attributed support for the right wing to the deteriorating economic situation of those working, like her, on assembly lines. "They never once said a racist word," she remarked of her white coworkers, but they still blamed her for their lifetime of disappointment when they voted.[23]

Counterexamples pointed to improvement and to entrepreneurial rebuilding even of communities where industrial and labor decline had taken hold. At the end of the nineteenth century and for the next few decades, Bilbao in Spain had enjoyed immense prosperity because of its mining and metallurgy industries. A thriving city life led to urban beautification and the construction of museums, railroads, and fine boulevards. Cafés and public parks became centers of sociability and solidarity. The Spanish civil war exacted its toll, however, and as resources were exhausted, the city entered a sad period of decay, unemployment, and outmigration. In 1991 city leaders and developers brought Bilbao's location and basically solid urban infrastructure to the attention of international investors; leading to the construction of Guggenheim Museum Bilbao (see the Picture Essay), whose opening in 1997 created 4,000 new jobs in the museum alone. The city entered a period of renovation, which led to its popularity as a center of tourism, conferences, and sporting events—a globalization success story in both human and economic terms.

The Cause of Human Rights

Human rights activists found much to lament in the face of global migration, economic restructuring, cutbacks in medical services, trafficking in human beings, and the decline in personal safety. Amnesty International, Doctors without Borders, Human Rights Watch, and other groups directed their attention to the violent power politics in post-Communist eastern Europe. Across this region in particular the underworld, hired assassins, government agents, and security forces exercised brutal censorship over the media and individual opposition leaders. In Russia, President Vladimir Putin closed down an important independent television station on which viewers had relied for information, and outspoken journalists were regularly beaten and even killed. Journalists faced brutality everywhere. In Belarus, critics and opponents of President Aleksandr Lukashenko regularly were found murdered or beaten, as were youthful demonstrators agitating on behalf of human rights. Lukashenko's government expelled European human rights observers from Belarus. In 2004, Ukrainian presidential candidate Viktor Yushchenko, a reformer and Western-oriented candidate, was poisoned (though not killed). Informed people believed the perpetrators to be the secret police of Ukraine or Russia or some other secret agent from those two countries. Yushchenko won the presidency in the third round of voting.

Journalists faced harassment and opposition everywhere. Silvio Berlusconi, center-right prime minister of Italy and himself a media mogul, menaced a television station that broadcast an endorsement of his electoral opponent by Roberto Benigni, director and star of the award-winning film *Life Is Beautiful.* "They have made criminal use of public television," Berlusconi charged, particularly enraged at the station's reporting about his personal business history. He called the journalists "seditious," and as the government brought suits against broadcasters who criticized him, newspapers countered by calling his policies "an abuse of power."[24]

Judges at the International Tribunal at the Hague addressed some of the worst human rights violations of the 1990s when they began the prosecution of some of those responsible for the Srebrenica massacre and other atrocities committed in the former Yugoslavia. Prosecutors obtained confessions from a number of leaders and used them to put Slobodan Milosevic on trial in February 2002 for crimes against humanity. Organizations such as Human Rights Watch began to address less dramatic abuses by expanding their definition of human rights to include the right to personal security, sufficient food, adequate shelter, and medical treatment. They charged that the barriers erected by the European Union against citizens of non-EU countries created a "Fortress Europe," and they worked to counter the harsh immigration policies of individual governments. Some states took pains to control migrants. The French government, for example, initially set up camps along the French Atlantic coast for migrants from Yugoslavia aiming to smuggle themselves to Britain. Then when the British made access increasingly difficult and the migrants remained in France, French officials tore down the camps and stopped providing even temporary shelter, medical care, or sustenance.

The Roma provide ample evidence of Europe-wide infractions. In the Netherlands some 20,000 Gypsies—Sinti people originally from Belgium, France, and Germany, and Roma originally from Romania and Hungary—found themselves the focus of a concerted effort to get them to settle down permanently. Dutch policy was forged by the belief, also held by the Nazis to justify extermination, that Gypsies would not work, were nomadic, and essentially were thieves. Restrictions had been placed on the number of Roma caravans and on the Romas' right to itinerant work in trade and the crafts. In the early twenty-first century, anyone considered a Gypsy was taken into custody, photographed, and fingerprinted, and photos of these individuals were circulated among the Dutch police. The Dutch government also paid and twisted arms to get some cities to provide living space for Gypsy groups. Human rights activists, whose efforts were often coordinated both locally and globally, stepped in to protect the Sinti and Roma from these policies.[25] The presence of skilled human rights workers constituted an ever more influential transnational element in European politics in the twenty-first century.

CULTURAL CHALLENGES FOR THE TWENTY-FIRST CENTURY

As the final years of the millennium unfolded into a global age, thinkers began to reimagine the future. Some saw the world's peoples rapidly absorbing Western cultural values as they adopted the sophisticated technology, representative government, and free-market institutions that characterized much of contemporary Europe. Others predicted a "clash of civilizations" between increasingly incompatible religions and cultures. For example, the power of Islam, as it gathered more than one billion followers, would confront rather than coexist with Western values. Such an argument was made, for example, in attempts to exclude Turkey from the European Union. Citizens of the growing number of small states populated by different ethnic and racial groups would simply refuse to live under a common national umbrella. Yet the migration that has occurred since the beginning of the human species, the movement of disease and climate, the information revolution, and the global sharing of culture argue against the cultural purity of any group: "Civilizations," Nobel Prize–winning economist Amartya Sen wrote after the terrorist attacks of September 11, 2001, "are hard to partition . . . , given the diversities within each society as well as the linkages among different countries and cultures."[26] In the 1980s and 1990s, European society changed as rapidly as it had when it came into intense contact with the rest of the globe hundreds of years earlier. Culture respected national boundaries less as East, West, North, and South became saturated with one another's cultural products.

Islam in Europe

Due to migration from both North and sub-Saharan Africa and from the Middle East, an estimated 50.8 million Muslims lived in Europe at the end of the twentieth century, integrating themselves into every walk of life and influencing the everyday habits of Europeans. Art and calligraphy, clothing and food, novels and poetry, patterns for design, and a large quantity of other cultural products modified European society just as influences from other cultures had done in the past. Mosques proliferated, and many women adopted Islamic garb. Islamic culture and traditions gained even greater hearing. Europeans became used to seeing Muslims worshipping in distinctive ways, and Muslim politicians and activists became

important to civil society. Debates over Muslim dress and Muslim worship sometimes erupted, as in the 1989 headscarf case when three young women were ejected
from a French high school for wearing "religious" dress in a secular institution.
France outlawed displays of any religious emblems in school, not only headscarves
but also crosses and yarmulkes. In 2003 and 2004 German authorities challenged
the right of a Muslim schoolteacher to wear her headscarf while teaching. The
teacher, however, won her battle to wear her headscarfs in the classroom.

The situation of Muslims in Europe—some 7 percent of the population—
was altered by the relationships among Middle Eastern and Western powers. The
Iran hostage crisis of 1979–1981 witnessed religion, nationalism, and the region's
increasing financial power combining to make the Middle East an arbiter of international order. The charismatic leaders of the 1980s—Iran's Ayatollah Ruhollah
Khomeini, Libya's Muammar Qaddafi, and Iraq's Saddam Hussein plus, from the
1990s on, Osama bin Laden—variously promoted a pan-Arabic or pan-Islamic
world order that garnered support. Khomeini's program—"Neither East, nor

◆ **Fereshta Ludin and the Headscarf Controversy**
Immigrants bring into Europe their own beliefs and
customs, which sometimes clash with those of the host
countries. As immigrants become citizens, governments
face issues such as the wearing of headscarfs in schools,
long established in several European countries as secular
institutions. Opponents argue that the presence of such
identifying marks of Islam in the schools undermines
the state's commitment to secularism. Advocates
counter that the government should not undermine
religious freedom. In 2003 a German court allowed
Fereshta Ludin, a Muslim schoolteacher, to wear her
headscarf in class. In 2004 the French government
banned the display of all religious emblems, including
yarmulkes, crosses, and headscarfs. *Michael Latz/ddp,
Berlin.*

West, only the Islamic Republic"—had wide appeal. Suddenly young Muslims in Europe and other regions of the world sensed the galvanizing force of their religion and became increasingly determined to reduce the power of the infidels, represented by European and U.S. society. Other Muslims, often more prosperous, created organizations to work in a more moderate way for rights and for increased acceptance of Islamic traditions and beliefs: the Muslim Council of Britain, founded in 1997 to promote unity among Muslims and an end to discrimination by non-Muslims, was one of these. More radical Muslim groups often accused these organizations of selling out to Westerners.

Religious beliefs and political ideals in Europe and the Middle East thus remained diverse, and Islam did not achieve the unifying goals of the various factions. Instead war plagued the region (Map 12.2), with repercussions for the West. A long-standing civil war in Lebanon involved both Israeli and Palestinian forces. In September 1980, Iraq's president, Saddam Hussein, launched an attack on Iran. Hussein feared that Iraq's Shi'ite Muslims might rebel against his regime, and he sought to channel their aggression through a patriotic crusade against the non-Arab Iranians. The Iraqi leader also coveted oil-rich territory in Iran. Eight years of combat led to stalemate and massive loss of life on both sides. To pay off the staggering debt from this war, Hussein attempted to annex neighboring Kuwait, whose 600,000 citizens enjoyed the world's highest per capita income. In 1990, he invaded the oil-rich country, dividing the allegiances of Muslims and the Arab world. Contrary to Hussein's expectations, the deployment of Iraqi troops on the Saudi Arabian border galvanized a UN coalition (joined by Russia) to stop the Iraqi invasion. A multinational coalition led by the United States pummeled the Iraqi army. Thereafter many Middle Eastern leaders worked to negotiate peaceful solutions to disputes, but the troubles in the Middle East remained, escalating because of Israel's treatment of Palestine and the subsequent resort to terrorism of some Palestinians.

Terrorism struck Europe with bombings of synagogues, public thoroughfares, and the Paris subway and massacres in airports and in Jewish neighborhoods in the 1980s and 1990s. Terrorists hijacked civilian airplanes and blew them out of the skies. As hopes for peace among Palestinians and Israelis receded after 2000 and as unemployment struck Middle Eastern youth particularly hard, armed clashes escalated, and terrorist cells mushroomed in Europe and the United States as well as in the Middle East, Africa, and the Mediterranean.

An unprecedented act of terrorism occurred against the United States on September 11, 2001, when militants from Arab countries hijacked four passenger airliners and flew two of them into the twin towers of the World Trade Center in New York City and crashed one of them into the Pentagon in Virginia. The fourth plane crashed in a field in Pennsylvania and not into the U.S. Capitol because of resistance from the passengers. Inspired by the radical leader Osama bin Laden, who sought to end the presence of U.S. armed forces in Saudi Arabia and other areas important to Islam, the hijackers had trained in bin Laden's terrorist camps in Afghanistan, constructed cohorts of suicide activists in cities around the world, and learned to pilot planes in the United States. The loss of some three thousand

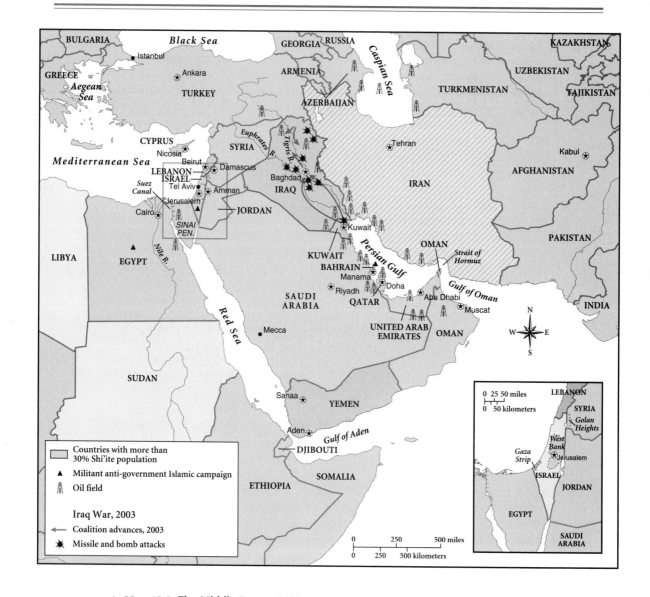

◆ **Map 12.2 The Middle East, c. 2003**

Europe's relationship with the Middle East was particularly troubled from the 1970s on when OPEC's Arab states tripled oil prices and enacted embargos against the West because of its support for Israel. Resenting ongoing European and U.S. interference in the region, Islamic terrorists acted in a variety of Western cities thereafter, including the notorious September 11, 2001, attacks. In 2003, the United States, Britain, Poland, Italy, and a coalition of other states invaded Iraq to rid that country of its supposed weapons of mass destruction. In 2006 Israel bombed Lebanon to challenge the military offensives of the political group Hezbollah. Although a cease-fire was soon in effect, the Middle East remains a murderous place for ordinary people even as the West continues to depend on its oil.

lives—Americans and citizens from dozens of other countries—led U.S. president George W. Bush to declare a "war on terrorism." His administration forged a multinational coalition with the vital cooperation of predominantly Islamic countries such as Pakistan. Although the coalition enjoyed quick successes in driving the terrorists and their backers in the ruling Taliban party out of Afghanistan, it became clear that terrorist cells existed throughout the world. In January 2003, as the United States prepared for an invasion to seize control of Iraq's "weapons of mass destruction," France and Germany spoke for the majority of European countries when they warned against what they saw as precipitous war. French president Jacques Chirac insisted that "an extra delay is necessary" to determine whether there were indeed any weapons of mass destruction, and he urged that the United Nations as a whole make the decision for war. The United States rejected both negotiation and collective decision making. Secretary of State Colin Powell asserted in a speech at the UN in February 2003 that Iraq's weapons of mass destruction posed a threat to humanity. Then, on March 20, 2003, the U.S. invasion of Iraq began. Poland and Italy supported the war with nominal aid; Britain provided more substantial military assistance. On May 1, 2004, President Bush declared "mission accomplished" even as terrorists from around the world headed for Iraq to resist the Americans. Terrorism continued against Western targets, with particularly devastating effects in Spain, where in March 2004 some two hundred commuters died in the bombing of a train leaving Madrid, and in Indonesia, where in October 2004 two bombings in Bali killed two hundred people, many of them on vacation. Further attacks occurred in July 2005 when terrorist bombers struck the London transport system, killing some fifty passengers and in July 2006 when a series of seven bomb blasts ripped through the Suburban Railway in Mumbai (formerly known as Bombay), the capital of the Indian state of Maharashtra and India's financial center. Two hundred people died and over seven hundred suffered injuries in the attacks. Some in the West and some among Islamic believers continued the drive for apocalyptic confrontations to force their own beliefs on others, while European governments in general continued to hunt down and prosecute terrorist cells on their soil.

The Global Diffusion of Culture

In this often heated international scene, cultural exchange continued and even intensified. Culture has long transcended political boundaries, and in fact archaeologists point to its diffusion as a constant over tens of thousands of years of human life. In the postwar period cultural exchange accelerated vastly thanks to new forms of transportation and communication. Tourism, for instance, was the largest single industry in Britain and in many other Western countries by the early 1990s. Four of the five top tourist destinations were in Europe. Throngs of visitors from Japan and elsewhere testified to the West's powerful hold on the world's imagination. Chinese students in Tiananmen Square had rallied around their own representation of the Statue of Liberty, which itself had been a gift from France to the United States erected in 1886.

In Japan, businesspeople wore Western-style clothing and watched soccer, baseball, and other Western sports and used English slang. They had a particular fondness for such products as the French "Beaujolais nouveau" wine. The exchange was mutual, as Europeans continued to be globally oriented and less provincial than almost any other people in the world: travel and tourism to Asia, Africa, and the Western Hemisphere filled their leisure and business hours.

Remarkable innovations in communications also integrated cultures and made the earth seem a much smaller place, though one with a distinctly Western flavor. Videotapes and satellite-beamed telecasts transported American television shows to Europe, Asia, and Africa, while Japanese and Hong Kong movies regularly played in European cities. In Russia people enjoyed English detective stories, Mexican soap operas, and Indian films from "Bollywood." On most European television screens at the end of the twentieth century one could watch news reported in multiple languages including Arabic and Chinese. American rock music sold briskly in Russia and elsewhere in the former Soviet bloc. When more than 100,000 Czechoslovakian rock fans, including President Václav Havel, attended a Rolling Stones concert in Prague in 1990, it was clear that despite a half century of supposedly insular Communist culture, Czechs and Slovaks had tuned in to the larger world. Sports stars such as the Brazilian soccer player Ronaldo and the American golf hero Tiger Woods became better known to countless people than their own national leaders. In today's world, millions of people, including Europeans, might even, at the same moment, be spectators at a "live" event anywhere on the planet, whether World Cup competition or an Academy Awards broadcast from Hollywood.

U.S. cultural influence remained strong in Europe, and the United States had a marketing edge, making English a dominant international language. English flourished and was the official language of EU institutions of higher education such as the European University Institute in Florence and the Central European University in Budapest. Europeans also devoured material from other cultures — African textiles, Indian music, Latin American pop culture. Film entrepreneurs marketed international blockbusters such as the Chinese *Crouching Tiger, Hidden Dragon* (2000) and the Mexican *Y Tu Mamá También* (2001).

Global literature won both popular and critical acclaim and exerted a strong influence on European writers. The lush, exotic fantasies of Colombian-born Nobel Prize winner Gabriel García Márquez (b. 1928), for example, attracted a vast European readership. His novels, including *One Hundred Years of Solitude* (1967) and *Love in the Time of Cholera* (1985), portray people of titanic ambitions and passions who endure war and all manner of personal trials. Another Nobel Prize recipient who won high regard in the West was Egyptian writer Naguib Mahfouz (1911–2006). Having immersed himself in his youth in great Western literature, Mahfouz authored more than forty books. His celebrated *Cairo Trilogy,* written in the 1950s, describes a middle-class family — its practice of Islam, the seclusion of women, and the business and cultural life of men in the family. British colonialism forms the trilogy's backdrop; it impassions the protagonists and shapes their lives and destinies. In the eyes of many Arab observers, Mahfouz was a "safe" choice for the Nobel Prize, not only because he produced a literature about the history of colonialism but also because he had adopted a European style. "He borrowed the novel from Europe; he imitated it," charged one fellow Egyptian writer. "It's not an Egyptian art form. Europeans . . . like it very much because it is their own form."

Musicians continued to base their compositions on non-Western and global patterns. To take just eastern European examples, Polish composer and percussionist Marta Ptaszynska (b. 1943) absorbed the global culture around her. Drawing on Asian art and Zen philosophy for inspiration, she composed *Concerto for Marimba and Orchestra* (1985). In *Moon Flowers* (1986), a work for cello and piano, she celebrated the astronauts killed when the U.S. space shuttle *Challenger* exploded. The internationally renowned Russian composer Sofia Gubaidulina (b. 1931), attracted to Asian mysticism, wrote for Asian instruments such as the Japanese koto and the Chinese shen. Her compositions straddled traditions, whether East or West, and were recorded worldwide by groups specializing in avant-garde and new music.[27]

Critics did not always approve of the direction artists took, and some artists became targets of international controversy and persecution at home. After Gao Xingjian (b. 1940) was harassed in China as an example of "intellectual pollution," his searing *Soul Mountain* (1990) about a ten-month contemplative trip by foot through his homeland became a European best seller when he finished writing it from exile in Paris. In 2000 the Nobel Prize committee awarded him its prize for literature—the first Chinese author to be so honored. Salman Rushdie (b. 1947), who had settled in Great Britain (from India), produced the novel *The Satanic Verses* (1988), which ignited outrage among Muslims around the world because it appeared to blaspheme the Prophet Muhammad. From Iran, Ayatollah Ruhollah Khomeini issued a fatwa promising both a monetary reward and salvation in the afterlife to anyone who assassinated the writer. In a display of Western cultural unity, international leaders worked together to protect Rushdie until the threat was lifted a decade later. Here was seen to be a potential "clash of civilizations" in which the right to free speech was contested by the right not to be slandered in one's religion (see Documents 12.3 and 12.4).

Writers dealt with other burning issues of the day, including the lingering and still haunting remnants of Europe's genocidal past. The most powerful of these authors was W. G. Sebald (1944–2001), who left his German homeland to teach in English universities. His novels were intense, bizarre mixtures of travel accounts, photographs, and stories pieced together with disturbing precision. *The Emigrants* (1993) is a painful account of wanderers from the Holocaust story, but none of these witnesses refers to the events behind the migration. In an age of professional memorialization by museums, Sebald examines the consequences in individual lives of lingering trauma, the intensity of forgetting, and other post-Holocaust phenomena. Tragically Sebald's life was cut short when he was killed in an automobile accident.

Some authors did not take up a single theme but rather explored the kaleidoscope of issues shaping contemporary life in Europe. English playwright Caryl Churchill (b. 1938) was one of these. Her internationally acclaimed plays ran the gamut, from considering what it takes for women to be successful (*Top Girls,* 1982) to replicating life in pre- and post-Communist Romania (*Mad Forest,* 1990). In *A Number* (2002), Churchill created one of her most disturbing if humorous works, portraying a cloned family that includes a father and some of his twenty cloned sons. "I don't set out to find a bizarre way of writing," Churchill commented in an interview.[28] But her plays extracted and then highlighted the bizarre side of the normal passage of society from one moment to another. In 1997, as Churchill was writing, a sheep named Dolly, cloned by a doctor in Scotland, was born. In November 2002, Italian gynecologist and embryologist Severino Antinori announced that three women were carrying human clones due to be delivered at the end of 2002 and the beginning of 2003. Although often called a "sorcerer's apprentice," Antinori defended himself: "Contrary to what my enemies say, I'm not a madman and, in my capacity as a doctor, I'm proud and happy to be able to participate in the development of science and progress."[29] Churchill drew out the imaginary consequences of science and the yearning of humans in the new millennium to push uncharted limits.

CONCLUSION

In an age of globalization the question of any geographic area's distinct heritage comes to the fore as boundaries lose their meaning and cultures continue to intermingle. There is no doubt, however, that Europe in the twentieth century had an important and specific history consisting of dramatic achievements and a horrendous legacy of war, imperialism, and genocide. Today many Europeans resist war because of that heritage and remain prosperous because of several decades of high-quality education, economic growth, political democracy, and technological development. These accomplishments are uneven across the British Isles and the European continent, but they now dominate people's lives.

Having shed colonies, Europe has not shed its tight connections with the rest of the world. Migrants flock to Europe's gates, although the enthusiasm for migration there diminishes with the rise of anti-immigrant parties. Europeans are among the most cosmopolitan of the world's peoples, absorbing foreign ways and undertaking global voyages more frequently than others do. They are among the most avid readers of non-European books and the most assiduous viewers of non-European films, causing Iranian, Indian, Japanese, and Hong Kong films to be really popular across cultural borders.

Europe's imperialist quest for foreign goods and foreign knowledge exacted a heavy price in the twentieth century, as colonies fought to establish their freedom and well-being apart from European masters. At the same time there was much cultural exchange the other way—from Europe to the rest of the globe—and some newly independent countries like India profess admiration for a variety of European institutions. Economic and political connections among Europeans and the world remain strong and vital, and Europeans are strong supporters of supranational institutions such as the United Nations and the World Trade Organization.

Many find the most hopeful sign of European progress in the expansion of the European Union, which promises to bring continuing economic growth and to foster peaceful problem solving among nations. Whether a United States of Europe would be good for individuals, for Europe's countries, or for the world remains much debated. Whatever one's opinion on the matter, most observers recognize that this "new Europe" populated with a substantial number of "new Europeans" is far in advance of the constellation of warring nations with which the twentieth century began. The harmony for which the European Union strives today and its stark contrast with the belligerent great power politics of 1900 suggest that Europe's fascinating history over the course of the past century has many lessons to offer.

D O C U M E N T S

Promoting Human Rights

IN THE 1990s THE QUESTION OF HUMAN RIGHTS took on a truly global dimension as civil wars, famines, and genocide spread around the world, creating a global refugee crisis. Whenever possible, refugees flocked to Western countries such as Britain, Germany, Canada, and the United States. From these countries where people enjoyed freedom of speech, access to resources, and good communications, activists established organizations to help mobilize assistance for those back home. They also saw that human rights issues had helped crystallize dissent in the Soviet bloc and had gained a worldwide hearing. Using human rights as a well-established currency, dozens of refugee organizations kept human rights issues in the public eye for the sake of people living in myriad countries where the situation was dire.

Fatima Ahmed Ibrahim, president of the Sudanese Women's Union, was rescued from Sudan in 1989 when her organization was banned. From exile in London she continued to pioneer for human rights on a global scale, calling attention to the plight of those living in southern Sudan. In so doing, she joined a growing cadre of activists from Iran, Iraq, the Democratic Republic of Congo, Zaire, and many other places who worked from exile in Europe to improve conditions in their native countries. In this article she calls for action on behalf of women refugees. The shocking percentage of refugees who are women and children has led some scholars to undertake a gendered analysis of the global refugee situation. Activists and officials at the Fourth World Conference on Women, held in Beijing in 1995 included in their final declaration many of the points made by Ibrahim and those who followed her in the leadership of Sudanese women. By the early twenty-first century the assault and rape of women in southern Sudan by the Sudanese military and their allies had come vividly to the world's attention thanks to the global media. Here Ibrahim focuses on the illiteracy, poor health, malnutrition, and routine abuse of women as well as on more dramatic though equally pervasive instances of violence.

There were many who believed that in light of cost cutting and the lack of funds for investment in human development at home, ameliorative efforts were unaffordable. Politicians judged that even the admission of refugees to the developed nations of Europe would strain the budgets of countries that were cutting back on health care and other necessary services to their own citizens. A single nation, it was thought, could not care for the entire global population. Human rights for people around the world became a hotly contested issue and one in the eyes of many in the West that drew attention away from important political battles at home. By 2006, even as conditions deteriorated in southern Sudan, there was little effective action from the world community.

Document 12.1

FATIMA AHMED IBRAHIM
The Global Refugee Crisis, 1995

It is only quite recently that the phenomenon of displacement and political asylum has reached a global crisis point. The increasing number of refugees worldwide make this an issue of paramount importance. It has become crucial to examine the reasons that have led to the spread of this phenomenon.

While some of the factors contributing to this situation are the lack of democracy and the denial of human rights in many countries around the world, the wave of military takeovers sweeping most of the developing countries, and the numerous outbreaks of civil wars globally, the roots of this problem lie in the historical situation of developing countries, and in particular the practice of colonialism and neo-colonialism.

Western countries have continued to influence the economies of many developing countries around the world in order to have control over resources, trade, prices, and over the movement of products. This control is reinforced by financial institutions of neo-colonialism like the World Bank and the International Monetary Fund (IMF), which plan and direct the economies in these countries. Many of these countries have borrowed from the World Bank and the IMF, which have subjected them to severe economic and financial management regimes, making them dependent on foreign loans, and unable to resist any conditions imposed on them by neo-colonialism. Western companies and institutions are encouraged to promote the sales of arms and weapons to developing countries at the expense of food and essential needs of the people. Huge arms sales to these countries are usually accompanied by plans to accentuate conflicts, civil wars, border clashes, uprisings, etc., which direct resources away from their proper use. To safeguard their interests, western countries, which claim to be democratic and defenders of human rights, do not hesitate to intervene in these countries by supporting reactionary regimes or even by staging military coups d'états, which often result in the defeat of democracy in these countries.

Western colonial and neo-colonial involvement in developing countries, and the effect that this has had on the national unity of these countries and on their economies, has contributed significantly to the phenomenon of displacement and political asylum and the burgeoning of the refugee population. Standards of living in developing countries have deteriorated to all-time lows, with considerable deterioration of social services, as well as significant increases in poverty, famine, and homelessness, leading to migration and the need for political asylum.

According to UN statistics, the number of refugees worldwide is about 20 million. Eighty per cent of these are women and children. The vast majority come from the poorest of the developing countries.

What are the solutions?

Solutions involve ensuring economic independence of developing countries and ending foreign interference in their national affairs, as well as preserving democracy and human rights based on principles of social justice. It is vital to give women equal rights with men and an equal role in development, policies, and decision making in all fields and at all levels. Illiteracy must be eradicated, especially among women and in rural areas.

Economic and social development initiatives should aim to alter the economic structure of the country if necessary. This depends on developing

SOURCE: Fatima Ahmed Ibrahim, "The Global Refugee Crisis," *Canadian Woman Studies/Les Cahiers de la Femme*, Vol. 15, Nos. 2 and 3 (Spring–Summer 1995), 138–139.

local resources by creating multiple production sectors, modernizing the agricultural sector, and creating a vast industrial base dependent on local raw materials, as well as commercial cooperation with other developing countries on equal bases.

The distribution of the national income should be based mainly on social justice. Minimum wage should be based on living expenses, and there should be fair working conditions in order to develop a strong work force which can become involved in managing production.

Solutions should also involve preserving peace, ending civil wars, disarming tribes, political parties, groups and individuals, as well as protecting the environment, offering health care and family planning services, and providing education for both sexes on equal footing. The achievement of these goals will promote higher standards of living, abolish illiteracy, and begin reducing unemployment.

These goals are not easy to achieve, but there are certain short-terms steps that could pave the way for radical solutions in the future. Human rights organizations worldwide should be strengthened, and organizations should be established in countries where they do not exist. Full cooperation should be developed between these organizations, women, children's organizations, and NGOS. An international campaign should peacefully press for the implementation of UN conventions concerning human rights, and the rights of women and children. An international campaign should be organized against governments which use violence, violate human rights, and repress women.

It is also important to contact UN organizations which deal with culture and education, as well as EEC countries, the Arab League, the OAU, and other international and regional bodies to work toward the inclusion of education on democracy and human rights in all curricula at all educational stages. Further educational programs, accompanied by campaigns against illiteracy, should be implemented. The media should disseminate continuous programs about human rights.

Public opinion in western countries should be mobilized to put peaceful pressure on western governments to stop supporting reactionary and military governments in countries which oppose democracy and violate human rights. The UN should be persuaded to introduce practical measures and appropriate sanctions against any government that violates human rights and opposes democracy. The UN should also make sure that such governments get no support from other governments.

Women should be encouraged to exercise their rights to vote and to stand for elections. The maximum number possible of women candidates should be nominated and encouraged to support women's and children's rights. Women should not vote for men unless they adopt a program supporting women's equality and the implementation of the UN conventions. Heads of governments, ministers, and national and international figures who are women should be contacted to enlist their support.

In my view, these suggestions are not difficult to carry out, especially if NGOS unite their efforts and create a network nationally, regionally, and internationally.

We must build an international community guided by democracy, peace, and social justice, in which every individual has the right to a decent standard of living in which he/she enjoys free medical care, free education, and pension benefits. Everyone must have freedom of belief, expression, and movement, without any racial, class, sex, religious, or political discrimination. Children must [be] secure and fully protected. Women of the world unite your efforts! We have had enough.

QUESTIONS FOR ANALYSIS

1. To what factors does Fatima Ahmed Ibrahim attribute the global refugee crisis?

2. In her view who is responsible for this crisis? Does she believe Europeans are part of the problem or part of the solution where refugees are concerned?

3. What might be the reaction of Europeans of the past decade to her analysis?

4. Would she be a welcome refugee in Europe?

Attacking Globalization

J OSÉ B OVÉ (B. 1953) HAS BEEN AN ACTIVIST since the mid-1970s when he joined a demonstration against the expansion of an army base in southern France and was jailed for his protest. After that, the French farmer lobbied for causes that increasingly opposed the power of global corporations. He went to jail again in the 1990s for destroying genetically altered crops and for protesting the presence of McDonald's in his region of France. His Confédération Paysanne (Peasant Confederation), which he founded in 1987, gathered support from around the world, including from farmers in the United States who said they shared Bové's concerns for "good food." When Bové was jailed in June 2003, President Jacques Chirac used his prerogative to issue pardons to free Bové on Bastille Day of that year. Joining antiglobalization forces at the WTO meeting in Seattle in 2000 and at subsequent economic meetings, Bové, a hero to many French people, became a world celebrity. He is adept at mobilizing huge numbers of people and provoking the government to rash actions, such as surreptitiously seizing him in the middle of the night to put him in jail. Many citizens of France urged him to run for public office but Bové rejected that idea in favor of fighting for the right to eat food that doesn't taste the same all the time everywhere around the world. In all his encounters with authorities—including his arrests and trials—Bové has been an eloquent if controversial spokesman for his cause. He made this oration in 1998 at his trial in France for destroying genetically modified crops.

Document 12.2

JOSÉ BOVÉ
Trial Testimony, February 3, 1998

The strength of our union movement rests on this determination to mobilize free individuals who accept all the consequences of their acts. . . .

Today, I am present in this court together with René Riesel and Francis Roux, accused of committing a serious crime according to the law.

The alleged crime is: the destruction of sacks of genetically modified maize.

Yes, this is serious, and that's why I assume full responsibility. I am not going to hide behind collective, anonymous responsibility. As a trade unionist in the Confédération Paysanne, I believe in the ability of everyone to act as an individual. There is no place in our trade union for a hierarchy of responsibility. Each member of the union plays a main part in her or his own future, and is fully engaged in this. The strength of our union movement rests on this determination to mobi-

SOURCE: SEMCOSH [Southeast Michigan Coalition for Occupational Safety and Health], 7752 W. Vernor, Detroit, MI 48209. 2004 SEMCOSH.

lize free individuals who accept all the consequences of their acts knowing fully the motive for them.

Yes, on January 8, I participated in the destruction of genetically modified maize, which was stored in Novartis' grain silos in Nerac. And the only regret I have now is that I wasn't able to destroy more of it.

I knew that by acting in this way I was doing something illegal. But it was necessary, and we had no other choice. The way in which genetically modified agricultural products have been imposed on European countries didn't leave us with any alternative.

When was there a public debate on genetically modified organisms? When were farmers and consumers asked what they think about this? Never.

The decisions have been taken at the level of the World Trade Organization (WTO), and state machinery complies with the law of market forces. The WTO dictates its own law on the opening of trade barriers. The obligation to import bovine somatotropin meat from the USA is a good example of this. The Panel of the WTO, the true policeman of world trade, decides what's "good" for both countries and their people, without consultation or a right of appeal.

The countries or groups of countries which refuse the importation of bovine somatotropin meat or genetically modified products have to prove that these are dangerous, and not the inverse! The Codex Alimentarius, the norm dictated by the multinationals, is there to fix the rules of the game!

Why refuse something which is presented as "progress"? It's not because of old-fashionedness, or regret for the "good old days." It's because of concern for the future, and because of a will to have a say in future development. I am not opposed to fundamental research. I think that it would be illusory and detrimental to want to curb it. On the other hand, I don't think that every application of research is necessarily desirable, at the human, social or environmental level.

The current discussion on cloning is like the one on genetic modifications. Is everything that is possible actually desired by and gainful for people?

Today, no intelligent person can say that genetically modified maize is an example of progress, neither for agriculture, nor for the economy. On the other hand, the greatest concerns surrounding genetically modified maize are equally important for human health as for nature.

Novartis' Bt maize is associated with multiple long-term risks because of the presence of the three introduced genes. Even the director of Novartis recognizes that a "zero risk" simply doesn't exist. Is this an admission of powerlessness, or a way in which to cast aside his future responsibility in case there are problems? The problems arising today with certain agricultural practices (such as animal-based feeds, the effects on bee populations, etc.) only serve to reinforce our caution when dealing with the sorcerer's apprentices.

The biggest danger which genetically modified maize represents, as well as all the other GMOs, is the impossibility of evaluating the long-term consequences of their use, and following their effects on the environment, animals and humans.

No separation of genetically modified and non-manipulated products is carried out. For example, non-manipulated and genetically modified soya are actually mixed together when they arrive in France. As a result, there is no way of tracing the genetically modified soya. There is no choice left, neither for the producer, of which I am one, nor for the consumer, amongst whom we all number.

This type of culture also poses a threat to the future of farmers. For some decades productionism has served to enslave farmers. From being a producer, the farmer has now become someone who is exploited, who can no longer decide on her or his way of managing the land, nor freely choose her or his techniques for this. However, a real revolution has been taking place for the last 15 years amongst members of the Confédération Paysanne, who have put this other type of agriculture back into action.

Either we accept intensive production and the huge reduction in the number of farmers in the sole interests of the World Market, or we create a farmer's agriculture for the benefit of everyone. Genetically modified maize is also the symbol of a system of agriculture and a type of society which I refuse to accept. Genetically modified maize is purely the product of technology, where the means become the end. Political choices are swept aside by the power of money.

Agriculture is a perfect illustration of this type of logic, which pervades every facet of food production. Agricultural production has now become the agro-industry. From the farmers who formed their small cooperatives, we have seen a conversion to the firms who have rationalized their systems of production in order to maximize profits on their investments. Since the 1920s, maize in the USA has been hybridized in order to oblige all farmers to buy seeds through a trust.

The trusts merged in order to invest in new techniques, which were capable of releasing new profits. Novartis, the world's leading pharmaceutical group, invests billions in order to remain number one: they sell seeds, herbicides, pesticides and medicines. But competition is strong, and as a result of the merger which took place between two of their main competitors last week, they have announced a plan to lay off 2000 employees in order to assure their shareholders of the profitability of the company.

Is it this kind of logic we want? No. I reject this lurch forwards where the aim of the economy isn't to satisfy needs, but is merely production for production's sake, without any link to the interests of the individual or the whole.

Do we need genetically modified maize in Europe?

No. In 1997 maize production increased yet again. It's overflowing the silos. The European Union has to stock the excess. And who's got to pay for this? Citizens. Who needs these new seeds? No one. It's only Novartis which wants to get the returns on its investment and remain the number one pharmaceutical group in the world!

By destroying the genetically modified maize seeds on January 8 at the Novartis factory in Nerac, we wanted to put this short-sighted logic into the spotlight.

Yes, this action was illegal, but I lay claim to it because it was legitimate.

A democratic debate simply doesn't exist. The conspiracy of silence organized by the companies and the sovereign states is the sole logic which prevails. As with blood contaminated with the HIV virus, or mad cow disease, the public mustn't be alarmed. Everything has to be allowed to continue in silence.

By appearing before you today, I'm aware of being in breach of the law which wants every citizen to be content with expressing her or his views by simply putting their vote in the urn every six years.

But it's not in this way that social and economic problems are resolved—on the contrary. Through the action which we undertook and for which we are being judged, we kicked off a vast citizen's movement which refuses the use of GMOs in foodstuffs for animals and for humans. These actions will stop when this mad logic comes to a halt.

Yes, this action was illegal, but I lay claim to it because it was legitimate. I don't demand clemency, but justice. Either we have acted in everyone's interest and you will acquit us, or we have shaken the establishment and in that case you will punish us.

There is no other issue.

QUESTIONS FOR ANALYSIS

1. To whom is Bové appealing in this speech?

2. What issues concern him most, and what are the solutions to them?

3. Assess the importance of Bové's actions and speeches in a globalizing world economy.

Fatwa and Free Speech:
The Rushdie Affair

E ARLY IN THE 1960S PARENTS OF THE YOUNG SALMAN RUSHDIE (b. 1947) sent their son from their home in Bombay to attend the Rugby boarding school in England. While Salman pursued his education there and subsequently at Cambridge University, his parents moved to Pakistan to escape anti-Muslim sentiment in India. Rushdie himself moved back to India but then returned to England in the 1970s to work as a journalist and to pursue his career as a novelist. In 1981 Rushdie published *Midnight's Children,* whose title referred to Prime Minister Jawaharlal Nehru's speech delivered at midnight of the day that India became independent from England. The novel won the 1981 Booker Prize for Fiction. Rushdie became an even more acclaimed author with the publication of *The Satanic Verses* in 1988 because of its rollicking, bizarre, and irreverent episodes, beginning with two Indian actors falling to earth from a jet blown apart in flight by terrorists.

The book's references to the Prophet Muhammad offended Muslims, who saw them as blasphemous, and the book was condemned and even burned by Muslims in Bradford, England. In February 1989, Ayatollah Ruhollah Khomeini, spiritual leader of Iran, issued a fatwa, a religious edict calling on Muslims to assassinate Rushdie. In response, British authorities sent him into hiding. Rushdie had both committed opponents and fervent defenders. Among the latter was his Norwegian publisher, William Nygaard, who was shot three times and gravely wounded in 1993. Assassins succeeded in murdering Rushdie's Japanese and Italian translators. Although the Iranian government professed to lift the fatwa in 1998 as part of its rapprochement with Britain, in January 2005, Ayatollah Ali Khamenei, supreme leader of Iran, reaffirmed the fatwa before pilgrims to Mecca, saying that it could be withdrawn only by Khomeini, who had issued it in the first place and died shortly thereafter.

Document 12.3 is the 1989 fatwa urging Rushdie's death. Document 12.4 is a speech by William Nygaard defending Rushdie before the EU Subcommittee on Human Rights in 1996. These documents are part of a media surge that made Rushdie one of the best known figures of the contemporary scene. The rock band U2 set to music and recorded a poem from one of Rushdie's later novels. His face appears on T-shirts and posters, and he himself shows up unannounced at rock concerts, television interviews, and symposia around the world.

Document 12.3

AYATOLLAH RUHOLLAH KHOMEINI
Fatwa against Salman Rushdie, February 14, 1989

In the name of God Almighty. There is only one God, to whom we shall all return. I would like to inform all intrepid Muslims in the world that the author of the book entitled *The Satanic Verses,* which has been compiled, printed, and published in opposition to Islam, the Prophet, and the Qur'an, as well as those publishers who were aware of its contents, have been sentenced to death. I call on all zealous Muslims to execute them quickly, wherever they find them, so that no one will dare insult the Islamic sanctions. Whoever is killed on this path will be regarded as a martyr, God willing. In addition, anyone who has access to the author of the book, but does not possess the power to execute him, should refer him to the people so that he may be punished for his actions. May God's blessing be on you all. Ruhollah Musavi Khomeini.

SOURCE: "The Fatwa on Salman Rusdie," http://experts.about.com/etf/fa/fatwa.htm (19 September 2006).

Document 12.4

WILLIAM NYGAARD
Speech to the Subcommittee on Human Rights of the European Union, April 25, 1996

THE FATWA AND THE PRICE OF FREEDOM OF EXPRESSION

Thank you for inviting me to this Public Hearing on something as natural to the West as freedom of expression. The EU should be saluted for the initiative—however tiresome such a topic may seem even for this assembly. There are few questions on which politicians, including EU politicians, produce more well-turned rhetoric and display more double standards than this.

Freedom of expression is, if truth be told, the great test of the real integrity and trustworthiness of politicians. And all too often it goes terribly wrong. The real, moral collapse becomes apparent when what we are taught about right and wrong in childhood comes into conflict with economic pragmatism.

In the spoken and written word alike politicians express their support for human values and freedom of expression. But inconsistency, weakness and inability to act manifest themselves when they are confronted with the concealed and open language of dictatorship, not to mention fatal self-censorship and the terrorist threat to life and limb.

THE MORAL STANDARDS OF THE WEST AT RISK

Words and neatly formulated attitudes are rarely translated into action, ethically motivated action. How then can we expect respect from others? Isn't

SOURCE: European Parliament, Brussels, April 25, 1996, http://www.europarl.europa.eu/hearings/19960425/droi/thef_en.htm.

this what we demand? Can we in the West be relied on? We scarcely live up to what we are taught in our childhood. In secret we—EU countries not least—sell arms to Iran, carry out clandestine training of their terrorist agents both at home and abroad. . . . We increase trade, while outwardly we make rhetorical attempts at indignant moral dialogue in meetings with foreign ministers in the capitals of the EU and more exotic locations, at which the fatwa, the death threat against Salman Rushdie, his publishers and translators, is condemned in the "appropriate" phrases in a dutiful effort to maintain a circle around freedom of expression. This is surely what we usually call double standards. . . .

The Rushdie affair is one of the most crucial tests of its moral standards the West has had to face for a long time. What is required of us?

Respect, or more precisely: mutual respect is always a prerequisite when equal parties wish to enter into dialogue—when there is a wish to maintain trusting, reliable communication between different societies and cultures. Certain assumptions and limitations are inherent in the term respect. For example: how long can respect be maintained if the views of one party are not accepted by the other? How pragmatic, not to say cynical, can a party allow itself to be in order to overlook such differences and permit continued dialogue?

Pragmatism—"realism"—have become favourite expressions with the so-called "goal-directed" politicians (in Norway at least). This type of politician has such a narrow perspective on what he is doing that he is guided by expedience and short-term economic interests alone; first and foremost he pursues individual cases uncritically instead of allowing an overall set of values to guide his actions.

SETTING LIMITS WHILE CONTINUING THE DIALOGUE

Dialogue without respect for the other party is worth little. Nevertheless, I believe that dialogue (even in the name of pragmatism) should be maintained as long as, that is, it does not undermine the limit of what we can tolerate in principle. Contact between the parties can, despite everything, contain hope.

But let me introduce a new dimension and a new term: setting limits. A dialogue without set limits between parties who are a long way apart is meaningless and undermines both our own self-respect and the possibility of obtaining respect from the other party if we compromise on human worth. Setting political limits is much more demanding to put into practice than dialogue because it requires both insight and the courage to act, whereas dialogue opens the way for the inherent talent which most politicians have for talk and deficient political action in difficult and unpleasant cases. Consequently dialogue, and so-called critical dialogue in particular, has been sneered at—and rightly so—as an inadequate device. This has at any rate been all too apparent in the Rushdie affair.

One example: the meeting in the winter of 1995 between Danish Foreign Minister Niels Helveg Petersen and Iranian Deputy Foreign Minister Vaezi. At the time Denmark was the only country in Scandinavia to choose to receive the Iranian politician in an ostensible defence of critical dialogue, despite strong protests from both the intellectual and political communities. The meeting became an embarrassment for Helveg Petersen because during his visit to Denmark the Deputy Foreign Minister made some cryptic statements about Iran not wanting to murder Salman Rushdie, a statement which the Danish Foreign Minister immediately tried to cash in on. Just a few hours later, during a stopover in Paris on his way home, Vaezi made a contradictory statement confirming the death sentence on Rushdie again.

This embarrassing episode was clearly instructive. According to press reports Helveg Petersen has been more critical of the dialogue with Iran during the past year. But what apart from words has happened in the EU's name? Are arms deals and the training of Iran's terrorist agents still going on?

BUILDING BRIDGES BETWEEN CULTURES HAS LIMITS

Building bridges between cultures is a long-term process. Building bridges between Islam and the Christian cultures of the West is probably possible within the foreseeable future, I believe. But building bridges with terrorist, fundamentalist regimes is far more demanding, as it is the goal of such regimes to combat the human values of the West: first and foremost freedom of expression. The Rushdie affair demonstrates this.

But even in this case I feel that the international community should maintain a two-pronged attack: it should set clear limits for what we can tolerate in the West and at the same time try to make its point of view understood by means of an ongoing dialogue through a variety of channels.

The question is how and with what patience the strategy should now be formed to make Iran understand that the West cannot tolerate a standing death sentence on one of its citizens, a death sentence contrary to all our ideas of human rights. How shall the West go on after prolonged diplomatic requests for the repeal of this death sentence have been made in vain?

Let me try to summarise.

The policy towards Iran and similar regimes must be part of a long-term, gradual process combining dialogue and the setting of limits. This applies both to the international community in general and Norway in particular. This is because Norway can genuinely be said to have its own responsibility, not only because we in particular have been affected by an act of revenge on the part of a foreign regime but also by virtue of our traditional defence of freedom of speech as a fundamental human right, our role as a peace broker in the international community and as a country which is independent of the EU. . . . Although we are a small nation, the international community could demand—and rightly so—that we, together with the other afflicted countries in the Rushdie affair, lead the way with the power of example as our motto.

Let me make my point of view clear as far as Norway is concerned. We have now been through several active stages in the name of dialogue. Every single time the fatwa has been confirmed in increasingly marked and provoking terms. The right to murder is still being claimed energetically.

Now only one natural solution in the gradual process remains—and allow me to go straight to the conclusion for reasons of time and without detailed justification: a limit has been reached for Norway. It must be marked in the belief in the power of example. A full diplomatic break with Iran is in our case the necessary next step, combined with a complete cessation of economic trade.

FOR AN ONGOING DIALOGUE THROUGH UN CHANNELS

Dialogue? What of it? Well, it should be maintained from now on through the UN and other international channels. And it is high time for the International Court of Justice in The Hague to be invited—gladly on the initiative of a small country such as Norway or the EU—to examine breaches of both international law and human rights in the Rushdie affair.

And what of the EU and its credibility now? Will the Troika seriously follow up the process it started in order to put a stop to the declared terrorist threat against European citizens? Or is the EU's latest initiative vis-à-vis Iran merely an obligatory exercise for the sake of outward credibility . . . ?

EUROPE'S GOAL: DEFENCE OF FREEDOM OF EXPRESSION IN THE RUSHDIE AFFAIR

The long-term goal must remain the same. It consists of building bridges between different cultures. The instantaneous, global isolation of Iran is not the way forward. But we should thank the U.S. government for its critical and consistent conduct—here too. I must not go too far, but do not allow the weakness displayed in the Iran situation to lead to a new Yugoslavia . . . , as far as

Europe's capacity for political inaction is concerned. The process should be gradual and consistent for us all. Well is it, I ask?

I ask again. Is there anyone who believes that our governments will adopt a consistent, action-oriented line in defence of freedom of expression in the Rushdie affair? I don't. In Norway we don't even get an open reply (from our government leaders). Is it so surprising then that we are struggling with a lack of mutual respect between the parties?

Finally, thank you again. It is initiatives such as this which can put the dramatic, political explosiveness of freedom of expression on the agenda, where openness can be ensured. It should produce results—if we believe in freedom of expression.

QUESTIONS FOR ANALYSIS

1. Describe the opposing positions on Rushdie's work expressed in the two documents.

2. What is the audience for each document?

3. What do the documents tell you about the presence of global standards when it comes to culture and the arts?

PICTURE ESSAY

Global City, Tourist City in a Rebuilt Europe

Cities at the turn of the twentieth century changed their look because of their burgeoning populations—the result of internal, international, and global migration—and the magnification of their global financial power. Many of the most important ones, such as Paris, Tokyo, Hong Kong, and New York, went skyward, fulfilling the dream of Le Corbusier for a radiant city of tall buildings always glowing with electric lights. These central cities gained importance as nodes of finance, services, research, transportation, and national administration and thus attracted millions of newcomers to serve at every level of activity—from sanitation workers who kept the cities clean to global entrepreneurs who ran massive businesses and influenced global policy with their decisions. These sites of financial and political power became architecturally more impressive than ever before, showcasing their status as centers of knowledge and unprecedented influence. In fact, politicians such as President François Mitterrand of France, one of the great urban builders of the 1980s and early 1990s, marked the global status of the city by encouraging a new round of urban renewal as the twentieth century drew to a close.

Among the buildings completed in Paris during Mitterrand's fourteen-year tenure as president of France were an enormous government office building designed in the shape of a new Arc de Triomphe, a massive music and science complex, a spectacular building where the Bastille had once been, a sports palladium, and the most modern library in the world for its day. After winning a competition headed by famed architect I. M. Pei, Dominique Perrault was selected to design the Bibliothèque de France (Library of France), with its four glass towers 79 meters (260 feet) tall holding some 395 kilometers (245 miles) of books (Figure 12.1). Perrault has built a reputation for impressive, sometimes controversial designs, and this one is no exception because its reading rooms accommodating several thousand readers are situated deep underground around a central interior garden of tall birches, pines, and ferns. It sometimes takes ten or more minutes to reach the actual research areas because of the numerous escalators and the long hallways. But the scale and ultimately the capacity of the library testify to the grandeur of the nation and the global city that house it. Interior conveyor belts move the books, ordered by computer, from the stacks to the reading rooms. More than 10,000 people per day use its online services, which include access to documents and books. An indication that the Bibliothèque receives visitors from around the world: Holiday Inn and Starbucks opened up nearby. The French government also introduced a new subway line to reach the library; the line itself is among the world's most up-to-date, featuring completely automated, driverless

◆ Figure 12.1 **Bibliothèque de France**
Annebicque Bernard/CORBIS/Sygma.

trains. Displaying the continuing preeminence of Paris as a center of enlightenment and global knowledge, Perrault's prizewinning structure quickly became a tourist attraction.

Both businesspeople and urban politicians chose internationally renowned architects to redesign nodal cities such as Hong Kong, Berlin, Paris, Tokyo, and New York—which gave their skylines a certain avant-garde sameness. The skyline of Hong Kong, once a British colony, rose precipitously in the last third of the twentieth century as international banks, industry, and financial and legal institutions rushed to this thriving hub of East Asia (Figure 12.2). Hong Kong businesses led and profited from the growth of the Pacific Tigers. Like Manhattan, Hong Kong is hemmed in by its location on an island, and its neighborhoods on the mainland are hemmed in by a mountain. To overcome these geographical limitations, it grew vertically. New York City, in contrast, has had skyscrapers—though modest ones by today's standards—since the late nineteenth century and became a center for flashy, tall buildings that even today remain world landmarks (Figure 12.3). Though housing businesses, skyscrapers such as the Empire State Building, the Chrysler Building, and the World Trade Center before the 2001 terrorist attacks are popular tourist destinations.

◆ **Figure 12.2 Hong Kong's Skyline**
Digital Vision/Getty Images.

◆ **Figure 12.3 New York City's Skyline, 1998**
L. Clark/CORBIS.

Berlin, becoming the capital of reunified Germany, underwent massive urban construction, especially on the extensive site of the former Berlin Wall. For most of the 1990s Berlin was a city of construction cranes, as high-rise office buildings and housing went up to satisfy the influx of migrants from across eastern Europe and to anticipate the needs of the new capital. The center of this construction was Potsdamer Platz, once a vibrant focal point of Berlin life that was almost completely leveled by Allied bombing in World War II. Some of the Berlin Wall covered Potsdamer Platz, and once the wall fell and the decision was made to rebuild, local and global businesses commissioned architects from around the world to reconstruct the area with their needs in mind. The architecture of the new Potsdamer Platz reflects global uniformity and global economic connections, as flashy skyscrapers like the Sony building replaced obliterated landmarks from the pre–World War II and cold war years (Figure 12.4). Yet the glassed-in courtyard of the Sony building has been made into a civic space by Berliners and tourists, who frequent its many delightful cafés and beer gardens. A gay-pride parade wends its way nearby, with the new Potsdamer Platz architecture forming a vibrant stage.

◆ Figure 12.4 **Sony Building at Potsdamer Platz**
Philip Wegener/Getty Images.

The rebuilding of Berlin also featured a spectacular redesign of the old Reichstag building in 1999 (featured on the cover of this book). The glass dome, which is atop the parliamentary chambers, allows the public to view from on high the work of its representatives. The copious use of glass is a symbol of transparency and openness, while the glass also serves as a solar collector, whereby energy can be stored and used for heating and cooling—a sign of the "green" values which Germans pioneered in European politics.

Whereas the new architecture of the Potsdamer Platz seems to eradicate Berlin's past as a national capital, the new Jewish Museum (Figure 12.5), which opened in Berlin in 2001, is very much about the past. Simultaneously it is also a centerpiece for modern global tourism because it presents not only the positive history of

◆ Figure 12.5 **Berlin's Jewish Museum**
AP Photo.

Jewish contributions to the rich history of Berlin but also a devastating evocation of the Holocaust. Architect Daniel Libeskind from Lodz, Poland, most of whose family was murdered in the Holocaust, designed the building to reflect the complexities of Jewish history through jagged lines running along the building's several interior pathways. The museum's windows are abrupt and violent slashes. One only experiences the new building's harsh architecture after passing through a comfortable old Baroque building and then being forced to follow underground passageways. Another theme of the architecture is the void, or feeling of absence of people who are missing through migration, death, or never having been born. There is a great deal of empty space in this museum, which is also a memorial. Libeskind so brilliantly conveyed the sense of a disjointed history—that is, unspeakable disaster amid vast accomplishment—that he was chosen to contribute to the rebuilding of "ground zero" in New York, helping to conceptualize it as a memorial to the dead. Like many of the architects working today, Libeskind crosses cultures and national barriers to present the world with architectural statements

◆ **Figure 12.6 St. Basil's Cathedral in Red Square**
Stone/Getty Images.

about our global humanity. To ensure a cultural liveliness that would attract entrepreneurial and other talent, global cities sponsored new theaters, operas, and museums—but few of them with the emotional resonance of Libeskind's design.

In Eastern Europe the collapse of communism and the prosperity in the 1990s brought about by the initial burst of post-Communist globalization led to accelerated reconstruction especially to attract tourist dollars, which were badly needed at a time when post-Soviet industry was hardly competitive. The satisfaction of the long pent-up demand of travelers to visit sites that were once difficult to reach came at just the right moment, paying for the importation of much-needed western European and U.S. technology. In the post-Communist east, capital cities like Moscow, Budapest, and Prague refurbished their historic city centers, repainting and repairing churches, hotels, and old public buildings. In Moscow, though communism was discredited, Lenin's tomb attracted visitors, as did St. Basil's Cathedral (Figure 12.6), built by Ivan the Terrible in 1522 to mark his capture of the city of

Kazan. Given that much Soviet architecture, with the notable exception of the Moscow subway, was often judged to be uninteresting if not downright ugly, the refurbishing of older structures was essential. Churches—which were kept in a state of decline during the Soviet years—were often foremost among these, but in the early twenty-first century Stalinist architecture received new attention. It too began to be restored.

There was also massive building of new structures on the site of the old. Prague gained a whimsical Frank Gehry building, affectionately nicknamed "Fred and Ginger" after the American dance team whose physical symbiosis the buildings seemed to mimic (Figure 12.7). Like Perrault, Libeskind, and Italian architect Renzo Piano, Gehry received commissions from around the world, but on this particular

◆ **Figure 12.7 The "Fred and Ginger" Building in Prague**
Ben R. Hays/brhphoto.com.

◆ **Figure 12.8 Twenty-First Century Bilbao**
Yann-Arthis Bertrand/CORBIS.

work he teamed up with local Czech architect Vlado Milunic. The new building replaced one that had been destroyed by U.S. bombing in World War II, rousing anger that an American architect would profit from destruction of the original. Once the building was finished, Czechs were even angrier, determining that it looked like a bent Coca-Cola can. For them, a design similar to that of the original structure would have been preferable, preserving the past rather than aiding the Americans in obliterating it. For all its power, global architecture in global cities could not eradicate local memory and values, and this is what supporters of "Fred and Ginger" themselves argued. The new structure was so jarring and incongruous that it would be hard to forget that it had replaced an old, prized building.

The prosperity connected to an expanding European Union also promoted the rebuilding of cities. Departing from the grim Franco years that mostly benefited the traditional landowners, Spain undertook dramatic expansion of business as part of its move to democracy, and it paid more attention to the needs of people in cities. Seville and Granada, for instance, became bustling, modern centers—attractive to both business people and tourists.

The most internationally renowned revival in Spain was that of Bilbao, a city that fell victim to deindustrialization for many decades. The opening of the Guggenheim Museum designed by Frank Gehry and built of luminescent titanium (Figure 12.8) pumped new energy into the city, whose neighborhoods—old and new—were among the most vital in all of Europe. Art lovers and tourists from around the world joined Bilbaoans in making an outdated industrial town into a vibrant place to live and an international cultural center. Bilbao's new architectural face, like that of other major cities, has come to symbolize the constant invention and renewal that have been a driving force of Europe's history in the contemporary world.

QUESTIONS FOR ANALYSIS

1. What were the purposes of the rebuilding of cities that began in the last third of the twentieth century?

2. What values are expressed in the new architecture? Are these values local and specific to the city and its citizens' wishes? Are they global and suited to a world where national borders are easily crossed?

3. Why do architects receive commissions from a range of nations and cultures?

4. What attractions do tourists find in global cities?

NOTES

1. International Organization for Migration, "Chinese Immigrants in Central and Eastern Europe: The Case of the Czech Republic, Hungary, and Romania," quoted in Gregor Benton and Frank N. Pieke, eds., *The Chinese in Europe* (New York: St. Martin's Press, 1998), 346.

2. Quoted in Allan Richard Pred, *Even in Sweden: Racisms, Racialized Spaces, and the Popular Geographical Imagination* (Berkeley: University of California Press, 2000).

3. United Nations Population Division, *Replacement Migration: Is It a Solution to Declining and Ageing Populations?* (New York: United Nations, 2001), 93–94.

4. Quoted in Jeffrey Cole, *The New Racism in Europe: A Sicilian Ethnography* (Cambridge: Cambridge University Press, 1997), 67–68.

5. Edmund Stoiber, Christian Social Union, quoted in *International Herald Tribune,* January 17, 2002.

6. "The Coming Hordes," *The Economist,* January 15, 2004.

7. Quoted in Catriona Kelly, "Popular Culture," in *Cambridge Companion to Modern Russian Culture,* ed. Nicholas Rzhevsky (Cambridge: Cambridge University Press, 1998), 152.

8. Quoted ibid., 152.

9. Quoted in Abby Peterson, *Neo-Sectarianism and Rainbow Coalitions: Youth and the Drama of Immigration in Contemporary Sweden* (Aldershot: Ashgate, 1997), 121.

10. Saranya Sukumaran, quoted in Saritha Rai, "India Is Regaining Contracts with the U.S.," *New York Times,* December 25, 2002, W7.

11. Bernard Cassen, quoted in *Libération,* January 20 and 21, 2002.

12. Quoted in *New York Times,* January 6, 2002.

13. Quoted in *Le Monde,* January 9, 2003.

14. Quoted in *Le Point,* May 24, 2002.

15. Baudouin Bollaert, "Rendez-vous à Thessalonique," *Le Figaro économie,* January 13, 2003.

16. "Czechs Lag behind Their Leaders in Embracing EU," *Guardian Weekly,* November 14–20, 2002, 32.

17. "La consommation de mass gagne les pays de l'Est," *Le Figaro,* May 27, 2002.

18. Georges Quioc, "La 'consomania' de l'Europe de l'Est électrise les distributeurs de l'Ouest," *Le Figaro économie,* January 13, 2003.

19. François Caron, *Les deux revolutions industrielles du XXe siècle* (Paris: Albin Michel, 1997).

20. David Coleman, ed., *Europe's Population in the 1990s* (Oxford: Oxford University Press, 1996); *State of the World Population: People, Poverty, and Possibilities* (New York: United Nations Publications, 2003).

21. Quoted in *Le Monde,* January 17, 2003.

22. Quoted in *Le Monde,* June 2, 2002.

23. Quoted ibid.

24. Quoted in *New York Times,* April 20, 2002.

25. Leo Lucassen et al., *Gypsies and Other Itinerant Groups: A Socio-Historical Approach* (New York: St. Martin's Press, 1998).

26. Amartya Sen, "A World Not Neatly Divided," *New York Times,* November 23, 2004.

27. Karin Pendle, ed., *Women and Music: A History* (Bloomington: Indiana University Press, 1991).

28. Quoted in *New York Times,* December 5, 2004.
29. Quoted in *Le Monde,* May 25, 2002.

SUGGESTED REFERENCES

The Perils and Possibilities of Globalization Europeans faced a range of global issues, some of them with more success than others. McNeill helps us understand European environmental issues in the context of the entire twentieth century and the entire world.

Baldwin, Peter. *Disease and Democracy: The Industrialized World Faces AIDS.* 2005.
Benton, Gregor, and Frank N. Pieke, eds. *The Chinese in Europe.* 1998.
Calleo, David P. *Rethinking Europe's Future.* 2001.
Connor, Walker. *Ethnonationalism: The Quest for Understanding.* 1993.
Geddes, Andrew. *Immmigration and European Integration.* 2000.
Haider, Jörg. *The Freedom I Mean.* 1981, 1995.
Hantrais, Linda. *Social Policy in the European Union.* 1995.
Ignatieff, Michael. *The Warrior's Honor: Ethnic War and the Modern Conscience.* 1998.
Kaldor, Mary. *Global Civil Society: An Answer to War.* 2003.
Manning, Patrick. *Migration in World History.* 2005.
McNeill, J. R. *Something New under the Sun: An Environmental History of the Twentieth-Century World.* 2000.
Osterhammel, Jürgen, and Niels P. Petersson. *Globalization: A Short History.* 2005.

Beyond the Nation-State: Integration and Fragmentation From the 1990s, Europeans had options of thinking locally, nationally, regionally, and globally, and these books chart the challenge to the nation-state in the recent past. Sassen describes in rich detail the workings of global cities, providing a contrast to the cities portrayed in Chapter 2 of this book.

Asmus, Ronald D. *Opening NATO's Door: How the Alliance Remade Itself for a New Era.* 2002.
Benson, Leslie. *Yugoslavia: A Concise History.* 2004.
Keating, Michael. *The New Regionalism in Western Europe: Territorial Restructuring and Political Change.* 1998.
Lebovics, Herman. *Bringing the Empire Back Home: France in the Global Age.* 2004.
Mazower, Mark. *The Balkans: A Short History.* 2000.
Olsen, Jonathan. *Nature and Nationalism: Right-Wing Ecology and the Politics of Identity in Contemporary Germany.* 1999.
Sassen, Saskia. *Cities in a World Economy.* 2006.
Sell, Louis. *Slobodan Milosevic and the Destruction of Yugoslavia.* 2002.
Urwin, Derek W. *The Community of Europe: A History of European Integration since 1945.* 1995.

The Future of European Society Historians have collected accounts from workers, migrants, and activists about the cause of democracy in Europe. The newly independent countries of eastern Europe face more specific challenges in regard to political rights, as Wilson's and Jack's books make clear.

Andall, Jacqueline. *Gender and Ethnicity in Contemporary Europe*. 2003.

Frieden, Jeffry A. *Global Capitalism: Its Fall and Rise in the Twentieth Century*. 2006.

Jack, Andrew. *Inside Putin's Russia: Can There Be Reform without Democracy?* 2004.

Pelagidis, Theodore, et al., eds. *Welfare State and Democracy in Crisis: Reforming the European Model*. 2001.

Piening, Christopher. *Global Europe: The European Union in World Affairs*. 1997.

Pred, Allan Richard. *Even in Sweden: Racisms, Racialized Spaces, and the Popular Geographical Imagination*. 2000.

Procoli, Angela. *Workers and Narratives of Survival in Europe: The Management of Precariousness at the End of the Twentieth Century*. 2004.

Ribas-Mateos, Natalia. *The Mediterranean in the Age of Globalization: Migration, Welfare, and Borders*. 2005.

Scott, Joan. *Parité!: Sexual Equality and the Crisis of French Universalism*. 2005.

Silverman, Maxim. *Deconstructing the Nation: Immigration, Racism, and Citizenship in Modern France*. 1992.

Wilson, Andrew. *Ukraine's Orange Revolution*. 2005.

Cultural Challenges for the Twenty-first Century Fiction offers vivid imaginings of contemporary life, and Smith's work offers prizewinning portraits.

Allievi, Stefano, and Jorgen Nielsen, eds. *Muslim Networks and Transnational Communities in and across Europe*. 2003.

Appiah, Kwame Anthony. *Cosmopolitanism: Ethics in a World of Strangers*. 2006.

Forrester, Sibelan, et al., eds. *Over the Wall/After the Fall: Post-Communist Cultures through an East-West Gaze*. 2004.

Kaldor, Mary, and Ivan Vejvoda, eds. *Democratization in Central and Eastern Europe*. 1999.

Karam, Azza. *Transnational Political Islam: Religion, Ideology, and Power*. 2004.

Lewis, Philip. *Islamic Britain: Religion, Politics and Identity among British Muslims*. 1994.

Ost, David. *The Defeat of Solidarity: Anger and Politics in Postcommunist Europe*. 2005.

Reid, T. R. *The United States of Europe: The New Superpower and the End of American Supremacy*. 2005.

Rifkin, Jeremy. *The European Dream: How Europe's Vision of the Future Is Quietly Eclipsing the American Dream*. 2005.

Rosefielde, Steven. *Russia in the 21st Century: The Prodigal Superpower*. 2006.

Smith, Zadie. *White Teeth*. 2001.

Selected Web Sites

These Web sites provide up-to-date news from NATO and the European Union as well as the histories of those complex transnational organizations. News Web sites often feature historical articles as well as breaking stories. British Broadcasting Co.: **bbc.co.uk.** European Union: **europa.eu.** NATO: **nato.int.** *Pravda,* English online version: **newsfromrussia.com.** Public Broadcasting Service: **pbs.org.**

Acknowledgments

[1.1] Serge Grafteaux. Excerpt from *Meme Santerre: A French Woman of the People*, translated by Louis A. Tilly and Kathryn L. Tilly. Copyright © 1985 by Louise A. Tilly and Kathryn L. Tilly. Reprinted with permission.

[1.3] Lothar von Trotha. "Proclamation" and excerpts from letters in *Absolute Destruction: Military Culture and the Practice of War in Imperial Germany*. Copyright © 2005 by Cornell University. Used with the permission of the publisher, Cornell University Press.

[2.1] Anthony Rhodes. Excerpt from *Louis Renault: A Biography* by Anthony Rhodes. Copyright © 1969 by Anthony Rhodes. Reprinted by permission.

[2.2] Wolfgang Sachs. Excerpt from *Allgemeine Automobil-Zeitung* (April 1914) in *For Love of the Automobile: Looking Back into the History of Our Desires*, translated by Don Reneau. Copyright © 1976 by the Regents of the University of California. Reprinted with the permission of the University of California Press via Copyright Clearance Center.

[2.5] F. W. Marinetti. "Manifesto of Futurism." From *Let's Murder the Moonshine: Selected Writings*, translated by R. W. Flint. Copyright © 1972 by R. W. Flint. Reprinted with permission of Farrar, Straus & Giroux LLC.

[2.6] Wassily Kandinsky. Excerpts from *Concerning the Spiritual in Art*, translated by M. T. H. Sadler. Published by Dover Publications, 1997.

[3.1] Johannes Haas. Excerpts from letters in *German Students' War Letters*, translated by Phillipp Witkop. Copyright © 2002 by Phillipp Witkop. Reprinted with the permission of Pine Street Books, an imprint of the University of Pennsylvania Press.

Figure 3.1. Manpower and Casualties of Major European Powers, 1914–1918. Adapted from *The Longman Handbook to the Twentieth Century Europe* by Chris Cook and John Stevenson. Copyright © 2003. Reproduced with permission of Pearson Education Limited.

[3.2] Khan Mahomed Khan. Excerpts from letters in *Indian Voices of the Great War: Soldiers Letters, 1914–1918*, edited by David Omissi. Copyright © 1999 by David Omissi. Reprinted with permission of Routledge UK.

[3.3] Maria Luisa Perduca. "A Hospital Year." From *Behind the Lines: Women Writers of World War I* by Margaret R. Higonnet, translated by Sylvia Notini. Copyright © 1999 by Sylvia Notini. Reprinted with the permission of the translator.

[4.1] Excerpts from *Mein Kampf*, translated by Ralph Manheim. Copyright © 1943 and renewed © 1971 by Houghton Mifflin Company. Reprinted with the permission of Houghton Mifflin Company. All rights reserved.

[4.2 and 4.3] "The Inwardness of Non-co-operation" and "Answers to Drew Pearson's Questions." Excerpt from *The Collected Works of Mahatma Gandhi*, Volume XX, by Mohandas K. Gandhi. Copyright © 1924. Reprinted with the permission of the Navajivan Trust.

[4.4] Aleksandra Kollontai. "Make Way for Winged Eros: A Letter to Working Youth." From *Aleksandra Kollontai, Selected Writings* by Aleksandra Kollontai. Copyright © 1977 by Aleksandra Kollontai. Reprinted with permission of Lawrence Hill Books/Chicago Review Press.

[5.1] Alva Myrdal. "Reliving Insecurity." From *Nation and Family: The Swedish Experiment in Democratic Family and Population Policy* by Alva Myrdal. Copyright © 1941 by Harper & Row, Publishers, Inc. Reprinted with the permission of HarperCollins Publishers.

[5.2] Anna Akhmatova. "Requiem." From *Poems*, edited and translated by Lynn Coffin. Copyright © 1983 by Lynn Coffin. Reprinted with the permission of W. W. Norton & Company, Inc.

[5.3] Ryusaku Tsunoda, William Theodore de Bary, and Donald Keene. "Draft of Basic Plan for Establishment of Greater East Asia Co-Prosperity Sphere." From *Sources of Japanese Tradition* by Ryusaku Tsunoda, William Theodore de Bary, and Donald Keene. Copyright © 1958 by Columbia University Press. Reprinted with the permission of the publisher.

[6.1] Anonymous. "London Diary, 1941." Excerpts from *Living Through the Blitz* by Tom Harrison. Copyright © 1976 by the Trustees of the Mass-Observation Archive. Reprinted by arrangement with the author, c/o Gelfman Schneider Literary Agents, Inc.

Figure 6.1. "Manpower and Casualities of Major European Powers, 1939–1945." Adapted from *The Longman Handbook to Twentieth Century Europe* by Chris Cook and John Stevenson. Copyright © 2003. Reproduced with permission by Pearson Education Limited.

[6.2] V. S. Kostrovitskaia. Excerpts from her diary, January 1942 through April 1943, translated by Cynthia Simmons. As published in *Leningrad: Women's Diaries, Memoirs, and Documentary Prose* by Cynthia Simmons and Nina Perlina. Copyright © 2002 by the University of Pittsburgh Press. Reprinted with the permission of the University of Pittsburgh Press.

[6.4] Nelly Sachs. "Already Embraced by the Arm of Heavenly Solace." From *Selected Poems including the verse play, Eli,* translated by Michael Hamburger, Christopher Holme, Ruth and Matthew Mead, and Michael Roloff. Originally published by Farrar, Straus & Giroux, 1957. In *Collected Poems I (1944–1949).* Reprinted with the permission of Green Integer Books, Los Angeles. www.greeninteger.com.

[7.1] Nikolai Novikov. "Report to Foreign Minister Molotov." From Soviet Foreign Ministry archives. Supplied by Bladimir Shustov and translated by John Glad. In *The Origins of the Cold War: The Novikov, Kennan, and Roberts 'Long Telegrams' of 1946* edited by Kenneth M. Jensen. United States Institute of Peace (1991). Reprinted by permission.

[7.2] Simone de Beauvoir. "What Is a Woman? . . . She Is the Other." From *The Second Sex,* translated and edited by H. M. Parshley. Copyright © 1952 and renewed 1980 by Alfred A. Knopf, a division of Random House, Inc. Used by permission of Alfred A. Knopf, a division of Random House, Inc.

[7.3 and 7.4] Karel Beran. "Official Account of the Trial of Dr. Milada Horáková." From *Pred soudem lidu* (Prague: 1950). Dr. Milada Horáková. Excerpt from a letter written by Dr. Milada Horáková to her daughter before her execution (1950). From *Women of Prague: Ethnic Diversity and Social Change from the Eighteenth Century to the Present* by Wilma Abeles Iggers. Reprinted with the permission of Berghahn Books.

[8.1] Carolyn Kay Steedman. "Childhood in the British Welfare State." Excerpts from *Landscape for a Good Woman: A Story of Two Lives* by Carolyn Kay Steedman. Copyright © 1987 by Carolyn Kay Steedman. Reprinted by permission of Rutgers University Press.

[8.2] Milovan Djilas. Excerpts from *The New Class: An Analysis of the Communist System* by Milovan Djilas. Copyright © 1957 by Harcourt, Inc. and renewed 1985 by Milovan Djilas and Harcourt, Inc. Reprinted with the permission of Harcourt, Inc.

[8.3] D. Belyaev. "Teen Culture in the Soviet Union." From "Stilyaga" in *Mass Culture in Soviet Russia: Tales, Poems, Songs, Movies, Plays, and Folklore, 1917–1953,* by James von Geldern and Richard Stites, eds. Copyright © 1949 by James von Geldern and Richard Stites. Reprinted with permission of Indiana University Press.

[9.2] Abena Adomako. "Mother: Afro-German, Father: Ghanaian." Memoir translated by George Busby from *Daughters of Africa: An International Anthology of Words and Writings by Women of African Descent from the Ancient Egyptian to the Present,* edited by Margaret Busby. Copyright © 1992. Capel & Land Ltd. London UK.

[9.3] Frantz Fanon. "A Powerful Voice of Decolonization." Excerpt from *The Wretched of the Earth* by Frantz Fanon. Copyright © 1963 by Presence Africaine. Used by permission of Grove/Atlantic, Inc.

[10.3] Petra Kelly. "Fighting for Hope," translated by Marianne Howarth. Copyright © 1984. South End Press. Reprinted by permission.

[11.1] Margaret Thatcher. "Speech to the Conservative Party Conference." Blackpool, October 16, 1981. From *The Collected Speeches of Margaret Thatcher* by Margaret Thatcher. Copyright © 1997 by Margaret Thatcher. Reprinted by permission of HarperCollins Publishers.

[11.2] Mikhail S. Gorbachev. "On Socialist Democracy." Excerpt from *Socialism, Peace, and Democracy* by Mikhail S. Gorbachev. Copyright © 1987 Mikhail S. Gorbachev. Reprinted by permission of Pluto Publishing Limited.

[11.3] Sara Bafo. "Between Despair and Hope: A Belgrade Diary." Excerpted from "Between Despair and Hope: A Belgrade Diary" from *Canadian Woman Studies/Les Cahiers de la Femme,* volume 16, (Winter, 1995) 6–8. Reprinted by permission.

[11.4] Julie Mertes. "Jelena, 9 years old, Sarajevo." Excerpt from *The Suitcase: Refugee Voices from Bosnia and Croatia* by Julie Mertes. Copyright © 1997 by Julie Mertes. Reprinted with the permission of the University of California Press via the Copyright Clearance Center.

[12.1] Fatima Ahmed Ibrahim. "The Global Refugee Crisis, 1995." From *Canadian Woman Studies/Les Cahiers de la Femme*, volume 15, Nos. 2 and 3 (Spring-Summer 1995), 138–39. Reprinted by permission.

Index